William Gunion Rutherford

Babrius

Edited with Introductory Dissertations, Critical Notes, Commentary, and Lexicon

William Gunion Rutherford

Babrius

Edited with Introductory Dissertations, Critical Notes, Commentary, and Lexicon

ISBN/EAN: 9783337017217

Printed in Europe, USA, Canada, Australia, Japan

Cover: Foto ©Thomas Meinert / pixelio.de

More available books at **www.hansebooks.com**

BABRIUS

EDITED

WITH INTRODUCTORY DISSERTATIONS,
CRITICAL NOTES, COMMENTARY,
AND LEXICON

BY

W. GUNION RUTHERFORD, M.A.,

OF BALLIOL COLLEGE, OXFORD ;

AUTHOR OF 'THE NEW PHRYNICHUS.'

παιδεία καὶ ἡ παιδιά.

London
MACMILLAN AND CO.
1883

PREFACE.

FROM a schoolmaster's lips the least considerate of readers will take the confession indulgently that the main attraction to re-edit these mythiambics lay in the belief that Babrius was one of the first to make schoolbooks interesting, and that the trim simplicity of his style and the careful regularity of his scazon have not only a literary value, but deserve a place in the history of educational methods. But besides this there were other reasons which tempted me to bring together into a connected whole the jots and tittles of illustration and correction which had accumulated during many pleasant hours of leisurely study, when other work had palled, and Babrius was taken up for recreation and amusement. The only manuscript of the larger parcel of the fables was easy of access, and had never been collated with accuracy, some of the readings given in previous editions not being found at all in the Codex itself, and some excellent emendations being the actual words of the manuscript. Moreover, the text at its best, notwithstanding the many important corrections which have been already made by different scholars, was still so manifestly corrupt as to court alteration; while the rigid rules of the choliambic metre as used by Babrius made the part of criticism unusually easy, not only by betraying the hand of the interpolating versifier and letting out the secret of corruption, but also by suggesting the means of restoration. In fact, I offer my text with some little confidence to the judgment of scholars. Although differing more than that of previous editors from the manuscript authorities, it differs in a different way. It is to be regretted that in textual criticism the τεχνῖται are so few, the αὐτοσχεδιασταί so many. Let a man's sagacity be as great as Bentley's, without laboriously acquired special knowledge it can do no better than produce a text of Milton that is the laughing-stock of Europe.

πρὸς σοφίᾳ μὲν ἔχειν τόλμαν μάλα σύμφορόν ἐστιν,
χωρὶς δὲ βλαβερὴ καὶ κακότητα φέρει.

Accordingly I have passed by unnoticed such conjectures as were either unnecessary or impossible, so as to give greater prominence to certain or probable corrections of corrupt passages. Had the choliambics passed through the fire of Cobet's criticism, the list of noteworthy emendations would have been much larger than it is; but for the present an editor can only hope that the late date of Babrius may not always deprive him of the Critic's countenance. Slight errors in transcription, due to careless reading or late pronunciation, I have not mentioned in the critical notes, contenting myself with classifying them in the chapter of the Introduction which treats of the text.

Of the other prefatory dissertations, that on the history of Greek Fable was written as much in the hope of supplying materials for students of folk lore as of illustrating Babrius. The facts have never, as far as I know, been accurately stated, and owing to this omission too easy credence has been yielded to the assumption of an oriental origin for the apologue.

The Lexicon Graecitatis Babrianae, with which this edition closes, I owe in great part to the kind assistance of my friend Mr. H. Duff, Fellow of All Souls College, who has found time in the intervals of an exacting profession to undertake so laborious and irksome a task. To another friend, also a Fellow of All Souls, Mr. W. P. Ker, I am indebted for a scholarly and accurate perusal of the revised sheets. The Lexicon is intended as an aid to the work which sooner or later must be undertaken, and to which so little has yet been done—the scientific lexicography of the Greek language. Towards that object my own favourite work on the Attic verb is primarily directed; and perhaps the interest which I take in the choliambics of Babrius has been augmented by the consciousness that an excursion into the regions of decaying Greek might bring in treasure for the Attic exchequer.

W. GUNION RUTHERFORD.

1 KING's BENCH WALK, TEMPLE,
January 1883.

ERRATA.

Page xxxiv, note 2, *for* σκόρπιον *read* σκορπίον.

,,   5ª, note on l. 6, *for* ἐπλήθω *read* ἐπιλήθω.

,,   62, Fab. 62, line 5, *for* ἐπαυσε *read* ἔπαυσε.

,,   72, Fab. 74, line 11, *for* ἡμῶν *read* ἡμῶν.

,,   73ᵇ, line 23, *for* ῥάζειν *read* ῥάζειν.

,,   90, Fab. 95, line 32, *for* παρεδρεύειν · *read* παρεδρεύειν

,,   102, Fab. 106, line 18, *for* βόρης *read* βορῆς.

,,   112, Fab. 116, line 1, *for* ἦδε *read* ᾖδε.

FOUR DISSERTATIONS

INTRODUCTORY TO

THE STUDY OF BABRIUS.

INTRODUCTION.

CHAPTER I.

BABRIUS.

FROM the beginning of the second century after Christ it be‑ came the practice of Italian writers to use either the Latin or the Greek language, according as personal inclination prompted, or the imperial court lent a more willing ear to the one or the other. Marcus Aurelius, Claudius Aelianus, and Dion Cassius were all of Italian descent; but all preferred to express them‑ selves in Greek.

From the second century after Christ Italian authors often preferred to write their works in Greek.

It is to this usage of the time that we owe a Greek Babrius, and had Bentley but given a little more attention to the Aesopic problem, it is credible that his rare sagacity would have tracked out the Roman versifier in his Greek guise, and proved, if not to the cul‑ tured admirers of literary impostures, at all events to men capable of reasoning, that the prose fables to which so much importance was attached, far from being the works of Aesop, were not even derived from a purely Greek source, but were the garbled paraphrases of an Italian versifier whom accident had brought to write in Greek.

Babrius followed this practice,

Whether the Child Branchus to whom the first preface of Babrius is addressed, and who is mentioned again in the close of the seventy-fourth fable, is identical with the son of the Emperor Alexander, to whom, as the second preface tells us, the fabulist dedicated a fresh parcel of his mythiambics, there is no evidence to show. But

and wrote in the time of Alex- ander Severus.

information so trivial is of no consequence when we know that one book at all events of the Babrian Fables was written in the times of Alexander Severus.

The paltry Lampridius,[1] who has left a biography of Alexander, takes unusual care to record that that emperor showed much more favour to the Greek than to the Latin language. The Roman Cassius, a Greek writer of Italian history, held high office under Severus, and Babrius was in good company when he followed the example of Dion, and chose the better approach to the ear of the court.

This Emperor himself preferred Greek to Latin.

In the dissertation on the diction of Babrius I shall discuss at length the characteristics of that late literary dialect which has so confused and perverted our notions of the Greek language. It will there be shown that although certain Latinisms of vocabulary and syntax in the Babrian choliambics may perhaps best be ascribed to the Italian origin of the writer, yet any one familiar with the mixo-barbarism of decaying Greek would readily account for them even in an author of acknowledged Greek parentage and education.

The Latinisms of Babrius.

But if there is little or perhaps nothing in the diction or style of Babrius which would be out of keeping in the writings of any Greek of his age, the case is different with his versification. As employed by Babrius the choliambic metre displays partialities markedly Italian. In other words, the Babrian scazon takes a place in the history of Latin metres and not of Greek. This point has been carefully and effectively treated by Otto Crusius

The choliambic metre as used by Babrius displays Italian partialities,

---

[1] Aelius Lampridius, 3, 2, 'in prima pueritia literatores habuit Valerium Cordum . . . grammaticum in patria Graecum Nehonem, rhetorem Serapionem . . . *Sed in Latinis non multum profecit* ut ex ejusdem orationibus apparet, quas in Senatu habuit vel in contionibus quas apud milites vel apud populum, *nec valde amavit Latinam facundiam*,' etc. Id. 27, 5, 'Facundiae *Graecae* magis quam Latinae nec versu invenustus et ad musicam pronus.' Id. 30, 1, 'Lectioni *Graecae* operam majorem dabat de Republica libros Platonis legens. Latina cum legeret, non alia magis legebat quam de Officiis Ciceronis et de Republica, nonnunquam et orationes et poetas in quis Serenum Sammonicum, quem ipse noverat et dilexerat, et Horatium.' Id. 34, 7, 'Habebat cum privatim convivaretur et librum in mensa et legebat, sed *Graece* magis.' Id. 38, 5, 'Hos versus cum ad eum quidam ex amicis detulisset respondisse ille dicitur *Graecis* versibus.'

in his learned monograph on the Date of Babrius; and such results of his patient investigation as are connected with this subject I shall reproduce as faithfully as I can.

A striking peculiarity of the Babrian choliambic is the manner in which the ictus of resolved feet is managed. From the nature of iambic verse it is manifest that if a foot is resolved the ictus is bound to fall upon the resolved syllables, and as a matter of fact its incidence is on the former of the two. The rule observed by Babrius in the case of resolved feet is to except the last syllable of a dissyllabic word and the two last syllables of a polysyllabic word from the incidence of the ictus. If the reader will turn to the fables themselves he will find examples by the score—

in the management of the ictus of resolved feet.

ἀσπονδ|ον ἀ|ει πὸλεμ|ον αἱμ|ατων | πληρη
καταβα|σα κοιτ|ης ἐπεδ|ιωκ|εν ἡ | νυμφη |
ἡρα | γυναικ|ων δύο | νεης | τε και | γραιης |;

while the spurious epimythia and interpolated lines which are given in the critical notes will provide him with verses not subject to this law—

ἀει | γαρ ἐν | γε τιλλ|ομένος | ἐγινμι|ουτο |.

Now it is true that neither Sophocles nor Aeschylus[1] allowed the ictus of a resolved foot to fall upon the last syllable of a polysyllabic word. They seem to have felt that syllables in so close metrical sympathy as the two last of a resolved foot ought not to be dissociated. Euripides,[2] however, fell away in some degree from this rule of his elders, and his successors in tragedy appear to have followed in his footsteps. Of the comic poets Aristophanes violated it within limits,[3] and even these limits were occasion-

The usage of Greek poets in this respect.

---

[1] Crusius refers to Bergk in Zeitschrift für Alterthumswissenschaft, 1835, pp. 946-948, and to Müller's monograph 'de pedibus solutis in dialogorum senariis,' p. 47, fin., and id. 80, 4.
[2] Müller, p. 56, 11. Rumpel, Philolog. xxiv. p. 412. Wecklein on Eur. Bacch. 940.
[3] 'R. Enger in commentatiuncula sic inscripta "Der Ictus auf der kurzen

Ultima eines mehrsilbigen Wortes im komischen Trimeter," tres exceptionum legitimarum statuit classes — primam enclitica si sequitur (velut ἐμέ γε), alteram in vocibus quae cum sequentibus sententia satis arte sunt conjunctae (velut αὐτίκα μάλα, ταχὺ πάνυ), tertiam in vocabulis ex monosyllabis compositis (velut ὥσπερ, ὅτι)—et praeterea interdum, in primo potissimum pede,

ally traversed by later comedians,[1] and by iambic writers of the Alexandrine[2] and Roman age.[3]

These facts being as they are, in what way are we to explain the circumstance that among the writers of Greek iambics Babrius holds the unique position of denying the ictus in resolved feet not only to the latter syllable of disyllables, but even to the last two syllables of polysyllabic words ?[4] How is it that he not only returned to the long neglected practice of refusing the ictus in resolved feet to a final syllable, but went one step further still in metrical severity ?[5] It is not from any rudi-

Babrius is unique among the writers of Greek iambics, (margin note)

legem illam sine ulla excusatione laedi concedit (v.c. una ἀλλά voce decem locis Aves, 1500, 1693; Lys. 463, etc.)' —Crusius, pp. 168-169.

[1] ' In Philemonis fragmentis, 1-100 et Menandri 1-150 duodecim regulae non observatae exempla invenies, ex quibus excusationem habent quattuor Philem. 84 οὔτε θε᾿ός, 88 ὥσπερ ἐν | ἀγρῷ, Men. 85 παρὰ τί᾿νι, 95 ὅστις ἁ δικεῖσθαι, caetera non habent Philem. 11 οὐχὶ μό᾿νον, 40 κοὐχὶ λο᾿πάδος, 42 οἶσθας ἁ᾿γαθόν, 64 ἐξὸν ἀ᾿ποσάττεσθαι, 67. 10 πλοῦτον ὑ᾿γίειαν, 74 οἶον ἀ᾿γοράξειν, Men. 97 εἰμὶ μὲν | ἄγροικος, 130. 11 αὐτὸν ἐ᾿πικουρεῖν.'—Crusius, p. 169.

[2] ' In tanta exemplorum paucitate exceptiones quinque inveni partim excusatas Callim. chol. fr. 3, 3 M. μήτι πα᾿ρά, Pytho trag. fr. 1. 11. p. 630 N. ὅτε μὲν | ἔφασκεν, Ezech. Exagōgê, ed. Philippson, 85 ἀρά γε μέγαν, partim non excusatas Ezech. 169 ἑπτὰ δι᾿οιδοπο- ροῦντες, 178 τετρὰς ἐ᾿πιλάμψει.'—Id. id.

[3] ' Lucianus in Tragœdopodagrae tri- metris fere 240 et Ocypodis 170 quin- quiens — bis licentia legitima Trag. 141 οὔτε χυ᾿θέν, Ocyp. 18 ὅτι τὸν | ἄπασιν, ter sine excusatione Trag. 172 ἄλλος ἐπ᾿αοιδαῖς, 178 τοῖσι δὲ | φρονοῦσι, Ocyp. 20 ἀλλὰ κατ᾿ | ἐμοῦ — legem neglexit.'—Id. id.

[4] ' Nihil ejus generis invenies neque apud choliambographos (Hippon. fr. 60 M. 'Ανα ξίβιος, Anan. 3, 1 μὲν | χρόμιος) aut dramaticos veteres (de Aeschylo cf. Rumpel, Philolog. xxv. p. 56, Müller p. 14. 16 al. ; de Sophocle Rumpel. l. s. s., Müller p. 30 ; de Euripide Rumpel, Philol. xxiv. p. 410, Müller p. 44. 48 al. ; de Aristo-

phane Rumpel, Philol. xxviii. p. 605 sq. 608 sq.), neque apud poetas Com- oediae novae (Philem. 39, ἄσμενος | ἔχεις, 41 τὸν | πατέρα, 46 ἀπὸ | στόματος, sim. 57. 58. 63. 75. 80. 84, 7. 89. 100, Men. 3 κηδεμόν' | ἀληθῶς, οὐκ | ἐφεδρον | ἕξεις, 67 Βύ᾿ξαντιον, sim. 71. 79, 6. 94. 109, 7. 110, 3. 4. 130, 9.) aut aetatis Alexandrinae (Phoen. 2. 5 M. πῦρ | ἱερόν, 18 ὁκόσον | ἔδαισα, Pytho fr. 1, 12 p. 630 N. ἱκανὸν | ἐδείπνοιν et χέδροπα | μόνον, 13 καὶ τὸν | μάραθον | ἔσθουσι, Lycophr. fr. 2, 2. p. 636. ὑδαρὲς | ὁ, 3 ἀτρέμα | παρεξεστηκός, Ezech. 11. πόλεσί | τε, 30 ὄνομα | δέ, 103 τῶν | ἔνεκεν | ἐλήλυθα, 150 πρωτ᾿όγονον | ἕξει νεκρόν) vel Romanae (Pomp. Mac. fr. 1. 3 p. 646 N. μητέρα | τι, Luc. Trag. 9 πνεύματι | βιαίῳ, 29 ἐλπίδι | ματαίᾳ [ep. ἐλπίσι ματαίαις· Babr. 79. 8 interpo- latum] 253 ἔθανε | δ' 'Αχιλλεύς, sim. 179, Ocyp. 65. 154.')

[5] Lycophron, indeed, in his Alex- andra never violates the Babrian rule, but neither can he be said to observe it. In its 1474 lines he only resolves the arsis eleven times — once in the fourth foot (l. 700, κρᾶτα Πολυδέγμων), and once in the second (l. 1204, δὲ μακάρων). The other nine instances (ll. 263, 680, 930, 1164, 1218, 1222, 1242, 1288, 1469) fall in the third foot. But as the instance in the fourth foot is due to a proper name, and the nine in the third are explicable by the fact that if the arsis was to be resolved at all the caesura almost required that it should be so resolved as it is, we have no right to see in Lycophron's usage an anticipation of that of Babrius. See Crusius, p. 170, note 1.

mentary difference between the scazon and the ordinary iambic
trimeter, or that the one in this respect gradually diverged
from the other. The analysis of Crusius embraces both species,
and in fact, as far as we can judge from the few fragments which
have come down to us, Hipponax[1] himself does not appear
to have attended even to the slight restraints which Aeschylus
and Sophocles were willing to impose upon themselves in the
management of resolved feet.

Supposing, however, that the Babrian scazon is made to
take its place in the historical sequence of Latin
rather than of Greek verse, the practice of Babrius
may be explained with ease. Plautus imitates
his Greek prototypes in now and again allowing the ictus
of resolved feet to fall upon the penultimate and even the
ultimate of polysyllables.[2] The versification of Lucilius and
Varro, however, was more severe, and Phaedrus followed in
their steps. These three, indeed, never violated the Babrian
rule, except in the case of dactyls at the beginning of the line.[3]
Even this exception disappeared in the verses of Catullus and
the writers of the Priapeia,[4] while Persius and Petronius were
equally careful.[5] From Petronius onwards the Latin writers
of iambics consistently observed the rule, the numerous verses
of Martial and Seneca[6] supplying not one instance of its
violation.

In another point still does the Babrian scazon show its
sympathy with Latin rather than with Greek versification. In the older writers of Greek choliambics
the anapaest is unheard of, and the tribrach and
dactyl are rare. The fragments of Hipponax,
consisting of 150 verses or more, supply no instance of the anapaest, and only three dactyls

*but holds a
natural position
among Latin
poets.*

*The Babrian
scazon further
falls in with the
historical se-
quence of Latin
metres in the
matter of trisyl-
labic feet.
The Greek usage.*

---

[1] Hipp. Fr. 13, 2 M. τοι δι̯ά, 54. 1
ἀπὸ σ' ο̣|λέσειεν.
[2] Crusius refers to Ritschl's prolegomena, pp. ccxxiv. sqq. Luchs. in
Studemund's Studien, I. p. 178 ; Brix
on Plautus, Mil. Glor. 27, and Men.
237 ; Spengel on Ter. Andr. 23, and
Christ's Metrik, § 74, 78, 379.
[3] Müller de Re Metrica, p. 418, sq.,
and Preface to Phaedrus, p. ix.

[4] Müller's Catullus, pp. lxx. and
lxxx.
[5] 'Idemque valet de Petronio (5. 3
le|ge poli|at) et Persio (prooem. 2
in | bicipi|ti, 9 picam|que docu|it).
Quamquam in tanta exemplorum pau-
citate proposuerintne sibi certam legem
dubitare possis.'—Crusius, p. 171.
[6] Müller de Re Metrica, pp. 155, sqq.
'Neque ab hac severitate saeculorum

and six tribrachs. Even these are for the most part due to the necessity of finding a *locus standi* for proper names.[1] The Alexandrine versifiers exhibit even greater severity. In the forty verses of Callimachus there are but two examples of a dactyl;[2] and in the fragments of his school, amounting in all to eighty lines, there is not a single instance of a trisyllabic foot except in a set of verses by Phoenix, in which several are intentionally employed, that, by producing emasculate and nerveless numbers, they may bring the metre into harmony with the morals pourtrayed by the words.[3] As far as we can judge from the scanty fragments of post-Alexandrine choliambics,[4] this dislike to trisyllabic feet was never overcome by Greek versifiers.

Even in Latin literature, up to the date of Petronius and The Latin usage. Persius, the Roman scazon was regulated by similar principles. The earlier writers, it is true, were a little less rigid than Hipponax and the Alexandrine School, for both Matius and Laevius[5] appear to have employed resolved feet with some freedom. But from Varro to Petronius[6] the Alexandrine

---

insequentium aut tituli choliambici recedunt a Buechlero Rh. M. xxvii. p. 142 sq. collecti (ciii. par|ce tumu|lis, dolo|ris titu|lus, num|quam dole|as; civ, 7 merc|tur ani|ma), aut choliamborum scriptores, velut Terentianus Maurus (2398 fe cit ali ter, sim. 2404, 2405) et Julius Valerius I, 42 (23 la|te spati a, sim. 5. 10. 11. 16), atque ne Boethius quidem sexti saeculi ineuntis (de Consol. II, 1, 5 non il|la mise|ra, 6 ultro|que gemi tus; iii. 11. 5 animum|que doce|at).'—Crusius, p. 171.

[1] Meineke, p. 90, compared with Bergk lyr., p. 756.

[2] Viz. 3, 3, and 10, 3.

[3] See Meineke, p. 90, and J. P. Rossignol, 'Fragments des choliambographes Grecs et Latins,' pp. 13, 14. In the 1st and 21st verses there is a tribrach in the third place, and in the 5th, 10th, 11th, and 16th, in the fourth. Theocritus' epitaph on Hipponax supplies an apt illustration. Rossignol rightly explains the two spondees which, contrary to the Alexandrine rule, it presents in the fifth place as due to a desire to recall the peculiarities of the Hipponactean scazon, p. 15.

[4] 'Neque apud Apollonidem Nicaeum, Tiberii aequalem (Mein. p. 171), ullus pes trisyllabus invenitur neque apud Diogenem Laertium saeculo III. incunte in frag. 1. 3 (= Anth. Pal. vii. 98) 4; fragmentum 2 autem, in quo legitur τὸν πόδα κολύμβων περιέπειρέ πως ἥλῳ diversi est generis, cum choliambi singuli cum singulis tripodiis dactylicis catalecticis compositi sint; in scitissimis denique 12 choliambis titulo aetatis Trajanae traditis Mein. p. 173 = Kaibel. Epigr. 549, unus admissus est | — βασι λέως dactylus v. 1 et 2 pede tertio, eadem qua nomina propria ratione is excusatus.'—Crusius, p. 173.

[5] 'Matius in versibus 13 quater (2, 2; 4, 1; 7), Laevius in 3 versibus bis (9, 18), arsin soluit.'—Crusius referring to Müller's Catullus, p. 91 and p. 78.

[6] 'Varro, qui ceteroquin haud nimis est severus—velut ne spondeum quidem in quinto pede semper vitavit, cf. Riesium p. 84 et Muellerum de re metrica, p. 414—arsin tamen in versibus fere 16 non soluit nisi semel (fr. 358 Buech. "hic badius"). Catullum autem et qui eum sequebantur Priapeorum scriptores ad ipsam Alexan-

model was carefully followed. With Petronius and Persius,
however, a change came. Not only were resolved feet admitted
with greater frequency, but the anapaest's right to the first
foot was recognised. In Martial we are confronted with the
same condition of things as in Babrius—anapaests in the first
place, and resolved feet everywhere, except in the fifth and
sixth. Of Martial's successors the same holds true.[1]

Although these facts would be of themselves sufficient to
prove that Babrius followed the traditions of   The Babrian
Latin rather than of Greek verse, there is still   scazon is Italian
                                                    in a third usage
another argument of even greater cogency which   even more im-
                                                    portant than the
will carry us to the same conclusion. The   preceding two.
                                                    Statement of this
mythiambic scazon of which its author was so   third particular.
proud must have presented some other features of originality
than those merely borrowed from Latin verse—the admission of the anapaest into the first place, the greater frequency
of trisyllabic feet, and the management of the ictus in resolved
arsis. Such a feature of the Babrian choliambic metre was
first pointed out by H. L. Ahrens in a monograph entitled

drinorum severitatem rediisse certum
est. Ille enim in versibus fere 115
duos dactylos habet et unum tribrachum,
hi in 80 fere versibus unum tribrachum
(51, 18) unumque dactylum (58, 4);
eademque Licinii Calvi fuit ars (Catull.
Muell. p. 84, 3) et Vergilii Catalept.
II, VII, qui in versibus fere 20 nullum
omnino pedem trisyllabum adhibuerunt.
Haec autem vincula Alexandrina laxata
videntur medio primo p. Chr. n. saeculo, nam Petronius et Persius etsi
arses haud saepe soluerunt (Petron. in
capite V versuum 8 semel, Persius in pro-
logo 14 versuum bis), tamen anapaestum
quasi legitima licentia primi omnium
in versus initium adhiuserunt (Petr.
Sat. 5, 8 sedeat | redemptus, Pers. Prol.
5 memini ut | , 6 Helico'nidasque, 8
hederae |).'—Crusius, pp. 174, 175.

[1] 'Hipponacteum autem ita mutatum
satis popularem posteriore quoque
tempore apud Romanos mansisse lapi-
des nonulli testantur a Buechlero Mus.
Rhen. xxvii p. 142 sq. et xxxii p. 479.
sq. enarrati. In carmine enim CIV
septem versuum Hadriani aetate con-
texto bis anapaestus in primo pede (v. 1.
3), semel vel bis arsis soluta (v. 7) in-

venitur, in inscriptione Antonino Pio
imperante concepta in tribus versibus
semel anapaestus et fortasse semel arsis
soluta (v. 2 et 3 extr.), in quattuor
versibus Caracallae tempore compositis
CIII semel tribrachys, bis dactylus.
De 7 illis choliambis CII Diocletiani
tempore conscriptis nihil quidem certi
dici potest, cum eorum nihil servatum
sit nisi misera pedum quinti et sexti
frustula ; sed exstant ejusdem aetatis
20 Terentiani Mauri hipponactei 2398-
2418, in quibus quamquam satis siccum
est argumentum duo tamen anapaesti
(2403, 2415), unus dactylus (2404), duo
tribrachi (2398, 2405) inveniuntur, et
25 Julii Valerii I, 42, qui Alexandri
majores enumerans semel anapaesto
(6), quater dactylo (23. 5. 10. 16 in
nom. propr.), semel tribracho (11) usus
est. Denique qui sexto saeculo in-
eunte ut alia metra, ita choliambum
restauravit, Boethius de Consol. II, 1
et III, 11 in paucis illis versibus neque
arsibus solutis abstinuit (II, 1, 5. 6.
III, 11, 5) neque anapaestis (II, 1, 4.
III, 11, 5 "animum que docce,at" :
anapaestus cum tribracho conjunctus).'
—Crusius, pp. 175, 176.

b

'de Crasi et Aphaeresi.' It consists in the unintermitting care with which the last word of the line is so chosen that its penultimate syllable must have the accent. In a Latin scazon this was bound to happen in all cases except when the line was closed by a monosyllable, because in Latin all disyllables not enclitics have the accent on the penultimate, and all polysyllables with a long penultimate have also a penultimate accent. In harmony with this tendency of the Latin language to force an accent on the penultimate syllable of a choliambic line, the writers of this metrical style avoided final monosyllables except in those cases in which it was possible to make them resign their own proper accent, and leave the penultimate syllable of the scazon in undisturbed possession. Accordingly, as far as the penultimate accent is concerned, all Latin choliambics must correspond with one or other of the following lines :—

> Petit Gemellus nuptias Maroníllae
> Et cupit et instat et precatur et dónat.
> Adeone pulchra est ? imo foedius níl est
> Optare utrumque pariter, improbi vótum est.

Final words of two or more syllables cannot help themselves in presenting a penultimate accent, and final monosyllables are not allowed except they coalesce with the preceding word or fall by enclisis into union with another monosyllable.

It was left for Otto Crusius to show that the Babrian *The bearing of this third particular on the Babrian question first observed by Crusius.* scazon derived its most singular characteristic from this natural law of Latin choliambics, and by Italian parentage to account for the presence in Greek verse of a feature so striking as a successful attempt to take accent into account in metrical composition.[1]

---

[1] Although Crusius is probably right in explaining the frequency of a penultimate accent in the hexameters of Nonnus and his school by their practice of ending the line with a long syllable rather than by any conscious desire to have the penultimate syllable accented, yet there is no question that in a certain sense Ahrens was right in regarding this feature of the Babrian metre as a first step in the direction of *versus politici*. The mere fact of an attempt to make Greek accents take to the ways of Latin shows conclusively that the Greek accent in Babrius' day was fast losing its purely chromatic nature, and was approximating to that of Latin or even English.

Of Babrius himself we know practically nothing. The
name is essentially Italian, and if he has any The name Bab-
right to that of Valerius as well, his title to Italian rius is Italian.
nationality is secured beyond dispute. Whether in the form
Barbius or Babrius, the word is found with some frequency in
Inscriptions.[1] It is derived from *barba*, as Fabius from *fuba*,
Naevius from *naevus*, Asinius from *asinus*, Valgius from *valgus*,
Plautius from *plautus*, and Licinius from *licinus*, the metathesis
in the form Babrius being readily paralleled in ferveo and
febris, Codrus and Cordus, Scodra and Scorda.[2]

The Athoan Codex begins with the words Βαλεβριου
μυθίαμβοι αἰσώπειοι, a corruption which can best The right of Bab-
be explained as due to running together the two rius to the prae-
genitives Βαλερίου and Βαβρίου— nomen of Vale-
rius.

ΒΑΛΕ[ΡΙΟΥΒΑ]ΒΡΙΟΥ.

The writer of the Notes which have found their way into
the Harleian Collection as part of the volume numbered
3521, has preserved the fifty-eighth fable. He began with the
intention of heading it

Βαλερίου Βαβρίου

but, leaving the former of the two names incomplete at the
epsilon, he erased it in that place and began a new line—

Βαλερίου χωριαμβικοὶ στίχοι ἐκ τῶν Αἰσώπου μύθων,

so that the whole citation is headed by the single name
Βαβρίου. At best the manuscript does not date earlier than
the seventeenth century, but, everything considered, there is
good reason to believe that the mythiambist has a right to
Valerius as well as to Babrius.

We are simply without evidence as to the position, if
any, which this Valerius Babrius held in the The position of
court of Alexander Severus. That home of Babrius in the imperial court.
spurious puritanism and artificial high-thinking appears to

---

[1] Cited by Crusius, pp. 190, 191.
The form Βαβρίας is nothing but a
corruption, or a wrong inference from
the genitive Βαβρίου.
[2] Crusius (p. 191), who cites other

instances from all sorts of authorities,
e.g., στέφρος στέρφος, νάρδηξ νάθραξ,
ἀγρυπνία ἀργυπνία, Δέρβη Δέβρη, Σίρβος
Σίβρος, Ἀργιόπη Ἀγριόπη.

have afforded unusual opportunities for literary effort, if I may apply the adjective literary to compositions of the class then prevalent. Babrius may have been an ordinary literary retainer of the court,—one of the *docti homines* whose *fabulae literatae* Severus was fond of asserting formed his meat, drink, and recreation[1]—or he may have acted as tutor to the Emperor's son. In the former case, the second preface, if not the first, would be a ceremonious dedication intended to conciliate the imperial favour; in the latter, it would be the more familiar address of a master to his pupil. Whatever the truth may be, —whether Branchus and the παῖς βασιλέως Ἀλεξάνδρου are identical or not,[2]—the fables found a ready audience and became well known.

I shall try to show in the next dissertation that the Babrian mythiambics are probably for the most part no more than a paraphrase in verse of some earlier prose collection of fables. But in his second preface our paraphrast distinctly states that he was the first to take this line. The assertion, however, must refer only to Greek[3] verse, as Babrius

Babrius was probably the first to exhibit Aesopic fables in a Greek metre. The date of the fables in other metres discussed.

---

[1] Aelius Lampridius, 34, 6, quoted on p. xii., *supra*, note. Cp. id. 3. 4, 'Amavit literatos homines vehementer, eos etiam reformidans, ne quid de se asperum scriberent. Denique quos dignos ad id esse videbat, singula quaeque, quae publice et privatim agebat, se ipso docente volebat addiscere, si forte ipsi non adfuissent, eosque petebat ut, si vera essent, in literas mitterent.' Id. 35, 1, 'Oratores et poetas non sibi panegyricos dicentes, quod exemplo Nigri Pescenii stultum ducebat, sed aut orationes recitantes aut facta veterum canentes libenter audivit, libentius tamen, si quis ei recitavit Alexandri Magni laudes aut meliorum retro principum aut magnorum Urbis Romae virorum,' etc. etc.

[2] For myself, I believe that the same boy is meant by both designations. There is never much made of the children of Roman emperors by their historians; and although Alexander was married at least three times, we learn the fact merely by slight references. Cp. Aelius Lampridius, 29, 2, and 49,

3, with J. Eckhel, 'Doctrina Nummorum veterum,' VII. p. 284. One of his wives—Sallustia Barbia Orbiana— may even have been related to our poet.

It shows a heart-breaking want of common sense to base a theory, as some have done, on the name Branchus, and to excogitate some connection with the Βραγχίδαι priesthood of Asiatic Ionia. Names were by this time as much mixed as races, and a Roman emperor, himself an Ἀλέξανδρος, might surely name a son Βράγχος, when his predecessor had actually been called Heliogabalus.

[3] It would be insane to lay any emphasis on the attempt of Socrates in the prison to throw into metre such fables as he could remember. The story may be no more than a Platonic myth, and at best Socrates was but trying, by the dull mechanic effort of versifying, to pass such weary hours of the thirty days as his friends were not able to spend with him. The announcement of the Thirty themselves, or even of Xanthippe and the baby, must have

cannot have been ignorant of the iambics of Phaedrus.
Taking it in this light, and grasping at the straw which
the use of the phrases σοφωτέρης μούσης and γρίφοις ὁμοίας
ποιήσεις offers, I incline to regard the few fragments of fables
that have come down to us in hexameter and elegiac verse as
specimens from the pens of the imitators whom Babrius repre-
hends in so strong language. They are printed in full below,[1]
in order that the reader may satisfy himself that the opinion

been a welcome interruption to such
labour. I need not add that I regard
with genuine suspicion the lines which
Laërtius assigns to this effort of Socrates—

Αἴσωπός ποτ' ἔλεξε Κορίνθιον ἄστυ νέμουσι
Μὴ κρίνειν ἀρετὴν λαοδίκῳ σοφίῃ.

[1] The words under which they appear in the lexicon of Suidas are printed
in spaced type, and the corresponding
Babrian fable is referred to by the
numerals on the left.

63, 1. ἠχήεις ἐτάνυσσε βαλὼν προ-
κάρηνον ἀήτης.

4. ἔστασαν οὐδὲ κόμας ψαφαρῇ
μεμίαντο κονίῃ.

64, 1. αἰπεινῇ ἐλάτῃ ἔρισεν βάτος·
ἡ μὲν ἔειπεν

5. καὶ ναῦς καὶ νηοὺς τεμνομένη
τελέειν.

7. αἰπεινὴν ἐλάτην ἔρις ὤρορεν
αἴσυλα φάσθαι.

66, 8. τοὔνεκα τὴν ἰδίην οὗτις ὄπωπε
δύην.

67, 1. ἐς βίοτον κοινωνὸς ὄνῳ γένετ'
ὠμοβόρος λίς.

5. τοῦτο μὲν οὖν πρῶτον λάχος
οἴσομαι.

93, 2. (?)   μετὰ δὲ σφίσι πιστώ-
σαντο
συνθεσίην.

4. πικροὶ μέν τε λύκοισιν, ἀτὰρ
χιμάροισιν ἀκηδεῖς.

95, 18. οὐδέ οἱ οὐδ' αἴθων ἅδε πάρδαλις, οὕνεκα θύμου
ἐμπλείη, τὸ δὲ πολλὸν
ἀγήνορα μέμφετο τίγριν.

37. κερδοῖ φηλωθεῖσα θοὴ κεμάς,
ἐγγύθι δ' ἔστη
ἠπεδανοῖο λέοντος.

59. ἡ δὲ πελιδνωθεῖσα καὶ ὄμμασι
λοξὸν ὑποδρὰξ
ὀσσομένη.

96. καὶ οἱ πορφύροντι διακριδὸν
ἀμφὶς ἕκαστα.

108, 1. θέντο μὲν ἀλλήλοισιν ἑται-
ρείην μύε δοιώ
οὐ καθ' ὁμὰ ζώοντες. ὁ μὲν
κατὰ νειὸν ἐρήμην

2. ἐτρέφεθ', ὃς δὲ δόμοισιν ἐν
ἀφνειῶν τρέφετ' ἀνδρῶν.

11. ἔνθ' ἵνα μοι βίος ἐστίν, Ἀμαλθείης κέρας αἰγός.

31. (?) λέξομαι ἐν μυχάτῳ κλισίη
δέ μοί ἐστιν ἑτοίμη.

115, 5. τίς γὰρ ἐμοὶ σεο μισθὸς ἐπάξιος,
ἤν σε διδάξω

6. ὑψοῦ ὑπὲρ πόντοιο μετα-
χρονίην ποτέεσθαι ;

9. ὅθι στυφελῶν ἐπὶ πετρῶν
ὀστρακόεντά τε νῶτα καὶ
ἀγκύλα γυῖα κεάσθη.

11. οὔτι δίκης ἀπάνευθεν ἀεικέι
δάμναμαι οἴτῳ.

122, 7. ἔκ μοι σκῶλον ἔρυσσον, ὅ μοι
κακὸν ἔμπεσεν ὁπλῇ.

141, 1. ὡς φάσαν· οὐδὲ ἄναξ ἄνεως
ἦν . . .
τί γὰρ σθένος ἔσκε σιδήρῳ,
ὑμείων εἰ μή οἱ ἐνὶ στειλειὸν
ἀρήρει ;

142, 1.   ἀλλὰ Λίβυσσα
στρουθὸς ἁλισκομένη πλάζε καὶ
ἀμφοτέρους.

Boissonade on Tzetz, Alleg. 2, p. 320,
quotes from a manuscript of John
Georgides' Gnomologia the fragment,

γαστέρα (δ' ?) ὄγκον ἔχουσαν
ἡ λεπτὴ χωρεῖν εἴσοδος οὐ δύναται,

which is from a version of the Babrian
86th. Eberhard has annotated these
fragments on p. 97 of his edition. I
reserve to my second volume the discussion of the possibility of restoring
such elegiac and hexameter fables from
the monkish prose versions, as also
the criticism of Gitlbauer's disastrous
attempt to do so.

of Babrius need not in any sense have been due to literary jealousy.

The fragment of a version in ordinary iambic trimeters of
Fables in ordinary iambic senarii are later than the choliambics of Babrius. the fable which appears in choliambics as the Babrian 115th has been preserved by Suidas under the words νῦν σωθείην—

$$νῦν δὲ σωθείην ἵνα$$
$$ᾖ μοι δίδαγμα τοῦτο τοῦ λοιποῦ χρόνου.$$

The lines may well have come in incidentally in some serious composition, and need not belong to a collection of fables in this metre; but as some of the late prose versions show traces of being adaptations from ordinary senarii, it is perhaps better to adopt the view that such a collection existed. The words of Babrius, however, make it plain that these senarii, if they ever had a real existence, must have been composed after his own choliambics; while the simplicity of the preserved fragment, short as it is, and of the prose versions, which are thought to have been derived from the same source, prevents us from including them among the γρίφοις ὁμοίας ποιήσεις which the poet's imitators published.

Accordingly there is some certainty in identifying with
Early popularity of the Babrian fables the Babrian mythiambics the *Aesopiam trimetriam* which Ausonius[1] tells us that one of the Titians[2] translated into Latin prose. If it was the elder Titian, then the verses of Babrius must have become popular almost immediately after they were published,—a conclusion confirmed by the fact that between the publication of the first and second parcels of the fables inferior men had thought it worth while to imitate them.

The favourable greeting which the fables received on their

---

[1] Ausonius, Epist. xvi. (addressed to Probus). 'Apologos Titiani . . . ad nobilitatem tuam misi'; and again,

'Apologos en misit tibi (Ausonius)
Aesopiam trimetriam
quam vertit exili stilo
pedestre concinnans opus
fandi Titianus artifex.'

See Crusius' note on p. 238.

[2] There is absolutely no evidence worthy of the name to indicate whether Ausonius meant father or son. It is quite possible that he did not himself know to which of the two the paraphrase in question was to be assigned. Those who care for the discussion of impracticable questions will find an able treatment of this in Crusius, pp. 242 ff.

first appearance seems to have passed into real and lasting popularity. About the middle of the succeeding century the Emperor Julian[1] refers to them in a way which suggests that they were well known and easily accessible. Avianus, whatever his date may be, recognised in Babrius a popular predecessor,[2] and Tzetz and Georgides display at a later date such familiarity with the mythiambics that we need not wonder that the lexicographer Suidas[3] so frequently cites them.

I have willingly forgotten the crude and fanciful theories on the age of Babrius which it was my duty to study, and which Otto Crusius has taken need-less pains to demolish in the introductory pages of his valuable dissertation. If the second preface of Babrius is genuine—and no critic has ventured to call it in question—it is beyond dispute addressed to the son of Alexander Severus.[4] Again

seems to have become perma-nent.

Fanciful theories as to Babrius.

---

[1] In Epist. 59 ad Dionysium : τὸν μῦθον ἀκήκοας—

γαλῆ ποτ᾽ ἀνδρὸς εὐπρεποῦς ἐρασθεῖσα,

τὰ δ᾽ ἄλλα ἐκ τοῦ βιβλίου μάνθανε.

The line is from Babrius 32, 1. The words τὸν Βαβρίου, which some codices insert after ἀκήκοας, are omitted in others. They are evidently a gloss. In another letter the Babrian 107th is referred to : Ep. 8, πάντως που καὶ παρὰ τῶν ἡττόνων εἶναί τι χρηστόν, ὁ μῦς τὸν λέοντα τῷ μισθῷ σώσας ἀρκούντως δείκνυσιν ; and in his Μισοπώγων the Emperor narrates the fable of the kite imitating the horse's neigh, cp. Babrius, 73. The two last instances may or may not have been taken from the Babrian collection.

[2] Avianus Theodosio, 'Has pro ex-emplo fabulas et Socrates divinis ora-culis indidit et poemati suo Flaccus aptavit, quod in se sub jocorum com-munium specie vitae argumenta con-tineant : quas Graecis iambis Babrius repetens in duo volumina coartavit, Phaedrus etiam partem aliquam quin-que in libellos resolvit.' Crusius would add Gregory of Nazianzus (see his note on p. 239) ; but considering that we have the certain testimony of his con-temporary Julian to the popularity of Babrius, we can afford to dispense with

Gregory, and prefer the Emperor to the Bishop.

[3] Perhaps Photius in the ninth, the author of the *Etymologicum Magnum* in the eleventh, and Zonaras in the twelfth century, ought also to be mentioned ; but in a work so easily interpolated as a lexicon, the less de-pendence put upon isolated glosses the less the liability to error.

[4] Since it has been shown that the choliambics,

ταῦτα δ᾽ Αἴσωπος
ὁ Σαρδιηνὸς εἶπεν, ὅντιν᾽ οἱ Δελφοί
ᾄδοντα μῦθον οὐ καλῶς ἐδέξαντο,

cited by Apollonius in his lexicon to Homer *sub vocabulo* ἄειδε, could not be by Babrius, as they violate the peculiar rules of his season, there is no author anterior to the age of Severus who quotes the Babrian fables except the grammarian Dositheus. Now, just as the citation of Apollonius would have been altogether worthless as evidence, even if the choliambics had been after the Babrian model, or had even in so many words referred to Babrius, so the appear-ance of a Babrian fable in the *Interpreta-menta* of Dositheus is no evidence either for or against any given date. The interpolation of Apollonius' Lexicon is allowed by its editors (see Villoison's *Prolegomena*, pp. xxxvii. sqq.) ; and any

and again does the term βασιλεύς occur in the pages of
Herodian and Dion as the most natural Greek equivalent for
emperor, and in referring to Severus the name Ἀλέξανδρος is
preferred by Herodian, as it would certainly be preferred by any
other Greek writer. It is the duty of every scholar to speak his
honest word on the side of self-control, and against the indulgence
of the fancy and love of novelty which the theories on the age of
Babrius so forcibly illustrate. Ignorance of an ancient language,
together with a dictionary of proper names, will yield material
enough to supply volumes of theories on the age and personality
of any author who has used that language. If I have
succeeded in clearing away the accumulations and obstructions
produced by such theorising, and have preferred the word of
Babrius himself to that of his scholiasts, I am well content to
remain ignorant of those incidents in the life of my author
which would be little likely to add anything worth knowing to
the sum of true learning, or to the history of human experience.
As it is, there may yet be some one who would emphasise
the last words in the Aristophanic citation—

$$\text{τοῦτο γάρ τοι καὶ μόνον}$$
$$\text{ἔτ' ἐστὶ λοιπὸν ἀγαθόν, εἰ καὶ τοῦτ' ἄρα,}$$

but for myself I would be loth to carry the line further than
the ἀγαθόν, or to allow sceptical indolence to overrule my
understanding.

---

one who will take the trouble to read
Böcking's edition of the Third Book of
the *Interpretamenta* of Dositheus will
find it difficult to credit how such a
congeries of corruption and interpolation found an editor at all. For
damning evidence of its authenticity
the reader is referred to Boucherie and
Crusius, in the latter's note on p. 238
of his dissertation.

CHAPTER II.

THE HISTORY OF GREEK FABLE.

HEAVY as is the blow which Benfey's edition of the Pantscha-
Tantra dealt on the theory[1] which derives the *The theories of Oriental origin*
fables of Greece from an Oriental source, it might *for the Aesopic fable now proved*
have been made much heavier by a discussion of the *to be erroneous.*
way in which the Greeks and the Orientals handle the fable in
their respective literatures. The first thought which will occur
to most English readers of the Pantscha-Tantra and the Kalilah
and Dimnah is the childishness of the whole, the indications
on all sides of the Oriental love of support, whether moral or
physical, and the absence of any great originality. Throughout the perusal of their contents the feeling will never be far
off that grown men who could derive any profit from such
writings are men on whom a great literature would have been
thrown away. Page follows page of weak moralising, capped
by a so-called fable. Κύνες πρὸς ἔμετον indeed !

[1] There is a very large collection of treatises bearing on this subject by Loiseleur des Longchamps, Wilson, Dubois, Silvestre de Sacy, Édélstand du Méril, A. Wagener, and others ; but they are all merely tentative, and have been quite superseded by Benfey's elaborate work on the Pantscha-Tantra and Kalilah and Dimnah. The study of Pali in the able hands of Mr. Rhys Davids and other scholars has reopened the question within recent years (see especially *Buddhist Birth Stories, or Jataka Tales, the oldest collection of Folk Lore extant, being the Jātakaa thavannanā for the first time edited in the original Pali by V. Fausböll, and translated by J. W. Rhys Davids*, 1880). I am sure, how-ever, that they will acknowledge that the facts to be stated in this essay make it plain that the Greeks were familiar with fable long before the Pali texts were written.

As late as 1880 Eugène Lévêque recurred to the wildest speculations of the earlier writers in his book, *Les Mythes et Légendes de l'Inde et la Perse dans Aristophane, Platon, Aristote, etc.*, which, by its great want of critical method and mad enthusiasm, gives the *coup de grâce* to the theory which it would fain support. Dr. J. Landsberger's book, *Die Fabeln des Sophos Syrisches Original der Griechischen Fabeln des Syntipas*, Posen, 1859, is still less critical.

It is among the professional rhetors of degenerate Greece, and their successors, the illiterate and trivial monks of the Middle Ages, that we must look for work at all corresponding to these Oriental books. The fabulists of India and of medieval Europe are tarred with the same stick. They have both tried to make a drink for strong men out of the sugared milk on which children thrive. If they found hearers it was because there was no vigorous intellectual vitality in the peoples whom they addressed.

The dotard juryman in Aristophanes, when reminded that

The Greeks of the best age evidently familiar with fable. there are men at his elbow who expect something worth listening to, begins first to babble of mythology. But his son cuts him short, and asks for matter in the quotidian vein ; and when the old man, with senile perversity, begins the fable of the Cat and the Mouse, his son's temper at last gives out. After a vocative, too irreverent even for democratic Athens, he launches the rude interrogation, 'Do you really mean to talk of cats and mice to grown-up men ?'

μῖς καὶ γαλᾶς μέλλεις λέγειν ἐν ἀνδράσιν ;

There is some difference here between the Greek and the Oriental. The Greeks, I believe, were as a nation steeped to the heart in fable. At their nurses' knees they learned the lore of birds and beasts and inanimate things endowed with the faculty of intelligible intercourse. It was the lowest stratum of their knowledge, underlying even that concerning the gods and heroes, and was as much a part of themselves as were the natural features of the country in which they grew up, the house in which they were born, the dove-cot and its occupants, the midden at the door.[1]

In fact, fable was a common background of knowledge

They used it for literary illustration, either directly or by allusion. Hesiod. for all, which might be made use of in literature for purposes of illustration in the same way as the other main constituent of that primitive learning which men drank in with their mother's milk — the familiar and loving knowledge of the beauty of

---

[1] Even in Attica, where there ran a stronger current of change than in any other part of Greece, the strength of these early associations is proved by

natural scenery.　In the noble age of Greek literature both sorts of lore are utilised in much the same way, whether directly or by that subtle form of allusion in which a single word or two aptly selected serve to flash upon the inner eye a mental landscape of associated memories.　The homely verse of Hesiod furnishes an example of the direct method of using fable in literature.　The true place which the lines ought to occupy in the *Works and Days* I believe to be doubtful; but the lesson which they are meant to enforce is plain enough :—

> ὧδ' ἴρηξ προσέειπεν ἀηδόνα ποικιλόδειρον,
> ὕψι μάλ' ἐν νεφέεσσι φέρων ὀνύχεσσι μεμαρπώς·
> ἡ δ' ἐλεόν, γναμπτοῖσι πεπαρμένη ἀμφ' ὀνύχεσσι,
> μύρετο· τὴν δ' ὅγ' ἐπικρατέως πρὸς μῦθον ἔειπεν·
> ' Δαιμονίη, τί λέληκας; ἔχει νύ σε πολλὸν ἀρείων·
> τῇδ' εἶς ᾗ σ' ἂν ἐγώ περ ἄγω καὶ ἀοιδὸν ἐοῦσαν·
> δεῖπνον δ', αἴ κ' ἐθέλω, ποιήσομαι ἠὲ μεθήσω.'
> ὣς ἔφατ' ὠκυπέτης ἴρηξ, τανυσίπτερος ὄρνις.—Op. et Di. 203.

Of the allusive method of using fable there are some notably fine instances.　In three words Solon brings home to the hearts of the Athenians that in allowing Pisistratus to make himself despot, they have been acting the part of the stag in the fable, and following at the heels of the crafty fox to the lion's den— *Instances of the allusive manner of employing fable in Greek literature. Solon, Sophocles.*

> ὑμέων δ' εἶς μὲν ἕκαστος ἀλώπεκος ἴχνεσι βαίνει,
> ξύμπασιν δ' ὑμῖν κοῦφος ἔνεστι νόος·
> εἰς γὰρ γλῶσσαν ὁρᾶτε καὶ εἰς ἔπος αἰόλον ἀνδρός,
> εἰς ἔργον δ' οὐδὲν γιγνόμενον βλέπετε.[1]

With somewhat less skill the fable of the north wind and the sun trying their power upon a wayfarer [2] is worked into an epigram of Sophocles addressed to Euripides.　It is stained too black with Greek manners to be cited here, but the learned will find it in Athenaeus.[3]

---

the way in which old Ionic names for domestic objects did not assume the Attic form.　Thus περιστερεών, 'dovecot,' did not pass into περιστερών, or βολεών, 'midden,' into βολών.
[1] Quoted by Diog. Laert. I. 51, ὅτε

τὸν Πεισίστρατον ἔμαθεν ἤδη τυραννεῖν, τάδε ἔγραψε πρὸς τοὺς Ἀθηναίους, see Babrius, 95.　[2] See Babrius, 18.
[3] Athen. xiii. 604 D, καὶ Ἱερώνυμος δ' ὁ Ῥόδιος ἐν τοῖς ἱστορικοῖς ὑπομνήμασὶ φησιν ὅτι Σοφοκλῆς κτε.

Tennyson has used fables after this fashion, sometimes with
dignity and effect, even in compositions of the
more elevated kind:—

> 'Refer my cause, my crown to Rome ! . . . The wolf
> Mudded the brook, and predetermined all.'

> 'Our wild Tostig,
> Edward hath made him Earl : he would be King:—
> The dog that snapt the shadow, dropt the bone.'

Perhaps better examples might be discovered than these two ;
but it would be impossible to find in English literature a bolder
or more effective instance of the illustrative value of fable than
the ἀλώπεκος ἴχνεσι βαίνει of Solon's elegiacs.

There is another point which must not be overlooked in
Did the Greeks
produce new
fables in the best
period of their
literature?
Plato. discussing the place which fable holds in the
nobler regions of Greek literature. The question
has to be asked, how far the Greeks went in
producing new fables after the pattern of the
old. A passage of Plato bears so directly upon this subject
that I will quote it in full without apology, especially as the
translator's English will make a pleasant break in our dull
discourse. 'And when Xanthippe was gone, Socrates, sitting
up on the couch, began to bend and rub his leg, saying as he
rubbed : How singular is the thing called pleasure, and how
curiously related to pain, which might be thought to be the
opposite of it ; for they never come to a man together, and yet
he who pursues either of them is generally compelled to take
the other. They are two, and yet they grow together out of
one head or stem ; and I cannot help thinking that if Aesop
had noticed them[1] he would have made a fable about God
trying to reconcile their strife, and when he could not, he
fastened their heads together ; and this is the reason why, when
one comes the other follows, as I find in my own case pleasure
comes following after the pain in my leg which was caused by
the chain.'[2] This passage, if taken along with the three purely
Platonic fables, all of a like philosophical cast to the apologue
here suggested—the fable of the Grasshoppers,[3] of Plenty and

---

[1] καί μοι δοκεῖ, ἔφη, εἰ ἐνενόησεν αὐτὰ
Αἴσωπος, μῦθον ἂν συνθεῖναι ὡς κτλ.

[2] Phaedo. 60, Jowett's translation.
[3] Phaedr. 259.

Poverty,[1] and of the Art of Government [2]—furnishes sufficient
evidence that fable was regarded, in the great age of Greek
literature, as a living organism, not merely as a fixed and
unalterable aggregate of traditional lore.

The Platonic pattern, however, was certainly not that on
which additional apologues were modelled by the
crowd, although it accords so well with the Greek
estimate of fable in one important respect—its employment
for the literary purposes of ornament and illustration. From
certain passages of Aristophanes and other writers, we learn
that it was a practice, not only to repeat, but also to invent,
new fables and stories of a sort likely to excite mirth at sym-
posia and other festive gatherings. He was a dull fellow and
an idler who neither knew the old fables nor had wit, at all
events, to pass the new into currency if he could not invent
them himself. 'Drinking is no joke,' says Philocleon in the
Wasps; 'to say nothing of the headache of the next morning, a
man has also to pay up for knocking somebody down.' 'There
is no difficulty at all,' replies his son, 'provided they are
gentlemen with whom you have been drinking. For either
they get your victim to let you off, or of yourself you win his
pardon, turning the whole affair into a joke by some happy tale
of Aesop or of Sybaris (αἰσωπικὸν γέλοιον ἢ συβαριτικόν)
which you have picked up during the evening.' A little
further on in the play we are supplied with an example of
the αἰσωπικὸν γέλοιον when Philocleon tries to check, by
means of an extempore fable of his own, the abuse of a woman
whose basket of loaves he has knocked over. It will be
observed that his λόγος δεξιός is not such as he would have
chosen in a soberer moment, or one likely to flatter the self-
love of the market woman.

Αἴσωπον ἀπὸ δείπνου βαδίζονθ' ἑσπέρας
θρασεῖα καὶ μεθύση τις ὑλάκτει κύων.
κἄπειτ' ἐκεῖνος εἶπεν, ὦ κύον, κύον,
εἰ νὴ Δί' ἀντὶ τῆς κακῆς γλώττης ποθὲν
πυροὺς πρίαιο, σωφρονεῖν ἄν μοι δοκεῖς.—Vesp. 1401.

But it is high time to inquire who this Aesop was whose

vein it had become the fashion to imitate. Of that broad

Who was Aesop? Bentley's dissertation. The evidence of Herodotus. current of genius, so commanding, so impatient of obstructions, with which Bentley cleansed the Augean stables of classical philology, one rivulet was turned our way. The dissertation upon the fables of Aesop demonstrated the insecurity of the fabulist's position, but it left him something more than a name. Modern criticism must go further still, and content itself with knowing nothing, or next to nothing. From a passing mention in Herodotus, the earliest author in whom his name appears, it is very evident that the Greeks even of that time knew little about him. After stating that the proverbial beauty Rhodôpis was the slave of the Samian Iadmon and a contemporary of Sappho, he adds that Aesop was also a slave of Iadmon's at the same time as Rhodôpis. His proof is not of the best, amounting only to this, that Iadmon's grandson was the only man who answered the proclamation which the oracle instigated the Delphians to make, setting forth that any man who chose might exact the penalty for Aesop's life.[1] It is, however, observable that the way in which this penalty is referred to,—the words actually leaving it doubtful whether the Delphians were themselves responsible for Aesop's death or not,—leads us to infer that Herodotus was counting on a fairly general tradition with regard to Aesop. A few lines of Aristophanes make it certain that this tradition credited the Delphians with the crime—

    A. Αἴσωπον οἱ Δελφοί ποτ'.
                          B. ὀλίγον μοι μέλει.
    A. φιάλην ἐπῃτιῶντο κλέψαι τοῦ θεοῦ·
      ὁ δ' ἔλεξεν αὐτοῖς, ὡς ὁ κάνθαρός ποτε.
    B. οἴμ' ὡς ἀπόλοι' αὐτοῖσι τοῖς σοῖς κανθάροις.—Vesp. 1446.

---

[1] Hdt. ii. 134, 135. All that we elsewhere learn from Plutarch, rhetors, and scholiasts regarding Aesop need be no more than an unsubstantial superstructure raised upon this unsubstantial foundation. The date of Rhodôpis Herodotus had probably means of authenticating from the votive offerings which in ch. 135 he states that she placed in the temple at Delphi. His theory as to Aesop being a fellow-slave of hers would, if accepted, at once make him a contemporary of Solon and Croesus; and the fabrications of Plutarch and Co. five centuries or so after Herodotus' time are easily explained. In fact the most reasonable explanation of the late statements as to Aesop's connection with Croesus is that offered here. Plutarch is for Aesop, even granting the date assigned by Herodotus, not so good an authority

On the whole Herodotus was probably not far out in the date which he assigned to Aesop. At all events the custom of referring fables to Aesop is unknown to Greek writers anterior to that date, so far as they have come down to us, whereas in later times it is general.

We have seen both Hesiod and Solon employing fable without any reference to Aesop, and the same is true of all writers between the two dates represented by their names. Thus Archilochus begins one fable with the words— The date suggested by Herodotus approximately correct. Archilochus never mentions the name of Aesop.

> Αἶνός τις ἀνθρώπων ὅδε,
> ὡς ἄρ' ἀλώπηξ καἰετὸς ξυνωνίην
> ἔμιξαν·

and another in a like general way—

> Ἐρέω τιν' ὑμῖν αἶνον, ὦ Κηρυκίδη·
> ἀχνυμένῃ σκυτάλῃ·
> πίθηκος ᾖει θηρίων ἀποκριθεὶς
> μοῦνος ἀν' ἐσχατιήν·
> τῷ δ' ἄρ' ἀλώπηξ κερδαλέη συνήντετο
> πυκνὸν ἔχουσα νόον.

and it is likely that we have also the opening of a fable in the words—

> Βοῦς ἐστὶν ἡμῖν ἐργάτης ἐν οἰκίῃ
> κορωνός, ἔργων ἴδρις.[1]

---

as a modern journalist would be for Dick Whittington; and as for the scholiasts on Aristophanes, there is not a single scholion which bears traces of being by even a moderately early hand, except a few words on Av. 651, which we shall afterwards make use of.

[1] The two first fragments are preserved in Ammonius, 'de voc. differentia,' ch. 6, and the third in Etym. Mag. sub voc. κορωνός. Two other portions of the first are also found—the one in a passage of Atticus cited by Eusebius, 'Praeparatio Evangelica,' xv. 795 A.

> ὁρᾷς ἵν' ἔστ' ἐκεῖνος ὑψηλὸς πάγος
> τρηχύς τε καὶ παλίγκοτος,
> ἐν τῷ κάθημαι, σὴν ἐλαφρίζων μάχην·

the other in Stobaeus, Eclog. Phys. i. 122—

> ὦ Ζεῦ, πάτερ Ζεῦ, σὸν μὲν οὐρανοῦ κράτος,
> σὺ δ' ἔργ' ἐπ' ἀνθρώπων ὁρᾷς
> λεωργὰ καὶ θεμιστά, σοὶ δὲ θηρίων
> ὕβρις τε καὶ δίκη μέλει.

The fable appears to have been in the Babrian collection, as there is a prose version in the Bodleian paraphrase No. 139, but evidently poverty - stricken when compared with the wealth of its original Archilochian shape.

The form which the second fable of the Fox and the Ape had when complete must remain obscure. It may have been the original of the miserable Babrian tetrastich 81; but if the words ἀχνυμένη σκυτάλη mean 'sad is its burden,' there is little likelihood in such a conjecture. According to Athenaeus (iii. 85 E), the critic Aristophanes had a treatise 'περὶ τῆς ἀχνυμένης σκυτάλης' and Apollonius Rhodius

An instance from Simonides of Amorgus teaches the same lesson—

> Ἐρῳδιὸς γὰρ ἔγχελυν Μαιανδρίην
> τρίορχον εὑρὼν ἐσθίοντ᾽ ἀφείλετο.[1]

Moreover the scholion,

> ὁ καρκίνος ὧδ᾽ ἔφα
> χαλᾷ τὸν ὄφιν λαβών.
> εὐθὺν χρὴ τὸν ἑταῖρον ἔμμεν
> καὶ μὴ σκολιὰ φρονεῖν,[2]

ought certainly to have a place here, as it has every appearance of age and simplicity.

---

discussed the question 'ἐν τῷ περὶ Ἀρχιλόχου' (Ath. x. 451 D.) These three are the only fragments of Archilochus which supply the beginnings of fables, although there are others which prove that Archilochus was fond of this manner of illustrating his verse. The words ῥόπτρῳ ἐρειδόμενον preserved in the *Etymologicum Magnum* sub voc. σκανδάληθρον may carry us back to the 130th Babrian fable, as do ὑφ᾽ ἡδονῆς σαλευμένη κορώνη (Schol. to Aratus, 1009) to the Babrian 77th. The Athenaean citations,

> χολὴν γὰρ οὐχ ἔχεις ἐφ᾽ ἥπατι (Ath. 3, 107 F.), and
> πάρελθε, γενναῖος γὰρ εἶς (Ath. 14, 653 D.),

have been with some probability referred by Bergk to the 95th in the Babrian collection, to which also it is not impossible that another fragment,

> πόδες δὴ κεῖθι τιμιώτατοι (Plut. de Garrulitate, ch. 2),

may belong. The line,

> τοιήνδε δ᾽, ὦ πίθηκε, τὴν πυγὴν ἔχων,

parodied by Aristophanes in Ach. 120, and preserved in a scholion *in loco* certainly falls into this note. I also see in the *senarius* (preserved in Orion's Lexicon, 37, 4),

> κατ᾽ οἶκον ἐστρωφᾶτο μισητὸς βάβαξ,

part of the original of the Babrian 135th, and recognise the remote possibility of the corrupt

> ἃ δέκα (var. ll. ἃ ἴαδ᾽ εἴς τε) ταύρους

belonging to the Babrian 44th.

The nursery antithesis between the hedgehog's single mode of avenging injuries and the legion at the fox's command, had by the time of Archilochus got summed up in the proverb—

> πόλλ᾽ οἶδ᾽ ἀλώπηξ ἀλλ᾽ ἐχῖνος ἕν μέγα,

as it is referred to in a fragment preserved by Bishop Theophilus 'ad Autolycum,' 2, 37—

> ἐν δ᾽ ἐπίσταμαι μέγα
> τὸν κακῶς με δρῶντα δεινοῖς ἀνταμείβεσθαι κακοῖς.

[1] Athen. 7, 299 C.
[2] Preserved by Athenaeus, 15, 695 A. Cp. Aristoph. Pax, 1083—

> οὔποτε ποιήσεις τὸν καρκίνον ὀρθὰ βαδίζειν.

Id. 1086—

> οὐδέποτ᾽ ἂν θείης λεῖον τὸν τρηχὺν ἐχῖνον.

Cp. Babrius, 109. Coraes (whom Benfey copies), in the preface to his edition of the Aesopic fables, wrongly sets it down to Alcaeus—not the only erroneous and uncritical statement in that long-winded dissertation.

Besides the authors quoted in the text, perhaps Theognis ought to be mentioned. The only passage, however, in which he uses fable is corrupt ; and at best the use is not direct but only allusive, l. 599—

> οὔ μ᾽ ἔλαθες φοιτῶν κατ᾽ ἀμαξιτόν, ἣν ἄρα καὶ πρὶν
> ἠλάστρεις, κλέπτων ἡμετέρην φιλίην.
> ἔρρε, θεοῖσίν τ᾽ ἐχθρὲ καὶ ἀνθρώποισιν ἄπιστε,
> ψυχρὸν ὃν ἐν κόλπῳ ποικίλον εἶχον ὄφιν.

This argument drawn from silence would be strengthened if the same were found to be true of the writers most closely following upon the date proposed by Herodotus for the patron saint of fable. But unfortunately in those portions of their works which have come down to us no apologues happen to be employed.[1] Certainly, even at a much later date, Herodotus makes no reference to Aesop in narrating the fable of the piper turned fisherman, which was the only reply vouchsafed by the victorious Cyrus to the prayer of the Ionians and Aeolians that they should serve him on the same conditions as they had served Croesus.[2]

The usage of other writers anterior to Herodotus and of Herodotus himself.

But when we come to Aristophanes, and writers subsequent to him, it is the exception if Aesop's name is not mentioned in introducing a fable. The passages already cited from the Attic comedian support this statement, and there are others which we will go on to quote.

The manner of introducing a fable with Aesop's name dates from the days of Aristophanes.

To his daughter's anxious inquiry—

τίς δ' ἡ 'πίνοιά σούστὶν ὥστε κάνθαρον
ζεύξαντ' ἐλαύνειν ἐς θεούς, ὦ παππία ;

I have adopted the correction of Sintenis. The manuscripts have δς and εἶχες.

Stesichorus is said by Aristotle (Plutarch and the grammarian Conon agree with him) to have addressed the story of the horse that asked a man to help it against a stag to the people of Himera when they were about to give a bodyguard to Phalaris.—Arist. Rhet. ii. 20 (1393ᵇ 10). Even although Aesop is not mentioned in Aristotle's account, we can infer nothing from his words as to the actual way in which Stesichorus introduced the fable in his prose address.

[1] It is true that Theon, in his Progymnasmata (Walz, i. 159), probably instances Hecataeus as having used some fable or other; but the historian's name rests only on a conjecture, and at best Theon's authority is of the poorest.

[2] Hdt. i. 141. The fable was also

known to Ennius, as is shown by a line preserved in Varro—

'Súbulo quondám marinas própter adstabát plagas.'

See Vahlen, 'Ennianae poesis Reliquiae,' p. 151.

The Babrian version (No. 9) differs in substituting a fisherman for a piper, which at first sight is a deterioration, but cp. Aelian, Nat. An. i. 39, θηρῶσι τὰς τρυγόνας οἱ καὶ τούτων ἀκριβοῦντες τὰ θήρατρα καὶ μάλιστα τῆς πείρας οὐ διαμαρτάνουσι τὸν τρόπον τοῦτον. Ἑστήκασιν ὀρχούμενοι καὶ ἄδοντες εὖ μάλα μουσικῶς. αἱ δὲ τῇ ἀκοῇ θέλγονται καὶ τῇ ὄψει τῆς ὀρχήσεως κηλοῦνται καὶ προσίασιν ἐγγυτέρω. οἱ δὲ ὑπαναχωροῦσιν ἡσυχῇ καὶ βάδην ἔνθα δήπου καὶ ὁ δόλος ταῖς δειλαίαις πρόκειται, δίκτυα ἐκπεπετασμένα. Cp. id. xvii. 18. The proverb ἄλλως ᾄδεις may be a condensation of this fable, Zenob. 1, 72. Aristaenetus founds a whole epistle upon the proverb, Ep. i. 27.

Trugaeus has an answer ready in a parody of an *Aesopic* fable—

> ἐν τοῖσιν Αἰσώπου λόγοις ἐξηυρέθη
> μόνος πετεινῶν ἐς θεοὺς ἀφιγμένος.
> ἦλθεν κατ' ἔχθραν ἀετοῦ πάλαι ποτέ,
> ᾧ' ἐκκυλίνδων κἀντιτιμωρούμενος.[1]

It is by an *Aesopic* fable that Pisthetaerus proves his assertion that the birds are primeval and more ancient than the Earth and Kronus himself. When his feathered audience greet his words with incredulous surprise, he answers disdainfully—

> ἀμαθὴς γὰρ ἔφυς κοὐ πολυπράγμων, οὐδ' Αἴσωπον πεπάτηκας,
> ὃς ἔφασκε λέγων κορυδὸν πάντων πρώτην ὄρνιθα γενέσθαι,
> προτέραν τῆς γῆς, κἄπειτα νόσῳ τὸν πατέρ' αὐτῆς ἀποθνῄσκειν·
> γῆν δ' οὐκ εἶναι, τὸν δὲ προκεῖσθαι πεμπταῖον· τὴν δ' ἀποροῦσαν
> ὑπ' ἀμηχανίας τὸν πατέρ' αὐτῆς ἐν τῇ κεφαλῇ κατορύξαι.[2]

Moreover, it is from *Aesop* that Pisthetaerus takes his objection to consorting with the birds—

> ὅρα νυν ὡς ἐν Αἰσώπου λόγοις
> ἐστὶν λεγόμενον δή τι, τὴν ἀλώπεχ', ὡς
> φλαύρως ἐκοινώνησεν ἀετῷ ποτέ.[3]

---

[1] Pax, 127. It is better to regard this as a parody of the fable found in Archilochus (see p. xxxi.; cp. Cor<es 1) than another version of it. The scholiasts take it in sober earnest, one presenting the note, 'Ἐν τοῖσιν Αἰσώπου· τοῦ μυθοποιοῦ. φέρεται γὰρ αὐτοῦ μῦθος, ἐχθρεῦσαι ἀετὸν καὶ κάνθαρον ἐκ τοῦ ἑκάτερον αὐτῶν θατέρου τὰ ᾠὰ διασπᾶν, and another manufacturing a suitable fable, ὁ λόγος τοιοῦτός ἐστιν. ἁρπάζοντος τοῦ ἀετοῦ τοὺς νεοττοὺς τοῦ κανθάρου, καὶ ὁ κάνθαρος τὰ ᾠὰ τοῦ ἀετοῦ ἐκκλέψας ἐξεκύλισεν ἕως τοσούτου, ἕως ἦλθεν πρὸς τὸν Δία. κατηγοροῦντος δὲ τοῦ ἀετοῦ προσέταξεν ὁ Ζεὺς τῷ ἀετῷ ἐν τῷ αὑτοῦ (τοῦ Διὸς) κόλπῳ νεοττεύειν. ἐπειδὴ δὲ τὰ ᾠὰ εἶχεν ὁ Ζεύς, περίπτα τὸν Δία ὁ κάνθαρος, ὁ δὲ ἐκλαθόμενος ἀνέστη ὡς σοβήσων ἐκ τῆς κεφαλῆς αὐτὸν καὶ κατέαξε τὰ ᾠά.—ὁ δὲ λόγος πρὸς τοὺς ἀδίκους ἐστίν, ὅτι οὐδεμία ἐστὶν αὐτοῖς ἀσφάλεια, οὐδ' ἂν εἰς τὸν κόλπον τοῦ Διὸς καταφύγωσι, διαφεύξονται τὴν τιμωρίαν.
[2] Av. 471. It would be rash to see in this more than an invention of Aristophanes himself. Uncritical and unreasoning as most of the compilers of fable were, none of them gave this a place in their collections until a modern Greek inserted it among them.

The phrase οὐδ' Αἴσωπον πεπάτηκας has given some trouble. In the *Phaedrus*, 273 A, Plato has its fellow—ἀλλὰ μὴν τόν γε Τισίαν αὐτὸν πεπάτηκας ἀκριβῶς. The explanation I believe to be this. Diogenian, 2, 95, has preserved the proverb Ἀρχίλοχον πατεῖς· ἐπὶ τῶν λοιδορούντων. τοιοῦτος γὰρ ὁ Ἀρχίλοχος· and Eustathius on Odyssey, 11, 277 (1684, 47), has the words καὶ παροιμία ἐπὶ τῶν σκώπτειν εὐφυῶν τό Ἀρχίλοχον πεπάτηκας ὡς εἴ τις εἴπῃ, σκόρπιον ἢ ὄφιν ἢ κακὴν ἄκανθαν. The phrase was first used of Archilochus for the reason given by Eustathius. But we have already seen that a prominent feature in the poems of Archilochus was his love for illustration by fable; and it was an easy thing for Aristophanes to transfer the phrase, with much of its significance already lost, from the one sphere to the other, and even from Archilochus himself to the rival whom the example of Aristophanes must, I believe, have done much to enthrone in his place. The saying once tampered with, and that too by Aristophanes, it was easy for Plato even further to extend the misuse.
[3] Aves, 651, see p. xxxi., and note there. Benfey believes that it passed

On this passage is found the one valuable scholion of all relating to Aesop in his Aristophanic connection—ὅτι σαφῶς ἀνετίθεσαν Αἰσώπῳ τοὺς λόγους, καὶ τοῦτον τὸν παρὰ Ἀρχιλόχῳ λεγόμενον καίτοι πρεσβυτέρῳ ὄντι. It bears the marks of being by one of the more ancient critics trained in the traditions of the early Alexandrine schools.

These facts, I believe, justify us in seeing in Aristophanes the mouthpiece of a tendency to exalt Aesop into the high priest of Fable, which appears to have been gradually[1] gathering strength, and to have reached a climax in the literary circles of Athens about the meeting-point of the fifth and fourth centuries before the Christian era. In my judgment it cannot be explained except by regarding Aesop as a real personage, imbued with the spirit of that primeval lore of fable which all peoples seem to have once possessed in a greater or less degree, and which the Greeks, if their place in intellectual history means anything at all, must have preserved with more than common

Results of the preceding evidence. Aesop a real personage.

into the Pantscha-Tantra through the Greek empire in Asia. See his edition, vol. i. p. 383.

The other passages of Aristophanes which show an intimate familiarity with fable do so in allusion merely. Vesp. 1240—

οὐκ ἔστιν ἀλωπεκίζειν
οὐδ' ἀμφοτέροισι γίγνεσθαι φίλον,

in which the word ἀλωπεκίζειν (probably coined by Aristophanes, cp. Bab. 95, 63) calls up a whole series of adventures in apologue, in which double-faced craft triumphs over innocence and strength. Pax, 1189—

ὄντες οἴκοι μὲν λέοντες
ἐν μάχῃ δ' ἀλώπεκες.

Both Vesp. 375—

τὸν περὶ ψυχῆς δρόμον δραμεῖν,

and Ran. 191—

δοῦλον οὐκ ἄγω,
εἰ μὴ νεναυμάχηκε τὴν περὶ τῶν κρεῶν,

imply an acquaintance with the original of the Babrian 69th. Cp. Zenobius, 4, 85, Λαγὼς τὸν περὶ τῶν κρεῶν τρέχων.

It would, however, be much too fine to see in Vesp. 1122—

οὔ τοί ποτε ζῶν τοῦτον ἀποδυθήσομαι
ἐπεὶ μόνος μ' ἔσωσε παρατεταγμένον
ὅθ' ὁ βορέας ὁ μέγας ἐπεστρατεύσατο,

any allusion, even the slightest, to the struggle between North Wind and Sun. The lines refer beyond dispute only to the great wind at Artemisium, or to some other campaigning experience.

[1] It is fully exemplified in Plato (see *supra*, p. xxviii.), *e.g.* Alc. 122 E, χρυσίον καὶ ἀργύριον οὐκ ἔστιν ἐν πᾶσιν Ἕλλησιν ὅσον ἐν Λακεδαίμονι ἰδίᾳ. πολλὰς γὰρ ἤδη γενεὰς εἰσέρχεται μὲν αὐτόσε ἐξ ἁπάντων τῶν Ἑλλήνων, πολλάκις δὲ καὶ ἐκ τῶν βαρβάρων, ἐξέρχεται δὲ οὐδαμόσε, ἀλλ' ἀτεχνῶς κατὰ τὸν Αἰσώπου μῦθον, ὃν ἡ ἀλώπηξ πρὸς τὸν λέοντα εἶπεν, καὶ τοῦ εἰς Λακεδαίμονα νομίσματος εἰσιόντος μὲν τὰ ἴχνη τὰ ἐκεῖσε τετραμμένα δῆλα, ἐξιόντος δὲ οὐδαμῇ ἄν τις ἴδοι. But Xenophon (Memorab. 2, 7, 13) introduces the fable of the sheep that found fault with their master's favouritism for the dog (the Babrian 128th) with a simple φασὶ γάρ.

precision. Moreover, this Aesop was able to extract from its traditional embodiment so much of the primitive naturalness and essential simplicity of fable that to the new apologues which he formed after the old types men were so partial that his name became associated with all. He was the children's Homer, and the willing lips of granddames and nurses preserved his λόγοι, μῦθοι, or αἶνοι, with as loving care as the ῥαψῳδοί devoted to the ἔπη of Homer.

The name Aesop is probably Greek, although its derivation
Origin of the name Αἴσωπος as yet unknown. is unknown.[1] One thing is certain—that Greek was the language which he used; and it is hardly less manifest that he was more at home in Greece than anywhere else. The suspicion of a foreign note would make inexplicable the warmth of the greeting which his apologues received throughout the Grecian world. He may have been a slave, as Herodotus says,—one of that large class of Greeks whom the fortune of war expatriated and forced to serve men of the same race and language with themselves. Even the date assigned to him by Herodotus may well be approximately true. As is shown above, it fairly agrees with such facts as we can glean from literature; while the two fragments of tradition which have been preserved in Herodotus and Aristophanes point to a date lying on the confines of oral and written history.

It were idle for me to discuss the origin of those tradi-
The question as to the ultimate sources of fable left in abler hands. tional myths from which Aesop drew his inspiration, and which are now blended in one aggregate with those consciously modelled after their pattern. There are able workers in this region of the origines of human thought from whom I am well content to await instruction, for the fine threads of primeval lore require handling more delicate than my rude fingers can give.

---

[1] Besides the Roman actor of the name, there is mentioned in literature an historian Αἴσωπος, whose life of Alexander the Great has been preserved in a Latin translation by Julius Valerius.

The whole story of Aesop's ill looks doubtless originated in a derivation of the name from αἰσχρός and ὤψ,—a conjecture which does not require the stupidity of the monk's *Life of Aesop* to confirm it, as even the best of ancient philologists confidently credited even lamer derivations. Even Eustathius derived the name from αἴθω and ὤψ.

The Progymnasmata of Aphthonius, Hermogenes, Theon, and the other rhetors, supply some statements which those who care to trust in such broken reeds will find repeated *ad nauseam* in the pages of Walz's edition. The only fact worth having which they have preserved is that Aeschylus spoke of one myth as Libyan in origin, and even that we have in a fuller shape in other writers. As preserved by a scholiast on Aristophanes, Av. 808, the lines of , the *Myrmidons* in which this important fact has been embalmed represent the Aeschylean equivalent of the 'Engineer hoist with his own petard '— The statements of the Greek rhetors. Aeschylus speaks of Libyan fable.

> ὧδ' ἐστὶ μύθων τῶν Λιβυστικῶν κλέος,
> πληγέντ' ἀτράκτῳ τοξικῷ τὸν αἰετὸν
> εἰπεῖν ἰδόντα μηχανὴν πτερώματος·
> τάδ' οὐχ ὑπ' ἄλλων, ἀλλὰ τοῖς αὐτῶν πτεροῖς
> ἁλισκόμεσθα.

Diogenian[1] even knows the name of the Libyan fabulist—οἱ δὲ Κύβισσαν (v. l. Κύβισαν) εὑρέτην γενέσθαι τοῦ εἴδους τούτου —a piece of erudition which has served to correct the Athoan λιβύσσης of the second Babrian preface into Κιβύσσης. The correction is right enough, but, for my part, I should not wonder if the Athoan misreading is simply the converse of what had happened at a much earlier date to the authorities on which Diogenian and Babrius had to depend, and that the black man's name originated in some corruption of Λίβυς, Λιβυκός, or Λιβυστικός.[2]

Our little masters, the rhetors, know many other sources of fable, but we will lose nothing if we leave them to cool their heels in the anteroom while we con- The rhetors again. The Alexandrine poets.

---

[1] P. 180. The statement also appears in Theon (Walz, I. p. 172), καὶ Κύβισσος ἐκ Λιβύης μνημονεύεται ὑπὸ τινων ὡς μυθοποιός.

[2] 'Mirum non est recentiores Graeculos graviter errare, quum constet ipsos *veteres* in ea re titubasse. Turpis error est Athenaei xi. p. 500, ubi de voce σκύφος disserens ex Ephoro haec affert : ἐκαλεῖτο δὲ καὶ Δερκυλίδας ὁ Λακεδαιμόνιος σκύφος, ὥς φησιν Ἔφορος ἐν τῇ ὀκτωκαιδεκάτῃ λέγων οὕτως·

Λακεδαιμόνιοι ἀντὶ Θίβρωνος Δερκυλίδαν ἔπεμψαν εἰς τὴν 'Ασίαν ἀκούοντες ὅτι πάντα πράττειν εἰώθασιν οἱ περὶ τὴν 'Ασίαν βάρβαροι μετ' ἀπάτης καὶ δόλου. Διόπερ Δερκυλίδαν ἔπεμψαν ἥκιστα νομίζοντες ἐξαπατηθήσεσθαι. ἦν γὰρ οὐδὲν ἐν τῷ τρόπῳ Λακωνικὸν οὐδ' ἁπλοῦν ἔχων ἀλλὰ πολὺ τὸ πανοῦργον καὶ τὸ θηριῶδες. διὸ καὶ Σκύφον αὐτὸν οἱ Λακεδαιμόνιοι προσηγόρευον. Perspexit Porsonus non ΣΚΤΦΟΝ sed ΣΙΣΤΦΟΝ in codice, quem legebat Athenaeus, scriptum fuisse.

verse with their betters. Even if they would attract attention
by shouting the lines of Callimachus—

> ἄκουε δὴ τὸν αἶνον· ἔγ κοτε Τμώλῳ
> δάφνην ἐλαίῃ νεῖκος οἱ πάλαι Λυδοὶ
> λέγουσι θέσθαι,

our wiser course is not to hear, as the οἱ πάλαι Λυδοὶ may be
no more than the Alexandrine's way of spelling Αἴσωπος. In
any case, Aristophanes would ill brook his librarian taking
precedence of himself.

In some lines from the *Wasps*, treated of on an earlier
page (xxix.), we found the adjectives Αἰσωπικός
and Συβαριτικός rubbing shoulders. The same
play furnishes two instances of the γέλοιον Συβαριτικόν—

[margin: What is signified by Sybaritic fable?]

> ἀνὴρ Συβαρίτης ἐξέπεσεν ἐξ ἅρματος,
> καί πως κατεάγη τῆς κεφαλῆς μέγα σφόδρα·
> ἐτύγχανεν γὰρ οὐ τρίβων ὢν ἱππικῆς.
> κἄπειτ᾽ ἐπιστὰς εἶπ᾽ ἀνὴρ αὐτῷ φίλος.
> ἔρδοι τις ἦν ἕκαστος εἰδείη τέχνην.

The other is of the same cast as the lines which the poet
fastens upon Aesop, quoted on p. xxix., *supra*—

> ἐν Συβάρει γυνή ποτε
> κατέαξ᾽ ἐχῖνον . . . . .
> οὐχῖνος οὖν ἔχων τιν᾽ ἐπεμαρτύρατο·
> εἶθ᾽ ἡ Συβαρῖτις εἶπεν, εἰ ναὶ τὰν κόραν
> τὴν μαρτυρίαν ταύτην ἐάσας ἐν τάχει
> ἐπίδεσμον ἐπρίω, νοῦν ἂν εἶχες πλείονα.

Such trivial follies are common among all peoples, and it
is needless to give instances of a custom so wide-
spread as that of imparting local colour to jocular
utterances, whether in prose or verse, by assigning them to
some particular neighbourhood. The Greeks selected their
colonies for this questionable honour just as we English put
it upon the sister isle; and Sybaris in the west, Miletus and
Cyprus in the east, were most frequently mentioned in this

[margin: by Milesian and Cyprian fable?]

Xenophon in Hellen. III. 1. 8. Δερκυλίδας ἄρξων ἀφίκετο ἐπὶ τὸ στράτευμα,
ἀνὴρ δοκῶν εἶναι μάλα μηχανητικός. καὶ

ἐπεκαλεῖτο δὲ Σίσυφος. Sed quis vel
sine Xenophonte poterat dubitare?'
—Cobet 'de Arte interpretandi,' p. 58.

connection.　A couplet of Timocreon, preserved by Hephaestion,[1]—

Σικελὸς κομψὸς ἀνὴρ
ποτὶ τὰν ματέρ' ἔφα,

implies that wider ground was sometimes taken by the con-
cocters of these *jeux d'esprits*; and from Plato we may perhaps
infer that the matter of them was sometimes grave. ' I think
that Euripides was probably right in saying—

" Who knows if life be not death, and death life ?"

for I think that we are very likely dead ; and I have heard a
wise man say that at this very moment we *are* dead, and that
the body is a tomb, and that the part of the soul which is the
seat of the desires is liable to be influenced and tossed about
in different ways ; and about this some ingenious man, probably
a Silician or Italian,[2] playing with the word, made a tale.　He
called the soul a vessel (πίθος), meaning a vessel of faith or
belief, and the ignorant he called the uninitiated or leaky ; and
the place in the souls of the uninitiated in which the desires are
seated, being the intemperate and incontinent part, he compared
to a vessel full of holes, because they can never be satisfied.'[3]

　All these different kinds of Greek story and fable, whether
forming part of Greek traditional heritage from It is now impos-
sible to trace
the earliest days of the human race, or in more with certainty
the origin of
self-conscious times produced by Aesops after the Greek fables.
model of the older lore, whether bred in the brains of philo-
sophers or revellers, came in the aggregate to be called by
the common name of Aesopic.　The day is long past for
making any attempt to decide the ultimate origin of any unit
in this aggregate.　Race borrowed from race, clan from clan,
author from author, and each time with some variation.　Fable
was condensed into proverb, and proverb extended into fable ;
and who will say how often the process has been repeated ?

---

[1] P. 71, τῷ καθαρῷ ἐφθημιμμερεῖ ὅλον
ᾆσμα Τιμοκρέων συνέθηκε · Σικελὸς κτλ.
[2] καὶ τοῦτο ἄρα τις μυθολογῶν, κομψὸς
ἀνήρ, ἴσως Σικελός τις ἢ Ἰταλικός, παρά-
γων τῷ ὀνόματι κ.τ.λ. It will not do
to consider Plato's phrase as referring

to Timocreon's lines.　We must rather
regard the Σικελὸς κομψὸς ἀνήρ as a recognised form of introduction which
Plato used to give a colour to his own
myth.
[3] Gorg. 492-493, Jowett's translation.

We do not know anything about the collection of fables
by Demetrius of (the Attic deme) Phalerus, who
lived about 300 B.C.   There is nothing to show
that he threw them into verse.   It is quite probable that by
his day had begun the paltry practice of making the study of
fable the first step in the teaching of rhetoric, which, if it has
preserved the fables of Greece and Rome, has at the same time
preserved them in a condition so artificial and corrupt that for
purposes of scientific research they are practically valueless.

The collection of fables by Demetrius of Phalerus.

The fable was put into schoolboys' hands· to be analysed,
to be rewritten, to be extended, to be abbrevi-
ated, and to be turned upside down by a thousand
rhetorical tricks.   Given a fable, write down its
moral.   Given a moral, write out a fable to illustrate it.
Given certain animals, compose a fable in which they act in
character.   Compose a fable illustrating the characteristic
marks of the Libyan species, the Lydian, the Carian, the
Sybaritic, the Asinine.   Poor lads ! poor masters !   The
system flourished, and no wonder, for the boy who best caught
the trick was there to fill his master's shoes when the old man
slipped them off, and to add another subtlety to his definition
of the μῦθος, or shed new light on the traditional ἦθος of
the ass.

Fable used as a progymnasma for rhetorical training.

The system was certainly in full use in the time of Babrius,
as will be clear to any one who cares to consult
the Progymnasmata of the rhetor Hermogenes,
whose old age probably overlapped the youth of
Babrius.   For the rhetor's purposes some school
textbook of fable was probably required, and Nicostratus, a
contemporary of Hermogenes, compiled a δεκαμυθία or ten books
of fables.   This is mentioned by Hermogenes himself περὶ
ἰδεῶν, II. 12, 3 (see also Rhodius, Rom. p. 326, adn. 1).

The practice well known in the time of Babrius. Text-book of fable by Nicostratus.

It is even possible that the fables of Babrius are nothing
more than a verse translation of this book of
Nicostratus, especially if Suidas' statement is
accepted, that Babrius' choliambics extended over
ten books.   Whether this be so or not, the verses
of Babrius are by themselves sufficient to prove that the term
Aesopic had been made still more comprehensive than it was

The Babrian collection may be a verse paraphrase of Nicostratus. Extension of the term Aesopic.

in the time of Aristophanes, and that in a collection of μῦθοι Αἰσώπειοι such stories as those of Procne and Philomela, Pandora and Zeus, and Prometheus creating man, were not regarded as out of place. There is hardly a fable in the whole collection which does not betray traces of an artificial age, in which all were more or less familiar from literature with the names and attributes of the ancient gods, as they were with the main features of the better known fables, but which lacked the unconscious naturalness and the creative informing fire of earlier days. The same is undoubtedly true of Phaedrus, but it is not in any degree so marked as in Babrius.

In nothing is the artificial and sceptical turn of the Babrian fable so manifest as in the way in which the old *Artificial charac-* mythology is handled. From fable in its primitive *ter of the Babrian fables.* natural condition nothing can be more alien than the sceptical spirit, and the obtrusive presence of that spirit in Babrius indicates that for scientific inquiry into the origines of fable his work has no value.

In the second fable a farmer is represented as carrying to town a gang of his labourers, one of whom he *Fables 2, 10, 12,* suspects of having stolen a spade, hoping to find *15, 20, 30, 48.* the town deities able to help him in detecting the thief, as the country gods are too simple by half. On entering the gates he hears a crier offering a reward for the discovery of sacrilege, and acknowledges the fruitlessness of his errand. There is little but art here, and poor art too, that carries us into the school of the rhetors. The farmer must go to town for his gods, and when there is surprised that they cannot leave their temples, to say nothing of the town, and make chase after a thief. Luckily the fable is not known elsewhere, although it has its fellows in the prose of Nevelet's and Furia's collections.[1] In the tenth fable Aphrodite takes the trouble

---

[1] Nevel. 254, πορευομένοις τισὶν ἐπὶ πρᾶξίν τινα κόραξ ὑπήντησεν τὸν ὀφθαλμὸν τὸν ἕτερον πεπηρωμένος. ἐπιστραφέντων δὲ αὐτῶν καί τινος ὑποστρέψαι παραινοῦντος τοῦτο σημαίνειν τὸν οἰωνὸν ἕτερος ὑποτυχὼν εἶπεν· καὶ πῶς οὗτος ἡμῖν δύναται τὰ μέλλοντα μαντεύεσθαι ὃς οὐδὲ ἰδίαν πήρωσιν προείδετο ἵνα φυλάξηται. Furia, 113, Μάντις ἐπὶ τῆς ἀγορᾶς καθεζόμενος ἠργυρολόγει. ἐλθόντος δέ τινος αἰφνίδιον πρὸς αὐτὸν καὶ ἀπαγγείλαντος ὡς τῆς οἰκίας αὐτοῦ αἱ θύραι ἀναπεπετασμέναι εἰσί, καὶ πάντα τὰ ἔνδον ἐκφορημένα (sic) ἐκταραχθεὶς ἀνεπήδησε, καὶ στενάξας ἀπῄει δρομαῖος, τὸ γεγονὸς ὀψόμενος. τῶν δὲ παρατυχόντων καὶ θεασαμένων τις εἶπεν· ὦ οὗτος, ὁ τὰ ἀλλότρια πράγματα προειδέναι ἐπαγγελλόμενος, ἑαυτοῦ οὐ

to inform a drab that a god's code of morals is actually lower than her own.[1] The twelfth is a frigid application of the story of Procne and Philomela to illustrate the truth that it is wiser for the unfortunate to keep away from those who have known them in prosperity. There is even a greater dash of artificiality in the fifteenth. It is a rhetorical combination of the commonplace antithesis between Attic loquacity and Theban stupidity,[2] with the late belief in the evil influence of heroes.[3] In the twentieth a waggoner, who is represented as a sceptic, except in so far as he made Herakles his patron-saint, serves as a peg for the reflection, 'God helps those who help themselves.'[4] The third decade ends with a fable in which Hermes is represented as deploring the uncertainty of his position in

προεμαντεύου. I have quoted these in full as an example of the way in which the rhetors varied the treatment of the same subject in μῦθος.

[1] This fable has another mark of its late origin in the mention of worship by means of lamps—a custom unknown before the imperial times. Crusius quotes two instances from inscriptions, —one published by Henzen, Ind. Arch. 1858, n. 113, p. 201 (vir . . . corpus uxoris mortuae)—

'ut numen colit anxius merentis ;
parcas, oro, viro puella parcas,
ut possit tibi plurimos per annos
cum sertis dare justa quae dicavit,
et semper vigilet lucerna nardo' ;

a second in Orelli, Inscr. 4838, 'Have Septima, sit tibi terra levis. Quisque huic tumulo possuit ardentem lucernam, illius cineres aurea terra tegat.'

[2] Crusius, p. 138.

[3] The same belief is plainly stated in the sixty-third fable, and accounts for the late proverb preserved in the collection of Zenobius and others (Zenob. v. 60), οὐκ εἰμὶ τούτων τῶν ἡρώων. Perhaps, however, the proverb is itself ancient, and has only been wrongly explained, the paroemiographi applying to heroes as a class qualities properly belonging only to some. See Aristoph. Av. 1490, where a scholiast makes the same mistake as we here suppose the paroemiographi to have done. The question is discussed by Crusius on pp. 235-237, where, among other authorities, he quotes Athenaeus,

xi. 461 C, χαλεπούς γάρ πλήκτας τούς ήρωας νομίζουσι καὶ μᾶλλον νύκτωρ ἢ μεθ' ἡμέραν.

[4] The proverb appears in different shapes both in authors and lexica, e.g. Aesch. Pers. 742—

ὅταν σπεύδῃ τις αὐτός, χώ θεὸς ξυνάπτεται.

Eurip. I. T. 911—

ἣν δέ τις πρόθυμος ᾖ
σθένειν τὸ θεῖον μᾶλλον εἰκότως ἔχει.

Id. El. 80—

ἀργὸς γὰρ οὐδεὶς θεοὺς ἔχων ἀνὰ στόμα
βίον δύναιτ' ἂν συλλέγειν ἄνευ πόνου.

Plaut. Cist. I. i. 51, 'Sine opera tua nil di horum facere possunt.' Plutarch, Instit. Lacon. 29, p. 239 A, has the proverb (also found in the paroemiographi and in Photius)—

τὰν χεῖρα ποτιφέροντα τὰν τύχαν καλεῖν.

Zenobius, v. 93, σὺν 'Αθηνᾷ καὶ χεῖρα κίνει (a form also found in other paroemiographi and in Hesychius, etc.) The explanation given by Zenobius is of a sort with that of our fable, whereas in Nevelet's collection (250) and in Schneider's (30) a different fable has been manufactured to account for it. If we were to sit down and make a fable on the theme 'Call on the saints if you list, but be your own best saint,' (Scott's Tales of the Crusaders), we might produce some trifle like this Babrian 20th.

these evil times—a complaint proved to be but too well founded by the next fable in which he appears. In that even the dogs show an inclination to take undue liberties with his reverence. This forty-eighth fable, however, may well be spurious, and at best is but an amplification of a proverb.[1]

It is ill done in these rhetors to let no chance pass of insulting their patron. The old tale of the descent of the Arabians from Hermes [2] is dished up in the fifty-seventh fable, in which the morals of sire and children make an equally poor show. The fifty-eighth is a garbled and absurd version [3] of the legend of Pandora. A little further on the late belief in the evil influence of heroes, referred to already in the fifteenth fable, reappears in an unmistakeable form in the sixty-third. Equally late is the manner of introducing the fable of the two bags by a reference to Prometheus [4]—

Fables 57, 58, 63, 66, 68.

$$\Theta\epsilon\hat{\omega}\nu\ \Pi\rho o\mu\eta\theta\epsilon\grave{\upsilon}s\ \mathring{\eta}\nu\ \tau\iota s\ \mathring{a}\lambda\lambda\grave{a}\ \tau\hat{\omega}\nu\ \pi\rho\acute{\omega}\tau\omega\nu.$$

In the sixty-eighth the Pagan Zeus has assumed the attributes of his counterpart in the Jewish or at all events the Orphic theology.[5]

---

[1] Macarius is the only paroemiographist who has preserved it, IV. 10, Ἑρμῆν μήτ' ἀλείψῃς μήτ' ἀπολείψῃς· ἐπὶ τῶν διὰ προσποιητῆς χάριτος ἀφαιρουμένων τι μᾶλλον ἢ διδόντων. ἐν βαλανείῳ γάρ τινι Ἑρμῆς ἦν ἱδρυμένος, ὃν οἱ πολλοὶ τῶν λουομένων ἤλειφον· πένης δέ τις προφάσει τοῦ ἀλείφειν ἐκεῖνον περιαιρούμενος τὸ ἔλαιον ἑαυτὸν ἤλειφεν. Macarius is late enough, and in lists of proverbs like his there is always the chance of interpolation; but at all events his explanation, compared with the Babrian(?) fable, shows very clearly the late method of manufacturing fables.

[2] Strabo, Geogr. I. 42, Ἡσίοδος δ' ἐν Καταλόγῳ φησί—

καὶ κούρην Ἀράβοιο, τὸν Ἑρμάων ἀκάκητα γείνατο καὶ Θρονίη, κούρη Βήλοιο Φάνακτος.

Οὕτω δὲ καὶ Στησίχορος λέγει. εἰκάζειν οὖν ἐστιν ὅτι ἀπὸ τούτου καὶ ἡ χώρα Ἀραβία ἤδη τότε ὠνομάζετο· κατὰ δὲ τοὺς ἥρωας τυχὸν ἴσως οὔπω.

[3] Pandora does not appear in the fable at all; the jar or box is said to contain blessings instead of curses, and nothing is said about the opening of it being forbidden. Cp. Anth. Pal. x. 71—

Πανδώρης ὁρόων γελόω πίθον οὐδὲ γυναῖκα μέμφομαι, ἀλλ' αὐτῶν τὰ πτερὰ τῶν ἀγαθῶν.
Ὡς γὰρ ἐπ' Οὐλύμποιο μετὰ χθονὸς ἤθεα πάσης πωτῶνται, πίπτειν καὶ κατὰ γῆν ὄφελον κτε.

It is difficult to understand how Hope passed out among men when it had the alternative of remaining under the lid or of flying off to heaven. See Crusius, p. 210.

[4] Catullus, 22, 21. Persius, 4, 29. Phaedrus, 4, 10. Themistius, Βασανιστής, 262 b. Cp. id. 359 d. Plutarch, Crassus, 32.

[5] See note on the passage.

The rhetors' insults to Hermes are all explained by the
Fables 119, 127. fable (119th) in which a craftsman discovers
the secret that the only means of enlisting Hermes on his
side is to browbeat him and knock him down. It is a secret
worth having, as it is Hermes who acts the part of recording
angel[1] in the one hundred and twenty-seventh, and few would
care to allow old-fashioned scruples about fair play to interfere
with the prospect of conciliating such an autocrat.

It was observed above that the twentieth fable is nothing
Many Babrian apologues merely extensions of proverbs. Fables 21, 29, 76, 98. but an extension of a proverb. There are in
Babrius many other manifest instances of this
method of manufacturing fables. The story of
the oxen and the butchers may well be a rhetorician's
attempt to explain the proverb εὔνους ὁ σφάκτης which is
found in Zenobius,[2] who offers three explanations. Babrius
was surely within his right in suggesting a fourth. In its
present shape the twenty-ninth is probably greatly shortened.
Aphthonius has a much longer and more sensible version, in
which the horse addresses the miller, and which served
Doxopatros[3] as an instance of μῦθος μικτός. Be that as it
may, the fable resembles the seventy-sixth in being based
upon the proverb ἀφ' ἵππων ἐπ' ὄνους.[4] Moreover, although
the apologue of the cat turned lover[5] probably dates from the
most primitive times, I still believe that in its Babrian form
it is no more than the proverb οὐ πρέπει γαλῇ κροκωτόν[6]
rehabilitated.

There is an obscure proverb ἀγόμενος διὰ φρατόρων
Fables 42, 56. κύων,[7] which Diogenian explains ἐπὶ τῶν ὅπου
μὴ δεῖ εὑρισκομένων καὶ τιμωρουμένων. Whether the ex-

---

[1] Cp. Zenobius, 4, 11, Ζεὺς κατεῖδε χρόνιος εἰς τὰς διφθέρας, and notes in loco ; also Crusius, p. 219.   [2] 3, 94.
[3] Walz, Rhetores, II. 173, μικτὸν δὲ τὸ ἐξ ἀμφοτέρων, ἀλόγου καὶ λογικοῦ, οἷός ἐστιν ὁ τοῦ ἵππου τοῦ μυλωροῦ.
[4] Zenobius, II. 33, ἀφ' ἵππων ἐπ' ὄνους· τὴν παροιμίαν ταύτην ἐροῦμεν ἐπὶ τῶν ἀπὸ τῶν σεμνῶν ἐπὶ τὰ ἄσεμνα ἠκόντων οἷον ἀπὸ γραμματικῶν ἐπὶ πράγματα ἢ εἰς ἄλλο τι τῶν ἀτιμοτάτων. The converse occurs in Zenobius, II. 5, ἀπὸ βραδυσκελῶν ὄνων ἵππος ὥρουσεν· ἐπὶ τῶν ἀπὸ εὐτελῶν ἐπὶ τὰ

μείζω μεταπηδώντων. Cp. Diogenian, I. 98, ἀπὸ κώπης ἐπὶ βῆμα· ἐπὶ τῶν ἀπὸ χειρόνων εἰς κρείττονα.
[5] For beasts falling in love with men and vice versa cp. Fab. 98. Athenaeus discusses the question in 13, 606 b, and Aristotle in Hist. Anim. 9, 48 (631 a8) ; Aelian, Nat. Anim. I. 6, II. 6, IV. 54, etc. Cp. Bleek's South African Fables.
[6] Zenobius, II. 93, who mentions that the fable was known to Strattis.
[7] Diogenian, II. 45, Suidas sub voc. ἀγόμενος.

planation be right or wrong, it has at least the support of
Babrius or the prosaist whom he paraphrased in the forty-
second fable. Even more instructive is the fifty-sixth—a
rhetor's amplification of a thought which had taken a proverbial
shape as early as the days of Epicharmus—

> Θαυμαστὸν οὐδὲν ἀμὲ ταῦθ' οὕτω λέγειν
> καὶ ἁνδάνειν αὐτοῖσιν αὐτοὺς καὶ δοκεῖν
> καλῶς πεφύκεν· καὶ γὰρ ἁ κύων κυνὶ
> κάλλιστον εἶμεν φαίνεται καὶ βοῦς βοΐ,
> ὄνος δ' ὄνῳ κάλλιστον, ὗς δέ θην ὑΐ.

To the rhetors in their capacity of fabulists the quality
λιχνεία or, as their late tongues will have it,
λιχνότης is the predominant mark of the μυῶν
ἦθος. From a combination of this tit-bit of
natural history with the Epicurean's proverb, γλυκὺ μέλι καὶ
πνιξάτω, the sixtieth fable has been concocted. Suidas[1] tells
us that it was a fig in Terpander's throat which started the
proverb, while Trypho[2] would make Terpes the victim. But
there can be no two ways of explaining the fable. Its suc-
cessor, the sixty-first, is also but an extension of the proverbial
εἰς ἀρχαίας φάτνας preserved by Zenobius[3] and other col-
lectors.

Fables more markedly in the rhetors' vein. Fables 60, 61.

In one of his works[4] Plutarch makes Aesop himself tell an
apologue of a mule. Ἡμίονος Λυδὸς ἐν ποταμῷ *Fables 62, 69.*
τῆς ὄψεως ἑαυτοῦ κατιδὼν εἰκόνα καὶ θαυμάσας τὸ κάλλος τε
καὶ τὸ μέγεθος τοῦ σώματος ὥρμησε θεῖν ὥσπερ ἵππος ἀνα-
χαιτίσας. εἶτα μέντοι συμφρονήσας ὡς ὄνου υἱὸς εἴη κατέ-
παυσε ταχὺ τὸν δρόμον καὶ ἀφῆκε τὸ φρύαγμα καὶ τὸν θυμόν.
But for my part I shall take Phrynichus' word for it that τοῦ
πατρὸς τὸ παιδίον[5] is an ancient proverb, and ask Plutarch's

[1] Τερπάνδρου ᾁδοντος καὶ κεχηνότος πρὸς τὴν ᾠδὴν ἐμβαλών τις εἰς τὸν φάρυγγα σῦκον ἀπέπνιξε.

[2] Anth. Palat. 9, 488—

Τέρπης εὐφόρμιγγα κρέκων σκιάδεσσιν ἀοιδάν
κάτθαν' ἀνοστήσας ἐν Λακεδαιμονίοις.
Οὐκ ἄορι πληγεὶς οὐδ' ἐν βέλει ἀλλ' ἑνὶ σύκῳ
χείλεα. φεῦ προφάσεων οὐκ ἀπορεῖ θάνατος.

Another form of the proverb is given by Diogenian, 4, 53, ἐν μέλιτι σαυτὸν καταπάττεις· ἐπὶ τῶν (τὸ) ἡδυπαθεῖν διωκόντων.

[3] Zenob. III. 50, εἰς ἀρχαίας φάτνας· ἐπὶ τῶν ἀπολαύσεώς τινος ἐκπεσόντων, εἶτα πάλιν ἐπὶ τὴν ἀρχαίαν ἐλθόντων δίαιταν.

[4] Mor. 178, 6.

[5] App. Soph. 65, 17, Τοῦ πατρὸς τὸ παιδίον· παλαιὰ ἡ παροιμία, τιθεμένη ἐπὶ τῶν ὅμοια ποιούντων τοῖς πατράσιν.

leave to take this fable out of Aesop's mouth and drop it like a fig into his own. Be this as it may, the rhetors have imported into the Babrian version their knowledge of a second proverb, which has been enshrined in an iambic line preserved by Galen [1]—

παχεῖα γαστὴρ λεπτὸν οὐ τίκτει νόον.

But of them all none bears so explicit marks of this manner of concoction as the sixty-ninth, which is a paltry attempt to account for the proverb Λαγὼς περὶ κρεῶν, which even in Aristophanes' time was so familiar as to admit of the obscure allusion in Ran. 192—

δοῦλον οὐκ ἄγω
εἰ μὴ νεναυμάχηκε τὴν περὶ τῶν κρεῶν.

There was a tale to much the same purpose as our Babrian fable current in early Attic times, but it was the proverb which that tale gave rise to, and not the tale itself, on which the Babrian version was based.

The seventy-fifth is a rhetorical exercise on the basis of the

Fables 37, 75, 87, 99, 100.

proverbial Ἀκεσίας ἰάσατο,[2] while the eighty-seventh in its present shape is hardly even an extension of the proverb λήθαργος κύων,[3] or the ninetieth of ὁ νεβρὸς τὸν λέοντα πυνθάνεται.[4] The proverb ἄρκτου παρούσης ἴχνη μὴ ζήτει[5] is as old as Bacchylides, and its rhetorical

---

[1] Galen, v. p. 878, who introduces it with the words πρὸς ἀπάντων σχεδὸν ἀνθρώπων ᾄδεται.

[2] Zenob. I. 52, 'Ἀκεσίας ἰάσατο· ἐπὶ τῶν ἐπὶ τὸ χεῖρον ἰωμένων. Ὅλην δὲ Ἀριστοφάνης ἐν τετραμέτροις ἐκφέρει λέγων Ἀκεσίας τὸν πρωκτὸν ἰάσατο. Ἀκεσίας γάρ τις ἐγένετο ἰατρὸς ἀφυὴς ὃς τὸν πόδα τινὸς ἀλγοῦντος κακῶς ἐθεράπευσεν. Cp. Diogen. II. 3; ps.-Plutarch, Prov. 98, et al. Cp. also Libanius, Ep. 319, συνήλγουν μὲν ἐπὶ τοῖς κακοῖς, συνηχθόμην δὲ τῇ πόλει πολλοὺς τρεφούσῃ τοὺς Ἀκεσίας. Id. Epist. 1134, fin. The Dosithean version differs slightly from the Babrian (Böcking, p. 30), but it is very corrupt. For χάροντος ἑστακέναι lege χάροντι εἶναι.

[3] Zenob. IV. 90, Λήθαργος κύων · ὁ προσσαίνων μέν, λάθρα δὲ δάκνων. Schol. ap. Arist. Eq. 1028, ἔπαιξε παρὰ τὴν πα-

ροιμίαν Σαίνεις δάκνουσα καὶ κύων λήθαργος εἶ· ἐπὶ τῶν ὑποκρινομένων δῆθεν εὐνοεῖν ἐπιβουλευόντων δὲ λάθρα. The origin of the term is not explained by the lines of Pisander given in Anth. Pal. 7, 304—

Ἀνδρὶ μὲν Ἱππαίμων ὄνομ' ἦν, ἵππῳ δὲ Πόδαγρος, καὶ κινὶ Λήθαργος, καὶ θεράποντι Βάβης.

Probably this proverb, like the other κάκιον ἢ Βάβης αὐλεῖ, was well known even in Pisander's time, and gave a point to his lines.

[4] Apostol. XIV. 58. Cp. Diogen. VI. 59—

μὴ πρὸς λέοντα δορκὰς ἀψώμαι μάχης.

[5] Zenob. II. 36, ἐπὶ τῶν δειλῶν κυνηγῶν εἴρηται ἡ παροιμία. μέμνηται δ' αὐτῆς Βακχυλίδης ἐν Παιᾶσιν. Cp. Diogen.

facing does little credit to Babrius or the preceding rhetor whom he follows. The saying ἐκ λύκου στόματος,[1] on the other hand, had probably never superseded the fable from which it sprang, and accordingly the Babrian version is simple and natural. The same may be the case with the ninety-ninth, which, as a fable, goes hand in hand with the proverb κύων ἐπὶ δεσμά,[2] just as the thirty-seventh is based upon the variation of the same proverb, namely, βοῦς ἐπὶ δεσμά. From the old apologue of the Fox and the Eagle the proverb ἀετὸς ἐν νεφέλαις crystallised out. This has been refaced by Babrius, the lion wrongly occupying the fox's place.[3] The fable of the Eagle and Tortoise is merely a rhetor's extension of ἄνευ πτερῶν ζητεῖς ἵπτασθαι,[4] if the minds of these literary triflers were really incapable of thought without something to suggest the line which they were to take.

There is a proverb in Zenobius[5] which has fur-   Fable 55.
nished such a suggestion to the framer of the fifty-fifth fable. Treating the business maxim,

$$\epsilon\grave{\iota} \ \mu\acute{\eta} \ \delta\acute{\upsilon}\nu\alpha\iota\sigma \ \beta o\hat{\upsilon}\nu \ \check{\epsilon}\lambda\alpha\upsilon' \ \check{o}\nu o\nu,$$

after the manner of his tribe, he has contrived to put upon it the face of an apologue.

There is, in fact, in the whole Babrian collection hardly one fable which literary tinkering has not deprived   Literary tinker-ing visible in all
of almost every mark of its primitive signifi-   the fables. Fable
cance in the history of folk lore. There is much   95.

II. 70. Plutarch, Lucullus, 8, p. 496, οὐκ ἔφη δειλότερος εἶναι τῶν κυνηγῶν ὥστε τὰ θηρία παρελθὼν ἐπὶ κενοὺς αὐτῶν τοὺς φωλεοὺς βαδίζειν. Aristaenetus, Ep. 2, 12, fin., where he makes up his mind to get rid of a bad wife—ἀπίτω τοίνυν ἡ θηριώδης. ἔστω, δεδόχθω. οὐδὲν ἀμφιβάλλω· κατάδηλος ἡ γυνή. ἄρκτου παρούσης οὐκ ἐπιζητήσω τὰ ἴχνη.
[1] Babrius, 94. Zenob. III. 48, ἐκ λύκου στόματος· ἐπὶ τῶν ἀνελπίστως τι λαμβανόντων. Longus founds an incident in his Pastoralia on this proverb, pp. 20, 21.
[2] Zenob. IV. 73, Κύων ἐπὶ δεσμά· ἐπὶ τῶν ἑαυτοὺς εἰς κόλασιν ἐπιδιδόντων, καὶ βοῦς ἐπὶ δεσμά.
[3] Babrius, 100. Zenobius has another

explanation: 'Αετὸς ἐν νεφέλαις· ἔστι μὲν οὖν χρησμός, εἴρηται δὲ ἐπὶ τῶν δυσαλώτων· πάροσον ὁ ἀετὸς ἐν νεφέλαις ὢν οὐχ ἁλίσκεται, which is due merely to a misunderstanding of Aristoph. Eq.1008. Cp. id. 1093 and Av. 979.
[4] Pseudo-Plutarch, Prov. 25.
[5] Zenob. III. 54, ἐπὶ τῶν ὃ κατὰ δύναμιν ἔχουσι πράττειν παρεγγυωμένων. Sometimes a proverb is preserved to which there is no literary fable-equivalent in existence, although from other sources we infer that such once existed ; e.g., the proverb ἀλώπηξ τὸν βοῦν ἐλαύνει (Diog. 2, 73) must be connected with the fable in the Kalilah and Dimnah of the jackal bringing the bull to the lion.

in the ninety-fifth fable which would tempt us to suppose that Babrius derived it from a purer source than the others. From a hint in a fragment of Solon we learned[1] that this apologue was well known in Greece at an early date. In its original shape it must have been a folk lore attempt to explain the slit in the ear of stags,[2] but in its Babrian presentment that falls into the background altogether, and is so little emphasised that Babrius may well have been ignorant of it himself. Everything considered, we can expect nothing else. Even

Hesiod had seen the literary use to which folk lore could be put, and by the time of Aristophanes it was looked upon as within an author's right to invent new tales and modify old ones for his own purposes. In the natural course of things the primitive complexion of all fable must have altered seriously, if not quite past recognition, in the many centuries which intervened between the best days of Athens and the degenerate times of Rome; especially when we reflect that during these centuries was developed that mixo-barbarism of races, beliefs, manners, and languages which reached its climax about the date when Babrius wrote. Add to this that for centuries sophists and rhetors had been accustomed to make fable the exercise-ground in which their youngest disciples should show their paces, and the condition of the Babrian fable will not appear so discreditable.

The literary ante-cedents of the Babrian fable explain its char-acteristics.

To my own mind there seem to be no data by which to determine the ultimate source of fable or the primi-tive form of any particular apologue which is not merely literary. According to Aulus Gellius,[3] the apologue of the Lark and its young, which is the eighty-eighth in our mythiambics, was versified by Ennius. But what means have we of deciding how Ennius obtained it? He may have followed some purely Latin form of a traditional fable running back into Indo-European times, or he may have borrowed it from some Greek author, or he may have invented it himself. When Ovid[4] explains the custom of tying torches to foxes' tails in the games of Ceres by the story that a

Certain fables discussed from this point of view.

---

[1] P. xxvii., *supra.*
[2] See Crusius, pp. 214-216. Cp. Bleek, *Reynard the Fox in South Africa.*
[3] *Noctes Atticae,* II. 29.
[4] Ovid, *Fasti,* IV. 681.

youngster of twelve in Carseoli of the Peligni once burned
down the grain of the neighbourhood in this way, whether
are we to believe that the poet invented the story to explain
the custom, or that the custom had for centuries preserved on
Italian soil the memory of some such fatal conflagration in the
inexperienced childhood of the Indo-European race? For
purposes of mischief the contrivance is too simple not to have
been often employed, and the corresponding story told of
Samson in Judges xv. has most probably no connection with
the Latin anecdote, although it is quite possible that the
pseudo-Lucian borrowed from the Jewish source one incident
in the life of his Ass.[1]

Diodorus Siculus is not wrong in calling the fable of the
lion turned suitor both ancient and traditional,[2] but neither his version nor the Babrian contains anything which might not have been produced by any literary fable-maker. The ordinary arguments used by inferior inquirers into the sources of fable are contemptible beyond imagination. The Babrian twenty-second is claimed by Landsberger[3] as a Hebrew story, on the plea that polygamy was intelligible to the Jews, whereas it would be absurd for a man to go with an aged hetaera! It would not be fairness of mind, but real disregard for truth, to speak in any but a severe and decisive manner about statements of this character, which are calculated still further to confuse the mind in that search after simple and ultimate truths which is bound, sooner or later, to bring simplicity and comprehensiveness into human knowledge. In fact, in the whole Babrian collection, as well as in that of Phaedrus, and in those parts of Avianus and the late prosaists which are not merely paraphrases of these earlier versifiers, there is not a single apologue which will shed any light upon the origines of fable, except so far as it demonstrates by its presence in a

---

[1] Asinus, 31. In return for a kick
his master loaded the ass with tow,
set fire to it, and let him go.
Gubernatis (Zoolog. Myth. II. 138)
finds phallic allusions in this fable.

[2] Diod. Sic. 19, 25, τῶν δὲ Μακε-
δόνων οὐ προσεχόντων τοῖς λόγοις ἀλλὰ

καὶ προσαπειλούντων τοῖς πρεσβυτάτοις,
Εὐμένης παρελθὼν ἐπῄνεσέ τε αὐτοὺς καὶ
λόγον εἶπε τῶν παραδεδομένων καὶ παλαιῶν, οὐκ ἀνοίκειον δὲ τῆς περιστάσεως
κτε. Cp. Georgius Pachymeres, Walz,
Rhetores Graeci, I. 551.

[3] Landsberger, Fabeln, p. xliii.

d

Graeco-Roman collection of the imperial times that it was either derived from one or other of the races which formed the empire, or was concocted by the collector himself or some literary predecessor.[1]

The interest of Babrius is mainly literary. The student

The merits of Babrius as a fabulist. of his choliambics will find in them the most attractive presentment which many of the so-called Aesopic fables have ever received; and if he will consent to judge them by the standard of the age in which they were produced, there is little fear of his contradicting the enthusiastic verdict of the poet's contemporaries.

---

[1] My notes on these questions I reserve for the second volume.

CHAPTER III.

THE LANGUAGE OF BABRIUS.

THE diction of Babrius has already supplied a subject for one
of those often elaborate and sometimes valuable *The subject has been already treated by Zachariae in reference to the date of Babrius.*
dissertations which the German universities require
from the candidates for their degrees. The essay
of Theodor Zachariae ' de dictione Babriana,' although of higher merit than most of these monographs, is,
however, far too uncritical to be of much service to more
mature inquirers. It is an attempt to determine the date
of Babrius by a method which, in the circumstances of the
case, is naturally inconclusive. It would be wrong to say
that this method can never be used with advantage ; but the
cases in which it may are peculiarly few. Fortunately there
is other evidence to decide the date of Babrius than that on
which Zachariae depended, or it could not be decided at all.
So much will incidentally appear from the following attempt
to investigate the leading characteristics in syntax, accidence,
and vocabulary, of the Babrian choliambics.

Scholars who have watched the recent development of the
study of language must look forward with con- *New methods of linguistic inquiry.*
fident interest to the position which the science
will have won for itself by the close of the century, in which it
has already grown from helpless childhood to self-dependent
and resolute adolescence. The same willing submission to the
reign of imperative law which is daily adding to our knowledge
of vocables and their morphology will also, if discreetly
yielded, produce much useful simplification in the study of
formed words and their syntactical collocations. As no
linguistic inquirer would dream of basing his investigations

into the Doric dialect upon the literary modification of it which appears in the choric portions of the Attic drama, or into Lowland Scotch upon its literary representative in the poems of Ramsay or Burns, so the lexicographer and the student of grammar, whether in its accidence or its syntax, has to draw a firm line, not only between the different dialects of a common language, but also between these dialects each in its self-centred and unconscious development, and the same when perverted by historical and literary influences,—historical, due to the movements and mixture of races produced by war or diplomacy; literary, arising from time-honoured artistic motives, or even from the fanciful conceits and imitative affectations of the Alexandrine and Byzantine ages of literature.

In every case the student of a language must, if possible, select for the starting point of his investigations a period in which men appear to have followed an instinctive and unconscious linguistic sense. Such a period need not be primeval, but may present itself in some particular language, even after centuries of its literature are already past. Certainly, whatever the cause may have been, the mature dialect of Attica furnishes an unequalled example of a tongue thus obedient to law so nearly inviolate as justly to be called instinctive, and consequently lends itself easily to scientific treatment. It would be unwise in the student to reject the foothold which, for these reasons, Attic is able to afford him in investigating the linguistic side of Greek literature, and in explaining the anomalies occurring in the works produced by Greek writers outside of Attica and in it during the long periods in which, with few important exceptions, literary effort ran in traditional and artificial grooves rather than in obedience to natural impulse. Even on Attic soil, and side by side with the purified and instinctive language, the higher poetry after its manner rejected quotidian usage and drew its vocabulary in great part from the abandoned synonyms of the undeveloped tongue; while in accidence and syntax its authors were not a little affected by conscious sympathy with the previous writers of their own order, and by the tendency to manipulate language to which all who use an artificial and unfamiliar mode of expression are more or less prone.

The necessity for a standard of usage. The value of the Attic dialect as such.

With a hand perhaps lacking in firmness I have attempted in a former work to draw this fundamental dis-tinction between language as an instinctive natural development and as a product of literary manip-ulation. For accurate philological inquiry some standard is quite necessary, and if Attic be accepted as such it will be found that great precision may be attained in Greek grammar, and the study of the language be simplified to an extent otherwise inconceivable. As this will be made clearer by an example or two, I shall briefly discuss, with Attic as my standard, the history of certain Greek words, inflections, and constructions,—namely, in vocabulary, the verbs ἀλέξειν and ἀμύνειν; in accidence, the endings of the third person plural of the imperative mood; in syntax, the constructions admissible after the verbs λέγειν, εἰπεῖν, and φάναι.

[margin note: Fundamental distinction between language as a natural development and as a product of literary manipulation illustrated.]

Of the verbs ἀλέξειν and ἀμύνειν, practically identical[1] in signification, the second alone was recognised by pure Attic usage; but in the higher poetry of the same date, whether in or outside of Attica, in the Pan-Hellenic prose of Xenophon, and, to speak generally, in all sorts of late writers not consciously Atticising, the two verbs were both employed. Even within itself the verb ἀλέξειν violated the rule of economy by forming the two futures ἀλέξειν and ἀλεξήσειν, and the two aorists ἀλέξαι and ἀλεξῆσαι, which were also capable of being further recruited by the aoristic ἀλκαθεῖν. The later Greeks transgressed the rule of economy still more idly, and offended incontinently against the classical usage by eliciting two new presents, ἀλέκειν and ἀλεξεῖν, from the future forms ἀλέξειν and ἀλεξήσειν respectively.

[margin note: The words ἀλέξειν and ἀμύνειν.]

As the painter of a portrait or an historical picture intro-duces into his design many odds and ends of antiquated bric-a-brac,—some to call up associations, others merely to harmonise the colours, but all serving to im-press the imagination,—so literary artists preserve the ἀλέξεινs and ἀλκαθεῖνs and other fragments from the wasteful abundance of primitive speech, that they may use them when occasion

[margin note: Poetical 'business.']

---

[1] I omit ἐρύκειν as not quite synonymous.

comes for purposes of ornamentation, or from a better motive, to touch some long silent chord of the human heart. In this way is to be explained the presence of ἀλέξειν and ἀλκαθεῖν in Attic tragic poets; but their occurrence in Xenophon and in late writers has to be accounted for in another manner. Xenophon's vocabulary is a cento of terms picked up in the various districts into which his active military life led him, and in some of which ἀλέξειν may have ousted ἀμύνειν, or even continued to co-exist with it. As to late writers it is impossible to say in any particular case whether they owed the word to their unappreciative study of classical authors or found it ready to their hand in the Pan-Hellenic or common dialect of their time. Did Plutarch, for example, employ ἀλέξειν as a term of familiar import in his day, or as a purple patch for the delectation of literary tinkers?

To take up the synonym ἀμύνειν, it accords with the business-like precision of Attic that it instinctively preferred the word with the fewest alternative forms, and after throwing aside the superfluous aorist ἀμυναθεῖν consistently adhered to the simplified mode of expression.

An example of economy in the Attic dialect.

Did schoolboys only know it, their Greek grammars are considerately compiled in order to prepare them for the corruptions of our Attic texts, and the usages of debased Greek. At all events, if certainty is to be trusted, the longer imperative forms in -σαν have little right to the place of honour which they have hitherto held, and no right at all to a place in the scheme of the Attic verb. Judging from inscriptions, they were unknown before Macedonian times. Imperative forms—Active, like λυέτωσαν, λυσάτωσαν ; Middle, like λυέσθωσαν, λυσάσθωσαν, λελύσθωσαν ; and Passive, like λυθήτωσαν, do not begin to occur in stone records till about 300 B.C., the same date at which the accusative plural of substantives in -ευς began to be represented by -εῖς in place of -έᾱς. After 300 B.C. they become more and more frequent, and in fifty years the shorter forms, which had once occupied the field alone,—λυόντων, λυσάντων, λυέσθων (or λύσθων), λυσάσθων, λελύσθων, λυθέντων,—completely disappear from stone monuments. The testimony of verse agrees with that of inscriptions.

The double forms in the 3d person plural of imperatives.

Homer[1] knows none but the shorter forms, and neither in Attic tragedy[2] nor comedy[3] do the longer occur. It is not till the New Comedy that the heavier endings are encountered in verse. In a passage from the 'Δεισιδαίμων' or 'Bigot' of Menander, quoted by the Alexandrine Clement in his *Stromateis* (VII. p. 303, 7, Sylb.), occur the lines—

περιμαξάτωσάν σ' αἱ γυναῖκες ἐν κύκλῳ
καὶ περιθεωσάτωσαν, ἀπὸ κρουνῶν τριῶν
ὕδατι περίρραν' ἐμβαλὼν ἅλας, φακούς·

[1] *e.g.* Iliad, 2, 430, ἀγειρόντων : 8, 517, ἀγγελλόντων : 521, καιόντων : 9, 47, φευγόντων : 67, λεξάσθων : 167, πιθέσθων : 170, ἐπέσθων : 18, 463, μελόντων, et al. freq. : 21, 467, δηριάσθων : 23, 643, ἀντιοώντων. Odyssey, 1, 340, πινόντων : 8, 36, κρινάσθων : 12, 50, δησάντων : 54, διδέντων : 17, 530, ἐψιαάσθων : 24, 485, φιλεόντων, etc. etc.

[2] Aesch. Cho. 714, κυρούντων : Supp. 669, φλεόντων (see Hermann *in loco*). Soph. O. C. 455, πεμπόντων : Aj. 100, ἀφαιρείσθων : 660, σωζόντων : 961, γελώντων κἀπιχαιρόντων. Eur. I. T. 1206, κάκκομιζόντων : H. F. 575, χαιρόντων. Two passages in which the manuscripts exhibit forms in -σαν are peculiarly instructive. It will be observed that there is only one verb, viz. εἰμί, in which the late form has the same number of syllables as the early. Accordingly, it is not suprising to find ἴτωσαν substituted for ἰόντων in I. T. 1480—

ἴτωσαν εἰς σὴν σὺν θεᾶς ἀγάλματι

The line originally ran—

Ἴτωσαν) εἰς σὴν ἰόντων σὺν θεᾶς ἀγάλματι·

and the gloss ἴτωσαν, according to the ordinary practice of the scholiasts with these imperatives, was added in the margin, thence to creep into the text by the simple process of omitting the Euripidean equivalent.

The second passage is Ion, 1130—

θύσας δὲ γενέταις θεοῖσιν ἦν μακρὸν χρόνον
μένω, παροῦσι δαῖτες ἔστωσαν φίλοις,

where δαῖτες ἔστωσαν is due to some commentator who did not understand

the Euripidean δαῖτας ἐστία, in concord with the sister imperative ἀνίστη, which occurs two lines before.

[3] Aristophanes, Ach. 186, βοώντων : Nub. 196, ἐπιμεινάντων : 438, χρήσθων : 453, δρώντων : 456, παραθέντων : 1142, δικαζέσθων : Vesp. 1530, ἐγγενέσθων : Av. 583, ἐκκοψάντων : Lys. 491, δρώντων : Thesm. 48, λυέσθων.

Prose texts are almost consistently corrupt, the copyist's habit of silent alteration of inflections to those of his own day being occasionally demonstrated in an instructive way, as in Xenophon, Hiero, 8, 3, where, as Cobet has shown, an imperative is taken for a participle, and the text altered to suit—ἰδὼν γὰρ πρῶτον προσειπάτω τινὰ φιλικῶς ὅ τε ἄρχων καὶ ὁ ἰδιώτης. ἐν τούτῳ τὴν προτέρου πρόσρησιν μᾶλλον εὐφραίνειν τὸν ἀκούσαντα νομίζεις ; ἵθι δὴ ἐπαινεσάντων ἀμφότεροι τὸν αὐτόν · τὸν ποτέρου δοκεῖς ἔπαινον ἐξικνεῖσθαι μᾶλλον εἰς εὐφροσύνην ; θύσας δὲ τιμησάτω ἑκάτερος · τὴν παρὰ ποτέρου τιμὴν μείζονος ἂν χάριτος δοκεῖς τυγχάνειν ; κάμνοντα θεραπευσάντων ὁμοίως · οὐκοῦν τοῦτο σαφὲς ὅτι οἱ ἀπὸ τῶν δυνατωτάτων θεραπεῖαι καὶ χάριν ἐμποιοῦσι μεγίστην ; δόντων δὲ τὰ ἴσα κτε. Of these four suppositional imperatives, each followed by a question, the first has been converted into a participle by reading ἀμφοτέρων for ἀμφότεροι, the second is in the singular, and the remaining two, in whose case such a process as that adopted with the first was impossible, have been altered in the usual way to δότωσαν and θεραπευσάτωσαν by critics of the type represented in scholia such as the following :—Ὥσπερ ἀπὸ τοῦ ἀφαιρείσθωσαν τὸ ἀφαιρείσθων κατὰ συγκοπήν, οὕτως καὶ ἀπὸ τοῦ λεγέτωσαν τὸ λεγόντων καὶ ὅσα τῆς ἀκολουθίας ταύτης (Schol. on Soph. Aj.

but the play cannot have been written before 322 B.C., and may well have been composed in the following century, so that the evidence of verse is significantly in harmony with that of inscriptions.

Accordingly, from this date onward, in the third person *Violation in late* plural of the imperative, contrary to the law of *Greek of the law of economy.* economy, two inflections were possible : one known to the vulgar and used also by the educated in ordinary life, another employed in the artificial literary products of the Alexandrine school and its successors, to give a savour of erudition to works which certainly stood· in want of every extrinsic aid which they could come by.

˙Our third instance to demonstrate the uncertainty of usage *The construction* in all late Greek was to be drawn from the *of the verb 'to say.'* domain of syntax, and will not occupy us long. The construction of the verbs signifying 'to say' in Attic is extremely regular. While λέγειν may be followed by the accusative and infinitive, or by ὅτι with the indicative or optative, and sometimes, although rarely, with ὡς, the other two verbs εἰπεῖν and φάναι admit of no such indifferency of use. Except in the sense of κελεύειν, the verb εἰπεῖν refuses any construction but that with ὅτι (or ὡς) ; while φάναι, on the contrary, will have none but that of the accusative and infinitive. In post-Attic writers,[1] however, both verbs send their Attic discipline to the winds, εἰπεῖν keeping company with the infinitive, and φάναι dallying with ὅτι.

Some of the causes which led to this want of accuracy *Causes of the de-* and refinement in the Greek language after *crease of accu-* Alexander's time have already been hinted at. *racy. The con-* *quests of Alex-* But I shall now briefly state the more important *ander necessarily* *impaired the pre-* of them. The conquests of Alexander led to a *cision of spoken* *Greek.* greater or less mixing of all the Greek dialects. The precision with which each little Greek community used

---

961). Τὴν μὲν προσφορὰν ὡς δυικὸν ἔχει τοῦ σχηματισμοῦ (τὸ χρῆσθον), πληθυντικῶς δὲ λέλεκται χρῆσθωσαν. Ἀττικῶν δὲ ἡ τοιαύτη σύνταξις, ποιούντων ἐκεῖνοι, φρονούντων ἐκεῖνοι ἀντὶ τοῦ ποιείτωσαν καὶ φρονείτωσαν (Schol. or Arist. Nub. 438). The notable corruption of κοινανεόντων into

κοινὰν ἐόντων, κοινὰν ἐχόντων, or κοινᾶν δ' ἐόντων, in the text of a treaty between Argos and Lacedaemon (Thuc. v. 79) is well known to have arisen from the same kind of ignorance. Valckenaer's emendation has long been accepted.
[1] In Xenophon there are several instances of φάναι followed by ὅτι or ὡς.

its own dialect was lost in a general medley of race and speech. Instead of accuracy in expression it was found that mere readiness to make oneself understood in any fashion had the highest value; and a man was best able to push his way in the new condition of things who could remember the most vocables, and so have a fairly adequate means of understanding others and making himself understood by them. Add to this that the Greek tongue began to be very widely spoken by foreigners, and, as always happens in such cases, accuracy was neglected so long as the purpose of communicating one's wishes was served, while foreign idiom gradually impaired the syntactical precision of earlier Greek. Suppose these influences to be left at work for centuries, during which Greek was constantly extending its bounds till it came to be widely spoken in the capital of the world itself, and it will be possible to imagine in some degree the condition of the spoken Greek language when Babrius wrote.

But important as it is for the student to keep constantly in mind the essential mixo-barbarism of the Greek tongue from the time of Alexander's conquests, A school of literary manipulators. still something more is required if he would properly appreciate the diction of such a book as the Babrian Aesop. He must remember, in fact, that Alexander founded Alexandria, and that the library shortly afterwards established there produced a literary class who set the example of playing strange tricks with language, and writing books in dialects of their own conception, many of the forms in which never existed except in their own minds, and many of the words received imaginary significations to which they never had any claim. A very large proportion of the anomalous forms registered in lexica and grammars are the merest absurdities, owing a literary existence to the inadequate critical methods of Alexandrine bookworms with an itch for authorship; and not a few of the meanings which lexicographers tabulate are to be ascribed to the like practice of endowing terms long obsolete with a sense to which they had no right. Lycophron's *Alexandra*, though written within a century after the foundation of Alexandria, is an extraordinary congeries of epic anomalies and debased inflections added to the tragic dialect, and thrown into a setting of tragic iambics. A little later, and Apollonius Rhodius utilised the labours of the Homeric critics in Alexandria to compose an epic after the manner of the ancients, which, with all its errors, is a *tour de force* that perhaps justifies his reputation. Such men had many imitators, and more than a thousand years after the date of Homer his ἅπαξ εἰρημένα and anomalous inflections became ordinary modes of expression with an Oppian or a Nonnus, and by false analogy supplied their employers with new terms, at which Homer would have shuddered or asked for an interpreter.

These two facts—mixo-barbarism in the spoken language and lettered affectation in the written—are suffi- *Two facts explain all the difficulties of Babrian Greek.* cient to explain all the anomalies of Babrian Greek. In the following pages of this essay I propose to discuss the language of the choliambics under the three heads of Vocabulary, Inflections, and Syntax, illustrating each section by a reference to the two divergent tendencies discussed above.

Vocabulary.

In using a foreign tongue a man chiefly errs in two ways. On the one hand he is apt to suppose that, because *Errors produced by a deficient acquaintance with a language.* a word in his adopted language corresponds in most of its significations to another in his native tongue, it therefore corresponds in all; on the other he husbands his vocabulary as much as possible, and to avoid the trouble of remembering more words than are absolutely necessary he supplies the place of genuine verbs by means of off-hand formations from the corresponding substantives and adjectives. With one or two generally applicable endings, such as the Greek -όω and -ζω, he can convert nouns and adverbs into verbs, and from these verbs produce new nouns, inelegant it may be, but still intelligible—nay, perhaps, even too expressive.

The former of these tendencies is seen in what have been called the Latinisms of Babrius, such as giving a *The Latinisms of Babrius.* plural number to ὕλη on the analogy of the Latin *silva*, the use of ξύειν in the sense of *radere* in ἠόνα ξύων, of διδόναι in that of *dare* in δρῦν ἔδωκε ποταμῷ, of πνεῦμα like *anima* of the soul when separated from the body in death, of Λιβυστῖνος for Λιβυκός. The Italian origin of Babrius, known to us in other ways, makes it natural to refer such usages to the influence of Latin; but except as a confirmatory test of the validity of more direct arguments, evidence of this kind resting upon language could not be conclusive in the case of a tongue so widely spoken as Greek was in its later stages. Indeed, before such reasoning became cogent it would be incumbent on the arguer to show that in none of the languages which Greek was overlaying had the word for *wood* a plural, and that Latin stood alone in the particular metaphorical uses of the other verbs affected.

In his employment of autoschediastic formations Babrius was only following the general tendency of men *Pro hac vice formations.* who are forced by circumstances to use a language other than their own. Greek, however, had by his day become so degenerate that even had Babrius, despite his name, been of the purest blood and straitest education a Greek of the Greeks, he might still have been overtaken by the fault as seriously as any foreigner. Under this head fall the words ταφρεύω in the sense of σκάπτω, ἀροτρεύω and ἀροτριῶ of ἀρῶ, ψαλίζω of κείρω, πωμάζω of κλείω, γομῶ, φορτίζω and ἀχθίζω for the classical τὰ σκεύη, τὸν φόρτον, etc., ἀνατίθημί τινι, μεσίτης (from μέσος on the false analogy of πολίτης) for διαιτητής, and μεσιτεύω for διαιτῶ or διαιτητὴς γίγνομαι.

I have purposely limited to the most striking and undoubted instances a list which every reader of Babrius *Caution in illustration demanded.* will be able to increase for himself. My reason for doing so was not only to satisfy my own sense of proportion, and to avoid insulting the understanding of my readers, but also because a grave practical difficulty interposes itself in this as in other reasoning of a like kind. As a fault of diction similar forms to the above are sometimes met with even in the purest Attic writers, and in Xenophon are not at all uncommon, but in no writer of the nobler age of Greek literature do they present themselves in such numbers as even in the best authors of a later age. In fact, of late Greek as opposed to classical, they are one of the most marked characteristics. Yet the instances in good authors, few though they be, are still sufficiently numerous to render futile any attempt to illustrate the general tendency of the baser sort by an enumeration of particular examples. The difference in the frequency of such violations of usage between a typical Attic writer and such an author as Babrius it would indeed be possible to represent numerically, but at a cost of labour quite incommensurate with the advantage.

Equally difficult is it to find concrete expression for another general characteristic of the Greek of Babrius and his fellows in its sad mixo-barbarism —I mean the want of precise significance in the terms used, manifesting itself in two contradictory ways. On the one hand, words etymologically very significant have a ridiculously commonplace meaning assigned to them; on the other, a special sense is given to words of generic import. The former of these manifestations of decay in verbal significance is most readily illustrated by its modern fellow in our own tongue—namely, slang or Americanism. As an American speaks of 'freezing' to a man, so the late Greeks used expressions like προσεκολλᾶτο τῷ ἀνδρί, and there is little to choose between the English vulgarism 'to put a knife in a man,' meaning 'to annoy him,' and πρίεσθαι or διαπρίεσθαι, the late equivalent for λυπεῖσθαι. How many Americanisms at once suggest themselves to illustrate the debased use of εὔριπος in the sense of a fish-pond or cistern, of σκόλοψ (a stake) in the same sense as ἄκανθα (a thorn), of φάραγξ (a ravine) for βόθρος (a hole), of μεθύσκειν as a synonym for θηλάζειν or βρέχειν, of πτύειν for ἐκβάλλειν, παρεδρεύειν for τρέφειν, ἁπλοῦν and its compounds for πετανννύναι and its compounds, of σύνεγγυς for the simple ἐγγύς!

Want of precise significance another characteristic of late Greek. Tendency to generalise meanings.

The inclination to specialise the signification of words is, on the whole, less common than this tendency to generalise it, but still a fair number of instances is to be found in Babrius. Of these the more important are ἀγρός, in the sense of cultivated and populated ground, δῶμα with the meaning of roof or house-top, ὁμιλεῖν as a synonym of προσαγορεύειν, and ἐντυγχάνειν of διαπράττεσθαι or διαλέγεσθαι; but the reader will have no difficulty in extending

Tendency to specialise.

the list if he has mastered the two types of verbal decay represented by these words.

If we turn to consider the question how far antiquated words were deliberately used by Babrius to Antiquated words in Babrius. heighten the effect of his εἰδύλλια, we are met by grave difficulties at the outset. The reference in his second preface to the unintelligibility of his imitators (see *supra*, xxi.) makes it improbable that he himself employed many obsolete terms. At the same time, his Homericisms in inflection indicate that he may also have used Homericisms in vocabulary. The facts seem to be that he kept his old words well in hand, and with genuine literary instinct made them serve either to give an old-world setting to an old-world tale like that of the contest between Zeus and Apollo, or to produce the humorous contrasts of parody as in the battle of the cats and the mice, and the story of the hares and the frogs. This latter practice is too common in all literatures to need illustration. A parallel to the former is best found in Chatterton :—

As Elinour by the green *lessel* was sitting,
  As from the sun's *heatë* she *harried*,
She said as her white hands white *hosen was* knitting,
  What pleasure it is to be married !

My husband, Lord Thomas, a forester bold
  As ever clove pin or the basket,
Does no *cherisaunces* from Elinour hold—
  I have it as soon as I ask it.

When I lived with my father in merry Cloud-dell,
  Though 'twas *at my lief* to mind spinning,
I still wanted something, but what *ne* could tell ;
  My lord-father's *barb'd* hall had *ne winning*.

Each morning I rise do I set my maidens,
  Some to spin, some to *cardle*, some *bleaking ;*
Gif any new entered do ask for mine *aidens*,
  Then *swithen* you find me a-teaching.

In these lines Chatterton has made more than one blunder in his antique vocables,[1] and if Babrius appears to us

[1] The blunders of this kind are legion in all the artificial epic poets. Thus epithets are used by themselves as substantives, *e.g.* χλούνης, ἀιζηός, μέροπες, νέποδες, ἐφημέριοι, τραφερή, μηκάδες, ἠριγένεια ; epithets as adjectives, διακ-

to be more correct it is possibly because we cannot be so
familiar with Greek as with English literature (see, however,
note on ξουθός, 118, 1). The more certain Babrian instances
are 25, 9, ἂψ νῦν ἴωμεν: 31, 9, ἴλας or φρήτρας: id. 16, φύζα,
also in 95, 41: 68, 3, ἠρίδαινε: 95, 49, βυσσόθεν: id. 90,
λαφύσσων: id. 95, ἐγκάτων: 103, 10, γῆρας λιπαρόν: 118,
10, θέμιστες: and I have enough confidence in my own
conjecture to add ἄντα (91, 4) to the number.

INFLECTIONS.

The dialect of the choliambics is conventional, and as such
Variety of end- admits not of scientific treatment in the matter
ings.   of forms. It is a sort of pseudo-Ionic, with an
Attic base, and is, moreover, further modified by that uncertainty in declension and conjugation which marks late
Greek, and by the occasional deliberate preference for antique
inflections. Though comparatively free from the late happy-
go-lucky disregard to which declension or conjugation a word
belonged, Babrius seems notwithstanding to have sometimes
slipped, as ἄλωνα in 11, 9, but ἄλω in 34, 2; θᾶσσον in 28,
9, but τάχιον in 45, 4; οἶδας in 95, 14. So κλείζων in 3,
1, may either be for κλείων or for κλήζων (= καλῶν).

Of antique forms there are about as many as of antique
Antique inflec- vocables, e.g. ποσσίν, οὐρανοῖο, πόσσον, τόσσος,
tions.   χωρίσσης, εἰρύσσας, ἐσσί, ἐών. To these may best
be added the imperfects and aorists without augment, as ἐλαφρύνθη in 111, 6: καθικέτευε in 95, 47: and perhaps φύλασσεν
in 33, 2, and ἔρυσσε in 68, 5: while the pluperfects without
augment should rather be referred to late carelessness.

τορος, ἀλλοπρόσαλλος, γλαυκῶπις, ἐνοσί-
χθων, etc. Significations are extended,
as ἰχθυόεσσα Ἐνύω, War between fishes,
δέμας ἰχθύοεν, διερὸς μόρος, death by
drowning, πόθῳ δενδρήεντι, love for trees,
διερὸς δρόμος, ὑδατόεις παρακοίτης, κη-
τώεσσα φάλαγξ, χόλῳ δασπλῆτι. Im-
possibilities of every kind due to false
analogy are also common, as ἠυδάξαντο,
ἀγέρονται, πλέγνυμαι (= πλέκω), ἔσπο-
μαι, ἵπταμαι, ἑλκύσσω, μέμβλονται,

βριδόντα, δέχνυμαι, λίτομαι, ἐδείδιες,
πιέσσω (for πιέσω), ἔρραφον from ῥάπτω,
μύχατος, etc. etc. Meanings are often
altogether mistaken, as δαιτρεύω =
devour; εὐρώεις = εὐρύς, οἰνοβαρείων, ex-
hausted; ἐριδμαίνω, contend; τοσσάτιος
= τόσσος, κεκασμένος, furnished with (a
mistake as early as Pindar). Two
similar words are sometimes confused,
as ἀγαίομαι used for ἄγαμαι.

The frequent use of pluperfects as ordinary pasts may, it is true, be an imitation of Homer, but the sparing way in which Babrius introduces Homericisms and the fact that late epic writers present very few instances of such a usage are strongly against this supposition. On the other hand, in writers of a later date than Babrius, an imperfect meaning is very commonly attached to the pluperfect, and this would lead us to infer that the necessities of his metre tempted Babrius to give a literary status to a vulgarism of his day. *Pluperfects for ordinary pasts.*

With the exception of the final letter in words like χώρη, the codex preserves the conventional dialect with surprising fidelity, even in its inconsistencies. It exhibits ἀεί but αἰετός, πράσσω, φυλάσσω, θαρσῶ, etc., but always ἡττᾶσθαι and ἧττα (cp. λιμώττω, 136, 3, note). It rarely slips in writing ἐς for εἰς before consonants, and never breaks the Babrian rule of using only σύν, not ξύν. It augments εὔχομαι and εὐστοχῶ, but εὑρίσκω only in the pluperfect. Much of this may be due to theories of manuscript editors, but when metre steps in we are on firmer ground. Two and three forms of the same word appear side by side, as πρόσω and πόρρω : χρύσειος, χρύσεος, χρυσοῦς : σιδήρειος, σιδήρεος, σιδηροῦς : χάλκειος, χάλκεος, χαλκοῦς : ἔρημος, ἐρημαῖος : ἐρημαίη, ἐρημίη : βαθείη, βαθέη : ὀξείη, ὀξέη : Ἑρμείης, Ἑρμῆς : ἀείδω, ᾄδω : μῦς and μύας : ζωγρῶ but ξωάγριος. The dual is not known either in nouns or verbs. *Illustrations of the conventional nature of the Babrian diction.*

SYNTAX.

As in Vocabulary and in Inflections, so in Syntax the choliambics bear traces of the two contending tendencies—the unconscious adoption of the modes of expression in use at the time, and the deliberate mimicry of antique style. A third principle, not worth considering in reference to diction, at once complicates the question of syntax. Prevented by the nature of his pseudo-Ionic medium from carrying Atticism into his vocabulary and accidence, Babrius seems certainly to have Atticised in Syntax. At all events, *Artificial nature of the syntax. Atticism.*

the general precision of his syntax is best to be explained in this way.

Leaving, however, a problem so difficult and intricate and unworkable, I will follow the same principle of arrangement as in the two previous heads.

Mixo-barbarism discovers itself even in the syntax. A few constructions are most naturally explained as Latinisms. *E.g.* ἐπέχειν absolutely, without νοῦν, like *advertere* without *animum*: ἐπιζητεῖν παρά τινος like *quaerere ab aliquo*: and in γνώσῃ πόσον τράγου μεταξὺ καὶ πόσον ταύρου the repetition of πόσον corresponding to that of *inter* in 'Nestor componere lites | inter Peliden festinat et inter Atriden.' Striking instances of Alexandrine or Byzantine uncertainty of construction are ever and anon presenting themselves. As late carelessness in the use of synonymous terms produced the ambiguous ἄνδρα καὶ πόλιν φεύγω (12, 20), so want of accuracy in the selection of tenses gave rise to sentences which might convey several meanings. For example, ὡς δ᾽ εἰσιόντες τὰς πύλας ἔνιζον τοὺς πόδας means in Attic only one thing; but as in late Greek, besides the Attic sense of *about to enter*, the participle may also bear those of εἰσβαίνοντες and εἰσελθόντες, the signification has to be settled by the context. Perhaps the choliambic metre may have affected the usage of the tenses to some extent by suggesting, among other things, a present participle for an aorist and an aorist for a present, but such evidence can never be conclusive. Thus the metre might be used to explain the indicative in εἰ μέλαιναν ηὑρήκει (22, 10), if we had not εἴ ποτ᾽ ᾐτήκει (33, 8) to show the fallacy of the reasoning. Metrically it was as easy to use the Attic construction εἴ ποτ᾽ αἰτοίη as the late equivalent in the indicative.

As will be seen from the Index Graecitatis, Babrius has the late confusion of οὐ and μή. He is un-Attic in the frequency with which he employs μή in dependent interrogative sentences, and also in preferring πῶς, πότερος, τίς, etc., to ὡς, ὁπότερος, ὅστις, etc. Further, in the clauses introduced by these words, and generally in all *oratio obliqua*, he does not consistently distinguish by the moods the difference between relative and absolute time.

[marginal notes]
Latinisms. Occasional uncertainty of meaning.

Instances of late usage in Syntax.

In prepositional usage he follows the later writers. The words ἀμφί, ἀνά, ἀντί, περί, do not occur at all, Prepositions. and ὑπέρ only twice. This oligo-prothesië accounts for the fact that the Attic practice of repeating the preposition of a compound verb with the substantive in regimen with it is even rarer in Babrius than in ante-Euripidean poets. The brachy-logic use of μετά, so notorious in writers later than Babrius, is met with in two passages of the 12th fable—μετὰ Θράκην for μετὰ τὰ ἐν Θράκῃ γενόμενα, and μετὰ τὰς 'Αθήνας for μετὰ τὰ 'Αθήνησι. In Babrius' day it may have been little better than a vulgarism, although the corresponding use of ἐπὶ occurs in the New Testament, Acts xi. 19, τῆς θλίψεως τῆς γενομένης ἐπὶ Στεφάνῳ, 'after the affair of Stephen.' [1]

To take wider ground, a reader of Babrius will be struck with the shortness of the sentences and the absence 'Ἀφέλεια. of all complexity in the arrangement of the clauses. Moreover, all the light connecting particles have disappeared with the exception of the most common and indispensable.[2] Of those which are left some are by Attic standard misused, e.g. τοιγάρ and τοιγαροῦν, which in classical Greek never get beyond the beginning of the sentence, are by Babrius placed second, third, fourth, or fifth. The place of the missing particles is supplied in two ways, namely, either by the repetition of a word from the preceding sentence or by a usage of the relative which some would derive from its Latin equivalent. Both sorts of attach-ment are too familiar to all readers of later Greek to require a detailed notice, but Babrius alone will furnish sufficient illustration.

For the discussion of the question whether Babrius did or did not import antique pre-Attic constructions Did Babrius em-into his choliambics there is as yet little material ploy obsolete constructions for ready, nor will it be supplied till the labours of literary effect? the young scholars now working in the field of historical syntax [3] be completed. With the possible exception of ὁρμῆς

---

[1] The instances of μετὰ, e.g. John xxx. 27, μετὰ τὸ ψωμίον, are not by any means so marked. Even Xenophon (An. 4, 8) has μετὰ τὰ πιστά for ἐπειδὴ τὰ πιστὰ ἐγένοντο.

[2] This is still more true of the Hom-eric particles in epic imitators.

[3] See the Preface to *Beiträge zur Historischen Syntax der Griechischen Sprache*, edited by M. Schanz. 1882.

c

ἀφ' ἱππείης (6, 3, see note) I have observed no examples of
literary imitation in the sphere of Syntax.   Certainly there is
not in Babrius anything so manifest as the late epic preference
for the optative instead of the subjunctive in sentences like

$$\sigma\tau\acute{\eta}\sigma\alpha\tau\acute{\epsilon} \; \mu o\iota \; \Pi\rho\omega\tau\mathring{\eta}\alpha \; \pi o\lambda\acute{\upsilon}\tau\rho o\pi ov \; \mathring{o}\phi\rho\alpha \; \phi\alpha\nu\epsilon\acute{\iota}\eta$$

—an imitation rather of a blunder of transliterators than of a
true Homeric construction.

CHAPTER IV.

THE HISTORY OF THE TEXT.

THE main parcel of the Babrian Fables were first published in 1844. But as many complete fables and many fragments were known before that date, so after it several fresh fables have been discovered. In the early pages of this dissertation I mean to describe the sources from which our knowledge of the text of Babrius must be derived, and afterwards to discuss the relation which they bear to each other, and the questions to which they give rise. The fables not all discovered at the same time.

In the year 1840 Abel Villemain, the head of the Department of Public Education in France, commissioned Μινωΐδης Μηνᾶς, a Macedonian Greek, who had for some years resided in the French capital, to explore his native country in search of rare manuscript books. In the library of the Monastery of St. Laura, on Mount Athos, Menas discovered a parchment codex[1] containing 122 fables in the The discovery of the main parcel. Menas.

[1] Menas thus tells of his discovery— 'Dans le couvent de *Laura*, à Mont-Athos, il y a deux bibliothèques, une petite et une grande. La première contient des manuscrits tout a fait abandonnés et jetés pêle-mêle, la plupart pourris par l'humidité et les ordures des animaux, au point que les Vies des hommes illustres par Plutarque, ouvrage manuscrit dont l'Allemand Zacharias parle dans le traité de son voyage qu'il fit il y a huit ans au Mont-Athos, manuscrit alors complet, je l'ai trouvé tout a fait abîmé ; il n'avait plus que dix cahiers ; en grande partie les feuilles étaient collées et pourries. Touts les autres manuscrits étaient dans un état pitoyable. Je travaillai dans cette bibliothèque quinze jours, accompagné d'un diacre, nommé Gabriel, en feuilletant tous les manuscrits, que j'ai nettoyés autant qu'il m'était possible ; et j'ai mis des étiquettes et des numéros a ceux qui m'ont paru de quelque intérêt. Il y avait un plancher, qui occupait le moitié du parterre de la bibliothèque en forme d'un sopha. Les planchesd'au-dessus étaient mouvantes, et le devant du plancher ouvert ; l'au-dessous était plein de poussière et des ordures d'animaux. Ayant examiné touts les manuscrits, je me suis fourré sous le plancher, malgré la résistance des moines, qui s y trouvaient. Ils me

Babrian choliambic verse. Being unable to procure the manuscript itself, he brought home a copy, comparatively accurate, and it was upon this copy that Boissonade had to depend in elaborating the text of the *editio princeps* [1] which was published

---

disaient qu'il n'y avait rien, et que je me salirais inutilement. Cependant j'eu ai extrait quinze manuscrits : un Denys d'Aréopage, grand in ⁻8°, *membr.*, avec des notes abrégées sur les marges ; un autre, Histoire des Animaux, par Élien, incomplet et pourri vers la fin, *chartaceus;* et autres treize encore, parmi lesquels se trouvait le manuscrit en question, abimé vers le commencement et vers la fin. La dernière feuille était un lambeau, qui contenait les six derniers vers ; le verso était embloqué d'un papier collé et pourri. La première partie de ce manuscrit contenait les Histoires fabuleuses dont Saint Grégoire de Nazianze fait mention dans quelques-uns de ses discours. La partie suivante contenait les Fables en quatre-vingt pages in⁻8°, de la même grandeur que la copie que j'eus l'honneur d'envoyer à M. le Ministre ; plusieurs de ses feuilles étaient réécrites. L'écriture m'a paru être du Xᵉ siècle. Le i n'y était pas souscrit sous les voyelles α η ω, mais placé du côté droit : par exemple, αι ηι ωι pour ᾳ ῃ ῳ. Toutes les affabulations étaient en lettres majuscules. Il y avait plusieurs mots, dont quelques lettres étaient effacées, que j'ai déchiffrées et transcrites avec beaucoup de peine.'

[1] Βαβρίου Μυθίαμβοι. *Babrii Fabulae Iambicae cxxiii jussu summi Educationis publicae Administratoris Abeli Villemain viri excell. nunc primum editae. Joh. Fr. Boissonade Litt. Gr. Pr. recensuit, Latine Convertit, Annotavit. Parisiis, apud Firmin Didot Fratres, 1844.* In the same year Boissonade also edited a text with some alterations. *Babrii Fabulae iambicae cxxiii Joh. Fr. Boissonade recensuit II. ed. novis curis expolitae. Parisiis, 1844.* In the next year several editions appeared. At Paris, *Fables, texte grec, publié avec des variantes par Théobald Fix;* also *Fables, Texte revu par Fr. Dübner, avec notes en français par C. Müller.* At Berlin, *Choliambica Poesis Graecorum,* in which Aug. Meineke edited the non-Babrian choliambics ;

while Charles Lachmann, assisted by G. Hermann, Meineke, Haupt, and Bekker, produced a text of Babrius, viz. *Fabulae Aesopeae. Carol. Lachmannus et amici emendarunt.* At Zurich, by Orelli and Baiter, *Fabulae iambicae cxxiii ex rec. J. Fr. Boissonadii passim reficta cum brevi adnotatione critica edid. J. C. Orellius et J. G. Baiterus, Turici 1845.* At Leipsig, by C. H. Weise, Μυθίαμβοι. *Babrii Fabulae Choliambicae cum fragmentis et fabulis aliunde notis. Cur. Car. Herm. Weise. Lipsiae, 1845.* In the following year was published in Oxford and London *Babrii Fabulae Aesopeae cum fabularum deperditarum fragmentis, Georgius Cornewall Lewis.* In 1853, *Babrii Fabulae Aesopeae, edidit F. G. Schneidewin. Lipsiae.* The *Anthologia Lyrica* of Theodor Bergk, which appeared in 1854, included a text of Babrius with some conjectures by the editor. In late years Alfred Eberhard's edition, *Babrii Fabulae ex recensione Alfredi Eberhard, Berolini,* 1875, has been deservedly popular with scholars ; and at the beginning of the present year appeared an edition by M. Gitlbauer, which sadly lacks that solid foundation of learning which the editor's native acuteness might make it worth his while to lay. *Babrii Fabulae, recensuit Michael Gitlbauer. Vindobonae, 1882.*

Besides these editions many very valuable critical notes on Babrius have been published by distinguished scholars. In a Latin letter to F. Jacobs, published in 1844 (*Viro Venerabili F. Jacobs gratulatur F. Duebner. Parisiis, 1844*) F. Duebner made some invaluable conjectures. There appeared also noteworthy articles by C. F. Hermann in the *Jahrbücher für Wissenschaftliche Kritik,* 1844, vol. ii. p. 801 ; by Théodor Fix and N. Piccolos in the *Revue de Philologie,* pt. 1, Paris, 1845 ; by Schneidewin in the *Göttingische gelehrte Anzeigen, Jan. 1845,* No. 136, p. 1361 *sqq.* The Monograph of H. L. Ahrens '*de Crasi et Aphaeresi,*' in 1844. In a subsequent journey to Greece Menas acquired the manuscript itself, and on the refusal of the Royal Library at Paris to purchase it on his terms he entered into negotiations with the Trustees of the British Museum, and transferred it to their hands in August 1857.[1]

The Codex, which carries the number 22,087 in the Additional Manuscripts, consists of forty parchment folios, and corresponds in its present shape to a low, broad octavo. Originally the folios were of a larger size, as is demonstrated by the fact that at the one hundred and third fable the epimythiast's couplet— *Description of the Athoan Codex.*

μακάριος ὅστις οὐ προλαμβάνει πταίσας
ἀλλ' αὐτὸς ἄλλων συμφοραῖς ἐπαιδεύθη,

appears again in the margin, scrawled in an ignorant hand by some reader, but without the final letters of the words nearest to the edge of the folio. The fables themselves are written throughout in cursive characters, which Menas assigned to the tenth century, Dindorf to the eleventh. The former date is perhaps nearer to the truth. The metrical epimythia are also in cursive letters, but in each the initial letter of the first line is placed a little in front to mark them off from the body of the fable. Sometimes a prose epimythium is attached even to those fables which already possess a metrical one. The prose epimythia are always written in accented uncials.

Stolberg, 1845, especially valuable in the history of the Babrian text, has had some worthy successors, especially the *Observationes Babrianae* (Berlin, 1865), and *Verbesserungsvorschläge zum text des Babrius* (Berlin, 1866) of Eberhard, and Hoch's *de Babrii Fabulis quae in codice Athoo leguntur corruptis atque interpolatis.* Halis, 1870. Within late years Nauck has been showing, by notes in the *Bulletin de l'Academie Impériale de Sciences de St. Pétersbourg*, the same fertile interest in Babrius as at an earlier date by articles in the *Philologus* and *Rheinische Museum.*

[1] The last fable (123d) printed by Boissonade had no more than its first line represented in the Codex. The remaining six had been concocted by Menas and added to the copy which he submitted to the Minister of Education. They run as follows—

θησαυρὸν ᾤεθ' ὁ δεσπότης ἐνευρήσειν
ἐν τῇσδε πλεῖστον ἐγκάτοις ἀγερθέντα·
κάκτεινε ταύτην, ἄθροον μέλλων λήψειν.
εὑρὼν δ' ὅμοια τἄνδον ὀρνέοις ἄλλοις,
ᾤμωξε πολλόν, ἐλπίδων ἀτευκτήσας·
πλείονος ἔρως γὰρ ἐστέρησε τῶν ὄντων.

The success with which these barbarities imposed upon the learned induced their author to concoct a new batch of 95 fables, a copy of which the Museum (Additional MSS. No. 22,088) also purchased along with the manuscript of the genuine apologues. To the eternal disgrace of English scholarship, these were actually edited by G. C. Lewis in 1859, but almost immediately exposed by Duebner, Cobet, and

The writing, whether cursive or uncial, is throughout very
The date of the
codex. beautiful and legible, with the iota adscript, and
with very few abbreviations, and these only of the
very commonest kind, as ἀνῶν in the epimythium of the eighty-
fourth, and σρίαν in the spurious line of the one hundred and
seventh fable. That they were familiar, however, to the scribe
is shown also by his writing ἀνῶν for ὤνων in the fifty-seventh.
The number of lines is not the same on every page, owing not
only to the unavoidable breaks between the fables, and to the
prose epimythia, but also to the practice of leaving a vacant
space after some of the fables which lack epimythia.

Besides that of the original scribe there are other two[1]
Diorthotae. hands evident in the Codex—one quite ancient,
using ink now of much the same colour as that of the text,
another[2] of a very different stamp, using a deep black ink.
In this way we have corrections of three kinds, namely, by
the original scribe, by the first hand, and by the second. The
alterations or alternative readings by the original hand are few,
the most important being εἰρηνεύει in the margin opposite
Fab. 39, 4, ἐκκλίνω opposite Fab. 91, 5, and λιμναίαις
opposite Fab. 115, 1. In each of these cases it is, of course,
impossible to say which reading εἰρηνεύει or ὁμηρεύοι, ἐκκλίνω
or ἐξωθῶ, λιμναίαις or λιμνάσιν appeared in the Codex which
the scribe followed, and no less impossible to determine
whether the reading in the text is anything more than a
clerical slip, as scribes often refused to injure their cali-
graphy by erasures and left a wrong word when once written

---

other scholars. Even in the last edition
of *Greek Verbs Irregular and Defective*,
however, Veitch quotes them as genuine.
They are all of a piece with the six lines
given above.

[1] I speak only of the text proper;
in the margin there is here and there a
good deal of scribbling in different
hands. Thus a lumbering, difficult
hand has written on the margin of the
first page a few almost illegible words
of which φίλε and ζῷων seem to have
been two. Again on the page which
begins with the third line of the sixty-
fifth fable, as also on the next page,
there is a great deal of unintelligible

writing. On the foot margin of
the last page five or six hands have
scrawled monkish trifles like ὦ χριστέ,
μακάριος ἵλεως, etc. Alongside of the
seventy-fifth fable some one has repeated the spurious line ὁ δ' ἀτεχνὴς
ἰατρὸς εἶπεν εἰσβαίνων.

[2] Dindorf wrongly jumped at the
conclusion that the third hand was
that of Menas. I believe there is little
to support this view—an opinion which
I am glad to find also stated by Pius
Knoell in his article on the Codex
Athous in *Wiener Studien* for 1881, pp.
184 ff. In any case, whether by Menas
or not, it is of no critical importance.

unerased, contenting themselves with adding the right one in the margin. The hand of the first diorthotes has made but few alterations and none of value. The second diorthotes with his black ink has affected the text most, and in a way little to his credit—inking over not only the fainter lines of the original hand, but in one case at all events (the correction χρη in Fab. 3, 1) even a suggestion of the first diorthotes. In this way a great number of lines have been retraced, generally without blundering, but in the case of very many single words the black ink has done its work effectually in concealing or obliterating the original letters, and the manuscript now exhibits what is undoubtedly not the original reading. Occasionally this second diorthotes suggests a poor variant for the primitive word, as τῆς ἰατρείας for τῶν ἰατρείων, in 94, 7, and in 98, 9, κλαύσει for κλαύσῃ.

The fables appear in alphabetical order, the first letter, as is usual in early works, being alone regarded ; The order of the fables. Traces of the true arrangement. when the letters change, the note ἀρχὴ τοῦ ἀ, etc. is inserted in the margin. The last page ends abruptly with the first line of the one hundred and twenty-third fable—

"Ορνιθος ἀγαθῆς ὠὰ χρυσᾶ τικτούσης,

which indicates that a considerable number of leaves have been lost, sufficient to contain all the fables beginning with the letters Π, Ρ, Σ, Τ, Υ, Φ, Χ, Ψ, Ω, and perhaps (certainly, as we now know) some in Ο.

Besides the fables there have also been preserved in the Athoan Codex two prooemia, one appearing in its proper place at the beginning of the whole, the other inserted among the fables beginning with Mu. The former, which itself begins with Gamma, is preceded on the top margin by the words, ΛΛΕΒΡΙΟΥ ΜΥΘΙΑΜΒΟΙ ΑΙΣΩΠΕΙΟΙ ΚΑΤ' ΣΤΟΙ-ΧΕΙΟΝ in accented uncials of the first hand, the initial letter of Βαλεβρίου being now illegible. The third hand has added
χ'   οι
στ χωλιαμβικ on the reader's right. An original faint α on the same margin in line with the top of the prooemium evidently means τμῆμα πρῶτον. This last fact is of some

interest when taken along with the original heading of the
second prooemium, which is ἀρχὴ τοῦ Β τμήματος, although
the first diorthotes has drawn a line round τμήματος and
changed B into μ. There can only be one explanation of these
circumstances, namely, that in some early manuscript the
fables were not arranged in their present order but fell into
at least two parts, each preceded by a preface. Whether the
Athoan scribe was the first to adopt the present arrangement,
or borrowed it from the codex which he followed, it is yet clear
that the second preface owes its present place to its initial
letter, and that the parcel of fables which it served to intro-
duce are confounded past extrication with those of the first
part.[1]

The manuscript which comes next in order as regards the
The Vatican Cod- number of fables which it contains is the Vatican.
ex. De Furia's
use of it.   In the collection of prose fables published by Fr.
de Furia[2] in 1809, a parcel of thirty-six[3] fables bear the
heading Ἐκ τῆς Βατανικῆς Βιβλιοθήκης. These Furia
extracted from a Vatican manuscript, or, as he thought,
manuscripts, of which a copy was made by one Hieronymus
Amatus, and sent him by Marini, who was at that time
custodian of the Vatican. Their editor, however, did not
observe that fifteen of the thirty-six were really in choliambic

---

[1] This evidence is confirmatory to
that of Avianus in his preface quoted
above, p. xxiii. note. Even the statement of Suidas (sub vocabulo Βαβρίας,
p. 699, C) that Babrius wrote ten books
of choliambics is quite compatible with
the evidence for two parts. Each part
might contain several books.

[2] Αἰσώπου μῦθοι, *Fabulae Aesopicae*
quales ante Planudem ferebantur ex vetusto Codice Abbatiae Florentiae nunc
primum erutae, Latina versione notis-
que exornatae cura ac studio Francisci
de Furia. Florentiae Typis Carlienis,
1809. It was reprinted in *the next year*
at Leipsic (with the omission of a fac-
simile specimen of the Codex Florentinus
which appears on p. xxviii. of the
Florence edition), along with Fabricius'
article on Aesop, Bentley's dissertation
on the Fables of Aesop, Tyrwhitt's on
Babrius, and Huschks' on the Fables

of Archilochus. A poor Index Graecitatis was added by C. E. C. Schneider.

[3] Furia's reference to this portion is
as follows :—'Uberrimam autem et
nunquam editam Fabularum seriem
Bibliothecae Vaticanae Codd. suppe-
ditarunt, quarum (sic) *exemplar* vir
doctiss. Caietanus Marinius, illius Bibliothecae Custos Primus, et Hieronymus
Amatus amicissime transmiserunt.
Dolendum tamen, horum Codd. scrip-
torem adeo imperitum atque rudem
fuisse, ut fere nulla in iis verba mendis
careant, ut ex fidelissimo *Amati apo-
grapho* apparet. Codd. itaque Vati-
canorum lectionem sarcire saepissime
necesse fuit ; opus mehercule plenum
aleae periculosae : in quo, etc. etc.
The mistake of considering that Furia
had the original manuscript in his own
hands has been made by Halm in his
collection of Aesopic Fables (Leipsic,

metre although written as prose. Uncritical and unscholarly as was Coray's edition of Aesopic Fables, published at Paris in the following year,[1] it nevertheless corrected this blunder, and led succeeding editors [2] to print in verse the fifteen fables affected. Niebuhr made search for the codex which had supplied Furia with the choliambics he appreciated so ill, but did not succeed in finding it, probably because he was misled by Furia's words concerning it, and imagined with Furia himself that the Vatican fables sent by copy to Furia were drawn from several manuscript sources, and that those in choliambics came from one codex containing only such.

At length in the year 1878 Pius Knoell, acting under a general commission from the Kaiserliche Akademie der Wissenschaften of Vienna, had the good fortune to discover the manuscript in question,[3] and he has described it at length in his article entitled 'Neue Fabeln des Babrius,' read before the Kaiserliche Akademie, and published in their *Sitzungsberichte* (xci. 2, 1878, pp. 659-690).   Re-discovery by Knoell.

The Codex (Codex Vaticanus Graecus, No. 777), a small paper manuscript of the second half of the fifteenth century, contains, from folio 15^r to folio 106^v, 242 fables, which, with the exception of the last ten, are arranged alphabetically by the initial letter. Not only does it contain different versions of the same fable, but also exhibits in monkish Greek the fable found in the Book of Judges (ix. 8).   Description of the Vatican Codex.

Teubner series, 1875, see Praefatio, p. iv.), and reproduced along with others in Pius Knoell's description of the Vatican Codex, which will be mentioned in the text.

[1] Μύθων Αἰσωπείων συναγωγή, ἐν Παρισίοις ΑΩΙ (1810), forming the second volume of an Ἑλληνικὴ Βιβλιοθήκη (Παρέργων Ἑλληνικῆς Βιβλιοθήκης Τόμος δεύτερος).

[2] The same Charles Ernest Christopher Schneider, who had supplied the Leipsic (1810) reprint of Furia's Florentine (1809) edition with an Index Graecitatis, himself edited the same fables, also in 1810, and in many places corrected Furia's text. Two years afterwards his namesake, Jo. Gottlob Schneider, in his edition of

the fables of the Augustan Codex, published an emended text of the Vatican choliambics with corrections by Buttmann and Niebuhr. They also appeared in other books and periodicals, and in 1835 were incorporated by Joach. Henr. Knoch in his elaborate work *Babrii Fabulae et Fabularum Fragmenta. Accedunt Metricae Fabularum Aesopicarum reliquiae. Halae.*

[3] There is no doubt upon the identity of Knoell's codex with that from which Furia's copy was taken, as the thirty-six fables printed by Furia are all found in the same shape in Knoell's, and further there is the same extraordinary gap in the fable of the lion and stag (Furia, 356).

Besides the fifteen Babrian fables published by Furia, the Codex contains fifteen more, of which nine were already known from the Athoan manuscript. Accordingly Knoell's discovery added only six new fables to the list.

These thirty choliambic fables of the Codex Vaticanus I *The Codex perhaps related to one described by Romulinus.* am inclined to identify with the thirty Aesop's Fables in 'versibus iambicis vel potius scazontibus,' which were observed by P. Romulinus[1] in a manuscript of the eleventh century, in the monastery at Grotta Ferrata some two miles from Frascati (the ancient Tusculum). From that manuscript they might very easily have been borrowed by the compiler of the Vatican Codex.

The following tables are taken, with the necessary modifications, from Knoell:—

1. Fables found both in the Vatican and in the Athoan Codex, those already published by Furia being marked with an asterisk.

Vatican.		Athoan.	Vatican.		Athoan.
17	=	21	114	=	114
18	=	20	*122	=	117
20	=	120	129	=	116
*30	=	27	*173	=	55
*64	=	68	*198	=	33
68	=	83	*211	=	28
88	=	90	216	=	12
*90	=	99	*217	=	88
*97	=	101	242	=	77

2. Fables not in the Athoan but already published by Furia.

Vatican.		Present Edition.	Vatican.		Present Edition.
133	=	126	137	=	129
134	=	127	141	=	125
136	=	128	155	=	124

---

[1] This discovery was reported from letters of Romulinus by Christoph. Gottlieb von Murr in Ephemerid. Noribergens., No. 1. 1789. 'Codex continet vitam Aesopi quae inscribitur Βίβλος ξανθοῦ φιλοσόφου καὶ αἰσώπου δούλου αὐτοῦ· περὶ ἀναστροφῆς Αἰσώπου, et incipit hisce verbis : ὁ πάντα βιω- φιλέστατος αἴσωπος, ὁ λογοποιός, Attico sermone conscripta prolixiorque quam Aesopi vita a Maximo Planude conscripta. Constat enim 72 paginis, misusculo charactere refertis cumaliquot correctionibus, et notulis in margino. Aesopi vitae proxime succedunt fabulae, hoc titulo, Αἰσώπου μῦθοι κατὰ στοιχεῖον

3. Fables first published by Knoell.

Vatican.		Present Edition.	Vatican.		Present Edition.
9	=	130	142	=	133
130	=	131	164	=	134
135	=	132	192	=	135

Like the rest of the Codex Vaticanus, these thirty fables teem with errors of all sorts, many of them merely mistakes of spelling to be passed by unnoticed by a sensible editor, but others unfortunately of a more grave kind. The most important will be discussed in their general aspect farther on, while the others are mentioned in the critical notes [1] attached to the fables.

Long before the discovery, however, either of the Vatican or the Athoan Codex, the choliambics of Babrius were not unknown to the learned. As early as 1505 Aldus issued, among the tetrastichs of Gabrias, the fable of the Swallow and the Nightingale (Fab. 12), but in a very curtailed shape, and with no reference to Babrius.[2] Noël Conti in his *Mythologia*, first published in 1551, quotes nine lines of the fable of Cybele's Priests and their Ass. The same lines, with the exception of two, are also quoted by Tzetz in his *Chiliads*, but are found nowhere else. In a codex of the Interpretamenta of Dositheus the grammarian, which has often changed hands, but is now at Leipsic under the name *Vossianus*,[3] appear two Babrian fables,

Portions of Babrius known at an earlier date. Aldus, Natalis Comes, Dositheus.

ὠφέλιμοι. Sunt No. 223 ordine Alphabetico dispositae, quae numero et verbis paullulum differunt a vulgatis. Postremo omnium fabulae 30, versibus iambicis, vel potius scazontibus concinnatae, hoc titulo τῶν Αἰσώπου μύθων Ιαμβοι."
The Vatican fables may indeed be actually a copy of the Grotta Ferrata set. The Vatican contains 245 fables, and at least three folios have been lost, so that the numbers must be very close. Grotta Ferrata Codex = 223 + 30 = 253 ; Vatican = 245 + fables in three missing folios.
[1] Besides Nauck's and other occasional notes I have used for these new fables the tentamina of Knoell and of Eberhard. The latter has published

his notes in a very inaccessible shape, as *Analecta Babriana* in the *Festschrift zur begrüssung der xxiv versammlung Deutscher Philologen und Schulmänner zu Thier*, 1879, pp. 177-194.
[2] Eberhard has also found the same fable in a manuscript of Marquard Gude's collection, but as the Gude manuscript seems to present a text identical with that found by Aldus in the two codices which he followed, our knowledge has not been bettered by Eberhard.
[3] From its having once belonged to Isaac Voss. When it was at Leiden I. C. Valckenaer studied it, and published therefrom the Babrian fable of the Ant and the Grasshopper (Miscell. Observ. vol. x. p. 109 *sqq.*), and from

that of the Gnat and the Lion, the Athoan eighty-fourth, and that of the Grasshopper and the Ant, which is not elsewhere known in choliambics. Tyrwhitt, in whose Dissertation on Babrius[1] the second of these fables was first published, also brought under the eye of scholars another,[2] No. 58, which has since been confirmed to Babrius by the Athoan manuscript.

But of all the minor sources from which our knowledge of the text of Babrius has to be derived, none has the same intrinsic importance as the lexicon of Suidas. Whatever the date of Suidas may have been, and whether we are to regard his lexicon as a compilation by one man, or as a body of glossological erudition steadily accumulating during many centuries, the fact remains that to the so-called Lexicon Suidianum we owe many invaluable readings, of which the ἀγγάρου in Aeschylus, Agam. 282, and the ἔλαιον in Aristophanes, Vesp. 702, are perhaps the best known, if not intrinsically the most convincing.

The Lexicon of Suidas.

Now Suidas has preserved about a hundred verses from choliambic fables, to a third of which he adds the name Babrius, and almost all of which are known from other sources to belong to the Babrian collection. It is not in their number but in their extraordinary divergence from the Athoan and Vatican versions that the immense critical importance of these lines rests.

The fragments preserved by him.

There is yet another mine from which critics have long been trying to extract Babrian ore—perhaps most strenuously within recent years. The magnificent insistance of Bentley's genius first convinced scholars of a fact which had already been observed before his

The prose para-phrases. Bent-ley, Nevelet, Tyrwhitt.

<hr/>

a copy supplied by Valckenaer Tyrwhitt derived the other Babrian fable. Valckenaer put an absurdly early date upon the codex, with which other scholars do not agree, see Böcking's *Dositlei Magistri Interpretamentorum Liber Tertius, Bonnae, 1832,* pp. xiv. *sqq.* The readings of a Paris Codex have also been recently published by A. Boucherie in his ' Ἑρμηνεύματα ' of Julius Pollux, Paris, 1872, p. 246. In any case, the Aesopic fables which the Vossian Codex contains, whether in prose or verse, are beyond question in-

sertions of a date much posterior to Dositheus, even if any part of the work is by Dositheus at all. See above, p. xxiii. note.

[1] *Dissertatio de Babrio Fabularum Aesopearum Scriptore. Inseruntur Fabulae quaedam Aesopeae nunquam antehac editae ex Codice MS. Bodleiano. Accedunt Babrii Fragmenta. Londini, 1776.*

[2] Brought under his own by Musgrave. For the codex in which it appears see *supra,* p. xix.

day, namely, that many of the prose fables in the ordinary
Aesopic collections were nothing but ill-made paraphrases from
choliambic versions.[1]　Tyrwhitt, on becoming acquainted with
the paraphrase,[2] which of all yet discovered is most nearly
allied to the metrical originals, attempted to go a little
farther than Bentley had done, and managed to restore a few
more lines to their Babrian shape.

In the Appendix to this dissertation I shall try to show that,
as at present understood, prose paraphrases, such as Small value of
the Bodleian which Tyrwhitt used, are principally the paraphrases.
valuable in showing generally what fables are still missing
from the Babrian collection, and are on the whole of very
little service indeed to the textual critic.　I fancy that neither
Bentley nor Tyrwhitt—μετρικωτάτω ὄντε ἄνδρε—would have
contented himself with a smile at the limping lines which
Gitlbauer[3] imagines he has restored to Babrius, but would
have been righteously angry in the poet's interest—

> Καὶ τόδε Δημοδόκου· Μιλήσιοι ἀξύνετοι μὲν
> οὐκ εἰσί, δρῶσιν δ᾽ οἷά περ ἀξύνετοι.

Putting aside for the present all the textual authorities
except the Athoan and Vatican Codices and the Relations of the
Suidian fragments, I now go on to discuss the Suidas.
general features of these three and their relations to each other.
It will be well in the first place to exhibit, in a tabular form,
their more important divergences.

---

[1] Isaac Nicolas Nevelet, son of a
French refugee (the better known Pierre
Nevelet, Sieur de Dosches), edited in
1610, from five manuscripts in the
Palatine Library, then at Heidelberg,
a collection of fables.　On fab. 175 he
has the note—'ἀρούρῃ παγίδας] Redolent
haec verba ut plurima alia harum fabularum loca versus iambicos: atque
utinam extarent hi versus unde haec
desumpta sunt ; Babrium ipsum, si
quid video, haberemus integrum, cujus
jam umbram et epitomen tantum ha-

bemus.'　Again, on Fab. 263, 'ὄνος
πατήσας σκόλοπα χωλὸς εἰστήκει] versus
iambicus scazon quales Babrius scripsit,
nec satis scio num Babrii ipsius.'

[2] Part of the Codex Bodleianus, 2906,
published in 1877 by Pius Knoell
(Fabularum Babrianarum Paraphrasis
Bodleiana edidit P. Knoell, Vindobonae,
1877), and described in the school
calendar for 1876 of the Staats Gym-
nasium in der Innern Stadt, Wien.

[3] See supra, p. lxviii. note.

PASSAGES COMMON TO THE ATHOAN CODEX AND SUIDAS.

ATHOAN.	SUIDAS.
'Αλεκτορίσκων ἦν μάχη Ταναγραίων οἷς θυμὸν εἶναί φασιν οἷον ἀνθρώποις 5, 1-2.	'Αλεκτορίσκων ἦν μάχη Ταναγραίων οἷς φασὶν εἶναι θυμὸν ὥσπερ ἀνθρώποις 3492 C, Ταναγραῖοι.
ἀμείνονα σχὼν τἀπίχειρα τῆς ἥττης 5, 9.	ἀμείνονα ἔχων τἀπίχειρα τῆς ἥττης 3496 A, τἀπίχειρα.
τί σοι τὸ κέρδος ἢ πόσου με πωλήσεις · 6, 6.	τί σοι τὸ κέρδος ἢ τίν' ὦνον[1] εὑρήσεις ; 2778 A, ὦνον.
αἰσχρῆς τις ἦρα καὶ κακορρύπου δούλης 10, 1.	αἰσχρᾶς[2] τις ἦρα καὶ κακοτρόπου δούλης 1682 A, ἦρα.
ἄρκτος φιλεῖν ἄνθρωπον ἐκτόπως ηὔχει 14, 1.	ἄρκος φιλεῖν ἄνθρωπον ἐκτόπως ηὔχει 1188 E, ἐκτόπως.
Βορέᾳ λέγουσιν ἡλίῳ τε τοιαύτην ἔριν γενέσθαι πότερος ἀνδρὸς ἀγροίκου ὁδοιποροῦντος τὴν σισύραν ἐκδύσει 18, 1-3.	Βορέῃ λέγουσιν ἡλίῳ τε τοιαύτην ἔριν γενέσθαι πότερος ἀνδρὸς ἀγροίκου ὁδοιποροῦντος τὴν σισύραν ἐκδύσῃ 3320 B, σισύρα.
καμοῦσα δ' ἄλλως οὐ γὰρ ἴσχυε ψαύειν παρῆλθεν οὕτω βουκολοῦσα τὴν λύπην 19, 6.	ὡς δ' οὐκ ἐφικνεῖτ' ἀλλ' ἔκαμνε πηδῶσα οὐδὲν κρεμαστῆς σχοῦσα πλεῖον αἰώρας παρῆλθεν οὕτω βουκολοῦσα τὴν λύπην 1108 C, αἰώρα.
τῶν οὖν τριχῶν ἑκάστοθ' ἡ μὲν ἀκμαία ἔτιλλεν ἃς ηὕρισκε λευκανθιζούσας . 22, 8, 9.	τῶν οὖν τριχῶν ἑκάστοθ' ἡ μὲν ἀκμαία ἔτιλλεν[3] ἃς εὕρισκε λευκανθιζούσας. 1159 D, ἑκάστοτε.
οὓς εἶπε παύσας φρῦνος, οὐχὶ παιάνων τοῦτ' ἔστιν ἡμῖν, φροντίδων δὲ καὶ λύπης 24, 4, 5.	ὁ δ' εἶπε κλαύσας φρῦνος, οὐχὶ παιάνος τοῦτ' ἔστιν ἡμῖν, φροντίδος δὲ καὶ λύπης. 2903, Παιάν.
ὃς γὰρ μόνος νῦν λιβάδα πᾶσαν αὐαίνει τί μὴ πάθωμεν τῶν κακῶν ἐὰν γήμας ὅμοιον αὐτῷ παιδίον τι γεννήσῃ ; 24, 6-8.	εἰ γὰρ μόνος νῦν λιβάδα πᾶσαν αὐαίνει τί μὴ πάθωμεν τῶν κακῶν ὅταν γήμας ὅμοιον αὐτῷ παιδίον τι γεννήσῃ ; 650 B, αὐήνας.
ὀθούνεκ' εἰσὶν ἀδρανέστατοι ζῴων ψυχάς τ' ἄτολμοι, μοῦνον εἰδότες φεύγειν. 25, 3, 4.	ὀθούνεκ' εἰσὶν ἀδρανέστατοι ζῴων ψυχὰς ἄτολμοι, μοῦνον[4] εἰδότες φεύγειν. 641 C, ἄτολμοι.
ἐπεὶ δὲ λίμνης ἐγγὺς ἦσαν εὐρείης 25, 5.	ἐπεὶ δὲ λίμνης ἐγγὺς ἦλθον γυρίης 857 A, γυρίης.
καὶ βατράχων ὅμιλον εἶδον ἀκταίων 25, 6.	καὶ βατράχων ὅμιλον εἶδον ἀκταίων. 166 C, ἀκταίη.
βαθέην ἐς ἰλὺν ὀκλαδιστὶ πηδώντων. 25, 7.	βαθεῖαν εἰς ἰλὺν ὀκλαστὶ πηδώντων. 2653 A, ὀκλαδίας.
γέρανοι γεωργοῦ κατενέμοντο τὴν χώραν ἐσπαρμένην νεωστὶ πυρίνῳ σίτῳ. 26, 1, 2.	γέρανοι γεωργοῦ κατενέμοντο τὴν χώρην ἐσπαρμένην νεωστὶ πυρίνῳ σίτῳ. 3187 A, πυρίνῳ σίτῳ.
γλύψας ἐπώλει λύγδινόν τις Ἑρμείην. 30, 1.	γλύψας ἐπώλει λύγδινόν τις Ἑρμείαν. 2349 A, λύγδινα.
οἱ σφᾶς ἐκόσμουν καὶ διεῖλον εἰς εἴλας λόχους τε καὶ φάλαγγας ὡς ἐν ἀνθρώποις. 31, 9, 10.	οἱ σφᾶς ἐκόσμουν καὶ διεῖλον ἐς φρήτρας λόχους τε καὶ φάλαγγας ὥσπερ ἀνθρώπους[5] 3844 A, φρήτρα.
ἄλλοι μὲν οὖν σωθέντες ἦσαν ἐν τρώγλαις. 31, 17.	ἄλλοι[6] μὲν οὖν σωθέντες ἦσαν ἐν τρώγλαις. 3628 A, τρώγλη.
ἰδὼν δ' ἐκεῖνος (ἐν μέρει γὰρ ἠλώκει) γαμεῖν ἔμελλεν. 32, 5.	ἰδὼν κἀκεῖνος (ἐν μέρει γὰρ ἠλώκει) γαμεῖν ἔμελλεν. 1273 A, ἐν τῷ μέρει.

---

[1] MSS., by dittographia, τίνων ὦνον.
[2] Some MSS. αἰσχρᾶς σαπρᾶς τις.
[3] vv.ll. ἔτελλεν and ἔτελεν.

[4] Some MSS. μᾶλλον.
[5] v.l. ἀνθρώποις.
[6] v.l. ἀλλ' οἱ.

ATHOAN.

ἡ δὲ τῆς βαθυστρώτου
καταβᾶσα κλίνης ἐπεδίωκεν ἡ νύμφη.
32, 7, 8.
καί τις γεωργὸς πυρὸν εἰς νεὸν ῥίψας
ἐφύλασσεν ἑστώς　　　33, 2, 3.
Δήμητρι ταῦρον ὄχλος ἀγρότης θύων
ἅλω πλατεῖαν οἰνάσιν κατεστρώκει.
34, 1, 2.
τάλας, ἐφώνει, μόχθον οἷον ὀτλεύεις.
37, 3.
ἐνεῖραν αὐτῇ σφῆνας ὡς διασταίη
38, 2.
ἐλθεῖν πρὸς αὐτὸν ἐπὶ τὸ δεῖπνον ἠρώτα.
42, 3.
παρῆν δὲ νέμεσις ἢ τὰ γαῦρα πημαίνει
43, 6.
ἤριζε τεφρὴ γέρανος εὐφύει ταῷ
κτλ.　　　65, 1.

ἐμοὶ γένοιτο κἂν ὁδῷ βαίνειν
ἄνευ γέλωτος μή τι κἂν χορῷ παίζειν
80, 3, 4.
κερδῷ πιθήκῳ φησίν, ἣν ὁρᾷς στήλην
ἐμὴ πατρῴα τ᾽ ἐστὶ κα᾽ μὴ παππῷα
81, 1, 2.
κοιμωμένου λέοντος ἀγρίης χαίτης
διέδραμεν μῦς· ὁ δὲ λέων ἐθυμώθη,
φρίξας δὲ χαίτην ἔθορε φωλάδος κοίτης.
82, 1-3.

ὁ δ᾽, οὐχὶ τὸν μῦν, εἶπεν, ὦ παλαμναίη
δέδοικα μή μου τὴν δορὴν κνίσῃ φεύγων,
κακὴν δὲ μελέτην ἐπ᾽ ἔμε τῆς ὁδοῦ τρίβει.
82, 6-8.
ἄλλοι μὲν ἡμῶν μέλανες οἱ δὲ τεφρώδεις
ἔνιοι δὲ λαμπροὶ καὶ διάργεμοι στήθη.
85, 14, 15.
ἐν τῇ δ᾽ ἔκειτο ῥωγὰς αἰπόλου πήρη
ἄρτων ἑώλων πᾶσα καὶ κρεῶν πλήρης.
86, 2, 3.
καὶ παῖδας εἶχε ληΐου κόμη θρέψας
λοφῶντας ἤδη καὶ πτεροῖσιν ἀκμαίους.
88, 3, 4.

SUIDAS.

τὸν δὲ τῆς βαθυστρώτου
καταβᾶσα κοίτης ἐπεδίωκεν ἡ νύμφη.
703 B, βαθύστρωτος κοίτη.
καί τις γεωργὸς πυρὸν εἰς νεὸν σπείρας
φύλασσεν ἑστώς.　　　2576 B, νεός.
Δήμητρι ταῦρον ὄχλος ἀγρότης θύων
ἅλω πλατεῖαν οἰνάροις ὑπεστρώκει.
3656 D, οἴναρα.
τάλας, ἐφώνει, μόχθον οἷον ὀτλεύω.
2731 C, ὀτλεύω.
ἐναφῆκαν τῇ δρυὶ σφῆνας ὡς διασταίη.
1237 D, ἐναφῆκαν.
ἐλθεῖν πρὸς αὐτὸν ἐπὶ τὸ δεῖπνον ἠρώτα.
1451 B, ἐρωτῶ σε.
παρῆν δὲ νέμεσις ἢ τὰ γῆς ἐποπτεύει. [1]
2572 A, νέμεσις.
Λίβυσσα γέρανος ἡ δὲ [2] ταὼς εὐπήληξ
χλωρὴν ἀεὶ βόσκοντο [3] χείματος ποίην.
810 C, γέρανος ; cp. 3495 C,
ἐμοὶ γένοιτο κἂν ὁδῷ βαίνειν
μὴ καταγέλαστον μή τε [4] πυρρίχην
παίζειν.　　　3187 C, πυρρίχη.
κερδῷ πιθήκῳ φησίν, ἣν ὁρᾷς στήλην
ἐμοὶ πατρῴη τ᾽ ἐστὶ κάτι παππῴη.
2985 A, πίθηκος.
κοιμωμένου λέοντος ἀγρίης χαίτης
διέδραμεν μῦς· ὁ δὲ λέων ἐθυμώθη,
φρίξας δὲ χαίτην ἔκθορε φωλάδος κοίλης.
3844 D, φριξότριχα, [5] also 3853
C, φωλάδος = σπηλαίου κρυπ-
τοῦ, and again in 1169 B,
ἔκθορεν, but with variant
κοίτης.
ὁ δ᾽, οὐχὶ τὸν μῦν, εἶπας ἡ παλαμναία,
δέδοικα μή μου τὴν δορὰν δάκοι φεύγων,
χαίτην δ᾽ ἔμελλε τὴν ἐμὴν καταισχύνειν.
2812 B, παλαμναῖος.
ἀλλ᾽ οἱ μὲν ὑμῶν μέλανες οἱ δὲ τεφρώδεις
ἕτεροι ξανθοὶ καὶ διάργεμοι στήθη.
957 A, διάργεμοι.
ἐν τῇ δ᾽ ἔκειτο ῥωγὰς αἰπόλων πήρα
ἄρτων ἑώλων πᾶσα καὶ κρεῶν πλήρης.
3226 C, ῥωγάς. [6]
καὶ παῖδας εἶχε ληΐου κόμη θρεψας
λοφῶντας ἤδη καὶ πτεροῖσιν ἀκμαίους.
2343 D, λόφος.

---

[1] Variant inserted thus—ἢ καὶ ἄλλως, τἄδικ᾽ ἐποπτεύει.
[2] v.l. ἠδὲ.
[3] v.l. βόσκοντος.
[4] v.l. μήτι.
[5] φριξότριχα· ὀρθοῦντα τὰς τρίχας is evidently a corruption of φρίξαι τὴν χαίτην· ὀρθοῦν τὰς τρίχας.
[6] Also 1310 C, ἔωλα· τὰ χθεσινά· καὶ ἔωλον ὁμοίως, τὸ ψυχρόν, μάταιον, ἀνωφελές, ἀνίσχυρον, τὸ εἰς τὴν ἔω λειπόμενον καὶ ἑώλων καὶ κρεῶν πλήρης, χθιζῶν· τὸ εἰς τὴν ἔω λειπόμενον. ἐπὶ ὄψων· ἔκειτο πήρα ἄρτων. The nonsensical latter part of this has to be corrected into—καὶ ἑώλων· χθιζῶν, τῶν εἰς τὴν ἔω λειπομένων, ἐπὶ ὄψων.
ἔκειτο πήρη
ἄρτων ἑώλων πᾶσα καὶ κρεῶν πλήρης
the scribe's eye having wandered from the first to the second ἑώλων.

ATHOAN.	SUIDAS.

ATHOAN.

νῦν ἐστὶν ὥρη, παῖδες, ἀλλαχοῦ φεύγειν
ὅτ' αὐτὸς αὐτῷ κού φιλοῖσι πιστεύει.
                                      88, 18, 19.
ὁ δ' ὠχριάσας γομφίους τε συγκρούων,
μή μοι χαρίζου, φησί.   92, 8, 9.

μωρὰ δὲ ποίμνη καὶ τὰ πάντ' ἀβληχρώδης
πέμπειν ἔμελλεν.   93, 5, 6.
         κάρχαρόν τι μειδήσας
σοὶ μισθὸς ἀρκεῖ, φησί, τῶν ἰατρείων
κεφαλὴν λυκείου στόματος ἐξελεῖν σώην.
                                      94, 6, 7, 8.
τοιαῦτα κοτιλλουσα τὴν ἀχαιΐνην
ἔπεισεν ἐλθεῖν δὶς τὸν αὐτὸν εἰς ᾅδην.
                                      95, 87, 88.

λέων μὲν αὐτὸς εἶχε δαῖτα παντοίην
σάρκας λαφύσσων, μυελὸν ὀστέων πίνων
καὶ σπλάγχνα λάπτων.
                                      95, 90-92.

πεινῶσα θήρης καρδίην δὲ νεβρείην
λάπτει πεσοῦσαν ἁρπάσασα λαθραίως.
                                      95, 93, 94.

λύκος παρήει θριγκόν, ἔνθεν ἐγκύψας
ἀρνειὸς αὐτὸν ἔλεγε πολλὰ βλασφήμως
                                      96, 1, 2.
κἀκεῖνος εἶπε τὰς σιαγόνας πρίων
                                      96, 3.
κοίλης ἔσω σπήλυγγος ὡς νόσῳ κάμνων
ἔκειτο δολίως οὐκ ἀληθῶς ἀσθμαίνων.
                                      103, 3, 4.

ποῦ δ' ὀσπρίων ἦν σωρὸς ἢ πίθοι σύκων
στάμνοι τε μέλιτος σώρακοί τε φοινίκων.
                                      108, 17, 18.
μικρόν τ' ἐπισχὼν εἶτ' ἔσωθεν ἐκκύψας
ψαύειν ἔμελλεν ἰσχάδος Καμειραίης
                                      108, 24, 25.
ἐγὼ δὲ λειτῆς οὐκ ἀφέξομαι βώλου
ὑφ' ἣν τὰ κρίμνα μὴ φοβούμενος τρώγω.
                                      108, 31, 32.
ὁ δ' ἐκλυθεὶς πόνων τε καὶ ἀναιδείης πάσης
τὸν κνακίαν χάσκοντα λακτήσας φεύγει.
                                      122, 11, 12.

SUIDAS.

νῦν ἐστὶν ὄντως, παῖδες, ἐκ τόπων φεύγειν
ὅτ' αὐτὸς ἁμᾷ κού φίλοισι πιστεύει.
                                      229 C, ἁμᾶν.
ὁ δ' ὠχριήσας γομφίους τε συγκρούσας,
μή μοί χαρίζου, φησί.
                                      835 C, γομφίους.
μωρὸς δὲ ποιμὴν καὶ τὰ πάντα βληχώδης
πέμπειν ἔμελλεν.   748 C, βληχώδης.
        καὶ κάρχαρόν τι μειδήσας,
σοὶ μισθὸς ἀρκεῖ, φησί, τῶν ἰατρείων
κεφαλὴν λυκείου φάρυγγος ἐξελεῖν σώαν.
                                      1957 B, καρχαρόδους.
τοιαῦτα κωτιλλουσα τὴν ἀχαιΐνην
ἔπεισεν ἐλθεῖν δὶς τὸν αὐτὸν εἰς ᾅδην
                                      690 A, ἀχαιΐνη, and
                                      2190 A, κωτίλλω.
λέων μὲν αὐτὸς εἶχε δαῖτα πανθοίνην
ἔγκατα λαφύσσων, μυελὸν ὀστέων πίνων
καὶ σπλάγχνα δάπτων.
                                      2833 A, πανθοίνην; cp.
                                      866 A, δάπτω.
πεινῶσα κερδὼ καρδίην δὲ νεβρείην
λάπτει πεσοῦσαν ἁρπάσασα λαθραίως.
                                      2569 A, νεβρός; cp.
                                      2568 C, νεβρείην καρδίην.
λύκος παρήει τριγχόν, ἔνθεν ἐκκύψας
ἀρνειὸς αὐτὸν ἔλεγε πολλὰ βλασφήμως
                                      3614 B, τριγχόν.
κἀκεῖνος εἶπε τὰς σιαγόνας πρίων
                                      3078 A, πρίων.
κοιώσω σπήλιγγος οἷά τις νοῦσῳ
κάμνων ἐβέβλητ' οὐκ ἀληθὲς ἀσθμαίνων.
                                      3383 C, σπήλιγξ. So from
                                      οἷά τις also at 605 A, ἄσθμα.
ποῦ δ' ὀσπρίων ἦν σωρὸς ἢ πίθος σύκων
στάμνοι τε μέλιτος σώρακοί τε φοινίκων.
                                      3373 B, σωράκους.
μικρὸν δ' ἐπισχὼν εὖτ' ἔσωθεν ἐκκύψας
ψαύειν ἔμελλεν ἰσχάδος Καμειραίας
                                      1967 B, Καμειραία ἰσχάς.
ἐγὼ δὲ λιτῆς οὐκ ἀφέξομαι βώλου
ὑφ' ἣν τὰ κρίμνα μὴ φοβούμενος τρώγω.
                                      2203 A, κρίμνον.
ὁ δ' ἐκλυθεὶς πόνων τε κἀνίης πάσης
τὸν κνηκίαν χάσκοντα λακτίσας φεύγει.
                                      2130 A, κνηκίας.

The above list, even if the numerous merely clerical errors are disregarded, still exhibits a fair number of very important discrepancies between the Athoan readings and those of the lexicon. These, I venture to say, will continue to be in great measure inexplicable till more materials for criticism are discovered. In the first place, there is no way

Discrepancies between the Athoan and Suidas. The fragments in Suidas not all inserted by the same man.

of determining whether the citations in the lexicon were all made from the same codex by the same man. There is even some evidence against this being the case. Is it possible, for instance, that within a few lines of each other the same scholar should have written the two articles—

1. Νεβρείην καρδιήν· Βάβριος
πεινῶσα κερδὼ καρδίην δὲ νεβρείην

and

2. Νεβρός· ἐλάφου γέννημα, οἱονεὶ νέον ἐπὶ τὴν βορὰν ἐξιὸν καὶ νεμόμενον· ἐτυμολογεῖται δὲ ὡς καὶ νεοβόρος τις ὤν. καὶ νεβρεία καρδία· Βάβριος

πεινῶσα κερδὼ καρδίην δὲ νεβρείην
λάπτει πεισοῦσαν, ἁρπάσασα λαθραίως ?

I believe that it is exceedingly improbable that these two glosses came from the same pen, and in any case consider the evidence quite inadequate to prove that the Babrian citations in Suidas are derived from the same recension. In the second place, one of the quotations presents a very manifest gloss :—

ἐναφῆκαν τῇ δρυί) ἐνεῖραν αὐτῇ σφῆνας ὡς διασταίη,

and if one does, surely the others may.

Further, the Suidian glossologists show themselves capable of inserting in the lexicon undoubted clerical corruptions, like γυρίης for εὐρείης and φωλάδος κοίλης for φωλάδος κοίτης, and if this can be proved, then the presence in Suidas, fortified by alphabetical order, of any particular variant cannot be used as evidence in favour of that variant. Again, the rules of Babrian verse prove the lexicon to be wrong in giving ἔγκατα λαφύσσων in place of the Athoan σάρκας λαφύσσων in 95, 91, and if the lexicon or its authority can in this case be shown to have improved upon Babrius by an Homeric reminiscence, then the Suidian φρήτρας (also an Homeric reminiscence) for the Athoan ἴλας in 31, 9, has not a very stable footing. The metre in the same way demonstrates that there is something wrong with the Suidian citation from the nineteenth fable, and it is not improbable that the lexicon lines—

Certain errors in Suidas.

ὡς δ᾽ οὐκ ἐφικνεῖτ᾽ ἀλλ᾽ ἔκαμνε πηδῶσα
οὐδὲν κρεμαστῆς σχοῦσα πλεῖον αἰώρας, 19, 6,

f

arose in somewhat the same way as the Athoan absurdity—

λαχὼν δ᾿ ὁ Φοῖβος χρυσέην τε κυκλώσας
τόξοιο νευρήν, ὀξέως ἀφεὶς πρῶτος.—68, 5.

Moreover, the Suidian ἐγγὺς ἦλθον γυρίης (25, 5), although not so long a blunder as the Athoan—

κακὴν δὲ μελέτην ἐπ᾿ ἐμὲ τῆς ὁδοῦ τρίβει, 82, 8,

is still certainly as deep. Lastly, both authorities agree in making the same unquestioned mistake of transposing κερδὼ πιθήκῳ φησίν and κερδοῖ πίθηκος εἶπεν in the eighty-first fable. The fact is that, with the exception of the one fable, the sixty-fifth, which the lexicon seems to have cited from a version of which the Athoan is a curtailment, there is not much to choose between the Codex Athous and the manuscript. or manuscripts employed by the compilers of Suidas. Each discrepancy has to be explained on its own merits, and in many cases cannot be explained at all. The use to which Prevalence of fables were put in the schools of the ancients alternative read- ings. must have led to a formidable number of glosses, and I feel sure that all our authorities for the text of Babrius have been seriously affected in this way. In a writer of any Byzantine age the difficulty of deciding with any approach to certainty which word is gloss and which word original, is in most cases quite insurmountable; but a few of the variants above tabulated lend a willing ear to an honest arbiter. Thus, of the three variants in 43, 6, viz. the Athoan ἢ τὰ γαῦρα πημαίνει, and the Suidian ἢ τὰ γῆς ἐποπτεύει, and ἢ τἄδικ᾿ ἐποπτεύει, the Athoan is evidently the Babrian lection, and the last a gloss upon it :—

παρῆν δὲ νέμεσις ἢ τὰ γαῦρα πημαίνει (τἄδικ᾿ ἐποπτεύει

the other being an attempt to restore the metre to the corrupt

παρῆν δὲ νέμεσις ἢ τἄδικ᾿ ἐποπτεύει.

Similarly, although it is difficult to decide between μὴ κατα-γέλαστον and ἄνευ γέλωτος in 80, 4, there is no question that πυρρίχην should be preferred to κἂν χορῷ, as in 82, 7, κνίσῃ to δάκοι, in 85, 15, λαμπροί to ξανθοί, and in 88, 18, ἀλλαχοῦ to ἐκ τόπων. Similarly I regard ἀμᾷ in 88, 19, to have arisen from a marginal note—

ὅτ᾽ αὐτὸς αὐτῷ κοὐ φίλοισι πιστεύει   (δηλονότι ἀ μ ᾷ.

Of all the Suidian divergences from the Athoan text there is only one—that on 103, 3, 4—which seems to support the hypothesis that there were two sets of readings both due to Babrius, one belonging to an earlier, the other to a later edition of the fables. Even that instance is weakened by the manifest blunder in the lexicon version. Were there two recensions by Babrius?

The same sort of conclusions are to be drawn from a comparison, first, of the passages common to the Vatican Codex and Suidas, and secondly, of those found in all three authorities. Passages common to the Vatican and Suidas.

PASSAGES COMMON TO THE VATICAN CODEX AND SUIDAS.

VATICAN.	SUIDIAN.
ὁ δὲ τοῦ τέγους κλαγγὴν εἶπε φωνήσας πόθεν μαθήσει πόσον εἰς ἕω λείπει τὸν ὡρομάτην ἀπολέσας ;	ὁ δ᾽ ἐκ πεταύρου κλαγγὸν εἶπε βοήσας πόθεν μαθήσῃ πόσον εἰς ἕω λείπει τὸν ὡρόνομον θύσας με ;
124.	2966 C, πέταυρα.

PASSAGES COMMON TO ATHOAN, VATICAN, AND SUIDAS.

ATHOAN.	VATICAN.	SUIDIAN.
καί τις γεωργὸς πυρὸν εἰς νεὸν ῥίψας ἐφύλασσεν ἑστώς	καί τις γεωργὸς ἐν κλήρῳ πυροὺς σπείρας ἐφύλαττεν ἑστώς.	καί τις γεωργὸς πυρὸν εἰς νεὸν σπείρας φύλασσεν ἑστώς.
εἶπε κορύδαλλος παῖσι νηπίοις ὄντως νῦν ἐστὶν ὥρη παῖδες ἀλλαχοῦ φεύγειν ὅτ᾽ αὐτὸς αὐτῷ κοὐ φίλοισι πιστεύει.	εἶπε κορυδὸς πᾶσι νηπίοις οὕτως νῦν ἐστὶν ὥρη παῖδες ἀλλαχοῦ φεύγειν ὅτ᾽ αὐτὸς αὐτῷ κοὐ φίλοισι πιστεύει.	νῦν ἐστὶν ὄντως παῖδες ἐκ τόπων φεύγειν ὅτ᾽ αὐτὸς ἀμᾷ κοὐ φίλοισι πιστεύει.

It is discernible that the discrepancies in these lines are all best explained by considering them as due either to glosses which have crept into the text or to clerical blunders. The Suidian βοήσας and θύσας με are as manifestly glosses upon φωνήσας and ἀπολέσας as the Vatican τοῦ τέγους upon ἐκ πεταύρων. There may be some question about ῥίψας and σπείρας, but there is none about ἐν κλήρῳ and εἰς νεόν.

Between the Athoan and the Vatican there is on the whole not much to choose, as the following table of the more important divergences will demonstrate :—

The Athoan and Vatican manuscripts compared.

ATHOAN.	VATICAN.
τί σε δροσίζει νυκτὸς ἔννυχος στείβῃ καὶ καῦμα θάλπει πάντα δ' ἀγρώτην τήκει ; 12, 16, 17.	τί σοι δροσίζει νῶτον ἔνδροσος κοίτη καὶ καῦμα θάλπει πάντα καὶ κατακαίει ;
σφάζουσι καὶ κτείνουσι χωρὶς αἰκίης 21, 7.	φάζουσι καὶ κόπτουσι χωρὶς αἰκίης.
γαλῆν δόλῳ τις συλλαβών τε καὶ πνίγων ἔπνιγεν ὑδάτων συναγγίᾳ κοίλῃ 27, 1, 2.	γαλῆν δόλῳ τις συλλαβών τε καὶ πνίγων ἔπνιγεν βαλὼν ὑδάτων συνεχεῖα.
ἔπνιγες ὄρνεις πάντα δ' οἶκον ἠρήμους 27, 6.	ἔπνιγες ὄρνεις πάντα δ' οἶκον ἠρήμους κρεῶν ἀνέψγας ἄγγος ὥστε τεθνήξῃ.
ψᾶρές τ' ὄλεθρος σπερμάτων ἀρουραίων 33, 5.	ψᾶρες ὀρύκται σπερμάτων ἀρουραίων.
θεοῖς Ἀπόλλων ἔλεγε μακρὰ τοξεύειν οὐκ ἂν βάλοι τις πλεῖον οὐδὲ τοξεύσει 68, 1, 2.	θεοῖς Ἀπολλὼν ἔλεγε μακρὰ τοξεύων οὐκ ἂν βάλλῃ τις πλεῖον οὐδὲ τοξεύσει
λαχὼν δ' ὁ Φοῖβος χρυσέην τε κυκλώσας τόξοιο νευρήν, ὀξέως ἀφεὶς πρῶτος 68, 5.	λαχὼν δὲ φοῖβος τὸ τόξον ἐκκυκλώσας
τυροῦ δ' ἀλώπηξ ἰχανῶσα κερδῴη 77, 2.	τυροῦ δ' ἀλώπηξ ἐρῶσα κερδῴη.
ἔτριβεν ἐκτένιζεν ἡμέρη πάσῃ 83, 2.	ἔψηχεν ἐκτένιζεν ἡμέρῃ πάσῃ
ὡς ξηρὸν εἶδε τὸ θέρος εἶπε νῦν ὥρη 88, 6.	ἀνθηρὸν ὃν εἶδε τὸ θέρος εἶπε νῦν ὥρῃ.
μισθὸν μὲν ἀμυντήρσιν αὔριον δώσειν 88, 15.	μισθὸν μὲν ἀμήτυρσιν αὔριον πέμπειν μισθὸν δὲ πᾶσι δραγματηφόροις δώσειν.
εἰπέν τις αὐτῷ βαῖον ἦν λύχνου πνεῦμα τῶν δ' ἀστέρων τὸ φέγγος οὐκ ἀποθνήισκει. 114, 6.	εἰπέν τις αὐτῷ φαῖνε λύχνε καὶ σίγα τῶν ἀστέρων τὸ φέγγος οὔποτ' ἐκλείπει.
τὸν ἀνδρ' ἑαυτῆς καταλιποῦσα κοιμᾶσθαι 116, 5.	τὸν ἀνδρ' ἑαυτῆς εὕδοντα ἐκλιποῦσα
ζητῶν ὑπουστὶ κοὺκ ἰδὼν δόμων εἴσω μηδὲν χανῶν τε καὐτὸς ἦλθεν εἰς οἶμας 116, 9, 10.	ζητῶν ἐφευρεῖν κοὺκ ἰδὼν δόμον ἴσω μηδὲν χαννῶν τε καὐτος ἦλθεν εἰς οἶκον.

Here both manuscripts present the same corruptions in the first lines of the sixty-eighth fable and the tenth of the hundred and sixteenth, and possibly also in the twenty-first and the twenty-seventh. It is also evident that in the fifth line of the sixty-eighth there was some corruption in both manuscripts, which the Athoan after its manner of making clean the outside tried to conceal as best it could by an audacious extension. In the twenty-first it is not unlikely that both *κτείνουσι* and *κόπτουσι* are merely glosses, as both codices exhibit undoubted corruption of this

Corruptions common to both.

kind. Thus in the twelfth fable the Vatican κοίτη is a
gloss upon the Athoan στίβη, the Athoan νυκτός is a gloss
upon ἔννυχος, while the Vatican ἔνδροσος is an attempt to
correct νυκτὸς ἔννυχος. In this case the seriation of corruptions may be thus represented—

τί σε δροσίζει νῶτον ἔννυχος στίβη   (νυκτός
τί σε δροσίζει νυκτὸς ἔννυχος στίβη   (ἔνδροσος
τί σε δροσίζει νυκτὸς ἔνδροσος στίβη (κοίτη
τί σε δροσίζει νυκτὸς ἔνδροσος κοίτη

Then by correction from another copy—

τί σε δροσίζει νῶτον ἔνδροσος κοίτη.

This one line is indeed quite sufficient to overthrow Knoell
and Gitlbauer's theories as to the relation of the Theories as to
two codices, as it suggests a continuity of corrupt- the relation of the Athoan and
ing influences, for which our study of the history Vatican.
of Greek fable has amply prepared us. The text of Babrius,
like that of almost every late Greek writer, must remain in
many respects uncertain. In the Vatican ὀρύκται (33, 5),
ἐρῶσα (77, 2), εὕδοντα ἐκλιποῦσα (116, 5), ἐφευρεῖν (116, 9),
we see glosses on the ὄλεθρος, ἰχανῶσα, καταλιποῦσα κοιμᾶσθαι, and ὅπουστί of the Athoan, while on the other hand the
Vatican ἔψηχεν (83, 2) is the original of the Athoan ἔτριβεν.
As to 88, 15, the explanation of the variants is on the whole
certain. The original reading was

μισθὸν μὲν ἀμητῆρσιν αὔριον δώσειν
μισθὸν δὲ πᾶσι δραγματηφόροις δώσειν.

In the Vatican the first δώσειν was changed to πέμπειν, while
the homoioteleuton led to the Athoan scribe missing the
second line (cp. 68, 1, 2, and 91, 4, 5).

The divergence in the one hundred and fourteenth fable
(and perhaps that in the seventeenth line of the Evidence of Va-
twelfth) suggests the hypothesis of two editions tican as to two editions of Bab-
of the fables, or at all events, of two editions of rius.
the former of the two parcels of fables versified by Babrius.
The strongest argument for this supposition is drawn from the
arrangement of lines in the twelfth fable. Both the Athoan

and the Vatican manuscripts exhibit in the text two sets
of lines—

> ἀλλ᾽ ἔλθ᾽ ἐς ἀγρὸν καὶ πρὸς οἶκον ἀνθρώπων·
> σύσκηνος ἡμῖν καὶ φίλη κατοικήσεις,
> ὅπου γεωργοῖς, οὐχὶ θηρίοις ἄσεις.

and—

> ὕπαιθρον ὕλην λεῖπε καὶ παρ᾽ ἀνθρώποις
> ὁμώροφόν μοι δῶμα καὶ στέγην οἴκει,

one or other of which must be an alteration from the pen
either of the author himself or of a grammarian. That the
former set was at some time or other in the margin is proved
by the fact that in the Vatican Codex the three lines have
been inserted in a wrong place—before instead of after a particular line (see critical note *in loco*). In any case the passage
is poor evidence upon which to base an hypothesis of such
import, and until more evidence is forthcoming it would be
rash to seek in so ill-established a supposition the explanation
of other variants. For my own part I deem it more discreet
to consider the Athoan

> βαιὸν ἦν λύχνου πνεῦμα

an audacious attempt to restore a half-obliterated hemistich, of
much the same sort as the notorious

> κακὴν δὲ μελέτην ἐπ᾽ ἐμὲ τῆς ὁδοῦ τρίβει,

than to throw the πνεῦμα before the βαιόν and refer the
restored words to Babrius himself. In any case the οὔποτ᾽
ἐκλείπει is most probably a gloss upon οὐκ ἀποθνήσκει.

The preceding pages must have prepared my readers for
the point of view which I take in regard to the
more general aspects of the Babrian text. There
is, I am convinced, no evidence worth considering
for two recensions from the author's pen. More-
over, to speak generally, it cannot be said that any of our three
authorities is markedly more trustworthy than its fellows.
The Vatican is in one respect inferior to both the others,
namely, in the number and gravity of its glosses and transcriber's blunders; but in the eyes of a critic searching for
traces of primitive readings, clerical errors are venial and

*The general as-
pects of all the
manuscripts.
Futility of all
theory as to their
genealogy.*

glosses often valuable. Generations of schoolmasters and their
pupils have left their thumb-marks on the pages of Babrius.
The ink is sometimes faint with age, and the characters blurred
with tears. The schoolboy's furtive pencillings between the
lines, as well as the teacher's explanations, have not seldom
worked their way into the text. Add to these sources of
corruption the tinkering of ignorant editors and the blundering
of copyists and the condition of the fables is not surprising.
To theorise about recensions and manuscript genealogies is in
such a case out of the question; and if my text approaches its
original in any degree it is because I have put theory aside and
tried by writing and rewriting the choliambics to get behind
the manuscripts and know Babrius himself.

Of the greater corruptions of the Athoan text the first to
strike the student are the interpolations. In
most cases these are easily detected by the violations therein presented of the rigid metrical rules
of the Babrian scazon. From very early times
this species of corruption has given trouble to textual critics.
In his Σοφιστικὴ Προπαρασκευή Phrynichus [1] tells us that the
verbs ἐπικαττύειν and πτερνίζειν were applied to the work of
the literary cobblers who put a patch on the Comic sock, or a
heel on the Tragic cothurnus. As was natural in the case of
short pieces like Aesopic fables, there are more πτερνίσματα
than ἐπικαττύματα in the Athoan recension of the choliambics.
Of these the attempts at metrical epimythia form by far the
largest number. More than fifty of the fables found in the
Athoan Codex have had one or more lines added to form a
moral, many of them very bad, and none of any literary value.
These I have remorselessly asked to take a lower place. It is
indeed difficult to understand why editors suffered them to
disfigure the book for so long, and inconceivable why they
thought it worth while to emend them. Eberhard was certainly
within his right in bracketing them all. They are never cited
by Suidas, and even the Vatican Codex is without them. Of

The greater cor-
ruptions of the
Athoan Codex.
Interpolations—
πτερνίσματα.
The Epimythia.

[1] Bekk. Anec. 39, 19, Ἐπικαττύειν
καὶ πτερνίζειν· τὸ παλαιὰ ἐπισκευά-
ζειν. ἡ μεταφορὰ ἀπὸ τῶν τοῖς παλαιοῖς
ὑποδήμασιν ἕτερα καττύματα καὶ πτέρνας

προσραπτόντων. λέγουσι δὲ ἐπὶ τῶν τὰ
παλαιὰ τῶν δραμάτων μεταποιούντων καὶ
μεταρραπτόντων.

the five manuscripts from which the twelfth fable has been edited the Athoan is the only codex which exhibits the four lines of moral. Every kind of error in metre, accidence, and syntax is represented in these epimythia, and it is perhaps a blot on this edition that they have found a place even in the critical notes. In fact, they have less right to be preserved than the prose epimythia [1] which I have not printed, but I judged that they would serve a purpose by indicating the kind of corruption which it was natural to expect in Babrius. Pius Knoell [2] considers them to be a characteristic of that recension of the fables to which the Athoan manuscript belongs ; but whether it is so or not, it is very plain that they enjoyed a great popularity in the later centuries. Writers like Tzetz and Georgides [3] are fond of citing them, and even a reader of the *Codex Athous* has tried to fix one [4] in his memory by scrawling it on the margin.

Besides the epimythia, however, there are other πτερνίσματα almost as readily detected. Most of these
resemble the epimythia in being attempts to
render more explicit the ethical gist of the fable to which they are appended. In the one hundred and fourth fable the Athoan scribe has actually written a ˙ spurious final couplet of this sort as a veritable epimythium, by beginning the former of the lines a little in front of the others. If my readers will turn to this apologue, and also to the thirty-third, forty-fifth, sixty-third, and ninety-eighth, I am sure that they will commend me for erasing in each case the one or more spurious lines at their close. Other fables have also suffered by the addition of one or more lines at the end, namely, the twenty-second, thirty-first, forty-second, seventy-ninth, eighty-sixth, ninety-fifth, one hundred and second, one hundred and nineteenth, and one hundred and thirty-fourth ; but in their case the spurious lines owe their existence to the fact that

(margin note:) Addition of lines to the close of the fables.

[1] Pius Knoell, *Neue Fabeln des Babrius*, pp. 667, 668. The tendency to moralising is too deep-rooted in human nature to require illustration. Even the Hesiodean Fable (*supra*, p. xxvii.) had its πτερνιστής, and its Lachmann too, as Aristarchus obelised the epimythium. There is generally a space left in the

Athoan Codex after such fables as have no epimythia.
[2] *Neue Fabeln*, p. 668. The *Etymologicum Magnum* (662, 27) exhibits a metrical epimythium to Fab. 140.
[3] He cites one to Fab. 136 which in the Vatican has none.
[4] Fab. 103.

Babrius had closed the apologues in a way which left an
opening for the cobblers.

Let me carry the quaint fancy of my ancient predecessors
a little further, and limit the term πτερνίζειν to 'Επικαττύματα.
the cobbling of the heels and toes of the fables, Their origin.
reserving the alternative verb ἐπικαττύειν for the like patches
on the uppers. The ἐπικαττύματα are almost as frequent as
the πτερνίσματα. There is a very ugly one after the second
line of the first prooemium, and others will be found by
turning to the critical notes on 3, 2; 12, 17; 27, 6; 50,
15; 57, 6; 58, 6; 72, 17; 76, 7; 88, 2; 95, 60; 126, 7;
128, 7; 131, 15. Sometimes they have originated in an
attempt to conceal either an imaginary or a real lacuna. Of
the former kind the sixty-fourth fable furnishes an example.
Possessed of too little Greek to understand the idiomatic καί
which begins the second last line, an early manuscript editor
rashly hit upon the expedient of inserting a line (compare 85,
4, note). The corruption of the seventy-fifth fable is similarly
traceable to the difficulty presented by a parenthesis.

But far more instructive are the lines which ancient
editors have concocted to conceal a manuscript Attempts to con-
corruption. The best instances come from the ceal corruptions.
sixty-eighth fable, which has been preserved both in the Athoan
and the Vatican manuscripts. The Vatican fifth line is corrupt,
but the editor has left it so, whereas the Athoan is patched up
into a show of meaning by the addition of a line. The note
on the passage will show how a half-obliterated verb was
misread as an adjective, and a substantive had to be supplied
for it even at the expense of a new scazon. I have traced
ἐπικαττύματα of this kind also in 23, 3 and 52, 3, and
have little doubt that the Suidian variant in the nineteenth
fable is due first to a misplacement of the first line, then to
further corruption, and lastly to an attempted cure.

Such early corruption in the text of Babrius is borne
witness to in a striking manner, not only by the instance
in the eighty-second fable, but also by Tzetz. In quoting
the one hundred and thirty-seventh Tzetz omits two lines
which are found in a corrupt shape in Noël Conti. Moreover, both writers exhibit the fable as beginning with Γάλλοις,

whereas its absence from what is left of the Athoan Codex
shows that in the Athoan recension the line now second came
first.

Almost all these additions, πτερνίσματα and ἐπικαττύματα

The faults of
the interpolators
in Greek and in
metre. alike, are marked by considerable offences against
the Greek language, and striking violations of the
Babrian and all other rules of metre. If the
student will read through the lines in spaced type in the
critical notes he will be surprised that they were not rejected
from the first. It would be wrong to assign them all to one hand.
It was stated above that the Vatican Codex has not a single
epimythiast's scazon, but notwithstanding it has other πτερνίσματα, e.g. the three last lines of 134. Of the Athoan
interpolations most are earlier, but some later (e.g. 45, 12;
98, 18; 119, 11) than the prose paraphrases. It would be
doing an injustice even to an interpolator to imagine the
author of the final couplet of the thirty-first fable capable of
writing the lines at the end of the twenty-second or forty-fifth,
or the epimythium of the ninth or the eighty-fourth.

At this point we are met by the question whether any

Were any entire
fables interpo-
lated? entire fables have been interpolated in the collection. The choliambics of Babrius were
addressed to a child, and I believe that this of itself would
almost be reason sufficient for denying the genuineness of the
forty-eighth, fifty-fourth, and one hundred and sixteenth fables,
and assigning them to some versifier as foul as the epimythiast
of the twenty-second. The one hundred and sixteenth,
moreover, in addition to its obscenity, bears another mark of
the interpolator's hand in those lines which end in a short
syllable. From the fact that in so many cases in which lines
end in short syllables it can be proved that they are not from
the hand of Babrius, I am inclined to consider the few short
final syllables still left unaccounted for as due to corruptions.
Both the Athoan scribe and the diorthotae were ignorant of
the Babrian metrical rules, and Suidas, or his authorities, were
equally so. Now, as it is plain that many glosses have crept
into the text, and that these cannot have been always detected,
it is not too rash to account for the short finals on the supposition that they belong to words which have taken the place

of the primitive expressions. The following instances still
defy the critic:—7, 2, τὸν φόρτον: 10, 6, πᾶσαν: 23, 5,
ταῦρον: 99, 4, πίστιν: 106, 4, ἐπειρᾶτο: 106, 16, μοῖραν:
106, 17, σιγῶσαν: 106, 18, ἀποσχοῦσαν: 106, 21, ψαῦσον:
106, 26, ἄλλος: 112, 9, μᾶλλον: 115, 4, ταῦτα: 116, 3,
παῖδα: 116, 7, πᾶσαν: 116, 10, οἶμον: 116, 13, κἀκεῖνος:
129, 19, εἶδον: 141, 1, 2, τίκτητε and εἶχε.[1] It will thus
be seen that out of nineteen defective lines, ten are met with
in the one hundred and sixteenth and the one hundred and
sixth fables, both of which have too much else against them
to allow of our doubting their spuriousness.

Curtailment also has done as much to deface the literary
merits of the choliambics as have interpolation and   Curtailment.
extension. The medieval monk Ignatius, who reduced many
of the apologues to four lines of ordinary iambics, has had predecessors who differed from him only in the metre they used.
It is also not unlikely that they occasionally insinuated a
tetrastich wholly their own, e.g. fable thirty-nine. There may
have been many hands employed in such curtailment, and at
different times. The age of one, however, is later than the
verse epimythia, as the epimythium actually occupies two lines
out of the four (Fab. 41). Curtailment, apart from the tetrastich craze, is proved by comparing the Babrian sixty-fifth with
the Suidian version of it; but whether this was due to the same
tendency that produced the tetrastichs, or originated in an
attempt to preserve in some shape or other a partially
obliterated fable, must for the present remain uncertain.

To pass to less important features of the Athoan copy, there
is evidence for believing that it is by no means so   The Athoan Codex mislead-
good as it looks, and that the beautiful and care-   ing. Its errors.
ful writing cloaks many corruptions. For example, the scribe
seems to have freely inserted syllables to correct metrical
deficiencies due to corruption. Thus in 102, 3, there is an
unmeaning ἄρα which owes its place to πρᾶος, having been
corrupted to πρός, and then πρὸς δὲ καὶ extended to πρὸς
δ᾽ ἄρα καί. So in 116, 10, ἀμηχανῶν both in the Athoan

and the Vatican has lost its alpha, and the μή been extended to μηδέν, so as to exhibit μηδὲν χανῶν. Sometimes also he seems to have followed a common practice of his tribe in converting words he did not know into those which he did without any regard to the sense demanded by the context, e.g. 30, 9, εἶεν to εἶδεν. I believe that in this way are to be explained the ἐμβάντα of 91, 4, and the πεινίη of 46, 7 (see notes *in loco*).

Instances of transposition—another frequent source of Transposition. error—are not uncommon. Two lines have been transposed in 21, 9, 10, and the words φοβερός and πικρός in 1, 15, 16 : πλήρεις and κερδώ in 19, 2, 3 : so in 53, 4, φησὶ νὴ τὸν Πᾶνα for νὴ τὸν Πᾶνα φησί : in 95, 8, εἰς χεῖρας for χεῖρας εἰς : in 100, 5, πῶς εἶπεν for εἶπε, πῶς : in 102, 7, πάντα ὡς δ' for πάντα δ' ὡς : in 117, 10, εἶναι | ὑμῶν for ὔμων | εἶναι : in 121, 3, σοι πάντα for πάντα σοι : and in 123, 1, ὠιὰ χρυσᾶ for χρύσε' ὠιά. In some of these cases the words were left in the wrong order simply to avoid erasures, the same reason which caused the blunder δεικνύει to be left unerased in the text of 13, 6 ; while the true reading σημαίνει was written in the margin (see *supra*, p. lxx.), but in 114, 5, the wrong ῥιπισθείς is in the margin.

The care with which the Athoan scribe has preserved one Inconsistency in of the most convincing proofs of the spuriousness preserving the conventional of the epimythia—I mean the spelling πράττω, spelling. etc., γίγνομαι, γιγνώσκω, ἄν in place of the Babrian πράσσω, γίνομαι, γινώσκω, ἤν—conveys a wrong impression of his accuracy in such things. Fortunately a comparison of the Athoan and the Suidian passages makes it plain that the scribes are not to be trusted for preserving the author's hand in other niceties of his conventional dialect. When the Athoan has η in words like χώρη, Suidas has a, and *vice versa*. In one line the Athoan will write χώρη, in another χώρα. Sometimes an original η is changed to an a by a diorthotes, as ἐλευθέρης to ἐλευθέρας in Prooem. 1, 16. Accordingly I have restored the η in the following words of the Athoan P. 1, 9, πέτρα : 3, 2, μιᾶς : 7, 16, χρεία : 10, 1, αἰσχρᾶς : 10, 2, ἰδίας : 4, πορφύραν : 7, ἡμέραν : 11, 1, ἐχθράν : 18, 1, βορέα : 4, βορέας : 5, βία : 22, 5, νέας, γραίας : 7, γραία : 8, ἀκμαία : 11, νέα, γραῖα : 23, 1, μακράν : 26, 1, χώραν :

28, 4, ὥρας: 37, 4, χώραν: 38, 1, ἀγρίαν: 43, 3, σκιάν: 44, 6, ῥᾳδίαν: 46, 6, πόας: 9, δευτέραν: 47, 8, μίαν: 14, μιᾷ: 48, 3, Ἑρμεία: 49, 1, ἀγνοίας: 4, αἰτία: 50, 13, παχείας: 57, 2, πανουργίας: 14, ἀληθείας: 59, 13, οἰκίας: 60, 1, χύτρα: 61, 5, θήραν: 9, συνηθείᾳ: 67, 3, λιαν: 68, 9, χώραν: 72, 16, Ἀθηναία: 81, 4, ἀληθείας: 2, πατρῴα, παππῷα: 84, 4, ποταμίας: 85, 1, ἔχθρα: 86, 7, ἑτέρα: 89, 2, βίᾳ: 3, ἔχθρας: 9, μητρῴα: 12, αἰτίαν: 93, 5, μωρά: 95, 80, γενναία: 85, κυρίαν: 97, 8, θύρα: 98, 1, ὡραίας: 102, 4, δυναστείας: [11, ἡμέραν]: 104, 1, λάθρα: 4, ἀγορᾶς: [106, 26, ἡμέραν]: Pr. 2, 9, θύρας: 10, σοφωτέρας: 115, 12, χρεία: [116, 4, λαμπρᾶς]: 119, 2, ἡμέραν: 6, Ἑρμεία: 124, 1, ὀρνιθοθήρᾳ. It is a more difficult question to decide which letter ought to be written in the middle of a word. Thus Suidas gives ὠχριήσας where the Athoan presents ὠχριάσας. Are we to abide by Suidas and alter on this principle all similar formations, or believe that as Babrius seems to have used ἡττᾶσθαι and ἧττα by the side of πράσσω, τάσσω, etc., and ἀεί by the side of αἰετός,[1] and πόρρω by the side of πρόσω, so he could write ἐπειράθην in 57, 11, κριθιάσας in 62, 2, ἤθρίασε in 45, 9, but ἰήσῃ in 120, 7 ? The question really admits of no certain answer for each case, but I have preferred the Suidian ὠχριήσας in 92, 8, and κνηκίαν (lege κνηκίην) in 122, 12, to the Athoan ὠχριάσας and κνακίαν, and have altered νεᾶνις to νεῆνις in 22, 6, κνακὸν to κνηκὸν in 113, 2, λίαν to λίην in 95, 76; 100, 1; [116, 4]: and ἂν (if) to ἢν in 6, 17; 7, 5; 47, 10; 48, 6; 53, 3; 71, 9; 84, 6; 95, 8; and 120, 4.

Like other late writers, Babrius also appears to have used ἐς only when the metre demanded, and accordingly I have felt justified in correcting ἐς to εἰς in 1, 11: 11, 5: and 108, 22, the only places in which the Athoan scribe has slipped.

Of other notorious faults of spelling the Athoan Codex supplies many instances. There appear two lambdas instead of one, Letters doubled. in 18, 5, συλλήσειν, 18, 11, ἄλλην (for ἀλῆν), and 111, Letters confounded. Iota 16, ἄλλας, and one instead of two in 6, 12, συλήψῃ adscript.

---

[1] As γιγνώσκω in 1, 16, is the only example outside of the epimythia of the spelling with two gammas of γίνομαι and γινώσκω, so ἀετός in 4, 7, is the only instance of the Attic form. In 112, 9, the third hand has changed ἀεί to αἰεί.

(corrected by a diorthotes), and βαλὼν for βάλλων in 26, 8. Lambda and delta are confounded in 32, 9, δέδιτο for λέλιτο, and perhaps in 95, 91, 93. An example of the confusion so often arising from τ and στ is found in φυγῆς τε for φυγή τε in 1, 3, and of βαλεῖν and λαβεῖν in βαλόντος for λαβόντος in 11, 5. The iota adscript is often added and often omitted wrongly. The codex throughout presents ζῶον or ζώιον, ζώω or ζώιω, θνήσκω or θνήισκω, indifferently. The iota has been forgotten in 33, 8, ἠτήκει: 50, 8, τῆδ᾽: 57, 5, ἑκάστω: 59, 5, ἠρέθη: 95, 74, βίη: id. 83, μόνη: Prooem. B. 13, λουκὴ: 15, πρηΰνας: 115, 11, δίκη: and in 148, 8, ζῆς, and has been wrongly added in 22, 5, ἥιρα, and 33 1, ὥρηι. It has given rise to a sigma in 10, 2, αἰτούσης for αἰτούσηι, and a nu has been mistaken for it in 116, 7, τῆι προθυμίηι (cp. 106, 27, βαῖνον for βαίνοι).

The constant interchange of πρό and πρός is exemplified in 57, 11, Interchange of πρό and πρός, etc. προσελθεῖν for προελθεῖν: 111, 7, προῆλθε for προσῆλθε: and 121, 1, προκύψας for προσκύψας. The confusion of the aorists of verbs in ίζω and έω is seen in 113, 3, φορτήσας for φορτίσας: and 122, 12, λακτήσας for λακτίσας.

The tendency to insert gamma in words like φάρὺξ in 94, 1, φάρυγγος, and 108, 13, ἀσφάλαγξι.

Most kinds of itacism and vowel confusion are represented:—6, 10, Itacism and other vowel confusion. θαλασσίων for θαλασσαίων: id. 15, ὀξείῃ for ὀξέῃ: 9, 3, ἡδυφωνέῃν for ἡδυφωνίην: id. 9, ὀρχεῖσθαι for ὀρχεῖσθε: 12, 16, στείβῃ for στίβῃ: 13, 2, συνειλήφῃ for συνειλήφει: id. 8, νοσιλεύω for νοσηλεύω: 18, 5, νομίζειν for νομίζωι: 29, 4, ἀλφίτοισι for ἀλφιτεῦσι: 22, 4, κώμας for κώμους: 28, 4, μήτηρ for μῆτερ: 31, 9, εἴλας for ἴλας: id. 12, τειχῶν for τοίχων: 32, 10, τῷ for τῇ: 34, 7, εἶμι or εἰμὶ for ἥμει: 35, 1, δύο for δίω: 37, 1, δάμαλις for δαμάλης: id. 10, πονεῖν for πονῶν: 41, 2, μήκους for μῆκος: 43, 4, ἔνεκε for ἕνεκα: 45, 1, ἔνειφεν for ἔνιφεν: 46, 2, βαθυσχοίνῳ for βαθυσχίνῳ: 47, 9, πειρᾶσθαι for πειρᾶσθε: 50, 14, ἀκάλλοισα for αἰκάλλοισα: 60, 1, ζωμῷ for ζωμοῦ: id. 4, τροφῆς for τριφῆς: 61, 5, ἀγρίην for ἀγρείην: id. 9, ἐξολεῖται for ἐξολεῖτε: 68, 4, κυνὶ for κυνῇ (κυνῇ m. rec.): id. 8, τοῦτο for ταὐτὸ: 77, 10, φωνέεις for φωνήεις (corr. man. sec.): 80, 2, αὐλῆς for αὐλοῖς(* αι*): 88, 8, πέδων for παίδων: 89, 4, τί for τοί: 89, 8, ἐκπέποκας(*ü*) for ἐκπέπωκας: 93, 9, ἡμιν for ὑμῖν: 94, 3, καθειμήσας for καθιμήσας: 95, 75, πλέον for πλεῖον: 95, 86, κοτίλλοισα for κωτίλλοισα: 97, 6, χαλκεῖα for χαλκία: 98, 16, χειρὸς for χερὸς: 100, 1, πημελὴς for πιμελής: id. 2, τράφῃς for τραφεὶς: 100, 6, σιδηρίω for σιδηρείω: 108, 7, βόλω for βώλω: id. 11, Ἀμαλθαίης for Ἀμαλθείης (corr. m. rec.): id. 27, ἀρουρείτης for ἀρουρίτης: id. 31, λειτῆς for λιτῆς: Pr. B, 13, λουκὴ for λευκῇ: 111, 8, μεισογεῖον for μεσόγεων: 120, 2, εὑρύποις for εὑρίποις: 119, 10, κεινὴν for καινὴν.

In the case of a few of these errors the change of vowel may not be due to pronunciation or palaeographic mistakes, but to another fertile source of corruptions—the habit of allowing the words in a sentence to attract one another perversely. Thus in 9, 9, ὀρχεῖσθαι may be due to the following κρεῖσσον ἦν, and ἐξολεῖται in 61, 9, to the preceding τὸ χρηστόν. To this cause is certainly to be ascribed θαρσῆσαι for θαρσήσας in 1, 4, because of the προυκαλεῖτο before it. So τῶν παρόντων for τις παρόντων in 2, 3: τάγηνον ὡραῖον¹ for τάγηνον ὡραίων in 6, 4: θεὸν ὕμνει for θεῶν ὕμνει in 15, 6: ἀτάκτους κινδύνους for ἀτάκτως κινδύνους in 31, 6: μῦς· ἡ δὲ for μῦς· τὸν δὲ in 32, 7: σε σωτῆρα for σε σωτήρων in 50, 3: δυσβάτου κρήνης for δυσβάτου κρήνη in 72, 5: ἐμῇ πατρῴα for ἐμοὶ πατρῴῃ in 81, 2: ἀγγέλου φήμῃ for ἄγγελος φήμη, in 103, 6: Σύρων παλαιῶν for Σύρων παλαιὸν, in Prooem. 2, 2: διαβρόχοις σίτους for διαβρόχους σίτου, in 108, 6.

Errors due to wrong collocation.

Others again of the vowel misspellings may well be alterations deliberately made by some editor ignorant alike of the conventional dialect and the metre of Babrius. The spelling of the following words may also be due to the same cause:—κατέαξε for κατῆξε in 3, 5: χωρίσης for χωρίσσης in 12, 21: ἐρύσας for ἐρύσσας in 121, 7: ἐξέρριψε for ἐξέριψε in 42, 5 (cp., however, διαρήσσει for διαρρήσσει in 38, 7. In 36, 1, the MS. has really αὐτόριζον, not αὐτόρριζον, as previously quoted).

Some mistakes possibly due to ancient editors.

Not seldom words are wrongly divided, syllables or letters belonging to one being attached to another, or a final letter being sometimes repeated with the following word, sometimes dropped when the next word begins with the same. 25, 3, ὅθ' οὕνεκ' for ὁθούνεκ': 28, 7, φυσῶσ' σεαυτὴν (pr. man.) for φυσῶσ' ἑαυτὴν: 31, 7, εἷλον τε for εἵλοντο (corr. diorth.): 36, 7, τε ων for τ' ἐών: 37, 7, ἀδμήσκειν ὃς for ἀδμὴς κεῖνος: 38, 2, αὐτῆσφήνας for αὐτῆς σφῆνας: 39, 4, τάχ' ὄπισθε for ταξόπισθε: 43, 3, δὲ αὐτοῦ for δ' ἑαυτοῦ: 50, 6, ὅδ' for ὁ δ': ὤμνυ for ὤμνυ': id. 11, ἤδ' for ἡ δ': id. 10, ἐδείκνυ for ἐδείκνυ': 50, 19, μ' ἔσωσας . . ἀπεκτείνας for με σώσας . . ἀποκτείνας: 54, 3, ὅτ' ἂν for ὅταν: 72, 12, καθ' ὑγρῶν for καθύγρων: 85, 10, εἰσιν οἴδ' for εἰσίν, οἱ δ': id. 14, ἄλλοι for ἀλλ' οἱ: 86, 8, σκώπτοισ' ἄμεινον (an early hand has written ἄν above the α!) for σκώπτοισα μεῖνον: 95, 55, ἀνωδήγει for ἂν ὡδήγει: id. 57, ἤδ' for ἡ δ': id. 59, ἐπέσχεν ὦτα for ἐπέσχε νῶτα: 102, 12, τὰ σθένῃ for τάσθενῇ: 103, 6, ἐπαυλὰς for ἐπ' αὐλὰς: 107, 14, τοῦτο for τοῦ τό: Pr. B. 14, ὀδόντας σου for ὀδόντας οὐ. If ἔπτισε μήτηρ in 6, 8, should be written ἔπτισ' ἡ μήτηρ, it belongs to this class of error, but if written ἔπτισεν μήτηρ to the next.

Wrong division of syllables.

The ephelkustic Nu is sometimes omitted unadvisedly, and sometimes added. It is often impossible to say whether Babrius used it or not, the codex not being consistent, e.g. before two consonants and the double letters. It does not follow that because Babrius could write ὅτε δροσώδης, etc., that he would not write εἶπεν δροσώδης preferentially to εἶπε. The circumstance that he leaves a syllable short before Zeta as readily as modern writers of Greek verse,

Ephelkustic Nu.

---

¹ In turn this caused the error ἐκ τῶν for οὐ τῶν which the Athoan exhibits.

complicates the question still further.   The Νυ is certainly wrongly
omitted in 10, 10, ἦλθε καθ (not in 7, 8, εἶρπε, as hitherto cited): 12,
9, ἔσχισε δαίμων: 16, 7, ἐλπίσι παρ: 28, 5, ἦλθε παχ: 43, 10, ἴχνεσι
κουφ: 75, 10, ποσὶ μόλις (ποσὶν m. rec.): 103, 10, κατήσθιε γηρ:
108, 9, πυθμέσι γῆς (corr. m. rec.), and is wrongly added in 14, 2,
ἔφασκεν μή: cp. 33, 13, ἔλθωσιν for ἔλθωσ'.   But which is right—
ἴσχνεν ψαύειν in 19, 6, or εἶπε προσελθών in 43, 3 ?   Probably we
should write ἴσχνε ψαύειν, but εἶπεν προσελθών.

Not a few blunders are due to crasis, viz. 6, 13, καὶ σπαίρων for
Errors due to κάσπαίρων: 20, 5, καὶ τίμα for κάτίμα: 62, 2, καὶ
crasis. φώνει for κἀφώνει: 81, 2, κα' 'μὴ for κἀμή: 116, 8,
ὠνὴρ for ἀνήρ.   These are sometimes to be explained by the Athoan
habit of writing the words in full, as 12, 23, καὶ ἐπίμιξις: 30, 5, καὶ ὁ:
33, 15, καὶ ἐνέμοντο: 37, 4, καὶ ὑπέτεμνε: 106, 7, καὶ ἐφίλει.

Syllables and letters have now and again dropped out, either from
Letters and syl- similarity of appearance or of pronunciation, as 2, 2,
lables dropped. ἀπολέσας ἐζήτει for ἀπολέσας ἀνεζήτει or ἐζητήκει: 6, 2,
λεπτῷ for λεπτῷ τε: 9, 4, ἑτέριζεν for ἑτερέτιζεν.

Miscellaneous errors of a like kind easily accountable for are:—4, 8,
Miscellaneous ἀμφίβαινε for ἀμφέβαινε: 6, 2, ζώων for σώζων: 9, 5,
errors. ἔκαμνε for ἔκαμε: 12, 21, ὀρχάδος for ὀργάδος: 20, 7,
κέντιζε for κέντριζε: 33, 12, ἡνίκα for ἡνίκ' ἄν: 36, 11, καμπτύμεθα
for καμπτόμεσθα: 55, 3, τετέλεστο for ἐτετέλεστο: 61, 5, ἠρέθιζεν for
ἠρέτιζεν: 85, 9, δὲ ἦλθον for δ' ἦλθον: 95, 11, μαλακῆς for μαλθακῆς:
96, 1, ἐγκύψας for ἐκκύψας: 102, 9, ἐλάφῳ for ἐλάφῳ δὲ: 106, 6,
θηρίων for θηρῶν: id. 12, δὲ for τε: id. 18, χεῖραν for χεῖρα: Pr. B. 6,
λιβίσσης for κιβίσσης: 111, 1, μικρὸς ἔμπορος for μικρέμπορος:
112, 5, ἔνθεν δὲ for ἔνθεν: 115, 12, τί γὰρ for τίς γὰρ: 116, 10,
εἰσοῖμας or εἰσοιμαι for εἰσ οἶμον (m. rec.): 117, 5, λέγοντες for
λέγοντος: 122, 5, δειπνήσει for δειπνήσεις.

Of the errors not mentioned in the critical notes there are very few
Uncial errors. that certainly date from uncial times, the most striking
being ΚΑΙϹΑΙΝΩ for ΚΑΙΙϹΑΙΝΩ in 84, 3 (cp. the
Suidian) ΙϹΛΛΥϹΑϹ for ΠΑΥϹΑϹ in 24, 4, and ΕΤΕΜΕΝ for
ΕΤΙΛΛΕΝ in 22, 9.   In two cases, namely, 2, 14, and 20, 6, an
Omicron has been lost before a Theta—ΟΟΕΟϹ.

The mistakes in accent are not very numerous.   The practice of this
Mistakes in codex, like so many others, is to write μὴ δέ and μὴ δ' for
accent. μηδέ and μηδ'.   I have silently altered this, and also the
cases of ἡμεῖς and ὑμεῖς at the end of a line, which are never written
ἥμεις, ὕμεις, etc.   Whether Babrius would have done so in the latter case
I consider a little doubtful.   Other errors in accent are—18, 11, ἄλλην
for ἀλῆν: 19, 4, θίγειν for θιγεῖν: 31, 9, σφὰς for σφᾶς: 32, 4, τις
for τίς: 33, 2, νέον for νεόν (corr. m. rec. νεών): id. 5, ψάρες τ' for
ψάρες τ': id. 7 and 15, ψάρες: 35, 4, κολποῖς for κύλποις: 36, 8, αὕτη
for αὐτή: τοσσὴ for τόσση: id. 12, βαῖον for βαιὸν (corr. m. rec.): 47,
1, ὑπέργγηρως for ὑπεργγήρως: 49, 5, σου for σοῦ: 54, 4, πιθῶρα for
πίθωνα: 65, 1, τέφρη for τεφρή: 89, 6, οὐκοῦν for οὔκουν: 92, 4,

ὦ for ὤ : νυμφῶν for νυμφῶν : 93, 7, μᾶλλον for μαλλὸν : 95, 53, που for πού : 100, 5, δέ σοὶ for δέ σοι : 106, 9, κερδῶ for κερδὼ : 107, 2, οἰκοτρὶψ for οἰκότριψ : Pr. B. 3, πρὶν πότ᾽ for πρίν ποτ᾽ : 111, 3, πριᾶσ- θαι for πρίασθαι : 116, 16, ἐκτίσαι for ἐκτῖσαι : 119, 8, ὠφελεῖς for ὠφέλεις : 121, 1, πότ᾽ for ποτ᾽.

I shall be pardoned for frankly saying that this enumera- tion of clerical errors would never have left my note-book if it had not been my duty to furnish more minute scholars with the readings of a manuscript to which they might not have easy access, and which hitherto had been collated with little care. To attempt the same for the Vatican Codex is not in my power, and, if it were, would be unnecessary, as Pius Knoell has so recently executed the task. Reasons for giv- ing details of Athoan lections.

In most respects my recension of the text may be called conservative. I have made it a rule to pass unnoticed those inanities or, to take a leaf from their own book, those insanities in conjecture which some critics The present recension.

ἀργαλεῆς αἰεὶ βάξιος ἱέμενοι,

supply in numbers that bear an inverse proportion to the knowledge they possess. My own tentamina I submit with some confidence to the judgment of riper scholars. In no case have I ventured upon emendation except after long and close study of the text, and if I have missed that touch at once bold and cautious which makes a good textual critic, it is not from ignorance of its value. The names of those critics who have done so much in restoring the text of the choliambics I have already mentioned, and in the critical notes have always written at length. If they have sometimes failed to convince it may be for a reason that is as good for our day as for Solon's—

ἔργμασιν ἐν μεγάλοις πᾶσιν ἀδεῖν χαλεπόν.

APPENDIX A.

The whole question of the prose fables belongs really to my second volume, but it is incumbent upon me here to state as briefly as possible my reasons for refusing to use the paraphrases with any freedom for the correction of the text of Babrius. It is true, as Knoell says, that the Bodleian paraphrast sometimes preserves a primitive lection corrupted in the Athoan Codex, but this does not necessarily prove that he had a better recension before him, but only that he did not always make the same blunder as the Athoan scribe. For example, when the paraphrast retains the original πρῷος δὲ in 102, 3, while the scribe has the corruption πρὸς δ᾽ ἄρα, both may still have had actually the same codex before them, but the one read the fading letters better than the other. Similarly it is leaning on a broken reed to draw any conclusion for the excellence of the paraphrast's copy of the choliambics from his presenting χλωρὸν in 120, 8, in place of the Athoan and Vatican χωλόν. In the first place, the Athoan scribe may well have misread χλωρόν into χωλόν (the blunder is bound to have had a beginning), and in the second place it is giving your paraphrast a poor character to think him incapable of so natural and easy a correction as χλωρόν for χωλόν in this passage. Moreover, both Knoell and Gitlbauer (who has entered into Knoell's labours) have built a house upon sand, and have taken no pains to lay a firm foundation for their speculations. Thus Knoell considers his recension of the Bodleian paraphrase to rest upon three manuscripts besides the Bodleian itself; but of these three one (Nevelet's fifth Palatine[1]) he consults at second hand, and of another he only infers the existence, while the third (that in St. Mark's) is plainly a curtailed Bodleian. His imaginary codex has had a strange origin. Coraes, whose edition of the fables has no critical merit, made the serious mistake of believing Hauptmann's collection to be in some extent

---

[1] It is quite possible that all Nevelet's five manuscripts survived the transference of the Palatine library, and are yet safe in Rome.

original. As a matter of fact Hauptmann did no more than
reproduce in Germany the beautiful Oxford edition of Hudson,
just as at a later date Furia's collection was reprinted at Leipsic.
With the exception of a sorry preface and a Latin life of Aesop,
Hauptmann's edition is identical with Hudson's. He inserts, it is
true, in the text the emendanda on the last page of Hudson's, but
he leaves the addenda as they were, and what is more, also, the
inserenda addendis and *inserenda annotatiunculis*. Hudson[1] prints
eighteen versions as from manuscripts, three being headed simply
ex MS., one *ex MSS. Gall*, one *ex alio MS. Gall*, and thirteen *ex MS.
Gall.* Coraes jumped at the conclusion that the thirteen were all
from the same manuscript, and further, that they were first printed
by Hauptmann. In these mistakes Knoell has acquiesced and
begotten a codex for his recension. As a matter of fact he might
have had an *MS. Gall* for the lifting, but not one which would have
assisted his theory. In *Notices et Extraits des Manuscrits de la Bibliothèque du roi* (Tome II., Paris, 1789) M. de Rochefort describes a
manuscript (Codex Paris. Nr. 1277) of the thirteenth or fourteenth
century which contains among much other matter twenty-eight
fables. These come in the same order as the Bodleian, but there are
no fables corresponding to the sixth, tenth, seventeenth, twentieth,
twenty-first, twenty-sixth, and thirty-second of the Bodleian. It
is extremely instructive to compare the two versions, as they lead
one to the inference, which I believe will be confirmed, that these
Aesopic paraphrases owe their existence to the practice, which has
injured the text of Babrius so materially, of using the fables to
impart the elements of rhetoric. The Babrian choliambics were
first used in this way, and were altered and added to, paraphrased
and rewritten from the paraphrase. Then the paraphrases themselves were subjected to the same treatment (cp. the extraordinary
popularity of Aphthonius as a school-book).

APPENDIX B.

SYNOPSIS of the Greek Paraphrases and Latin Versions of such Fables as still survive in Choliambics.

Note.—The versions of Ignatius are referred to by the numbers which they bear in the collection of Coraes.

1	2	3	4	5	6	7	8	9	10	11	12	13
Babrian.	Vatican.	Bodleian.	Rochefort.	Augustan.	Florentine.	Aphthonius.	Syntipas.	Ignatius.	Coraes.	Halm.	Phaedrus.	Avianus.
1	...	11	9	...	...	...	...	279	279	403	...	17
2	...	...	...	...	...	...	...	...	...	91	...	...
3	...	4	4	...	...	5	...	151	151	17	App. 22	...
4	...	8	7	...	...	...	...	...	154	26	...	...
5	...	7	6	...	119	12	7	...	145	21	...	...
6	...	...	...	18	20	...	...	...	124	28	...	20
7	...	12	10	177	24.133	...	...	...	125	177	...	...
8	...	...	...	...	...	...	...	...	...	68	...	...
9	...	...	...	11	34	33	...	...	130	27	...	...
10	...	...	...	...	...	...	...	353	...	73	...	...
11	...	9	8	...	...	38	...	...	163	61	...	...
12	216	2	2	...	...	...	...	...	149	10	...	...
13	...	14	12	190	76.147	14	...	172	172	100	...	...
14	...	13	11	...	25	...	...	...	165	69	...	...
15	...	...	...	...	...	...	...	...	...	50	...	...
16	...	1	1	155	104	39	...	...	138	275	...	...
17	...	...	...	16	15	...	...	...	6	14	...	1
18	...	17	...	46	...	...	55	...	306	82	...	4
19	...	18	15	15	5.170	...	...	156	156	33	4, 3	...
20	18	...	...	...	...	...	...	...	335	81	...	32
21	17	...	...	...	...	...	...	...	...	80	...	...
22	...	15	13	31	199	...	...	162	162	56	...	...
23	...	16	14	49	31	...	12	...	131	83	...	...
24	...	21	...	...	...	...	...	350	350	77	1, 6	...

SYNOPSIS—*Continued.*

	1	2	3	4	5	6	7	8	9	10	11	12	13
	Babrian.	Vatican.	Bodleian.	Rochefort.	Augustan.	Florentine.	Aphthonius.	Syntipas.	Ignatius.	Coraes.	Halm.	Phaedrus.	Avianus.
25	...	101	...	...	137	89.150	23	...	57	57	237	...	...
26	...	...	...	...	...	...	...	...	...	...	93	...	...
27	30	...	...	...	...	...	...	...	...	...	89	1, 22	...
28	211	...	...	...	...	...	...	...	...	...	84	1, 24	...
29	...	22	17	...	...	...	13	...	...	193	174	App. 19	...
30	...	...	...	...	...	...	...	...	...	...	265	...	23
31	...	20	...	...	163	115.175	...	51	...	242	291	4, 6	...
32	...	19	16	...	50	48	...	...	169	169	88	...	...
33	198	...	...	...	...	...	...	...	...	...	99	...	...
34	...	...	...	...	47	40	...	...	262	262	348	...	...
35	...	30	24	...	215	182	...	...	...	267	366	...	35
36	...	29	...	...	213	81	30	...	143	143	179	...	16
37	...	24	19	...	...	61	...	...	...	174	113	...	36
38	...	28	22	...	...	174	...	...	...	179	123	...	...
39	...	...	...	...	72	53	...	...	...	177	116	...	...
40	...	25	20	...	...	...	...	...	...	342	181	...	...
41	...	...	...	...	...	...	...	...	...	...	388	...	...
42	...	27	21	...	...	22	...	...	...	129	62	...	...
43	...	34	27	...	75	66	18	15	181	181	128	1, 12	...
44	...	36	28	...	...	...	16	13	296	296	394	...	18
45	...	37	...	...	...	...	...	...	...	150	12	...	...
46	...	...	...	...	...	...	...	20	...	377	131	...	...
47	...	38	...	...	53	52	...	...	...	171	103	...	...
48	...	...	...	...	...	...	...	...	...	...	139	...	...
49	...	33	26	...	169	62	...	...	...	252	316	...	...
50	...	41	...	...	22	10	...	...	...	127	35	App. 26	...
51	...	39	...	...	208	168	...	...	...	288	382	...	...
52	...	32	...	...	45	39	...	...	...	168	79	...	...
53	...	31	25	...	156	...	...	...	...	...	271	...	...
54	...	...	...	...	...	...	...	...	...	...	143	...	...
55	173	...	...	...	...	...	...	...	...	...	104	...	...
56	...	...	...	...	...	...	...	...	...	...	364	...	14
57	...	40	...	...	...	...	...	...	...	...	141	...	...
58	...	44	...	...	...	...	...	...	...	...	132	...	...
59	...	43	...	...	100	...	...	...	...	190	155	...	...
60	...	...	...	...	...	117	...	...	...	243	292	...	...
61	...	...	...	...	...	...	...	...	...	...	220	...	...
62	...	46	...	...	...	83	...	...	...	140	157	...	...
63	...	...	...	...	109	80	...	...	...	399	161	...	...
64	...	48	...	...	...	...	...	...	...	180	125	...	19
65	...	47	...	...	219	...	...	...	...	357	397	...	15
66	...	50	...	...	...	...	...	...	...	337	359	4, 10	...
67	...	52	...	...	...	...	...	...	225	225	258	1, 5	...
68	64	...	...	...	103	...	...	...	...	187	151	...	...
69	...	...	...	...	...	...	...	...	...	...	238	...	...
70	...	51	...	...	...	...	...	...	...	361	162	...	...
71	...	54	...	...	166	...	...	...	...	247	94	...	...
72	...	59	...	...	101	78	31	...	188	188	200	...	...

APPENDIX B.

Synopsis—*Continued.*

1 Babrian.	2 Vatican.	3 Bodleian.	5 Augustan.	6 Florentine.	7 Aphthonius.	8 Syntipas.	9 Ignatius.	10 Coraes.	11 Halm.	12 Phaedrus.	13 Avianus.
73	...	55	...	...	3	...	...	...	170	...	...
74	...	58	104	...	...	...	...	194	173	...	...
75	...	53	...	...	...	...	...	192	168	...	...
76	...	57	...	...	...	...	...	...	178	...	...
77	242	61	123	...	29	...	204	204	204	1, 13	...
78	...	63	...	87	...	...	...	132	208	...	...
79	...	66	132	...	35	28	209	209	233	1, 4	...
80	...	...	...	...	...	...	...	...	182	...	...
81	...	...	14	...	...	14	...	...	43	...	...
82	...	65	144	95	...	...	218	218	257	...	...
83	68	67	...	...	...	...	...	...	176	...	...
84	...	70	136	...	...	47	213	...	235	...	...
85	...	86	...	...	...	...	...	...	267	...	...
86	...	64	24	12	...	...	158	158	31	...	...
87	...	68	135	...	...	50	...	...	229	...	...
88	217	...	...	...	...	...	...	...	210	...	21
89	...	83	152	101	...	...	229	229	274	1, 1	...
90	88	74	...	...	...	...	348	...	252	...	...
91	...	72	214	181	...	40	277	277	396	...	13
92	...	79	45	39	...	...	...	168	114	...	...
93	...	80	...	...	...	...	...	238	269	...	...
94	...	84	153	94.102	25	...	144	144	276	1 8	...
95	...	75	...	...	...	...	...	358	243	...	...
96	...	81	...	75	...	...	139	139	135	...	...
97	...	...	141	92	...	...	...	227	262	...	...
98	...	76	138	110	7	...	...	221	249	...	...
99	90	...	...	...	...	...	...	...	245	...	...
100	...	...	...	...	...	...	...	...	278	...	37
101	97	...	...	...	...	...	...	...	272	...	cp.40
102	...	78	...	...	...	...	...	...	242	4, 3	...
103	...	73	140	91	8	37	...	137	246	...	...
104	...	71	...	...	...	...	...	210	224	...	7
105	...	85	...	...	...	52	...	234	279	...	...
106	...	...	...	...	...	...	...	...	244	...	...
107	...	77	148	98	...	...	...	217	256	...	...
108	...	...	...	121	24	...	...	...	297	...	...
109	...	91	...	...	4	...	295	...	187	...	3
110	...	...	...	...	...	...	...	...	227	...	...
111	...	92	176	122	...	...	254	...	322	...	...
112	...	...	...	...	...	...	...	...	299	...	31
113	...	89	...	...	...	...	...	271	371	...	...
114	114	90	...	...	...	...	...	239	285	...	...
115	...	...	229	193	...	...	61	61	419	...	2
116	129	...	...	...	...	...	...	...	54	...	...
117	122	95	...	...	...	...	...	...	118	...	...
118	...	96	225	190	...	...	286	286	418	...	...
119	...	97	...	21	...	...	...	128	66	...	...
120	20	113	...	154	24	...	...	135	78	...	6

Synopsis—*Continued.*

1	2	3	5	6	7	8	9	10	11	12	13
Babrian.	Vatican.	Bodleian.	Augustan.	Florentine.	Aphthonius.	Syntipas.	Ignatius.	Cornes.	Halm.	Phaedrus.	Avianus.
121	...	111	7	14	...	...	152	152	16		...
122	...	106	{183 227}	{134 140}	9	...	259	259	334		...
123	...	112	88	153	...	27	136	136	343		33

End of Athoan Fables.

1	2	3	5	6	7	8	9	10	11	12	13
124	155	...	...	...	...	...	...	...	341	...	...
125	141	...	...	...	...	...	...	...	338	...	...
126	133	98	...	...	...	...	...	...	314	...	...
127	134	105	...	...	...	...	...	...	152	...	...
128	136	...	...	...	...	...	...	...	317	...	...
129	137	...	92	...	...	...	...	212	331	...	...
130	9	...	...	...	...	...	...	...	...	...	...
131	130	...	...	123	...	...	...	248	304	...	...
132	135	...	...	107	...	...	...	228	273	...	42
133	...	109	178	135	...	...	257	257	324	...	...
134	164	116	...	...	...	...	...	260	344	...	...
135	192	...	...	197	...	...	...	291	423	...	...
136	...	146	...	{195 198}	1	43	134	134	401	...	34
137	...	...	...	...	...	...	...	...	...	...	...
138	...	135	...	187	...	...	...	264	349	...	...
139	...	...	162	...	...	...	...	241	290	...	...
140	...	5	...	...	...	...	...	...	122	...	...

ΒΑΒΡΙΟΥ

ΜΥΘΙΑΜΒΟΙ ΑΙΣΩΠΕΙΟΙ.

ΠΡΟΟΙΜΙΟΝ.

Γενεὴ δικαίων ἦν τὸ πρῶτον ἀνθρώπων,
ὦ Βράγχε τέκνον, ἣν καλοῦσι χρυσείην.   2
ἐπὶ τῆς δὲ χρυσῆς καὶ τὰ λοιπὰ τῶν ζώων   6
φωνὴν ἔναρθρον εἶχε καὶ λόγους ᾔδει.
ἀγοραὶ δὲ τούτων ἦσαν ἐν μέσαις ὕλαις.
ἐλάλει δὲ πέτρη καὶ τὰ φύλλα τῆς πεύκης,
ἐλάλει δὲ – ͂, Βράγχε, νηὶ καὶ ναύτῃ,   10

---

1. Me piget tantas in critices difficultates e vestigio delabi ; sed aliquot prooemii locos adeo corruptos codex exhibet ut de iis desperare liceat. 2. Post vocabulum χρυσείην tres versus Athous habet et sensu et numero carentes, quos plurimi editores sanare temptaverunt, sapientior Lachmannus omisit.   Interpolatoris verba tibi habe :—

> τρίτη δ' ἀπ' αὐτῶν ἐγενήθη χαλκείη,
> μεθ' ἣν γενέσθαι φασὶ θείαν ἡρώων.
> μεμπτὴ σιδηρὰ ῥίζα καὶ γένος χεῖρον.

6. verbi χρυσῆς priores duo literae Chi et Rho in Athoo paene evanuerunt, tertia upsilon omnino ; sed de adjectivo dubitare non licet. 10. Post ἐλάλει in codice apparet evanida quaedam litera, deinde quatuor vel quinque literarum lacuna, postea ἰχθὺς.   Editores plurimi δὲ πόντος

---

2. The spurious lines which the critical genius of Lachmann first discarded are an ἐπικάττυμα of some grammarian, who was better acquainted with the description of the five ages in Hesiod's *Works and Days* (109 ff.) than with the laws of the Babrian seazon. The third hand of the codex has written a superlineal τις after αὐτῶν to supply the lacking syllable, and Burges altered ἐγενήθη into ἐγεγένητο. Eberhard solved the metrical difficulty of the next line by substituting δῖαν for θείαν, and in the last it

would be easy to read γόνος or γονὴ χείρων to obviate the short ultimate. In any case μεμπτὴ is to be corrected to πέμπτη, πέμπτης, or πέμπτῃ, if the lines deserve attention, and a line marked wanting between χρυσείην and ἐπὶ τῆς. Lachmann's further correction of ἐπὶ τῆς δ' ἐπίσης will be condemned by every reader conversant with authors like Longus and Heliodorus, in whom the practice of repeating a word instead of using a relative is even more common than in Babrius himself.

στρουθοὶ δὲ συνετὰ πρὸς γεωργὸν ὡμίλουν.
ἐφύετ᾽ ἐκ γῆς πάντα μηδὲν αἰτούσης,
θνητῶν δ᾽ ὑπῆρχε καὶ θεῶν ἑταιρείη.
μάθοις δ᾽ ἂν οὕτω ταῦτ᾽ ἔχοντα καὶ γνοίης
ἐκ τοῦ σοφιστοῦ τοῦ γέροντος Αἰσώπου   15
μύθους φράσαντος τῆς ἐλευθέρης μούσης.
ὧν νῦν ἕκαστον – ⏑ – ⏑ –   μνήμῃ
μελισταγές σοι τοῦτο κηρίον θήσω,
πικρῶν ἰάμβων σκληρὰ κῶλα θηλύνας.

I.

Ἄνθρωπος ἦλθεν εἰς ὄρος κυνηγήσων,
τόξου βολῆς ἔμπειρος· ἦν δὲ τῶν ζώων

dederunt, neglecto ἰχθύς. Ego satius esse putavi nihil decernere quam cum iis errare aut cum Knoelio δὲ κίχθυς scribere. 14. De novo codex deficit, μαθ δ᾽ ἃ οὕτω exhibens, sed cum editoribus μάθοις δ᾽ ἂν malo legere quam cum Knoelio μαθὼν δ᾽ ἄρ᾽. 15. Gitlbauero duce, σοφιστοῦ τοῦ pro σοφοῦ ἡμῶν dedi. 17. Manifeste errat Athous, verbis ἂν θείης ἐμῃ post ἕκαστον lectis ; de conjecturis criticorum silere mallem, si auderem. Lachmannus ἂν θέλῃς ἑνὶ proposuit, Duebnerus ἵνα τιθῇς ἑνὶ, Gitlbauerus ἀντιθεὶς ἐμῇ. Mihi placet Babriana de lectione ignorare, sed fortasse in ἂν θείης latet casus aliquis vocabuli ἄνθος, et in ἐμῃ μνήμῃ participii μεμνημένος pars. 18. Minima cum fiducia Athoum ροῦτὸ in τοῦτο mutavi. 19. θηλύνας editoribus debeo, verbi enim Babriani tantum θη manet quod manus recentissima in θηλῶσαι (sic) extendit.

15. Gitlbauer's correction of this line is not certain, but I have adopted it preferentially to the impossible σοφοῦ γέροντος ἡμῖν Αἰσώπου of Eberhard, and I have done so the more readily because in most cases it will be necessary to disregard Gitlbauer's work, which fails rather from want of knowledge and judgment than of native acuteness.

16. The reading ἐλευθέρης ought never to have been called in question. By μῖθοι τῆς ἐλευθέρης μούσης Babrius meant fables narrated in prose. Μοῦσα is applicable to any kind of composition in which the imagination has more share than the intellect, and ἐλεύθερος bears the natural meaning of 'unfettered,' i.e. 'not bound by the ties of verse.'

18. Lit. 'refining the harsh iambics' rugged limbs.' The reference in these words is plainly to modifications introduced by Babrius into the scazon.

l. 1. κυνηγήσων. The Attic word for hunter was κυνηγέτης, and the verb 'to hunt' κυνηγετεῖν. The tragic κυναγός was, however, atticised by later writers into κυνηγός, and a verb κυνηγεῖν formed from it. See Phryn. p. 496.

2. τόξου βολῆς ἔμπειρος, 'skilled in shooting with the bow,' an extraordinary expression equivalent to ἔμπειρος τοῦ τοξεύειν. Such a signification of βολή is unknown in good Greek, although the word itself is in other meanings familar to classical poetry.

ἦν δὲ . . πλήρης, 'and there was hurrying and scurrying of all the

φυγή τε πάντων καὶ φόβου δρόμος πλήρης.
λέων δὲ τοῦτον προὐκαλεῖτο θαρσήσας
αὐτῷ μάχεσθαι. 'μεῖνον' εἶπε 'μὴ σπεύσῃς'   5
ἄνθρωπος αὐτῷ 'μηδ' ἐπελπίσῃς νίκῃ·
τῷ δ' ἀγγέλῳ μου πρῶτον ἐντυχὼν γνώσῃ
τί σοι ποιητέ' ἐστίν'· εἶτα τοξεύει

I. 8. Bergkium et Seidlerum secutus sum, verbo quod Athous profert
ποιητόν in ποιητέ', mutato. Scribae ποιητεεστιν male intelligenti culpa
est referenda.

beasts, and full of panic was their
running.'
6. **μηδ' ἐπελπίσῃς νίκη**, 'and place
not thy hope in victory.' Cp. Eur.
Hipp. 1011, σὸν οἴκησειν δόμον ἐπήλ-
πισα if ἔτ' ἤλπισα should not be there
read. In Attic Greek proper there
are no compounds of ἐλπίζω, unless
ἐπελπίζω, in the sense of 'inspire with
hope,' is regarded as such. The preposition ἐπί sometimes confers a causative meaning upon intransitive verbs.
There is in Homer one instance. In
Od. 20, 85—

ὁ γάρ (sc. ὕπνος) τ' ἐπέλησεν ἁπάντων
ἐσθλῶν ἠδὲ κακῶν, ἐπεὶ ἄρ βλέφαρ' ἀμφι-
καλύψῃ,

the active ἐπλήθω has the sense of
'cause to forget.' (Although to Il. 2,
234—

οὐ μὲν ἔοικεν
ἀρχὸν ἐόντα κακῶν ἐπιβασκέμεν υἷας
Ἀχαιῶν,

the Hesychian gloss Ἐπιβασκέμεν·
ἐπιβιβάζειν must be referred, yet in that
passage the ἐπί governs the genitive,
and has probably nothing to do with
the causative sense of βασκέμεν.) Thucydides has ἐπαληθεύειν twice in the sense
of 'verify,'—4, 85, τὴν αἰτίαν ἐπαληθεύ-
ουσα ; and 8, 52, τὸν Ἀλκιβιάδου λόγον
ἐπηλήθευσεν ὁ Λίχας. Aristophanes
gives this value of the preposition a
comic turn in Nub. 1147, where he
uses ἐπιθαυμάζειν of opening the eyes
of a schoolmaster with a fee—χρὴ γὰρ
ἐπιθαυμάζειν τι τὸν διδάσκαλον. Suidas,
quoting the passage, explains the verb
by the gloss δώροις τιμᾶν, which misses
the point. Aristophanes supplies a
second example in Vesp. 704, κᾆθ'
ὅταν οὗτός σ' ἐπισίξῃ | ἐπὶ τῶν ἐχθρῶν

τιν' ἐπιρρύξας ἀγρίως αὐτοῖς ἐπιπηδᾷς,
where ἐπιρρύξας has the meaning of
'making to snarl at.' To give ἐπί the
same force in ἐπισίζω and ἐπιρρύζω is
to convict the poet of tautology in
grammar, and to convert the master of
the dog Demus into a dog himself, or
at best a cynic. The ultimate sense
of ἐπισίζειν and ἐπιρρύξειν is almost the
same, but the two meanings of ἐπί are
to be carefully kept distinct. ἐπισίζειν
is to be compared with ἐπιρροιζεῖν 'to
whistle (a dog) on,' ἐπιρρύζειν with ἐπελ-
πίζειν, ἐπαληθεύειν, etc. The writer
of the *Oeconomicus* (11, 13) has
ἐπισχύω 'make strong,' φίλους ἐπ-
ωφελεῖν καὶ πόλιν ἐπισχύειν. A similar
force of κατά I shall here only refer to
by naming the verbs κατασιωπῶ, κατασ-
τασιάζω, καταστρατοπεδεύω.
It is also interesting to observe how
an early causative meaning of certain
verbs, which was lost in Attic to the
simple forms, was yet preserved in the
compounds with ἐπί and κατά ; *e.g.*
ἐπιρρέπω and καταρρέπω, ἐπισπέρχω
and κατασπέρχω. These facts will
confirm the causative sense generally
assigned to ἐποικτίζω in Soph. O. R.
1296, θέαμα δ' εἰσόψει τάχα | τοιοῦτον
οἷον καὶ στυγοῦντ' ἐποικτίσαι, and to
κατοικτίζω in O. C. 1282, ῥήματ' ἢ
τέρψαντά τι | ἢ δυσχεράναντ' ἢ κατοικ-
τίσαντά πως, where δυσχεραίνω is as
naturally transitive as χαλεπαίνω, etc.
On the other hand, lexicographers are
wrong in translating by 'ply with
drink' the verb ἐπισκυθίζω in Hdt. 6,
84, where it really is equivalent to
Σκυθιστὶ ἐπιχεῖν, according to the usage
of Greek in regard to verbs in -ζω.
7. **τῷ δ' ἀγγέλῳ . . γνώσῃ**, 'but
first discuss the matter with my envoy ;
after that thou wilt decide.' This use

μικρὸν διαστάς. χὣ μὲν οἰστὸς ἐκρύφθη
λέοντος ὑγραῖς χολάσιν· ὁ δὲ λέων δείσας　　　　10
ὥρμησε φεύγειν εἰς νάπας ἐρημαίας.
τούτου δ᾽ ἀλώπηξ οὐκ ἄπωθεν εἰστήκει.
ταύτης δὲ θαρσεῖν καὶ μένειν κελευούσης
᾽ οὔ με πλανήσεις᾽ φησίν ᾽ οὐδ᾽ ἐνεδρεύσεις·
ὅπου γὰρ οὕτω πικρὸν ἄγγελον πέμπει　　　　15
πῶς αὐτὸς ἤδη φοβερός ἐστι γινώσκω.᾽

II.

Ἀνὴρ γεωργὸς ἀμπελῶνα ταφρεύων
καὶ τὴν δίκελλαν ἀπολέσας ἀνεζήτει
μή τις παρόντων τήνδ᾽ ἔκλεψεν ἀγροίκων.
ἠρνεῖθ᾽ ἕκαστος. οὐκ ἔχων δ᾽ ὃ ποιήσει
εἰς τὴν πόλιν κατῆγε πάντας ὀρκώσων·　　　　5
τῶν γὰρ θεῶν δοκοῦσι τοὺς μὲν εὐήθεις

of ἐντυγχάνω is common in late Greek. Polyb. 4, 30, 1, οἱ δ᾽ ἐξαποσταλέντες πρέσβεις πρὸς τοὺς συμμάχους, ἀφικόμενοι πρῶτον εἰς Ἀκαρνανίαν, ἐνετύγχανον τούτοις. Id. 76, 9, ἐντυχόντων δ᾽ αὐτῶν τῷ βασιλεῖ περὶ τούτων.
10. λέοντος ὑγραῖς χολάσιν 'in the soft' or 'yielding bowels of the lion.' The adjective ὑγρός corresponds to the Latin 'mollis' in its connotation, though not in its denotation. It has very wide associations in all periods of Greek, and admits of no accurate rendering here. For the form χολάδες, see Phryn. p. 364.
12. ἄπωθεν with long penultimate as always in Attic. See Phryn. p. 60.
II. 1. ἀνὴρ γεωργός. Such combination of a generic with a specific substantive is known to be very frequent in Homer—σῦς κάπρος, βοῦς ταῦρος, ἔρηξ κίρκος, μόσχοισι λίγοισι, γυνὴ δέσποινα, etc.—but in Attic to be almost confined to cases in which ἀνήρ, ἄνθρωπος, and γυνή are the generic terms. Even in tragedy there is no approach to the freedom of the Homeric usage.
ταφρεύων means 'trenching' in classical Greek, and though the δίκελλα could be used for this purpose as is known from the Antigone of Sophocles and the Phoenissae of Euripides; yet

trenching a vineyard would go far to ruin the vines, and we must here give the word its late sense of 'digging.'
2. In Λέξεις Ῥητορικαί, Bekk. An. p. 240, 3, δίκελλα is explained as τὸ ἐργαλεῖον ᾧ τὴν γῆν οἱ σκαπανεῖς ἀνορύττουσιν.
ἀνεζήτει μή τις .. ἔκλεψεν. This usage of μή is frequent in Babrius as in all late Greek. It is very rare in Attic. In tragedy it is not found before Euripides, and even he employs it very sparingly—Heracl. 482, θέλω πυθέσθαι μὴ 'πὶ τοῖς πάλαι κακοῖς | προσκείμενόν τι πῆμα σὴν δάκνει φρένα. It is not found at all in Aristophanes, and in Attic prose there is perhaps no example earlier than Plato, who supplies one or two,—Phaedr. 273 A., εἰπάτω τοίνυν καὶ τόδε ἡμῖν ὁ Τισίας μή τι ἄλλο λέγει τὸ εἰκὸς ἢ τὸ τῷ πλήθει δοκοῦν.
5. ὀρκώσων, see Phryn. p. 466. ὀρκῶσαι is found in an Attic inscription of a good age, Corp. Inscr. Attic. iv., Suppl. p. 11.
6. δοκοῦσι τοὺς μὲν .. κατοικεῖν. The history of this use of δοκεῖν is instructive. In Ionic prose it is quite common, and naturally far from rare in tragedy. In Attic, however, it is somewhat restricted. Aristophanes prefers δοκῶ μοι to δοκῶ = 'I think';

ἀγροὺς κατοικεῖν, τοὺς δ' ἐσωτέρω τείχους
εἶναί τ' ἀληθεῖς καὶ τὰ πάντ' ἐποπτεύειν.
ὡς δ' εἰσιόντες τὰς πύλας ἐπὶ κρήνῃ

II. 9. verbum κρήνῃ tertia manus atramento obduxit ita ut κρήνης nunc appareat sed utrum κρήνης an κρήνηι Athoo scribae reddenda sit prorsus incertum.

---

but both expressions are found, whether the subject of the following infinitive is identical with the subject of δοκῶ or not. Eq. 1311, καθῆσθ' ἄν μοι δοκῶ, ' I think that we will sit.' Vesp. 250, τῳδὶ μοι δοκῶ τὸν λύχνον προβύσειν, 'I think I will stop.' Ach. 994, τρία δοκῶ γ' ἂν ἔτι προσβαλεῖν, 'I think I would add.' On the other hand σοι δοκεῖς is never met with, but always δοκεῖς. Ran. 188, ποῖ σχήσειν δοκεῖς, ' Where do you mean to put in?' Vesp. 1198, ποῖον ἂν λέξαι δοκεῖς, 'What do you think you would say?' Av. 1652, ἢ πῶς ἄν ποτε | ἐπίκληρον εἶναι τὴν Ἀθηναίαν δοκεῖς, 'Or how do you think that A. could ever be an heiress?' Eccl. 777, οἴσειν δοκεῖς τινά, 'Do you think any one will carry?' Av. 355, πῶς γὰρ ἂν τούτους δοκεῖς ἐκφυγεῖν, 'How do you think you will avoid them?' All these sentences are interrogative (cp. Ach. 775). The participle is found in Pl. 1068, λανθάνειν δοκῶν ἐμέ, 'fancying that he escapes my notice'; and the imperative once, Thesm. 208 A, ποιήσεις ταῦτα; B, μὴ δόκει σύ γε. The use of the imperfect in Vesp. 15 is very bold, ἐδόκουν ἀετὸν φέρειν, 'I thought an eagle bore.' The future is met with in the second person in Pl. 328, βλέπειν γὰρ ἀντικρυς δόξεις μ' Ἄρη, 'you will think that I look.' δοκεῖν, 'think,' absolutely, without following infinitive, is used only in the phrases πόσον δοκεῖς (Eccl. 399) and πῶς δοκεῖς (Pl. 742, Nub. 881, Ach. 24), both always at the end of the line, except in Ach. 12, πῶς τοῦτ' ἐσεισέ μου δοκεῖς τὴν καρδίαν. The Ionic, Tragic, and late usage is, however, found in an Ionian's lips in Pax 47, δοκέω μέν ἐς Κλέωνα τοῦτ' αἰνίσσεται. The later comedy reverted towards the Ionic use, Antiphanes ap. Suidam, s. v. ῥαγδαῖος,— ῥαγδαῖος, ἄμαχος, πρᾶγμα μεῖζον ἢ δοκεῖς. Anaxandrides ap. Athen. v. 222 B, χρὴ γὰρ εἰς ὄχλον φέρειν ἄπανθ' ὅσ' ἄν τις καινότητ' ἔχειν δοκῇ. The practice of

Plato corresponds with that of Aristophanes, whereas Thucydides keeps much nearer the Ionic. The difference between the Attic and the late construction is well illustrated by Pollux. He twice quotes the same passage of Metagenes — in vi. 103, δίμυξον, ὡς ἐμοὶ δοκεῖ ; in x. 115, δίμυξον ὡς ἐγὼ δοκῶ. Of course the comic poet wrote neither, but ὡς ἐμοὶ δοκῶ.

7. τοὺς .. ἐσωτέρω τείχους. The misuse of the comparative is to be marked. It cannot be defended as ἐξωτέρω in Aesch. Cho. 1022, ξὺν ἵπποις ἡνιοστροφῶ δρόμου ἐξωτέρω, 'somewhat wide of the course,' and in a few passages of Aristotle, Rhet. 3, 9 (1409, b23), ὥσπερ οἱ ἐξωτέρω ἀποκάμπτοντες τοῦ τέρματος. Pol. 4, 11 (1295,"32), καὶ γὰρ ἃς καλοῦσιν ἀριστοκρατείας τὰ μὲν ἐξωτέρω πίπτουσι ταῖς πλείσταις τῶν πόλεων, τὰ δὲ γειτνιῶσι τῇ καλουμένῃ πολιτείᾳ.

9. εἰσιόντες incorrectly for εἰσελθόντες, of a piece with the ἐσωτέρω. If the one expression is correct, the other may also be.

ἐπὶ κρήνῃ, I believe that the dative is here the more probable reading. The correct Attic usage is very simple, the best writers of prose and comedy limiting ἐπί with the genitive to position or motion upon an object or surface, and ἐπί with the dative to position or motion at or near. Thus a floating body is ἐπὶ ποταμοῦ, a city ἐπὶ ποταμῷ. A wounded man may be carried home ἐπὶ θρῶν, a beggar sits ἐπὶ θύραις. In tragedy this distinction is not observed, and ἐπί with the dative is also used to convey the sense which prose writers confine to the genitive. In Thucydides the prose usage has not yet become absolute, and although several deviations from the rule, such as ἀκάτιον ἐπὶ ἁμάξῃ κατακομίζειν (4, 67) admit of easy correction, yet the undoubted dative in 2, 80, τοὺς ὁπλίτας ἐπὶ ναυσὶ πέμπουσι. 4, 10, ἐπὶ ταῖς ναυσὶ ῥᾷστοί εἰσιν ἀμύν-

τοὺς πόδας ἔνιζον κἀπέθεντο τὰς πήρας,　　　　　10
κῆρυξ ἐφώνει χιλίας ἀριθμήσειν
μήνυτρα σύλων ὧν ὁ θεὸς ἐσυλήθη.
ὁ δὲ τοῦτ᾽ ἀκούσας εἶπεν. ᾽ὡς μάτην ἥκω·
κλέπτας γὰρ ἄλλους πῶς ὁ θεὸς ἂν εἰδείη,
ὃς τοὺς ἑαυτοῦ φῶρας οὐχὶ γινώσκει,　　　　　15
ζητεῖ δὲ μισθοῦ μή τις οἶδεν ἀνθρώπων ;᾽

III.

Αἰγάς ποτ᾽ εἰς ἔπαυλιν αἰπόλος κλείζων
μιῆς ἀπειθοῦς, ἐν φάραγγι τρωγούσης
κόμην γλυκεῖαν αἰγίλου τε καὶ σχίνου,
τὸ κέρας κατῆξε μακρόθεν λίθῳ πλήξας·
τὴν δ᾽ ἱκέτευε ᾽μή, χίμαιρα συνδούλη,　　　　　5

15. οὐχὶ retinui, Babrio hoc in versus loco usitatissimum neque
unquam in οὔτι mutavi, quamvis haud sim ignarus quantulum haec
vocabula manu scripta inter se discrepent.

III. 2. Secundum post versum Athous alium praestat hunc—

ἐπὶ σηκὸν ἄγειν θ᾽ ὡς αἱ μὲν ἦλθον αἱ δ᾽ οὔπω

cujus in paraphrasi Bodleiana non est vestigium. Uncis inclusit Schneidewin, recte. Codicis diorthotes antiquus post versum primum locare

　　　　　　　　　　　　　　　　　　　χρη
voluit, literis β α γ adscriptis, et χρη supra κλει (κλείζων) scripto.

εσθαι,—proves that such emendation is as uncalled for in the immature Attic of Thucydides as it would be in Herodotus or Xenophon. The Ionic and poetical laxity also crops up in the *Symposium,* where Plato allows himself a poet's licence, and in the same paragraph (212 E) are found the poetical ἐπὶ τῇ κεφαλῇ ἔχων τὰς ταινίας, and the prosaic ταινίας ἔχοντα ἐπὶ τῆς κεφαλῆς. In no writer, however, is the genuine prose signification of ἐπί with the dative ever accredited to ἐπί with the genitive, although the meaning, 'in the direction of,' sometimes brings ἐπί close to that of 'near.'

11. κῆρυξ ἐφώνει, (cp. 76, 12, *infra*) = Attic ὁ δ᾽ ἀνηγόρευε. The future infinitive follows, because the sense is κῆρυξ φωνῶν ὑπισχνεῖτο. Χιλίας, sc. δραχμάς, cp. Andoc. 6, 26, μήνυτρα κεκηριγμένα ἑκατὸν μνᾶς.

·12. σύλων . . ἐσυλήθη. This sense of σῦλα is unknown except in late writers, and may have been due to confusion with σκῦλα. Dion Cassius, xxxvi. 22, 3, τὰ σῦλα ὅσα ἐλάμβανον ἀδεῶς διετίθεντο. Heliodorus Aethiopica, i. 33, ἀγανακτήσαντες ὅτι τῶν ἀλλοτρίων ἐστέρηντο, καὶ τὴν ἀφαιρεσιν τῶν σύλων ὡς ἰδίων περιαλγήσαντες. v. 5, τὸν ἀπὸ σύλων πλοῦτον βέβηλον ἐδοκίμαζον. In fact it is sometimes corrupted into σκῦλα in the manuscripts of Heliodorus.

III. 1. αἰγάς . . κλείζων. In late Greek like that of our author it is impossible to say whether κλείζων is an instance of incorrect form and meaning combined, namely, κλείζων for κλῄζων for καλῶν, or of incorrect form alone, namely, κλείζων for κλείων. A student of late Greek has to accept such uncertainty.

5. χίμαιρα. The meaning of this

πρὸς τοῦ σε Πανὸς ὃς νάπας ἐποπτεύει,
τῷ δεσπότῃ, χίμαιρα, μή με μηνύσῃς·
ἄκων γὰρ ηὐστόχησα τὸν λίθον ῥίψας.'
ἡ δ' εἶπε 'καὶ πῶς ἔργον ἐκφανὲς κρύψω;
τὸ κέρας κέκραγε κἂν ἐγὼ σιωπήσω.'   10

IV.

Ἁλιεὺς σαγήνην ἥν νεωστὶ βέβληκει
ἀνείλετ'· ὄψου δ' ἔτυχε ποικιλου πλήρης.
τῶν δ' ἰχθύων ὁ λεπτὸς εἰς βυθὸν φεύγων
ὑπεξέδυνε δικτύου πολυτρήτου,
ὁ μέγας δ' ἀγρευθεὶς εἰς τὸ πλοῖον ἡπλώθη.   5

IV. Epimythium addit codex versus tres :—

σωτηρία πώς ἐστι καὶ κακῶν ἔξω
τὸ μικρὸν εἶναι· τὸν μέγαν δὲ τῇ δόξῃ
σπανίως ἴδοις ἂν ἐκφυγόντα κίνδυνον.

Eadem sententia ut promythio utitur paraphrasta Bodleianus.

---

term is perhaps best ascertained by a comparison with the Latin adjectives *bimus, trimus,* and *quadrimus,* applied to beasts, wine, etc., and derived from the same root as χεῖμα and hiemps. χίμαιρος and χίμαιρα will then be equivalent to the English *yearling.* This is consistent with the note of Aristophanes, the grammarian, preserved by Eustathius, p. 1625, ·τῶν αἰγῶν οἱ μὲν τέλειοι, τράγοι καὶ ἴξαλοι, ἡ δὲ ἐχομένη ἡλικία, χίμαροι, τὰ δὲ νεώτατα, ἔριφοι, and with a scholium on Theocr. 1, 5, ἔριφοι μέχρι τριῶν μηνῶν ἢ καὶ τεττάρων· χίμαροι ἐπὶ θηλυκοῦ ἕως ἐνιαυτοῦ, τουτέστιν ἕως ἂν τέκωσι καὶ ἀμελχθῶσιν ; but there the ἐπὶ θηλυκοῦ is of course an error due to the rare feminine χίμαρος employed by Theocritus. The rest of the scholium is worthless.

The derivation from root χι, *hi,* is very natural when we remember that kids are dropped in the spring ; but it is worth while comparing the English *fortnight* for a space of fourteen *days.*

6. νάπας. Anydale among hills might be called νάπη. Arist. Av. 740 (ch.), νάπαισί τε κορυφαῖσίν τ' ἐν ὀρείαις.

Thesm. 998 (ch.), μελάμφυλλά τ' ὄρη δάσκια καὶ νάπαι, —'hills and dales,' —but the word connotes wood and water.

IV. 1. νεωστὶ βέβληκει. Babrius very rarely omits the augment of the pluperfect except after a long vowel, in which case it may be regarded as elided. In Attic poetry such a license as νεωστὶ βέβληκει is impossible, and whenever it occurs in prose texts it ought to be corrected. The Attic ear was, however, exceptionally sensitive to the collision of vowels, and what sometimes happened to ἐθέλω and ἐκεῖνος after a long vowel happened also to pluperfects with the syllabic augment. Thuc. 1, 89, πολλαὶ 'πεπτώκεσαν. Dem. 299, εὖ 'πεπόνθεσαν. Even when a short vowel precedes the augment appears to be omitted ; but in these cases it ought to be retained while the other vowel is elided. Thuc. 7, 71, παραπλήσιά τ' ἐπεπόνθεσαν. The mere fact of the gradual disappearance of the augment from the pluperfect after Macedonian times is sufficient to explain the state of the manuscripts.

V.

Ἀλεκτορίσκων ἦν μάχη Ταναγραίων,
οἷς θυμὸν εἶναί φασιν οἷον ἀνθρώποις.
τούτων ὁ λειφθείς (τραυμάτων γὰρ ἦν πλήρης)
ἔκυπτ' ἐς οἴκου γωνίην ὑπ' αἰσχύνης·
ὁ δ' ἄλλος εὐθὺς εἰς τὸ δῶμα πηδήσας   5
ἐπικροτῶν τε τοῖς πτεροῖς ἐκεκράγει.
καὶ τὸν μὲν αἰετός τις ἐκ στέγους ἄρας
ἀπῆλθ'· ὁ δ' ἀδεῶς ἀμφέβαινε θηλείαις,
ἀμείνονα σχὼν τἀπίχειρα τῆς ἥττης.

VI.

Ἁλιεὺς θαλάσσης πᾶσαν ἠόνα ξύων
λεπτῷ τε καλάμῳ τὸν γλυκὺν βίον σώζων
μικρόν ποτ' ἰχθὺν ὁρμίης ἀφ' ἱππείης

V. 4. Palmariam Hauptii emendationem ἔκυπτ' ἐς in textum recepi. Codex ἐκρύπτετ' habet. 8. Paraphrastas secutus, ἀδεῶς Eberhard scripsit, Athoo ἄλλος bene ejecto. 9. Post hunc versum habet epimythium Athous, tres versus :—

ἄνθρωπε, καὶ σὺ μή ποτ' ἴσθι καυχήμων,
ἄλλου σε πλεῖον τῆς τύχης ἐπαιρούσης·
πολλοὺς ἔσωσε καὶ τὸ μὴ καλῶς πράττειν.

---

2. ἔτυχε . . πλήρης. For the omission of οὖσα see Phryn. p. 342.

3. τῶν δ' ἰχθύων ὁ λεπτὸς . . ὁ μέγας. Such a combination of collective singular and the plural number I have never elsewhere met with. It is a solecism of a grave kind.

4. The generic word δίκτυον is here used, although we know from the first line that the specific net employed was the σαγήνη.

V. 1. 'Galli Tanagraei a Paus. ix. 22, § 4, et Plinio H. N. X. 24, memorantur; vide Müller, Orchomen. p. 26.' G. C. Lewis.

3. 'Of these the vanquished crouched into a corner of the house.'

5. ὁ δ' ἄλλος for class. ὁ δ' ἕτερος.

The late use of δῶμα for house-top is well known to readers of the New Testament. Matthew xxiv. 17; Mark xiii. 15; Luke v. 19; xvii. 31. So Lxx. 2d Samuel xvi. 22.

VI. 1. ἠόνα ξύων a Latinism 'litus radens.'

3. ὁρμίης ἀφ' ἱππείης. This instrumental use of ἀπό is uncommon, and is here to be regarded as an imitation of Homer (Il. 24, 605, τοὺς μὲν Ἀπόλλων πέφνεν ἀπ' ἀργυρέοιο βιοῖο) rather than as a late fault. There are several exact parallels in the Homeric poems, but I know of none elsewhere, although the usage is sometimes approached outside of Attic, especially in Xenophon and late writers. The notorious tendency

ἤγρευσεν, οὐ τῶν εἰς τάγηνον ὡραίων.

ὁ δ' αὐτὸν οὕτως ἱκέτευεν ἀσπαίρων·　　　　5
'τί σοι τὸ κέρδος ; ἢ τίν' ὦνον εὑρήσεις ;
οὐκ εἰμὶ γὰρ τέλειος, ἀλλά με πρῴην
πρὸς τῇδε πέτρῃ φυκὶς ἔπτυσ' ἡ μήτηρ.
νῦν οὖν ἄφες με, μὴ μάτην μ' ἀποκτείνῃς.
ἐπὴν δὲ πλησθεὶς φυκίων θαλασσαίων　　　　10
μέγας γένωμαι, πλουσίοις πρέπων δείπνοις,
τότ' ἐνθάδ' ἐλθὼν ὕστερόν με συλλήψῃ.'
τοιαῦτα μύζων ἱκέτευε κάσπαίρων,
ἀλλ' οὐκ ἔμελλε τὸν γέροντα θωπεύσειν·
ἔφη δὲ πείρων αὐτὸν ὀξέῃ σχοίνῳ　　　　15
'ὁ μὴ τὰ μικρά, πλὴν βέβαια, τηρήσας
μάταιός ἐστιν ἣν ἄδηλα θηρεύῃ.'

VI. 6. Pro verbis ἢ τίν' ὦνον εὑρήσεις, quae citat Suidas sub ὦνος
vocabulo, alia dat Athous ἢ πόσου με πωλήσεις ; quae nescio cui gram-
matico referre velim.

---

of copyists to confuse ἀπό (ἄπο) and ὑπό (ὕπο) Bast., pp. 794, 823) has no place in the case of ἀφ' and ὑφ'.

6. In the phrase ὦνον εὑρήσεις the verb εὑρίσκω bears a natural signification, which in Attic is almost confined to poetry (εὑρίσκειν κλέος, ἀρετήν, δόξαν, etc.), except in the phrases τοῦ εὑρίσκοντος and τοῦ εὑρόντος, 'at the price which gets an article *for the buyer*.'

This usage is to be carefully distinguished from the more common one illustrated by the sentence ὁ ἀγρὸς πένθ' ἡμιτάλαντα εὑρίσκει, 'the field fetches two and a half talents *for the seller*.' In colloquial Attic the Homeric ἀλφάνω survived with this latter meaning.

To alter εὑρήσεις to εὑρήσω with Naber, or to ἀλφήσω with Eberhard, is conjecture of the worst kind, as is proved by common sense and by Xen. Vect. 4, 29, ὁ μὲν γὰρ εὑρὼν ἀγαθὴν ἐργασίαν πλούσιος γίγνεται, ὁ δὲ μὴ εὑρὼν πάντα ἀπόλλυσιν ὅσα ἂν δαπανήσῃ. Id. 25, εἴ τινες ἔτι εἰσὶ τῶν μεμνημένων ὅσον τὸ τέλος εὕρισκε (ἡ πόλις) τῶν ἀνδραπόδων. Cp. id. 40.

8. 'It was but yesterday my mother hake cast me out by this rock-side.' Such a meaning of πτύω is not rare in late writers. Oppian. Hal. 5, 597, τὰ δ' ἠόσιν ἔπτυσαν αὐταῖς | κύματα. Leon. Tar. Anth. Pal., 7, 283, θάλασσα, τί μ' οὐκ . . τηλόσ' ἀπὸ ψιλῆς ἔπτυσας ἠιόνος.

14. θωπεύσειν, 'deceive,' a rare but good use of the verb.

15. ὀξέῃ σχοίνῳ. Babrius employs the Ionic feminine at pleasure. The only form of this kind known to Attic, whether verse or prose, is ἡμισέα, a rare bye-form for ἡμίσεια, and to be reckoned with ἡμίσεας for ἡμίσεας, and ἡμίση for ἡμίσεα. Moreover, in accent ἥμισυς stands by itself. The Antiatticist in Bekk. Anecd. 99, 24, fathers θρασέα upon Philemon. Θρασέα· Φιλήμων Γάλλῳ (lege Γάμῳ) θρασέα γυνή : but the Antiatticist ought to be studied in full by any one to whom he is cited.

16, 17. These lines are awkwardly expressed, but are intended to mean : 'If a man has once secured a return for his labour, be it ever so small, he is unwise to throw it away and start anew on a doubtful quest.'

VII.

Ἄνθρωπος ἵππον εἶχε. τοῦτον εἰώθει
κενὸν παρέλκειν, ἐπετίθει δὲ τὸν φόρτον
ὄνῳ γέροντι. πολλὰ τοιγαροῦν κάμνων
ἐκεῖνος ἐλθὼν πρὸς τὸν ἵππον ὡμίλει
' ἤν μοι θελήσῃς συλλαβεῖν τι τοῦ φόρτου,   5
τάχ' ἂν γενοίμην σῶος· εἰ δὲ μή, θνήσκω.'
ὁ δ' ' οὐ προάξεις ;' εἶπε ' μή μ' ἐνοχλήσῃς.'
εἶρπεν σιωπῶν, τῷ κόπῳ δ' ἀπαυδήσας
πεσὼν ἔκειτο νεκρός, ὡς προειρήκει.
τὸν ἵππον οὖν παρ' αὐτὸν εὐθέως στήσας   10
ὁ δεσπότης καὶ πάντα τὸν γόμον λύων
ἐπ' αὐτὸν ἐτίθει τὴν σάγην τε τοῦ κτήνους,
καὶ τὴν ὀνείην προσεπέθηκεν ἐκδείρας.
ὁ δ' ἵππος ' οἴμοι τῆς κακῆς ' ἔφη ' γνώμης·
οὐ γὰρ μετασχεῖν μικρὸν οὐκ ἐβουλήθην,   15
τοῦτ' αὐτό μοι πᾶν ἐπιτέθεικεν ἡ χρείη.'

_____

VII. 7. Athoi verba μὴ δ' ἐνοχλήσῃς cum Schneidewino in μή μ'
ἐνοχλήσῃς mutare malo quam cum Halmio notissimum Atticæ dialecti
idioma μηδ' ἐνοχλήσεις Babrio adscribere.

_____

VII. 2. **κενὸν παρέλκειν.** The phrase
was properly applied to a groom mounted
on one horse, and leading another
without a rider. Aristophanes gives
it a grotesque turn in Pax 1306, ὑμῶν
τὸ λοιπὸν ἔργον ἤδη 'νταῦθα τῶν μενόν-
των | φλᾶν ταῦτα πάντα καὶ σποδεῖν
καὶ μὴ κενὰς παρέλκειν. The French
scholiast Biset has the sensible note,
κενὰς παρέλκειν· τὰς γνάθους δηλονότι; but such a violent ellipse must
have a reason. This is found in a
proverb preserved by Phrynichus,
Soph. App. 45, 23, Κενὰ τῆς γνάθου
πολλὰ χωρία· ἐπὶ τῶν οὐκ ἐχόντων
δαψιλῶς, ὥστε τὴν γνάθον ἐμπλῆσαι.
The comic poet was in this way enabled
to say μὴ κενὰς παρέλκειν, 'You have
got to work both (mares) hard,' as the
proverb at once suggested τὰς γνάθους
instead of τὰς ἵππους.
3. **πολλὰ τοιγαροῦν . . ὡμίλει,** 'wherefore oftentimes in his weariness the ass
would come to the horse and commune

with him.' ὡμίλει = Attic ἂν ὡμίλει—
not 'wherefore, when sore foredone,
the ass came.'
11. Join **πάντα τὸν γόμον λύων . .
τὴν σάγην τε.** To take **ἐκδείρας** with
τὴν σάγην by zeugma is wrong.
15. **οὐκ ἐβουλήθην.** The metre here
settles the ever recurring difficulty of
augment, as it also does in the other
passages (111, 1, and 124, 12) in which
Babrius uses an historical tense. Here
and in 111, 1, the Athoan codex has
the correct syllabic augment, as has
the Vatican in 124, 12 : but the tran-
script of Menas gave ἠβουλήθην here,
and the edition of Furia ἠβουλήθη in
the third passage. These corruptions
ought to prepare us for the like in
other texts.
There are three verbs which are said
to employ, indifferently, either the
temporal or the syllabic augment,
namely, βούλομαι, δύναμαι, and μέλλω.
Let us consider the only evidence

VIII.

"Ἄραψ κάμηλον ἀχθίσας ἐπηρώτα
πότερ' ἀναβαίνειν μᾶλλον ἢ κάτω βαίνειν
αἱροῖτο. χὼ κάμηλος οὐκ ἄτερ μούσης
εἶφ' 'ἡ γὰρ ὀρθὴ τῶν ὁδῶν ἀπεκλείσθη;'

IX.

Ἁλιεύς τις αὐλοὺς εἶχε καὶ σοφῶς ηὔλει·
καὶ δή ποτ' ὄψον ἐλπίσας ἀμοχθήτως

VIII. Fabulam vix e Babrio profectam esse judico ; si minus recte, utique tamen a Tetrastichistâ pessime est depravata. Una certe quaerenti manet opinio auctorem camelo suo totum ipsius ingenium deposuisse.

which we have—metrical laws and stone records. In the case of βούλομαι inscriptions give no help, as before Euclid either form would be written in the same way, and no augmented tense is found in later inscriptions of the true Attic period. The remaining evidence is, however, very strong. *There is not a single line of Attic verse in which the Eta augment is required, but there are many which demand the form with Epsilon.* Arist. Vesp. 706, εἰ γὰρ ἐβούλοντο βίον πορίσαι τῷ δήμῳ ῥᾴδιον ἦν ἄν. Vesp. 960, ἐγὼ δ' ἐβουλόμην ἂν οὐδὲ γράμματα. Eur. Hec. 1211, τί δ' οὐ τότ', εἴπερ τῷδ' ἐβουλήθης χάριν. Hipp. 476, τόλμα δ' ἐρῶσα· θεὸς ἐβουλήθη τάδε. Anaxandrides ap. Arist. Nic. Eth. vii. 11 (1152, ⁰23), ἡ πόλις ἐβούλεθ' ᾗ νόμων οὐδὲν μέλει. In the decline of Attic the temporal augment was allowed, as is proved by ἠβούλοντο in an inscription of the third century (C. I. A. II. 314, 25, p. 137) 284/3 B.C. There is a better case for Eta with μέλλω and δύναμαι. Aristophanes uses ἤμελλον in anapaestic verse (Eccl. 597, Ran. 1038), and Aeschylus ἠδυνήθην *in senarii* (P. V. 206) ; while even in comic iambics οὐκ ἠδύνω ends a line of Philippides (ap. Athen. xv. 700 c). The evidence, however, for the superiority of Epsilon is overpowering. For ἔμελλον, Comic Iambics, Aristophanes,

Plut. 1103 ; Nub. 1301 ; cp. Eq. 267. Tragic Iambics, Soph. O. R. 967, 1385 ; Aj. 443, 1287 ; Eur. Hec. 1204 ; cp. Or. 1445. For ἐδυνάμην, ἐδυνήθην, Comic Iambics, Arist. Eccl. 316, 343 ; Plut. 672 ; and inscriptions of the best period. C. I. A. II. 89, 5, p. 40 [cp. a doubtful ἐδύνατο in id. 301, 15, p. 125]. Philippides is really outside the Attic period, and ἠδύνω is as natural in his verse as ἠδύναντο in C. I. A. II. 331, 42, p. 155. So ἠδύνατο and ἠδύναντο in id. 420, 12 and 37. Of course ἔθελον and ἤθελον stand on an entirely different footing.

IX. 2. ἐλπίσας.. ἥξειν. Whether Babrius wrote ἥξειν or not (see Not. Crit.) the verb he employed was in the future, as he is very careful in this portion of syntax—the tense of infinitives. Goodwin has treated the question of the tense after ἐλπίζω with little of his usual care (see *Moods and Tenses*, § 15, 2, note 2; § 23, 2, note 2; § 27, note 3). The apparent exceptions to the legitimate construction—the future infinitive or the aorist infinitive with ἄν—are due to three causes—(1) confusion between the two meanings of ἐλπίζω, 'I hope' and 'I conceive' or 'believe'; (2) importing into the question phrases with ἐλπίς ; (3) well known and acknowledged errors of copying. To take these in detail—(1) It must be remembered that ἐλπίζω never lost its original

πολὺ πρὸς αὐλῶν ἡδυφωνίην ἤξειν,
τὸ δίκτυον θεὶς ἐτερέτιζεν εὐμούσως.

IX. 3. Verbum ἤξειν retinui utpote loco diutius usum. De prima codicis manu una aegre lineola manet, a scriba recentiore ἤξειν delineato. Ignorare placet.

---

meaning of 'wish' or 'am pleased,' which is especially visible in some uses of the Homeric ἔλποπαι (Fέλπ, *volupe*, *voluptas*), and that by the side of *hope* was another definite meaning, 'believe,' which will be found best to translate ἐλπίζω as often as an infinitive indisputably present follows. *E.g.* Plato, Rep. 573 C, καὶ μὴν ὅ γε μαινόμενος καὶ ὑποκεκινηκὼς οὐ μόνον ἀνθρώπων ἀλλὰ καὶ θεῶν ἐπιχειρεῖ τε καὶ ἐλπίζει δυνατὸς εἶναι ἄρχειν—'tries and believes that he is able to rule.' Rep. 451 A, ἐλπίζω γὰρ οὖν ἔλαττον ἁμάρτημα ἀκουσίως τινὸς φονέα γενέσθαι ἢ ἀπατεῶνα καλῶν κτλ.— 'I believe that it is a more venial sin.' Anon. ap. Clement of Alexandria, Stromateis, vii. p. 305, τίς ὦδε μωρὸς . . ὅστις ἐλπίζει θεοὺς χαίρειν ἀπαρχαῖς. Aesch. Sept. 76, ξυνὰ δ' ἐλπίζω λέγειν. Aesch. ap. Plat. Rep. 383 B, κἀγὼ τὸ Φοίβου θεῖον ἀψευδὲς στόμα | ἤλπιζον εἶναι μαντικῇ βρύον τέχνῃ.

(2) The phrases ἐλπίς ἐστιν, ἐλπίδα ἔχειν, ἐν ἐλπίδι εἶναι, εἰς ἐλπίδα ἥκειν, etc., are, however, very frequently, perhaps preferentially, followed by the present or aorist infinitive without ἄν, which is then to be regarded as the genitive case of a substantive. With this usage may be compared that of ἀξιοῦν, referring to future time, but notwithstanding followed by a present or aorist infinitive, the verb being regarded as equivalent to such a phrase as ἄξιόν τινα νομίζειν τοῦ ποιεῖν or τοῦ ποιῆσαι.

(3) The source of error arising from copying will be best understood by the following analysis of the Thucydidean usage. In more than forty passages he employs ἐλπίζω, *hope*, and the rule is never broken in any codex except in cases in which the true form differs from the false by more than one or two letters; and in every case some codex has preserved the genuine lection, viz.— 1, 11, ἤλπιζον βιοτεύσειν (*v. l.* βιοτεύειν); 4, 24, ἤλπιζον χειρώσεσθαι (*v. l.* χειρώσασθαι); 4, 80, ἤλπιζον ἀποτρέψειν (*v. l.* ἀποτρέψαι); 5, 28, ἐλπίσαντες ἡγήσεσθαι (*v. l.* ἡγήσασθαι); 7, 21, ἐλπίζειν κατερ-

γάσεσθαι (*v. l.* κατεργάσασθαι*). The only passage which offers the least difficulty is 4, 13, ἐλπίζοντες τὸ κατὰ τὸν λιμένα τεῖχος ὕψος μὲν ἔχειν, ἀποβάσεως δὲ μάλιστα οὔσης ἑλεῖν μηχαναῖς, where ἐλπίζοντες in the first case certainly means *believe*, but for the second clause *hope*. If the corruption does not lie much deeper, we must read μάλιστ' ἄν for μάλιστα (a very frequent corruption), even if the order of the words somewhat fights against it. Only in one place has Thucydides the very rare construction with ὡς and the future indic.—8, 54, ἐλπίζων ὡς καὶ μεταβαλεῖται, which is also found in Soph. El. 963, μηκέτ' ἐλπίσῃς ὅπως τεύξει.

A less general error of transcription than those already named is seen in Eur. H. F. 746, πάλιν ἔμολεν ἃ πάρος οὔποτε διὰ φρενὸς ἤλπισεν παθεῖν γᾶς ἄναξ. Euripides wrote ἤλπισ' ἄν παθεῖν. One more caution before dismissing the subject. Aristophanes twice uses ἐλπίζω, *hope*, with an infinitive,—Thesm. 195, ἐλπ. ὑφέξειν; and Lys. 257, ἐπεὶ τίς ἄν ποτ' ἤλπισ' ἀκοῦσαι γυναῖκας. In the second place the ἄν belongs to the ἀκοῦσαι by the notorious Greek idiom in which ἄν is attracted to interrogatives, negatives, and superlatives.

3. πολύ, 'in shoals.'

4. τὸ δίκτυον θεὶς as opposed to βαλὼν σαγήνην in l. 6.

---

* I would fain call attention here to the wise words with which Dr. Arnold closes the Preface to the First Edition (1832) of the 4th and 5th Books of Thucydides. "My increased acquaintance with the manuscripts of Thucydides has greatly lessened my respect for their authority; and I should not hesitate to alter the text in spite of them, whenever the grammarians who laboured to keep alive a knowledge of the genuine Attic Dialect amidst the growing barbarisms of their times require or sanction the correction." Throughout his noble edition he everywhere shows that soundness of judgment and dislike to fanciful renderings which marks the best work of English scholars; and had he started his task even with that knowledge of Greek which he acquired in its execution, his Thucydides would have made an epoch in Greek scholarship.

ἐπεὶ δὲ φυσῶν ἔκαμε καὶ μάτην ηὔλει, 5
βαλὼν σαγήνην ἔλαβεν ἰχθύας πλείστους.
ἐπὶ γῆς δ' ἰδὼν σπαίροντας ἄλλον ἀλλοίως,
τοσαῦτ' ἐκερτόμησε τὸν βόλον πλύνων·
'ἄναυλα νῦν ὀρχεῖσθε. κρεῖσσον ἦν ὔμας
πάλαι χορεύειν, ἡνίκ' εἰς χοροὺς ηὔλουν.' 10

X.

Αἰσχρῆς τις ἦρα καὶ κακορρύπου δούλης
ἰδίης ἑαυτοῦ καὶ παρεῖχεν αἰτούσῃ
ἄπανθ' ἑτοίμως· ἡ δὲ χρυσίου πλήρης,
σύρουσα λεπτὴν πορφύρην ἐπὶ κνήμας
πᾶσαν μάχην συνῆπτεν οἰκοδεσποίνῃ. 5
τὴν δ' Ἀφροδίτην ὥσπερ αἰτίην τούτων
λύχνοις ἐτίμα, καὶ καθ' ἡμέρην πᾶσαν
ἔθυεν ηὔχεθ' ἱκέτευεν ἡρώτα,
ἕως ποτ' αὐτῶν ἡ θεὸς καθευδόντων

Epimythium adjecit codex, quo chartam foedare pudet—

οὐκ ἔστιν ἀπόνως οὐδ' ἀλύοντα κερδαίνειν·
ὅταν βαλὼν δὲ τοῦτο θέλῃς ὅπερ βούλει
τὸ κερτομεῖν σοι καιρός ἐστι καὶ παίζειν.

Latet in ἀλύοντα vocabulum non minus ametrum αὐλοῦντα.
X. 1. Suidas sub voc. ἦρα laudavit, codicibus aliquot σαπρᾶς τινός pro
αἰσχρῆς τις exhibentibus. Quinetiam pro κακορρύπου Suidas et paraphrasta Bodleianus κακοτρύπου habent. 4. κνήμας ego, κνήμης alii.
In Athoo ita est verbum atramento recentiori oblitum ut aegre appareat
terminatio. 5. πάση μάχην habet Athous. Latet corruptio.

6. ἰχθύας, see Phryn. p. 234, note.
8. τοσαῦτ' ἐκερτόμησε. There is no
reason why editors should have accepted
Sauppe's conjecture, τοιαῦτ'. 'He threw
them as he washed his net a taunt or
two.'
9. κρεῖσσον ἦν. For the idiomatic
omission of ἄν see Goodwin, Moods and
Tenses, § 49, 2, note 2.
10. ἡνίκα. See Phryn. p. 122.
εἰς χορούς. The plural of a substantive
here, as so often, takes the place of the
infinitive of the corresponding verb.
Thus, 4, 55, ἀτολμότεροι δι' αὐτὸ ἐς τὰς
μάχας ἦσαν (= ἐς τὸ μάχεσθαι), where
Cobet's alteration to ἦσαν is not required.

X. 1. ἦρα. Babrius follows the Attic
usage in regard to this verb (see Index),
the aorist being supplied by ἔραμαι.
3. χρυσίου πλήρης, 'loaded with
ornaments of gold.' The plural is
regularly found in this sense, as in an
apt sentence of Plutarch, ἐδόκεις τις
εἶναι διὰ τὰ χρυσία καὶ τὴν πορφύραν.
4. The correction κνήμας is necessary,
see note on 2, 9, supra.
5. If πᾶσαν is right—and certainly
the Athoan πάση is almost inexplicable
if it is—it must equal παντοίαν.
9. αὐτῶν .. καθευδόντων. The simple
εὕδω occurs in the spurious 116th fable.
In Attic the compound verb is the more

ἦλθεν καθ' ὕπνους, καὶ φανεῖσα τῇ δούλῃ   10
'μή μοι χάριν σχῇς ὡς καλήν σε ποιούσῃ·
τούτῳ χολοῦμαι' φησίν 'ᾧ καλὴ φαίνῃ.'

XI.

'Αλώπεκ' ἐχθρὴν ἀμπέλων τε καὶ κήπων
ξένῃ θελήσας περιβαλεῖν τις αἰκίῃ
τὴν κέρκον ἅψας καὶ λίνον τι προσδήσας
ἀφῆκε φεύγειν· τὴν δ' ἐπίσκοπος δαίμων
εἰς τὰς ἀρούρας τοῦ λαβόντος ὠδήγει   5
τὸ πῦρ φέρουσαν. ἦν δὲ ληίων ὥρη
καὶ καλλίπαις ἀμητὸς ἐλπίδων πλήρης.
ὁ δ' ἠκολούθει τὸν πολὺν κόπον κλαίων
οὐδ' εἶδεν αὐτοῦ τὴν ἄλωνα Δημήτηρ.

---

12. Quod verbum Athous habet κεχόλωμαι, praesens in tempus convertit Meineke. Epimythium claudum, ut solet, addit Athous—

ἅπας ὁ τοῖς αἰσχροῖς ὡς καλοῖς χαίρων
θεοβλαβής τίς ἐστι καὶ φρένας πηρός.

XI. 5. Lectionem Athoam βαλόντος cum Abrensio in λαβόντος mutavi, neque ignoro tamen vocabulum rejectum in paraphrastis apparere. Saepius in codicibus sunt λαβεῖν et βαλεῖν confusa. Exhibet hic quoque Athous Epimythium—

χρὴ πρᾶον εἶναι μηδ' ἄμετρα θυμοῦσθαι.
ἔστιν τις ὀργῆς νέμεσις ἣν φυλαττοίμην
αὐτοῖς βλάβην φέρουσα τοῖς δυσοργήτοις.

---

frequently met with, but the simple is also used in prose and comedy (Arist. Av. 82; Nub. 12; Plat. Rep. 571 C; Phaedr. 267 A; Legg. 807 E, 823 E, 824 A; Symp. 203 B, etc. The future is καθευδήσω, the imperfect καθηῦδον or ἐκάθευδον, according to the period; while the place of aorist is filled by κατέδαρθον, and of perfect by καταδεδάρθηκα. From the earliest period the verbs were used to complement each other; e.g. Od. 20, 141, οὐκ ἔθελ' ἐν λέκτροισι καὶ ἐν ῥήγεσσι καθεύδειν, | ἀλλ' ἐν ἀδεψήτῳ βοέῃ καὶ κώεσιν οἰῶν | ἔδραθ' ἐνὶ προδόμῳ; and in Attic there are many striking instances. Ar. Nub. 38 A, ἔασον, ὦ δαιμόνιε, καταδαρθεῖν τί με. B, σὺ δ' οὖν κάθευδε. Plato Symp. 219 C, καταδεδαρθηκώς ..

καθηῦδον. Id. 223 B, κατθηῦδον . . καταδαρθεῖν . . καθεύδοντας . . καταδαρθεῖν. Id. Apol. 40 D, καθεύδων . . κατέδαρθεν.

ἡ θεὸς, see Cobet, Mnem. iv. 122 (1855).

XI. 2. ξένῃ . . αἰκίῃ. It is idle to mention the conjectures which have been proposed for ξένῃ. They are due to ignorance of a rudimentary fact in Greek—the possession of an active and passive signification by such adjectives as ξένος. These are equivalent in meaning to the larger class of privative words like ἀπείρατος, ἀόρατος. Thus Sophocles (O. R. 219) could say ἐγὼ ξένος μὲν τοῦ λόγου ξένος δὲ τοῦ πραχθέντος, 'knowing nothing of the story,

XII.

Ἀγροῦ χελιδὼν μακρὸν ἐξεπωτήθη,
εὗρεν δ' ἐρήμοις ἐγκαθημένην ὕλαις
ἀηδόν' ὀξύφωνον· ἡ δ' ἀπεθρήνει
τὸν Ἴτυν ἄωρον ἐκπεσόντα τῆς ὥρης.
ἐκ τοῦ μέλους δ' ἔγνωσαν αἱ δύ' ἀλλήλας,   5
καὶ δὴ προσέπτησάν τε καὶ προσωμίλουν.
χἠ μὲν χελιδὼν εἶπε ' φιλτάτη, ζώεις ;
πρῶτον βλέπω σε σήμερον μετὰ Θρᾴκην·

XII. De hac fabula valde despero, si unquam ad ipsissima Babrii verba accedere licebit. Non desunt codices, sed inter se multum differunt. Primus inter tetrasticha edidit Aldus, anno 1505, p. 57, ex duobus exemplaribus, quibus paene dimidium fabulæ deest, videlicet, versus 5, 6, 9, 10, 14, 15, 16, 17, 18, 21, 22. Continet etiam codex Vaticanus. Codex Gudianus ab Eberhardo conlatus recensionem prope eundem atque Aldini exhibet.

and knowing nothing of the deed,' as he might also have said ξένος αἰκίης, 'knowing nothing of the affront.' The passive meaning is no less natural— ξένη αἰκίη, 'an unheard-of affront'— and appears in all lexica.

4. ἐπίσκοπος δαίμων, 'overseeing providence.' The expression might have been used by a classical writer, as is seen from Plato, Legg. 872 E, ἡ τῶν συγγενῶν αἱμάτων τιμωρὸς δίκη ἐπίσκοπος νόμῳ χρῆται τῷ νῦν δὴ λεχθέντι.

5. τοῦ λαβόντος. There can be little question about the necessity of this reading. The verb βάλλω can be used of driving animals, as ll. 23, 572, τοὺς ἵππους πρόσθε βαλών ; Theocr. 4, 44, βάλλε κάτωθε τὰ μοσχία ; but in these cases the added adverb makes all the difference, as does the following preposition in βάλλ' ἐς κόρακας and similar phrases, in which βάλλω is intransitive.

7. ἀμητός. I have here retained the accent of the manuscript, which, following Boissonade, all editors change to ἄμητος. The question must, I fear, remain unsettled. See Chandler's Greek Accentuation, § 324.

8. τὸν πολὺν κόπον κλαίων, 'bewailing his great affliction.'

9. οὐδ' εἶδεν, 'visited not.' This

sense of ἰδεῖν (Lat. visere) is very rare. It does not seem to have any right to be called an Atticism, although Thucydides once uses it, 4, 125, τὸν Περδίκκαν ἠνάγκασαν πρὶν τὸν Βρασίδαν ἰδεῖν προαπελθεῖν. So Xen. An. 2, 4, 15, ἠρώτησε τοὺς προφύλακας ποῦ ἂν ἴδοι Πρόξενον ἢ Κλέαρχον. Pseudo-Xen. Oec. 11, 14, ἀνίστασθαι μὲν ἐξ εὐνῆς εἴθισμαι εἴ τινα δεόμενος ἰδεῖν τυγχάνοιμι. Philemon ap. Stob. Flor. 113, 10, τί ποτ' ἐστὶν ἆρα διότι βούλεταί μ' ἰδεῖν ; | ἧ καθάπερ οἱ νοσοῦντες ἀλγοῦντες σφόδρα, | τὸν ἰατρὸν ἂν ἴδωσιν οὐκ ἀλγοῦσ' ἔτι. Dio. Cass. 71, 35, 4, ἠσπάζετο τοὺς ἀξιωτάτους πρὶν τὸν πατέρα ἰδεῖν.

ἄλωνα. To a late Greek this substantive might follow any one of the types, λεώς, ἥρως, ἀγών, or αἰδώς.

XII. 1. ἀγροῦ. In late Greek ἀγρός is often opposed to ἡ ἐρημία, ἡ ἔρημος, and has the sense of cultivated land. New Test., Luke ix. 12, ἀπόλυσον τὸν ὄχλον ἵνα ἀπελθόντες εἰς τὰς κύκλῳ κώμας καὶ τοὺς ἀγροὺς καταλύσωσιν καὶ εὕρωσιν ἐπισιτισμόν· ὅτι ὧδε ἐν ἐρήμῳ τόπῳ ἐσμέν.

4. 'Itys deprived of his beauty before his time.'

6. For προσέπτησαν see Phryn. p. 373.

8. μετὰ Θρᾴκην = μετὰ τὰ ἐν Θρᾴκῃ γενόμενα, like μετὰ τὰς Ἀθήνας in line

C

ἀεί τις ἡμᾶς πικρὸς ἔσχισεν δαίμων,
καὶ παρθένοι γὰρ χωρὶς ἦμεν ἀλλήλων.   10
ἀλλ' ἔλθ' ἐς ἀγρὸν καὶ πρὸς οἶκον ἀνθρώπων·
σύσκηνος ἡμῖν καὶ φίλη κατοικήσεις,
ὅπου γεωργοῖς, οὐχὶ θηρίοις ἄσεις.   13
τί σε δροσίζει νῶτον ἔννυχος στίβη,   16
καὶ καῦμα θάλπει, πάντα καὶ κατακναίει;'
τὴν δ' αὖτ' ἀηδὼν ὀξύφωνος ἠμείφθη·
' ἔα με πέτραις ἐμμένειν ἀοικήτοις,   20
καὶ μή μ' ὀρεινῆς ὀργάδος σὺ χωρίσσῃς.
μετὰ τὰς Ἀθήνας ἄνδρα καὶ πόλιν φεύγω·

10. Hunc versum post tertium decimum ponit Vaticanus codex. Causam explicabo. Versui tertio decimo et in Athoo et in Vaticano succedunt duo.
14.   ἵπαιθρον ὕλην λεῖπε καὶ παρ' ἀνθρώποις
15.   ὁμώροφόν μοι δῶμα καὶ στέγην οἴκει.

quos ego quamvis incertus extrusi. Si vere sunt Babriani, certe tamen ad diversam recensionem referre opportet. Hoc propter versus 11-13 in marginem expulsi, postea in sedem non suam a Scriba Vaticano redditi sunt. 16. Ex Athoo edidi, nisi quod Vaticanum νῶτον pro Athoo νυκτὸς substitui. Sed pro ἔννυχος στίβη in Vaticano ἔνδροσος κοίτη apparet. 17. Ex Vaticano edidi, κατακναίει modo pro κατακαίει lecto. Quem in modum lectio Athoa πάντα δ' ἀγρώτην τήκει orta sit non video. 17. Hunc post versum exhibent alium manifeste suppositum Athous et Vaticanus—

ἄγε δὴ σεαυτήν, σοφὰ λαλοῦσα, μήνυσον, Athous.
ἄγε μήνυσον σεαυτὴν σοφή περ οὖσα, Vaticanus.

Quid velit Crusii conjectura μή σίνου pro μήνυσον viro sobrio non liquet.

22. To any one accustomed to the later Greek authors this usage is very familiar. Thus it occurs eight times in the first book of Nonnus' Dionysiaca, and Heliodorus, Longus, etc., have only to be opened to supply instances.
13. For the late future ἄσω see Phryn. p. 377.
17. The phrase καὶ καῦμα θάλπει may be modelled on καὶ καῦμ' ἔθαλπε in Soph. Ant. 417, or it may not. It is really no more striking in Greek than 'the sun-heat warms' is in English, and may well have been used independently by Babrius. The compound κατακναίειν is not so common as διακναίειν, but such a signification as

it here bears—wear out, destroy—is as legitimate for the compound with κατά as for that with διά.
19. ἠμείφθη is rare even in late Greek.—Theocr. 7, 27; pseudo-Oppian. Cyn. 1, 19. Pindar and Xenophon anticipated the usage. See Phryn. p. 187.
20. 'Suffer me to abide in the desolate rocks, and sever me not from the mountain-meadow.' Ὀργὰς καλεῖται τὰ λοχμώδη καὶ ὀρεινὰ χωρία καὶ οὐκ ἐπεργαζόμενα, ὅθεν καὶ ἡ Μεγαρικὴ ὀργὰς προσωνομάσθη τοιαύτη τις οὖσα περὶ ἧς ἐπολέμησαν οἱ Ἀθηναῖοι Μεγαρεῦσιν.—Harpocration.
22. ἄνδρα = ἄνθρωπον.

οἶκος δέ μοι πᾶς κἀπίμιξις ἀνθρώπων
λύπην παλαιῶν συμφορῶν ἀναξαίνει.'

XIII.

Αὔλαξι λεπτὰς παγίδας ἀγρότης πήξας
γεράνους σποραίων πολεμίας συνειλήφει.
τοῦτον πελαργὸς ἱκέτευε χωλεύων
(ὁμοῦ γὰρ αὐταῖς καὶ πελαργὸς ἡλώκει)·
' οὐκ εἰμὶ γέρανος, οὐ σπόρον καταφθείρω.   5
πελαργός εἰμι (χὴ χρόη με σημαίνει),
πτηνῶν πελαργὸς εὐσεβέστατον ζῴων·

24. Cum Athoo, Vaticano, et paraphrasi Bodleiana λύπην scribere
malo quam μνήμην cum Aldinis et Gudiano. Epimythium Athous habet
aliis codicibus ignotum—

παραμυθία τίς ἐστι τῆς κακῆς μοίρης
λόγος σοφὸς καὶ μοῦσα καὶ φυγὴ πλήθους·
λύπη δὲ πᾶσ' ὅταν τις εὐθενῶν ὀφθῇ
τούτοις ταπεινὸς αὖθις ὧν συνοικήσῃ.

quod eruditi varie emendare temptarunt. Severitas mea vix patitur ut
istas Graeculi sordes typis de novo tradam.

24. One of the Aldine copies reads
ἀναφλέγει, the other ἀναφλέξει, for the
Athoan and Vatican ἀναξαίνει. The
former is a gloss changed into the
future to restore the metre lost with
the displaced ἀναξαίνει.
XIII. 2. σποραίων πολεμίας, 'foes of
things sown,' or rather ' of things that
relate to sowing.' The adj. σποραῖος is
found only in this place ; but notwithstanding this and the difficulty in its
meaning, it is quite in keeping with
much of the diction of Babrius. Certainly Fix's conjecture σποράων is not
an emendation.
4. ὁμοῦ .. αὐταῖς. This use of ὁμοῦ
with the dative is familiar to scholars
from its occasional appearance in
Homer, Herodotus, and the Tragedians ; but in late Greek it occurs with
great frequency, e.g. Oppian, Hal. 1,
508, 636, 650 ; 3, 484, 486 ; 4, 357 ;
pseudo-Oppian, Cyn. 4, 258 ; Quintus
Smyrnaeus, 7, 363, etc. We find even
αὐτῇ ὁμοῦ σύριγγι in Nonnus, Dionys.
1, 417.

ἡλώκει. From the index it will
be seen that Babrius has used both
forms of the aorist, ἑάλων and ἧλων,
but only one of the pluperfect. The
augmentation of the imperfect of ἁλίσκομαι is the same in all Greek, ἡλι-
σκόμην ; but the best Attic forms of the
aorist and perfect are subject to dispute.
That ἑάλων was excellent Attic can be
proved, for it is required by the metre
in Arist. Vesp. 355, ἵεις σαυτὸν κατὰ
τοῦ τείχους ταχέως ὅτε Νάξος ἑάλω ; and
occurs in an Attic inscription of the
first half of the fourth century, C. I.
A. II. 38, 14, ἑάλωσαν ἂν αἱ πολέμιαι ;
αἱ πολέμιαι. But was ἧλων un-Attic ?
The length of the alpha, and the
analogy of the accusative plural
of substantives in -εύς, makes ἧλων
an improbable Attic form, although
Homer may have used it, as did
Herodotus. In the former it is found
only in one passage (Od. 22, 230),
and there ἑάλω might stand by syn-
izesis, σῇ δ' ἧλω βουλῇ Πριάμου πόλις
εὐρυάγυια. The perfect stands on a

τὸν ἐμὸν τιθηνῶ πατέρα καὶ νοσηλεύω.'
κἀκεῖνος ' ὦ πελαργέ, τίνι βίῳ χαίρεις
οὐκ οἶδα' φησίν, ' ἀλλὰ τοῦτο γινώσκω,   10
ἔλαβόν σε σὺν ταῖς ἔργα τἀμὰ πορθούσαις.
ἀπολῇ μετ' αὐτῶν τοιγαροῦν μεθ' ὧν ἥλως.'

XIV.

Ἄρκος φιλεῖν ἄνθρωπον ἐκτόπως ηὔχει·
νεκρὸν γὰρ αὐτοῦ σῶμ' ἔφασκε μὴ σύρειν.

XIII. Epimythium addit codex, versus duo—

κακοῖς ὁμιλῶν ὡς ἐκείνοις μισηθήσῃ,
κἂν μηδὲν αὐτὸς τοὺς πέλας καταβλάψῃς.

XIV. In dubio manet utrum quatuor hi versus Babrio ipsi sint tribuendi an ex pluribus contraxerit tetrastichista. 1. Athous ἄρκτος exhibet ; ego autem ἄρκος scripsi, Suidae codices secutus, quorum omnes in vocabulo ἄρκος, aliquot etiam in vocabulo ἐκτόπως formam breviorem habent.

---

different footing, as in it the alpha is short, just like the o in ἑόρακα. In this way contraction might more easily take place, and both forms be in use. Verse does not help us at all, as in Aesch. Ag. 30, ἑάλωκεν might be replaced by ἥλωκεν, and ἥλωκε by ἑάλωκε in Antiphanes ap. Athen. 3, 103 E, ἢ τριηραρχῶν ἀπήγξατ', ἢ πλέων ἥλωκέ ποι; as also ἥλωκέναι by ἑαλωκέναι in Xenarchus ap. Athen. 6, 225, D, εἴποις ἂν αὐτοὺς ἀρτίως ἡλωκέναι. The facts are probably these, that in Attic of the best age ἑάλων and ἑάλωκα were the recognised forms, and that while ἑάλων held out much longer than ἑάλωκα, which towards the close of the period was being replaced by ἥλωκα, on the other hand ἀναλίσκω, whether connected or not with ἁλίσκομαι, always augmented in eta, ἀνήλωσα, ἀνηλώθην, etc.

In pure Attic ἁλίσκομαι is practically the only passive of αἱρῶ, for although Thucydides (2, 94) uses ᾑρῆσθαι, and Plato (Soph. 261 C) ᾑρημένον εἴη, as also (Phaedr. 253 C) αἱρεθῇ and αἱρεθείς (Rep. 613 D,) αἱρεθέντες, and (Phaed. 81 B) αἱρετός, still so few instances as these count as nothing against the numerous

examples of ἑάλων and ἑάλωκα. Of αἱροῦμαι, ᾑρούμην, αἱρήσομαι, with the meaning 'be taken,' there are no instances at all. These words signified respectively, 'I choose' or 'I am chosen,' 'I was choosing' or 'being chosen,' 'I shall choose' or 'be chosen,' as ᾑρέθην meant 'I was chosen,' and ᾕρημαι 'I have chosen' or 'been chosen.' One must go to tragedy to find αἱροῦμαι and its tenses taking the place of ἁλίσκομαι and its tenses. [Eur. Med. 624 ; Soph. O. C. 1148 ; Eur. Supp. 635, etc.]

XIV. 1. ἐκτόπως φιλεῖν 'bore a strange love.' Suidas quotes this line after the gloss Ἐκτόπως· μεγαλῶς, ἀπρεπῶς, παρηλλαγμένως, and also adds a sentence from Procopius, in which the adverb bears the same signification, εἶθ' ὕστερον αὐτοῦ ἐρασθεῖσα ἐκτόπως. The word is frequent in late Greek.

2. νεκρὸν . . σῶμα. Observe the unclassical use of νεκρός as an adjective.

ἔφασκε μὴ σύρειν. I have forborne to mention the reading of the codex—ἔφασκεν—as it is more likely due to a simple dittographia (cursive or uncial), or to the late love of the ephelkustic Nu, than a remnant of an original ἔφασκεν οὐ. Any one who is acquainted

πρὸς ἣν ἀλώπηξ εἶπε 'μᾶλλον ἠρούμην
εἰ νεκρὸν εἷλκες, τοῦ δὲ ζῶντος οὐχ ἥπτου.'

XV.

Ἀνὴρ Ἀθηναῖός τις ἀνδρὶ Θηβαίῳ
κοινῶς ὁδεύων, ὥσπερ εἰκός, ὡμίλει.
ῥέων δ' ὁ μῦθος ἦλθε μέχρις ἡρώων·
μακρὴ μὲν ἄλλως ῥῆσις οὐδ' ἀναγκαίη·
τέλος δ' ὁ μὲν Θηβαῖος υἱὸν Ἀλκμήνης   5
μέγιστον ἀνδρῶν, νῦν δὲ καὶ θεῶν ὕμνει·

---

4. Omnino fere hic parcit lectori epimythiasta, mox tribus fabulis ingenium suum negaturus—

ὁ ζῶντα βλάπτων μὴ νεκρόν με θρηνείτω.

with late Greek must acknowledge that the tendency to substitute μή for οὐ in classical texts must have been very strong during certain periods of their transmission. There is a telling instance of a corruption due to this cause in a passage of Alexis quoted by Athenaeus, i. 21 D—

ἓν γὰρ νομίζω τοῦτο τῶν ἀνελευθέρων
εἶναι τὸ βαδίζειν ἀρρύθμως ἐν ταῖς ὁδοῖς,
ἐξὸν καλῶς· οὗ μήτε πράττεται τέλος
μηδὲν ἡμᾶς μήτε τιμὴν δόντα δεῖ
ἑτέρων λαβεῖν, φέρει δὲ τοῖς μὲν χρωμένοις
δόξης τιν' ὄγκον κτε.

Suidas, s. v. ἀναλαμβάνειν, reads v. 3 thus—

ἐξὸν καλῶς οὐ μήποτε πράττεται τέλος
μηδεὶς γὰρ ἡμᾶς κτε.

The words of Alexis were of course—

ἐξὸν καλῶς· ὡς οὐδὲ πράττεται τέλος
οὐδὲν παρ' ἡμῶν οὐδὲ τιμὴν δόντα δεῖ
ἑτέρων λαβεῖν κτε.

The ὡς was lost through the preceding καλῶς, the οὐ converted into οὐ to supply the connecting link ; while the missing negative was inserted according to late usage, and assimilated the following negatives to itself.

Notwithstanding this, Babrius may well have written μή here, as he belonged to the offending age, or at worst the fault may be ascribed to the tetra-stichist to whom the fable probably owes its present shape. In classical Greek οὐ was required after φημί or φάσκω as certainly as in the rather more numerous cases in which it precedes the verb (Xenophon as usual is an exception). In one point Babrius deserves credit. He never commits the fault of Xenophon, and of modern imitators of Attic Greek, in putting a ὅτι or ὡς after φημί or φάσκω, although in 97, 4, he falls as low as they do, and employs an infinitive after εἰπεῖν, 'to say.'

3. μᾶλλον ἠρούμην. For this use of the imperfect without ἄν, so well known in the case of ἐβουλόμην, see Goodwin, § 49, 2 (C).

XV. 3. 'And flowing on, their conversation turned upon heroes,' lit. 'came as far as.' For the late form μέχρις, see Phryn. p. 64.

4. 'Tedious in other respects was their talk and nothing to the purpose, but at last the Theban lauded the son of Alcmené as (once) the greatest of men, and now-a-days one of the gods. But the man from Athens would have it that Theseus was far the better of the two, and had in truth been granted a lot divine, whereas Herakles had that of a servant.' The younger student must be careful to avoid translating ὕμνει, 'began to laud.' The imperfect tense in Greek has never such a signification, although the aorist may.

ὁ δ' ἐξ Ἀθηνῶν ἔλεγεν ὡς πολὺ κρείσσων
Θησεὺς γένοιτο, καὶ τύχης ὁ μὲν θείης
ὄντως λέλογχεν, Ἡρακλῆς δὲ δουλείης.
λέγων δ' ἐνίκα· στωμύλος γὰρ ἦν ῥήτωρ.   10
ὁ δ' ἄλλος ὡς Βοιωτὸς οὐκ ἔχων ἴσην
λόγοις ἄμιλλαν εἶπεν ἀγρίῃ μούσῃ·
' πέπαυσο· νικᾷς. τοιγαροῦν χολωθείη
Θησεὺς μὲν ἡμῖν, Ἡρακλῆς δ' Ἀθηναίοις.'

XVI.

Ἄγροικος ἠπείλησε νηπίῳ τίτθη,
κλαίοντι ' παῦσαι, μή σε τῷ λύκῳ ῥίψω.'

---

7. ἔλεγεν ὡς . . γένοιτο . . λέλογχεν.
Observe the idiomatic change of mood.
In direct speech we should have ἐγένετο
and λέλογχεν. The latter is to all
intents and purposes a present, being
often joined with such a word as ἔχω.
The form is poetical and late, the
Attic word being εἴληχα. The most
common construction of λέγω in this
sense is a following infinitive, but it is
also frequently followed by ὅτι. The
present construction with ὡς is the
rarest of the three.

9. δουλείης. Herakles married Hebe,
the waiting woman of Olympus.

13. πέπαυσο, 'stop! stop!' The
perfect imperative passive or middle is
very rare in the second person, and
hardly used at all except in verbs
whose perfect has the force of a present,
as μέμνησο, *remember thou*; κεῖσο, *be
thou placed*; ἔρρωσο, *farewell*; πέπαυσο,
quiesce. Arist. Vesp. 142, σὺ δὲ τῇ
θύρᾳ πρόσκεισο. Dem. 721, 6, ἀκούετε,
ὦ ἄνδρες δικασταί; λέγε αὐτοῖς αὐτὸ
τοῦτο πάλιν . . . πέπαυσο. Such perfects
are found in all moods co-ordinated
with presents, Soph. Phil. 1279, εἰ δὲ
μή τι πρὸς καιρὸν λέγων | κυρῶ, πέπαυ-
μαι. Bato, comicus, ap. Athen. xiv.
662 C, τὰς νύκτας οὐ καθεύδομεν, | οὐδ'
ἀναπεπαύμεθ', ἀλλὰ κάεται λύχνος, | καὶ
βιβλί' ἐν ταῖς χερσί, καὶ φροντίζομεν—
where ἀναπεπαύμεθ' is a certain emendation of Cobet for ἀναγεγράμμεθ'.
Pherecrates ap. Athen. iii. 75 b, κάθευδε
τῆς μεσημβρίας, | κᾆτα σφακέλιζε καὶ
πέπρησο καὶ βόα. Brunck. Analecta,
II. 413, τοὔνεκά μοι, βέλτιστε, τόδε ζῷον

πεφύλαξο. Arist. Nub. 294, αὐτὰς
τετρεμαίνω καὶ πεφόβημαι. Thuc. 6,
17, μὴ πεφόβησθε.
Of cases in which the present force
of the perfect is not so well established
there are extremely few, as λέλυσο in
Arist. Thesm. 1208, 'have your liberty
at once'; and Xen. Cyr. 4, 2, 7, καὶ
σὺ ἡμῖν πιστὰ θεῶν πέποιησο καὶ δεξιὰν
δός, 'offer assurances once for all.' But
not even Xenophon could have used
δέδωκε instead of δός in this sentence.
For till late Greek there is not one
case of a perfect imperative active,
except when the perfect indicative is
regularly used as a present tense, and
even then the ending of the imperative
is always -θι. Six of these occur in
Attic verse or prose—Arist. Av. 206,
ἕσταθι; Soph. El. 50, ἑστάτω; Il. 22,
365, τέθναθι; Plat. Legg. 933 E,
τεθνάτω; Arist. Vesp. 198, Ach. 335,
Thesm. 692, κέκραχθι; Vesp. 415, κεκρά-
γατε; Eq. 230, Vesp. 373, δέδιθι;
Ach. 335, κεχήνατε; Aesch. Eum. 598,
πέπισθι. A seventh is found in Homer
and Hesiod—Od. 20, 18; Il. 5, 382;
1, 586; Hesiod. Op. 718, τέτλαθι; Od.
16, 275, τετλάτω.
The best proof of the difference between the active and the passive in
this respect is, that nowhere does the
third person of the perfect imperative
active occur in the construction so
frequent in the corresponding part of
the passive, e.g. Lys. 168, 24, περὶ μὲν
οὖν τούτων τοσαῦτά μοι εἰρήσθω.

XVI. 2. παῦσαι, μή σε . . ῥίψω. It
has been too little observed that an im-

ὁ λύκος δ' ἀκούσας τήν τε γραῦν ἀληθεύειν
νομίσας ἔμεινεν ὡς ἕτοιμα δειπνήσων,
ἕως ὁ παῖς μὲν ἑσπέρης ἐκοιμήθη,   5
αὐτὸς δὲ πεινῶν καὶ λύκος χανὼν ὄντως
ἀπῆλθε νωθραῖς ἐλπίσιν παρεδρεύσας.
λύκαινα δ' αὐτὸν ἡ σύνοικος ἠρώτα
' πῶς οὐδὲν ἄρας ἦλθες ὥσπερ εἰώθης;'
ὁ δ' εἶπε ' πῶς γάρ, ὃς γυναικὶ πιστεύω;'   10

XVI. 9. Duo ultimi versus fortasse sunt corrupti, sed nihil aliud
in Athoo mutavi quam γυναικὸς in γυναικί. Eberhardus pro ὥσπερ
emendavit ὧνπερ, et Naberus πῶς γὰρ οὐ γυναικὶ πιστεύσας; legendum
esse statuit. Incertioribus incerta antepono.

---

perative influences constructions only
in a less degree than a negative or an
interrogative. The most striking example is the collocation πρὸς ταῦτα,
meaning 'wherefore,' which in Attic is
found only with imperatives. The
present line supplies an instance of a
similar Attic refinement, which the
index will show that Babrius did not
always observe. Unlike Homer and
even their own tragedians, the Athenian writers of prose and comedy
avoided μή = lest, except the clause
introduced by it followed an imperative
or a construction equivalent to an
imperative. Arist. Vesp. 162, ἴθ' ἀντι-
βολῶ σ' ἔκφρες με μὴ διαρραγῶ. Eccl.
28, φέρε νυν ἐπαναχωρήσω πάλιν, | μή καί
τις ὢν ἀνὴρ ὁ προσιὼν τυγχάνει. Cratinus ap. Zonaram, II. 1168, τὴν χεῖρα
μὴ 'πίβαλλε, μὴ κλάων κάθῃ. Eubulus
ap. Athen. xiv. 622 F, ἔπειγ' ἔπειγε,
μή ποθ' ὡς λύκος χανὼν | καὶ τῶνδ'
ἁμαρτὼν ὕστερον συχνὸν δράμῃς. Antiphanes ap. Athen. viii. 338 E, οὐ βαλεῖς
πάλιν | εἰς τὴν θάλατταν καὶ πλυνεῖς;
μὴ φῶσί σε κτε. Arist. Thesm. 529, ὑπὸ
λίθῳ γὰρ παντί που χρὴ μὴ δάκῃ ῥήτωρ
ἀθρεῖν. Menander, Monost. 358, μὴ
σπεῦδε πλουτεῖν μὴ ταχὺς πένης γένῃ.
Xenophon of course violates this, as all
other peculiarly Attic rules, e.g. Anab.
4, 4, 21 ; Cyr. 1, 4, 25 ; 2, 4, 12 ; and
in Thucydides it is not by any means
absolute, 4, 22, ὁρῶντες δὲ οἱ Λακεδαιμόνιοι οὔτε σφίσιν οἷόν τε ὂν ἐν πλήθει
εἰπεῖν . . μὴ ἐς τοὺς ξυμμάχους διαβλη-
θῶσιν εἰπόντες καὶ οὐ τυχόντες. It is
also an Attic tendency—the exceptions

are too many to allow of my calling
it a rule—to confine ὡς ἄν, and ὅπως
ἄν, in final clauses to such as follow
an imperative mood or its equivalent.

6. λύκος χανὼν ὄντως, 'a gaping
wolf if ever there was one.' The proverb is found in Aristophanes, Lys.
629, λύκος κεχηνώς, and in many other
writers. Cp. Diogenianus, vi. 20,
Λύκος ἔχανεν· ἐπὶ τῶν τῆς ἐλπίδος
ἀποτυγχανόντων. Οἱ γὰρ λύκοι ἀθηρίᾳ
περιπεσόντες, χαίνουσι διερχόμενοι, where
Leutsch has an exhaustive note.

7. νωθραῖς ἐλπίσιν παρεδρεύσας.
This may be translated in two ways,
according as we decide to regard the
metaphor as derived from a lecture-
room or a sick bed :—(1) 'after lending
an ear to stupid hopes.' Suidas sub
vocabulo Χοιρίλος Σάμιος· Ἡροδότῳ τῷ
ἱστορικῷ παρεδρεύσαντα λόγων ἐρασθῆναι.
(2) 'after nursing stupid hopes,' infra,
95, 31. Diod. 14, 71, οἱ τοῖς κάμνουσι
παρεδρεύοντες.

9. I have here retained the manuscript reading, εἰώθης, as probably the
form written by Babrius. Although
in his day the late ending -εις may
have been general, yet his verses are so
plainly the work of a lettered grammarian that Atticising is always to be
looked for. At the same time this
fact makes certainty in such a case all
the more impossible, and I have not
altered the manuscript throughout so
as to make it consistent in the matter
of the pluperfect active inflections.
See Phryn. pp. 229 ff.

XVII.

Αἴλουρος ὄρνεις οἰκίης ἐνεδρεύων
ὡς θύλακός τις πασσάλων ἀπηρτήθη.
τὸν δ᾽ εἶδ᾽ ἀλέκτωρ πινυτὸς ἀγκυλογλώχιν,
καὶ ταῦτ᾽ ἐκερτόμησεν ὀξὺ φωνήσας·
'πολλοὺς μὲν οἶδα θυλάκους ἰδὼν ἤδη·   5
οὐδεὶς δ᾽ ὀδόντας εἶχε ζῶντος αἰλούρου.'

XVIII.

Βορέῃ λέγουσιν ἡλίῳ τε τοιαύτην
ἔριν γενέσθαι, πότερος ἀνδρὸς ἀγροίκου
ὁδοιποροῦντος τὴν σίσυρναν ἐκδύσει.

XVIII. 3. Editores caeteros secutus, σισύραν, quod dant Athous et
Suidas, in σίσυρναν mutavi. Ultimo autem in versu σίσυραν pro σισύραν
dedi utpote minus in numeros Babrii offendens. Alios tres versus, sine
dubio suppositos, addit Athous, quorum duo posteriores ut epimythium
proponit, vocabulo λέγει paullulum extra ordinem scripto—

Βορρᾶς μὲν οὕτως συγκριθεὶς ἐνικήθη,
λέγει δ᾽ ὁ μῦθος 'πρᾳότητα, παῖ, ζήλου,
ἀνύσεις τε πειθοῖ μᾶλλον ἢ βίᾳ ῥέζων.'

XVII. 1. **ὄρνεις οἰκίης.** Athenaeus
(ix. 373 A, ff.) has a long note on ὄρνις,
showing that in his time ὄρνιθες and
ὀρνίθια were only used of hens, and
ἀλεκτρυόνες and ἀλέκτορες (H. Stephanus,
for MS. ἀλεκτορίδες) of cocks ; whereas
in classical times ὄρνεις and ὄρνιθες were
used of both genders and all kinds of
birds ; while ἀλεκτρυών was applied to
a domestic fowl, and might be either
masculine or feminine.
In place of the Babrian phrase
Aeschylus (Eum. 866) has ὄρνις ἐνοίκιος ;
and ὄρνις ἡ κατὰ οἶκον, ὄρνις κατοικίδιος,
ὄρνις ἥμερος, are also found.
3. **ἀγκυλογλώχιν** is met with only
here in all Greek. It refers to the beak
and not to the spurs. Homer applies
ταννγλώχις and τριγλώχις to an arrow,
and his late epic imitator Nonnus is
fond of similar compounds, 1, 151,
πυριγλώχινος ὀϊστοῦ ; Id. 295, πυριγλώ-
χινι κεραυνῷ ; 2, 676, πολυγλώχινα
κεραίην ; 5, 256, πολυγλώχινα καλύπ-

τρην ; 6, 23, ἰσογλώχινι τριγώνῳ ; 138,
λιθογλώχινα ὀχῆα.
4. **ταῦτα** for classical τάδε, as τοσαῦτα
for τοσάδε, supra, 9, 8, see Index.
5. 'Many bags do I remember to have
seen ere now.' The perfect (English)
signification conferred upon aorists by
collocation with the χρονικὰ ἐπιρρήματα,
ἤδη, πολλάκις, οὔπω, is too well known
to require illustration.
XVIII. 1. 'They say that between
north wind and sun this quarrel arose,
which of them should strip the cloak
from a countryman on the road.'
3. If we are to credit Pollux, σίσυρνα is not merely a late form of σισύρα,
but was used by Aeschylus—Poll. 10,
186, φαίης δ᾽ ἂν καὶ σίσυρναν, Αἰσχύλου
ἐν Κήρυξι σατύροις λέγοντος, Καὶ τῆς
σισύρνης τῆς λεοντείας. If σισύραν
is the right reading in l. 13, it must be
written proparoxytone, as it sometimes
is in the texts of grammarians. Aristophanes often employs the word, but

BABRIUS.

βορέης δ' ἐφύσα πρῶτος οἷος ἐκ Θράκης,
βίῃ νομίζων τὸν φοροῦντα συλήσειν·   5
ὁ δ' οὐ μεθῆκε μᾶλλον, ἀλλὰ ῥιγώσας

always in a part of the line which admits of either a long or a short ultimate. If the latter is the true quantity, the word can hardly be genuine Greek, connected with τίτυρος, but of foreign origin. Gregorius Corinthius, p. 540, σίσυρνα(?)· βαρβαρικὸς χιτών. Pollux, 7, 70, explains σισυρα as χιτὼν σκύτινος, ἔντριχος, χειριδωτός· Σκυθικὸν τὸ χρῆμα· ἡ σισυρα περίβλημα ἂν εἴη ἐκ διφθέρας. Other grammarians and lexicographers simply confuse. In short, whether σίσυρνα, σισύρα, or σίσυρα, the article was plainly a rug which might be worn as a rude wrap, either as it was or with appurtenances of strings and buckles.

5. νομίζων . . συλήσειν. Babrius is as accurate in the construction of verbs of thinking as of hoping and expecting (supra, 9, 2). In other words, he wrote as a reasonable man must. There are in Attic at all events no genuine exceptions to the law that verbs of thinking, when referring to the future, must be followed by the future infinitive (or more rarely ὅτι, very rarely ὡς, with future). Of those mentioned by Goodwin—who himself plainly does not think much of them—there is none which is not due to mistakes in copying of the most familiar kind. proved to be mistakes over and over again, as often as a single valuable manuscript has been preserved by the side of inferior ones. (N.B.—The quotation from Aesch. Sept. 429, is misleading and has no business there. σχεθεῖν does not refer to future time, as is shown by the following προσήκασεν.) All other cases I have met with are of the same kind.

6. ὁ δ' οὐ μεθῆκε μᾶλλον. 'He did not let it go the more for that.' The more usual expression is οὐδὲν μᾶλλον. Thuc. 2, 70, αἱ ἐς τὴν Ἀττικὴν ἐσβολαὶ οὐδὲν μᾶλλον ἀπανίστασαν τοὺς Ἀθηναίους. Aristot. Eth. Nic. 9, 5, 1167, "4, μὴ γὰρ προσοηθεὶς τῇ ἰδέᾳ οὐθεὶς ἐρᾷ, ὁ δὲ χαίρων τῷ εἴδει οὐθὲν μᾶλλον ἐρᾷ, ἀλλ' ὅταν καὶ ἀπόντα ποθῇ καὶ τῆς παρουσίας ἐπιθυμῇ. οὕτω δὴ καὶ φίλους οὐχ οἷόν τ' εἶναι μὴ εὔνους γενομένοις, οἱ δ' εὖνοι οὐθὲν μᾶλλον φιλοῦσι.

ῥιγώσας, 'shivering and clutching with his hands his skirts all round, he sat with his back resting on a projecting rock.' The two verbs ῥιγόω and ἱδρόω stand by themselves among verbs in -οω, both in meaning and in form. Ῥιγόω in Attic certainly contracted in ω instead of ου. Moeris has the glosses: (1) Ῥιγῶντος Ἀττικοί, ῥιγοῦντος Ἕλληνες; (2) Ῥιγῶν Ἀττικοί, ῥιγοῦν κοινῶς, ῥιγοῖ Ἕλληνες (correct ῥιγῷ Ἀττικοί, ῥιγοῖ Ἕλληνες).

The scholiast on Arist. Vesp. 446, makes the same statement, and ῥιγῶν has to be read in Av. 935 ; Ach. 1146 ; Nub. 443 ; Plat. Rep. 440 C. Also ῥιγῷ subj. in Plat. Phaed. 85 A ; Gorg. 517 D. ῥιγῶσι indic. in Phil. 45 B ; ῥιγῷ, Theat. 152 B. In some of these cases the best MSS. already present the true forms. The other, ἱδρόω, was similarly anomalous, but it does not happen to occur in Attic, in which ἱδίω took its place ; Arist. Ran. 237 ; Pax. 85 ; Av. 791 ; Plat. Tim. 74 C ; cp. ἀνιδιτί, Plato, Legg. 718 E. I leave it to comparative philologists to explain the origin of the -όω of these verbs, which will perhaps be found to differ from that of other verbs with this ending. Their other anomaly, however,—that of a neuter signification,—is shared by μεσόω. The great name of Shilleto is in favour of translating περαιώσειν as active in Thuc. 2, 67 ; but in his note* on the passage that scholar has forgotten ἱδρόω, ῥιγόω, and μεσόω. Most of the forms of μεσόω which occur might come from μεσέω as well as μεσόω, but there remains the recalcitrant infinitive μεσοῦν in Plato, Phaedr. 241 D ; Symp. 175 C ; Rep. 618 B. The anomaly probably arose from false analogy, and μεσῶν, μεσοίη, μεσούσης, μεσοῦν (partc.), etc., may have produced a false present μεσόω. The question of the confusion of σκηνάω, σκηνέω, σκηνόω, is too long to be treated here.

---

* The note belongs to the portion that really came from the pen of Shilleto. With many scholars I regret that the second book of his Thucydides was not published just as he left it, ἔχουσ' αἴσθησιν οἱ τεθνηκότες.

καὶ πάντα κύκλῳ χερσὶ κρίσπεδα σφίγξας
καθῆστο, πέτρης νῶτον ἐξοχῇ κλίνας.
ὁ δ᾽ ἥλιος τὸ πρῶτον ἡδὺς ἐκκύψας
ἀνῆκεν αὐτὸν τοῦ δυσηνέμου ψύχους,   10
ἔπειτα δ᾽ αὖ προσῆγε τὴν ἀλῆν πλείω·
καὶ καῦμα τὸν γεωργὸν εἶχεν ἐξαίφνης,
αὐτὸς δὲ ῥίψας τὴν † σίσυραν ἐγυμνώθη.

XIX.

Βότρυς μελαίνης ἀμπέλου παρωρείη
ἀπεκρέμαντο. τοὺς δὲ ποικίλη πλήρεις
ἰδοῦσα κερδὼ πολλάκις μὲν ὡρμήθη
πηδῶσα ποσσὶν ᾽πορφυρῆς θιγεῖν ὥρης·
ἦν γὰρ πέπειρος κεἰς τρυγητὸν ἀκμαίη.   5
κάμνουσα δ᾽ ἄλλως (οὐ γὰρ ἴσχυε ψάυειν),

XIX. 6. Pro hoc versu habet sub vocabulo αἰώρα Suidas duo—

ὡς δ᾽ οὐκ ἐφικνεῖτ᾽ ἀλλ᾽ ἔκαμνε πηδῶσα
οὐδὲν κρεμαστῆς σχοῦσα πλεῖον αἰώρας,

de quibus alio jam disserui.

---

11. **ἀλῆν** for ἀλέαν, like κωλῆ for κωλέα, and νῆ for νέα.

12. **καῦμα** . . **εἶχεν** = ἐθερμαίνετο ὁ γεωργός. Babrius is fond of this periphrase with εἶχον. Had he meant to convey the aorist force he would have used ἔσχον, according to the distinction between the two words constantly observed in Greek. Eberhard suggests εἶλεν in this and the other passages, often ruining the sense, and evidently ignorant of the above distinction. The confusion between λ and χ is notorious (Bast. pp. 724, 738, etc.); but so consistent a mistake is impossible.

13. **αὐτός** = sponte.

XIX.1. 'Bunches of grapes were hanging from a swarthy vine on a hill-side. A crafty fox, seeing them ripe to bursting, tried with many a bound to reach the fresh purple fruit.' Why a difficulty should have been made of παρωρείη passes my comprehension. The conjectures are all as bad as they are

futile. The word bears the sense required here in many authors, and the absence of ἐν is only an instance of the oligoprothesié so common in Babrius and other late Greek writers. In Attic prose of course the dative of place, like the dative of time, is not found without ἐν, except in a small class of frequently occurring words (in Thuc. 4, 26, ὅσοι δὲ γαλήνῃ κινδυνεύσειαν, we should read δ᾽ ἐγ γαλήνῃ·); but Babrius is neither an Attic writer nor a prosaist.

3. **ὡρμήθη.** Babrius is always correct in his use of this class of passives, and does not employ absurdities like ὡρμησάμην, ἐφοβησάμην, ἐῳχησάμην, which disfigure the diction of most late writers of Greek down to our own day. (See Phryn. p. 188 ff.)

5. **τρυγητὸν.** For accent see 11, 7, supra.

6. **ἴσχῠε ψάυειν.** Babrius elsewhere makes the upsilon long before a vowel (see Index), and Nauck would here

παρῆλθεν οὕτω βουκολοῦσα τὴν λύπην·
'ὄμφαξ ὁ βότρυς, οὐ πέπειρος, ὡς ᾤμην.'

XX.

Βοηλάτης ἄμαξαν ἦγεν ἐκ κώμης.
τῆς δ' ἐμπεσούσης εἰς φάραγγα κοιλώδη,
δέον βοηθεῖν αὐτὸς ἀργὸς εἱστήκει,
τῷ δ' Ἡρακλεῖ προσηύχεθ', ὃν μόνον πάντων
θεῶν ἀληθῶς προσεκύνει τε κἀτίμα.   5
ὁ θεὸς δ' ἐπιστὰς εἶπε 'τῶν τροχῶν ἅπτου
καὶ τοὺς βόας κέντριζε. τοῖς θεοῖς δ' εὔχου,
ὅταν τι ποιῇς καὐτός, ἢ μάτην εὔξῃ.'

XXI.

Βόες μαγείρους ἀπολέσαι ποτ' ἐζήτουν
ἔχοντας αὐτοῖς πολεμίην ἐπιστήμην.
καὶ δὴ συνηθροίζοντο πρὸς μάχην ἤδη
κέρατ' ἀποξύνοντες, εἷς δέ τις λίην
γέρων ἐν αὐτοῖς, πολλὰ γῆς ἀροτρεύσας,   5
'οὗτοι μὲν ἡμᾶς' εἶπε 'χερσὶν ἐμπείροις

---

7. Pro παρῆλθεν levi et usitata mutatione ἀπῆλθεν proposuit Burges in Aesch. Supp. 920, sed παρῆλθεν aeque bonum est.

XXI. 5. Manifesta fraude πολλὰ γὰρ ἦν Athous habet, πολλὴν γῆν Vaticanus. In πολλὰ γῆν Lachmannus correxit, πολλὰ γῆς ego.

substitute ἔσθενεν, but needlessly. The class of verbs in ύω is a very small one, and consists of the following members: —(1) with υ always short, ἀρύω, βρύω, κλύω(Impte.κλῦθι,long),μεθύω, πληθύω; (2) with υ always long, δακρύω, καττύω, κνύω, μηρύομαι, ξύω, τρύω, ὕω, βρενθύομαι; (3) with υ long or short before a vowel, long before a consonant, γηρύω, δύω, ἱδρύω, ἰσχύω, κωκύω, κωλύω, λύω, μηνύω, φιτύω, φύω, ὠρύομαι. The others, ἀρτύω, θύω, κύω, πτύω, must have their quantities learned by use, and even of the three classes named several vary in quantity with the dialect in which they occur.

XX. 1. ἄμαξαν ἦγεν = 'plaustrum agebat,' a Latinism.
2. φάραγγα κοιλώδη appears to be much too strong an expression.
XXI. 4. Knoell's preference for the Vatican reading ἀποξύναντες here, as for Nauck's conjecture καμοῦσα in 19, 6, is baseless. Even in classical Greek the present would be more natural here; and as for the other passage, I hold that the metre proves that Babrius often used a present where in classical Greek an aorist would be necessary, and that conjecture of this quality in a writer of a late conventional style is of no value.

σφάζουσι καὶ κτείνουσι χωρὶς αἰκίης·
ἢν δ᾽ εἰς ἀτέχνους ἐμπέσωμεν ἀνθρώπους,
διπλοῦς τότ᾽ ἔσται θάνατος· οὐ γὰρ ἐλλείψει
τὸν βοῦν ὁ θύσων κἂν μάγειρος ἐλλείψῃ.'   10

XXII.

Βίου τις ἤδη τὴν μέσην ἔχων ὥρην
(νέος μὲν οὐκ ἦν, οὐδέπω δὲ πρεσβύτης)
λευκαῖς μελαίνας μιγάδας ἐκλόνει χαίτας,
εἶτ᾽ εἰς ἔρωτας ἐσχόλαζε καὶ κώμους.
ἦρα γυναικῶν δύο, νέης τε καὶ γραίης,   5
νέον μὲν αὐτὸν ἡ νεῆνις ἐζήτει
βλέπειν ἐραστήν, συγγέροντα δ᾽ ἡ γραίη.

7. σφάζουσι καὶ κτείνουσι cum Athoo legere malo, quam cum Knoellio
κόπτουσι καὶ σφάζουσι, [φάζουσι καὶ κόπτουσι Vat.], vel σφάζουσι
κάκτείνουσι cum Nabero. Epimythium jamdudum a Lachmanno saeptum
in Vaticano non invenitur—

ὁ τὴν παροῦσαν πημονὴν φεύγειν σπεύδων
ὁρᾶν ὀφείλει μή τι χεῖρον ἐξεύρῃ.

XXII. 3. Accusativum λευκὰς in λευκαῖς dativum mutavi, hujus-
modi asyndeti haud patiens.

7. **σφάζουσι καὶ κτείνουσι,** 'cut our
throats and kill us.' σφάζω (Att.
σφάττω) is a butcher's word. Arist.
Pax. 1018, εἶθ᾽ ὅπως μαγειρικῶς σφάξεις
τὸν οἶν.
10. **ὁ θύσων.** The idiom is too common to require illustration—Soph. Ant.
261, οὐδ᾽ ὁ κωλύσων παρῆν.
ἐλλείψῃ = defecerit.
XXII. 1. 'A certain man, already
in the mid-season of life—young he
was not, but not yet old—was blending
his dark hair with a sprinkling of
white.' *Lit.* 'was confusing his dark
hair mixed (*i.e.* by a mixture) with
white.' The alteration generally adopted by editors, viz. λευκὰς μελαίναις, is
to me incomprehensible without proof
that in those days hair became black
with age. The Greek idiom, by which
a person is said himself to produce the
changes of physical and mental state
which take place in him, is never
sufficiently attended to by editors, who

do not carry it further than its simplest
form seen in phrases like φῦσαι ὀδόντας
(ὀδοντοφυεῖν), φῦσαι πτερά (πτεροφυεῖν),
στῆσαι τρίχας, φρίξαι χαίτην, τὸν
ὀφθαλμὸν κατακλᾶν, φρένα πάλλειν.
It will be sometimes found to explain
otherwise inexplicable verbal constructions, as ἀμέρδειν in βίον ἀμέρσας (Eur.
Hec. 1029).
5. **γυναικῶν δύο.** Phryn. pp. 289-
290.
7. **βλέπειν ἐραστήν** (see Index). This
poetical use of βλέπω occurs even in
prose in late Greek, as Polyb. 12, 24, 6,
τὸν ἥλιον βλέπειν. In Attic prose and
comedy it means *to look*, and is construed with εἰς, πρὸς, ποι, ἐνταῦθα, etc.;
κάτω, ἄνω, ὀξύ, δριμύ, νᾶπυ, ἀπιστίαν,
etc.; or if absolute, signifies *to have
one's sight.* In Pax. 208 Aristophanes
uses it as here, but in para-tragedy,
ἵνα μὴ βλέποιεν μαχομένους ὑμᾶς ἔτι.
The scholiast on Av. 296 also quotes
as from the Νῆσοι the words τί σὺ

τῶν οὖν τριχῶν ἑκάστοθ' ἡ μὲν ἀκμαίη
ἔτιλλεν ἃς ηὕρισκε λευκανθιζούσας,
ἔτιλλε δ' ἡ γραῦς εἰ μέλαιναν ηὑρήκει,   10
ἕως φαλακρὸν ἡ νέη τε χἠ γραίη
ἔθηκαν ἄνδρα, τῶν τριχῶν ἀποσπῶσαι.

XXIII.

Βοηλάτης ἄνθρωπος εἰς μακρὴν ὕλην
ταῦρον κεράστην ἀπολέσας ἀνεζήτει.
ἔθηκε δ' εὐχὴν ταῖς ὀρεινόμοις νύμφαις
ἄρν' ἂν παρασχεῖν εἰ λάβοι γε τὸν κλέπτην.
ὄχθον δ' ὑπερβὰς τὸν καλὸν βλέπει ταῦρον   5

12. Graviter corruptum hunc versum exhibet Athous ἔθηκαν ἑκάστη
τῶν τριχῶν ἀποσπῶσα. Correxi ego, ἄνδρα pro ἑκάστη scripto. ἔθηκαν
δρα similem in modum medebatur scriba atque 91, 4, infra. Versus in
Athoo accedit plane ab eodem fictus qui hanc ceterasque fabulas epimythiis
ornavit—

ἀεὶ γὰρ ἔν γε τιλλόμενος ἐγυμνοῦτο.
μῦθος φάσκει τοῦτο πᾶσιν ἀνθρώποις·
ἐλεεινὸς ὅστις εἰς γυναῖκας ἐμπίπτει·
ἀεὶ γὰρ ἔν γε δακνόμενος γυμνοῦται.

Pro μῦθος φάσκει codicis diorthotes φάσκει δὲ μῦθος scripsit.

XXIII. Tertium post versum habet Athous verba spuria haec, quae
ratione et metro carent—

Ἑρμῆ νομαίῳ, Πανί, τοῖς πέριξ, ἄρνα
λοιβὴν

Lautae certe erant epulae et optatae non modo nymphis aliquot et
Mercurio et Pani, sed etiam τοῖς πέριξ, unus agnus parvulus, idemque in
libamentum liquefactus. 5. Pro Athoo λάβοιτο cum Duebnero λάβοι
γε legere malo. Epimythium plus solito foedum—

ἐντεῦθεν ἡμᾶς τοῦτ' ἔοικε γινώσκειν,
ἄβουλον εὐχὴν τοῖς θεοῖσι μὴ πέμπειν
ἐκ τῆς πρὸς ὥραν ἐκφορουμένης λύπης.

λέγεις; εἰσὶν δέ που | αἰδὶ κατ' αὐτὴν
ἣν βλέπεις τὴν εἴσοδον; but if the
passage is not para-tragedic, it is corrupt. In the New Comedy, however,
βλέπω is used just as in the higher
poetry.

9. Observe ηὕρισκε and ηὑρήκει in
place of the classical εὑρίσκοι or εὗροι.
XXIII. 1. Join εἰς μακρὴν ὕλην . .
ἀπολέσας.
3. ἔθηκεν εὐχὴν, the well-known poetical periphrasis = ηὔξατο.

λέοντι θοίνην· δυστυχὴς δ' ἐπαρᾶται
καὶ βοῦν προσάξειν εἰ φύγοι γε τὸν κλέπτην.

XXIV.

Γάμοι μὲν ἦσαν Ἡλίου θέρους ὥρη,
τὰ ζῷα δ' ἱλαροὺς ἦγε τῷ θεῷ κώμους,
καὶ βάτραχοι δὲ λιμνάδας χοροὺς ἦγον·
οὓς εἶπε παύσας φρῦνος ' οὐχὶ παιάνων
τοῦτ' ἔστιν ἡμῖν, φροντίδων δὲ καὶ λύπης·   5
ὃς γὰρ μόνος νῦν λιβάδα πᾶσαν ἀναίνει,

XXIV. 3. Verbum λιμναίους quod Athous exhibet correxit Fixius,
λιμνάδας scripto; confer 115, 1, infra, sed ἦγον ultima syllaba brevis
plus corruptionis minari videtur. 4. Accusativum οὓς Athous habet, sed
ita recentiore atramento oblitum ut editores οἷς dederint. Sub παιάν
vocabulo offert Suidas ὁ δ' εἶπε κλαύσας κτε. Epimythium sanius—

χαίρουσι πολλοὶ τῶν ὑπερβολῇ κούφων
ἐφ' οἷς ἄγαν μέλλουσιν οὐχὶ χαιρήσειν.

---

7. This last sentence is very puzzling.
In what sense can ἐπαρᾶται with a
future infinitive be used? If it means
τῷ λέοντι ἐπαρώμενός φησι προσάξειν,
then Greek is a strange language. The
Athoan reading βοῦς is probably due to
the misconception of a copyist, who
imagined the point lay in bringing the
cows of the herd as well as the bull to
the lion, instead of in increasing the
prize to the nymphs from a lamb to an
ox. The text of the fable is probably
more corrupt than the critical note
indicates.

XXIV. 3. λιμνάδας is predicative.
'The frogs also danced in the pools.'
If the line is not corrupted from one in
which λιμναίους formed the last word,
the conjecture of Fix is certain. The
diphthong of λιμναίους could not be
shortened as that of the differently
accented δείλαιος, παλαιός, γεραιός.

4. The antecedent of οὓς is βάτραχοι,
not χορούς.

6. ἀναίνει. Observe the late spiritus
lenis. Thus the Attic ἀφαναίνω is in
late writers ἀπαναίνω, and though they
do not use the corresponding compound
of αὔω, its late form would have been
ἀπαύω. The Attic tendency to aspirate

(ἀσφάραγος, σφόγγος, φιδάκνη, σχινδαλ-
μός, λίσφοι, σφονδύλη) has been too
rashly used by some editors of Attic
texts. Thus Cobet insists (Var. Lect.
588) upon ἄνιτω being everywhere
written in tragedy, and has altered
(Nov. Lect. 340) καταννύσαι into καθαννύσαι in Xenophon (Hell. 7, 1, 15), rely-
ing upon the Hesychian gloss καθαννύ-
σαι· συντελέσαι. Now Xenophon
may have used καθαννύσαι, but he was
more likely to use the non-Attic καταννύσαι, just as the tragic dialect would
prefer the early ἀνύτειν to the more
modern ἀνύτειν. The evidence of καθ-
είργω is very good. It is the regular
form in comedy and Attic prose proper,
while κατείργω is preferentially used in
tragedy and early prose. Further
ἀπείργω had so come to be regarded as
a simple verb that the labial never
suffered aspiration. On these grounds
I must maintain that in no single
passage of tragic verse or of Xenophon's
prose can we be certain whether the
aspirated or unaspirated form of εἴργω
or ἀνύτω was employed, because the
diction was in the former case a conventional mixture of new and old, in
the latter a particoloured tissue of Attic

τί μὴ πάθωμεν τῶν κακῶν, ἐὰν γήμας
ὅμοιον αὐτῷ παιδίον τι γεννήσῃ;'

XXV.

Γνώμη λαγωοὺς εἶχε μηκέτι ζώειν
πάντας δὲ λίμνης εἰς μέλαν πεσεῖν ὕδωρ,
ὁθούνεκ' εἰσὶν ἀδρανέστατοι ζώων,
ψυχάς τ' ἄτολμοι, μοῦνον εἰδότες φεύγειν.
ἐπεὶ δὲ λίμνης ἐγγὺς ἦσαν εὐρείης   5

and Hellenic. Of course the differentiation of the meaning of εἴργω according to the breathing is only a figment of inferior grammarians.

I have carefully abstained from the etymological side of the question, which does not concern the grammarian. ἀνύτω may be the same word as the English 'send,' and αὖος be correctly identified with the English 'sere,' and still the aspirate in Attic have nothing to do with the primitive spirant.

7. **τί μὴ πάθωμεν.** There would be no occasion to draw attention to these words if editors had not, in obedience to rules of syntax and canons of criticism quite unintelligible to me, changed the legitimate μή into the impossible μὴ οὔ. With the deliberative subjunctive μή is the negative used, Soph. El. 1276, τί μὴ ποιήσω; Aj. 668, ἄρχοντές εἰσιν ὥσθ' ὑπεικτέον, τί μή; sc. ὑπείκωμεν. Aesch. Agam. 672, λέγουσιν ἡμᾶς ὡς ὀλωλότας, τί μή; sc. λέξωσιν.

XXV. 1. **γνώμη .. εἶχε** = οἱ λαγωοὶ ἐγίγνωσκον. After verbs of resolving upon a course and fulfilling a duty, μή is the *regular* negative. See Kühner, § 514, where the instances are, even more than usually, ill arranged and carelessly selected.

2. 'But to throw themselves in a body into the wan water of a pool, because of living things they are the most feeble and craven of spirit, skilled in nothing but flight.' Observe the idiomatic πεσεῖν—the equivalent of the passive of βάλλω. I say 'passive' because the Greeks used the passive, not the middle, in cases of this kind when a neuter like πίπτω was not to be had. Many neuter verbs in Greek are intelligible only when we have

discovered the transitive verb to which they serve as passive. βάλλω, πίπτω: ἐκβάλλω, ἐκπίπτω: μεταβάλλω, μεταπίπτω: ἐμβάλλω, ἐμπίπτω: συμβάλλω, συμπίπτω: περιβάλλω, περιπίπτω. Nothing is more common than phrases like περιβάλλειν τινὰ κακοῖς, συμφοραῖς, etc., but we never find περιεβλήθην or περιβέβλημαι κακοῖς, always περιέπεσον, περιπέπτωκα. No Athenian said ἐξεβλήθην θύραξε, always ἐξέπεσον θύραξε. In dice τρὶς ἓξ βαλεῖν, etc.; but *the* cast is τὰ πεσόντα. There is no end to the passive uses of ἰέναι, ἐλθεῖν, ἥκω, πλέω, etc., both simple and compound. κατάγω, κατέρχομαι: εἰσάγω, εἰσέρχομαι: παράγω, παρέρχομαι: διώκω, φεύγω: ἀποκτείνω, ἀποθνήσκω: λέγω, ἀκούω: διδάσκω, μανθάνω: λείπω, μένω: ποιῶ, πάσχω. If any one has tried to read an Attic writer without knowing that γίγνομαι is the passive of the most frequent sense of ποιῶ, he must lamentably have misunderstood his author. Due to the same feeling is the other method of forming the passive in Attic, seen in phrases like λόγον, ὄνειδος, τιμήν, ἔπαινον, ψόγον ἔχειν, and for aorist, σχεῖν or λαβεῖν. Thuc. 6, 60, ὁ δῆμος χαλεπὸς ἦν ἐς τοὺς περὶ τῶν μυστικῶν αἰτίαν λαβόντας. Dem., ὥστε πολὺ μᾶλλον προσήκειν ἐμὲ τούτους ἐγκαλεῖν ἢ αὐτὸν ἐγκλήματ' ἔχειν. Plat. Rep. 565 B, αἰτίαν ἔσχον ὑπὸ τῶν ἑτέρων .. ὡς ἐπιβουλεύουσι τῷ δήμῳ. Anaxandrides, τὸ γὰρ κολακεύειν νῦν ἀρέσκειν ὄνομ' ἔχει. The passive of ἐλεῶ is hardly used, ἐλέου τυγχάνειν and τυχεῖν being used instead.

5. Nauck has pointed out an instructive blunder in Suidas as to this line. Ῥυρίης· περιφερούς.
ἐπεὶ δὲ λίμνης ἐγγὺς ἦλθον γυρίης.

καὶ βατράχων ὅμιλον εἶδον ἀκταίων
βαθέην ἐς ἰλὺν ὀκλαδιστὶ πηδώντων,
ἐπεστάθησαν, καί τις εἶπε θαρσήσας,
' ἄψ νῦν ἴωμεν· οὐκέτι χρεὼν θνήσκειν·
ὁρῶ γὰρ ἄλλους ἀσθενεστέρους ἥμων.'   10

XXVI.

Γέρανοι γεωργοῦ κατενέμοντο τὴν χώρην
ἐσπαρμένην νεωστὶ πυρίνῳ σίτῳ.
ὁ δ' ἄχρι πολλοῦ σφενδόνην κένην σείων
ἐδίωκεν αὐτάς, τῷ φόβῳ καταπλήσσων.
αἱ δ' ὡς ἐπέσχον σφενδονῶντα τὰς αὔρας,   5
κατεφρόνησαν λοιπὸν ὥστε μὴ φεύγειν,
ἕως ἐκεῖνος, οὐκέθ' ὡς πρὶν εἰώθει,
λίθους δὲ βάλλων ἠλόησε τὰς πλείους.
αἱ δ' ἐκλιποῦσαι τὴν ἄρουραν, ἀλλήλαις
' φεύγωμεν ' ἐκραύγαζον ' εἰς τὰ Πυγμαίων.   10

Of course there is no such word as γύριος, but ΓΥΡΙΗΣ arose from ΕΥΡΕΙΗΣ. Zonaras also (Lexicon, p. 459) has either got his gloss from Suidas or copied from the same source. Γυρίης· περιφεροῦς. See also note on Fab. 88, 11, *infra*.

6. 'And had seen a company of frogs from its strand leaping with a hop into the deep mud.' How far Babrius intended to magnify his humble actors by the use of words like ἀκτή, ἀκταῖος, and heroic phrases like the following, ἄψ νῦν ἴωμεν, cannot be safely decided in a writer of his date. ἰλύς has here its correct meaning. Phryn. p. 147. ὀκλαδιστί, of gathering the legs up under one, in this case for a fresh spring. The form is late, as if from ὀκλαδίζω, instead of ὀκλάζω. The Attic adverb was ὀκλάξ, which by a certain emendation Bekker restored for ὁ βλάξ in a line of Pherecrates, ἀδράφραξιν ἔφουσ', εἶτ' ὀκλὰξ καθημένη. See lexica, and cp. Phryn. App. Soph. 56, 1, ὀκλάσαι· τὸ τὰ γόνατα κάμψαι ἐγκαθίζοντα.
XXVI. 3. 'For a long time to chase them off he shook an empty sling, cowing them by the fear of it.' What ψόφῳ, a conjecture of Seidler's, uni-

formly accepted by the editors, can possibly mean is to me incomprehensible. Where was the *noise* to come from?

10. Hom. Il. 3, 3 :—

ἠΰτε γὰρ κλαγγὴ γεράνων πέλει οὐρανόθι πρό,
αἵτ' ἐπεὶ οὖν χειμῶνα φύγον καὶ ἀθέσφατον ὄμβρον,
κλαγγῇ ταί γε πέτονται ἐπ' Ὠκεανοῖο ῥοάων,
ἀνδράσι Πυγμαίοισι φόνον καὶ κῆρα φέρουσαι.
ἠέριαι δ' ἄρα ταί γε κακὴν ἔριδα προφέρονται.

The myth is also mentioned by Aristotle, Strabo, Gellius, Athenaeus, and others, who evidently knew no more than we do about its origin. Two facts are to be reached. In Homer's time the existence of a race of dwarfs was believed in, a πυγμή in height. The cranes led them a sorry life. The word πυγμαῖος originally conveyed a definite idea of size, but the attempts of late writers to explain the size meant by πυγμή are futile. The late accessories to the myth are such as might have sprung from the Homeric facts.

ἄνθρωπος οὗτος οὐκέτ' ἐκφοβεῖν ἥμας
ἔοικεν, ἤδη δ' ἄρχεταί τι καὶ πράσσειν.'

XXVII.

Γαλῆν δόλῳ τις συλλαβών τε καὶ δήσας
ἔπνιγεν ὑδάτων ἐν συναγκίῃ κοίλῃ.
τῆς δ' αὖ λεγούσης 'ὡς κακὴν χάριν τίνεις
ὧν σ' ὠφελοῦν θηρῶσα μῦς τε καὶ σαύρας,'
'ἐπιμαρτυρῶ σοι' φησίν, 'ἀλλὰ καὶ πάσας   5
ἔπνιγες ὄρνεις, πάντα δ' οἶκον ἠρήμους,
βλάπτουσα μᾶλλον ἤπερ ὠφελοῦσ' ἥμας.'

XXVII. Fabula magis corrupta et in Athoo codice et Vaticano.
1. Per dittographiam habent πνίγων Athous et Vaticanus; δήσας ex
paraphrasi Boissonadius dedit. 2. Athoam lectionem vix mutavi, vocula
ἐν post ὑδάτΩΝ restituta et συναγκίη pro συναγγίᾳ lecto: Saepissime
in codicibus confusa sunt ἄγγος et ἄγκος. Tria modo verba Vaticanus
offert, βαλὼν ὑδάτων συνεχεία, sed alio etiam συνάγκεια et συνέχεια inter
se confundi solent, e.g. ap. Diod. 3, 68. Conjecit Butmannus ἔπνιγε
βάπτων et Bernhardius ὕδατος ἐν συναγκείῃ. 4. Adderunt σ' Fix.
aliique. 6. Post hunc versum addit alium Vaticanus sine dubio fictum—

κρεῶν ἀνέῳγας ἄγγος ὥστε τεθνήξῃ.

Oppian uses the myth in a simile, probably directly suggested by Homer's lines, Hal. 1, 620 :—

ὡς δ' ὅτ' ἀπ' Αἰθιόπων τε καὶ Αἰγύπτοιο
ῥοάων
ὑψιπετὴς γεράνων χορὸς ἔρχεται ἠερο-
φώνων,
Ἀτλάντος νιφόεντα πάγον καὶ χεῖμα
φυγοῦσαι,
Πυγμαίων τ' ὀλιγοδρανέων ἀμενηνὰ γέ-
νεθλα.

XXVII. 2. Homer (Il. 4, 452) applies μισγάγκεια to the place where several gullies meet, and unite the waters of their streams—

ὡς δ' ὅτε χείμαρροι ποταμοὶ κατ' ὄρεσφι
ῥέοντες
ἐς μισγάγκειαν συμβάλλετον ὄβριμον ὕδωρ
κρουνῶν ἐκ μεγάλων κοίλης ἔντοσθε χαρά-
δρης.

Late writers used συνάγκεια in the same sense, and joined it with a genitive expressing whether the meeting glens had their sides wooded or their gullies filled with water, or both. Diod. Sic. 3, 67 fin., εἶναι τῆς νήσου τὴν μὲν πρώτην εἰσβολὴν αὐλωνοειδῆ, σύσκιον ὑψηλοῖς καὶ πυκνοῖς δένδρεσιν, ὥστε τὸν ἥλιον μὴ παντάπασι διαλάμπειν διὰ τὴν συνάγκειαν, αὐγὴ δὲ μόνην ὁρᾶσθαι φωτός, where a long valley is meant with lateral valleys running into it. Id. 4, 84, ἐν ταύτῃ τῇ χώρᾳ συναγκείας δένδρων οὔσης θεοπρεποῦς. In the Λέξεις 'Ρητορικαί, Bekk. Anec. p. 226, 5, there is a note on βῆσσα which incidentally explains συνάγκεια. Βῆσσαν· κοιλάδα ὕδωρ ἔχουσαν καὶ μεσότητα ὀρῶν· τὴν συνάγκειαν. ἄλλοι τὸ ἔνυδρον. On the other hand, συναγγίη receives some support from Soph. O. C. 159, νάπει | ποιέντι, κάθυδρος οὗ | κρατὴρ μειλιχίων ποτῶν | ῥεύματι συντρέχει.

D

XXVIII.

Γέννημα φρύνου συνεπάτησε βοῦς πίνων.
ἐλθοῦσα δ' αὐτόν (οὐ παρῆν γάρ) ἡ μήτηρ
παρὰ τῶν ἀδελφῶν ποῦ ποτ' ἦν ἐπεζήτει·
' τέθνηκε, μῆτερ· ἄρτι γάρ, πρὸ τῆς ὥρης,
ἦλθεν πάχιστον τετράπουν ὑφ' οὐ κεῖται   5
χηλῇ μαλαχθέν.' ἡ δὲ φρῦνος ἠρώτα,
φυσῶσ' ἑαυτήν, εἰ τοιοῦτον ἦν ὄγκῳ
τὸ ζῷον. οἱ δὲ μητρί ' παῦε, μὴ πρίου·

XXVIII. 1. 'An ox in drinking trod upon one of a toad's brood. His mother came, and as he was not to be seen, asked of his brothers where in the world he was.' The idiomatic αὐτόν appears to have given trouble to some editors, who have quite changed the point of οὐ παρῆν γάρ by reading αὐτόσ'. Observe ποῦ ποτ' ἦν in place of the Attic ὅπου ποτ' εἴη or ὅπου ποτ' ἐστί.
4. πρὸ τῆς ὥρης, 'an hour ago.' This use of πρό first became frequent in late Greek and was possibly due to Latin influence, although it occurs in classical writers. For the division of the day into twelve hours of equal length, see lexica. We should have expected the omission of τῆς.
7. εἰ τοιοῦτον ἦν ὄγκῳ, 'whether he was like that in size.' I believe that Babrius wrote τοιοῦτον here and ποιότητα in the last line. The treatment which the sober words of this fable have received at the hands of editors is really vexatious. I have printed it as it stands in the Athoan codex with the change of only two letters, μῆτερ for μήτηρ in l. 4, and ἑαυτήν for σεαυτήν in l. 7, and I doubt if ever a like poem of the nursery or schoolroom was more naturally expressed. The ὄγκῳ makes all the difference, and τοιοῦτον ὄγκῳ = τοσοῦτον. Moreover, it is late Greek we have to do with, as ποιότητα shows.
8. παῦε. This use of the second person singular of the imperative active of παύω is found as early as Hesiod, unless for παῦε μάχης in Scut. 449, we ought to read παῦε μάχην (cp. Hom. Il. 1, 282; Od. 24, 543). Homer, however, uses the middle, Il. 9, 260, παῦε', ἔα δὲ χόλον θυμαλγέα, as ἐάω in Homer's time at all events had no initial

spirant. Attic appears always to employ the active (Arist. Ran. 122, 270, 581; Ach. 864; Av. 889, 1243, 1504; Eq. 821, 919; Vesp. 37, 518, 1194, 1208; Pax. 326, 648; Eccl. 161; Plato, Phaedr. 228 E; Soph. Phil. 1275). Accordingly in Ephippus ap. Athen. 8, 347 B, for παύου φυσῶν, Μακεδὼν ἄρχων, we should probably read παῦε σὺ φυσῶν. On the other hand, no other part but the second person singular is so used intransitively. The plural is παύεσθε (Arist. Lys. 461), and the aorist παῦσαι (Arist. Ach. 1111; Vesp. 652; Pax. 1229; Av. 209, 859, 1381; Eccl. 129; Thesm. 173, 1076; Plut. 360. Frag. Comic. frequently. Plato, Phaedr. 262 E; Gorg. 486 C; Phil. 19 E; Soph. Aj. 1353; Ant. 280); and παύσασθε (Arist. Nub. 934; Pax. 442; Lys. 762; Thesm. 571; Ran. 241, Trag. frequently); and παύσασθον (Arist. Ran. 1364). In Soph. O. C. 1777, ἀλλ' ἀποπαύετε μηδ' ἔτι πλείω θρῆνον ἐγείρετε, the ἀπό is intensive, and θρῆνον the object of both imperatives. In the fragment of Euripides preserved by a schol. on Arist. Thesm. 1018,

προσαυδῶ σε τὰν ἐν ἄντροις
ἀπόπασον (sic) ἔασον ἁ –
χοῖ με σὺν φίλαισιν
γόου πόθον λαθεῖν,

Seidler restores ἀπόπαυσον, but by so doing he makes a poor sense and violates a rule of Greek. Certainly in Eur. Hec. 918,

ἦμος ἐκ δείπνων ὕπνος ἡδὺς ἐπ' ὄσσοις
κίδναται, μολπᾶν δ' ἀπο καὶ χοροποιῶν
θυσιᾶν καταπαύσας
πόσις ἐν θαλάμοις ἔκειτο,

the verb is not intransitive, even if we

θᾶσσον σεαυτήν᾽ εἶπον ᾽ἐκ μέσου ῥήξεις,
ἢ τὴν ἐκείνου ποιότητα μιμήσῃ.᾽   10

XXIX.

Γέρων ποθ᾽ ἵππος εἰς ἀλητὸν ἐπράθη·
ζευχθεὶς δ᾽ ὑπὸ μύλην πᾶσαν ἑσπέρην – –,
καὶ δὴ στενάξας εἶπεν ᾽ἐκ δρόμων οἵων
καμπτῆρας οἵους ἀλφιτεῦσι γυρεύω.᾽

XXIX. Fabula Babriana a tetrastichista misere decurtata est et corrupta. Versum secundum ἄμετρον codicis Athoi diorthotes recentior verbo τάλας in fine auxit ; melius Eberhard ἤλει adjecit. Ridicule Gitlbauer εἶλεθ᾽ ἑσπέρην πᾶσαν; neque minus absurde versum quartum verbo mirabili ἀλφιτογυρεύω idem criticus ornavit. Eheu, Babri, tui equi sedem ipse occupas ! Epimythium metro caret—

μὴ λίαν ἐπαίρου πρὸς τὸ τῆς ἀκμῆς γαῦρον.
πολλοῖς τὸ γῆρας εἰς πόνους ἀνηλώθη.

do not read μολπᾶν σ᾽ ἄπο. Paris had not been dancing a *pas seul.* Cp. Od. 23, 297—

αὐτὰρ Τηλέμαχος καὶ βουκόλος ἠδὲ
  συβώτης
παῦσαν ἄρ᾽ ὀρχηθμοῖο πόδας παῦσαν δὲ
  γυναῖκας,
αὐτοὶ δ᾽ εὐνάζοντο κατὰ μέγαρα σκιόεντα.

A similar explanation holds for Xen. Hell. 5. 1, 21, ἐπειδὴ δὲ ἀπεῖχε πέντε ἢ ἐξ στάδια τοῦ λιμένος ἡσυχίαν εἶχε καὶ ἀνέπαυε. So in Thuc. 4, 11, οἱ δὲ κατ᾽ ὀλίγας διελόμενοι καὶ ἀναπαύοντες ἐν τῷ μέρει τοὺς ἐπίπλους ἐποιοῦντο, the active is used because the subject of ἐποιοῦντο is the relieving party (οἱ ἀεὶ ἀναπαύοντες), and in partitive apposition to οἱ . . διελόμενοι, which is a reciprocal middle, including both οἱ ἀεὶ ἀναπαύοντες as well as οἱ ἀεὶ ἀναπαυόμενοι, as its aorist time proves. Thucydides is often very nice in this way, as another instance may show. The only passage in which σπένδω is used in the sense of ᾽make a truce,᾽ is one in Thucydides (4, 98), σαφῶς τε ἐκέλευον σφίσιν εἰπεῖν μὴ ἀπιοῦσιν τῆς Βοιωτῶν γῆς, . . ἀλλὰ κατὰ τὰ πάτρια τοὺς νεκροὺς σπένδουσιν ἀναιρεῖσθαι. The Athenians asked the Boeotians for permission to bury their dead under the protection of mutual libations, but deprecating the necessity of first evacuating Boeotian territory. Now σπένδομαι, ᾽to make a truce,᾽ is really a reciprocal middle, ᾽make mutual libations,᾽ and implies two parties (οἱ σπένδοντες). Thucydides still felt the origin of the signification, and, because grammatically only one of the parties was referred to, used the active instead of the middle voice. Poppo's conjecture, σπεύδουσιν, is of the worst type, palaeographically almost impossible, and quite without meaning.

In the fragment of a late anonymous comic poet quoted by Diod. Sic. in 12, 14, there is a certain instance of κατάπαυσον used intransitively :—

εἶτ᾽ ἐπέτυχες γάρ, φησί, γήμας τὸ πρότερον
εὐημερῶν κατάπαυσον· εἶτ᾽ οὐκ ἐπέτυχες,
μανικὸν τὸ πεῖραν δευτέρας λαβεῖν πάλιν.

The reference is to the law of Charondas forbidding second marriages (Diod. Sic. 12, 12), ἔφη γὰρ τοὺς μὲν πρῶτον γήμαντας καὶ ἐπιτυχόντας δεῖν εὐημερεῦντας τῷ γάμῳ παύειν· τοὺς δὲ ἀποτυχόντας τῷ γάμῳ καὶ πάλιν ἐν τοῖς αὐτοῖς ἀμαρτάνοντας ἄφρονας δεῖν ὑπολαμβάνεσθαι. There must be some reason for such an exceptional use of the active appearing both in Diodorus and the comedian ;

XXX.

Γλύψας ἐπώλει λύγδινόν τις Ἑρμείην.
τὸν δ' ἠγόραζον ἄνδρες, ὃς μὲν εἰς στήλην
(υἱὸς γὰρ αὐτῷ προσφάτως ἐτεθνήκει),
ὁ δὲ χειροτέχνης ὡς θεὸν καθιδρύσων.
ἦν δ' ὀψέ, χὠ λιθουργὸς οὐκ ἐπεπράκει,   5
συνθέμενος αὐτοῖς εἰς τὸν ὄρθρον αὖ δείξειν

XXX. 6. Athoum δεῖξαι in δείξειν cum Eberhardo lubenter mutavi,
nec non εἶδεν (v. 10) cum Gitlbauero in εἶεν.

---

and I take it to have been a misunderstanding of the wording of the law, unless we are to explain κατάπαυσον like the historical ϹΙϹΤΦΟϹ for ϹΙϹΤΦΟϹ in Athen. 11, 500, as a very early blunder for κατάλυσον.

XXX. 1. 'A man desired to sell a Hermes which he had carved in marble, and two men were thinking of buying it, the one for a tombstone, as his son was lately dead, and the other, who was a craftsman, to set it up as a god.' Cobet (Mnem. vii. p. 187) has rightly distinguished between πωλῶ and ἀποδίδομαι. 'Πωλεῖν dicitur qui emptorem quaerit, ἀποδίδοσθαι qui reperit, ut Latine vendilare et vendere. Hinc intelligitur quomodo accipienda sint verba in Symposio, viii. 21 : ὁ ἐν ἀγορᾷ πωλῶν καὶ ἀποδιδόμενος. Hinc etiam melius constituenda sunt quae de formis usitatis verborum πωλεῖν et ἀποδίδοσθαι annotavimus. Ἀποδίδομαι enim habet ἀποδώσομαι et ἀπεδόμην, sed perfectum πέπρακα, et in forma passiva πέπραμαι, ἐπράθην, πεπράσομαι, et praesens πιπράσκομαι.'

3. For προσφάτως see Phryn. p. 70. I do not remember having seen the perfect τέθνηκα compounded with ἀπό or κατά even in poetry. Certainly in Attic prose it never was, but even in the same sentence it stands by the side of ἀποθνήσκω, ἀπέθανον, or ἀποθανοῦμαι as Plato, Phaed. 64 A, ἀποθνήσκειν τε καὶ τεθνάναι. On the other hand the simple form is unknown in the other tenses, except very rarely in the present and imperfect in the early prose of Thucydides or the poetical dialogues of Plato. So also προαποθνήσκω, προαποθανοῦμαι, προαπέθανον, but προτέθνηκα

and προύτεθνήκη ; ἐναποθνήσκω, but ἐντέθνηκα ; συναποθνήσκω, but συντέθνηκα; ὑπεραποθνήσκω, but ὑπερτέθνηκα; ἐπαποθνήσκω, but ἐπιτέθνηκα.

Of the writers of the true Attic period Lysias violates Attic usage by using the aorist ἐνθανόντων for ἐναποθανόντων in 147, 13 ; but I have elsewhere (Phryn. p. 202) shown that Lysias' diction was naturally far from pure. My friend Mr. Gow, Fellow of Trinity College, Cambridge, has drawn my attention to the fact that French critics saw in Victor Hugo's works written during his sojourn in Jersey an absence of 'la malice et la délicatesse l'arisienne,' and a similar nescio quid I have always felt the want of in Lysias' Attic.

4. I have retained with confidence the manuscript reading χειροτέχνης in preference to the conjecture χειροτέχνημ', which injures the sense, and is grammatically inelegant. The second buyer was a business man who wanted the statue of the god for some contract he had in hand. The ὡς goes with the participle as ἠγόραζον does not imply motion, and Babrius never violates the Attic rule that, except after verbs of motion, a future participle expressing purpose must be preceded by ὡς, 'intending to set him up the god he was.'

6. Although the aorist infinitive is permissible after a verb denoting the making of an agreement, yet the future is more common, and makes so much better an ending to a Babrian scazon, that I have adopted it here. εἰς τὸν ὄρθρον (Phryn. p. 341), here = τῇ αὔριον.

BABRIUS.

37

ἐλθοῦσιν. ὁ δὲ λιθουργὸς εἶδεν ὑπνώσας
αὐτὸν τὸν Ἑρμῆν ἐν πύλαις ὀνειρείαις
‘ εἶεν ’ λέγοντα ‘ τἀμὰ νῦν ταλαντεύῃ·
ἐν γάρ με, νεκρὸν ἢ θεόν, σὺ ποιήσεις.’   10

XXXI.

Γαλαῖ ποτ’ εἶχον καὶ μύες πρὸς ἀλλήλους
ἄσπονδον ἀεὶ πόλεμον αἱμάτων πλήρη·
γαλαῖ δ’ ἐνίκων. οἱ μύες δὲ τῆς ἥττης
ἐδόκουν ὑπάρχειν αἰτίην σφίσιν ταύτην,
ὅτι στρατηγοὺς οὐκ ἔχοιεν ἐκδήλους,   5
ἀεὶ δ’ ἀτάκτως ὑπομένουσι κινδύνους.
εἵλοντο τοίνυν τοὺς γένει τε καὶ ῥώμῃ
γνώμῃ τ’ ἀρίστους, εἰς μάχην τε γενναίους,
οἳ σφᾶς ἐκόσμουν καὶ διεῖλον εἰς ἴλας
λόχους τε καὶ φάλαγγας, ὡς ἐν ἀνθρώποις.   10
ἐπεὶ δ’ ἐτάχθη πάντα καὶ συνηθροίσθη,
καί τις γαλῆν μῦς προὐκαλεῖτο θαρσήσας,
οἵ τε στρατηγοὶ, λεπτὰ πηλίνων τοίχων
κάρφη μετώποις ἁρμόσαντες ἀκραίοις,
ἡγοῦντο, πάντος ἐκφανέστατοι πλήθους,   15
πάλιν δὲ φύζα τοὺς μύας κατειλήφει.
ἄλλοι μὲν οὖν σωθέντες ἦσαν ἐν τρώγλαις,

XXXI. 14. Egregie Duebner verbum quod exhibet Athous ἀχρεῖα
emendavit, ἀκραίοις lecto.

7. ὑπνώσας. It is unnecessary to
save Babrius' credit by referring this
to the Homeric ὑπνώω instead of the
late intransitive ὑπνόω. Babrius was
a late writer if one of the best of them.
See *supra*, 18, 6, note.
8. Hom. Od. 4, 808 :—
περίφρων Πηνελόπεια
ἡδὺ μάλα κνώσσουσ’ ἐν ὀνειρείῃσι πύλῃσιν.
9. ‘Well! my fate now wavers in
thy hands ; one or other thou wilt
make me, a dead man or a god.’ The
manuscript reading is excellent.—‘One
thing only you can make of me ; which
is it to be, dead man or god?’ The
conjectures as usual miss the point.

XXXI. 5. ὅτι . . οὐκ ἔχοιεν . . ἀεὶ
δ’ . . ὑπομένουσι. Observe the combination of the regular and graphic constructions, known in Attic and sometimes effectively employed by Babrius.
Cp. *supra*, 15, 8.
11. ‘And when the whole host was
set in array and gathered together, a
mouse also took heart and challenged
a cat.’ There is no necessity to suppose with Duebner that a line has
been lost between συνηθροίσθη and καί
τις.
13. ‘And the generals, with fine
morsels of mud-walls fitted on the tops
of their foreheads, led them on, most
conspicuous of all the host.’

τοὺς δὲ στρατηγοὺς εἰστρέχοντας οὐκ εἴα
τὰ περισσὰ κάρφη τῆς ὀπῆς ἔσω δύνειν.

XXXII.

Γαλῆ ποτ' ἀνδρὸς εὐπρεποῦς ἐρασθείσῃ
δίδωσι σεμνὴ Κύπρις, ἡ πόθων μήτηρ,
μορφὴν ἀμεῖψαι καὶ λαβεῖν γυναικείην,
καλῆς γυναικός, ἧς τίς οὐκ ἔχειν ἦρα;

19. Hunc post versum alii tres interpolati sunt—

μόνοι θ' ἑάλωσαν αὐτόθι μυχῶν πρόσθεν,
νίκη δ' ἐπ' αὐτοῖς καὶ τρόπαιον εἱστήκει,
γαλῆς ἑκάστης μῦν στρατηγὸν ἑλκούσης.

fortasse eidem reddendi qui epimythium adjecit—

λέγει δ' ὁ μῦθος· εἰς τὸ ζῆν ἀκινδύνως
τῆς λαμπρότητος ἐντέλεια βελτίων.

Locos pejores emendaverunt critici, ἑᾶλον, αὐτόθεν et ἠντέλεια scriptis.
Οὐ φροντὶς Ἱπποκλείδῃ.
XXXII. 4. Athoum participium ἔχων cum Seidlero in infinitivum
ἔχειν mutavi malo quam cum Lachmanno legere ἑκών.

19. The fable closes naturally at
δύνειν, and what remains in the Athoan
codex is as near nonsense as it well
can be.
XXXII. 2. ἡ πόθων μήτηρ. This
use of πόθοι is very common in late
Greek, and has given unnecessary
trouble to some critics in this passage.
3. 'To change her form and take
that of a woman, a lady fair whom
every one was fain to wed.' The
idiomatic apposition γυναικείην, καλῆς
γυναικός, is best known in the case of
the possessive pronouns, though even
then it occasionally escapes commen-
tators, as in Homer, Od. 21, 383,
ἣν δέ τις ἢ στοναχῆς ἠὲ κτύπου ἔνδον
ἀκούσῃ | ἀνδρῶν ἡμετέροισιν ἐν ἕρκεσι,
where the ἀνδρῶν is wrongly taken
with the preceding line, and really
goes with ἕρκεσι, 'in the courts of us
men.' Xenophon supplies an instance
not unlike the Babrian in Anab. 4, 7,
22, γέρρα δασειῶν βοῶν ὠμοβόεια, where
Cobet rashly omits the genitives.

4. However awkward the interrogative in a relative clause appears in
English, it is very idiomatic Greek.
See Kühner, § 587, 5, p. 1020. Nothing has injured scholarship more
than the attempt to illustrate the
idioms of an ancient language by those
of a modern. As in the science of
language, so in the science of philology,
striking coincidences are most easily
found by the ignorant, and almost
always contravene the facts of one of
the languages concerned. It is only
when a man puts from him his own
notions of the meaning of moods, and
tenses, and everything else, and presents his mind as a tabula rasa to the
true Greek way of regarding things,
that he begins to know Greek. Take
for example the phrase which has
troubled so many Ἑλληνισταί, and no
few Ἕλληνες—the nauseating οἶσθ' οὖν
ὃ δρᾶσον. To any one who regards the
Greek imperative as a mood of the
same quality as the English, the sen-

ἰδὼν δ' ἐκεῖνος (ἐν μέρει γὰρ ἡλώκει)   5
γαμεῖν ἔμελλεν. ἡρμένου δὲ τοῦ δείπνου
παρέδραμεν μῦς· τὸν δὲ τῆς βαθυστρώτου
καταβᾶσα κλίνης ἐπεδίωκεν ἡ νύμφη.
γάμου δὲ δαίτη 'λέλυτο καὶ καλῶς παίξας
Ἔρως ἀπῆλθε· τῇ φύσει γὰρ ἡττήθη.   10

XXXIII.

Δυσμαὶ μὲν ἦσαν Πλειάδων, σπόρου δ' ὥρη,
καί τις γεωργὸς πυρὸν εἰς νεὸν ῥίψας

tence is difficult; but for one who knows that to a Greek δρᾶσον corresponds more nearly to the English 'thou must do,' 'thou hast to do,' δρασάτω 'he must do,' δράσατε 'you must do,' δρασάντων 'they must do,' there is no difficulty whatever. The Greeks used the imperative freely in any person after relatives and relative adverbs, and might add a subject with the definite article no less to the second than to the third person. ἄνδρας πέμπει οἱ δρασάντων, 'he sends men who have got to do.' οἶσθ' οὖν δ ποίησον, 'Dost know what thou hast got to do'? ἐπεὶ λέξον εἰ τοιοῦτόν ἐστι τὸ ἔργον, 'since thou must tell me.' οἱ Θρᾷκες ἴτε δεῦρ', οὓς Θέωρος ἤγαγεν, 'you Thracians must come forward.'

6. 'When dinner had been brought in.' The phrase αἴρειν τράπεζαν is common in comedy, and generally in the sense of 'bring in,' as Eubulus ap. Athen. 15, 685 E, ὡς γὰρ εἰσῆλθε τὰ γερόντια τότ' εἰς δόμους, | εὐθὺς ἀνεκλίνετο· παρῆν στέφανος ἐν τάχει· | ᾕρετο τράπεζα παρέκειθ' ἅμα τετριμμένη | μᾶζα. In the Λέξεις χρήσιμοι (Β. Α. 359, 23) is found the accurate note Αἴρειν τράπεζαν· παρατιθέναι. Occasionally, however, it appears also to be used of 'taking away,' but in the fragments in which are left us it is often impossible without the context to decide upon the rendering. The sense 'bring in' was the more frequent. Suïdas, Αἴρειν· αὔξειν· ἢ τράπεζαν παρατιθέναι ἢ ἀπαίρειν (correxi. αἴρειν MSS.) ; and again, Αἴρειν· καὶ τὸ προσφέρειν δηλοῖ—

αἴρ', αἶρε μᾶζαν ὡς τάχιστα καν-

θάρῳ | Ἀριστοφάνης Εἰρήνη ... Ἐτίθεσαν δὲ τὴν λέξιν ὡς καὶ ἡμεῖς ἐπὶ τοῦ παρακειμένην ἀφελεῖν τὴν τράπεζαν. Μένανδρος Κεκρυφάλῳ, εἶτ' εὐθὺς οὕτω τὰς τραπέζας αἴρετε· | μύρα, στεφάνους ἑτοίμασον, σπονδὰς ποίει. καὶ Σιναριστώσαις—Ἂν ἔτι πιεῖν μοι δῷ τις· ἀλλ' ἡ βάρβαρος | ἅμα τῇ τραπέζῃ καὶ τὸν οἶνον ᾤχετο | ἄρασ' ἀφ' ἡμῶν.

9. 'Love had played his pretty game, and was gone, vanquished by Nature.' Such a use of φύσις is familiar to students of late Greek, and is found in Aristotle, if not earlier.

XXXIII. 1. 'The Pleiads were setting in the time of seed-sowing, and a husbandman, after casting his wheat into the ground, set himself to watch it. For the black race of noisy daws had come in untold numbers, and starlings, the ruin of field seeds.'

3. ἑστώς, Babrius uses only this form of the participle of ἕστηκα, and also only the corresponding form from τέθνηκα. In Attic both the longer and the shorter forms were in use, and, as comic verse proves, might be employed side by side in the same sentence. The two perfects, throughout their moods, very closely correspond, except that in the participle both forms are trisyllabic, τεθνηκώς and τεθνεώς (on τεθνώς see infra, 45, 9) ; in the other not so, ἑστηκώς and ἑστώς. In the singular of both perfect and pluperfect indicative the forms in kappa are alone known—ἕστηκα, ἕστηκας, ἕστηκε(ν), τέθνηκα, τέθνηκας, τέθνηκε(ν), εἰστήκη, εἰστήκης, εἰστήκει(ν), ἐτεθνήκη, ἐτεθνήκης,

ἐφύλασσεν ἑστώς· καὶ γὰρ ἄκριτον πλήθει
μέλαν κολοιῶν ἔθνος ἦλθε δυσφώνων,
ψαρές τ' ὄλεθρος σπερμάτων ἀρουραίων.   5

XXXIII. 5. Pro ὄλεθρος habet Vaticanus codex ὀρύκται. Quam saepe hunc in modum scribae ὄλεθρος explicent satis constat, vide Mehler. apud Mnemosynem, vol. iii. p. 22 seq.

ἐτεθνήκει(ν) ; while in the optative and imperative both agree in using only the shorter forms, although in neither verb are they of frequent occurrence. In ἴστημι the perfect optative is non-existent, the corresponding tense of the aorist being used instead. In subjunctive and infinitive the two verbs diverge. There is only one instance known of a subjunctive to τέθνηκα, viz. τεθνήκωσι in Thuc. 8, 74 ; but of that from ἕστηκα there are a good many examples, and they are all of the shorter kind, ἑστῶ, ἑστῶσι, etc. For infinitive τεθνηκέναι and τεθνάναι are both legitimate ; but ἑστάναι has almost crushed ἑστηκέναι out of existence. The verbs again correspond in the dual and plural numbers of the two indicative tenses and in the participle, in exhibiting double sets of forms side by side, except that in the pluperfect of ἴστημι the shorter as now edited have no augment. The Attic tendency was rather towards the shorter words, but the longer never became actually rare.

Besides these there were other so-called syncopated perfects, some of which were known only to the higher poetry, and others only to comedy. In tragedy the forms of βέβηκα corresponding to ἑστῶσι, ἑστώς, ἑστῶσα, ἑστῶτες, etc., might be used ; and in choric parts even βεβᾶσι, βεβάναι, etc., are found, but in prose they are unknown except in such as touches upon the confines of poetry. There is also the participle γεγώς, which in Attic never finds its way out of tragedy except to cause a comic effect in comedy. Hephaestion, moreover (de Syll. pp. 17,18), cites from tragedy (Achaeus) and from comedy (Cratinus) the forms ἐλήλυμεν and ἐλήλυτε ; but these are doubtful, and at best have still less right than γεγώς to a place in the discussion of so-called syncopated forms of perfects in -κα. That ἐλήλυμεν and ἐλήλυτε are

not found in complete plays is a side-proof of the judgment of the great grammarians who made our selections for us ; but we have reason to congratulate ourselves that they let the Antigone survive even with such a flaw as βεβρῶτες for βεβρωκότες (in l. 1022). The form is as absurd as if the poet had coined πέπως from πεπωκώς, or δεδώς from δεδωκώς. In comedy, however, no extant play contains the forms which colloquial Attic had forged on the analogy of τέθναμεν, ἑστάναι, etc. They are enumerated by Athenaeus in X. 422 E, εἴρηκε δὲ οὕτως Ἄλεξις ἐν Κουρίδι· ἐπεὶ πάλαι δεδείπναμεν· Εὔβουλος Προκρίδι, ἡμεῖς δ' οὐδέπω δεδείπναμεν· καὶ πάλιν· ὃν χρὴ δε-δειπνάναι πάλαι. καὶ Ἀντιφάνης ἐν Λεωνίδῃ, ἀλλὰ πρὶν δεδειπνάναι ἡμᾶς, παρέσται. καὶ Ἀριστοφάνης ἐν Προαγῶνι—

ὥρα βαδίζειν μοι 'στὶ πρὸς τὸν
    δεσπότην,
ἤδη γὰρ αὐτοὺς οἴομαι δεδειπνάναι.

καὶ ἐν Δαναΐσιν—

ἤδη παροινεῖς εἰς ἐμέ, πρὶν δεδειπ-
    νάναι.

καὶ Πλάτων Σοφιστῇ, καὶ Ἐπικράτης ὁ Ἀμβρακιώτης (μέσης δ' ἐστὶ κωμῳδίας ποιητής) ἐν Ἀμαζόσιν—

δεδειπνάναι γὰρ ἄνδρες εὐκαίρως
    πάνυ
δοκοῦσί μοι.

καὶ ἠρίσταμεν δ' εἴρηκεν Ἀριστοφάνης ἐν Ταγηνισταῖς—

ὑποπεπώκαμεν γάρ, ὦνδρες, καὶ
    καλῶς ἠρίσταμεν.

καὶ Ἕρμιππος ἐν Στρατιώταις—

ἠριστάναι καὶ παρεστάναι τουτωί.

Θεόπομπος Καλλαίσχρῳ—

ἠρίσταμεν, δεῖ γὰρ συνάπτειν τὸν
    λόγον.

τῷ δ' ἠκολούθει σφενδόνην ἔχων κοίλην
παιδίσκος. οἱ δὲ ψᾶρες ἐκ συνηθείης
ἤκουον εἰ τὴν σφενδόνην ποτ' ᾐτήκει,
καὶ πρὶν λαβεῖν ἔφευγον. εὗρε δὴ τέχνην
ὁ γεωργὸς ἄλλην τόν τε παῖδα φωνήσας   10
ἐδίδασκεν· ' ὦ παῖ, χρὴ γὰρ ὀρνέων ἥμας
σοφὸν δολῶσαι φῦλον· ἡνίκ' ἂν τοίνυν
ἔλθωσ', ἐγὼ μέν ' εἶπεν ' ἄρτον αἰτήσω,
σὺ δ' οὐ τὸν ἄρτον, σφενδόνην δέ μοι δώσεις.'
οἱ ψᾶρες ἦλθον κἀνέμοντο τὴν χώρην.   15
ὁ δ' ἄρτον ᾔτει καθάπερ εἶχε συνθήκην·
οἱ δ' οὐκ ἔφευγον· τῷ δ' ὁ παῖς λίθων πλήρη
τὴν σφενδόνην ἔδωκεν· ὁ δὲ γέρων ῥίψας
τοῦ μὲν τὸ βρέγμα, τοῦ δ' ἔτυψε τὴν κνήμην,
ἑτέρου τὸν ὦμον, οἱ δ' ἔφευγον ἐκ χώρης.   20

XXXIV.

Δήμητρι ταῦρον ὄχλος ἀγρότης θύων
ἅλω πλατεῖαν οἰνάσιν κατεστρώκει.

---

20. De versibus qui sequuntur primus dubitavit Eberhardus, et recte—

γέρανοι συνήντων καὶ τὸ συμβὰν ἠρώτων.
καί τις κολοιῶν εἶπε 'φεύγετ' ἀνθρώπων
γένος πονηρόν, ἄλλα μὲν πρὸς ἀλλήλους
λαλεῖν μαθόντων, ἄλλα δ' ἔργα ποιούντων.'

Meliores tamen sunt quam versus qui in Athoo codice sequitur—

ὅτι δεινὸν τὸ φῦλον τῶν δόλῳ τι πραττόντων.

In Vaticano non reperitur. In versu 24 et Vaticanus et Athous δὲ
ποιούντων exhibent.
XXXIV. 2. Lectiones Athoas, ut soleo, Suïdianis antepono.

6. 'And a lad ran at his heels with a sling. But the starlings from long use would listen if he ever asked for the sling, and made off before he had it in his hand.' κοίλην is untranslatable except by *big*, *capacious*, or some such word, which says too much, as the epithet is constant, and refers to the shape. Observe ᾐτήκει or rather ποτ' ᾐτήκει for the Attic αἰτοίη or αἰτήσειεν. There is no reason for pre-ferring βαλεῖν, the reading of a poor codex like the Vatican, to the λαβεῖν of the Athoan.
16. καθάπερ εἶχε συνθήκην = εἶχε συνθέμενος = συνέθετο.
19. For ἔτυψε see Phryn. pp. 257 ff.
20. Observe ἑτέρου by late usage for ἄλλου.
XXXIV. 2. The reading of Suïdas, οἰνάροις ὑπεστρώκει, could only mean 'had strewed a flat threshing-floor under

κρεῶν τραπέζας εἶχε καὶ πίθους οἴνου.
ἐκ τῶν δὲ παίδων ἐσθίων τις ἀπλήστως
ὑπὸ τῶν βοείων ἐγκάτων ἐφυσήθη,   5
κἀπῆλθ᾽ ἐς οἴκους γαστρὸς ὄγκον ἀλγήσας.
πεσὼν δ᾽ ἐφ᾽ ὑγραῖς μητρὸς ἀγκάλαις ἤμει
καὶ ταῦτ᾽ ἐφώνει ᾽ δυστυχὴς ἀποθνήσκω·
τὰ σπλάγχνα γάρ, τεκοῦσα, πάντα μου πίπτει.᾽
ἡ δ᾽ εἶπε ᾽ θάρσει κἀπόβαλλε, μὴ φείδου·   10
οὐ γὰρ σά, τέκνον, ἀλλ᾽ ἐμεῖς τὰ τοῦ ταύρου.᾽

XXXV.

Δύω μὲν υἱοὺς ἡ πίθηκος ὠδίνει,
τεκοῦσα δ᾽ αὐτοῖς ἐστὶν οὐκ ἴση μήτηρ,
ἀλλ᾽ ὃν μὲν αὐτῶν ἀθλίης ὑπ᾽ εὐνοίης
θάλπουσα κόλποις ἀγρίοις ἀποπνίγει,

3. Errat Lachmannus, arbitratus versum post κατεστρώκει excidisse ;
errat etiam praeter solitum Gitlbauer ὑπεστρώκει κρεῶν τραπέζας dis-
tinguens. 7. ἤμει ego. Athous nota culpa εἰμὶ vel εἶμι, quod ridicule in
οἴμοι mutavit manus recentissima. Epimythium supra solitum imbecillum—

          ὅταν ὀρφανοῦ τις οὐσιάν ἀναλώσας
          ἔπειτα ταύτην ἐκτίνων ἀποιμώζῃ,
          πρὸς τοῦτον ἄν τις καταχρέοιτο τῷ μύθῳ.

vine-tendrils,' and is plainly wrong.
Here, as in so many other cases, the
Athoan codex has been misrepresented
by previous editors. It reads, not
οἴνασι, but οἴνάσιν.
7. ἤμει καὶ ταῦτ᾽ ἐφώνει. For the
collocation of words see 17, 4 ; 43, 13.
I edit ἤμει with confidence, as, to any
one who is familiar with the rudiments
of palaeography, it will present itself,
not as a conjecture, but as a fact,
especially as it restores the line to the
true Babrian metre. The form is of
course excellent, Macrob. Saturn. v.
18, ' Aristophanes vetus comicus in
Comoedia Cocalo sic ait, ἤμουν ἄγριον
βάρος· ἤγειρεν γάρ τοί μ᾽ οἶνος οὐ μεγεὶς
᾽Αχελώῳ (πόμ ᾽Αχελώῳ MS.)᾽ Xen.
Anab. 4, 8, 20, καὶ τῶν κηρίων ὅσοι
ἔφαγον τῶν στρατιωτῶν πάντες ἄφρονές

τε ἐγίγνοντο καὶ ἤμουν καὶ κάτω διεχώρει
αὐτοῖς κτε.
I have retained ἐφ᾽ ὑγραῖς ἀγκάλαις
as a late construction. Though ἐν and
ἐπί are in certain circumstances liable
to confusion in copying, ἐν and ἐφ᾽
never are.
9. τεκοῦσα. This participle used
substantivally has in Attic always ὦ
before it in the vocative. For πίπτει
see supra, 25, 2, note. Put actively the
phrase would be, τὰ σπλάγχνα μου βάλ-
λομαι, or rather ἐκβάλλομαι. Perhaps
μου ᾽κπίπτει should actually be read
here, but its look does not recommend
it.
11. Babrius uses the late future ἐμῶ
for ἐμοῦμαι here, as in 12, 13, ἄσω for
ἄσομαι, see Phryn. p. 401. The Attic
form has survived in Aesch. Eum. 730.

τὸν δ' ὡς περισσὸν καὶ μάταιον ἐκβάλλει. 5
κἀκεῖνος ἐλθὼν εἰς ἐρημίην ζώει.

XXXVI.

Δρῦν αὐτόριζον ἄνεμος ἐξ ὄρους ἄρας
ἔδωκε ποταμῷ· τὴν δ' ἔσυρε κυμαίνων,
πελώριον φύτευμα τῶν πρὶν ἀνθρώπων.
πολὺς δὲ κάλαμος ἑκατέρωθεν εἰστήκει
ἐλαφρὸν ὄχθης ποταμίης ὕδωρ πίνων. 5
θάμβος δὲ τὴν δρῦν εἶχε πῶς ὁ μὲν λίην
λεπτός τ' ἐὼν καὶ βληχρὸς οὐκ ἐπεπτώκει,
αὐτὴ δὲ τόσση φηγὸς ἐξεριζώθη.
σοφῶς δὲ κάλαμος εἶπε ‘ μηδὲν ἐκπλήσσου.
σὺ μὲν μαχομένη ταῖς πνοαῖς ἐνικήθης, 10
ἡμεῖς δὲ καμπτόμεσθα μαλθακῇ γνώμῃ,
κἂν βαιὸν ἡμῶν ἄνεμος ἄκρα κινήσῃ.’

XXXV. Exhibet Athous epimythium—

τοιοῦτο πολλῶν ἐστὶν ἦθος ἀνθρώπων,
οἷς ἐχθρὸς ἀεὶ μᾶλλον ἢ φίλος γίγνου.

XXXVI. Accedit epimythium hoc—

κάλαμος μὲν οὕτως· ὁ δέ γε μῦθος ἐμφαίνει
μὴ δεῖν μάχεσθαι τοῖς κρατοῦσιν ἀλλ' εἴκειν.

XXXVI. 2. ἔδωκε ποταμῷ, 'fluvio dedit,' 'in fluvium dedit.' Editors have not observed the Latinism, and have suggested all sorts of absurdities in place of ἔδωκε. Any Latin dictionary will furnish the younger student with examples of this well-known use of 'dare,' if his memory fails him.

3. πελώριον . . ἀνθρώπων = πελώριόν τι ὑπὸ τῶν πρὶν πεφυτευμένον. 'The boiling river swept it on, a giant planted by the men of former time. And on either side were set thickets of reeds, drinking up the still water of the river's bank. And the oak tree wondered how the reeds, exceeding slender and weak though they were, had not been cast down, whereas an oak in her strength she herself was rooted up.'

5. The conjecture ἐλαφρός, though connected with the great name of Lachmann, is a good instance of the fatality which seems to await upon critics in dealing with Babrius. It materially injures the fable, in which the antithesis is very carefully handled, viz.—(1) unbending oak: yielding reeds. (2) boiling current : lapping water. The adjective is frequently applied to still water, Aelian, N. A. 9, 49, τῶν κητῶν τῶν μεγίστων αἰγιαλοῖς καὶ ῥόσι καὶ τοῖς ἐλαφροῖς καλουμένοις καὶ βραχέσι χωρίοις προσπελάζει οὐδέν, οἰκεῖ δὲ τὰ πελάγη. Polyb. 16, 17, 7, ὁ ποταμὸς τὰς μὲν ἀρχὰς ἐλαφρός, εἶτα λαμβάνων αὔξησιν κτε.

6. θάμβος . . εἶχε = ἡ δρῦς ἐθαύμαζε, not θάμβος ἔσχε, which would give the same unapt sense as if ἡ δρῦς ἐθαύμασιν had been used. For πῶς ἐπεπτώκει a classical writer would have employed ὅπως πέπτωκεν or ὅπως πεπτωκοίη (πεπτωκὼς εἴη).

9. Although σοφός, the correction of

XXXVII.

Δαμάλης ἐν ἀγροῖς ἄφετος, ἀτριβὴς ζεύγλης,
κάμνοντι καὶ σύροντι τὴν ὕνιν ταύρῳ
'τάλας' ἐφώνει 'μόχθον οἷον ὀτλεύεις.'
ὁ βοῦς δ' ἐσίγα χὐπέτεμνε τὴν χώρην.
ἐπεὶ δ' ἔμελλον ἀγρόται θεοῖς θύειν,   5
ὁ βοῦς μὲν ὁ γέρων εἰς νομὰς ἀπεζεύχθη,
ὁ δὲ μόσχος ἀδμὴς κεῖνος εἵλκετο σχοίνῳ
δεθεὶς κέρατα, βωμὸν αἵματος πλήσων,
κἀκεῖνος αὐτῷ τοιάδ' εἶπε φωνήσας·
'εἰς ταῦτα μέντοι μὴ πονῶν ἐτηρήθης·   10
ὁ νέος παρέρπεις τὸν γέροντα καὶ θύῃ,
καὶ σοῦ τένοντα πέλεκυς, οὐ ζυγὸς τρίψει.'

XXXVIII.

Δρυτόμοι τινὲς σχίσαντες ἀγρίην πεύκην
ἐνεῖραν αὐτῇ σφῆνας, ὡς διασταίη,

XXXVII. Epimythium addit Athous, de quo editores adhuc silent—
ἔργοις ἔπαινος, ἀργία δὲ κινδύνοις.

manu autem recentiore κινδύνοις in κίνδυνος mutatum est.

XXXVIII. 2. Pro ἐνεῖραν αὐτῇ vocabulis exhibet Suidas ἐναφῆκαν τῇ

---

a διορθωτής, is plainly wrong, yet lines
6, 7 prove that κάλαμος even in its collective sense has the masculine gender.
XXXVII. 2. κάμνοντι καὶ σύροντι,
'hard at work dragging.' Even the
best Attic writers illogically connect
participles related like κάμνοντι and
σύροντι here, by a superfluous καί,
especially when they come close together in a sentence. The instances
are too numerous for the conjunctions
to be explained as mere 'putida em-
blemata,' and occasionally critics, by
so treating them, fall into serious error
—as, for example, Cobet in Thuc. 4,
30, Κλέων δ' ἐκείνῳ τε προπέμψας ἄγγελον ὡς ἥξων καὶ ἔχων στρατιὰν ἣν
ἡγήσατο ἀφικνεῖται ἐς Πύλον, where the
καί is demanded by the preceding τε,
and connects ἔχων with προπέμψας, the
message ending with ἥξων.
'ὕνις priorem corripit in epigrammate Philippi ap. Anth. Pal. vi. 104.

Antiphili, ib. vii. 175. Isidori, ib. vii.
280. Secundum Suidam, priorem pro-
ducit. Vide Jacobs ad Anth. Pal. vol.
3, p. 147.'—C. Lewis.
6. εἰς νομάς. Observe the force of
the plural, = εἰς τὸ νέμεσθαι. For the
form ἀπεζεύχθην, and a discussion of
the verbs which admit of both passive
aorists, that in -ην and that in -θην,
see Veitch, Greek Verbs, sub ἀλάσσω.
10. The metre in this case estab-
lishes the late use of μή. The Athoan
πονεῖν, if not merely the transcriber's
slip that I have judged it to be, may
be referred to the Atticising diorthotes,
through whose hands the Athoan recension of the Babrian text has undoubtedly passed. The question of
the encroachment of μή on οὐ in later
Greek has been ably discussed by Mr.
Gildersleeve in the American Journal
of Philology, No. I.
XXXVIII. 2. The rarity of εἵρω and

γένοιτο δ' αὐτοῖς ὁ πόνος ὕστερον ῥᾴων.
πεύκη στένουσα ' πῶς ἄν ' εἶπε ' μεμφοίμην
τὸν πέλεκυν, ὅς μου μὴ προσῆκε τῇ ῥίζῃ,
ὡς τοὺς κακίστους σφῆνας ὧν ἐγὼ μήτηρ ;
ἄλλος γὰρ ἄλλῃ μ' ἐμπεσὼν διαρρήσσει.'

5

XXXIX.

Δελφῖνες ἀεὶ διεφέροντο φαλλαίναις.
τούτοις παρῆλθε καρκίνος μεσιτεύων,
ὡς εἴ τις ὢν ἄδοξος ἐν πολιτείαις
στάσιν τυράννων μαχομένων εἰρηνεύει.

δρυΐ. Utrum glossa in ἐνείραν sit ἐναφῆκαν judicanda an ipsa vox ἐναφῆκαν ex ἐνέφρηκαν corrupta sit alii dubitent. Epimythium ex iambis plus aequo σκάζουσιν constat—

ὁ μῦθος δ' ἡμῖν τοῦτο πᾶσι μηνύει,
ὡς οὐδὲν οὕτω δεινὸν ἄν ὑπ' ἀνθρώπων
πάθοις τι τῶν ἔξωθεν ὡς ὑπ' οἰκείων.

XXXIX. Fabulam tetrastichista decurtavit. 4. Verbum εἰρηνεύει Athoi in margine codicis prima manu scriptum legere malo quam ὁμηρεύοι quod ipsum versum occupat. Hoc sensu caret et locum habet meliorem

its compounds in late Greek (practically they did not exist) is a strong argument in favour of the Athoan reading here. If ἐναφῆκαν is not a corruption of ἐνέφρηκαν, it is just the word which would be used to explain ἐνείραν, as in late writers the compounds of ἀφίημι take the place of those of εἴρω or φρήμι. The two verbs, φρῆμι and ἀφίημι, are in certain forms very like each other, and have been more than once confused in Attic texts. In these it is not easy to decide in every case between the two, and in debased Greek it is of course impossible. In his diction Xenophon anticipates the later Greek usage, and accordingly it would be rash to substitute, as one would naturally do in an author of Attic purity, εἰσέφρηκαν for εἰσαφῆκαν in Cyrop. 4, 5, 14, ἐπεὶ δ' ἐγένοντο πρὸς τῷ στρατοπέδῳ, οἱ φύλακες, ὥσπερ εἰρημένον ἦν ὑπὸ Κύρου, οὐκ εἰσαφῆκαν αὐτοὺς πρὸ ἡμέρας. See also Phryn. p. 220.

7. The verb ἐμπίπτω, which in such a context signifies ' to be driven in ' or ' home,' has here also its other meaning of ' attack ' alluded to.

XXXIX. 1. I have restored from the codex the true spelling of φαλλαίναις, which, for reasons best known to themselves, previous editors have changed to φαλαίναις. 'Ad mensuram syllabae primae quod attinet, longam eam postulant Nicandri, Nonni, ac Juvenalis versus, et admittunt Aristophanis et Lycophronis loci, ex quo colligi potest veram nominis scripturam esse φάλλαινα quam utroque in versu Aristophanis servavit codex Ravennas, apud Aristotelem, Lycophronem et Aelianum praebent libri optimi, Philostrato et Nonno imprudenter exemerunt editores recentiores. Eadem brevioris formae φάλλη, ἡ, ratio est, κτλ.'—Hase apud Steph. vol. 8, 614.

2. Eberhard suggests μεσιτεύσων, but in a writer of this date the correction would be rash.

XL.

Διέβαινε ποταμὸν ὀξὺν ὄντα τῷ ῥείθρῳ
κυρτὴ κάμηλος, εἶτ᾽ ἔχεζε. τοῦ δ᾽ ὄνθου
φθάνοντος αὐτὴν εἶπεν ᾽ἢ κακῶς πράττω.
ἔμπροσθεν ἤδη τἀξόπισθέ μου βαίνει.᾽

XLI.

Διαρραγῆναί φασιν ἐκ μέσου νώτου
δράκοντι μῆκος ἐξισουμένην σαύραν.
βλάψεις σεαυτὸν κοὐδὲν ἄλλο ποιήσεις
ἂν τὸν σὲ λίαν ὑπερέχοντα μιμήσῃ.

XLII.

Δεῖπνόν τις εἶχε λαμπρὸν ἐν πόλει θύσας·
ὁ κύων δὲ τούτου κυνὶ φίλῳ συναντήσας

---

quod scriba lituris parcere voluit. Serior erat hujus fabulae tetrastichista quam qui paraphrases fecerunt. His fretus novos tres choliambos Gitl- bauer concoxit—

εἰς δ᾽ ὑπολαβὼν πρὸς αὐτὸν εἶπεν ᾽ἀλλ᾽ ἡμῖν
διαφθαρῆναι μαχομένοις ὑπ᾽ ἀλλήλων
ἀνεκτότερον ἢ σοῦ τυχεῖν διαλλάκτου.᾽ (sic!)

XL. Fabulam, si revera a Babrio scriptam, tetrastichista serior foedavit. Sed talia Babrio adjudicare nolo. Epimythium sequitur hoc—

πόλις ἄν τις εἴποι τὸν λόγον τὸν Αἰσώπου
ἧς ἔσχατοι κρατοῦσιν ἀντὶ τῶν πρώτων.

XLI. Huic fabulae epimythium accedere sino ut melius videatur omnes versus eidem pseudo-Babrio esse adscribendos qui tot fabulas revera Babrianas τετραστίχοις fecit.

XL. 3. Observe the rare φθάνοντος for the classical φθάσαντος and πράττω for πράσσω, a spelling of this class of verbs which elsewhere occurs only in the epimythia, with the uniform ex- ception of ἧττα and ἡττᾶσθαι.

XLII. 1. 'A certain man in a city had made sacrifice and was giving a splendid dinner.' The practice hardly

needs illustration. Paul ad. Corinth. Ep. 1, 10, 27, εἰ δέ τις καλεῖ ὑμᾶς τῶν ἀπίστων καὶ θέλετε πορεύεσθαι, πᾶν τὸ παρατιθέμενον ὑμῖν ἐσθίετε, μηδὲν ἀνακρί- νοντες διὰ τὴν συνείδησιν. ἐὰν δέ τις ὑμῖν εἴπῃ ᾽τοῦτο ἱερόθυτόν ἐστι᾽ μὴ ἐσθίετε.

2. συναντήσας. According to the law of parsimony (Phryn. p. 29) ἀπαντᾶν occupied alone in Attic the

ἐλθεῖν πρὸς αὐτὸν ἐπὶ τὸ δεῖπνον ἠρώτα.
κἀκεῖνος ἦλθε· τὸν δὲ τοῦ σκέλους ἄρας
ὁ μάγειρος ἐκτὸς ἐξέριψε τοῦ τοίχου.　　5

XLIII.

Ἔλαφος κεράστης ὑπὸ τὸ καῦμα διψήσας
λίμνης ὕδωρ ἔπινεν ἡσυχαζούσης,
ἐκεῖ δ᾽ ἑαυτοῦ τὴν σκιὴν θεωρήσας
χηλῆς μὲν ἕνεκα καὶ ποδῶν ἐλυπήθη
ἐπὶ τοῖς δὲ κέρασιν ὡς καλοῖς ἄγαν ηὔχει.　　5

XLII. Ut fine magis ad suos mores idoneo hanc fabulam coronaret,
serior aliquis tres versus addidit, quorum alter a metro Babriano abhorret,
et tertius paene caret intellectu—

εἰς τὴν ἄγυιαν· τῶν κυνῶν δ᾽ ἐρωτώντων
ὅπως ἐδείπνησ᾽ εἶπε ʽπῶς γὰρ ἂν κρεῖττον
ὃς οὐδὲ ποίαν ἀναλύειν με γινώσκω.ʼ

Paraphrastis sunt noti ; sed utrum ab iis fictum additamentum postea in
versum redderetur an culpa illis esset antiquior, non satis liquet.

---

ground which in poetry, and in inferior
and late prose, was divided between it
and other words, the simple verbs
ἄντομαι, ἀντάω, ἀντιάω, ἀντιάζω, and
their compounds. The Aristophanic
exceptions to the Attic rule are very
instructive. In Plut. 41 ξυναντήσαιμι
occurs, and in id. 44 ξυναντᾷς, the
former being given as part of an
oracular response, and the latter being
used in reference to the same. The
present ξυναντᾷ is also found in Ach.
1187, but in a passage which, for other
reasons, both Blaydes and Meineke
regard as spurious. The participle
ξυναντῶν in Av. 137 helps us to the
true way of considering the passage in
which it is met with. The Epops asks
his visitors what sort of city they
should like to reside in. Euelpides'
answer contains the adaptation of a
proverbial mode of invitation to a
merrymaking (cp. Lys. 1066), and
Pisthetaerus is also plainly modelling
his response on some proverb now
unknown to us when he begins it with
the words ὅπου ξυναντῶν μοι ταδί τις
μέμψεται.

3. ἠρώτα. The late sense of ʽinviteʼ

is well known from the New Testament.
Suidas quotes the present line to illustrate it. Ἐρωτῶ σε· παρακαλῶ σε,
ἱκετεύω σε, δέομαί σε. Μύθοις (codd.
ΔΕΟΜΑΙΚΑΙΑΥΘΙΣ)—
ἐλθεῖν πρὸς αὐτὸν ἐπὶ τὸ δεῖπνον ἠρώτα,
ἀντὶ τοῦ παρεκάλει.

XLIII. 1. ὑπὸ τὸ καῦμα, ʽas the
heat of the day came on.ʼ
4. χηλῆς . . ποδῶν. The combination of singular and plural is worth
observing. The writer might have
said any of four things—χηλῆς, ποδῶν :
χηλῶν, ποδός: χηλῆς, ποδός: χηλῶν,
ποδῶν.
5. ἐπὶ τοῖς δὲ κέρασιν. The position
of the δὲ is quite legitimate, and there
is no cause to read with almost all
critics ἐπὶ τοῖς κέρασι δ᾽. They have
read Greek to little purpose who make
alterations of this stamp. Cp. 34, 4,
supra. So ἐς τὸν δὲ φαλακρόν in Eupolis,
and ἀπὸ τῶν δὲ τεγῶν in Pherecrates.
The index will show that Babrius
adapted the quantity in κέρας to the
demands of his verse, and any lexicon
how, in a literary style like his, this
was quite justifiable.

παρῆν δὲ νέμεσις ἢ τὰ γαῦρα πημαίνει·
κυνηγέτας γὰρ ἄνδρας εἶδεν ἐξαίφνης
ὁμοῦ σαγήναις καὶ σκύλαξιν εὐρίνοις,
ἰδὼν δ' ἔφευγε, δίψαν οὐδέπω παύσας,
καὶ μακρὸν ἐπέρα πεδίον ἴχνεσιν κούφοις.   10
ἐπεὶ δὲ δὴ σύνδενδρον ἦλθεν εἰς ὕλην,
κέρατα θάμνοις ἐμπλακεὶς ἐθηρεύθη,
καὶ ταῦτ' ἔφη ' δύστηνος ὡς διεψεύσθην.
οἱ γὰρ πόδες μ' ἔσωζον οἷς ἐπηδούμην,
τὰ κέρατα δὲ προὔδωκεν οἷς ἐγαυρούμην.'   15

XLIV.

Ἐνέμοντο ταῦροι τρεῖς ἀεὶ μετ' ἀλλήλων,
λεών δὲ τούτους συλλαβεῖν ἐφεδρεύων
ὁμοῦ μὲν αὐτοὺς οὐκ ἔδοξε νικήσειν,
λόγοις δ' ὑπούλοις διαβολαῖς τε συγκρούων

XLIII. 6. Citat Suidas sub νέμεσις vocabulo, duas lectiones proponens
—(1) ἢ τἄδικ' ἐποπτεύει; (2) ἢ τὰ γῆς ἐποπτεύει, quarum prior est glossa
in Athoa verba, altera glossae in numeros reductio. Qua de causa ab
Athoo codice discedam non video. Epimythium accedit hoc—

περὶ τῶν σεαυτοῦ πραγμάτων ὅταν κρίνῃς,
μηδὲν βέβαιον ὑπολάβῃς προγινώσκων
μηδ' αὖτ' ἀπογνῷς μηδ' ἀπελπίσῃς· οὕτω
σφάλλουσιν ἡμᾶς ἐνίοθ' αἱ πεποιθήσεις;

ubi μὴ τ' αὖ . . μὴ δ' codex.
XLIV. 4. Nauckius interpolatorem indagat et λόγοις ὑπούλοις χωρίσας
ἀπ' ἀλλήλων legere mavult, quia in paraphrasi (vide Halm, 394) nihil verbis

6. τὰ γαῦρα πημαίνει, ' who punishes
pride.' Cp. Agathias, Hist. 5, 23, p.
169, ὁ δὲ οὐ πρότερον ἀνῆκε πρὶν σφόδρα
πημῆναι τὸ δυσμενές.
8. ὁμοῦ, see supra, 13, 4.
11. ἐπεὶ δὲ δὴ is in Attic more
common than ἐπειδὴ δέ.
XLIV. 2. συλλαβεῖν ἐφεδρεύων, here
simply 'lying in wait to catch,' without any reference to the technical
meaning of ἔφεδρος. In Thuc. 4, 71,
the technical sense has not been
sufficiently recognised—αἱ δὲ τῶν Με-
γαρέων στάσεις φοβούμεναι, οἱ μὲν μὴ
τοὺς φεύγοντας σφίσιν ἐσαγαγὼν αὐτοὺς
ἐκβάλῃ, οἱ δὲ μὴ αὐτὸ τοῦτο ὁ δῆμος

δείσας ἐπιθῆται σφίσι καὶ ἡ πόλις ἐν
μάχῃ καθ' αὑτὴν οἶσα ἐγγὺς ἐφεδρευ-
όντων Ἀθηναίων ἀπόληται, οὐκ ἐδέξαντο.
'The Athenians being close at hand
waiting their turn.'
3. The alteration of αὐτοὺς into ἔντας
proposed by Seidler improves the sense,
but is very difficult to account for, and
certainly not required.
4. λόγοις .. ὑπούλοις. I cannot believe that the accepted derivation of
ὕπουλος is the true one, and that an
adjective formed from ὑπό and οὐλή
could ever have the primary meaning
'still sore under the scar.' Sore ought
to form an important part of the com-

ἐχθροὺς ἐποίει, χωρίσας δ᾽ ἀπ᾽ ἀλλήλων 5
ἕκαστον αὐτῶν ἔσχε ῥᾳδίην θοίνην.

XLV.

Ἔνιφεν ὁ Ζεύς· αἰπόλος δέ τις φεύγων
εἰς ἄντρον εἰσήλαυνε τῶν ἀοικήτων
τὰς αἶγας ἀδρῇ χιόνι λευκανθιζούσας.
εὑρὼν δ᾽ ἐκεῖ τάχιον εἰσδεδυκυίας
αἶγας κερούχους ἀγρίας, πολὺ πλείους 5
ὧν αὐτὸς ἦγε, μείζονάς τε καὶ κρείσσους,
ταῖς μὲν φέρων ἔβαλλε θαλλὸν ἐξ ὕλης,
τὰς δ᾽ † ἰδίας ἀφῆκε μακρὰ λιμώττειν.

omissis respondet. Bodleianam tamen confer:—ὑπούλοις δὲ λόγοις
διαβαλὼν ἐχώρισεν ἀπ᾽ ἀλλήλων. Epimythium aliquis hoc addidit—

    ὅταν μάλιστα ζῆν θέλῃς ἀκινδύνως
    ἐχθροῖς ἀπίστει, τοὺς φίλους δ᾽ ἀεὶ τήρει.

XLV. 3. Duebneri conjecturam incertus recepi, ἀδρῇ pro ἄκρῃ lecto.
Quo modo ἀδρῇ in ἄκρῃ transire potuerit, non video. 8. Athoam
lectionem τὰς δ᾽ ἰδίας mutare nolo. Ego certe facilius crediderim
Babrium primam syllabam longam fecisse quam criticorum tentamina
scripsisse, τὰς δ᾽ ἄρ᾽ ἰδίας, τὰς δὲ τιθασοὺς, τὰς δ᾽ ἐνδίους, τὰς δὲ γ᾽ ἰδίας,
τὰς δ᾽ ἐννύχας (sic). Viro sobrio talia placere nequeunt.

pound instead of not being represented
at all. At first the word signified no
more than 'just short of whole,' being
the diminutive of the adjective οὖλος,
and this sense has been preserved in
the gloss of Photius, ὕπουλοι· οἱ ἐγγὺς
τοῦ κατουλωθῆναι μώλωπες. The signification 'unsound beneath' rests on a
false derivation from οὐλή, and is to be
regarded as the product of an age when
men began to read their own ideas into
words which their fathers had formed
correctly in obedience to an instinctive
and almost unconscious linguistic sense.

XLV. 3. ἀδρῇ χιόνι is a pretty conjecture, but not convincing. Hdt. 4,
31, ἤδη ὧν ὅστις ἀγχόθεν χιόνα ἀδρὴν
πίπτουσαν εἶδε, οἶδε τὸ λέγω.
4. τάχιον. For this late form see
Phryn. p. 149.
7. θαλλὸν ἐξ ὕλης, 'young boughs
from the forest'; θαλλός collectively like
ἄμπελος, κάλαμος, etc.

8. ἰδίας. I am inclined to think that
Babrius really wrote the word with
the iota long. It is also long in Aesch.
P. V. 543, ἰδίᾳ γνώμῃ σέβει, which corresponds to ἀλλά μοι τοῦτ᾽ (τόδ᾽ MSS.)
ἐμμένοι. Most editors have rightly
tried to alter it in that passage, but
with as little success there as here.
The conjectures αὐτόνῳ, οἰόφρων, αὐτό-
βουλος ὤν, μουνάδι, recommend themselves to nobody but the fathers who
begat them, and Verrall's special plead-
ing for ἠλεᾷ is too baseless and too
brilliant to convince sober critics.
λιμώττειν as a late verb, never known
in the form λιμώσσω, retains the ττ.
Its formation is of course quite irregular,
but may be paralleled even in Attic by
the Aristophanic λαιμάττουσι (Eccl.
1176), formed from λαιμός, as λιμώττω
from λιμός. Another late formation is
αἰθριάω in the next line. Cp. Phryn.
p. 155.

E

ὡς δ᾽ ἠθρίασε, τὰς μὲν εὗρε τεθνώσας,
αἱ δ᾽ οὐκ ἔμειναν, ἀλλ᾽ ὁρῶν ἀβοσκήτων   10
ἀνέμβατον δρυμῶνα ποσσὶν ἠρεύνων.

XLVI.

Ἔλαφος καθ᾽ ὕλην γυῖα κοῦφα ναρκήσας
ἔκειτο πεδίων ἐν χλόῃ βαθυσχίνῳ,
ἐξ ἧς ἑτοίμην χιλὸν εἶχε πεινήσας.
ἤρχοντο δ᾽ ἀγέλαι ποικίλων ἐκεῖ ζῴων
ἐπισκοπούντων· ἦν γὰρ ἀβλαβὴς γείτων.   5
ἐλθὼν δ᾽ ἕκαστος τῆς πόης τ᾽ ἀποτρώγων
ᾔει πρὸς ὕλας οὐδ᾽ ἐπῇεν εἰ θνήσκει·

11. Alios tres versus Athous exhibet, quorum primus paraphrastae Augustano ignotum est, alter et tertius Bodleiano et Furiano—

ὁ δ᾽ αἰπόλος γελάσας ἦλθεν εἰς οἴκους
αἰγῶν ἔρημος· ἐλπίσας δὲ τὰς κρείσσους,
οὐκ ὤνατ᾽ οὐδ᾽ ὧν αὐτὸς εἶχεν ἐκ πρώτης.

Indicare sufficit interpolatoris indicia, γελάσας et ὤνατ᾽ pro γελάσας et ὤνητο.

XLVI. 7. Pro οὐδ᾽ ἐπῇεν εἰ θνήσκει exhibet Athous perperam ὁ δὲ πεινίῃ θνήσκει. Ego vestigia sequor Gitlbaueri quo οὐδ᾽ ἐπῇι᾽ εἰ θνήσκει

9. **τεθνώσας.** Perhaps τεθνεώσας ought to be written here. 'It is said that τεθνεώς is never syncopated τεθνώς; but Herodian's expression "τεθνεὼς διῃρημένως" proves that τεθνώς was in use; indeed it actually occurs in the lately-discovered Fab. of Babrius, τεθνώσας, 45, 9; in an epigram edited by Welcker, see Hermann's Opusc. 4, 313; (Luc.) Trag. 9 (MSS. Dind.); Eur. Supp. 273, hexamet. (Heath, Nauck); and Dindorf with a "recte fortasse" rather approves, but edits with Reiske τεθνεώς.'—Veitch.

XLVI. 1. 'In a forest, with his nimble limbs stiff and numb, a stag was lying among meadow grass deep with mastich, off which when hungered he had food for the taking.' The πεδίων shows that by ὕλη is here meant a *forest*, not a *wood*; whereas the ὕλαι in verse 7 refers to the wooded parts of the ὕλη. The gender of χιλός is not easily determined. No pure Attic writer uses

the word, the term preferred being χόρτος ; but Xenophon twice makes it masculine (An. 1, 9, 27 ; 4, 5, 33), as does Arrian (1, 12, 17, etc.) The feminine does not occur in any writer but Babrius, although there are many places in which the gender is left indeterminate (Hdt. 4, 140 ; Xen. Cyr. 5, 4, 40 ; Anab. 1, 5, 7, etc.) The Etym. Mag. expressly states the gender as feminine, p. 811, 47, χιλός θηλυκῶς λέγεται· σημαίνει δὲ τὴν τροφήν ; and so does Choeroboscus (Cram. Anecd. 2, 276, 23) ; but the two evidently quote from the same source.

4. In **ἤρχοντο .. ἐκεῖ** Babrius allows himself ἐκεῖ in the sense of ἐκεῖσε ; see Index.

6. **ἀποτρώγων** is best to be regarded as equivalent to the classic ἀποτραγών, and an instance of the way in which the inflexible metre interfered with choliambic syntax.

7. **οὐδ᾽ .. θνήσκει,** 'and observed

ἔλαφος δὲ λιμῷ κοὺ νόσῳ κατεσκλήκει,
μή πω κορώνην δευτέρην ἀναπλήσας,
ὃς εἰ φίλους οὐκ ἔσχε κἂν γεγηράκει.　　　10

XLVII.

Ἐν τοῖς παλαιοῖς ἦν ἀνὴρ ὑπεργήρως,
εἶχεν δὲ πολλοὺς παῖδας· οἷς ἐπισκήπτων
(ἔμελλε γὰρ δὴ τὸν βίον τελευτήσειν)
ἐκέλευε λεπτῶν, εἴ τις ἔστι που, ῥάβδων
δέσμην ἐνεγκεῖν· ἧκέ τις φέρων ταύτην.　　　5
'πειρᾶσθε δή μοι, τέκνα, σὺν βίῃ πάσῃ
ῥάβδους κατᾶξαι δεδεμένας σὺν ἀλλήλαις.'
οἱ δ' οὐ γὰρ ἠδύναντο· 'κατὰ μίην τοίνυν

---

egregie proposuit. Idem si unquam Graece scire didicerit, et aliquid impetus et temeritatis deposuerit, de Graecis fortasse literis bene merebitur.

---

not that he was dying,' not 'and cared not if he died,' a sense which ἐπᾴειν could not give.

9. Refers to the lines of Hesiod quoted by Plutarch de Orac. defectu, 11 (p. 415 C), ὁ δὲ Ἡσίοδος οἴεται καὶ περιόδοις τισὶ χρόνων γίνεσθαι τοῖς δαίμοσι τὰς τελευτάς· λέγει γὰρ ἐν τῷ τῆς Ναΐδος προσώπῳ, καὶ τὸν χρόνον αἰνιττόμενος—

ἐννέα τοι ζώει γενεὰς λακέρυζα κορώνη
ἀνδρῶν ἡβώντων· ἔλαφος δέ τε τετρακόρωνος·
τρεῖς δ' ἐλάφους ὁ κόραξ γηράσκεται.
αὐτὰρ ὁ φοῖνιξ,
ἐννέα τοὺς κόρακας· δέκα δ' ἡμεῖς τοὺς
φοίνικας
νύμφαι εὐπλόκαμοι, κοῦραι Διὸς αἰγιόχοιο.

Rhunken's note on the passage is as follows:—'Hesiodum imitantur Aratus Dios, 200. Oppianus (lege pseudo-Oppianus) Cyneg. II. 291. Automedon Epigrammate apud Dorvil. Sicul. Cap. 16, p. 271. Synesius Epist. 110 et plures alii, quos laudat Io. Davisius ad Cicer. T. Q. III. 28. Ut vocem τετρακόρωνος ab Hesiodo sumpsit Oppianus l. c., sic eadem forma πεντακόρωνος pro vetulo dixit Myrinus

Anthol. II. 9, p. 193. τρικόρωνος Lucilius ibid.'

XLVII. 1. ὑπεργήρως. With one or two exceedingly rare exceptions, such as ὑπέρπολυς and ὑπέρσοφος, classical Greek compounded ὑπέρ with the substantive, and not with the adjective, to form superlatives of this kind, e.g. ὑπέρβιος, ὑπέρφοβος, ὑπέρκομπος, ὑπερμήκης, ὑπέρχολος, ὑπέρκοτος, ὑπεραλγής, ὑπεραχθής, etc. In late Greek the converse is true, and for the classical ὑπερμεγεθής, ὑπέρπλουτος, ὑπερπλήθης, etc., were used ὑπέρμεγας, ὑπερπλούσιος, ὑπερπλήρης, etc.

2. ἐπισκήπτω is the regular word for the exhortations and injunctions of the dying. Lys. 138, 35, ἀποθνήσκοντες ἡμῖν ἐπέσκηψαν καὶ ὑμῖν καὶ τοῖς ἄλλοις ἅπασι τιμωρεῖν ὑπὲρ σφῶν αὐτῶν· Ἀγόρατον τουτονί. Hdt. 3, 65, καὶ δὴ τελευτῶν τὸν βίον, Ὦ Πέρσαι, ὑμῖν τάδε ἐπισκήπτω κτε.

5. Here the first hand accents δεσμὴν, which a diorthotes has changed to δέσμην. See Chandler, Greek Accentuation, §§ 131, 132, 2d ed. In the preceding line I have diffidently retained εἴ τις ἔστι που as perhaps defensible. See id. §§ 973 seq.

πειρᾶσθ'· ἑκάστης δ' εὐχερῶς καταγείσης,
'ὦ παῖδες, οὕτως' εἶπεν 'ἢν μὲν ἀλλήλοις   10
ὁμοφρονῆτε πάντες, οὐδ' ἂν εἰς ὕμας
βλάψαι δύναιτο κἂν μέγιστον ἰσχύῃ·
ἢν δ' ἄλλος ἄλλου χωρὶς ἦτε τὴν γνώμην,
πείσεσθ' ἕκαστος ταὐτὰ τῇ μιῇ ῥάβδῳ.

XLVIII.

Ἐν ὁδῷ τις Ἑρμῆς τετράγωνος εἱστήκει,
λίθων δ' ὑπ' αὐτῷ σωρὸς ἦν. κύων τούτῳ
εἶπεν προσελθών 'χαῖρε πρῶτον, Ἑρμείη·
ἔπειτ' ἀλεῖψαι βούλομαί σε, μηδ' οὕτω
θεὸν παρελθεῖν καὶ θεὸν παλαιστρίτην.'   5
ὁ δ' εἶπεν 'ἤν μοι τοῦτο μὴ 'πολιχμήσῃς

XLVII. Epimythium accedit hoc et claudicat—

φιλαδελφία μέγ' ἀγαθὸν ἀνθρώποις
ἢ καὶ ταπεινοὺς ὄντας ἦρεν εἰς ὕψος.

XLVIII. Fabulam hanc Babrio adjudicem an non, incertus sum. Pro
Athoo 'πιλιχμήσῃς cum Bergkio 'πολιχμήσῃς scripsi.

---

9. καταγείσης. The Attic quantity of the alpha in κατεάγην does not admit of being settled by pure grammar. Aristophanes has the tense three times. In Vesp. 1428 the metre leaves the vowel doubtful—

καί πως κατεάγη τῆς κεφαλῆς μέγα σφόδρα.

Another line is quoted by Pollux, 2, 39.—

ἵνα μὴ καταγῇς σκάφιον πληγεὶς ξύλῳ,

where Toup is probably right in inserting τὸ before σκάφιον; but a scholar is rash indeed who allows an isolated line quoted by a grammarian to decide any point. In the third place the optative aorist is exhibited by the manuscripts with the alpha long—

οὐκ ἂν καταγείη ποτ', εἰ—Ach. 944;

but Cobet's conjecture κατεάγοιη somewhat invalidates the testimony. On the whole the evidence tends to make the vowel long, and the spurious Homeric line, Il. 11, 559—

νωθής, ᾧ δὴ πολλὰ περὶ ῥόπαλ' ἀμφὶς ἐάγη,

points in the same way, especially if we regard it, like so much else in Homer, as the outcome of the Attic recension. The text of the Iliad and Odyssey is still too unsettled to supply any trustworthy evidence in a case of this sort.

11. οὐδ' ἂν εἰς, the true Attic collocation for οὐδεὶς ἄν. Of οὔτις nothing is known to Attic proper except οὔτι used adverbially.

12. μέγιστον ἰσχύῃ, the superlative of μέγα ἰσχύω.

XLVIII. 1. 'De Ἑρμαῖς τετραγώνοις vide Thuc. vi. 27. de acervo lapidum ad Mercurii statuas, Hom. Od. xvi. 471. de more statuas ungendi, Lucian Contempl. c. 22. et de Mercurio palaestrarum praeside, Diod. v. 75, Aristoph. Plut. 1162, quae omnia contulit Boissonade.' C. Lewis.

6. The conjecture of Bergk, μὴ 'πολιχμήσῃς, certainly gives the best sense, if there is really any sense worth having in these unsavoury lines. Canis

τοὔλαιον ἐλθών μηδέ μοι προσουρήσῃς,
χάριν εἴσομαί σοι· καὶ πλέον με μὴ τίμα.'

XLIX.

Ἐκάθευδε νύκτωρ ἐργάτης ὑπ' ἀγνοίης
φρέατος ἐγγύς. τῆς Τύχης δ' ἐπιστάσης
ἔδοξ' ἀκούειν· 'οὗτος, οὐκ ἐγερθήσῃ ;
μὴ σοῦ πεσόντος αἰτίη παρ' ἀνθρώποις
ἐγὼ λέγωμαι καὶ κακὴν λάβω φήμην.   5
ἐμοὶ γὰρ ἐγκαλοῦσι πάντα συλλήβδην,
ὅσ' ἂν παρ' αὐτοῦ δυστυχῇ τις ἢ πίπτῃ.'

L.

Ἔφευγ' ἀλώπηξ, τῆς δ' ὄπισθε φευγούσης
κυνηγὸς ἐτρόχαζεν. ἡ δ' ἐκεκμήκει,
δρυτόμον δ' ἰδοῦσα 'πρὸς θεῶν σε σωτήρων
κρύψον με ταύταις αἷς ἔκοψας αἰγείροις,
καὶ τῷ κυνηγῷ' φησί 'μή με μηνύσῃς.'   5
ὁ δ' οὐ προδώσειν ὤμνυ· ἡ δ' ἀπεκρύφθη.

'unctionem' ait 'a me habebis' [*i.e.* cacaberis], 'atque tantillum aliud' [*i.e.* mingeris]. Cui respondet Hermes, 'Si quod habeo unguentum manere passus sis, et aliud istud tibi servaveris, ego certe contentus sum.'

XLIX. 3. The future ἐγερθήσομαι often presents itself in later writers,—as N. T., Mark, 13, 8 ; Matthew, 24, 11,— but is not found in Attic any more than ἐγεροῦμαι, which also first occurs in debased Greek. I believe, however, that ἐγεροῦμαι was the Attic form, not only for the simple verb, but also for its four Attic compounds, ἀνεγείρω, διεγείρω, ἐξεγείρω, and ἐπεγείρω. The forms of the verb were these,—ἐγείρω, ἐγερῶ, ἤγειρα, for the active ; and for the passive, ἐγείρομαι, ἐγεροῦμαι, ἠγρόμην, and ἐγρήγορα. The aorist ἠγέρθην and the perfect ἐγήγερμαι are just found. The active had probably to do without a perfect, as so many other verbs, especially the whole classes in -ύνω and -αίνω. The aorist indicative

active was saved from confusion with that of ἀγείρω by συνέλεξα taking the place of the latter in the doubtful mood.

5. λέγωμαι for ἀκούω or κλύω is unidiomatic, but tolerable even in Attic. κακὴν λάβω φήμην. Babrius might also have said κακὴ λάβῃ φήμη, just as we have νόσος λαμβάνει τινά, φόβος ἔλαβέ τινα, by the side of νόσον λαμβάνειν and φόβον λαβεῖν.

7. There is no cause to change πίπτῃ into πταίῃ with Duebner and Meineke.

L. 6. Here Babrius uses ὤμνυε, and in the tenth verse ἐδείκνυε, as if the presents were ὀμνύω and δεικνύω. In late Greek ὀμνύω and δεικνύω were employed as naturally as ὄμνυμι and δείκνυμι ; but in Attic proper they were long looked upon askance. The present subjunctive and optative of verbs in -υμι were at a very early date assimilated to those of -ω verbs, although isolated instances of the older formations are once or twice

ἦλθεν κυνηγός, καὶ τὸν ἄνδρ' ἐπηρώτα
μὴ τῇδ' ἀλώπηξ καταδέδυκεν ἢ φεύγει.
' οὐκ εἶδον' εἶπε, τῷ δὲ δακτύλῳ νεύων

met with [as Plato, Phaed. 77 B, διασκεδάννυται; id. C, διασκεδάννυσιν [or διασκεδαννύηται and διασκεδαννύῃ]; but the indicative, both in present and imperfect, the imperative, the infinitive, and the participle, both active and passive, were in Attic long retained in their original form. This is conclusively proved by the evidence of verse both of tragedy and old comedy. To confine ourselves first to the class of verbs to which ὄμ-νυ-μι and δείκ-νυ-μι strictly belong, the following are the extant forms which concern the inquiry :—

Of οἴγνυμι and its compounds διοίγνυμι, παροίγνυμι, ὑποίγνυμι, ἀνοίγνυμι, διανοίγνυμι, ἐξανοίγνυμι, παρανοίγνυμι, and ὑπανοίγνυμι, there occur only the imperative διοίγνυτε (Ar. Eccl. 852), the indicative passive ἀνοίγνυται (Eur. Ion. 923), and the participle ἀνοιγνυμένων (Ar. Eq. 1326).

Of ἄγνυμι and its compounds κατάγνυμι and περικατάγνυμι, are found—ἄγνυται (Eur. Hel. 410), κατάγνυται (Soph. Synd. fr.), and καταγνύμενον (Ar. Pax, 703).

Of ἄρνυμαι occur—ἄρνυμαι (Soph. Ant. 903; Tr. 711; Eur. Alc. 55): ἄρνυται (Soph. Phil. 838, ch.; Eur. And. 696): ἀρνύμενος (Hec. 1073).

Of γάνυμαι occur — γάνυμαι (Ar. Vesp. 612; Aesch. Eum. 970; Eur. Cycl. 502): γάνυται (Eur. I. T. 1239).

Of δαίνυμι and its sole compound συνδαίνυμι are found—δαίνυται (Soph. Trach. 1088): ἐδαινύμην (Eubul. ap. Athen. 2, 63 E): ἐδαίνυτο (Soph. Trach. 771): δαίνυσθε imperative (Eur. Tro. 770): δαινύμενος (Cratinus ap. Schol. ad Ar. Vesp. 710; Eur. Cycl. 325, 371): δαίνυντο in epic parody, ap. Pax, 1280-82.

Δείκνυμι is more frequent, and of the simple verb and its fourteen Attic compounds there are over thirty instances —δείκνυμι (Soph. O. C. 1145): ἐνδείκνυμι (Ar. Eq. 278): δείκνυσι (Ar. Av. 1080; Soph. El. 425; O. R. 1258; Ant. 254; Eur. Med. 1120; Ion. 1099 (ch.); and thrice in frag.): ἐνδείκνυσιν (Aesch. P. V. 405 ch.): ἐδείκνυμεν, Eur. Alc. 763: δεικνύς, Ar. Nub. 54; Av. 52; Ran. 912; Soph. Tr. 1250: ἐπιδεικνύς, Ar. Eq. 349: προδεικνύς, Soph. O. R. 456: δεικνῦσα,

Ar. Thesm. 499 : δεικνύτω, Soph. O. C. 1532: ἀναδείκνυται, Ar. Nub. 303 (ch.) : ἐδείκνυτο, Thesm. 629: ἐπεδείκνυτο, Ran. 771 : δεικνυμένων, Eur. Her. 905 (ch.) : ἐνδεικνύμενος, Ar. Plut. 785. Besides these are found, unfortified by metrical requirements, the imperative ἐπιδείκνυ in Ar. Av. 666: the infinitives δεικνύναι, Soph. O. R. 1427; Eur. Med. 744; H. F. 1215: ἀναδεικνύναι, Soph. El. 1458: and the indicative δείκνυσιν, Soph. O. R. 614. In Eur. Ion, 1341, either δείκνυμεν or ἐδείκνυμεν may stand, while ἀποδεικνύμενα in Aesch. P. V. 1087 is critically insecure.

Of ζεύγνυμι and its thirteen Attic compounds, only five of the parts in question have come down in verse, viz. —ζεύγνυσιν, Aesch. Pers. 191 : ζευγνῦσι for ζευγνύασι, Eur. El. 1323 (ch.): ζεύγνυτε, impte. pseud-Eur. Rhes. 33 : ζευγνύς, Frag. inc. : κἀποζεύγνυμαι, Eur. H. F. 1375.

Μίγνυμι and its compounds ἀνα-, ἐμ-, ἐπι-, ἐγκατα-, ἐγκατα-, σιγκατα-, παρα-, συμπαρα-, προσ-, συμπροσ-, ὑπο-, supply only twelve forms—μιγνύς, Ar. Ran. 944; Eq. 1399 : σιγκαταμιγνύς, Eur. H. F. 674: καταμιγνύντας, Ar. Lys. 580: συμπαραμιγνύων, Plut. 719: μίγνυται, Aesch. Eum. 69; Eur. Andr. 174; El. 756: ἀναμίγνυσθαι, Eur. Suppl. 592: μιγνυμένας, Ar. Ran. 1081; Eur. Ion, 1233 (ch.): ξυμμιγνυμένων, Ar. Av. 701.

Of ὄμνυμι and twelve Attic compounds are found—ὄμνυμι, Ar. Av. 445; Thesm. 274; Soph. Tr. 1188; Eur. Med. 752; Hipp. 713, 1026: κατόμνυμι, I. A. 473: ἐπόμνυς, I. A. 747: ὄμνυσι, Ar. Vesp. 1046; Av. 521; Aesch. Sept. 529: ὄμνυτε, Ar. Nub. 248: συνεπόμνυτε, Lys. 237: ἀπώμνυν, Eq. 424: ἐπώμνυς, Nub. 1227: ὤμνυμεν, Eccl. 823: ξυνώμνυτε, Eq. 478: ὄμνύς, Nub. 1135: ὑπομνύς, Soph. Camic. frag. : ὀμνύντες, Phil. 357: διόμνυσθε. Eur. Phil. frag. : διώμνυτο. Soph. Trach. 378. Besides these occur in places where the other forms might stand—present ὀμνύοσι, Pherecr. ap. Ath. xi. 481 D: the imperfect ὤμνυ, Ar. Av. 520: the imperative ὄμνυ, Soph. Trach. 1185; Eur. I. T. 743; Med. 746:

τὸν τόπον ἐδείκνυ ' οὗ πανοῦργος ἐκρύφθη. 10
ὁ δ' οὐκ ἐπισχών, τῷ λόγῳ δὲ πιστεύσας,
παρῆλθε. θερμοῦ δ' ἐκφυγοῦσα κινδύνου

and the infinitive ὀμνύναι, Ar. Lys.
207 ; Eur. Supp. 1188. They have,
however, escaped the altering hand of
the copyist, except in the one case of
Pherecrates.

Of ὁμόργνυμι and its compounds with
ἀπό and ἐκ, none of the parts affected
are met with in verse ; but of ὄρνυμι
and its compound with ἐπί occur—
ὄρνυται (Aesch. Sept. 90, 419 ; Soph.
O. C. 1320) : ἐπόρνυται (Aesch. Supp.
187) : ὀρνύμενος (Ar. Ran. 1529, ch. ;
Soph. O. R. 165 ch. ; Eur. I. T. 1149).
Of πετάννυμι and its eight compounds,
with ἀνά, διά, ἐκ, ἐν, ἐπί, κατά, περί,
πρό, only two forms are met with—
διαπετάννυ in Ar. Lys. 733, and
ἐξεπετάννυτο in Eq. 1347 ; and in the
former case the metre would allow of
διαπετάννυε.

Of πήγνυμι and its eleven compounds
the following are found :—ἀποπήγνυσι,
Ar. Ran. 126 : ἀναπηγνύασι, Eccl. 843 :
ἐπηγνύμην, Eq. 1310 : προσπηγνύναι,
Eur. Sci. frag. In Aesch. Pers. 496,
πήγνυσιν is not demanded by the
metre.

Πτάρνυμαι does not occur in verse.
'Ρήγνυμι presents nine instances—
ῥήγνυσιν, Aesch. Pers. 199 : καταρρήγ-
νυσι, Soph. Ant. 675 : ἀνερρήγνυ, Aj.
236, ch. : ῥηγνύτω, O. R. 1076 : ῥηγνύς,
Tham. frag. : ἀναρρηγνύς, Ar. Eq. 626 :
ῥήγνυσα, Eur. Bacch. 1130 : ῥήγνυνται,
Ar. Nub. 378 : περιρρηγνυμένων, Aesch.
Sept. 329 (ch.) The remaining verb
στόρνυμι [or στρώννυμι] exhibits—στόρ-
νυσι, Eur. Her. 702 : στόρνυ, Ar. Pax,
844 : στορνύναι (στρωννύναι), Aesch.
Agam. 909 : στορνύντα, Soph. Trach.
902. Of the other similar classes,—viz.
of ἀμφιέννυμι, σβέννυμι, and their compounds ; κεράννυμι, κρεμάννυμι, σκεδάν-
νυμι, and their compounds ; ζώννυμι
and its compounds,—none of the forms
in question occur in verse of the required period except ἀνεκεράννυ in Ar.
Ran. 511. The presents κορέννυμι and
ῥώννυμι are not Attic at all.

As to ὄλλυμι and its compounds
διόλλυμι, ἐξόλλυμι, ἀπόλλυμι, ἀνταπόλλυμι,
ἐναπόλλυμι, ἐξαπόλλυμι, παραπόλλυμι,
προαπόλλυμι, προσαπόλλυμι, and συνα-
πόλλυμι, they present more than a

hundred of the forms concerned, and
in only nine cases (Ar. Pax, 250 ;
Aesch. Pers. 461 ; Soph. O. C. 394 ;
Phil. 686 ; O. R. 1441 ; Eur. Or. 569,
395 ; I. A. 405 ; Heracl. 950) unfortified by metre.

We have thus recognised that in all
Attic verse down to the Plutus of
Aristophanes, there is no instance, outside the subjunctive and optative, of an
-ω inflection demanded by the metre
for the present and imperfect active
and passive of verbs in -νμι. In that
play συμπαραμιγνύων is met with, and
after that date inflections of the same
kind become more and more common,
till by Menander they seem even to be
preferred. We may therefore alter
with complacency ὀμνύωσι in Pherecrates to ὀμνύασι, especially if we
remember that even the necessity of
metre did not preserve ἀπώμνυν in Ar.
Eq. 424, but that in all the MSS.
ἀπώμνυον has taken its place, and had
to be expelled by Bentley. It is true
that ὤμνυον occurs in Thucydides three
times, in v. 19, 23, and 24 ; notwithstanding that, in all other places except
4, 25 (where ἀπολλύουσι is wrongly
exhibited by all), some or other of the
codices have preserved the true form
from -μι. In these three cases I believe that ὤμνυον is right, as it forms
part of a treaty drawn up for the
Athenians and Spartans in common ;
and outside of Attica the -ω inflections
were unquestionably used in verbs in
-νμι at quite an early date, as many
passages of Pindar prove ; and even if
for the present the text of Homer is to
be regarded as unsettled, still the existence of the -ω forms in the received
text is all that is required to prove
their exoteric legitimacy. It need
hardly be added that a large proportion
of the forms above quoted from tragedy
would naturally be preferred in its
rigid iambics.

12. θερμοῦ .. κινδύνου. The metaphor
is best illustrated by Plutarch, Mor.
p. 517 F, οὐχ ἕωλα κακά, ἀλλὰ θερμὰ
καὶ πρόσφατα. Cp. Philostratus, Vita
Apoll. p. 165, 3, πηνίκα οἱ γάμοι ;
θερμοὶ καὶ ἴσως αὔριον.

κερδὼ παχείης ἐξέκυπτεν αἰγείρου,
σεσηρὸς αἰκάλλουσα. τῇ δ' ὁ πρεσβύτης
' ζωαγρίους μοι χάριτας ' εἶπεν ' ὀφλήσεις.'   15
' πῶς οὐκ ἄν ' εἶπεν ' ὧν γε μάρτυς εἰστήκειν ;
ἔρρωσο τοίνυν, καὶ τὸν "Ορκον οὐ φεύξῃ
φωνῇ με σώσας, δακτύλῳ δ' ἀποκτείνας.'

LI.

Ἐν τῷ ποτ' οἴκῳ πρόβατον εἶχέ τις χήρη,
θέλουσα δ' αὐτοῦ τὸν πόκον λαβεῖν μείζω
ἔκειρεν ἀτεχνῶς, τῆς τε σαρκὸς οὐ πόρρω
τὸν μαλλὸν ἐψάλιζεν ὥστε τιτρώσκειν.
ἀλγοῦν δὲ πρόβατον εἶπε ' μή με λυμαίνου.   5
πόσην γὰρ ὁλκὴν τοὐμὸν αἷμα προσθήσει;
ἀλλ' εἰ κρεῶν, δέσποινα, τῶν ἐμῶν χρήζεις,
ἔστιν μάγειρος ὅς με συντόμως θύσει·
εἰ δ' εἰρίων πόκου τε κοὐ κρεῶν χρήζεις,
πάλιν ἔστι κουρεὺς ὃς κερεῖ με καὶ σώσει.'   10

L. 15. Post hunc versum, Athoo in codice alter reperitur—

ἐρρυσάμην σε' φησίν, 'ἀλλά μου μνήσκου,'

quem Bergkius et Eberhardus tanquam alterius recensionis jam uncis
incluserunt ; ego manifeste spurium duco, neque melius quam epimythium—

σοφὸν τὸ θεῖον κἀπλάνητον· οὐδ' ἄν τις
λαθεῖν ἐπιορκῶν προσδοκᾷ Δίκην φεύγει,

ubi φεύγειν exhibet Athous.

---

13. παχείης .. αἰγείρου. This signification of παχύς—dense—seems to be
very late. Himerius, Or. 23, 17 (p. 794),
has the phrase παχυδένδροις ἄλσεσιν ;
and Constantinus Manasses, Chronic.
p. 8 Λ, l. 330, of the fall, ἔρραψαν
περιζώματα φύλλων ἐκ παχυφύλλων. It
cannot bear its ordinary sense of thick,
stout, in the present passage.
14. σεσηρὸς αἰκάλλουσα, 'with a
winning grin.' The neuter participle
is similarly used by Theocritus (?), 20,
14, καί τι σεσαρός | καὶ σοβαρόν μ'
ἐγέλασσεν.
15. 'Thanks you will owe me for
saving your life.' ' Yes, that I will.

I saw it all ; so fare thee well.' In
debased Greek ὀφλισκάνω was employed
like ὀφείλω.
LI. 1. Lachmann's conjecture, ἕν τῷ
ποτ' οἴκῳ, is unnecessary, see supra, 43,
5, note.
2. 'And wishing to make more of
its fleece, she sheared it and no mistake ; clipping the fleece close to the
flesh, and hurting the poor beast.'
To substitute ἀτέχνως for the Athoan
ἀτεχνῶς is to injure the sense seriously.
τῆς σαρκὸς οὐ πόρρω, cp. the phrase
ἐν χρῷ κείρειν, Phryn. p. 132. ψαλίζω,
'scissor,' a late formation.
9. 'But if thou wouldst have wool,

LII.

Εἰς ἄστυ τετράκυκλον ἀτρέμας ταῦροι
ἅμαξαν ὤμοις εἷλκον· ἡ δ' ἐτετρίγει.
καὶ τὸν βοώτην θυμὸς εἶχ', ἔφη δ' οὕτως·
'ὦ παγκάκιστον κτημάτων, τί δὴ κρώζεις,
ἄλλων ἐπ' ὤμοις φερομένη σιωπώντων;'   5

LIII.

Εἰς λύκον ἀλώπηξ ἐμπεσοῦσα δειλαίη
ζωγρεῖν ἐδεῖτο μηδὲ γραῦν ἀποκτείνειν.
ὁ δ' 'ἢν λόγους μοι τρεῖς ἀληθινοὺς εἴπῃς,
ἐγώ σε νὴ τὸν Πᾶνα' φησί 'ζωγρήσω.'
ἡ δ' 'εἴθε μέν μοι πρῶτα μὴ συνηντήκεις,   5
ἔπειτα δ' εἴθε τυφλὸς ὢν ὑπηντήκεις,—
τρίτον δ' ἐπ' αὐτοῖς' εἶπε 'μὴ σύγ' εἰς ὥρας
ἵκοιο, μηδέ μοι πάλιν συναντήσῃς.'

LII. Fabulam non esse Babrianam judicat Eberhardus, corruptam
ego. 1. Pro Athoo ἄρρενες ego ἀτρέμας conjeci. 3. Conjecturam Eberhardi non sine fiducia in textum recepi qui, verbis εἶχε, τῇ δ' οὕτως in
εἶχ', ἔφη δ' οὕτως mutatis, sequentem versum—

ἐγγὺς προσελθὼν εἶπεν ὡς ἀκουσθῆναι,

intrusum esse credit a scriba εἶχε τῇ pro εἶχ', ἔφη legente, nisi quod
perverso ingenio Eberhard εἷλε pro εἶχε substituerit. Certe de versu
dubitato nemo paraphrasta non ignorat. Epimythium nemo retinebit—

κακοῦ πρὺς ἀνδρός ἐστι μακρὸν οἰμώζειν
ἄλλων ποιούντων ὡσείπερ αὐτὸς κάμνων,

quod critici varios in modos ad metrum et sensum reddere temptarunt.

---

and my fleece, not my flesh.' The
conjecture σὺ for τε at once obliterates
the point of the line, a function which
very many of the so-called emendations
of the Babrian text gratuitously fulfil.
LII. 2. ὤμοις εἷλκον is a natural
enough mode of expression, but the ἐπ'
ὤμοις φερομένη of the fifth line cannot
be defended.
3. This late use of βοώτης, = βοηλάτης
or 'waggoner,' is best to be explained as

a literary extension of the astronomical
term (Odys. 5, 272). θυμὸς εἶχε = ἐθυ-
μοῦτο.
LIII. 1. 'A fox, poor thing, fell in
with a wolf, and besought him to spare
her life, and not to kill her in her old
age.'
4. νὴ τὸν Πᾶνα is almost equivalent
to a phrase like ' What a fright you are
in,' ' By the fright I have given you.'
5. Lachmann was quite wrong in

LIV.

Εὐνοῦχος ἦλθε πρὸς θύτην ὑπὲρ παίδων
σκεψόμενος. ὁ θύτης δ᾽ ἀγνὸν ἧπαρ ἁπλώσας
'ὅταν μὲν εἶπε ' ταῦτ᾽ ἴδω, πατὴρ γίνῃ,
ὅταν δὲ τὴν σὴν ὄψιν, οὐδ᾽ ἀνὴρ φαίνῃ.'

LV.

῎Ενα βοῦν τις εἶχε, τὴν ὄνον δὲ συζεύξας
ἠροτρία, πτωχῶς μέν, ἀλλ᾽ ἀναγκαίως.
ἐπεὶ δὲ τοὔργον ἐτετέλεστο καὶ λύειν
ἔμελλεν αὐτούς, εἶτ᾽ ὄνος διηρώτα
τὸν βοῦν ' τίς ἄξει τῷ γέροντι τὰ σκεύη;'   5
ὁ δὲ βοῦς πρὸς αὐτὴν εἶπεν ' ὅσπερ εἰώθει.'

LVI.

Εὐτεκνίης ἔπαθλα πᾶσι τοῖς ζῴοις
ὁ Ζεὺς ἔθηκε, πάντα δ᾽ ἔβλεπεν κρίνων.

LIV. Ejusmodi nugas illepidas et subobscoenas ad Babrium referre
nolo, sed causa non est cur omnino abjudicem. 2. Certa emendatione
Athoum ἀγνοεῖν παραπλώσας Lachmannus in ἀγνὸν ἧπαρ ἁπλώσας
mutavit.
LV. 4. Lachmanno duce, εἶτ᾽ ὄνος pro manuscripto ἤτ᾽ ὄνος scripsi.
LVI. 2. Exhibet Athous ἔβλεπε, forsan ex proposito, sed quamvis
incertus malo nu addere. Epimythium plus solito imbecillum—

> ὁ λόγος δοκεῖ μοι πᾶσι τοῦτο σημαίνειν.
> τὸν αὐτὸς αὐτοῦ πᾶς τις εὐπρεπῆ κρίνει,

ubi pro αὐτὸς Athous αὐτοὶ legit.

---

changing εἶπε in the seventh verse into
εἴθε. It is plainly required by the
current of the verse succeeding it, and
does not injure the preceding lines.
LV. 2. πτωχῶς . . ἀναγκαίως, 'a
beggarly team, but the best he could
command.'
6. ὅσπερ εἰώθει, 'Why change the
carrier?' In some such way as this
we have to bring out in English the
force of the masculine ὅσπερ. The

conjecture δς πρὶν substitutes a tautology for the expressive ὅσπερ, in which
the περ gives just the sense required,
'Surely there is no need to change the
carrier.'
LVI. 1. ἔπαθλα, a late word for ἆθλα.
Pollux, 3, 143, καὶ τὰ μὲν ὀνομαζόμενα
ὑπὸ τῶν πολλῶν ἔπαθλα, ἆθλα καλοῖτ᾽
ἂν κοινῶς ἐπ᾽ ἀμφοῖν (i.e. ἀγώνοιν γυμνι-
κοῖν τε καὶ σκηνικοῖν) καὶ νικητήρια καὶ
ἐπίχειρα καὶ γέρα.

ἦλθεν δὲ καὶ πίθηκος ὡς καλὴ μήτηρ,
πίθωνα γυμνὸν σιμὸν ἡρμένη κόλποις.
γέλως δ' ἐπ' αὐτῷ τοῖς θεοῖς ἐκινήθη·   5
ἡ δ' εἶπεν οὕτω ' Ζεὺς μὲν οἶδε τὴν νίκην,
ἐμοὶ δὲ πάντων οὗτός ἐστι καλλίων.'

LVII.

Ἑρμῆς ἄμαξαν ψευσμάτων τε πληρώσας
ἀπάτης τε πολλῆς καὶ πανουργίης πάσης
ἤλαυνε διὰ γῆς, ἄλλο φῦλον ἐξ ἄλλου
σχέδην ἀμείβων καὶ μέρος τι τῶν ὤνων
νέμων ἑκάστῳ μικρόν· ὡς δὲ τῷ χώρῳ   5
τῶν Ἀραβίων ἐπῆλθε καὶ διεξῄει,
ἐκένωσαν αὐτὴν οὐδ' ἀφῆκαν εἰς ἄλλους   10

LVII. 4. Athoum lectionem σχεδίην Lachmannus recte in σχέδην
mutavit.   6. Athons τῷ τῶν Ἀράβων per dittographiam exhibet, quod
ego cum Duebnero in τῶν Ἀραβίων mutavi. Post hunc versum alios
tres interpolator supposuit—

λέγουσιν αὐτοῦ συντριβεῖσαν ἐξαίφνης
ἐπισταθῆναι τὴν ἄμαξαν· οἱ δ' ὥσπερ
πολύτιμον ἁρπάζοντες ἐμπόρου φόρτον.

---

3. The extraordinary conjectures
which the words ὡς καλὴ μήτηρ have
called forth suggest the suspicion that
their authors were ignorant of the
common idiomatic use of ὡς, = νομί-
ζουσα καλὴ μήτηρ εἶναι.
4. 'With the snub-nosed naked son
of an ape in her bosom.' Phrynichus,
App. Soph. 59, 13, has the note Πίθων·
ὁ πίθηκος, ὑποκοριστικῶς. Pindar uses
the term, Pyth. 2, 72, καλός τοι πίθων
παρὰ παισίν, αἰεὶ καλός.
ἡρμένη. This middle use of ἦρμαι
is found in Soph. El. 54, and occurs in
other late writers besides Babrius.
LVII. 1. 'Hermes filled a waggon
with lies and loads of deceit and all
villany, and drove it the world
through.'
4. σχέδην· ἡσυχῇ, βάδην, Hesychius. Eberhard's correction of ἀυῶν
to ὤνων is quite certain, but ὤνοι in the

sense of 'wares' is unexampled. It
does not really bear that meaning in
Apollonius Rhodius, 2, 1007, where
he describes the Black Country of the
Ancients and its inhabitants, the
Chalybes— ἀλλὰ σιδηροφόρον στυφελὴν
χθόνα γατομέοντες ὦνον ἀμείβονται βιοτή-
σιον. 'For all their labour they get in
exchange the price that brings them
food,' τῆς τροφῆς τίμημα, schol. in loco.
6. The objection to Ἀραβίων, that it
is not the Greek form of the name, will
not recommend itself to any one who
reads late authors. The emendation is
quite certain, as Ἀρράβων, the only
other possible suggestion, cannot be
defended by Arabiae in Propertius, or
Ἀρραβίη, the form found regularly in
Nonnus.
In addition to their metrical faults
the three interpolated lines stultify the
rest of the fable. Γλαῦκ' Ἀθήναζε.

ἔτι προελθεῖν καίπερ ὄντας ἀνθρώπους.
ἐντεῦθεν Ἄραβές εἰσιν, ὡς ἐπειράθην,
ψεῦσταί τε καὶ γόητες ὧν ἐπὶ γλώσσης
οὐδὲν κάθηται ῥῆμα τῆς ἀληθείης.

LVIII.

Ζεὺς ἐν πίθῳ τὰ χρηστὰ πάντα συλλέξας
ἔθηκεν αὐτὸν πωμάσας παρ' ἀνθρώπῳ.
ὁ δ' ἀκρατὴς ἄνθρωπος εἰδέναι σπεύδων
τί ποτ' ἦν ἐν αὐτῷ καὶ τὸ πῶμα κινήσας
διῆκ' ἀπελθεῖν αὐτὰ πρὸς θεῶν οἴκους.   5
μόνη δ' ἔμεινεν ἐλπίς, ἣν κατειλήφει   7
τεθὲν τὸ πῶμα· τοιγὰρ ἐλπὶς ἀνθρώποις
μόνη σύνεστι, τῶν πεφευγότων ἥμας
ἀγαθῶν ἕκαστον ἐγγυωμένη δώσειν.   10

LIX.

Ζεὺς καὶ Ποσειδῶν, φασί, καὶ τρίτη τούτοις
ἤριζ' Ἀθηνᾶ, τίς καλόν τι ποιήσει.
ποιεῖ μὲν ὁ Ζεὺς ἐκπρεπέστἀντον ζώων
ἄνθρωπον, ἡ δὲ Παλλὰς οἶκον ἀνθρώποις,
ὁ δ' αὖ Ποσειδῶν ταῦρον. ᾑρέθη τούτοις   5
κριτὴς ὁ Μῶμος· ἔτι γὰρ ἐν θεοῖς ᾤκει.

---

11. Qua de causa verba καίπερ ὄντας eruditi emendare temptaverint,
ego certe non video. Ecce tentamina ! καὶ περιόντας Ahrens, γειτνιῶντας
Fix, γῆν πολοῦντας idem, καὶ περᾶν πρόσω ῥώπους Bergk, κάμελοῦντας
Gitlbauer. Talia neglegere soleo, neque poenitet.

LVIII. Versum sextum, quem saepsit recte Eberhardus, ego et inferius
descendere jussi—

κἀκεῖ πέτεσθαι τῆς τε γῆς ἄνω φεύγειν.

---

13. ὧν ἐπὶ γλώσσης κτλ. Cp.
Soph. O. C. 1052, ὧν καὶ χρυσέα κλῂς
ἐπὶ γλώσσᾳ βέβακε προσπόλων Εὐμολ-
πιδᾶν. Aesch. Agam. 36, βοῦς ἐπὶ
γλώσσῃ μέγας βέβηκε.
LVIII. 2. πωμάσας, a late word for
κλείω, as ἀροτριάω for ἀρῶ.

5. διῆκε, 'let them out.'
7. ἔμεινεν, here as passive of καταλείπω.
LIX. 1. Join τρίτη τούτοις.
6. ἔτι γὰρ . . ᾤκει is added to
suggest the fate which his free criticism brought upon him.

κἀκεῖνος, ὡς πέφυκε, πάντας ἐχθραίνων,
πρῶτον μὲν εὐθὺς ἔψεγεν τὸ τοῦ ταύρου,
τῶν ὀμμάτων τὰ κέρατα μὴ κάτω κεῖσθαι,
ὡς ἂν βλέπων ἔτυπτε· τοῦ δὲ κἀνθρώπου,   10
μὴ σχεῖν θυρωτὰ μηδ' ἀνοικτὰ τὰ στήθη,
ὡς ἂν βλέποι τὸ τοῦ πέλας, τί βουλεύοι·
τῆς οἰκίης δέ, μὴ τροχοὺς σιδηρείους
ἐν τοῖς θεμελίοις γεγονέναι, τόπους ἄλλους
συνεξαμείβειν δεσπόταισιν ἐκδήμοις.   15

LX.

Ζωμοῦ χύτρῃ μῦς ἐμπεσὼν ἀπωμάστῳ
καὶ τῷ λίπει πνιγόμενος ἐκπνέων τ' ἤδη
'βέβρωκα' φησί 'καὶ πέπωκα καὶ πάσης
τρυφῆς πέπλησμαι· καιρός ἐστί μοι θνήσκειν.'

LIX. 10. Ego pro γ' ἀνθρώπου non sine fiducia κἀνθρώπου scripsi.
12. Pro Athoa lectione βλέποιτο τὸν Gitlbaueri conjecturam βλέποι τὸ
τοῦ in textum incertus recepi. 14. Voculam δ' ante ἄλλους cum editore
principe omisi ut ab aliquo male erudito suppositam. 15. E paraphrasi
editores alium versum concoxerunt ; ὡς τὸν πονηρὸν γείτον' ἦν ἂν ἐκφεύ-
γειν Lachmannus, neque melius alii. Babrii verba, si revera aliquando
extiterunt, sine dubio nemo redintegravit. Epimythium quoque alii alium
in modum emendaverunt, sed οὐ φροντὶς Ἱπποκλείδῃ—

τί οὖν ὁ μῦθός φησιν ἐν διηγήσει;
πειρῶ τι ποιεῖν τὸν φθόνον μὴ κρίνειν.
ἀρεστὸν ἁπλῶς οὐδέν ἐστι τῷ Μώμῳ.

LX. Fabula certe Babrio est digna, si non Babriana. Epimythium
longe aliud—

τότ' ἂν λίχνος γένοιο μῦς ἐν ἀνθρώποις
ἐὰν τὸ κατάβλαπτον ἡδὺ μὴ παραιτήσῃ.

---

7. It would not be necessary to point out the idiomatic use of πέφυκε if Eberhard had not altered ἐχθραίνων to ἐχθραίνειν. The Greek synonyms signifying *to hate* are an interesting study. By the law of parsimony Attic prose abandoned ἐχθαίρω and στυγῶ, and retained μισῶ alone. Ἐχθραίνω is Xenophontean and late. Like all other verbs in -ρω, except αἴρω, εἴρω, and φθείρω, the form ἐχθαίρω was denied a perfect active. So was ἐχθραίνω, like

all other verbs in -αίνω. These same two classes of verbs rarely possess a perfect passive, and neither ἐχθαίρω nor ἐχθραίνω had that tense. That it does not occur in μισῶ shows that the Attics preferred a periphrasis.
10. ὡς ἂν βλέπων ἔτυπτε, see Goodwin, § 44, 3, note 1. The καί which I have imported into the following clause not only ejects τό γε τὸ πάγχρηστον, but betters the sense.
LX. 3. As ἔδω had not been alto-

LXI.

Ἦιει κυνηγὸς ἐξ ὄρους κυνηγήσας,
·'ει δὲ γριπεὺς κύρτον ἰχθύων πλήσας.
καί πως συνηβόλησαν οἱ δύ' ἀλλήλοις,
χὤ μὲν κυνηγὸς ἰχθύων ἁλιπλώων,
θήρην δ' ὁ γριπεὺς ἠρέτιζεν ἀγρείην,   5
τά τ' εἶχον ἀντέδωκαν. εἶτα τὴν θήρην
ἤμειβον ἀεί, δεῖπνα δ' εἶχον ἡδίω,
ἕως τις αὐτοῖς εἶπεν· ' ἀλλὰ καὶ τούτων
τὸ χρηστὸν ἐξολεῖτε τῇ συνηθείῃ,
πάλιν δ' ἕκαστος ἃ πρὶν εἶχε ζητήσει.'   10

LXII.

Ἡμίονος ἀργῆς χιλὸν ἐσθίων φάτνης
καὶ κριθιάσας ἐτρόχαζε κἀφώνει
τένοντα σείων ' ἵππος ἐστί μοι μήτηρ,
ἐγὼ δ' ἐκείνης οὐδὲν ἐν δρόμοις ἥττων.'
ἄφνω δ' ἔπαυσε τὸν δρόμον κατηφήσας.   5
ὄνου γὰρ εὐθὺς πατρὸς ὢν ἀνεμνήσθη.

gether crushed in Attic by ἐσθίω, so
βέβρωκα picked up the crumbs thrown
to it by ἐδήδοκα. If there were shades
of meaning between the terms, I for one
do not care to discuss them.
4. πέπλησμαι. The rarity of this
form is to be partly explained by the
fact that in Attic at all events the old
aorist ἐνεπλήμην supplied all the moods
of ἐμπέπλημαι except the indicative.
LXI. 3. 'And as chance would have
it the two men met.' The verb συναβολέω only occurs in this passage,
although the Hesychian gloss συνηβό-
λησεν· ἀπήντησεν indicates that it
appeared in some work now lost. Liddell and Scott make a strange slip in
giving συνηβολέω as the present. The
verb ἀβολέω is as naturally formed
from ἄβολος, thrown together (α = ἅμα)
as ξυμβολέω from ξύμβολος, or ἀντιβολέω
from ἀντίβολος, and though known to
us only from Apollonius Rhodius and
Callimachus, is undoubtedly much
earlier than they. By Babrius' time
the force of the ἀ was lost, and he was
able to use συναβολέω.

6. ἀντέδωκαν has the same sense here
as the Attic law-term ἀντιδιδόναι =
ἀντίδοσιν ποιεῖσθαι.
7. The plural δεῖπνα is not poetical,
but is to be rendered as a plural, 'their
dinners.'
LXII. 1. 'A mule eating fodder from
a lazy crib.' There is no reason for
the conjecture ἀργός. For the un-Attic
feminine, see Phryn. p. 185. The Attic
equivalents of χιλός and χιλόω were
χόρτος and χορτάζω. The distinction
between ἡμίονος and ὀρεύς as between
mulus and mula (hinnus) is not always
observed. Here, however, we have
ἡμίονος properly used of the offspring
of a mare and he-ass.
2. κριθιάσας, see Phryn. p. 155.
Cp. Aristoph. Vesp. 1305 :—ὥσπερ κα-
χρύων ὀνίδιον εὐωχημένον | ἐνήλλετ'
ἐσκίρτα 'πεπόρδει κατεγέλα | κάτυπτε δὴ
με νεανικῶς κτε.
4. δρόμοις, obs. pl. = τῷ τρέχειν.
5. κατηφήσας. Aristotle, Anim.
Hist. 8, 24, 604, ᵇ12, mentions this as
one of the indications of νυμφιᾶν in
mares, and seemingly uses κατωπιᾶν as

LXIII.

Ἢν τις κατ᾿ οἴκους ἀνδρὸς εὐσεβοῦς ἥρως
ἔχων ἐν αὐλῇ τέμενος. ἔνθα δὴ θύων
στέφων τε βωμοὺς καὶ καταβρέχων οἴνῳ
προσηύχετ᾿ ἀεί ᾿ χαῖρε, φίλταθ᾿ ἡρώων,
καὶ τὸν σύνοικον ἀγαθὰ δαψιλῆ ποίει.᾿   5
κἀκεῖνος αὐτῷ νυκτὸς ἐν μέσαις ὥραις
᾿ ἀγαθὸν μέν ᾿ εἶπεν ᾿ οὐδ᾿ ἂν εἷς τις ἡρώων
ὦ τᾶν παράσχοι· ταῦτα τοὺς θεοὺς αἴτει·
κακῶν δὲ πάντων ἅτε σύνεστιν ἀνθρώποις
δοτῆρες ἡμεῖς. τοιγὰρ εἰ κακῶν χρῄζεις,   10
εὔχου· παρέξω πολλά, κἂν ἐν αἰτήσῃς.᾿

LXIV.

Ἤριζον ἐλάτη καὶ βάτος πρὸς ἀλλήλας.
ἐλάτης δ᾿ ἑαυτὴν πολλαχῶς ἐπαινούσης
᾿ καλὴ μέν εἰμι καὶ τὸ μέτρον εὐμήκης,

LXIII. 7. Versui claudo Meinekius εἷς adjecit, an recte incertum.
8. G. Hermannum sequor, pro Athoa οὔτ᾿ ἂν lectione vocativo ὦ τᾶν
scripto. 9. Qua de causa ἅτε σύνεστιν eruditi emendare voluerint, viro
sobrio non liquet. Certe cum πᾶσίν ἐσμεν Gitlbauerus legit, facit
mendam non movet. Attice non scripsit Babrius et in tali ἅτε non
offendit lectori. Versum manifeste e Christiano epimythiasta profectum
et ab editoribus male junctum fabulae ego removi—

πρὸς ταῦτα λοιπὸν αὐτὸς οἶδας ἂν θύσῃς.

a synonym. τό τε νυμφιᾶν καλούμενον,
ἐν ᾧ συμβαίνει κατέχεσθαι ὅταν αὐλῇ τις,
καὶ κατωπιᾶν· καὶ ὅταν ἀναβῇ τις προ-
χάζει, ἕως ἂν μέλλῃ κατά τινας θεῖν.
κατηφεῖ δ᾿ ἀεὶ κἂν λυττήσῃ. Just before he has described the conditions of
τὸ κριθιᾶν.
LXIII. 4. 'He would from time to
time address him in prayer, "Hail,
hero beloved, and work thy house-mate
plenteous blessings." And in the mid-
seasons of night the hero spake to him,
"A blessing indeed no hero of us all
can bestow."' I have thought it more
discreet to accept Meineke's and Hermann's conjectures in this passage than

to make a violent change. The corruption, however, lies much deeper,
and perhaps

οὐ δύναιτ᾿ ἂν ἡρώων
οὐδεὶς παρασχεῖν

would most nearly approach the primitive reading.
12. In addition to the more cogent
reasons for fathering this line upon an
interpolator are the blunders οἶδας for
οἶσθα, and ἂν θύσῃς for εἰ θύσεις, and
πρὸς ταῦτα with an indicative.
LXIV. 3. τὸ μέτρον εὐμήκης, lit. 'as
to the measure, tall.' In Greek of a
good age the phrase, if used at all,

καὶ τῶν νεφῶν σύνοικος ὀρθίη φύω,
στέγη τε μελάθρων εἰμὶ καὶ τρόπις πλοίων,   5
δένδρων τοσούτων ἐκπρεπεστάτη πάντων,'
βάτος πρὸς αὐτὴν εἶπεν ' ἢν λάβῃς μνήμην   7
καὶ τῶν πελύκων τῶν ἀεί σε τεμνόντων,   9
βάτος γενέσθαι καὶ σὺ μᾶλλον αἱρήσῃ.'

LXV.

Ἤριζε τεφρὴ γέρανος εὐφυεῖ ταῷ
σείοντι χρυσᾶς πτέρυγας ' ἀλλ' ἐγὼ ταύταις'
ἡ γέρανος εἶπεν ' ὧν σὺ τὴν χρόην σκώπτεις,
ἄστρων σύνεγγυς ἵπταμαί τε καὶ κράζω.
σὺ δ' ὡς ἀλέκτωρ ταῖσδε ταῖς καταχρύσοις   5
χαμαὶ πτερύσσῃ' φησίν ' οὐδ' ἄνω φαίνῃ.'

LXIV. 7. Post hunc versum exhibet Athous alium, alicui referendum
qui voculae καὶ ante τῶν πελύκων positae suam vim adscribere nesciret—

τῶν πελέκεων τῶν ἀεί σε κοπτόντων,

in quo Fixius τε post πελέκεων addidit.   Epimythium tibi habe—

ἅπας ὁ λαμπρὸς τῶν ἐλαττόνων μᾶλλον
καὶ δόξαν ἔσχε χὑπέμεινε κινδύνους·

LXV. Quantum mutata sit Athoa fabula a Babriana videre licet si
quis fragmentum animadverterit a Suida sub γέρανος vocabulo servatum
infra No. 142. Qua de causa ταῷ in ultima versus sede retinui. 4. Verba
καὶ κράζω Gitlbauerus οὐκ ἄτερ μούσης in κἀκρίζω mutavit. Epimythium
fabula ipsa etiam pejus—

θαυμαστὸς εἶναι σὺν τρίβωνι βουλοίμην
ἢ ζῆν ἀδόξως πλουσίᾳ σὺν ἐσθῆτι.

---

would mean, 'Measure me and great is
my stature.' In late Greek it may
have that meaning, or else simply 'tall
in stature.' Such difficulties are always presenting themselves in all Alexandrine and Byzantine ages, and really
admit of no settlement. The Hermann
School of Greek scholarship owed its
transitory success to the fact that man-
kind in general will not believe in
Attic precision of language.

4. τῶν νεφῶν σύνοικος. This substantival construction is occasionally
used even by the best writers, but the
dative is the case regularly employed.
In late writers φύω may be intransitive,
not even meaning 'I put forth shoots,'
but 'I grow.' Pseudo-Oppian. Cyneg.
2, 567, βένθεσιν αὐτόρρεκτα φύει καὶ
ἀμήτορα φῦλα, | ὄστρεά τ' ἠπεδαναί τ'
ἀφύαι κτε.

LXV. 4. σύνεγγυς, a late and de-
praved use of the adverb, see Phryn.
p. 119. For ἵπταμαι, see id. p. 373.

5. ἀλέκτωρ, see supra, Fab. 17, 1,
note.

LXVI.

Θεῶν Προμηθεὺς ἦν τις ἀλλὰ τῶν πρώτων.
τοῦτον πλάσασθαί φασι δεσπότην ζώων
ἄνθρωπον ἐκ γῆς, ἐκ δὲ τοῦ δύω πήρας
κρεμάσαι φέροντα πᾶσι τῶν ἐν ἀνθρώποις
κακῶν γέμουσας, τὴν πρόσω μὲν ὀθνείων,   5
ἰδίων δὲ τὴν ὄπισθεν ἥτις ἦν μείζων.
διό μοι δοκοῦσι συμφορὰς μὲν ἀλλήλων
βλέπειν ἀκριβῶς, ἀγνοεῖν δὲ τὰς οἴκοι.

LXVII.

Θήρης ὄναγρος καὶ λέων ἐκοινώνουν,
ἀλκῇ μὲν ὁ λέων, ὁ δ᾽ ὄνος ἐν ποσὶν κρείσσων.
ἐπεὶ δὲ λείην ἔσχον ἄφθονον ζώων,
ὁ λέων μερίζει, καὶ τίθησι τρεῖς μοίρας,

LXVI. 4. Fabulam ex codice edidi nisi quod quarto in versu πᾶσι
pro φασι cum Gitlbauero scripsi, et in sexto δὲ τὴν ὄπισθεν ἥτις ἦν μείζων
pro δ᾽ ὄπισθεν ἥτις ἦν πολὺ μείζων cum Fixio et aliis dedi. Manet mihi
tamen in incerto quatenus φασί iteratum debeat in seriore reprehendi.
Minus recte Eberhardus de duobus ultimis versibus dubitat. Longe alii
sunt quam quos epimythiasta concoquere solet et cum Fab. 57, 12-14,
comparari debent.

LXVI. 3. ἐκ δὲ τοῦ. For this collocation and the usage of the article, cp.
Aesch. Eum. 693 :—ἔνθεν ἔστ᾽ ἐπώνυμος
| πέτρα πάγος τ᾽ Ἄρειος· ἐν δὲ τῷ σέ-
βας | κτλ. Meineke's conjecture, ἐκδέ-
τους, is grotesque, and, what is worse,
uncalled for. The following φέροντα is
idiomatic, and Lachmann's conjecture,
τένοντος, unnecessary and palaeographically impossible.

4. If πᾶσι is right, then κακῶν was
preferred to κακοῖς to avoid confusion
with ἀνθρώποις.

6. ἥτις. We should expect ἥπερ
here ; but in a late writer it would be
too fanciful to press the meaning of
ἥτις, and to say that it suggests its
size as a reason for hanging the wallet
behind.

LXVII. 1. For late forms like ὄναγρος, see Phryn. p. 476.

2. Editors have fallen foul of this
simple and straightforward line. The
omission of ὧν is not rare even in
Attic, and the presence of the preposition only in the second clause,
though belonging to both, is too well
known to require illustration. For ἐν
with κρείσσων we may compare 62, 4,
ἐν δρόμοις ἥττων.

3. ἐπεὶ δὲ λείην ἔσχον. It is strange
that editors have wrongly corrected
εἶχον into ἔσχον so often in Babrius,
and not done so in this, the only
passage in which such a correction
would have been just. As a matter
of fact the Athoan codex has been
hitherto cited incorrectly, and really
exhibits the necessary aorist.

F

καὶ ' τὴν μὲν αὐτός ' φησί 'λήψομαι πρώτην.　　5
βασιλεὺς γάρ εἰμι· λήψομαι δὲ κἀκείνην
ὡς ἐξ ἴσου κοινωνός. ἡ τρίτη δ' αὕτη
κακόν τι δώσει μὴ θέλοντί σοι φεύγειν.'

LXVIII.

Θεοῖς Ἀπόλλων ἔλεγε μακρὰ τοξεύων,
' οὐκ ἂν βάλοι τις πλεῖον † οὐδὲ τοξεύσει.'
ὁ Ζεὺς δὲ παίζων ἠρίδαινε τῷ Φοίβῳ.
Ἑρμῆς δ' ἔσειεν Ἄρεος ἐν κυνῇ κλήρους.
λαχὼν δ' ὁ Φοῖβος τόξ' ἔρυσσε κυκλώσας　　5

LXVII. 5. Ex tetrastichis πρώτην pro Athoo πρῶτος restitui, duce
Eberhardo. Epimythium accipe—

μέτρει σεαυτόν· πρᾶγμα μηδὲν ἀνθρώπῳ
δυνατωτέρῳ σύναπτε μηδὲ κοινώνει.

LXVIII. 2. Versui mederi non valeo. Aut in τοξεύων aut τοξεύσει
vitium latet. Si cum aliquot editoribus τοξεύσαι legeris, multum non
proficies, minus si τοξεύων cum Gitlbauero in δοξάζων mutaveris. 5. Hic
etiam pravissime Athous—

λαχὼν δ' ὁ Φοῖβος χρυσέην τε κυκλώσας
τόξοιο νευρὴν ὀξέως ἀφεὶς πρῶτος
τὸ βέλος ἔπηξεν,

minus prave Vaticanus—

λαχὼν δὲ Φοῖβος τὸ τόξον ἐκκυκλώσας
τὸ βέλος ἔπηξεν.

Vitia satis nota scribarum uterque codex exhibet — Athoa culpa ex
τόξ' ἔρυσσε orta est, verbo χρυσέην pro veris litteris paene oblitis lecto,
et postea toto versu addito ut χρυσέην aliquid daret cum quo congrueret.
Mea fiducia Babrio ipsius verba reddidi.

---

5. τὴν μὲν αὐτός λήψομαι πρώ-
την, 'the first I shall take to myself.'
The Athoan reading could mean nothing but ' I shall be the first to take
the one to myself'; and this inadequacy,
if not absurdity, of signification, combined with the metrical fault in πρῶτος,
makes the reading πρώτην absolutely
certain.
　　LXVIII. 2. The sense demanded is,
' No one will send a bolt further than

1—at all events from a bow,' there
being a sly hit at Διὸς βέλη. It is
tempting to read οὔ γε τοξεύων with
hyperbaton of γε, but I remember no
instance of a hyperbatic γε following
the negative. It should be remembered that τοξεύσει may be the dative
of a substantive.
　　5. It is needless to point out the
absurdity of the Athoan reading. A
golden string, and that string in shoot-

τὸ βέλος τ᾽ ἔπηξεν ἐντὸς Ἑσπέρου κήπων.
ὁ Ζεὺς δὲ διαβὰς ταὐτὸ μέτρον εἱστήκει,
καὶ ' ποῦ βάλω, παῖ ;' φησίν ' οὐκ ἔχω χώρην.'
τόξου δὲ νίκην ἔλαβε μηδὲ τοξεύσας.

LXIX.

Θάμνου λαγωὸν δασυπόδην ἀναστήσας
κύων τις ἐδίωκ᾽ οὐκ ἄπειρος ἀγρεύειν,
δρόμῳ δ᾽ ἐλείφθη· καί τις αἰπόλος σκώπτων ·
' ὁ πηλίκος σου' φησίν ' εὑρέθη θάσσων.'
ὁ δ᾽ εἶπεν ' ἄλλως ἄλλον ἁρπάσαι σπεύδων   5
τρέχει τις, ἄλλως δ᾽ αὐτὸν ἐκ κακοῦ σώζων.'

LXIX. 1. Ahrensius δασυπόδην pro Athoo δασύποιν recte restituit.
2. Dedi κύων τις ἐδίωκ᾽ sed minus fidenter, quia munere eodem atque τις
alia verba fungi possunt, ut Seidleri μέν et Hochii ποτ᾽. Culpa manifesta
κύων ἐδίωκεν Athous exhibet. Certe, vocula post κύων elapsa, in posteriore
sede syllaba accessit, sed vocula elapsa, quis ? 6. Editores αὐτὸν pro
Athoo ἄλλον. Scholiasta in Thucydidem, 4, 92, hunc locum cum citat
vitiavit neque hanc mendam omisit.

ing forming the arc of a circle! Add
to this the metrical fault in πρῶτος,
and the spuriousness of the rejected
line is demonstrated, even apart from
the evidence of the Vatican codex, to
which I should be loth to attach
weight. The unaugmented Homeric
form ἔρυσσε is quite in keeping with
the Babrian diction.

6. ἐντὸς Ἑσπέρου κήπων, 'inside the
Gardens of the West.' The phrase is
as indefinite as 'over the Mountains of
the Moon,' except that the writer intended it as the extreme western limit
of the world. Even then the distance
of the arrow-flight is not given, as the
place in which the gods were is not
mentioned. Probably Olympus—the
Homeric Olympus in Thessaly—is intended as the scene of the dispute. It
would be idle here to reproduce the
confusions and contradictions of the
ancients themselves as to the Hesperides, the Gardens of the Hesperides,
the Gardens of the West, the Islands
of the West, and the Islands of the
Blest. It would be less futile to discuss

the whereabouts of the Mountains of
the Moon.

7. διαβὰς ταὐτὸ μέτρον. To readers
of Nonnus this notion of Zeus is familiar,
cp. Dionys. 7, 312 :—

ἀστερόεν τότε δῶμα παρέστιχεν αἰθέριος
    Ζεὺς
εἰς Σεμέλης ὑμέναιον, ἀτεκμάρτῳ δὲ
    πεδίλῳ
ἅλμα θορὼν πρώτιστον ὅλην παρεμέτρεε
    ταρσῷ
ἀτραπὸν ἠερίην· τὸ δὲ δεύτερον ἵκετο
    Θήβην
ὡς πτερὸν ἠὲ νόημα κτε.

LXIX. 1. δασυπόδην. Eberhard
gives a list of similar forms, ὠκυπόδης,
αἰγιπόδης, ἀελλοπόδης, ἀερσιπόδης, ἀκα-
μαντοπόδης, ἀργιπόδης, εἰλιπόδης, ὀρθο-
πόδης, πουλυπόδης, ὑψιπόδης. The three
words τριπόδης, ἑπταπόδης, and ὀκταπόδης, occur in one passage of Hesiod
(Op. 423-425), meaning 'three-feet-,
seven-feet-, eight-feet-long.' Homer has
ἑπταπόδης θρῆνυς, 'with seven legs,' and
Nonnus ὀκταπόδης, 'with eight feet.'
For either meaning the only Attic forms

LXX.

Θεῶν γαμούντων ὡς ἔκαστος ἐζεύχθη,
Ἄρης ἔγημεν Ὕβριν ἐσχάτῳ κλήρῳ·
ταύτης περισσῶς ὡς λέγουσιν ἠράσθη,
ἕπεται δὲ ταύτῃ πανταχοῦ βαδιζούσῃ.

LXXI.

Ἰδὼν γεωργὸς νῆα ναυτίλων πλήρη
βάπτουσαν ἤδη κῦμα κυρτὸν ἐκ πρῴρης,

LXX. Fabulam manifeste corruptam et fortasse insanabilem liberius tractavi. In codice Athoo versus octo se praestant, quorum tres ultimi epimythiastae referendi sunt—

Θεῶν γαμούντων ὡς ἔκαστος ἐζεύχθη
παρῆν ἐφ᾽ ἅπασι Πόλεμος ἑκάστῳ κλήρῳ
Ὕβριν δὲ γήμας ἦν ἄρης κατειλήφει ἄρης
ταύτης περισσῶς ὡς λέγουσιν ἠράσθη,
ἕπεται δὲ ταύτῃ πανταχοῦ βαδιζούσῃ.
μὴ γοῦν ἔθνη που μὴ πόλεις τας ἀνθρώπων
ὕβρις ἐπελθοι προσγελῶσα τοῖς δήμοις,
ἐπεὶ μετ᾽ αὐτὴν πόλεμος εὐθέως ἥξει.

Talia medendo aegrescunt ; scalpello egent. Fabula primo longior, deinde in tetrastichon decurtata, tandem in quinque versus vitiis producta est. Dittographiae pravissimae signa non latent : παρην, αρης, αρης, εκαστος, εκαστω, αρης κατειληφει. Si cui mea non placent, ecce eruditorum tentamina. ἐφ᾽ ἅπασι Πόλεμος ἐσχάτῳ παρῆν κλήρῳ, Ὕβριν δὲ γήμας ἦν ἄρ᾽ ὕστατ᾽ εἰλήφει, ἣν μόνην κατειλήφει, ἣν πάρος κατειλήφει et alia. Quot editores tot conjecturae, neque ipse editoris officio deesse volui.

LXXI. 2. Pro Athoo πρώτης cum Duebnero πρῴρης scripsi.

---

were ἑπτάπους, ὀκτώπους, etc. As a rule the -δης forms are late, but there are secure enough instances in Hesiod and Homer to prove wrong the explanation of Οἰδιπόδης as a patronymic. It is only a bye-form of Οἰδίπους.
LXXI. 2. βάπτουσαν .. κῦμα. Such a use of βάπτω is unexampled, although other passages show how it arose. The verbs βάπτω and βαπτίζω acquired in late Greek the sense of drawing liquids, and could be used with an accusative

of the liquid drawn and a dative of the vessel employed. Theocr. 5, 127, ἁ παῖς ἀνθ᾽ ὕδατος τᾷ κάλπιδι κηρία βάψαι, where a scholiast has the true gloss ἀντλῆσαι. Eratosthenes ap. Athen. xi. 482 B, ἀποσπείσαντες τοῖς θεοῖς ἐκ τῆς φιάλης, ᾠνοχόουν ἐφεξῆς, τὸν νεοκράτα βάπτοντες τῷ κυμβίῳ. Nicander, Alexipharmaca, 514, αὐτὴν ἅλα βάπτε. This sense, if not really Attic, was very nearly reached in some passages. The Hesychian gloss, βαπτάν·

' ὦ πέλαγος ' εἶπεν ' εἴθε μήποτ' ἐπλεύσθης,
ἀνηλεὲς στοιχεῖον, ἐχθρὸν ἀνθρώποις.'
ἤκουε δ' ἡ θάλασσα, καὶ γυναικείην   5
λαβοῦσα φωνὴν εἶπε ' μή με βλασφήμει·
ἐγὼ γὰρ ὑμῖν οὐδὲν αἰτίη τούτων,
ἄνεμοι δὲ πάντως, ὧν ἐγὼ μέση κεῖμαι.
τούτων δὲ χωρὶς ἢν ἴδης με καὶ πλεύσης,
ἐρεῖς με τῆς σῆς ἠπιωτέρην γαίης.'   10

LXXII.

Ἰρίς ποτ' οὐρανοῖο πορφυρῆ κῆρυξ
πτηνοῖσι κάλλους εἶπεν ἐν θεῶν οἴκοις

---

8. Baitero duce, Athoum πάντες in πάντως mutavi. Epimythium plus solito claudicat—

ὅτι πολλὰ χρηστὰ πράγμαθ' αἱ κακαὶ φύσεις
τρέπουσιν εἰς τὸ χεῖρον ὡς δοκεῖν φαῦλα.

LXXII. 2. Duebnerum fidenter secutus sum, οὐρανοῖο pro Athoo οὐρανοῦ substituto.

ἀντλουμένην, refers to Eurip. Hipp. 123—

βαπτὰν κάλπισι ῥυτὰν
παγὰν προϊεῖσα κρημνῶν·

but the scholiast from whom it was taken read into the word too much of his own age; and although in strict grammar the construction βάπτειν κάλπιδας εἰς ὕδωρ could not give rise to ὕδωρ βαπτὸν κάλπισι, still the βαπτὰν κάλπισι παγάν of Euripides has as much to do with that as with βάπτειν ὕδωρ κάλπισι. The constructions of these verbals is often very vague in poetry, and when ῥιπτὸς μόρος and others like it can be elucidated by strict rules of grammar, it will be time to insist upon taking βαπτὰν κάλπισι as an early instance of βάπτω, draw. In Eur. Hec. 610, often cited for this sense, the ordinary signification is demanded, and the lines of Antiphanes cited by Athenaeus, iii. 123 C, κατασκεδῶ, νὴ τὴν φίλην Δήμητρα, τὴν μεγίστην | ἀρύταιναν ὑμῶν ἐκ μέσου βάψασα τοῦ λέβητος |

ξέοντος ὕδατος, may be translated almost equally well by keeping to the recognised Attic meaning of βάπτω.

In the present line of Babrius, however, we encounter not only the late sense of draw, but a further extension still. The ship is represented as taking in the arched waves at the bows. ἐκ πρῴρης = πρῴραθεν, like ἐκ νώτου, ἐκ πλαγίου, ἐκ τοῦ ὄπισθεν, etc.

3. ἐπλεύσθης. Although the passive of πλέω is extremely rare in Attic, it could be used in this way. Demosthenes has πλοῦς πεπλευσμένος, and θάλαττα ἐπλεύσθη was doubtless possible also.

8. ἄνεμοι δὲ πάντως. Here as elsewhere Gitlbauer mistakes the paraphrase, and in giving the Bodleian οἱ ἐκταράσσοντές με ἄνεμοι as his authority for the conjecture ἄνεμοι δ' ἐλῶντες, has not observed that ἐκταράσσοντες is really the paraphrase of ὧν ἐγὼ μέση κεῖμαι.

LXXII. 2. Here εἶπεν has the construction of ἀνεῖπεν.

ἀγῶνα κεῖσθαι· πᾶσι δ' εὐθὺς ἠκούσθη,
καὶ πάντα θείων ἔσχεν ἵμερος δώρων.
ἔσταζε πέτρης αἰγὶ δυσβάτου κρήνη,   5
καὶ θερινὸν ὕδωρ καὶ διαυγὲς εἰστήκει·
πάντων δ' ἐπ' αὐτὸ φῦλον ἦλθεν ὀρνίθων,
πρόσωπα δ' αὐτῶν ἐξέλουε καὶ κνήμας,
ἔσειε ταρσούς, ἐκτένιζε τὰς χαίτας.
ἦλθεν δ' ἐκείνην καὶ κολοιὸς εἰς κρήνην,   10
γέρων, κορώνης υἱός, ἄλλο δ' ἐξ ἄλλου
πτερὸν καθύγρων ἐντὸς ἁρμόσας ὤμων,
μόνος τὰ πάντων ποικίλως ἐκοσμήθη,
καὶ πρὸς θεοὺς ἤϊξεν αἰετοῦ κρείσσων.
ὁ Ζεὺς δ' ἐθάμβει καὶ παρεῖχε τὴν νίκην,   15
εἰ μὴ χελιδὼν αὐτόν, ὡς Ἀθηναίη,
ἤλεγξεν ἑλκύσασα τὸ πτερὸν πρώτη,
τά τ' ἄλλ' ὁμοίως καὶ κολοιὸς ἐγνώσθη.

---

4. Restituit Duebnerus pro Athoo θεῖον ἔσχεν ἵμερον ζώων. 17. Hunc
post versum habet Athous codex alios quatuor, quorum nullum est in
paraphrasis vestigium, manifesta fraudis indicia prae se ferentes—

ὁ δ' εἶπεν αὐτῇ 'μή με συκοφαντήσῃς'
τὸν δ' ἄρα τρυγὼν ἐσπάραττε καὶ κίχλα
καὶ κίσσα καὶ κορύδαλλος οὖν τάφοις παίζων
χὠ νήπιος δ' ἔφηβος ὀρνέων ἴρηξ.

Talia sarcire non placet, neque epimythium laudo—

ὦ παῖ, σεαυτὸν κόσμον οἰκεῖον κόσμει·
τοῖς ἑτέρων γὰρ ἐμπρέπων τούτων στερηθήσῃ.

---

4. ἔσχεν ἵμερος. Here the aorist is
really required, and the codex presents
it.

5. 'A spring trickled from a rock
which a goat could scarce climb, and
the water lay summer-like and clear.'
Some editors would change θερινόν, but
the word is natural and used in a sense
quite legitimate. Εἰστήκει has the sense
of the more common καθειστήκει.

8. Eberhard would exhibit the Attic
imperfect by reading the impossible
ἐξέλου τε καί, but in Babrius ἐξέλουε is
not offensive. For the Attic forms of
λούειν see Phryn. p. 274.

11. κορώνης υἱός, see supra, Fab.
46, 8.

16. This is a parody on the Homeric
metamorphosis of Athene into a swallow, and not due to confusion in the
mind of the writer. 'The swallow
making herself out to be Athene,' i.e.
'in the guise of Athene.'

17. ἑλκύσασα—the true Attic form
of the aorist. The verbs ἕλκω and ἕρπω
coincide in the peculiarity of having a
present and future—ἕλκω, ἕλξω, ἕρπω,
ἕρψω, but an aorist—εἵλκυσα, εἷρπυσα.
Forms like ἑλκύω, ἑρπύω, are as incorrect as are εἷλξα, ἦλξα, εἷρψα, or ἦρψα.
The verdict of Aristophanes alone is
conclusive—ἕλκω, Nub. 12, 18 ; Pax,
470 : ἕλκεις, Thesm. 618 ; Eccl. 1037,
1050 : διέλκεις, Thesm. 618 : ἕλκει, Nub.

LXXIII.

Ἴκτινος ἄλλην ὀξέην εἶχε κλαγγήν
ἵππου δ' ἀκούσας χρεματίσαντος εὐφώνως,
μιμούμενος τὸν ἵππον οὔτε τὴν κρείττω
φωνὴν θελήσας ἔσχεν οὔτε τὴν πρώτην.

LXXIV.

Ἵππος τε καὶ βοῦς καὶ κύων ὑπὸ ψύχους
κάμνοντες ἦλθον οἰκίην ἐς ἀνθρώπου.
κἀκεῖνος αὐτοῖς τὰς θύρας ἀναπλώσας
παρῆγεν ἔνδον καὶ παρ' ἑστίῃ θάλψας
πυρὸς γεμούσῃ παρετίθει τι τῶν ὄντων,   5
κριθὰς μὲν ἵππῳ, λάθυρα δ' ἐργάτῃ ταύρῳ·
ὁ κύων † γὰρ αὐτῷ συντράπεζος εἱστήκει.

LXXIII. Fabellam plane a tetrastichista decurtatam et depravatam editores frustra emendare tentaverunt. Desperare et in luto relinquere satius est.

LXXIV. 7. De vocabulo γὰρ dubito, sed neque Eberhardi δ' ἄρ', neque Gitlbaueri παρ' satis placet.

233, 235; Vesp. 694: ἀνέλκει, Vesp. 568: ἕλκετε, Pax, 504: ἕλκουσι, Pax, 464, 478, 481; Lys. 727: ἐξέλκουσι, Nub. 713; Pax, 511: ἕλκῃς, Eq. 366: ἕλκωσι, Lys. 161; Eccl. 259: ἕλκε, Eq. 107: ὕφελκε, Vesp. 187; Av. 365: ἕλκετε, Pax, 469: ἀφέλκετε, Ach. 1005; Pax, 427: ἕλκειν, Av. 443; Eccl. 1020: παρέλκειν, Pax, 1306: καθελκείν, Eccl. 197: ἕλκοντε, Eccl. 1087: ἕλκοντες, Lys. 1073: διέλκων, Pax, 1131: ἕλκομαι, Eccl. 1066: ὑφέλκομαι, Eccl. 319: ἑλκοίμην, Eq. 772: ἕλκοιτο, Pax, 452: ἑλκόμενος, Nub. 1004; Eccl. 1094: ἑλκόμενον, Eccl. 1055: εἷλκον, Eq. 665; Vesp. 793; Pax, 475: καθείλκετε, Ach. 544: ἕλξω, Eq. 710, 711: ἕλξει, Plut. 955: ἕλξετε, Lys. 459: ἀφέλξομεν, Pax, 361: ἐξέλξω—a certain emendation of Porson's for ἐξελέγξω or ἐξελῶ in Eq. 365.
On the other hand, in the aorist are found—εἵλκυσεν, Nub. 540: παρείλκυσεν, Nub. 553: διελκύσαις, Plut. 1036: συνέλκυσον, Pax, 416: ἑλκύσαι,

Pax, 295, 315, 506: ἀνελκύσαι, Pax, 307: εἰσελκύσας, Ach. 379: ἀνελκύσας, Ach. 687: καθελκύσας, Eq. 1315: συνελκύσας, Nub. 585: ἀφελκύσωμαι, Ach. 1120. The other tenses follow the aorist, not the present and future. εἵλκυκα, εἵλκυσμαι, εἱλκύσθην; but the verbal has both forms—ἑλκτέος as well as ἑλκυστέος—a fact which may be compared with the co-existence of θρεκτέον and δραμητέον, ἀλωτός and αἱρετός, and others. The simple ἕρπω was not a pure Attic word (see Phryn. p. 50), but its compounds were in use—ἀνέρπω, ἐξέρπω, ἐφέρπω, καθέρπω, παρέρπω, προσέρπω; while ἕρπω, ἀφέρπω, διέρπω, and ὑφέρπω, are met with in tragedy. In no case do we find the analogy with ἕλκω contravened, except that the perfect does not occur. But even εἵλκυκα, which belongs to a verb in much more frequent use, has barely escaped oblivion, and there is little doubt that εἵρπυκα is a legitimate form.

ξενίης δ' ἀμοιβὴν ἀντέδωκαν ἀνθρώπῳ
μερίσαντες αὐτῷ τῶν ἐτῶν ἀφ' ὧν ἔζων,
ὁ μὲν ἵππος εὐθύ· διόπερ ἐν χρόνοις πρώτοις   10
ἕκαστος ἥμῶν γαῦρός ἐστι τὴν γνώμην·
ὁ δὲ βοῦς μετ' αὐτόν· διόπερ εἰς μέσους ἥκων
μοχθεῖ φίλεργός τ' ἐστιν ὄλβον ἀθροίζων.
ὁ κύων δ' ἔδωκε, φασί, τοὺς τελευταίους·
διὸ δυσκολαίνει, Βράγχε, πᾶς ὁ γηράσας   15
καὶ τὸν διδόντα τὴν τροφὴν μόνον σαίνει,
ἀεὶ δ' ὑλακτεῖ καὶ ξένοισιν οὐ χαίρει.

LXXV.

Ἰατρὸς ἦν ἄτεχνος. οὗτος ἀρρώστῳ
(πάντων λεγόντων ' μὴ δέδιχθι, σωθήσῃ·

LXXV. Fabulam in Athoo codice valde corruptam ex paraphrasi
Bodleianâ restitui.   2. Verbum δέδιχθι non sine fiducia scripsi, Otto
Schneidero duce, qui apud Nicandrum (Alexiph. 443) eandem formam ex

LXXIV. 9. 'Giving him a share in
the years of their life.' *Lit.* 'the
years on which they lived.' The years
are regarded as the basis of their life, a
point of view required to give the fable
point. A man's early life is generous
and high spirited because it is composed
of the years with which the horse presented him, and so with its other
portions. The conjecture ἐθῶν misses
the point, and τῶν ἐτῶν ἐφ' ὧν ἔζων is
impossible.

10. It would be easy to read εὐθύς,
but in late Greek like the Babrian
such emendations are unwarranted, see
Phryn. p. 222. ἐν χρόνοις πρώτοις, 'at
the beginning of his life.' In Attic
proper the plural number of χρόνος is
very rare except in phrases like κατὰ
τούτους τοὺς χρόνους, ἐν τούτοις τοῖς
χρόνοις, etc., in which the plural adds
to the notion of indefiniteness. In
tragedy it is more rare still, although
in Sophocles it is twice met with in the
sense of *periods* (O. R. 561 and 1137),
—a usage also found in prose, Plato,
Legg. 798 B. In Thuc. 1, 97, it means
dates.

15. πᾶς ὁ γηράσας, 'every one that
groweth old.' Moeris, whom Thomas

Magister follows, is wrong in preferring
γηρᾶναι to γηράσαι, as the aorist of
γηράσκω. The former is an old form occurring in tragedy, but never in comedy
or prose, as ἐγήρασαν, κατεγήρασαν, are
proved by γηράσαντι in Plato, Legg. 958
D, and καταγηράσω (subj.) in id. Symp.
216 A, to belong to the weak aorist.
That Aeschylus could give ἐγήρασα a
transitive meaning I do not believe,
and am inclined to think Supp. 894
corrupt, οὐ γάρ μ' ἔθρεψαν οὐδ' ἐγήρασαν
τροφῇ. If ὁ θεός με γηράσκει is Greek,
then anything may be. The correction
to οὐδ' ἐγήρασ' ἐν τροφῇ is simple, and
gives an equally good sense. The true
accent of the strong infinitive of tragedy
is γηρᾶναι, not γηράναι, if βιῶναι is
right and not βιώναι, ἀποδρᾶναι and not
ἀποδράναι, etc. etc. It would be unnecessary to state this had not W.
Dindorf edited γηράναι, and defended it
in the Paris Thesaurus, 3, 609. The
abundance of his work has given his
name a predominance to which, if
linguistic tact and careful scholarship
are of value, it has little right.

LXXV. 2. There can really be no
question about the restoration of δέδιχθι
in this passage, especially when the

πάθος μέν ἐστι χρόνιον, ἀλλ᾽ ἔσῃ ῥᾴων)
'ἀπατῶ σε' φησίν 'οὐδέν, οὐδ᾽ ἐνεδρεύω·
ἕτοιμα δεῖ σε πάντ᾽ ἔχειν· ἀποθνήσκεις· 5
τὴν αὔριον γὰρ μακρὸν οὐχ ὑπερβήσῃ.'

codice restituit. Hic vero Athous codex δέδειθι nunc exhibet; at tamen literae ε et ει incertae sunt, recentiore atramento obductae, et eaedem, quaecunque sint, a primo scriba super alias erasas ductae esse videntur. 3. Post tertium versum omnia turbat codex—

ὁ δ᾽ ἀτεχνὴς ἰατρὸς εἶπεν εἰσβαίνων 4
'ἕτοιμα δεῖ σε πάντ᾽ ἔχειν· ἀποθνήσκεις· 5
οὐκ ἐξαπατῶ σε' φησίν 'οὐδ᾽ ἐνεδρεύω, 6
τὴν αὔριον γὰρ τὸ μακρὸν οὐχ ὑπερβήσῃ. 7

Ex iis primum interpolavit aliquis, cui parenthesis turbas dedit, ipse turbas daturus. Hoc enim facto, justum duum versuum proximorum ordinem mutare necesse fuit. 4. Ita codicis verba transposui ut lex Babriana metrica servetur. Vitium forsan altius latet, versu decimo quinto collato, sed Mendelsohni ἐγὼ οὐ πλανῶ nemini placebit. 6. Ex versu articulum τὸ fidenter extrusi. Si emendare est errare, tum emendator fit Mendelsohnus, τλῆμον pro τὸ μακρὸν scripto.

order of the words has not preserved the chi even in Hesychius, in whose lexicon the gloss

δέδιθι· εὐλαβοῦ, φοβοῦ

stands between δεδίσσεσθαι and δεδμάων. True, it is a spurious form, but a form produced in a semi-legitimate way. No perfect in -κα forms any imperative at all in classical Greek, and consequently δέδοικα should have none. But δέδιχθι is the outcome of applying to perfects of this class the rules which produced the true classical imperatives, the vowel change being the same as in ἴσθι from οἶδα, and πέπισθι from πέποιθα. Similarly δείδιθι is not really the imperative of δείδια, but of δείδοια, which, by regular loss of the intervocalic vowel, affords δείδω (through δείδοα, which is perhaps the true Homeric form). δείδοια : δείδιθι : : οἶδα : ἴσθι : : πέποιθα : πέπισθι : : δείδοικα : δείδιχθι. So since δείδοια gave the plural δείδιμεν, and ἔοικα εἴξασι, and the same vowel change produced ἧκει, the Aristophanic past of ἔοικα corresponding to the Homeric passive ᾔκτο :—

ἔοικα : (ἤικ-σε(ν)). ἧκειν
ἤικ-το, (ᾖκτο).

3. This sense of ῥᾴδιος is confined to

the comparative, Greek thus agreeing with English. The corresponding verb ῥᾴζω must therefore be referred to ῥᾴων, not to ῥᾴδιος. There are in classical Greek eight verbs formed from adjectives in the comparative degree—ἐλασσόω, ἡσσάομαι, μειόω, νεωτερίζω, πλεονάζω, προτερέω, ῥᾴζω, and ὑστερέω; and three from adjectives in the superlative—ἀγχιστεύω, ἀριστεύω, and καλλιστεύω; for λωτίζω, with its compound ἀπολωτίζω, is from λωτός, not λῶστος. Notwithstanding the gloss of Hesychius,

ῥᾶισαι· τρισυλλάβως Ἀττικοί,

I have written ῥᾴξειν, not ῥαΐξειν, as the tendency to write the word with the diaeresis is proved by another gloss of the same lexicographer, where, although the order of the words calls for ῥᾴξειν (between ῥαδ and ῥάξειν), ῥαΐσας is presented by the manuscripts. In Attic, at all events, ῥᾴξειν (i.e. ῥαΐξειν, not ῥαΐξειν) was the true form.

6. There is no more difficulty in μακρὸν applied to time here than in its corresponding local use in Fab. 12, 1, supra. It is not classical, but in late Greek like the Babrian passes well enough. 'You will not long survive the morrow.'

74   SCRIPTORES FABULARUM GRAECI.

ταῦτ᾽ εἶπε, καὶ τὸ λοιπὸν οὐκέτ᾽ εἰσήει.
χρόνῳ δ᾽ ἐκεῖνος ἐκ νόσων ἀνασφήλας,
προῆλθεν ὠχρός, τοῖς ποσὶν μόλις βαίνων.
ὁ δ᾽ ἰατρὸς αὐτῷ ʼχαῖρʼ ʼ ἔφη συναντήσας,   10
καὶ πῶς ἔχουσιν οἱ κάτω διηρώτα.
κἀκεῖνος εἶπεν ʻ ἠρεμοῦσι τῆς Λήθης
πίνοντες. ἡ Κόρη δὲ χὠ μέγας Πλούτων
πρῴην ἰατροῖς δεινὰ πᾶσιν ἠπείλουν
ὅτι τοὺς νοσοῦντας οὐκ ἐῶσ᾽ ἀποθνήσκειν.   15
ἀνέγραφον δὲ πάντας, ἐν δὲ τοῖς πρώτοις
καὶ σὲ γράφειν ἔμελλον· ἀλλ᾽ ἐγὼ δείσας
εὐθὺς προσῆλθον ἡψάμην τε τῶν σκήπτρων,
κἀπώμασ᾽ αὐτοῖς ὅτι σὺ ταῖς ἀληθείαις
ἰατρὸς οὐκ εἶ καὶ μάτην διεβλήθης.ʼ   20

LXXVI.

Ἱππεὺς τὸν ἵππον ἄχρι μὲν συνειστήκει
ὁ πόλεμος, ἐκρίθιζε, κἄτρεφεν χόρτῳ,
παραστάτην γενναῖον ἐν μάχαις κρίνων·
ἐπεὶ δ᾽ ἐπαύσατ᾽, ἦν δὲ λοιπὸν εἰρήνη
καὶ μισθὸν ἱππεὺς οὐκέτ᾽ εἶχεν ἐκ δήμου,   5
τότ᾽ ἐκεῖνος ἵππος πολλάκις μὲν ἐξ ὕλης ·

---

15. Ex paraphrasi recepit Gitlbauerus : vix recte Athous—
ἐπὶ τῷ θεραπεύειν τοὺς νοσοῦντας ἀνθρώπων.

---

11. This line could in Attic have only one meaning—ʻput the question, "How are the folks below?"ʼ In late Greek we may write it either so, καί ʻ πῶς ἔχουσιν οἱ κάτω ʼ διηρώτα, or, as in the text, take it as equivalent to the Attic ὅπως . . κάτω.
13. There is no reason for preferring πινόντες till it can be proved that the dead could only drink of the waters of Lethé once.
19. The phrase ταῖς ἀληθείαις in place of the classical singular is often met with in late authors. Polybius, 10, 40, 5, βασιλικὸς μὲν ἔφη βούλεσθαι καὶ λέγεσθαι παρὰ πᾶσι καὶ ταῖς ἀληθείαις

ὑπάρχειν. Galenus, v. 393, ταῖς δ᾽ ἀληθείαις οὐδὲν αὐτῶν οὕτω γίγνεται καθάπερ καὶ ὁ θειότατος Ἱπποκράτης εἶπεν· ἡμῖν μὲν αὐτόματον, ἐτεῇ (sic Cobet, αἰτίαι MSS.) δ᾽ οὐκ αὐτόματον. The earliest instance extant is probably one from Philemon—εἰ ταῖς ἀληθείαισιν οἱ τεθνηκότες | αἴσθησιν εἶχον κτε. It is of a piece with the late use of the plural generally. Σνναγ. λέξεων χρησίμων, p. 376, 4, Ἀληθῇ καὶ τὰς ἀληθείας πληθυντικῶς λέγουσι. Μένανδρος Ἀφροδισίῳ·
εἰ τὰς ἀληθείας ἁπλῶς τίς σοι λέγει.
Polyb. 23, 14, 2, πέμψειν ἵνα πύθηται παρὰ τούτου τὰς ἀληθείας ἡ σύγκλητος.

κορμοὺς παχεῖς κατῆγεν εἰς πόλιν βαίνων,
τὸ πνεῦμα σώζων ἐπ' ἀχύροισι δυστήνοις,   9
σάγην δὲ νώτοις ἔφερεν οὐκέθ' ἱππεύων.
ὡς δ' αὖ πρὸ τειχῶν πόλεμος ἄλλος ἠκούσθη,
σάλπιγξ τ' ἐφώνει πᾶσιν ἀσπίδα σμήχειν
ἵππους τε κοσμεῖν καὶ σίδηρον ὀξύνειν,
κἀκεῖνος αὖ τὸν ἵππον ἐγχαλινώσας
ὁ δεσπότης παρῆγεν ὡς ἐφιππεύσων.   15
ὁ δ' ὀκλάσας ἔπιπτεν οὐκέτ' ἰσχύων.
' ἔντασσε πεζοῖς σαυτόν ' εἶπεν ' ὁπλίταις.
σὺ γάρ μ' ἀφ' ἵππων εἰς ὄνους μεταστήσας,
πῶς αὖθις ἵππον ἐξ ὄνου με ποιήσεις;'

LXXVI. 7. Hunc post versum exhibet Athous alium (cujus in Bodleiano non est vestigium) metri Babriani legi certissimae offendentem—

μισθῷ τε φύρτον ἔφερεν ἄλλοτ' ἀλλοῖον.

Eberhardus, paraphrasi Coraesiana male intellecta, φόρτοις ἀλλοίοις legere voluit. 10. Pro Athoo ἵππεινιν cum Gitlbauero ἱππεέων scribere malo quam cum Ahrensio et aliis ἱππείην. 12. Secundum paraphrasem pro ἐκέλευε Athoo ego cum Bergkio ἐφώνει scripsi.

LXXVI. 7. There may be an emphasis on βαίνων, 'at a walking pace,' as opposed to 'at the gallop.' In addition to its metrical fault the rejected line presents μισθῷ instead of μισθοῦ.

9. δύστηνος is often enough used of things in classical Greek to make the conjecture δυστήνως quite unnecessary.

10. The reason for preferring ἱππεύων to ἱππείην is obvious, as the latter would not be in accordance with the facts. In 7, 12, σάγη is used of the harness of a beast of burden; and if ἱππείην were read here, σάγη would have to be restricted to the trappings of a charger. The participle supplies an excellent sense. 'Harness he carried on his back, but a saddle no longer.' ἱππεύειν of a horse is met with in Xen. de re Eq. 1, 6, εἰκάζοις ἂν καὶ ἱππεύοντα τὸν πῶλον ὑγρὰ ἕξειν τὰ σκέλη. 10, 3, ἐάν τις διδάξῃ τὸν ἵππον ἐν χαλαρῷ τῷ χαλίνῳ ἱππεύειν.

12. For σμήχειν see Phryn. p. 321.

14. τὸν ἵππον ἐγχαλινώσας is a

curiously brief expression for τὸ τοῦ ἵππου στόμα ἐγχαλινώσας, i.e. ἐν τῷ τοῦ ἵππου στόματι χάλινον ἐνθείς.

17. ἔντασσε πεζοῖς. In Attic the practice was to repeat the preposition ἐν in cases of this kind. In fact it is just not always done. A good many of the prose exceptions are of a kind which must always be doubtful: Plato, Rep. 610 B, ἀλλοτρίου δὲ κακοῦ ἐν ἄλλῳ γιγνομένου, τοῦ δὲ ἰδίου ἑκάστῳ μὴ ἐγγιγνομένου, where ἐν has probably dropped out before the ἐκ. as 'γ before the γιγνομένου; as also in Phileb. 38 A, ἀγνοίας πολλάκις ἑκάστοις ἡμῶν ἐγγιγνομένης. In Plato, Tim. 29 E, ἀγαθῷ δὲ οὐδεὶς ἐγγίγνεται φθόνος; and in Phaedr. 256 B, δουλωσάμενοι μὲν ᾧ κακία ψυχῆς ἐνεγίγνετο, are we to read ἦν ἐν ἀγαθῷ δέ and μὲν ἐν ᾧ respectively? In Rep. 371 E, perhaps κἂν τίνι is to be read for καὶ τίνι; and in Polit. 273 C, κἂν τοῖς for καὶ τοῖς. At the beginning of a sentence there appears, however, to have been a tendency to omit the ἐν with the dative.

LXXVII.

Κόραξ δεδηχὼς στόματι τυρὸν εἰστήκει·
τυροῦ δ' ἀλώπηξ ἰχανῶσα κερδώη
μύθῳ τὸν ὄρνιν ἠπάτησε τοιούτῳ·
'κόραξ, καλαί σοι πτέρυγες, ὀξέη γλήνη,
θεητὸς αὐχήν· στέρνον αἰετοῦ φαίνεις,   5
ὄνυξι πάντων θηρίων κατισχύεις·
ὁ τοῖος ὄρνις κωφός ἐσσι κοὐ κρώζεις.'
κόραξ δ' ἐπαίνῳ καρδίην ἐχαυνώθη,
στόματος δὲ τυρὸν ἐκβαλὼν ἐκεκράγει.
τὸν ἡ σοφὴ λαβοῦσα κερτόμῳ γλώσσῃ   10
'οὐκ ἦσθ' ἄφωνος' εἶπεν 'ἀλλὰ φωνήεις.
ἔχεις, κόραξ, ἅπαντα, νοῦς δέ σοι λείπει.'

LXXVIII.

Κόραξ νοσήσας εἶπε μητρὶ κλαιούσῃ
'μὴ κλαῖε, μῆτερ, ἀλλὰ τοῖς θεοῖς εὔχου
νόσου με δεινῆς καὶ πόνων ἀνασφῆλαι.'
καὶ 'τίς σε' φησί 'τῶν θεῶν, τέκνον, σώσει;
τίνος γὰρ ὑπὸ σοῦ βωμὸς οὐκ ἐσυλήθη;'   5

LXXVII. 10. Athoum τὸν magis quam Vaticanum ὅν scribere malo, nec non in ultima fabula lectionem Athoam retinui, nam σ' ἐλλείπει quod temere Lachmannus conjecit Vaticano σε λείπει non confirmatur, illo codice omnes vocales et diphthongos inter se semper confundente.

LXXVII. 1. In good Greek δάκνω is confined in the active to the present and aorist, as its future has the inflections of the middle voice. In the passive the aorist and perfect tenses are in frequent use. Even in debased Greek the perfect active is perhaps not found elsewhere; but δεδείχασι appears in Hesychius, the order of words proving that the ει is a mistake of the lexicographer himself. Nauck's conjecture τούτου δ' for τυροῦ δ' in the next line could never have been made by any one conversant with late Greek, or even with Babrius. In Longus, Heliodorus, and others, this repetition of the substantive where in good Greek a pronoun

would be employed is very frequent. I have retained ἰχανῶσα, although palaeographically it differs so little from ἰσχανῶσα, as glosses in Hesychius show that the non-sigmatic form was known long before cursive writing was in use and the confusion possible.
3. μύθῳ.. τοιούτῳ. Even in Attic τοιοῦτος is not seldom met with where τοιόσδε would be more regular.
11. οὐκ ἦσθ' ἄφωνος = οὐκ ἄρ' ἦσθ' ἄφωνος, 'so after all you are not.'
LXXVIII. 3. The word ἀνασφάλλω has already occurred in 75, 8. It is a striking example of a very rare use of the preposition ἀνά in composition with a verb. In a certain sense ἀνασφάλλω

LXXIX.

Κρέας κύων ἔκλεψεν ἐκ μαγειρείου,
καὶ δὴ παρῄει ποταμόν· ἐν δὲ τῷ ῥείθρῳ
πολὺ τοῦ κρέως ἰδοῦσα τὴν σκιὴν μείζω,
τὸ κρέας ἀφῆκε, τῇ σκιῇ δ' ἐφωρμήθη.
ἀλλ' οὔτ' ἐκείνην εὗρεν οὔθ' ὃ βεβλήκει.   5

LXXX.

Κάμηλον ἠνάγκαζε δεσπότης πίνων
ὀρχεῖσθ' ὑπ' αὐλοῖς κυμβάλοις τε χαλκείοις.
ἡ δ' εἶπ' 'ἐμοὶ γένοιτο κἂν ὁδῷ βαίνειν
μὴ καταγέλαστον, μήτι πυρρίχην παίζειν.'

LXXIX. 5. Versum sextum in inferiorem locum descendere jussi,
utpote aliis male congruentem—

   πεινῶσα δ' ὀπίσω τὸν πόρον διεξῄει.

Nulla in paraphrasi apparet. Accedit epimythium hoc—

   βίος ἀβέβαιος παντὸς ἀνδρὸς ἀπλήστου
   ἐλπίσι ματαίαις πραγμάτων ἀναλοῦται.

LXXX. Utrum a tetrastichista brevior facta sit an non, valde incertum. 3. A verbis ἐμοὶ γένοιτο ad finem habet Suidas sub πυρρίχῃ
vocabulo. Versum quartum multo deteriorem exhibet Athous—

   ἄνευ γέλωτος μήτι κἂν χορῷ παίζειν.

Pro μήτι codices aliquot in Suida μήτε praebent.

---

stands alone, as it implies an intransitive signification to σφάλλω. (Here
a transitive sense *might* be given to it,
but not in 75, 8, or in other writers.)
In classical Greek the nearest approach
to it is ἀνακαλύπτω, 'uncover,' Lat.
'detego,' although ἀναδιδάσκω, 'de-
doceo,' is also very near it. In other
words, the action of the verb is reversed
by compounding it with ἀνά ; καλύπτειν,
'to furnish with a covering;' ἀνακαλύπ-
τειν, 'to deprive of a covering;' [σφάλ-
λειν, 'to be cursed with failing health ;']
ἀνασφάλλειν, 'to be blest with returning
health.' In any case the word is
extraordinary, and is happily found
only in later authors, especially the

latest. Synesius, ἐὰν ἀνασφήλω, ἐπὶ
τὴν Ἀλεξάνδρειαν εὐθὺς ἵεμαι. Clemens
Alexandr. Paed. p. 146, καλὸν δὲ καὶ
τὸ ἀνασφῆλαι τῆς νόσου. By itself it
would damn the Axiochus, pseudo-
Plato, Axioch. 364 C, καὶ γὰρ ἤδη πολλάκις αὐτῷ γέγονε συμπτώματος ἀνασφῆλαι. Younger students must be
careful not to confuse with this class of
compounds verbs like ἀνομοιῶ, which
are quite regularly formed ; ἀνόμοιος,
'unlike ;' ἀνομοιοῦν, 'to make unlike.'
LXXIX. 2. παρῄει ποταμόν, 'was
passing along a river's bank.' The
spurious sixth line was added by some
one who preferred the other version, in
which the dog was crossing a bridge.

LXXXI.

Κερδοῖ πίθηκος εἶπεν ' ἢν ὁρᾷς στήλην,
ἐμοὶ πατρῴη τ' ἐστὶ κάτι παππῴη.'
κερδὼ πιθήκῳ φησίν· ὡς θέλεις ψεύδου,
ἔλεγχον οὐκ ἔχουσα τῆς ἀληθείης.'

LXXXII.

Κοιμωμένου λέοντος ἀγρίης χαίτης
διέδραμεν μῦς· ὁ δὲ λέων ἐθυμώθη,
φρίξας δὲ χαίτην ἔθορε φωλάδος κοίτης.
κερδὼ δ' ἐπεχλεύαζεν, ὡς ἐκινήθη
πρὸς μῦν ὁ πάντων θηρίων τυραννεύων.   5

LXXXI. Versum unum et alterum habet Suidas sub πίθηκος vocabulo.
Hemistichia primi et tertii versus male transposuerunt Suidae codices et
Athous, verbis κερδὼ πιθήκῳ φησίν fabulae initio locatis cum in versu
tertio κερδοῖ πίθηκος εἶπεν exhibet Athous. A tetrastichista pravata est
fabula, neque e peritiore profectum est epimythium—

κακοῦ πρὸς ἀνδρός ἐστι μὴ φεύγειν ψεῦδος,
κἂν λανθάνειν ψευδόμενος εὐχερῶς μέλλῃ.

ubi λανθάνηι in Athoo videre licet.

LXXXII. Primos tres versus habet Suidas sub φριξότριχα vocabulo,
tertium quoque sub ἔκθορε et φωλάδι. Pro ἔθορε ter ἔκθορε dant Suidae
codices, quamvis unus liber plane contra Suidae animum ἔθορε semel
prae se ferat. Hoc esse potest documento quantillum de metro Babriano
intellexerit Suidas. Idem κοίλης pro κοίτης male scripsit, lectione sub
φωλάδι per interpretationem confirmata. 5. Lachmanni conjecturam in
textum recepi, verbis θηρίων τυραννεύων pro βασιλεῖων θηρίων lectis.

What sense can be got out of it in any
way? If ὀπίσω is to be translated by
'thereafter,' the use is questionable; if
by 'back,' the behaviour of the dog is
unaccountable, and the words τὸν πόρον
διεξήει unintelligible. With the former
sense of ὀπίσω they may just mean
'went through with' or 'completed
the crossing.'
LXXXII. 3. Suidas is wrong in
giving φωλάς as a substantive. He
quotes no passage but this, and the
reading of the copy he used was corrupt. Nonnus, Dionys. 1, 63, φωλάδα

πέτρην ; 2, 142, φωλάδες ὕδραι ; 242,
φωλάδες εὐναί ; 6, 270, φωλάδος ἄκρης.
This method of forming feminine adjectives occurs very rarely in classical
Greek (ἱππάς = ἱππική, λαμπάς = λαμ-
πρά, and a few others in addition to
race names like Ἰάς, Λακωνίς, etc.), but
is of extraordinary frequency in later
authors, e.g. ῥωγὰς πήρη λυσσάδες
ἄρκτοι, πενθάδι φωνῇ, ὀρεστιὰς φήμη,
ἐρημάδος Ἰοχεαίρης, ἠθάδος ἄγρης, κοιλάδι
γαίῃ, κοιλάδι κίστῃ, φοιτὰς Ἀγαίῃ, διψάδα
νύμφην, λευκάδα χαίτην, θυιάδι φωνῇ,
μυστίδι τέχνῃ, etc. etc.

ὁ δ' ' οὐχὶ τὸν μῦν' εἶπεν, ' ὦ παλαμναίη,
δέδοικα μή μου τὴν δορὴν κνίσῃ φεύγων.
χαίτην δ' ἔμελλε τὴν ἐμὴν καταισχύνειν.'

LXXXIII.

Κριθάς τις ἵππου πᾶσαν ἑσπέρην πίνων
ἔτριβεν, ἐκτένιζεν ἡμέρῃ πάσῃ.
ὁ δ' εἶπεν ' εἰ θέλεις με ταῖς ἀληθείαις
καλὸν γενέσθαι, τὸ τρέφον με μὴ πώλει.

6. Ultimos tres versus Suidas servavit sub παλαμναῖος vocabulo.
7. Athoam lectionem κνίσῃ sequi malo quam δάκῃ aut δάκοι Suidianam.
8. Tibi habe Athoum! κακὴν δὲ μελέτην ἐπ' ἐμὲ τῆς ὁδοῦ τρίβει, corruptionem ante paraphrases Bodleianam et Coraesianam ortam. Epimythium hoc—

ἀρχόμενον ἄρτι τὸ θρασὺ τῶν ὑβριζόντων,
κᾶν μικρὸν ᾖ κώλυε μηδὲ συγχώρει
εὐκαταφρόνητον σαυτὸν εἶναι τοῖς φαύλοις.

LXXXIII. Fabulae Babrianae pauca modo vestigia supersunt. Codicem Athoum secutus sum nisi quod in primo versu ἑσπέρην pro ἡμέρην ex Vaticano duxi, et in secundo ἡμέρῃ pro ἡμέρῃ scripsi. Ex paraphrasi Bodleianâ Gitlbauerus Babrii verba restituere conatus, tetrastichistam fortasse revocavit, aut tetrastichistarum unum—

κριθάς τις ἱπποκόμος ἔκλεπτε κἀπώλει,
τὸν δ' ἵππον ἐκτένιζεν ἡμέρην πᾶσαν.
ὁ δ' εἶπεν κτλ.,

sed ipsius Babrii leges metricas violavit. Ut epimythium pedestre, addit Athous choliamborum tentamina haec—

τῶν καιρίων δεῖ τὸν φιλοῦντα φροντίζειν
καὶ συμφερόντων· κόσμος γὰρ οὐδὲν ὠνήσει (sic)
. . . τὸν ἀποροῦντα τῶν ἀναγκαίων.

quae vix memorari merentur.

8. 'Luculentum exemplum licentiae, quam sibi in locis hiulcis aut corruptis sumebant Graeculi, mihi nuper oblatum est in fabula Babriana, quae recens ex Athoo codice prodiit . . . Poeta ipse scripserat in fabula 82, vs. 8—

χαίτην δ' ἔμελλε τὴν ἐμὴν καταισχύνειν.

Monachus aliquis iu vetusto libro longo

usu aut situ detrito reperit ΧΑΙΤΗΝ-ΔΕΜΕΛΛΕΤΗΝ . . . reliqua oculorum aciem fallebant. Itaque inde pulcherrimum choliambum eruit et supplevit hunc—

κακὴν δὲ μελέτην ἐπ' ἐμὲ τῆς ὁδοῦ τρίβει.

Quid interpretibus futurum fuisset, ni vera lectio apud Suidam servata exstitisset?'—Cobet.

LXXXIV.

Κώνωψ ἐπιστὰς κέρατι καμπύλῳ ταύρου
μικρόν τ᾽ ἐπισχὼν εἶπε ταῦτα βομβήσας·
‘εἴ σου βαρύνω τὸν τένοντα καὶ κλίνω,
καθεδοῦμ᾽ ἀπελθὼν ποταμίης ἐπ᾽ αἰγείρου.’
ὁ δ᾽ ‘οὐ μέλει μοι’ φησίν ‘οὔτ᾽ ἐὰν μείνῃς   5
οὔτ᾽ ἢν ἀπέλθῃς· οὐδ᾽ ὅτ᾽ ἦλθες ἐγνώκειν.’

LXXXV.

Κυσίν ποτ᾽ ἔχθρη καὶ λύκοις συνειστήκει.
κύων δ᾽ Ἀχαιὸς ᾑρέθη κυνῶν δήμου
στρατηγὸς εἶναι. καὶ μάχης ἐπιστήμων
ἔμελλεν, ἐβράδυνεν· οἱ δ᾽ ἐπηπείλουν.   4
‘ἀκούσατ᾽’ εἶπεν ‘οὗ χάριν διατρίβω,   6
τί δ᾽ εὐλαβοῦμαι· χρὴ δ᾽ ἀεὶ προβουλεύειν.
τῶν μὲν πολεμίων τὸ γένος ὂν ὁρῶ πάντων
ἕν ἐστιν· ἡμῶν δ᾽ ἦλθον οἱ μὲν ἐκ Κρήτης,
οἱ δ᾽ ἐκ Μολοσσῶν εἰσίν, οἱ δ᾽ Ἀκαρνάνων,   10
ἄλλοι δὲ Δόλοπες, οἱ δὲ Κύπρον ἢ Θρᾴκην
αὐχοῦσιν, ἄλλοι δ᾽ ἄλλοθεν. τί μηκύνω;
τὸ χρῶμα δ᾽ ἡμῖν οὐχ ἕν ἐστιν ὡς τούτοις,

LXXXIV. 3. Alio in loco de κλίνω disserui. Vide ea quae de
codicibus Babrianis scripsi. 6. Tyrwhitto praeeunte, οὐδ᾽ ὅτε pro οὔθ᾽
ὅτε dedi. Plus solito claudicat epimythium, et typis committere me
pudet—

γελοῖος ὅστις οὐδὲν ὢν κατ᾽ ἀνθρώπων
τῶν κρειττόνων θρασύνεται ὥς τις ὤν.

Addit manus recens σφόδρα ut versus exeat.

LXXXV. 4. Post hunc versum fidenter omisi alium de quo paraphrastae Bodleiani et Coraesiani silent. Eundem utpote intellectu carentem
Duebnerus primus culpavit—

εἰ μὴ προάξῃ τὴν μάχην τ᾽ ἐνεδρεύσει.

Critici alii aliter emendare frustra conati sunt.

LXXXV. 12. ‘And others pride themselves in Cyprus or in Thrace.’ This
construction of αὐχῶ is unknown to classical Greek, but not rare in baser styles.

ἀλλ' οἱ μὲν ἡμῶν μέλανες, οἱ δὲ τεφρώδεις,
ἔνιοι δὲ λαμπροὶ καὶ διάργεμοι στήθη,   15
ἄλλοι δὲ λευκοί. πῶς ἂν οὖν δυνηθείην
εἰς πόλεμον ἄρχειν᾽ εἶπε ʽ τῶν ἀσυμφώνων
πρὸς τοὺς ὅμοια πάντ᾽ ἔχοντας ἀλλήλοις;᾽

LXXXVI.

Κοίλωμα ῥίζης φηγὸς εἶχεν ἀρχαίη·
ἐν τῇ δ᾽ ἔκειτο ῥωγὰς αἰπόλου πήρη,
ἄρτων ἑώλων πᾶσα καὶ κρεῶν πλήρης.
ταύτην ἀλώπηξ εἰσδραμοῦσα τὴν πήρην
ἐξέφαγε· γαστὴρ δ᾽, ὥσπερ εἰκός, ὠγκώθη,   5
στενῆς δὲ τρώγλης οὐκέτ᾽ εἶχεν ἐκδῦναι.
ἑτέρη δ᾽ ἀλώπηξ ὡς ἐπῆλθε κλαιούσῃ,
σκώπτουσα ʽ μεῖνον᾽ εἶπεν ʽ ἄχρι πεινήσῃς.᾽

---

15. Athoum λαμπροὶ retinui. Misere Suidas ἕτεροι ξανθοὶ exhibet.
Addit Athous epimythium pro hac vice in uncialibus literis scriptum—

συμφωνία μέγιστον ἀγαθὸν ἀνθρώποις
τὸ δὲ στασίαζον ἀσθενές τε καὶ δοῦλον.

LXXXVI. 8. Post hunc versum duo alios a Babrio certe abjudicandos
Athous exhibet—

οὐδ᾽ ἐξελεύσῃ πρότερον ἄχρι τοιαύτην
τὴν γαστέρα σχῇς, ἡλίκην ὅτ᾽ εἰσῄεις.   10

---

15. The word διάργεμος is only met with in this passage. It is here explained by Suidas as meaning πῇ μὲν λευκοί, πῇ δὲ μέλανες. The simple ἄργεμος is not found at all as an adjective; but if Babrius could use διάργεμος for shot with white, he might have used ἄργεμος for white. The preposition has the same force in διάλευκος, διέρυθρος, διαπόρφυρος, διάχλωρος, and apparently even διαποίκιλος in Arist. Hist. Anim. 4, 1, 525, a12, τὰ γὰρ πρανῆ τοῦ κύτους πάντα μελάντερα τῶν ὑπτίων τραχύτερά τε ἔχει ὁ ἄρρην τῆς θηλείας καὶ διαποίκιλα ῥάβδοις.
LXXXVI. 10. The form εἰσῄεις is late, its Attic equivalent being εἰσῄησθα. In the New Phrynichus (p. 227) I had not yet determined altogether to deny

the form ᾔεισθα as second person singular of ᾖα in Attic. Further consideration, however, has led me to conclude that the genuine Attic form was ᾖσθα only, and that ᾔεις and ᾔεισθα are as corrupt as ᾔδης or ᾔδεις for ᾔδησ'α, ᾖς for ᾖσθα, ἔφης for ἔφησθα, οἶδας for οἶσθα. Unfortunately the second person singular, either of simple or compound, occurs nowhere in Attic verse. Athenaeus indeed quotes from Antiphanes the line—

φαινίνδα παίζων ᾔεις ἐν Φαινεστίου,

but ᾔεις will not scan, and gives no sense. Perhaps we should re-write—

φαινίνδα παίζων ἦν ἐγὼ 'ν Φαινεστίου,

but its emendation is of little conse-

G

LXXXVII.

Κύων λαγωὸν ἐξ ὄρους ἀναστήσας
ἐδίωκε, δάκνων αὐτὸν εἰ κατειλήφει,

LXXXVII. Fabulam ex Athoo dedi. Fortasse a Babrio longior primo evasit. Ea quae critici proposuerunt valde incerta. Tertio in versu

quence. As metrical evidence thus breaks down, and as I have naturally searched for the word in vain in inscriptions, we are thrown back on more general evidence. The imperfect tense of εἰμί has throughout suffered so sadly from the hand of ignorance and time, that its primitive forms have been almost superseded by the debased coinage of decaying Greek. The only genuine Attic forms were, to my belief, ἦα, ἦσθα, ἦει(ν), ἦτον, ἦτην, ἦμεν, ἦτε, ἦσαν ; but the manuscripts present ἦειν, ἦεις, ἦεισθα, ἦειμεν, ἦειτε, etc. Some accept both forms as genuine, and make ἦα a perfect, and ἦειν a pluperfect—a theory which is refuted by being stated. As far as verse goes, its authority tends to establish the shorter forms in all cases, and beneath the corruptions of transcribers a glimpse of the true reading may be sometimes caught. The Attic ἦα is simply the ἦια of the Homeric poems—

καὶ τότε δὴ παρὰ θῖνα θαλάσσης εὐρυπόροιο
ἦια, πολλὰ θεοὺς γουνούμενος κτε.

There are no instances of a first person ἦειν in Attic verse ; but ἦα is found in a line of Aristophanes used by Photius to establish the genuine form, and it also occurs uncorrupted in several passages of Plato (Apol. 21 D, 36 C; Charm. 153 A ; Theaet. 180 C ; Rep. 449 A). In fact ἦειν does not occur in Plato at all, and the oldest and best manuscripts confirm the shorter forms in the dual and plural—ἦτην, Euthyd. 294 D ; ἦμεν, Alc. i. 124 E ; εἰσῆμεν, Phaed. 59 D ; ἀπῆμεν, Rep. 327 B ; Prot. 362 A ; περιῆμεν, Prot. 311 A ; προσῆμεν, Prot. 516 B. The paragraph of Photius bears every mark of being an excerpt from one of the earlier and better grammarians. ἦα· δισυλλάβως τὸ ἐπορευόμην σὺν τῷ ι γράφεται· οἱ γοῦν Ἴωνες ἦια λέγουσι· καὶ ἦσαν τὸ ἦσαν· καὶ παρὰ Θουκυδίδη οὕτως ἀναγνωστέον· ὅτι ἀκμάζοντές τε ἦσαν ἐς αὐτόν·

ol δὲ Ἴωνες ἦισαν (ἦεσαν καὶ ἦισαν, codd. emend. Cobetus). Ἀριστοφάνης Ὁλκά-σιν—

ἐπεὶ δ' ἐγενόμην οἷπερ ἦ' ἐπὶ ξύλα.

In addition to the mere manuscript authority for the dual and plural forms given above, there are the following lines in which the dissyllabic forms are required by metre. Arist. Eq. 605, ταῖς ὁπλαῖς ὤρυττον εὐνὰς καὶ μετῆσαν στρώματα. Plut. 659, ἔπειτα πρὸς τὸ τέμενος ἦμεν τοῦ θεοῦ. Moreover, the Etymologicum Magnum, in remarking upon these forms, quotes from the Gerutidés of Aristophanes ἦσαν εὐθὺ τοῦ Διονύσου· and in another place εἰσῆμεν from the Prisoners of Callias, and εἰσῆσαν from the Acropé of Agathon. So also ἐπῆμεν occurs in a fragment of the Oedipus of Aeschylus, preserved by a scholiast on Sophocles, O. R. 733. The lines are these—

ἐπῆμεν τῆς ὁδοῦ τροχήλατον
σχιστῆς κελεύθου τρίοδον ἔνθα συμβολὰς
τριῶν κελεύθων Ποτνιάδων ἠμείβομεν·

but the manuscripts exhibit only ἐπείημεν, just as some codices read μετῆσαν in the line from the Knights, and a good codex omits the iota from the ἦμεν in the Plutus, the gloss ὑπήρχομεν being added to show that it was not merely a slip. In fact the dissyllabic forms were unintelligible to late Greeks, as is demonstrated by the frequency of explanatory glosses like ἐπορευόμεθα, ἐπορεύοντο. The evidence of the grammarian in Photius with regard to ἀκμάζοντές τε ἦσαν in the first chapter of Thucydides is not to be lightly passed over, and ἦσαν has an excellent case in its favour. These genuine imperfect forms of ἰέναι were frequently replaced by those of εἶναι, and this fact is by itself the best of evidence for the shorter forms. The verb παρέρχομαι is used of a speaker passing up the floor of a place of assembly to the ordinary

BABRIUS. 83

μεταστραφεὶς τ' ἔσαινεν ὡς φίλῳ ψαύων.
χὼ λαγωός ‘ ἁπλοῦν ' εἶπε ' θηρίον γίνου:
φίλος εἶ; τί δάκνεις; ἐχθρὸς εἶ; τί οὖν σαίνεις; '   5

LXXXVIII.

Κορυδαλλὸς ἦν τις ἐν χλόῃ νεοσσεύων,
καὶ παῖδας εἶχε ληίου κόμῃ θρέψας,   3
λοφῶντας ἤδη καὶ πτεροῖσιν ἀκμαίους.

diorthotes μεταστραφεὶς τ' in μεταστραφεὶς δ' mutavit, Eberhardus in εἶτ' αὖ στραφεὶς. Stultior epimythiasta—

ἀμφίβολος οὗτός ἐστι νοῦς ἐν ἀνθρώποις
οἷς οὔτ' ἀπιστεῖν ἔχομεν οὔτε πιστεύειν.

LXXXVIII. Fixio praeeunte, de versu valde dubito qui in Athoo sequitur—

ὁ τῷ χαραδριῷ πρὸς ὄρθρον ἀντᾴδων,

Exhibet codex ὃς τὸ χαραδραίῳ, et non minus delirat Vaticanus, ὃς κορυδαλλῷ hic lecto ut in priore χαραδρεὺς.

spot of vantage, and is of frequent occurrence in the orators. As its present was παρέρχομαι and its aorist παρῆλθον, so its future was πάρειμι and its imperfect παρῆα. But in Dem. 11, 10, παρῆσαν occurs without a variant for παρῆσαν. εἰ γάρ, ὅθ' ἥκομεν Εὐβοεῦσι βεβοηθηκότες καὶ παρῆσαν Ἀμφιπολιτῶν Ἱέραξ καὶ Στρατοκλῆς ἐπὶ τουτὶ τὸ βῆμα κτε. In Xenophon, Hell. 2, 1, 18, Λύσανδρος ἐξ Ἀβύδου παρέπλει καὶ ἄλλοι παρῆσαν πεζῇ, all manuscripts give the corrupt παρῆσαν. The converse corruption is also met with, as in Thuc. 4, 39, περὶ εἴκοσιν ἡμέρας ἐν αἷς οἱ πρέσβεις περὶ τῶν σπονδῶν ἀπῆσαν κτε. Id. 42, ἐν Λευκαδίᾳ ἀπῆσαν αὐτῶν πεντακόσιοι φρουροί, in both of which passages the codices present the unmeaning ἀπῆσαν. As to the second person, ᾔεισθα occurs twice in Plato—διῄεισθα in Tim. 26 C, and ἐπεξῄεισθα in Euthyphro, 4 B; and in the Orators διεξῄεις is presented by the manuscripts in Dem. 232, 22, and περιῄεις in Aesch. 77, 11. In all cases I believe that ᾖσθα ought to be restored. The second person is the only part in which we are left wholly dependent upon manuscript authority, —are we to accept it in this case when it

has been proved untrustworthy in the others? In the third person even the Ravenna gives the ridiculous προσῄει γ' for the genuine προσῄειν in Arist. Plut. 696 A, ὁ δὲ θεὸς ὑμῖν οὐ προσῄειν ; B, οὐδέπω; and in Plato the nu has dropped out of all passages but one or two, as—ᾔειν, ἑπτά, Tim. 38 C; and ᾔειν ἐν κύκλῳ τεῖχος, Critias, 117 E.

LXXXVII. 2. A classical writer would have used εἰ καταλάβοι for εἰ καταειλήφει.

3. The dative after ψαύω is quite possible in a late writer, for even if the dative is to be explained otherwise in Homer, ll. 13, 132, and 15, 216, yet Quintus Smyrnaeus (8, 349) has it where there can be no doubt—ἄνω δ' ἔψανε νέφεσσι | θεσπεσίη τριφάλεια ; and if Quintus could misunderstand Homer, so could Babrius. Moreover, the dative in Pindar, Pyth. 9, 213, is almost certain ; and there is no doubt at all about the Pindaric construction of θιγγάνω with a dative. If recourse is had to conjecture, φίλος is worth suggesting as preferable to Sauppe's φίλου.

LXXXVIII. 4. Although λοφᾶν occurs in classical Greek only in a comic sense (Arist. Pax, 1211), there

ὁ δὲ τῆς ἀρούρης δεσπότης ἐποπτεύων   5
ὡς ξηρὸν εἶδε τὸ θέρος, εἶπε ' νῦν ὥρη
πάντας καλεῖν μοι τοὺς φίλους ἵν' ἀμήσω.'
καί τις δὲ κορυδοῦ τῶν λοφηφόρων παίδων
ἤκουσεν αὐτοῦ τῷ τε πατρὶ μηνύει,
σκοπεῖν κελεύων ποῦ σφέας μεταστήσει.   10
ὁ δ' εἶπεν ' οὔπω καιρός ἐστιν ἀλλύειν
ὃς γὰρ φίλοις πέποιθεν οὐκ ἄγαν σπεύδει.'
ὡς δ' αὖτις ἦλθεν, ἡλίου δ' ὑπ' ἀκτίνων
ἤδη ῥέοντα τὸν στάχυν θεωρήσας
μισθὸν μὲν ἀμητῆρσιν αὔριον δώσειν,   15
μισθὸν δέ φησι δραγματηφόροις δώσειν,
κορυδαλλὸς εἶπε παισὶ νηπίοις ' ὥρη
νῦν ἐστὶν ὄντως, παῖδες, ἀλλαχοῦ φεύγειν
ὅτ' αὐτὸς αὐτῷ κοὐ φίλοισι πιστεύει.'

---

6. Pro vera lectione ὡς ξηρὸν, quam Athous habet, Vaticanus codex
ἀνθηρὸν praebet, signo tachygraphico pro ὡς male intellecto vel lecto.
8. Vocula δὲ Eberhardo debetur. Errat Athous, κοροιδοῦ scripto ut
versus evadat. 11. De hoc versu infra Anglice disputabo. Pro Athoo
ἐστι νῦν φεύγειν ego ἐστιν ἀλλύειν lubenter dedi. Suidae verba ἐστιν
ἥια λύειν quamvis ipsa corrupta certe lectionem Babrianam servaverunt,
quo modo infra Anglice monstrabo. 16. Versus deest Athoo, et in
Vaticano πᾶσι pro Fixii φησι apparet. Praeterea Eberhardi conjecturam
κορυδαλλὸς εἶπε magis quam Athoum εἶπε κορυδαλλὸς aut Vaticanum
εἶπε κορυδός dedi. Prorsus displicent versus neque multum prodest
quod πέμπειν pro priore δώσειν obtrudat Vaticanus. 17. Lachmannum
sequor verbis ὥρη et ὄντως inter se mutatis, cum praesertim ὄντως post
ἐστὶν posuerit Suidas sub ἀμᾶν vocabulo. 18. Codicum ἀλλαχοῦ Suidiano
ἐκ τόπων anteponere malo ; nec non αὐτῷ pro Suidae ἀμᾷ scripsi.

---

is nothing in the form of the word to
make the Babrian use incorrect. Λοφᾶν,
in the signification ' grow a crest,' is as
natural as γενειᾶν, κομᾶν, λιπᾶν, ὀργᾶν,
and others.

9. The aorist ἤκουσεν is necessary,
and is read by both codices, the imperfect of the editors being a mistake.
The imperfect could not mean ' caught
what he said,' ' overheard him.'

11. Zonaras and Suidas, both plainly
citing from the same source, give under
ἤτων the words οὔπω δὲ καιρός ἐστιν ἥια
λύειν as a line of Babrius. Toup
corrected the metrical fault by reading
ἥι' ἀλλύειν, and J. G. Schneider referred

the citation to this fable. For myself
I believe that Babrius wrote as I have
edited, and that ἥια λύειν and νῦν φεύγειν
are both corruptions. In any case ἥια
λύειν will not do, ἥι' ἀλλύειν hardly
betters it, and οὔπω νῦν is at best incorrect, and not supported by the
Vatican, which has τοῦ φεύγειν. With
the meaning ' go away,' ἀναλύειν is not
rare in late authors—Polyb. 2, 32, 3,
ἀνέλυσαν ἐκ τῶν τόπων ; 3, 69, 14, οἱ
'Ρωμαῖοι βραχὺν ἐπισχόντες χρόνον ἀνέλυσαν, et id. freq. Appian. B. C. 4, 18,
ἀναλύοντα δὲ ἐκ μέθης στρατιῶται προσ-
κρούσαντές τι ἔκτειναν. A case in
which Suidas and Zonaras are both

LXXXIX.

Λύκος ποτ' ἄρνα πεπλανημένον ποίμνης
ἰδὼν βίῃ μὲν οὐκ ἐπῆλθεν ἁρπάξων,
ἔγκλημα δ' ἔχθρης εὐπρόσωπον ἐζήτει.
' σύ τοί με πέρυσι μικρὸς ὢν ἐβλασφήμεις.'
' ἐγὼ οὐ περυσινός· οὐκ ἐπ' ἔτος ἐγεννήθην.'   5
' οὔκουν σὺ τὴν ἄρουραν ἣν ἔχω κείρεις;'
' οὔπω τι χλωρὸν ἔφαγον οὐδ' ἐβοσκήθην.'
' οὐδ' ἄρα πηγὴν ἐκπέπωκας ἣν πίνω;'
' θηλὴ μεθύσκει μέχρι νῦν με μητρῴη.'
τότε δὴ τὸν ἄρνα συλλαβών τε καὶ τρώγων   10
' ἀλλ' οὐκ ἄδειπνον ' εἶπε ' τὸν λύκον θήσεις,
κἂν εὐχερῶς μου πᾶσαν αἰτίην λύσῃς.'

XC.

Λέων ἐλύσσα. τὸν δὲ νεβρὸς ἐξ ὕλης
ἰδὼν ἔφησεν ' ἡμέων ταλαιπώρων·
τί γὰρ μεμηνὼς οὗτος οὐχὶ ποιήσει,
ὃς ἦν φορητὸς οὐδὲ σωφρονῶν ἥμιν;'

LXXXIX. 5. Post περυσινός ego inserui οὐκ ita ut ἐπ' ἔτος aliquid sensus capiat, et versus numerosus sit.
XC. Fabellam decurtavit tetrastichista.

found tripping in the same way has already been observed in the note to Fab. 25. 5, supra.
LXXXIX. 5. The former οὐ may have led to the omission of the second; but whatever the loss was due to, the insertion of οὐκ restores the hand of Babrius. The ludicrous πέρυσιν ὅς γ' ἐπ' ἔτος has been proposed by more than one critic, but the lexicon will show how rarely Babrius employed the particle γε. The prevalence of this word and of prepositions in the choliambics (let the term have a connotation as well as a denotation), which Gitlbauer has the temerity to father upon Babrius, is in itself sufficient to prove that his attempt to restore the prose fables to their original metrical form has been abortive. Later authors use γε very rarely,—so rarely, indeed, that one is led to believe that they recognised their inability to employ it correctly. Greek scholars might take a lesson from the Graeculi.

7. Of the two aorists ἐβοσκήθην and ἐβοσκησάμην the former is the more correct, as βόσκομαι is passive, not middle. No classical writer could have said βοσκήσασθαι. If βοσκηθῆναι does not occur, it might have. Here, of course, it is tautological with ἔφαγον.

9. θηλὴ μεθύσκει. Μεθύει ὁ Βάβριος τῷ μεθύσκειν οὕτω χρώμενος. Νήφων δ' οἶνος.

XCI.

Λέοντα φεύγων ταῦρος εἰς ἐρημαίην
σπήλυγγα κατέδυ ποιμένων ὀρειφοίτων,
ὅπου τράγος τις χωρὶς αἰπόλου μείνας
τὸν ταῦρον ἄντα τοῖς κέρασιν ἐξώθει.
ὁ δ᾽ εἶπεν ‘οὐ σέ, τὸν λέοντα δ᾽ ἐκκλίνω.   5
ἀνέξομαί σου μικρὰ τῆς ἐπηρείης·
ἐπεὶ παρελθέτω με, καὶ τότε γνώσῃ
πόσον τράγου μεταξὺ καὶ πόσον ταύρου.᾽

XCII.

Λέοντά τις κυνηγὸς οὐχὶ τολμήεις
ἴχνευεν ὀρέων ἐν βαθυσκίοις ὕλαις·

XCI. 4. Ego ἄντα scripsi pro Athoo ἐμβάντα, quod participium finxit scriba tum Graecitatis tum numerorum ignarus. Quid ἐμβὰς sibi velit, editores quibus placet forte sciunt ; ego nescio. 5. Athous ἐξωθῶ in textu prae se fert, sed ἐκκλίνω in margine. Nota est haec scribarum consuetudo per quam lituras vitabant.

XCI. 4. The absence of the augment in ἐξώθει is a mark of un-Attic Greek. In Attic verse there is no instance of the unaugmented forms, the two so given by Veitch being really presents —one from a fragment of the *Tereus* of Sophocles, preserved in Stobaeus, Flor. 68, 19, the other from the *Iphigenia in Tauris* of Euripides. In the former a woman finds fault with good fortune—

ὅταν δ᾽ ἐς ἥβην ἐξικώμεθ᾽ ἔμφρονες,
ὠθούμεθ᾽ ἔξω καὶ διεμπολώμεθα,
θεῶν πατρῴων τῶν τε φυσάντων ἄπο,
αἱ μὲν ξένους πρὸς ἄνδρας, αἱ δὲ βαρβάρους,
αἱ δ᾽ εἰς ἀληθῆ δώμαθ᾽, αἱ δ᾽ ἐπίρροθα.
καὶ ταῦτ᾽ ἐπειδὰν εὐφρόνη ζεύξῃ μία
χρεὼν ἐπαινεῖν καὶ δοκεῖν καλῶς ἔχειν.

In these lines ὠθούμεθα is as little past as the discontent which they depict. The passage of Euripides is a fine instance of his manner of combining the historic present with aorists and imperfects—

οἱ δὲ στεναγμὸν ἡδὺν ἐκβρυχώμενοι
ἔπαισαν ἅλμην· ναῦς δ᾽ ἕως μὲν ἐντὸς ἦν
λιμένος ἐχώρει, στόμα διαπερῶσα δὲ
λάβρῳ κλύδωνι συμπεσοῦσ᾽ ἠπείγετο.
δεινὸς γὰρ ἐλθὼν ἄνεμος ἐξαίφνης νεὼς
ὤθει πάλιν πρυμνῇσι᾽· οἱ δ᾽ ἐκαρτέρουν,
κτε.

It is a trick of style which, to their misfortune, critics have often failed to mark. In Plato, Charm. 155 C, ἐώθει must replace ὤθει, and in Thuc. 2, 84, διωθοῦντο must give way to διεωθοῦντο. 6. For the construction of μικρά see note on Fab. 75, 6, *supra*. 8. Although not actually corresponding to Latin idiom, the un-Greek construction of this line is probably due to Latin influence. Cic. Laelius, 25, 95, ‘Contio . . judicare solet, quid intersit inter popularem civem et inter constantem et severum et gravem.’ Id. de Fin. 1, 9, 30, ‘interesse enim inter argumentum conclusionemque rationis et inter mediocrem animadversionem atque admonitionem.’ Hor. Sat.

δρυτόμῳ δὲ μακρῆς ἐγγὺς ἐντυχὼν πεύκης
'ὦ πρός σε νυμφῶν' εἶπεν 'ἆρα γινώσκεις
ἴχνη λέοντος ὅστις ὧδε φωλεύει;' 5
κἀκεῖνος εἶπεν 'ἀλλὰ σὺν θεῷ βαίνεις·
αὐτὸν γὰρ ἤδη τὸν λέοντά σοι δείξω.'
ὁ δ' ὠχριήσας γομφίους τε συγκρούων
'μή μοι χαρίζου' φησί 'πλεῖον οὐ χρήζω,
τὸ δ' ἴχνος εἰπέ· τὸν λέοντα μὴ δείξῃς.' 10

XCIII.

Λύκων παρῆσαν ἄγγελοί ποτ' εἰς ποίμνην
ὅρκους φέροντες καὶ βέβαιον εἰρήνην
ἐφ' ᾧ λάβωσι τοὺς κύνας πρὸς αἰκίην.
δι' οὓς μάχονται καὶ κοτοῦσιν ἀλλήλοις.
μωρὴ δὲ ποίμνη καὶ τὰ πάντα βληχώδης 5
πέμπειν ἔμελλεν. ἀλλά τις γέρων ἤδη
κριὸς βαθείῃ φρικὶ μαλλὸν ὀρθώσας
'καινῆς γε ταύτης' εἶπε 'τῆς μεσιτείης.
ἀφύλακτος ὑμῖν πῶς ἐγὼ συνοικήσω,
δι' οὓς νέμεσθαι μηδὲ νῦν ἀκινδύνως 10
ἔξεστι, καίτοι τῶν κυνῶν με τηρούντων.'

XCII. 8. συγκροῦσας quod male habet Suidas ex aoristo praecedente
ortum est.
XCIII. 5. Pro πάντα βληχώδης, quod Suidas profert, Athous habet
πανταβληχρώδης seriore manu in πάντ' ἀβληχρώδης mutatum.

1, 7, 11, 'inter | Hectora Priamiden
animosum atque inter Achillem | ira
fuit,' etc. etc.

XCII. 5. The beginner should mark
the force of ὅστις, which is here used
because its clause really gives a reason
for the question. A preceding negative or interrogative or imperative is
apt to conceal the idiomatic significance
of this pronoun.

10. 'Tell me where the tracks are ;
bring not the lion into my ken.'

XCIII. 5. The reading βληχώδης cannot be doubted, and receives additional
support from a similar mode of expres-

sion in 16, 6, supra, αὐτὸς δὲ πεινῶν καὶ
λύκος χανὼν ὄντως. The gloss of Suidas,
however, presents a slight error. Βλη-
χώδης· προβάτοις τὸν νοῦν ὅμοιος—

μωρὸς δὲ ποίμην καὶ τὰ πάντα βληχώδης
πέμπειν ἔμελλεν.

The nu and eta in ποίμνη had been ac-
cidentally transposed, and μωρὴ adapted
to the new word.

6. 'But a ram now far advanced iu
years set his thick fleece all a-bristling,
and exclaimed, "Truly, a new sort of
reconciliation this !"'

XCIV.

Λύκῳ ποτ᾽ ὀστοῦν φάρυγος ἐντὸς ἠρείσθη.
ἐρωδιῷ δὲ μισθὸν ἄξιον δώσειν
ἔταξε, τὸν τράχηλον εἰ καθιμήσας
ἀνελκύσειε καὶ πόνων ἄκος δοίη.
ὁ δ᾽ ἑλκύσας τὸν μισθὸν εὐθέως ᾔτει.　　　5
κἀκεῖνος αὐτῷ κάρχαρόν τι μειδήσας
'σοὶ μισθὸς ἀρκεῖ' φησί 'τῶν ἰατρείων
κεφαλὴν λυκείου φάρυγος ἐξελεῖν σῴην.'

XCV.

Λέων νοσήσας ἐν φάραγγι πετραίῃ
ἔκειτο νωθρὰ γυῖα γῆς ἐφαπλώσας,

XCIV. 3. Athonm ἔταξε in ἔφασκε mutaverunt Fixius et Seidlerus.
8. Tenui cum fiducia Suidianum φάρυγος pro Athoo στόματος scripsi.
Suidae codices φάρυγγος (ut Athous quoque in primo versu) vitio sollenni
exhibent. Epimythium plus solito claudum—

κακοῖς βοηθῶν μισθὸν ἀγαθὸν οὐ λήψῃ,
ἀλλ᾽ ἀρκέσει σοι μή τι κακὸν πάθοις.

Recentiore manu κακὸν in τῶν κακῶν mutatum est.

XCIV. 3. Such a use of τάσσω
appears to be unexampled; but it is
probably a Latinism for statuit or
constituit. The conjecture ἔφασκε is
hardly worth notice, even though it is
based upon παρέξειν εἶπε or ἔφη of
the paraphrases. The verb ἱμάω, with
its two compounds ἀνιμάω and καθιμάω,
is often said to contract in eta; but the
only authority for the statement is a
dubious gloss of Photius, which is repeated by Suidas—ἱμᾶν καὶ ἱμῆν·
ἀντλεῖν, ἀνέλκειν, ἀνασπᾶν. The manuscripts of Aristophanes (Vesp. 379,
καθῖμα, imperative, 396, καθιμᾷ), and
Xenophon (Eq. 7, 2, ἀνιμάτω), are
plainly against the eta contraction,
which is a figment of grammarians due
to misunderstanding certain forms of
the perfect passive. The word is also
said to be formed from ἵμας by some
unaccountable process, ἱμάσσω being
the true verb of ἵμας. The root of

ἱμῶ is however the same as that of
ἵμας, ἱμάσσω, μάστιε, μάστιξε, μάστιξ,
etc. (see Curtius, Gr. Et. 602); and the
words ἱμονιά and ἱμαῖος both point to
the existence of other substantives
besides ἵμας. Καθιμᾶν alone has Attic
authority, but probably ἱμᾶν was also
in use where later and less correct
writers preferred ἀνιμᾶν. At all events,
Xenophon's use of ἀνιμᾶν for ἀνέλκειν
must not be regarded as Attic.
6. κάρχαρόν τι μειδήσας, 'with a
smile that showed his teeth,' lit. 'with
a jagged smile.'
7. This plural substantive ἰατρεῖα is
not met with till late, but its formation
is defensible by such classical instances
as ἀριστεῖα, καλλιστεῖα, ἀγχιστεῖα, 'the
wages or rights of being the bravest,
the most beautiful, the next of kin.'
XCV. 2. Hartung's conjecture, γῆς
ἐφ᾽ ἁπλώσας, disregards the Babrian
usage with reference to such compound

φίλην δ' ἀλώπεκ' εἶχεν ἦ προσωμίλει.
ταύτῃ ποτ' εἶπεν 'εἰ θέλεις με σὺ ζώειν·
πεινῶ γὰρ ἐλάφου τῆς ὑπ' ἀγρίαις πεύκαις   5
κεῖνον τὸν ὑλήεντα δρυμὸν οἰκούσης,
καὶ νῦν διώκειν ἔλαφον οὐκέτ' ἰσχύω·
σὺ δ' ἢν θελήσῃς, χεῖρας εἰς ἐμὰς ἥξει
λόγοισι θηρευθεῖσα σοῖς μελιγλώσσοις.'
ἀπῆλθε κερδώ, τὴν δ' ὑπ' ἀγρίαις ὕλαις   10
σκιρτῶσαν εὖρε μαλθακῆς ὑπὲρ ποίης
ἔκυσσε δ' αὐτὴν πρῶτον, εἶτα καὶ χαίρειν
προσεῖπε χρηστῶν τ' ἄγγελος λόγων ἥκειν.
'ὁ λέων,' ἔφασκεν, 'οἶδας, ἔστι μοι γείτων,
ἔχει δὲ φαύλως, κἀγγύς ἐστι τοῦ θνήσκειν.   15
τίς οὖν μετ' αὐτὸν θηρίων τυραννήσει
διεσκοπεῖτο. σῦς μέν ἐστιν ἀγνώμων,
ἄρκος δὲ νωθής, πάρδαλις δὲ θυμώδης,
τίγρις δ' ἀλαζὼν καὶ τὸ πᾶν ἐρημαίη.
ἔλαφον τυραννεῖν ἀξιωτάτην κρίνει.   20
γαυρὴ μὲν εἶδος, πολλὰ δ' εἰς ἔτη ζώει,

XCV. 9. Nauckius θηρευθεῖσα male in φηλωθεῖσα mutavit, Graecitatis certe ignarus. 12. Pro Athoo ἔσκυε (sic) cum Lachmanno ἔκισσε
legere malo quam cum Bergkio προσέκισσε, sed forsan neuter recte.
14. Ipse Athous οἶσθας ἔφασκε exhibet, sed manus recentior a β supra
scripsit, οἶσθας etiam in οἶδας mutato. Scripsit forte Babrius—

'ὁ λέων' ἔφασκεν 'ἐγγύς ἐστι τοῦ θνήσκειν.'

---

verbs—cp. Nonnus, Dionysiaca, 20,
385, δίκτυα μὴ νεπόδεσσιν ἐφαπλώσητε
θαλάσσης.
4. The protasis εἰ θέλεις με σὺ ζώειν
is taken up again in the eighth line,
σὺ δ' ἢν θελήσῃς, and ἦ θέλεις .. ζώειν ;
the conjecture of Boissonade is wrong.
12. The Athoan ἔσκυε is an easy
uncial corruption.
13. The construction is equivalent
to καὶ προσέτι χαίρειν εἶπε, χρηστῶν τ'
ἔφη ἄγγελος λόγων ἥκειν, but made more
easy by the late construction of εἰπεῖν,
with an infinitive, not only when it
means 'tell,' 'bid,' as with χαίρειν here,
but also when it has the sense of 'say,'
as with ἥκειν. Even in Attic the sense
of φάναι is sometimes elicited from
εἰπεῖν, 'bid,' in sentences of this cast.
15. The manifest laceration of the

manuscript reading, and the fact that
the questionable οἶδας elsewhere occurs
in the Fables only in a spurious line
(63, 12), suggest corruption here also—
perhaps to be removed by the omission
of the two half lines from οἶδας to καί.
This is better than reading οἶσθα, σούστι
μέν γείτων, which is questionable Greek.
21. 'De longa cervorum vita vide
fab. 46, 9, et pro epitheto γαῦρος confer
fab. 43, 6, 15. De cervorum cum ser-
pentibus inimicitia vide Plin. H. N.
viii. 50, xxii. 37.'—C. Lewis. Oppian
regards the latter fact as so familiar that
he uses it for a simile, Hal. 2, 289—
ὡς δ' ὅτ' ἀνὰ ξυλόχους ὀφίων στίβον ἐξε-
ρεείνων
βριθοκέρως ἔλαφος ῥινήλατον ἴχνος ἀνεῦρε,
χειὴν δ' εἰσαφίκακε, καὶ ἑρπετὸν εἴρυσεν
ἔξω κτε.

κέρας δὲ φοβερὸν πᾶσιν ἑρπετοῖς φύει,
δένδροις ὅμοιον, κοὐχ ὁποῖα τῶν ταύρων.
τί σοι λέγω τὰ πολλά; πλὴν ἐκυρώθης,
μέλλεις τ᾽ ἀνάσσειν θηρίων ὀρειφοίτων.   25
τότ᾽ οὖν γένοιτο τῆς ἀλώπεκος μνήμη,
δέσποινα, τῆς σοι τοῦτο πρῶτον εἰπούσης.
ταῦτ᾽ ἦλθον. ἀλλὰ χαῖρε, φιλτάτη. σπεύδω
πρὸς τὸν λέοντα, μὴ πάλιν με ζητήσῃ
(χρῆται γὰρ ἡμῖν εἰς ἅπαντα συμβούλοις)·   30
δοκῶ δὲ καὶ σέ, τέκνον, εἴ τι τῆς γραίης
κεφαλῆς ἀκούεις· ἔπρεπέ σοι παρεδρεύειν·
ἐλθοῦσαν αὐτῷ καὶ πονοῦντα θαρσύνειν.
τὰ μικρὰ πείθει τοὺς ἐν ἐσχάταις ὥραις·
ψυχαὶ δ᾽ ἐν ὀφθαλμοῖσι τῶν τελευτώντων.'   35
ὡς εἶπε κερδώ. τῆς δ᾽ ὁ νοῦς ἐχαυνώθη
λόγοισι ποιητοῖσιν, ἦλθε δ᾽ εἰς κοίλην
σπήλυγγα θηρός, καὶ τὸ μέλλον οὐκ ᾔδει.
λέων δ᾽ ἀπ᾽ εὐνῆς ἀσκόπως ἐφορμήσας
ὄνυξιν οὔατ᾽ ἐσπάραξεν ἀκραίοις,   40

---

26. Athoum τότ᾽ ἄν cum Lachmanno in τότ᾽ οὖν mutavi ; fortasse tamen pristina lectio stare potest. Certe Seidlerus errat, τότ᾽ αὖ lecto. 27. Verbum ταῦτο omisit Athous, sed recentiore manu in versu extremo additum post σοι posuit Minas. 29. Quare πάλιν in πάλαι mutem et in v. 32, ἔπρεπέ σοι in ἔπρεπεν ego non video. Volo reputetis, editores.

22. On φύει, = 'sprouts,' see Fab. 64, 4, note.
24. πλὴν ἐκυρώθης. I know no other instance of such a use of κυροῦν, 'your election was ratified,' 'your claims were acknowledged.'
29. μὴ πάλιν με ζητήσῃ. The conjecture πάλαι has nothing to recommend it. The words are naturally rendered, 'lest he look for me back again,' a sense of πάλιν and ζητεῖν quite in keeping with Babrian usage.
31. δοκῶ δὲ καὶ σέ scilicet σπεύσειν.
35. Compare Nonnus, Dionysiaca, 3, 225, ἀριφραδέων γὰρ ἀνάκτων | αὐτόματοι κήρυκες ἀναυδέες εἰσὶν ὀπωπαί.'
36. ἐχαυνώθη. Plutarchus, Caes. 29, de Pompeio quem falsae de Caesare narrationes vana impleverant spe—ἐπὶ τούτοις Πομπήιος ἐχαυνοῦτο.' — Boissonade.

40. Zachariae,'de Dictione Babriana,' p. 35, explains ψαύειν ὠτός, in line 70, of a particular kind of kiss. 'ψαύειν ὠτός, aurem vellicare, 'auriculis prehendere' (Plaut.) significat i.q. osculari, cf. v. 73, κνίσμα χειρὸς ἀρρώστου ; 87, 3, ἔσαινεν ὡς φίλῳ ψαύων.—τῶν ὤτων καθαιρεῖν dixit Theocritus, 5, 133, τῶν ὤτων λαβέσθαι Aristaenetus,1, 24; ibique cf. interpretes 552 (Bois.) de illo delicatissimo osculorum genere, quod χίτρα, osculum Florentinum, vocatur. Crusius, however, 'de Babrii Aetate, p. 185, rightly rejects this view. 'At pater moriens num his osculis utetur? Num utetur rex moriens, qui excitaturus est regni heredem ex pristina ignavia et edocturus, quo modo imperium acceptum tueatur ? Apage tam ridicula. Vera interpretatio repetitur ex Romano antestandi more, ex quo ubi testem

σπουδῇ διωχθείς· τὴν δὲ φύζα δειλαίην
θύρης κατιθὺς ἦγεν εἰς μέσας ὕλας.
κερδὼ δὲ χεῖρας ἐπεκρότησεν ἀλλήλαις,
ἐπεὶ πόνος μάταιος ἐξανηλώθη.
κἀκεῖνος ἐστέναξε τὸ στόμα βρύχων   45
(ὁμοῦ γὰρ αὐτὸν λιμὸς εἶχε καὶ λύπη),
πάλιν δὲ κερδὼ καθικέτευε φωνήσας
ἄλλον τιν' εὑρεῖν δεύτερον δόλον θήρης.
ἡ δ' εἶπε κινήσασα βυσσόθεν γνώμην·
'χαλεπὸν κελεύεις αὖθις ἀλλ' ὑπουργήσω.'   50

---

45. Aoristum ἐστέναξε jamdudum a criticis aliquot propositum Athous
re vera exhibet, non ἐστέναζε. 50. Claudicat in Athoo versus et, ut
exeat metrum, αὖθις supra lineam addidit manus recentior. Tyrwhittus
ἀλλ' ὅμως, Eberhardus δέσποτ', ἀλλ', Nauckius ἔργον legere mavult.
Non est quo decernam.

---

aliquem esse volebant, imam ejus aurem
tangebant "memento" dicentes. Quod
—ut in jus vocationem et mancipationem
omittam—etiam in testamento facie-
bant per aes et libram i. e. per mancipationem facto. Hanc testamenti formam, quae postrema fuit, usque ad
ultimum tempus servatam esse Clemens
Alexandrinus testatur loco maxime
memorabili Stromat. V. 8, extr.:—καὶ τὰ
παρὰ Ῥωμαίοις ἐπὶ τῶν καταθηκῶν γινό-
μενα τάξιν εἴληχε (in iis quae de sym-
bolis dixerat) τὰ κατὰ δικαιοσύνην ἐκεῖνα
ζύγα καὶ ἀσσάρια καρπισμοί τε (manci-
pationes) καὶ αἱ τῶν ὤτων ἐπιψαύ-
σεις. τὰ μὲν γάρ, ἵνα δικαίως γίνηται·
τὰ δὲ εἰς τὸν τῆς τιμῆς μερισμόν· τὸ δ'
ὅπως ὁ παρατυχὼν ὡς βάρους τινὸς
αὐτῷ ἐπιτεθειμένου ἑστὼς ἀκούσῃ
καὶ τάξιν μεσίτου λάβῃ.'
As a matter of fact the ceremony by
which the fox would fain explain the
lion's precipitancy was nothing but the
ordinary touching of the ear to request
attention and remembrance (see Con-
nington's Note on Vergil, Eclogue 6, 3),
and Crusius has erred from ill-digested
erudition as much as Zachariae from
ignorance.
42. The meaning of κατιθύς is difficult to settle. In Quint. Smyrnaeus,
7, 136, ῥιπῆς κατιθύς has the sense of
'facing the blast;' but here it is
better to take θύρης as a genitive of
place from, and translate κατιθύς with

εἰς ὕλας—'carried her out of doors
straight to the midst of the woods in
front.' In any case the adverb is late,
see Phryn. p. 117 ff.
43. The conjecture ἐκρότησεν is wrong,
as ἀλλήλαις could not be translated
with the simple verb.
45. The words τὸ στόμα βρύχων are
difficult of interpretation. Boissonade
translates 'leo dentibus infrendens,' and
would refer to this passage the gloss of
Suidas—βρύχων τοὺς ὀδόντας ὁ λεών.
But the sense ' biting his lips,' or ' with
his mouth working,' is equally plausible
for a writer like Babrius. Although
grammarians identify βρύχω and βρύκω,
making the latter an Attic variety of
the former, the fact remains that, except
in late writers, βρύχω means 'gnash,'
and βρύκω 'bite,' 'devour'; and it is
not unlikely that the confusion of
signification no less than of form
belongs to the decaying language.
Certainly 'gnashing the mouth' is a
strange modification of 'gnashing the
teeth,' as στόμα may mean much the
same as our 'lip' or 'lips,' but not
'teeth.'
47. It is much more likely that
Babrius omitted the augment in this
passage, as in others, than that he used
the accusative κερδοῦν, by Meineke's
conjecture κερδοῖν ἱκέτευε. The conjecture δ' ἀλώπεχ' ἱκέτευε does not
commend itself either.

καὶ δὴ κατ' ἴχνος ὡς σοφὴ κύων ᾔει,
πλέκουσα τέχνας καὶ πανουργίας πάσας,
ἀεὶ δ' ἕκαστον ποιμένων ἐπηρώτα
μή πού τις ἔλαφος ἡματωμένη φεύγει.
τὴν δ' ὥς τις εἶδε, δεικνύων ἂν ὡδήγει,　　　　55
ἕως ποθ' εὗρεν ἐν κατασκίῳ χώρῳ
δρόμων ἀναψύχουσαν. ἡ δ' ἀναιδείης
ὀφρὺν ἔχουσα καὶ μέτωπον εἰστήκει.
ἐλάφου δὲ φρὶξ ἐπέσχε νῶτα καὶ κνήμας,
χολὴ δ' ἐπέζει καρδίην, ἔφη δ' οὕτως·　　　　60
ἀλλ' ὦ στύγημα, νῦν μὲν οὐχὶ χαιρήσεις
ἤν μοι προσέλθῃς καὶ γρύσαι τι τολμήσῃς.
ἄλλους ἀλωπέκιζε τοὺς ἀπειρήτους,
ἄλλους δὲ βασιλεῖς ὑπερέθιζε καὶ ποίει.'

---

60. χολὴ in χολῇ mutavit Duebnerus Graecitatis parum peritus.
Post hunc versum habet Athous fraude manifesta—

σὺ νῦν διώκεις πανταχοῦ με καὶ φεύγω

quem non noverat Bodleianus paraphrasta. 62. Ut metro satis faciam
γρύσαι pro Athoo γρῦξαι scripsi. Serioris Graecitatis est γρύσαι vix
alienum. 63. Pro dativo ἄλλοις τοῖς ἀπειρήτοις recte conjecit accusativum
Cobetus. Male autem idem ὑπερέθιζε in αἱρέτιζε mutavit.

57. The earliest instance of the active
of ἀναψύχω thus used in the sense of
the classical passive is recorded by the
Antiatticist (80, 29), as from Diphilus
—Ἀνέψυξα ἀντὶ τοῦ ἀνεπαυσάμην.
Δίφιλος Φιλαδέλφῳ. Nor is the simple
verb or either of the two other Attic
compounds, ἀποψύχω and διαψύχω,
thus employed in Attic.
60. Of ζέω and its compounds, viz.
ἀναζέω, ἀποζέω, ἐκζέω, ἐξαναζέω, ἐπιζέω,
and συζέω, it will be found that in Attic
ἐπιζέω alone has the causative sense
here exhibited. Eur. Cycl. 392, καὶ
χάλκεον λέβητ' ἐπέζεσεν πυρί. (In Eur.
I. T. 987, however, the accusative is to
be differently explained—δεινή τις ὀργὴ
δαιμόνων ἐπέζεσε | τὸ Ταντάλειον σπέρμα,
διὰ πόνων τ' ἄγει, 'boiled over,' 'came
surging over.') This is in accordance
with the facts discussed in Fab. 1, 6,
supra. In late writers, on the contrary, the causative sense is attached to
the others. In Aesch. P.V. 370, Liddell
and Scott wrongly assign it to ἐξαναζέω,
where the cognate accusative construc-

tion with the intransitive meaning is
to be preferred :—τοιόνδε Τυφὼς ἐξανα-
ζέσει χόλον.
62. Babrius employs γρύσαι here for
the classical γρῦξαι (for accent see
Cobet, Mnem., New Series, 4, 276),
just as he uses συρίσαντος in 114, 4,
infra, for συρίξαντος. This tendency to
convert verbs in -ζω into -ττω, as γρύζω
into γρύττω, συρίζω into συρίττω, is
humorously referred to by Lucian in
the Δίκη Φωνηέντων (c. 10), where Zeta
accuses Tau of robbing him of 'συρίζειν
καὶ σαλπίζειν, ὡς μηκέτ' αὐτῷ ἐξεῖναι
μηδὲ γρύζειν.' It would hardly be
necessary to remind the student of the
frequent phrase γρύζειν τι τολμᾶν, if
Gitlbauer had not flaunted his ignorance
in our face by making the conjecture
κάγριόν τι τολμήσῃς. Cp. γρυκτός and
ἄγρυκτος, to the latter of which L. and
S. give a wrong sense ; see Συναγ. λεξ.
χρησ., 339, 33.
64. The only reason for Cobet's
alteration of the excellent ὑπερέθιζε
into the superfluous αἱρέτιζε in this

τῆς δ' οὐκ ἐτρέφθη θυμός, ἀλλ' ὑποβλήδην   65
' οὕτως ἀγεννής ' φησί ' καὶ φόβου πλήρης
πέφυκας; οὕτω τοὺς φίλους ὑποπτεύεις;
ὁ μὲν λέων σοι συμφέροντα βουλεύων
μέλλων τ' ἐγείρειν τῆς πάροιθε νωθείης
ἔψαυσεν ὠτός, ὡς πατὴρ ἀποθνήσκων·   70
ἔμελλε γάρ σοι πᾶσαν ἐντολὴν δώσειν,
ἀρχὴν τοσαύτην πῶς λαβοῦσα τηρήσεις·
σὺ δ' οὐχ ὑπέστης κνίσμα χειρὸς ἀρρώστου,
βίῃ δ' ἀποσπασθεῖσα μᾶλλον ἐτρώθης.
καὶ νῦν ἐκεῖνος πλεῖον ἢ σὺ θυμοῦται,   75
λίην ἄπιστον πειράσας σε καὶ κούφην,
βασιλῆ δέ φησι τὸν λύκον καταστήσειν.
οἴμοι πονηροῦ δεσπότου. τί ποιήσω;
ἅπασιν ἡμῖν αἰτίη κακῶν γίνῃ·
ἀλλ' ἐλθὲ καὶ τὸ λοιπὸν ἴσθι γενναίη,   80
μηδ' ἐπτόησο, πρόβατον οἷον ἐκ ποίμνης.
ὄμνυμι γάρ σοι φύλλα πάντα καὶ κρήνας,
οὕτω γένοιτο σοι μόνῃ με δουλεύειν,
ὡς οὐδὲν ἐχθρὸν ὁ λέων ἀλλ' ὑπ' εὐνοίης
τίθησι πάντων κυρίην σε τῶν ζῴων.'   85
τοιαῦτα κωτίλλουσα τὴν ἀχαιίνην
ἔπεισεν ἐλθεῖν δὶς τὸν αὐτὸν εἰς ᾅδην.
ἐπεὶ δὲ λόχμης εἰς μυχὸν κατεκλείσθη,
λέων μὲν αὐτὸς εἶχε δαῖτα πανθοίνην,

---

65. Certam Bergkii et Fixi conjecturam in textum recepi, ἐτέρφθη in ἐτρέφθη mutato.   77. Certa emendatione Fixius βασιλῆ pro βασιλέα scripsit.   84. Temere Lachmannus οἶδεν pro ὁ λέων proposuit.   89. Recte Suidas sub vocabulo πανθοίνην servavit, ab Athoo in παντοίην corruptum.

passage must be that in another (61, 5, supra), ἠρέτιζεν has been corrupted into ἠρέθιζεν. The position of the βασιλεῖς is peculiar, but it has its force, 'seek others to fire with the love of rule; seek others to make kings.'

76. Till something really is known about the Homeric text, I venture to consider πειράζω as one of the many spurious presents of decaying Greek, produced by misunderstanding forms like πεπειράσθω and πεπειρᾶσθαι. In late prose it is impossible to decide the intended quantity of words like πειρά-

σας, as the writer may have known the true present or may not.

81. For ἐπτόησο see note on 15, 13, supra.

84. Lachmann's generally accepted conjecture of οἶδεν has little to recommend it. Οὐδὲν ἐχθρόν is a strong οὐκ ἐχθρόν by a familiar Greek idiom, and the neuter is used for the masculine by a more familiar still, although it often puzzled copyists and led them astray, as it has done Lachmann here. (See Verrall's Medea, 1197, 1375, notes.)

89. The πανθοίνην of Suidas is certain

σάρκας λαφύσσων, μυελὸν ὀστέων πίνων   90
καὶ σπλάγχνα δάπτων· ἡ δ' ἀγωγὸς εἰστήκει
πεινῶσα θήρης, καρδίην δὲ νεβρείην
λάπτει πεσοῦσαν ἁρπάσασα λαθραίως,
καὶ τοῦτο κέρδος εἶχεν ὧν ἐκεκμήκει.
λέων δ' ἕκαστον ἐγκάτων ἀριθμήσας   95
μόνην ἀπ' ἄλλων καρδίην ἐπεζήτει,
καὶ πᾶσαν εὐνὴν πάντα δ' οἶκον ἤρευνα.
κερδὼ δ' ἀπαιολῶσα τῆς ἀληθείης
'οὐκ εἶχε πάντως' φησί·' 'μὴ μάτην ζήτει.'

90. σάρκας cum Athoo legere malo quam cum Suida ἔγκατα quod
leges metricas Babrianas violat.   91. Contra Suidianum δάπτων Athoo
λάπτων praeposui.   92. Pro θήρης habet Suidas κερδὼ sub νεβρός et
νεβρεία καρδία.   99. Adjecit Athous versus spurios duos—

> ποίην δ' ἔμελλε καρδίην ἔχειν ἥτις
> ἐκ δευτέρου λέοντος ἦλθεν εἰς οἴκους;

qui etiam ante paraphrastas interpolati sunt.

(cp. Oppian, Hal. 2, 221, μηδ' ἐπὶ
πανθοίνοισι νόον τέρποιτο τραπέζαις);
but his ἔγκατα in the next line violates
one of the most stringent rules of the
Babrian metre, and has crept in from
the Homeric passages which preserve
the old word λαφύσσω, and handed it
down to form part of the highly artificial diction of the later Greek styles.
Even before their day Aristophanes
made use of the substantive λαφυγμός
for comic effect (Nub. 52), and after
him Eupolis in his Κόλακες, adding the
verb thereto—

λαφύσσεται λαφυγμὸν ἀνδρεῖον πάνυ.

96. Eberhard's conjecture ἀπάντων,
for the Athoan ἀπ' ἄλλων, makes a
difficulty of a very common Greek
idiom, and has nothing to recommend
it.
98. The Bodleian paraphrase and
the Vatican [Fur. 356], which is from
the same original, supplant ἀπαιολῶσα
by σταθεῖσα and στᾶσα respectively,
and insert an ἀληθῶς with the εἶχε,
showing that ἀπαιολῶσα was misunderstood, and ταῖς ἀληθείαις substituted
for τῆς ἀληθείης. In any case the verb
is far from easy, and admits of at least
two renderings in Greek of this age.
First, ἀπαιολῶσα τῆς ἀληθείης need be
no more than a highly-coloured Greek
equivalent for 'swerving from the
truth.' Αἰόλος = 'changing,' αἰολάω =
'am changeable,' 'am a will o' the
wisp ;' the ἀπό really going with the
genitive according to the Babrian habit.
On the other hand, there is no doubt
about the existence of another αἰολάω
of the type of τιμάω, not of ὀργάω, and
with a transitive signification. Hippo-
crates is cited for the passive αἰολᾶται
(= πλανᾶται) of the simple verb, and
Euripides has the compound in Ion,
549, τοῦτο κάμ' ἀπαιολᾷ. Moreover,
the substantives ἀπαιόλησις and ἀπαιό-
λημα both corroborate the transitive
sense, left doubtful by ἀπαιόλη ; and
lexicographers show that they regarded
the verb as a synonym of πλανῶ or
ἀποπλανῶ. On the whole the better
course is to take it so here also, and to
translate 'misleading him from the
truth.'

XCVI.

Λύκος παρῄει θριγκόν, ἔνθεν ἐκκύψας
ἀρνειὸς αὐτὸν ἔλεγε πολλὰ βλασφήμως.
κἀκεῖνος εἶπε τὰς σιαγόνας πρίων,
'ὁ τόπος μ' ἐλοιδόρησε· μὴ σὺ καυχήσῃ.'

XCVII.

Λέων ποτ' ἐπεβούλευεν ἀγρίῳ ταύρῳ,
καὶ προσποιηθεὶς μητρὶ τῇ θεῶν θύειν
τὸν ταῦρον ἐλθεῖν ἐπὶ τὸ δεῖπνον ἠρώτα.
κἀκεῖνος ἥξειν εἶπεν οὐχ ὑποπτεύσας.
ἐλθὼν δὲ καὶ στὰς ἐπὶ θύρας λεοντείους   5
ὡς εἶδε θερμοῦ πολλὰ χαλκία πλήρη,
σφαγίδας, μαχαίρας βουδόρους νεοσμήκτους,
πρὸς τῇ θύρῃ δὲ μηδὲν ἀλλὰ δεσμώτην
ἀλεκτορίσκον, ᾤχετ' εἰς ὄρος φεύγων.
ἐμέμφεθ' ὁ λέων ὕστερον συναντήσας.   10
ὁ δ' 'ἦλθον' εἶπε 'καὶ τὸ σύμβολον δώσω·
ᾤμην ὅμοιον θῦμα τῷ μαγειρείῳ.'

XCVI. 1. Primos tres versus Suidas citat, τριγχὸν pro θριγκόν dato.
Lateat epimythium—

ὁ μῦθος ὀρθῶς πᾶσι τοῦτο μηνύει,
μηδεὶς διὰ καιρὸν ἰσχύων τι γαυρούσθω.

XCVII. 2. Cum Lachmanno τῇ scripsi pro Athoo τῶν. 8. Athoum
ἀλλ' ἤ cum Schneidewino in ἀλλὰ mutavi. 12. Pro Athoo οὐκ ἦν
summa cum fiducia ego ᾤμην dedi, quamvis vocula τὸ, quam codex ante
θῦμα exhibet, alteram emendationem suggerat, ὅμοιον ἦν τὸ θῦμα τῷ
μαγειρείῳ.

XCVII. 2. For the tendency to replace aorists middle by aorists passive, as προσποιηθείς here for the
classical προσποιησάμενος, see Phryn.
p. 186 ff.
4. For the late construction ἥξειν
εἶπεν, see supra, Fab. 95, 13.
7. The old punctuation σφαγίδας
μαχαίρας, βουδόρους has been rightly
abandoned. In any case νεοσμήκτους
goes both with σφαγίδας and μαχαίρας.

For the spelling νεόσμηκτος, see Phryn.
p. 321 ff.
8. μηδέν = classical οὐδέν.
12. It is tempting to replace τῷ by
σὸν, but I have thought it best to make
no alteration which is not warranted by
palaeography. The confusion of kappa
and mu is best known in the case of the
prepositions κατά and μετά. The transi-
tion from ωικην to ουκην is very easy.
For μαγειρεῖον, see Phryn. p. 341.

XCVIII.

Λέων ἁλοὺς ἔρωτι παιδὸς ὡραίης
παρὰ πατρὸς ἐμνήστευε. τῷ δ' ὁ πρεσβύτης
οὐδέν τι δύσνουν οὐδ' ὕπουλον ἐμφήνας
'δίδωμι γῆμαι' φησί 'καὶ διδοὺς χαίρω.
τίς οὐ δυνάστῃ καὶ λέοντι κηδεύσει;   5
φρένες δὲ δειλαὶ παρθένων τε καὶ παίδων.
σὺ δ' ἡλίκους μὲν ὄνυχας, ἡλίκους δ' ἥμιν
φέρεις ὀδόντας, τίς κόρη σε τολμήσει
ἀφόβως περιλαβεῖν; τίς δ' ἰδοῦσα μὴ κλαύσῃ;
πρὸς ταῦτα δὴ σκόπησον εἰ γάμου χρῄζεις,   10
μηδ' ἄγριος θὴρ ἀλλὰ νύμφιος γίνου.'
ὁ δὲ πτερωθεὶς τῇ δόσει τε πιστεύσας
ἐξεῖλε τοὺς ὀδόντας, εἶθ' ὑπὸ σμίλης
ἀπωνυχίσθη, τῷ δὲ πενθερῷ δείξας
τὴν παῖδ' ἀπῄτει. τὸν δ' ἕκαστος ἡλόια,   15
ῥοπάλῳ τις ἢ λίθῳ τις ἐκ χερὸς παίων.
ἔκειτο δ' ἀργός, ὥσπερ ὗς ἀποθνήσκων.

XCVIII. 10. Decimum post versum lacunam temere statuerunt Bergk
et Hartung.   17. In codice accedunt versus spurii tres et epimythium.
Illos Eberhard saepsit, hoc Lachmann—

γέροντος ἀνδρὸς ποικίλου τε τὴν γνώμην
σοφίῃ διδαχθεὶς ὡς ἄμικτον ἀνθρώποις
ἐρᾶν λεόντων ἢ λέοντας ἀνθρώπων.   20
αὐτός τις αὐτὸν λανθάνει κακῶς δράσας,
ὧν οὐ πέφυκε μεταλαβεῖν ὅταν σπεύδῃ.

XCVIII. 3. 'Making no sign of ill-
feeling or hidden dislike.'
6. 'But timorous is the heart of
maidens and young things. Think of
the claws, think of the teeth thou hast!
what maid so bold as clasp thee to her
bosom without fear? who could see thee
and keep back her tears?' The second
hand has wrongly altered the deliberative
κλαύσῃ into κλαύσει. The negative μή
confirms the first hand (see note on Fab.
24, 7, supra). If κλαύσει were right,
then μή would be wrong. Cp. line 5.
10. For the late σκοπήσω, ἐσκόπησα,
etc., see Veitch sub σκοπέω.
12. πτερωθείς. This metaphorical
signification is in Attic confined to the
compound ἀναπτεροῦν. Cp. πλέως and
ἀνάπλεως.
13. ὑπὸ σμίλης ἀπωνυχίσθη, 'had

his nails cut out by a surgeon's knife.'
This rendering is demanded by the
context ἐξεῖλε τοὺς ὀδόντας, and it is
evident that the lion was inveigled by
a Biblical stratagem, so as to fall an
easy prey when sore with self-inflicted
injuries. To take it as, 'had his nails
pared with a penknife,' is certainly
wrong. Σμίλη is often used of a surgeon's knife for cutting out mortified
flesh, tumours, etc.; and ἀπονυχίζω,
like other verbs in -ζω, has its meaning determined by the context. Here
ἀπωνυχίσθη = τοὺς ὄνυχας ἀφῃρέθη.
The codex contradicts the schismatic
accentuation σμιλῆ.
16. Gitlbauer's εὐχερῶς has more to
recommend it than most of his conjectures, but ἐκ χερός is excellent.
17. There should be no comma after

XCIX.

Λέοντι προσπτὰς αἰετῶν τις ἐξήτει
κοινωνὸς εἶναι. χὢ λέων ' τί κωλύει ;'
πρὸς αὐτὸν εἶπεν ' ἀλλ' ἐπ' ἐνεχύρῳ δώσεις
τὠκυπτέρω σου μὴ μεθιέναι πίστιν·
πῶς γὰρ φίλῳ σοι μὴ μένοντι πιστεύσω ;'   5

C.

Λύκῳ συνήντα πιμελὴς κύων λίην.
ὁ δ' αὐτὸν ἐξήταζε ποῦ τραφεὶς οὕτως
μέγας κύων ἐγένετο καὶ λίπους πλήρης.
' ἄνθρωπος ' εἶπε ' δαψιλής με σιτεύει.'
ὁ δέ σοι τράχηλος, εἰπέ, πῶς ἐλευκώθη ;   5
' κλοιῷ τέτριπται σάρκα τῷ σιδηρείῳ,
ὃν ὁ τροφεύς μοι περιτέθεικε χαλκεύσας.'

XCIX. Fabulam habet Vaticanus. Corrupti sunt versus tertius et quartus. Pro manuscripto ἀλλ' ἐνέχυρον ego ἀλλ' ἐπ' ἐνεχύρῳ dedi ; et τὠκυπτέρω fidenter restitui. Athous τὰ ὠκύπτερα exhibet, τὠκυπτέρῳ Vaticanus. Manu scriptum μεθεῖναι τὴν cum Eberhardo in μεθιέναι mutavi. Fabulae manifeste in brevius contractae forte metri culpa relinquenda est ; forte altius latet menda et versus in hunc modum e tetrastichista profectus est—

τὠκύπτερ' ὥς σοι μὴ μεθετέα τὴν πίστιν.

ῦς. Cp. Fab. 95, 70. 'He was laid low without an effort to save himself, like a swine under the slaughterer's knife.'

The three spurious lines I have given as they stand in the codex. The fact that they are not found in the prose versions, together with their syntactical errors, is conclusive proof of their late origin.

XCIX. 3. The conjecture ἐπ' ἐνεχύρῳ δώσεις is to my mind certain, although perhaps there is no need to go further than ἐν ἐνεχύρῳ δώσεις. Palaeographically either reading is easy. The preposition once dropped, the dative naturally passed into the accusative. What editors can mean by adopting

Lachmann's τὠκύπτερον, I do not see. The substantive is confined to the dual and plural.

C. 1. If the line is not corrupt, it is a good instance of the way in which the exigencies of the Babrian metre warp the order. The natural order would be λύκῳ κύων συνήντα πιμελὴς λίην. The κύων in the third verse is added for clearness' sake, and Eberhard's ' dubito de verbo κύων ' is uncalled for.

4. σιτεύω, Attic πιαίνω.

5. 'And the bare patch on your neck, how came it there ?' For this sense of λευκοῦν, cp. Maccius in Anth. Pal. 9, 403, 3, λεύκωσα πόδα γαῦρον. It is rare that the connotation of a word so masters the denotation.

λύκος δ' ἐπ' αὐτῷ καγχάσας ' ἐγὼ τοίνυν
χαίρειν κελεύω' φησί ' τῇ τρυφῇ ταύτῃ,
δι' ἣν σίδηρος τὸν ἐμὸν αὐχένα τρίψει.' 10

CI.

Λύκος τις ἁδρὸς ἐν λύκοις ἐγεννήθη,
λέοντα δ' αὐτὸν ἐπεκάλουν· ὁ δ' ἀγνώμων
τὴν δόξαν οὐκ ἤνεγκε, τῶν δὲ συμφύλων
ἀποστατήσας τοῖς λέουσιν ὡμίλει.
κερδὼ δ' ἐπισκώπτουσα ' μὴ φρενωθείην ' 5
ἔφη ' τοσοῦτον ὡς σὺ νῦν ἐτυφώθης·
σὺ γὰρ ὡς ἀληθῶς ἐν λύκοις λέων φαίνῃ,
ἐν δ' αὖ λεόντων συγκρίσει λύκος γίνῃ.'

CII.

Λέων τις ἐβασίλευεν οὐχὶ θυμώδης
οὐδ' ὠμὸς οὐδὲ πάντα τῇ βίῃ χαίρων,
πρᾶος δὲ καὶ δίκαιος ὥς τις ἀνθρώπων.
ἐπὶ τῆς ἐκείνου φασὶ δὴ δυναστείης
τῶν ἀγρίων ἀγυρμὸς ἐγεγόνει ζώων, 5
δίκας τε δοῦναι καὶ λαβεῖν παρ' ἀλλήλων.

CI. Fabulam habet codex Vaticanus. Ultimo in versu Nauckium
sequor, verbo γίνῃ pro codicum lectione φαίνῃ scripto.
CII. 3. Verba πρᾶος δὲ ex Tyrwhitti (i.e. Bodleiana) paraphrasi restituit
Boissonade, Athoo πρὸς δ' ἄρα rejecto.

---

8. καγχάσας, Attic καχάσας.
Cl. 2. 'Lion they gave him for nickname.' The old English 'eke-name,'
corrupted into 'nickname,' exactly
expresses the force of the preposition
in ἐπικαλεῖν, ἐπώνυμος, etc.
5. There is no reason for altering the
manuscript reading φρενωθείην into
'κφρενωθείην, with Coraes and subsequent editors. Μέγα or τοσοῦτον φρε-
νοῦσθαι is in late Greek a legitimate
equivalent for the classical μέγα or τοσοῦτον φρονεῖν. If no instance is found it
might be. Certainly ἐκφρενοῦν is never

found either. ' God forbid that I
should be so high-minded.'
There is a Hesychian gloss φρενώσας·
παραλογισάμενος, ἀπατήσας, but before
believing it to be correct I desire to
see the context.
6. The aorist ἐτυφώθης is placed for
the present to satisfy the requirements
of the Babrian season.
8. Phrynichus, p. 344, justly condemns
this use of σύγκρισις in late writers.
CII. 5. The word ἀγυρμὸς is very rare,
having apparently survived elsewhere
only in grammatical writings and lexica.

τὰ ζῶα πάντα δ' ὡς ὑπέσχον εὐθύνας,
λύκος μὲν ἀρνί, πάρδαλις δ' ἐπ' αἰγάγρῳ,
ἐλάφῳ δὲ τίγρις, πάντα δ' εἶχεν εἰρήνην,
ὁ πτὼξ λαγωὸς εἶπεν ' ἀλλ' ἐγὼ ταύτην   10
τὴν ἡμέρην ἀεί ποτ' ηὐχόμην †ἤτις
καὶ τοῖς βιαίοις φοβερὰ τἀσθενῆ θήσει.'

CIII.

Λέων ἐπ' ἄγρην οὐκέτι σθένων βαίνειν
(πολλῷ γὰρ ἤδη τῷ χρόνῳ 'γεγηράκει)
κοίλης ἔσω σπήλυγγος ὡς νόσῳ κάμνων
ἔκειτο, δόλιον οὐκ ἀληθὲς ἀσθμαίνων,
φωνὴν βαρεῖαν προσποιητὰ λεπτύνων.   5
θηρῶν δ' ἐπ' αὐλὰς ἦλθεν ἄγγελος φήμη,
καὶ πάντες ἤλγουν ὡς λέοντος ἀρρώστου,
ἐπισκοπήσων δ' εἰς ἕκαστος εἰσῄει.
τούτους ἐφεξῆς λαμβάνων ἀμοχθήτως
κατήσθιεν, γῆρας δὲ λιπαρὸν ηὑρήκει.   10

8. Fidenter Athoum secutus sum. Mendas sibi finxerunt editores δέ
γ', δέ τ', δ' ὑπ'. 11. Brevis syllaba in ultimo loco versum corruptum
arguit. Vertit Bodleianus ὁ πτὼξ δὲ ἔφη· ηὐχόμην ἰδεῖν τὴν ἡμέραν
ταύτην. Forte in hunc modum scazon e Babrio evasit—τὴν ἡμέρην ἀεί
ποτ' ηὐχόμην βλέψαι (vel βλέψειν) ἢ τοῖς κτλ. Sed valde dubito.
CIII. 3. Cui Babrii verba corrupta legere libet, Suidam sub vocibus
σπηλύγξ et ἄσθμα consulito. Idem tamen veram lectionem ἀληθὲς
servavit, codice Athoo ἀληθῶς aeque ac δολίως male exhibente.

7. I have preferred to regard the
Athoan reading πάντα ὡς δ' ὑπέσχον as
a merely accidental transposition, not
worthy of critical annotation ; Gitlbauer, however, would read πανταχῶς.
This, like Eberhard's correction ὑπέσχεν,
is, in my judgment, wrong.
8. The ignorant consensus of editors
in rejecting the adverbial ἐπί forces me
to illustrate a usage which ought to be
familiar to boys. In this collocation
(the δέ preceding) it is found, among
other passages, in Il. 18, 527, ὦκα δ'
ἔπειτα | τάμνοντ' ἀμφὶ βοῶν ἀγέλας καὶ
πώεα καλὰ | ἀργεννέων ὀΐων, κτεῖνον δ'
ἐπὶ μηλοβοτῆρας. So τ' ἐπί in Soph. O.
R. 181, ἐν δ' ἄλοχοι πολιαί τ' ἐπὶ ματέρες.
More usually the ἐπί precedes the con-

junction. Pseudo-Hesiod. Op. et Di.
590, ἀλλὰ τότ' ἤδη | εἴη πετραίη τε
σκιὴ . . , ἐπὶ δ' αἴθοπα πινέμεν οἶνον.
Il. 5, 705, ἀντίθεον Τεύθραντ', ἐπὶ δὲ
πλήξιππον Ὀρέστην | Τρῆχόν τ' αἰχμητὴν
Αἰτώλιον, Οἰνόμαόν τε | κτλ.
CIII. 1. Like στένω and πένομαι,
σθένω is only found in the present and
imperfect tenses.
6. It is observable that the peculiarly
Greek notion of φήμη is here used of
animals spoken of in the guise of men.
For a discussion of the notion, the long
note to Grote's *History of Greece*, ch.
xlii., ought to be consulted.
7. 'And all were sore at the thought
that the lion was ailing.'
10. λιπαρὸν γῆρας is a phrase of com-

σοφὴ δ' ἀλώπηξ ὑπένοησε καὶ πόρρω
σταθεῖσα 'βασιλεῦ, πῶς ἔχεις ;' ἐπηρώτα.
κἀκεῖνος εἶπε 'χαῖρε, φιλτάτη ζῴων·
τί δ' οὐ προσέρχῃ, μακρόθεν δέ με σκέπτῃ ;
δεῦρο, γλυκεῖα, καί με ποικίλοις μύθοις   15
παρηγόρησον ἐγγὺς ὄντα τῆς μοίρης.'
'σώζοιο' φησίν 'εἰ δ' ἄπειμι, συγγνώσῃ·
πολλῶν γὰρ ἴχνη θηρίων με κωλύει,
ὧν ἐξιόντων οὐκ ἔχεις ὅ μοι δείξεις.'

CIV.

Λάθρη κύων ἔδακνε· τῷ δὲ χαλκεύσας
ὁ δεσπότης κώδωνα καὶ προσαρτήσας
πρόδηλον εἶναι μακρόθεν πεποιήκει.
ὁ κύων δὲ τὸν κώδωνα δι' ἀγορῆς σείων
ἠλαζονεύετ'. ἀλλὰ δὴ κύων γραίη   5
πρὸς αὐτὸν εἶπεν 'ὦ τάλαν, τί σεμνύνῃ ;'

---

17. Cum Duebnero σώζοιο dedi pro Athoo ζώοιο, et cum Boissonadio
εἰ pro ἦν. Accedit epimythium—

μακάριος ὅστις οὐ προλαμβάνει πταίσας
ἀλλ' αὐτὸς ἄλλων συμφοραῖς ἐπαιδεύθη.

CIV. 6. Post hunc versum duos exhibet codex mala fraude Babrio
adscriptos—

οὐ κόσμον ἀρετῆς τοῦτον οὐδ' ἐπιεικείης,
σαυτοῦ δ' ἔλεγχον τῆς πονηρίης κρούεις,'

quorum extra ordinem initium ponit Athous, quasi epimythium. Pro
Athoo ἐπιεικείης Boissonadius ἐπικείης scripsit.

mon occurrence. Homer, Od. 11, 136;
19, 368 ; 23, 283. Pind. Nem. 7, 99.
Even Cratinus employs it, ap. Plutarch,
Vita Cimonis, ch. 10. Homer has also
λιπαρῶς γηράσκεμεν in Od. 4, 210.
19. Eberhard's conjecture of ἐξιόντος
is quite uncalled for.
CIV. 5. ἠλαζονεύετο. The so-called
deponents in -ενομαι present some difficulties. In one class of them the termin-
ations are certainly passive, not middle,
e.g. ἑβδόμενομαι, 'I am seventh-dayed,'
i.e. 'undergo the ceremony of the seventh
day after birth.' πεντηκοστεύομαι, 'am

taxed with the πεντηκοστή'; πραγματεύ-
ομαι, 'am involved in affairs.' Others
illustrate the usages of the middle voice,
as ἐπιδαψιλεύομαι, 'give freely from my
store' ; ἐπικηρυκεύομαι, 'negotiate by
herald,' a reciprocal middle. In others
the middle inflections only serve to
accentuate the fact of personal activity
in a particular character, as ἀλαζονεύομαι,
νεανιεύομαι, νεανισκεύομαι, βωμολοχεύ-
ομαι, πονηρεύομαι, φιλανθρωπεύομαι,
δημοτεύομαι, εἰρωνεύομαι, μαντεύομαι,
τερατεύομαι, μαιεύομαι, τερθρεύομαι,
ξενιτεύομαι, κοβαλικεύομαι (Ar. Eq. 270).

CV.

Λύκος ποτ' ἄρας πρόβατον ἐκ μέσης ποίμνης
ἐκόμιζεν οἴκαδ'. ᾧ λέων συναντήσας
ἀπέσπασ' αὐτό· καὶ λύκος σταθεὶς πόρρω
'ἀδίκως ἀφείλω τῶν ἐμῶν' ἐκεκράγει.
λέων δὲ τερφθεὶς εἶπε τὸν λύκον σκώπτων   5
'σοὶ γὰρ δικαίως ὑπὸ φίλων ἐδωρήθη.'

CVI.

Λέων ποτ' ἀνδρῶν βίον ἄριστον ἐζήλου.
καὶ δὴ κατ' εὐρὺν φωλεὸν διατρίβων,
ὅσων ἀρίστην ὀριτρόφων φυὴν ἔγνω,
φιλοφρονεῖσθαι γνησίως ἐπειρᾶτο.
πολὺς δ' ὑπὸ σπήλυγγι θαμινὰ παντοίων   5
θηρῶν ὅμιλος ἡμέρως συνηυλίσθη.

CV. 3. Pro Athoo αὑτοῦ scripsi αὐτό, praecunte Eberhardo, cui tamen
latuit vitii causa, quae in versu secundo prodit οἴκαδε lecto, videlicet,
οἴκαδε· χὦ λέων . . αὑτοῦ. 5. Athoum τερφθεὶς temere in τρεφθεὶς
Hartung mutavit.
CVI. Fabula mala fraude Babrio est supposita. Non latent indicia,
praesertim syllaba brevis in versuum sex exitu. De ea etiam paraphrastae
silent.

Even νωθρεύομαι may perhaps be so
explained. Στραγγεύομαι, ' I twist and
turn,' may be regarded either as the
passive or the middle of the active
στραγγεύω preserved in lexica.
CV. 4. For the late aorist ἀφειλάμην,
see Boissonade's note, and Veitch.
5. ' But the lion made merry with
a joke at the wolf's expense. "'T was
an honest present from thy friends, I
trow."'
CVI. I would call the reader's attention to the fable as a whole. A
careful perusal will confirm the suspicion of its spuriousness, already
expressed in the critical notes. After
writing and re-writing it many times,
I am convinced that my judgment
is correct. Were ever twenty-nine
lines written to lead up to so poor a
point in the thirtieth? I am glad to
find that C. F. Hermann and F. W.
Hoch have already expressed strong
opinions against this fable. Naber,
who requires the final trochees to bolster
a theory, is yet forced to admit that
the fable is a fragment, and is without
point as it stands. Crusius makes the
same admission, and suggests that the
missing conclusion is to be sought for
in some fable in which a fox takes
vengeance on an ape, e.g. Fab. 255,
and 44 in Halm's collection. Crusius'
note (p. 144) is a typical example of
the attempt to gain a point by first
obfuscating, or at all events fatiguing
the reason. You may get a man to
allow that he sees a non-existent object
by taking care that there is a haze
when he looks.

ὁ δ᾽ εἰστία τε κἀφίλει νόμῳ ξείνων
ἄδην τιθεὶς ἅπασι δαῖτα θυμήρη·
φίλην δὲ κερδὼ καὶ σύνοικον εἰλήφει
μεθ᾽ ἧς τὰ πολλὰ μειλίχως συνεζήκει,   10
γέρων δέ τις πίθηκος ἦν ὁ δαιτρεύων
κρεῶν τε συσσίτοισι διανέμων μοίρας,
ὃς εἴ τις ἦλθεν οὐχὶ τῆς συνηθείης,
ταὐτὸν παρετίθει δεσπότῃ τε κἀκείνῳ,
ὅπερ εἶχεν ὁ λέων νεοδρόμῳ λαβὼν θήρῃ·   15
κερδὼ δ᾽ ἑώλων ἔφερεν οὐκ ἴσην μοῖραν
καὶ δή ποτ᾽ αὐτὴν προσποιητὰ σιγῶσαν
δείπνου τε χεῖρα καὶ βόρης ἀποσχοῦσαν
λέων τίν᾽ εἶχεν αἰτίην διηρώτα·
'κερδοῖ σοφή, λάλησον ὥσπερ εἰώθης·   20
φαιδρῷ προσώπῳ δαιτός, ὦ φίλη, ψαῦσον.'
ἡ δ᾽ εἶπεν 'ὦ φέριστε θηρίων γέννης,
πολλῇ μερίμνῃ καρδίην διαξαίνω·
οὐ γὰρ τὰ νῦν παρόντα μοῦνον ἀλγύνει,
τὰ δ᾽ ἔπειτα᾽ φησί 'προσκοπουμένη κλαίω.   25
καθ᾽ ἡμέρην γὰρ εἴ τις ἄλλος, εἶτ᾽ ἄλλος
ξένος πελάζοι, τοῦτο δ᾽ εἰς ἔθος βαίνοι,
τάχ᾽ οὐδ᾽ ἑώλων γεύσομαι κρεῶν μούνη.'
ὁ λέων δὲ τερφθεὶς ὡς λέων τε μειδήσας.
εἶπεν 'πιθήκῳ ταῦτα μηδ᾽ ἐμοὶ μέμφου.'   30

CVII.

Λέων ἀγρεύσας μῦν ἔμελλε δειπνήσειν·
ὁ δ᾽ οἰκότριψ κλὼψ ἐγγὺς ὢν μόρου τλήμων
τοιοίσδε μύθοις ἱκέτευε τονθρύζων·

---

8. Scripsi cum Boissandio ἄδην, quod vitio frequenti ἄλην exhibet
codex.   10. Fixio praeeunte Athoum συνεζήτει in συνεζήκει mutavi.
18. Versus 18 et 19 Athous codex ordine 19, 18 exhibet.
CVII. Plus solito corrupta est fabula.   3. Pro Athoo τὸν θῆρα summa
cum fiducia ego τονθρύζων scripsi.

CVII. 3. The verb whose participle
I have here substituted for the corrupt
and unmetrical τὸν θῆρα, is used of any
inarticulate sound expressive of the

feelings. Aristophanes applies it to a
slave's grumbling after a whipping
(Ran. 747); to a servant's mutterings
in performing a distasteful task (Vesp.

' ἐλάφους πρέπει σοι καὶ κερασφόρους ταύρους
θηρῶντα νηδὺν σαρκὶ τῇδε πιαίνειν·   5
μυὸς δὲ δεῖπνον οὐδ' ἄκρων ἐπιψαύσει
χειλῶν ἄμειβον· ἀλλὰ λίσσομαι, φείδου.
ἴσως χάριν σοι τῆσδε μικρὸς ὢν τίσω.'
γελάσας δ' ὁ θὴρ παρῆκε τὸν ἱκέτην ζώειν·
καὶ θηραγρεύταις ἐμπεσὼν νεηνίσκοις   10
ἐδικτυώθη καὶ σφαλεὶς ἐδεσμεύθη.
ὁ μῦς δὲ λάθρη χηραμοῦ προπηδήσας,
στερρόν τ' ὀδοῦσι βραχυτάτοις βρόχον κείρας,
ἔλυσε τὸν λέοντα, τοῦ τὸ φῶς βλέψαι
ἐπάξιον δοὺς μισθὸν ἀντιζωγρήσας.   15

---

5. Cum Fixio θηρῶντα pro Athoo θηρῶν δὲ dedi. 6. Quod codex exhibet ἄκρον ἐπιψαῦσαι χειλῶν ἀμέσων ego fidenter emendavi. 9. Fixio
praecunte, Athoum ζῶντα in ζώειν mutavi. 10. Athoum φιλαγρευταῖς
ego correxi. De hac literarum confusione vide Gregorium de Dialectis ed.
Schaefer, p. 269. 11. Hunc post versum interpolatum habet Athous κάν-
τεῦθεν ἀπεγνώκει ὁ θὴρ τὴν ὄριαν sed super ultima verba τι ὄρα diorthotes
scripsit. Haec et epimythium tu ejicito—

σαφὴς ὁ μῦθος εὐνοοῦσιν ἀνθρώποις
σώζειν πένητας μηδὲ τῶν ἀπελπίζειν
εἰ καὶ λέοντα μῦς ἔσωσ' ἀγρευθέντα.

---

614); to the whine of helpless age
(Ach. 683); Lucian to the whispered
murmurs of the gods when their common dignity is offended (Conc. Deor.
1) ; the pseudo-Oppian to a bear's cubs
whimpering when their dam licks
them (Cyn. 3, 169), etc. etc. In the
present passage it expresses the whine
or whimper of deprecation. As to the
spelling τονθορύζω, τονθορίζω, τονθρύζω,
τονθρίζω, grammarians contradict each
other. As to Attic, the authority of
Aristophanes is decisive for the quadri-
syllable ; but the late form is more in
keeping with the Babrian diction. The
conjecture is corroborated—if a confirmatory proof is wanted—by the set
of the line which corresponds to that
of 6, 5, ἱκέτευεν ἀσπαίρων ; 6, 13, τοιαῦτα
μύζων ἱκέτευε κάσπαίρων ; 13, 3, ἱκέτευε
χωλεύων ; 95, 47, καθικέτευε φωνήσας;
136, 3, ἱκέτευε λιμώττων, cp. 134, 13.
I have given only those lines in which
ἱκετεύω comes.
6. 'But a mouse is a meal that in

passing thy lips will scarce touch their
surface.' The conjectures of previous
editors are these—ἄμεινον, Lachmann ;
ἄφες μ' οὖν, Seidler; θέμις σῶν, Schneidewin ; ἄλις σῶν or ἀποχρῶν, Eberhard ;
ἀμέτρων, Gitlbauer.
7. The corruption of ἄμειβον into
ἄμεσον or some like vox nihili, is anterior to the Bodleian paraphrase, which
has ἐγὼ γὰρ οὐδὲ τὸ χεῖλός σου ἀλείψω
αἵματος ; but the ἀλείψω indicates
that ἐπιψαύσει had not been replaced
by ἐπιψαῦσαι.
8. τῆσδε, videlicet χάριτος, Boissonade.
Eberhard prefers τήνδε, Fix τῶνδε.
11. 'He was caught in the toils,
tripped up, and bound fast.' Perverse
ingenuity has been expended on the
participle as if a net was expected to
hold a lion long. The δίκτυον was
employed only to put the lion at the
mercy of the θηράγρευται ; and σφαλεὶς
is natural, if not necessary. Meineke
reads σφαλοῖς, Ahrens κάσφαλῶς, and
Eberhard κάλψς.

ΠΡΟΟΙΜΙΟΝ Β.

Μῦθος μέν, ὦ παῖ βασιλέως Ἀλεξάνδρου,
Σύρων παλαιόν ἐστιν εὕρεμ' ἀνθρώπων,
οἳ πρίν ποτ' ἦσαν ἐπὶ Νίνου τε καὶ Βήλου·
πρῶτος δέ, φασίν, εἶπε παισὶν Ἑλλήνων
Αἴσωπος ὁ σοφός, εἶπε καὶ Λιβυστίνοις   5
λόγους Κιβύσσης. ἀλλ' ἐγὼ νέῃ μούσῃ
δίδωμι, φαλάρῳ χρυσέῳ χαλινώσας

Prooemium B. Haec libri secundi praefatio inter fabulas secundum
alphabetum dispositas locum habet; sed in codice etiam nunc dilucet origo,
verbis ἀρχὴ τοῦ Β τμήματος praepositis. (Serior tamen manus et lineam
circum τμήματος duxit et literam B in μ mutatit.) Ex quo si reputaveris
licet forsan colligere scribam Athoum ante oculos librum habere in quo
fabulae Babriano ipsius in ordine collocati sunt, atque inde secundum
alphabetum descripsisse. 4. Fixio praecunte φασίν pro Athoo πᾶσιν dedi.
5. Athoum λίβυς τινὸς emendavit Schneidewinus, et λιβύσσης Ahrensius.
7. Conjectura palmaria pro Athoo καθαρῷ Duebnerus φαλάρῳ scripsit.

Prooem. 1. The person intended by
παῖς Ἀλεξάνδρου is discussed in the
introductory essay on the age of Babrius.
2. For the form εὕρεμα, see Phryn. p.
501. Between παλαιῶν of the codex
and Fix and Lachmann's παλαιὸν, I
have allowed the sense to decide, as in
this case manuscript authority is valueless. The line is offered as a bait to
the scion of a Syrian house. Athough
Lampridius, in his life of Alexander
Severus, tells us that the Emperor was
best pleased to be regarded as of Roman
descent, yet his son must have been
aware of his oriental extraction.
As a matter of fact, however, Ninus
and Belus were not Syrians, but
Assyrians.

6. The meaning of Κιβύσσης has
been discussed in the introductory
dissertation on Greek Fable.
'For me, I throw them into a new
form, bridling the mythiambus like an
armed horse with trappings of gold.'
7. Palaeographically the corruption
of φαλάρῳ into καθαρῷ is inexplicable,
and something is to be said for Boissonade's simpler correction of χρυσέῳ
into χρυσίῳ. Χρυσίῳ would give practically the same sense as φαλάρῳ, but the
emphatic attributive adjective would
be out of place. In any case the
reference is not to yoking the fable to
the metre, but to the ornamentation of
the verse itself. Χαλινός may be applied
loosely to housings as a whole. 'This

τὸν μυθίαμβον ὥσπερ ἵππον ὁπλίτην.
ὑπ' ἐμοῦ δὲ πρώτου τῆς θύρης ἀνοιχθείσης
εἰσῆλθον ἄλλοι, καὶ σοφωτέρης μούσης   10
γρίφοις ὁμοίας ἐκφέρουσι ποιήσεις,
μαθόντες οὐδὲν πλεῖον ἢ γεγωνίσκειν.
ἐγὼ δὲ λευκῇ μυθιάζομαι ῥήσει,
καὶ τῶν ἰάμβων τοὺς ὀδόντας οὐ θήγω,
ἀλλ' εὖ πυρώσας, εὖ δὲ κέντρα πρηύνας,   15
ἐκ δευτέρου σοι τήνδε βίβλον ἀείδω.

---

12. Neque minus perite Nauckius ἢ γεγωνίσκειν pro Athoo ἢ με γινώσκειν.

mythiambus of mine is meant to catch the ear, as a prancing war-horse with jingling trappings takes the ear and eye of childhood.'

9. 'After the door had been first opened by me others entered thereat, and publish poems like to the riddles of more learned verse, skilled in nothing but the making of noise. But transparent is the style in which I recount my fables ; and I whet not the teeth of the iambics, but, carefully fining the points as with fire, carefully tempering them, I write for thee this second book.'

The difficulties of these lines—themselves a riddle not easy to read—are very great. Babrius claims to have been the first to write fables in choliambics,—in fact to have invented the μυθίαμβος, and versified Aesop's Fables in a transparent and simple style. After his first essay appeared others tried to imitate him, but missed the simplicity and gaiety which is the chief charm of such composition. Studied epigram is not in place in anything which aims at amusing the young ; and his imitators made the mistake of being too clever. For his part he refined his cleverness, and brought it down to the level of a child's comprehension.

τῆς θύρης ἀνοιχθείσης. Boissonade has a long note on this metaphor ; to my thinking it may well have been in use before the Flood.

10. ''T is true they caught the jingle of my verse, but they missed the transparency of my style.' Athenaeus has a long discussion on γρίφοι, x. 448 ff. A typical one is the line

Ἕκτορα τὸν Πριάμου Διομήδης ἔκτανεν ἀνήρ,

which is not intelligible till one knows that Diomedé succeeded Briseis in the affections of Achilles. Babrius asserts that his imitators used conceits of this sort. Γριφώδης, γριφότης, and γρίφωσις, are all applied to crabbed, conceited, or difficult styles.

There is no difficulty in σοφωτέρης μούσης, except what editors make. Μοῦσα is applicable to any composition in its literary aspect, and by σοφωτέρη μοῦσα is signified any writing suited to wiser heads than children's.

13. The term λευκός is applied as early as Homer to water in the sense of 'clear,' 'transparent,' 'limpid,' and in late writers is sometimes found along with σαφής applied to style. Boissonade also quotes instances of μέλας and μελαίνω being used of opposite qualities, cp. Latin 'albus' and 'ater.'

14, 15. 'Art I have used, but in toning down my natural smartness, not in exaggerating it.'

16. The line might be taken to mean that the present prooemium is that to a new edition, not to a new book, but the latter alternative is probably right.

CVIII.

Μυῶν ὁ μέν τις βίον ἔχων ἀρουραίων,
ὁ δ' ἐν ταμείοις πλουσίοισι φωλεύων,
ἔθεντο κοινὸν τὸν βίον πρὸς ἀλλήλους.
ὁ δ' οἰκόσιτος πρότερος ἦλθε δειπνήσων
ἐπὶ τῆς ἀρούρης ἄρτι χλωρὸν ἀνθούσης·　　　　5
τρώγων δ' ἀραιὰς καὶ διαβρόχους σίτου
ῥίζας μελαίνῃ συμπεφυρμένας βώλῳ
' μύρμηκος ' εἶπε ' ζῆς βίον ταλαιπώρου,
ἐν πυθμέσιν γῆς κρίμνα λεπτὰ βιβρώσκων.
ἐμοὶ δ' ὑπάρχει πολλὰ καὶ περισσεύει·　　　　10
τὸ κέρας κατοικῶ πρὸς σὲ τῆς Ἀμαλθείης.
εἴ μοι συνέλθῃς, ὡς θέλεις ἀσωτεύσῃ,
παρεὶς ὀρύσσειν ἀσφάλαξι τὴν χώρην.'
ἀπῆγε τὸν μῦν τὸν γεηπόνον πείσας
εἰς οἶκον ἐλθεῖν ὑπό τε τοῖχον ἀνθρώπου.　　　　15
ἔδειξε δ' αὐτῷ ποῦ μὲν ἀλφίτων πλήθη,

CVIII. 1. Pro Athoo ἀρουραῖον ego ἀρουραίων scripsi. 12. Sub-
junctivum legere malo. συνελθῇς^{οι} codex. 16. Baitero praeducente,
Athoum πλήρη in πλήθη mutavi.

CVIII. 1. The emendation ἀρουραίων
needs no defence, sc. μυῶν.

4. For the classical sense of οἰκόσιτος,
see Phryn. p. 285.

5. The line admits of two renderings
in a writer of this date—(1) 'When the
land was just bursting into verdure';
(2) 'In the fields which were just
bursting into verdure.'

9. Here and in line 32 I have
followed the codex in writing κρίμνα—
an accent generally given by the manuscripts. Other editors prefer the accent
properispomenon here, but there is no
evidence for that. In fact the tendency
to use the circumflex in such cases is
so strong that its absence is in favour
of the acute.

10. 'I have plenty and to spare, and,
compared with thee, house in the horn
of Amalthea.' 'De Amalthcae cornu
pervulgata omnia. Vide quae monui

ad Anecd. Graec. t. 3, p. 12; quae
monuerunt Jacobs. ad Callicterem
Anal. t. 9, p. 151, et Anthol. 11, 5;
Walz. ad Arsen. p. 49; Fischer ad
Anacr. Fragm. 5; et ceteri. Joannes
Pediasimus bonam mulierem esse ait
παροιμιακὸν τῆς Ἀμαλθείας κέρας. Hip-
podamus Stobaei Tit. 103, 26, p. 341,
de civitate bene constituta : ταῦτα μὲν
ἐγὼ φημὶ ἤμεν τὸ ὀνομαζόμενον Ἀμαλθείας κέρας· ἐν εὐνομίᾳ γὰρ τὰ πάντα
ἐντί.'—Boissonade.

12. It is quite impossible to decide
between subjunctive and optative here.
Babrius may have written either. For
ἀσωτεύομαι, see note on Fab. 104, 5,
supra.

16. πλήθη is a Latinism, viz. copiae.
The supposition that πλήρη is right,
and that a line has been lost, beginning with ἀγγεῖα or some such word,
is indefensible.

ποῦ δ' ὀσπρίων ἦν σωρὸς ἢ πίθοι σύκων
στάμνοι τε μέλιτος σώρακοί τε φοινίκων.
ὁ δ' ὡς ἐτέρφθη πᾶσι καὶ παρωρμήθη
καὶ τυρὸν ἦγεν ἐκ κανισκίου σύρων,   20
ἀνέῳξε τὴν θύρην τις· ὁ δ' ἀποπηδήσας
στεινῆς ἔφευγε δειλὸς εἰς μυχὸν τρώγλης,
ἄσημα τρίζων τόν τε πρόξενον θλίβων.
μικρὸν δ' ἐπισχὼν εἶτ' ἔσωθεν ἐκκύψας
ψαύειν ἔμελλεν ἰσχάδος Καμειραίης·   25
ἕτερος δ' ἐπῆλθεν ἄλλο τι προαιρήσων·
οἱ δ' ἔνδον ἐκρύβοντο. μῦς δ' ἀρουρίτης
'τοιαῦτα δειπνῶν' εἶπε 'χαῖρε καὶ πλούτει,
καὶ τοῖς περισσοῖς αὐτὸς ἐντρύφα δείπνοις.
ἔχων τὰ πολλὰ ταῦτα μεστὰ κινδύνων.   30
ἐγὼ δὲ λιτῆς οὐκ ἀφέξομαι βώλου
ὑφ' ἣν τὰ κρίμνα μὴ φοβούμενος τρώγω.'

CIX.

Μὴ λοξὰ βαίνειν ἔλεγε καρκίνῳ μήτηρ
ὑγρῇ τε πέτρῃ πλάγια κῶλα μὴ σύρειν.
ὁ δ' εἶπε 'μῆτερ ἡ διδάσκαλος, πρώτη
ὀρθὴν ἄπελθε καὶ βλέπων σε ποιήσω.'

CIX. Fabulam decurtavit tetrastichista μούσης ἄτερ. Meliorem
recensionem sequi videtur paraphrasta Bodleianus, pro ἄπελθε verbo
βάδιζε, pro ποιήσω verbo ζηλώσω lecto.

---

25. The Rhodian figs were valued.
Athenaeus, iii. 75 E; Pliny, Nat.
Hist. xiii. 8, § 59. Σῦκα τρώγειν was
used proverbially as the equivalent of
τρυφᾶν.
27. The incorrect aorist ἐκρυβόμην is
very rare even in late Greek.
CIX. 1. Even in Attic λέγειν is
sometimes thus construed with the
sense of εἰπεῖν or κελεύειν. Pherecrates,
τοῖς δὲ κριταῖς τοῖς νυνὶ κρίνουσι λέγω, μὴ
ἐπιορκεῖν μηδ' ἀδίκως κρίνειν. Eupolis,
ἀλλ' οὖν ἔγωγέ σοι λέγω Μαρικᾶντα μὴ
κολάζειν. The most frequent instances

are of the type χαίρειν σοι λέγω. To
write 'μὴ λοξὰ βαίνειν' and 'ὑγρῇ τε . .
σύρειν' with the editors is certainly
wrong.
3. I would prefer the nominative:
μήτηρ ἡ διδάσκαλος πρώτη ἄπελθε by
the Attic idiom referred to in the note
on Fab. 32, 4, supra, if the words were
really by Babrius; but even Babrius
may have written the late construction
as it stands.
4. 'I will do it with my eye on thee';
i.e. 'I will keep my eye on thee and
do it too.'

CX.

Μέλλων ὁδεύειν τῆς κυνός τις ἑστώσης
εἶπεν 'τί χάσκεις; πάνθ' ἕτοιμά σοι ποίει·
μετ' ἐμοῦ γὰρ ἥξεις.' ἡ δὲ κέρκον οὐρείην
ἄρασά φησι 'πάντ' ἔχω· σὺ βαρδύνεις.'

CXI.

Μικρέμπορός τις ὄνον ἔχων ἐβουλήθη,
τοὺς ἅλας ἀκούων παρὰ θάλασσαν εὐώνους,
τούτους πρίασθαι, φορτίσας τε γενναίως
τὸν ὄνον κατῆγε. τῆς δ' ὁδοῦ προκοπτούσης
ὤλισθεν ἄκων εἴς τι ῥεῖθρον ἐξαίφνης   5
καὶ συντακέντων τῶν ἁλῶν ἐλαφρύνθη,
ῥάων δ' ἀνέστη καὶ παρῆν ἀμοχθήτως
εἰς τὴν μεσόγεων· τοὺς ἅλας δὲ πωλήσας
πάλιν γομώσων τὸν ὄνον ἦγε καὶ πλείω
ἔτ' ἐπετίθει τὸν φόρτον. ὡς δὲ μοχθήσας   10
διέβαινε τὸν ῥοῦν, οὗπερ ἦν πεσὼν πρῴην,
ἑκών κατέπεσε, καὶ πάλιν δ' ὅλους τήξας

CX. Fabellam subobscenam et male lepidam Babrio tribuere nolo. Certe
manum inertem applicavit tetrastichista. Serius Gitlbauer depravavit
Graecitatem, σὺ δ' ἀρτύνεις pro σὺ δὲ βραδύνεις lecto. Idem tamen bene
οὐρείην pro οὐραίης emendavit. Sed si Babrius ita scripsit magister,
discipuli me miseret Branchi. 4. Ahrensio debeo σὺ βαρδύνεις pro Athoo
σὺ δὲ βραδύνεις, quod tamen e tetrastichista proficisci potuit. Lachmanni
σὺ δ' ἀβρύνῃ non placet.
CXI. 10. Lachmannus ἔτ' addidit ut versus exiret. 12. Ego literulam
δ' inserui. Schneidewinus ὅλους etiam in ἅλας mutare mavult. Acute
Meinekius πάλιν δόλους τεύξας.

CXI. 4. Here and in verse 15 κατά-
γειν means 'carry home,' and has not
the signification natural in this context. Of the late sense of προκόπτειν
in the next clause the lexica supply
examples.
8. For μεσόγεως, see Phryn. pp. 356-
358.
12. Meineke's conjecture is ingenious

but untrue, as on the first occasion the
fall was accidental. The manuscript
reading ὅλους implies that the first
time all the load had not been lost, as
the ass, unconscious of the effect of his
slip, did not persist in keeping down
long enough to melt all. The second
time he deliberately lay down in the
water.

κούφως ἀνέστη γαῦρος ὥς τι κερδήσας.
ὁ δ' ἔμπορος μὲν ἐπενοεῖτο καὶ πλείστους
σπόγγους κατῆγεν ὕστερον πολυτρήτους   15
ἐκ τῆς θαλάσσης τοὺς δ' ἅλας μεμισήκει.
ὁ δ' ὄνος πανούργως, ὡς προσῆλθε τῷ ῥείθρῳ,
ἑκὼν κατέπεσεν· ἀθρόως δὲ τῶν σπόγγων
διαβραχέντων πᾶς ὁ φόρτος ὠγκώθη,
βάρος δὲ διπλοῦν ἦλθε βαστάσας νώτοις.   20

CXII.

Μῦς ταῦρον ἔδακεν. ὁ δ' ἐδίωκεν ἀλγήσας
τὸν μῦν· φθάσαντος δ' εἰς μυχὸν φυγεῖν τρώγλης
ὤρυσσεν ἑστὼς τοῖς κέρασι τοὺς τοίχους,
ἕως κοπωθεὶς ὀκλάσας ἐκοιμήθη

13. Eberhardum libens sequor. Male Athous exhibet ἀνέστη γαῦρος κοῦφος, quae verba in ordinem γαῦρος ἀνέστη κοῦφος posuit manus recens. 14. Athoum ὁ δ' ἔμπορος τέχνην μὲν ἐπενοεῖθ καὶ πλείστους cum Eberhardo emendavi. Scriba recentior, μὲν deleto, ἐπινοεῖ dedit. 16. Recte τοὺς δ' pro Athoo τοὺσθ Eberhardus scripsit. Epimythium addit Athous—

πολλάκις ἐν οἷς τις ηὐτύχησε καὶ πταίει.

13. It is not necessary to defend Eberhard's emendation of this line. It is simply the correction of a clerical error, and commends itself. Most grotesque is Gitlbauer's παλιμβόλως τήξας γάρους ἀνέστη κοῦφος. The aorist ἐκέρδησα, rashly altered by the editors in this passage, is a well-known late form. Even in Demosthenes traces are to be found of the tendency to allow the overwhelming numbers of vowel-verbs to affect the inflections of the consonantal. Thus in Dem. 521, 2, is found ἠσελγημένα as a perfect participle of ἀσελγαίνω—a formation assisted by the extreme rarity of perfect passive forms from verbs in -αίνω. The non-existence in Attic of perfects active from the same class of verbs may be an apology for Demosthenes employing κεκέρδηκα, but it is not a defence. Earlier writers did without a perfect altogether.

14. The deponent form and absolute

sense of ἐπενοεῖτο can both be well supported from the lexica.
18. This signification of ἀθρόως is very familiar to students of late Greek. It has its counterpart in English slang, so uniform are the processes of decay.
20. The late misuse of βαστάζω is here prominent. Cp. Batrachomach. 78, οὐχ οὕτω νώτοισιν ἐβάστασε φόρτον ἔρωτος. J. H. Schmidt, with his usual absence of appreciation of the history of the Greek language, allows this passage of the spurious Batrachomachia to vitiate his conclusions as regards βαστάζω (Synonymik der Griechischen Sprache, vol. iii. p. 185). The change of meaning which this verb underwent is illustrated by the fact that in Attic it is not compounded with any preposition but ἐπί, while in late Greek it is compounded with most.
CXII. 3. Eberhard's suggestion to replace ὤρυσσεν by ἤρασσεν will be re-

παρὰ τὴν ὀπὴν ὁ ταῦρος· ἔνθεν ἐκκύψας   5
ὁ μῦς ἐφέρπει καὶ πάλιν δακὼν φεύγει.
ὁ δ᾽ ἐξαναστὰς οὐκ ἔχων ὃ ποιήσει,
διηπορεῖτο· τῷ δ᾽ ὁ μῦς ἐπιτρύξας
'οὐχ ὁ μέγας ἀεὶ δυνατός· ἔσθ᾽ ὅπου μᾶλλον
τὸ μικρὸν εἶναι καὶ ταπεινὸν ἰσχύει.'   10

CXIII.

Μάνδρης ἔσω τις πρόβατα συλλέγων δείλης
κνηκὸν μετ᾽ αὐτῶν λύκον ἔμελλε συγκλείειν.
ὁ κύων δ᾽ ἰδὼν πρὸς αὐτὸν εἶπε 'πῶς σπεύδεις
τὰ πρόβατα σῶσαι, τοῦτον εἰσάγων ἥμιν;'

CXIV.

Μεθύων ἐλαίῳ λύχνος ἑσπέρης ηὔχει
πρὸς τοὺς παρόντας ὡς ἑωσφόρου κρείσσων
ἅπασι φέγγος ἐκπρεπέστατον λάμπει.

CXII. 8. Pro ἐπιτρύξας ego ἔφη τρύξας legere malim, de prae-
positionis virtute hoc in loco dubius.
CXIV. Fabulam habet codex Vaticanus. 3. Eberhardo praeeunte,
lectionem emendavi Athoam λάμπειν ἅπασιν ἐκπρεπέστατον φέγγος,

---

jected by every one who remembers
his Aristophanes.
7. The same editor also errs, and
from the same cause, defective general
knowledge of Greek, in preferring ὀργί-
λως to οὐκ ἔχων. 'The bull sprang up,
only to recognise his helplessness, and
was at his wits end.'
CXIII. The fable has otherwise so
little point that it is tempting to consider it the spurious addition of some
monk playing upon the two meanings
of μάνδρα, 'a sheepfold' and 'a monastery,' and the Christian metaphor of
τὰ πρόβατα and οἱ λύκοι, rather than as
a tetrastich abridgment of a longer
piece.
3. Although the prose paraphrase
has πῶς τὰ πρόβατα θέλων σῶσαι τοῦτον
εἰσάγεις ἔσω, it is better not to accept
here Bergk's suggestion of σπεύδων and
εἰσάγεις. The Athoan reading is the

idiomatic Greek equivalent for the
English 'Little you effect to make us
secure if you let this fellow in amongst
us.'
CXIV. 1. 'De metaphora verbi μεθύω
in sensu plenitudinis monui ad Theo-
phylactum Simoc. p. 218. Antiphilus
de torrente Anth. 9, 277: μεθύεις
ὄμβροισι. Ibi Jacobs. Philippus Anth.
6, 38: κώπην ἅλμης τὴν μεθύουσαν ἔτι,
Suida interpretante μεθύουσαν, πεπληρω-
μένην.'—Boissonade. Here it does not
mean 'full' except in the Scotch sense
of 'fou.' The lamp was drunk to make
such a statement. Of a man you may
use μεθύων οἴνῳ: μεθύων ἐλαίῳ is the
corresponding phrase for a personified
lamp.
3. Although λάμπει admits of being
translated as an intransitive here, it is
better to make it transitive—a sense
which is quite common in late writers.

ἀνέμου δὲ συρίσαντος εὐθὺς ἐσβέσθη
πνοῇ ῥαπισθείς· ἐκ δὲ δευτέρης ἅπτων   5
εἰπέν τις αὐτῷ ' φαῖνε, λύχνε, καὶ σίγα·
τῶν ἀστέρων τὸ φέγγος οὐκ ἀποθνήσκει.'

CXV.

Νωθὴς χελώνη λιμνάσιν ποτ' αἰθυίαις
λάροις τε καὶ κήυξιν εἶπεν ἀγρώσταις·
' κἀμὲ πτερωτὴν εἴθε τις πεποιήκει.'
τῇ δ' ἐκ τύχης ἔλεξεν αἰετὸς — --
' πόσον, χέλυμνα, μισθὸν αἰετῷ δώσεις,   5
ὅστις σ' ἐλαφρὴν καὶ μετάρσιον θήσω ;'
' τὰ τῆς Ἐρυθρῆς πάντα δῶρά σοι δώσω.'
' τοιγὰρ διδάξω ' φησίν. ὑπτίην δ' ἄρας
ἔκρυψε νέφεσιν, ἔνθεν εἰς ὄρος ῥίψας
ἤραξεν αὐτῆς οὖλον ὄστρακον νώτων.   10
ἡ δ' εἶπεν ἐκψύχουσα ' σὺν δίκῃ θνήσκω.
τίς γὰρ νεφῶν μοι καὶ τίς ἦν πτερῶν χρείη,
τῇ καὶ χαμᾶζε δυσκόλως προβαινούσῃ ;'

---

quam haud invitus retinuit Gitlbauer quo facilius ipse choliambos ex
paraphrasi effingeret. Emendationem, si necesse sit, Bodleianus fulcit,
ἐκαυχᾶτο ὡς ὑπὲρ ἥλιον πλέον λάμπει. 6. Athoo inest vitium non
minus ridiculum quam ea in Fab. 54, 2, atque 82, 8. Pro lectione
Vaticana φαῖνε λύχνε καὶ σίγα exhibet Athous βαῖον ἦν λύχνου πνεῦμα,
sed pro Vaticano οὔποτ' ἐκλείπει recte idem οὐκ ἀποθνήσκει.

CXV. 4. In Athoo ταῦτα, quo exit hic versus, latet participium
aliquod quod ego supplere nequeo. Conantor peritiores. Schneidewini
conjectura κλίων in metrum offendit.

---

5. For ῥαπίζειν see Phryn. p. 264.

6. The Athoan readings of this line
are evidently attempts to preserve a
mutilated or partly obliterated text.

CXV. 5. The form χέλυμνα only
occurs here. In a case like this criticism is powerless, and the conjectures
χέλυννα, χέλυνα, χελύνη, and χελώνη,
do nothing but prove it.

6. The terms Ἐρυθρὸς πόντος, Ἐρυθρὰ
θάλασσα, Ἐρυθρά, Ἐρυθραῖος πόντος, etc.,
corresponded rather to the ' Indian
Ocean ' than to our ' Red Sea.'

10. The word οὖλος is a favourite with
Theophrastus, in whose writings it is
sometimes to be translated by ' crisp,'
sometimes by ' brittle.' Pl. Hist. 10, 4,
3, φύλλον οὖλον, 'a crisp leaf;' 5, 5, 1,
ξύλα οὖλας ἔχοντα συστροφάς, 'with
brittle knots ;' Pl. Caus. 6, 11, 8, ἡ
οὐλότης καὶ πυκνότης τῶν ξύλων, 'the
brittleness and density of the wood.'
For other examples see Schneider's
Lexicon.

13. Observe χαμᾶζε by late usage for
χαμαί, and δυσκόλως for χαλεπῶς.

CXVI.

Νυκτὸς μεσούσης ἦδε παῖς τις εὐφώνως.
γυνὴ δ᾽ ἀκούει τοῦδε κἀξαναστᾶσα
θυρίδων προκύπτει καὶ βλέπουσα τὸν παῖδα
λαμπρῆς σελήνης ἐν φάει καλὸν λίην,
τὸν ἄνδρ᾽ ἑαυτῆς καταλιποῦσα κοιμᾶσθαι 5
κάτω μελάθρων ἦλθε καὶ θύρης ἔξω
ἐλθοῦσ᾽ ἐποίει τὴν προθυμίην πᾶσαν.
ἀνὴρ δὲ ταύτης ἐξανίστατ᾽ ἐξαίφνης
ζητῶν ὅπου᾽στί, κοὐκ ἰδὼν δόμων εἴσω
ἀμηχανῶν τε καὐτὸς ἦλθεν εἰς οἶμον 10
καὶ τῇ συνεύνῳ φησί ῾μηδὲν ἐκπλήσσου,
τὸν παῖδα δ᾽ ἡμῖν πεῖσον εἰς δόμους εὕδειν.᾽
ὃν καὶ λαβὼν παρῆγεν· εἶτα κἀκεῖνος,
ἄμφω θελόντων δρᾶν τι, τῇδ᾽ ἐραθύμει.

CXVII.

Νεὼς ποτ᾽ αὐτοῖς ἀνδράσιν βυθισθείσης,
ἰδών τις ἔλεγεν ἄδικα τοὺς θεοὺς κρίνειν·
ἑνὸς γὰρ ἀσεβοῦς ἐμβεβηκότος πλοίῳ,
πολλοὺς σὺν αὐτῷ μηδὲν αἰτίους θνήσκειν.
καὶ ταῦθ᾽ ὁμοῦ λέγοντος, οἷα συμβαίνει, 5
πολλῶν ἐπ᾽ αὐτὸν ἑσμὸς ἦλθε μυρμήκων,
σπεύδοντες ἄχνας πυρίνας ἀποτρώγειν.
ὑφ᾽ ἑνὸς δὲ δηχθεὶς συνεπάτησε τοὺς πλείους.

CXVI. Fabulam Babrio vere indignam editores plerique rejiciunt. Est certe aetatis serioris, ingenii magis corrupti. Exhibet codex Vaticanus. 7. Pro Athoo πλήρη Vaticanum πᾶσαν dedi. 9. Vaticanus ἐφευρεῖν pro ὅπου᾽στί habet. 10. Verbum ἀμηχανῶν ex Athoo μηδὲν χανὼν et Vaticano μηδὲν χαννὼν cum Ahrensio elicui. Knoellii μηδὲν χαλῶν (nihil remittens) non placet, quamvis codicis Athoi diorthotes supra χανὼν verbum μελήσας forte pro μελλήσας scripsit. Epimythium forsan ipsa fabula est serius, numeris aeque caret—

τουτὶ μὲν οὕτως· ἔμφασις δὲ τοῦ μύθου
κακὸν ἐπιχαίρειν ὅταν ἔχῃ τις ἐκτῖσαι.

CXVII. Fabulam exhibet Vaticanus.

Ἑρμῆς δ' ἐπιστὰς τῷ τε ῥαβδίῳ παίων
εἶτ' 'οὐκ ἀνέξῃ' φησί 'τοὺς θεοὺς ὕμων   10
εἶναι δικαστὰς οἷος εἶ σὺ μυρμήκων;'

CXVIII.

Ξουθὴ χελιδών, ἡ πάροικος ἀνθρώπων,
ἦρος καλιὴν ηὐθέτιζεν ἐν τοίχῳ,
ὅπου γερόντων οἶκος ἦν δικαστήρων·
κἀκεῖ νεοσσῶν ἑπτὰ γίνεται μήτηρ,

---

10. Paraphrasi neglecta, εἶτ' 'οὐκ ἀνέξῃ' κτλ; distinxi ego.
CXVIII. Codicem Athoum totus in hac fabula secutus sum, nisi quod
in extrema φεύγει manifestum vitium in φεύγω mutavi. Editores caeteri
alia vitia codici invito aggerunt.

CXVIII. 1. The meaning of ξουθὴ
in this passage is evidently 'twittering.'
The adjective seems to be used of
colour, motion, and sound—an argument against its identification with
ξανθός, which is only used of colour.
Curtius would derive the Vedic
çk'andras, later k'andras, ξανθός, ξουθός
(= ξονθός), Latin candeo, candidus,
etc., all from the same root.
Soberly the meaning of the term
is still to be discovered. The ancient
lexicographers are worthless in a case
of this kind, viz. Hesychius, ξουθόν·
λεπτόν, ἁπαλόν, ἐλαφρόν, ὑγρόν, πυρρόν,
χλωρόν, ἄργυρος, ξανθόν, πυκνόν, ὀξύ·
τινὲς δὲ ποικίλον, εὐειδές, διαυγές. He
might as well have said that the word
could mean anything. As for ἀργυρός,
it is evidently a corruption of a Latin
word 'argutus,' and has come from
some Graeco-Latin glossologist. In
Suidas and Photius the same absurdities
appear.
In Attic the word occurs sixteen
times, and in all cases in the higher
poetry or in parodies thereof. It is
applied to the nightingale in Aesch.
Agam. 1142, ἀμφὶ δ' αὐτᾶς θροεῖς νόμον
ἄνομον οἷά τις ξουθά, ἀκόρετος βοᾶς, φεῦ,
ταλαίναις φρεσὶν Ἴτυν Ἴτυν στένουσ'
ἀμφιθαλῆ κακοῖς ἀηδὼν βίον. Eur. Hel.
1109, ἀναβοάσω σὲ τὰν ἀοιδοτάταν ὄρνιθα
μελῳδὸν ἀηδόνα δακρυόεσσαν, ἐλθ' ὦ διὰ
ξουθᾶν γενύων ἐλελιζομένα θρήνοις ἐμοῖς

ξυνεργός. It is applied to the bee
in Soph. Polyid. 365, τὸ ποικιλώτατον
ξουθῆς μελίσσης κηρόπλαστον ὄργανον.
Eur. I. T. 165, ξουθᾶν πόνημα μελισσᾶν.
Id. 634, τῆς ἐρείας ἀνθεμόρρυτον γάνος
ξουθῆς μελίσσης. So Plato (?) in Anth.
Pal. 16, 210 (cp. ξουθόπτερος μέλισσα
in Eur. H. F. 487; Cress. 470).
Aeschylus spoke of ξουθὸς ἱππαλεκτρυών;
and if Athenaeus (xiii. 608 D) is to b
trusted, Chaeremon wrote the lines—
κόμαι δὲ κηροχρῶτες ὡς ἀγάλματος
αὑτοῖσι βοστρύχοισιν εὖ πεπλασμένου
ξουθαῖσιν ἀνέμοις ἐνετρίφων φορούμεναι.
Finally, Herodian, περὶ λέξεως μονήρους,
p. 8, 35, quotes as from Sophocles
Polyidus, ξουθὸς Φαμενὸς Τειρεσίου παῖς.
Aristophanes parodies the passage from
the Helena in Av. 211, 743, and (less
markedly) 676, and ridicules the Aeschylean ξουθὸς ἱππαλεκτρυών in Pax,
1177, Av. 800, and Ran. 932. Antiphanes parodies the Euripidean application of the word to bees in a γρῖφος,
quoted by Athenaeus in x. 449 B. In
none of these passages is there any
necessity to understand the word as
referring to colour. In fact so to
translate it is to violate the harmony
of sense in Agam. 1142 and Hel. 1109.
In Chaeremon, if the true word has
been preserved, it may refer to colour,
or to motion, or to sound; while, as
for Herodian's quotation, the context

I

οὔπω πτερίσκοις πορφυροῖς ἐπανθούντων.   5
ὄφις δὲ τούτους ἑρπύσας ἀπὸ τρώγλης
ἅπαντας ἑξῆς ἔφαγεν. ἡ δὲ δειλαίη
παίδων ἀώρων συμφορὰς ἀπεθρήνει,
'οἴμοι' λέγουσα 'τῆς ἐμῆς ἐγὼ μοίρης·
ὅπου νόμοι γὰρ καὶ θέμιστες ἀνθρώπων,   10
ἔνθεν χελιδὼν ἠδικημένη φεύγω.'

CXIX.

Ξύλινόν τις Ἑρμῆν εἶχεν· ἦν δὲ τεχνίτης,
σπένδων δὲ τούτῳ καὶ καθ' ἡμέρην θύων
ἔπρασσε φαύλως· τῷ θεῷ δ' ἐθυμώθη,
χαμαὶ δ' ἀπεκρότησε τοῦ σκέλους ἄρας.
χρυσὸς δὲ κεφαλῆς ἐρρύη καταγείσης,   5
ὃν συλλέγων ἄνθρωπος εἶπεν ''Ἑρμείη,
σκαιός τίς ἐσσι καὶ φίλοισιν ἀγνώμων,
ὃς προσκυνοῦντας οὐδὲν ὠφέλεις ἥμας,
ἀγαθοῖς δὲ πολλοῖς ὑβρίσαντας ἠμείψω.
τὴν εἰς σὲ καινὴν εὐσέβειαν οὐκ ᾔδειν.'   10

CXIX. 7. Ahrensio duce, τίς ἐσσι pro τις εἶ scripsi. 10. Hoc de
versu fortasse interpolato paraphrases silent. Epimythium primus saepsit
Eberhard—

καὶ τοῖς θεοῖς Αἴσωπος ἐμπλέκει μύθοις,
βουλόμενος ἡμᾶς νουθετεῖν πρὸς ἀλλήλους.
πλέον οὐδὲν ἕξεις σκαιὸν ἄνδρα τιμήσας,
ἀτιμάσας δ' ἂν αὐτὸν ὠφεληθείης.

---

would probably show that he had
quoted negligently.

The late Greek usage permits of any
of the three meanings, but with none
of them well defined. In short, the
history of the word is probably this.
Originally possessing a precise signification (hence perhaps the proper name
Ξοῦθος), it afterwards dropped out of use
till it was taken up by the higher poetry
to which the indefiniteness of meaning
produced by time had a literary value.
The passages in which it was embalmed

being few, and supplying no necessary
clue to the sense intended, led to misconception, and the late literary schools
ended by assigning to the word the
meanings which they fancied best
suited the two or three classical passages,
but to which the word may or may not
originally have had any claim.

CXIX. 1. 'Subjicit poeta hominem
fuisse opificem, ut significet eum pau-
pertate laborare, conf. v. 3.'—Lewis.

5. For καταγείσης compare note on
Fab. 47, 9, supra.

CXX.

Ὁ τελμάτων ἔνοικος, ὁ σκιῇ χαίρων,
ὁ ζῶν ὀρυκτοῖς βάτραχος παρ' εὐρίποις,
εἰς γῆν παρελθὼν ἔλεγε πᾶσι τοῖς ζῴοις
'ἰατρός εἰμι φαρμάκων ἐπιστήμων,
οἵων τάχ' οὐδεὶς οἶδεν, οὐδ' ὁ Παιήων,   5
ὃς Ὄλυμπον οἰκεῖ καὶ θεοὺς ἰατρεύει.'
'καὶ πῶς' ἀλώπηξ εἶπεν 'ἄλλον ἰήσῃ,
ὃς σαυτὸν οὕτω χλωρὸν ὄντα μὴ σώζεις;'

CXXI.

Ὄρνις ποτ' ἠσθένησε. τῇ δὲ προσκύψας
αἴλουρος εἶπε 'πῶς ἔχεις; τίνων χρῄζεις;
ἐγὼ παρέξω πάντα σοι· μόνον σῴζου.'
ἡ δ' 'ἢν ἀπέλθῃς' εἶπεν 'οὐκ ἀποθνήσκω.'

CXXII.

Ὄνος πατήσας σκόλοπα χωλὸς εἱστήκει·
λύκον δ' ἰδὼν παρόντα καὶ σαφῆ δείσας

CXX. Fabulam habet codex Vaticanus. 4. Cum Vaticano magis
'ἰατρός εἰμι' quam cum Athoo ἰατρὸς εἶναι legere malo. 8. Paraphrasi
Bodleiana et Aviano fretus, verbum χλωρὸν dedi. Corrupte codices
χωλὸν exhibent.

CXXI. Fabula a tetrastichista in brevius contracta est. Versum
quintum

χρονιώτερον γὰρ δορκάδος βίον ζήσω

temere supplevit Lachmannus : Nam quod exhibent paraphrases aliquot—
ζωὴν γὰρ ζήσω δορκάδος ὑπερτέραν vel verba similia—talia sunt qualia
non raro ad finem fabularum addiderunt interpolatores.

CXX. 2. The use of εὔριπος for an
artificial receptacle for water—aqueduct,
canal, fish-pond, cistern, etc.—is frequent in late Greek authors and in
Latin. Cp. 'Nilus.'
6. 'Who has a house in Olympus
and is physician to the Gods.' 'Ιατρεύω
is not merely a late synonym for ἰάομαι,
but there is a natural distinction between the two words which occasioned
their early co-existence.
8. 'Pallida caeruleus cui notat ora
color.'—Avianus. The mistake probably originated from Fab. 122, l. 15.
CXXII. 1. σκόλοψ =classical ἄκανθα,
as often in late Greek. St. Paul, Ep.
ad. Cor. 2, 12, 7, ἐδόθη μοι σκόλοψ τῇ
σαρκὶ ἄγγελος Σατᾶν.

ὄλεθρον οὕτως εἶπεν· ' ὦ λύκε, θνήσκω,
μέλλω τ' ἀποπνεῖν· σοὶ δὲ συμβαλὼν χαίρω.
σὺ μᾶλλον ἢ γὺψ ἢ κόραξ με δειπνήσεις.   5
χάριν δέ μοι δὸς ἀβλαβῆ τε καὶ κούφην,
ἐκ τοῦ ποδός μου τὴν ἄκανθαν εἰρύσσας,
ὥς μου κατέλθῃ πνεῦμ' ἀναλγὲς εἰς ᾅδου.'
κἀκεῖνος εἰπών ' χάριτος οὐ φθονῶ ταύτης '
ὀδοῦσιν ἀκροῖς σκόλοπα θερμὸν ἐξῇρει.   10
ὁ δ' ἐκλυθεὶς πόνων τε κἀνίης πάσης
τὸν κνηκίην χάσκοντα λακτίσας φεύγει,
ῥῖνας, μέτωπα, γομφίους τ' ἀλοιήσας.
' οἴμοι' λύκος ' τάδ' ' εἶπε ' σὺν δίκῃ πάσχω.
τί γὰρ ἄρτι χωλοὺς ἠρξάμην ἰατρεύειν   15
μαθὼν ἀπ' ἀρχῆς οὐδὲν ἢ μαγειρεύειν;'

CXXIII.

Ὄρνιθος ἀγαθῆς χρύσε' ᾠὰ τικτούσης

CXXIV.

Ὀρνιθοθήρῃ φίλος ἐπῆλθεν ἐξαίφνης
μέλλοντι θύμβρα καὶ σέλινα δειπνήσειν.

CXXII. 11. Pro Athoo καὶ ἀναιδείης editores κανίης receperunt ex
Suidae Lexico sub κνηκίας vocabulo.

CXXIII. Hoc in versu desinit codex Athous. Versiculos, quos
pedestri fretus paraphrasi in fabulam conficiendam Minerva sua Gitlbauer
confinxit, ego non recepi. Talia Βαβριάζοντά τινα revocant eundemque
imperitum, non Βάβριον, neque ab ipso mythographo libenter suscepti
essent. Versus quoque a Minoida Mena mala fraude additos in suam
ipsorum sedem abire volo. Ecce paraphrasem Bodleianam exhibebo.
Ὄρνιν τις εἶχε καλὴν χρυσᾶ ᾠὰ τίκτουσαν. νομίσας δὲ ἔνδον αὐτῆς
ὄγκον χρυσίου εἶναι καὶ θύσας εὗρεν οὖσαν ὁμοίαν τῶν λοιπῶν ὀρνίθων.
ὁ δὲ ἀθρόον πλοῦτον ἐλπίσας εὑρεῖν καὶ τοῦ μικροῦ κέρδους ἐστέρητο.

CXXIV. Fabulam habet codex Vaticanus.

3. The οὕτως goes with the εἶπεν,
and is not equivalent to ἅτε χωλὸς
ὤν.
4. In late writers ἀποπνεῖν may be
used absolutely like the classical ἐκπνεῖν.
10. 'The feverish thorn.' Lach-

mann's conjecture θερμός has not re-
commended itself even to the editors.
12. 'Ere yellow-boy's mouth is shut
he kicks him and makes off.' There is
a side play on λύκος χανών. See Fab.
16, 6, supra.

ὁ δὲ κλωβὸς εἶχεν οὐδέν· οὐ γὰρ ἠγρεύκει.
ὤρμησε δὴ πέρδικα ποικίλον θύσων,
ὃν ἡμερώσας εἶχεν εἰς τὸ θηρεύειν. 5
ὁ δ' αὐτὸν οὕτως ἱκέτευε μὴ κτείνειν·
'τὸ λοιπόν' εἶπε 'δικτύῳ τί ποιήσεις,
ὅταν κυνηγῇς; τίς δέ σοι συναθροίσει
εὐωπὸν ἀγέλην ὀρνέων φιλαλλήλων;
τίνος μελῳδοῦ πρὸς τὸν ἦχον ὑπνώσεις;' 10
ἀφῆκε τὸν πέρδικα καὶ γενειήτην
ἀλεκτορίσκον συλλαβεῖν ἐβουλήθη.
ὁ δ' ἐκ πεταύρου κλαγκτὸν εἶπε φωνήσας
'πόθεν μαθήσῃ πόσσον εἰς ἔω λείπει,
τὸν ὠρόμαντιν ἀπολέσας με; πῶς γνώσῃ 15
πότ' ἐννυχεύει χρυσότοξος Ὠρίων,
ἔργων δὲ τίς σε πρωινῶν ἀναμνήσει,
ὅτε δροσώδης ταρσός ἐστιν ὀρνίθων;'

---

6. κτείνειν pro κτεῖναι scripsi. 7. εἶπε addidit Schneider. 13. Verbum πεταύρου ex Suida (sub voc.) receptum Vaticano τοῦ τέγους praeposui, et κλαγγὸν in κλαγκτὸν mutavi, Vaticano κλαγγὴν neglecto. Male tamen Suidas βοήσας pro Vaticano φωνήσας dedit, et θύσας pro ἀπολέσας.

CXXIV. 3. The word κλωβὸς is quite late. It means a cage, generally of wood, used for keeping netted game alive till wanted by the cook. Antipater in Anth. Pal. 6, 109, 3, has κλωβοὺς ἀμφίρρωγας, in which the adjective implies that such cages were reticulated on the sides at least. The top may have been roofed.
6. The text of this fable has come down to us, like all dependent upon the Vatican codex alone, in so corrupt a state—as far as spelling goes—that I have not hesitated to better the metre by substituting κτεῖναι by κτείνειν. The change leaves the sense as it was.
7. For the use of partridges as decoy birds see Aristotle, Anim. Hist. 10, 8, (614 ᵃ8) ff.
9. εὐωπὸς refers to the keen sight, not to the beauty of the eyes.
10. 'To what songster's strain will you close your eyes?' For ὑπνοῦν see note on Fab. 30, 7, supra.
11. In grammatical writers γένειον and πώγων are used like the French 'barbe' of the wattles of the cock and

like birds. In Arist. also, Anim. Hist. 10, 7 (613, ᵃ31), πώγων seems to have this sense—οἱ τῶν στρουθίων ἄρρενες οὐ φαίνονται ἔχοντες εὐθὺς τὰ περὶ τὸν πώγωνα μέλανα, ὕστερον δ' ἴσχουσιν. The correct Greek word was κάλλαιον or κάλλαια (Aristoph. Eq. 497). Ammonius explains κάλλαια as οἱ τῶν ἀλεκτρυόνων πώγωνες, and Moeris has the note, κάλλαια τὰ ὑπὸ τὰ γένεια τῶν ἀλεκτρυόνων, οὓς κάλλωνας οἱ Ἀττικοὶ λέγουσιν, in which Pierson has rightly shown that χελλῶνας (labrones) should be read. In Aristotle the emended word has similarly been corrupted to χάλλωνες.
13. Here and in 135, 3, I have written the verbal κλαγκτὸν according to the conjecture of Jacobs on this passage. The form κλαγγὴν presented by the Vatican in both places is metrically absurd, and the Suidian κλαγγὸν leads us half-way to the intelligible reading.
15. 'How wilt thou know what hour Orion of the golden bow takes up his nightly station, and who will remind

118   SCRIPTORES FABULARUM GRAECI.

κἀκεῖνος εἶπεν ' οἶδα χρήσιμόν σ' ὥραις,
ὅμως δὲ δεῖ σχεῖν τὸν φίλον τί δειπνήσει.'   20

CXXV.

Ὄνος τις ἀναβὰς εἰς τὸ δῶμα καὶ παίζων
τὸν κέραμον ἔθλα, καί τις αὐτὸν ἀνθρώπων
ἐπιδραμὼν κατῆγε τῷ ξύλῳ παίων.
ὁ δ' ὄνος πρὸς αὐτόν, ὡς τὸ νῶτον ἠλγήκει,
' καὶ μὴν πίθηκος ἐχθές ' εἶπε ' καὶ πρώην   5
ἔτερπεν ὑμᾶς αὐτὸ τοῦτο ποιήσας.'

CXXVI.

Ὁδοιπορῶν ἄνθρωπος εἰς ἐρημαίην
ἑστῶσαν εὗρε τὴν Ἀληθίην μούνην
καί φησιν αὐτῇ ' διὰ τίν' αἰτίην, †γραίη,
τὴν πόλιν ἀφεῖσα τὴν ἐρημίην ναίεις;'
ἡ δ' εὐθὺ πρὸς τάδ' εἶπεν ἡ βαθυγνώμων   5
†' ψεῦδος παρ' ὀλίγοις ἦν τὸ πρῶτον ἀνθρώποις,†

19. Vaticanum χρησίμους ὥρας ego non sine fiducia emendavi.
CXXV. Fabulam servavit codex Vaticanus. 5. Cum Buttmanno ὁ
πίθηκος χθές in πίθηκος ἐχθές mutavi.
CXXVI. Hos mythiambos deterrime servatos habet codex Vaticanus,
cujus minuta vitia lectori apud Knoellium, p. 683 legere licet. Non
meum est talia iterum scribere. 6. Versum sextum hunc in modum
exhibet Vaticanus—

ὅτι ποτὲ παρ' ὀλίγοισιν ἦν ψεῦδος,

et septimum addit—

νῦν εἰς πάντας βροτοὺς ἐλήλυθε ψεῦδος,

quod facile erat sic corrigere—

νῦν εἰς ἅπαντας ἐξελήλυθ' ἀνθρώπους,

sed reputanti spurium esse videbitur.

thee of thy morning tasks when the
dew lies thick on the wings of birds?'
Whatever the natural facts may be,
ἐννυχεύει cannot bear the meaning of
'set' as the lexica say. Moreover,
there is an antithesis intended here
between evening and morning.

19. χρήσιμόν σ' ὥραις. The necessary change I have made is little more
than a correction of spelling.
CXXV. 1. δῶμα, cp. note on Fab.
5, 5, supra.
5. For ἐχθές καὶ πρώην see Phryn.
p. 370 ff.

εἰ δ' ἐστὶν εἰπεῖν καὶ κλύειν τι βουλήσῃ
ὁ νῦν βίος πονηρός ἐστιν ἀνθρώπων.'

CXXVII.

†Ὁ Ζεὺς γράφοντ' ἐν ὀστράκοισιν Ἑρμείην
τὰ τῶν ἁπάντων ἀμπλακήματ' ἀνθρώπων†
ἐκέλευσεν εἰς κιβωτὸν αὐτὰ σωρεύειν
σταθεῖσαν αὐτοῦ πλησίην, ἐρευνήσας
ὅπως ἑκάστου τὰς δίκας ἀναπράξει.   5
τῶν ὀστράκων δὲ κεχυμένων ἐπ' ἀλλήλοις
τὸ μὲν βράδιον τὸ δὲ τάχιον ἐμπίπτει
εἰς τοῦ Διὸς τὰς χεῖρας, εἴ ποτ' εὐθύνοι.
τῶν οὖν πονηρῶν οὐ προσῆκε θαυμάζειν
ἢν θᾶσσον ἀδικῶν ὀψέ τις κακῶς πράσσῃ.   10

8. Vaticanum καὶ βεβούλησαι κλύειν emendavit Gitlbauer, qui etiam adjecit epimythium ex paraphrasi Bodleiana—

τὸ ψεῦδος ὅτι νῦν πρόκριτόν ἐστ' ἀληθείης,

quod sibi habere satius fuit.

CXXVII. Fabulam praeter duo primos versus moderate bene servavit Vaticanus codex, ex quo a Furia edito restituerunt editores priores. Nuper Knoellius lectiones Vaticanas accuratius edidit p. 683. Eberhardi recensionem suscepi nisi quod alios in versibus primo et secundo secutus sum, in altero Lachmannum, altero M. Schmidtium. 1, 2, ὀστράκῳ γράφοντι τὸν Ἑρμῆν ἐκέλευσεν ὁ Ζεὺς εἰς κιβωτὸν ταύτας σωρεύειν— Vaticanus. ὁ Ζεὺς τὰς τῶν ἀνθρώπων ἁμαρτίας ἐν ὀστράκοις τὸν Ἑρμῆν ὥρισε γράφειν καὶ εἰς κιβώτιον ἀποτιθέναι πλησίον αὐτοῦ—Bodleianus.

ὁ Ζεὺς τὸν Ἑρμῆν ἐγγράφειν ποτ' ἀνθρώπων
ἐν ὀστράκοισι τὰς ἁμαρτίας πάσας—Eberhard.

ὁ Ζεὺς τὸν Ἑρμῆν ἀμπλακήματ' ἀνθρώπων
ἅπαντ' ἐν ὀστράκοισιν ὥρισεν γράψαι—Gitlbauer.

5. Vaticanum ἀναπράσσει in ἀναπράξει mutavi.

CXXVII. 7. 'And as the potsherds are heaped one upon the other, they fall into the hands of Zeus, some late, some soon, for him to give judgment thereon.' Zeus is regarded as the εὔθυνος or scrutineer, not of each man's complete account, but of the separate items which compose it. The system of book-keeping is not simple but only primitive. There is not even a day book, much less a ledger. For τάχιον and βράδιον see Phryn. p. 149.

8. εἴ ποτ' εὐθύνοι· almost 'if he should ever give judgment thereon.' The form of phrase suggests the possibility of some of the potsherds never reaching the scrutineer's hand.

9. In οὐ προσῆκε θαυμάζειν the im-

CXXVIII.

Οἷς εἶπε †μύθους πρὸς νομῆα †τοιούτους·
κείρεις μὲν ἡμᾶς καὶ πόκους ἔχεις κέρσας,
τὸ γάλα δ' ἀμέλγοντ' ἐστί σοι φίλον πῆξαι,
ἡμῶν δὲ τέκνα μῆλά σοι περισσεύει.
πλέον οὐδὲν ἡμῖν ἀλλὰ χ᾽ τροφὴ γαίης   5
πᾶσ᾽ ἦν ἐν ὄρεσιν εὐτελές τι γεννήσῃ,
†φέρβεις δὲ τὴν κύν᾽ ἧμιν ἐν μέσαις ταύτην,†
τρέφων ὁποῖα σαυτὸν εὐθαλεῖ σίτῳ.᾽
†ἤκουσε τούτων ἡ κύων ἔφη δ᾽ οὕτως·†   10
'εἰ μὴ παρήμην κἂν μέσοις ἐπωλεύμην,

CXXVIII. Haec fabula, in codice Vaticano servata, manifestis scatet erroribus, quos ego pedetentim amovere conatus sum alios mea ipse Minerva alios editoribus fretus. 1. Vaticanum οἷς τις εἶπε πρὸς νομέα τοιάδε ego correxi. 6. Vaticanum πᾶσα in πᾶσ᾽ ἦν cum Gitlbauero mutavi. 7. Pro Vaticano εὐθαλές ego εὐτελες scripsi et proximum versum—

ὡραία βοτάνη καὶ δρόσου γεμισθεῖσα,

ex verbo εὐθαλές ortum esse putare malo quam in talia mutare—

βοτάνην ἀραιὴν καὶ δρόσου γεμισθεῖσαν.

8. Sordes in melius revocavi Vaticanas φέρβοις δ᾽ ἂν ἡμῖν ἐν μέσοις κένα ταύτην. 10. Verba Vaticana ταῖθ᾽ ὡς ἤκοισεν ἡ κύων ἔφη τοῖα Lachmannus rescripsit nisi quod ego ἔφη δ᾽ pro ἔφη θ᾽ dedi.

perfect answers to the English 'it were not right to marvel.'
CXXVIII. 3. There is something corrupt in this line, but Lachmann did not remove it by replacing φίλον by φλέον. Besides rennet (πυετία, πυαρ, τάμισος) the ancients used the juice of plants to curdle milk, most commonly that of the fig-tree, and especially the wild fig-tree. Dioscorides 1, 184, ὁ δὲ ὀπὸς τῆς ἀγρίας καὶ τῆς ἡμέρου συκῆς πηκτικός ἐστι γάλακτος, ὥσπερ ἡ πιτία. The κνῆκος was also so employed.
5. I had re-written this line
ἡμῖν μὲν οὐδὲν ἄλλο πλὴν τροφὴ γαίης,
from a feeling that the sheep wished to emphasise the difference between their own condition and that of the dog.

But the words are right as they stand in the codex, 'Great as our services are, they profit us nothing. All the food we have is but the trash that mother earth makes to grow on the hills, and you feed the dog here in our midst, giving him fare as rich as your own.' I am confident that the conjecture εὐτελές restores the text, and that it will be accepted.
11. The word παρήμην is an excellent instance of the sort of difficulty which artificial Greek, such as the Babrian, is always presenting. There is no way of deciding whether it is the past of πάρημαι or of πάρειμι, as on the one hand Babrius may well have used the corrupt form of παρήν, common in his own day, and on the other may have been harking back to the πάρημαι of classical

οὐκ ἄν ποθ' ὑμεῖς ἔσχετ' ἄφθονον ποίην.
ἐγὼ δὲ περιτρέχουσα πάντα κωλύω
λῃστῶν †πανούργων καὶ λύκων διωκτήρων.'

CXXIX.

†"Ονον τις εἶχε κύνα τε τῶν τραπεζήων·
κύων δ' ἔχαιρεν εὐρύθμως ἀεὶ παίζων†
τὸν δεσπότην τε ποικίλως περισκαίρων.
κἀκεῖνος αὖ κατεῖχεν αὐτὸν ἐν κόλποις·
ὄνος δὲ τὴν μὲν νύκτ' †ἔμειν' ἀλετρεύων   5

13. Hunc versum Matthiae restituit, proximum ego : περιτρέχουσα
δ' ἐγὼ πάντοθεν κωλύω δρηστῆρα λῃστὴν καὶ λύκον διωκτῆρα Vaticanus.
De meo largius Anglice disputabo.
CXXIX. Fabulam in initio male pravatam servavit Vaticanus codex.
1. Versum primum restituere tentavi ex paraphrasi apud Coraem, p. 137,
ἔχων τις κύνα Μελιταῖον καὶ ὄνον ; versum secundum ex Vaticano (ὄνον
τις ἔτρεφε καὶ κυνίδιον πάνυ ὡραῖον) κυνίδιον δὲ χάριν ὂν εὐρύθμους
παῖζον, sed de τραπεζήων dubito. 4. Vaticanus habet ἐκεῖνος δ' αὐτὸ
κατέχων ἐν τοῖς κόλποις, quod ego correxi. 5. Summa cum fiducia ego
ἀλετρεύων proposui, de ἔμεινε dubitans. Corrupte Vaticanus ὁ δέ γ'
ὄνος τὴν μὲν νύκτα λατρεύων.

poetry, just as he does in ἐπωλεύμην.
For ἤμην, the late form of ἦν, see Phryn.
p. 240.
14. I believe that δρηστῆρα of the
codex is a poor paraphrase of πανούρ-
γον, itself substituted for the genitive
plural πανούργων by a scribe to whom
the partitive genitive after πᾶς was
not familiar. To make a δρηστήρ from
διδράσκω, as Dindorf does, to suit this
passage, or rather not to suit it, is a
paltry shift, although it has been accepted by Liddell and Scott.
CXXIX. 1. The conjecture τραπεζήων
is a bold one ; but the uncertainty of
the paraphrasts suggests some word
which would give them trouble, and
I cannot help thinking that my correction hits the mark. The term is
applied to dogs in Homer, and Ibycus
used τραπεζῆται in the same way.
Etym. Mag. 763, 46, τὸ δὲ παρ' Ἰβύκῳ
λεγόμενον τραπεζῆτα ν κυνᾶν ἐστιν
ὡς πλείων πλήων.
Against τῶν Μελιταίων, which readily

offers itself, the objection of quantity
is final. It is true that in a line of
Lycophron Μελίτη once stood, but it
has now been corrected from the best
manuscripts by the insertion of δέ.
Alexandra, 1027—

ἄλλοι δὲ Μελίτην νῆσον Ὀθρωνοῦ πέλας.

5. It is remarkable that the simple
conjecture ἀλετρεύων has escaped being
made already. Hom. Odys. 7, 104, αἱ
μὲν ἀλετρεύουσι μύλης ἐπὶ μήλοπα καρπόν.
Others besides Babrius had made it
part of their motley diction, giving it
even the derived sense of 'rub.'
Lycophron, 159, λευρὰν ἀλετρεύσοντα
Μόλπιδος πέτραν. Apol. Rhod. 4,
1093, χαλκὸν ἀλετρεύουσα. Nonnus has
it more than once in its simple meaning, Dionys. 20, 242, καρπὸν ἀλετρεύουσα μύλης τροχοειδέι πέτρῃ. Id. 26, 64,
κεῖνον (i.e. χέδροπα) ἀλετρεύουσι μύλης
τροχοειδέι κύκλῳ. The principal verb
has still to be restored, as I put little
value on my own attempt to do so.

πυρὸν φίλης Δήμητρος, ἡμέρης δ' ὕλην
κατῆγ' ἀφ' ὕψους ἐξ ἀγροῦ θ' ὅσων χρείη.
ὡς δ' ἦν ἐν αὐλῇ παρὰ φάτναισι δεσμώτης
ἔτρωγε κριθάς, χόρτον, ὥσπερ εἰώθει.
δηχθεὶς δὲ θυμῷ καὶ περισσὸν οἰμώξας,   10
σκύμνον θεωρῶν ἁβρότητι †σὺν πάσῃ,
φάτνης ὀνείης δεσμὰ καὶ κάλους ῥήξας
εἰς μέσσον αὐλῆς ἦλθ' ἄμετρα λακτίζων.
σαίνων δ' ὁποῖα καὶ θέλων περισκαίρειν
τὴν μὲν τράπεζαν ἔθλασ' εἰς μέσον βάλλων   15
ἅπαντα δ' εὐθὺς ἠλόησε τὰ σκεύη.
δειπνοῦντα δ' εὐθὺς ἦλθε δεσπότην κύσσων
νώτοις ἐπεμβάς· ἐσχάτου δὲ κινδύνου
θεράποντες ἐν μέσοις ἔσωσαν ὡς εἶδον.
κρανέης δὲ κορύναις ἄλλος ἄλλοθεν κρούων   20
ἔθεινον ὥστε καὐτὸς ὕστατ' ἐκπνείων
' ἔτλην ' ἔλεξεν ' οἷα χρή με δυσδαίμων·
τί γὰρ παρ' οὐρήεσσιν οὐκ ἐπωλεύμην,
βαιῷ δ' ὁ μέλεος κυνιδίῳ παρισούμην;'

CXXX.

Πάγης ἀλώπηξ οὐκ ἄπωθεν εἰστήκει
βουλάς τ' ἐκίνει ποικίλας τί ποιήσει.

---

7. κατῆγ' Schneiderus pro ἦγεν bene scripsit. 8-9. Versus 8 et 9
post v. 1, ponit Vaticanus. 8. ὡς δ' ego pro καὶ scripsi. Mali origo aut
versuum in codice transpositio aut per notam culpam literae tachygraphicae
confusae. 11. Nauckio duce, ἁβρότητι σὺν pro ἐν ἁβρότητι scripsi, sed
versus corruptus manet. 15. Vaticanum ἐς μέσον βαλὼν Ολάσεν Eberhardus emendavit. 17. Lachmanni conjecturam κύσσων libenter Vaticano
κροίνων praeposui. 19. Versus corruptus. Ita edidit Gitlbauer. Pravius
Vaticanus θεράποντες ἐν μέσοισι ὡς εἶδον ἐσάωσαν.
CXXX. Fabulam ex Vaticano codice primus edidit Knoell. p. 685.
Versum primum Eberhardus correxit. ἀλώπηξ πάγης οὐκ ἄποθεν ἑστῶσα
βουλὰς ἐκίνει Vaticanus.

---

8. As in Homer the αὐλή here har-
bours the cattle.
10. θυμῷ = dolore.
16. The plural σκεύη is furniture in
the widest sense, fittings of ships,
houses, temples, etc. In Thucydides

(4, 52) this plural has once been
strangely corrupted into a singular
noun of the first declension :—καὶ ἦν
αὐτῶν ἡ διάνοια τάς τε ἄλλας πόλεις τὰς
Ἀκταίας καλουμένας ἐλευθεροῦν καὶ πάντων
μάλιστα τὴν Ἄντανδρον, καὶ κρατινάμενοι

λύκος δὲ ταύτην πλησίον θεωρήσας
ἐγγὺς προσελθὼν τὸ κρέας λαβεῖν ἤτει.
ἡ δ᾽ εἶπεν ᾽ἧκε τῇδε καὶ δέχου χαίρων·   5
φίλος γάρ εἰμι τῶν ἄγαν ἀναγκαίων.᾽
ὁ δ᾽ ἀθρόως ἐπῆλθεν· ὡς δὲ προσκύψας
αὐτὴν σκυταλίδ᾽ ἔσεισε, καὶ χαλασθείσης
ῥάβδου μέτωπα σύν τε ῥῖνας ἐπλήγη
᾽ἀλλ᾽ εἰ τοιαῦτα᾽ φησί ᾽τοῖς φίλοις δώσεις   10
τὰ δῶρα, πῶς σοί τις φίλος συναντήσει ;᾽

CXXXI.

Νέος ἐν κύβοισιν οὐσίην ἀναλώσας
στολὴν ἑαυτῷ κατέλιπεν μίην μούνην,
χειμῶνος ὄντος μὴ πάθοι τι ῥιγώσας.

---

5. Versus 5 et 6 secundum ordinem 6, 5 exhibet codex. Recte
transposuit Gitlbauer. 8. Idem pro Vaticano τὴν scripsit αὐτὴν et in
10 Knoellius δίδως in δώσεις mutavit. Qui alias codicis sordes vult scire
apud Knoellium reperiet.
CXXXI. Fabulam ex Vaticano codice primus edidit Knoell. 2. Vaticanum μίαν καταλελοίπει ita correxit Knoell.

αὐτήν—ναῦς τε γὰρ εὐπορία ἦν ποιεῖσθαι
αὐτόθεν ξύλων ὑπαρχόντων καὶ τῆς Ἴδης
ἐπικειμένης καὶ τῇ ἄλλῃ σκευῇ (lege τὰ
ἄλλα σκεύη)—ῥᾳδίως ἀπ᾽ αὐτῆς ὁρμώμενοι
τήν τε Λέσβον κακώσειν καὶ κτλ. ᾽They
purposed to liberate the cities of the
Strand, and especially Autandros; and
after strengthening it—for there was
every facility both for building ships
and providing their equipment also—
they hoped, with such a base of opera-
tions, to find little difficulty in crush-
ing Lesbos,᾽ etc. The conjecture καὶ τῇ
ἄλλῃ παρασκευῇ, adopted by the editors,
cannot explain the corruption of the
text. How has the παρα so completely
disappeared?
CXXX. 8. The mechanism of the
πάγη here referred to can only be con-
jectured. I regard the σκυταλίς as a
bar of wood or metal, which, when
trodden upon, displaced a spring which
sent some cruelly armed rod or staff in
the face of the victim as it stooped to
the bait. Philo of Byzantium, in his

Βελοποιϊκά, p. 85 A, speaks of the
σκιτάλη of a military engine: Δώδεκα
γάρ ἐστι πηχῶν τοῦ ταλανταίου πετρο-
βόλου ἡ σῦριγξ. ἡ δὲ σκιτάλη τεσσάρων
πηχῶν. I believe that the σῦριγξ there
means the tube through which the
missiles were discharged to give them
the true direction, and that the σκιτάλη
was the spring bar by which the impetus was imparted. The meanings of
σκιτάλη there and σκυταλίς in this
passage are not identical, if my explanation is correct, but they help to
illustrate one another.
CXXXI. 1. Eberhard, while support-
ing his uncalled-for conjecture ἐψιλώθη
for ἐνικήθη in the eleventh line, well
illustrates the fable from Alciphron, 3,
42, ἀπέδωσε γάρ με Παταικίων ὁ παμ-
πόνηρος δεξιαῖς χρώμενος ταῖς καλινδήσεσι
τῶν κύβων . . . καθ᾽ ἓν γὰρ ἕκαστον τῶν
ἱματίων ἐκ προκλήσεως ἀποτιθεὶς τέλος
ἁπάντων ἐψιλώθην τῶν ἐνδυμάτων.
3. ῥιγώσας, see note on Fab. 18, 6,
supra.

ἀλλ᾽ αὐτὸν ὁ χρόνος ἐξέδυσε καὶ ταύτης·
πρὸ γὰρ εἴαρος λιποῦσα τὰς κάτω Θήβας   5
ἐφάνη χελιδὼν ἐκπεσοῦσα τῆς ὥρης·
ταύτης ἀκούσας μικρὰ τιττυβιζούσης
' τί μοι περισσῶν ' εἶπεν ' ἐσθέων χρείη;
ἰδοὺ χελιδὼν ἥδε καῦμα σημαίνει.'
ὡς δ᾽ εἶπεν, ἐλθὼν τοῖς κύβοισιν ὡμίλει   10
καὶ σμικρὰ παίξας τὴν στολὴν ἐνικήθη.
νιφετὸς δ᾽ ἐπῆλθε καὶ χάλαζα φρικώδης,
κροκύδος δὲ καινῆς πᾶσιν ἦν τότε χρείη.
γυμνὸς δ᾽ ἐκεῖνος τῆς θύρης ὑπεκκύψας
καὶ τὴν λάλον χελιδόν᾽ αὖ κατοπτεύσας   15
' τάλαινα ' φησίν ' εἴθε μοι τότ᾽ οὐκ ὤφθης·
ὡς γὰρ σεαυτὴν κἀμὲ νῦν διεψεύσω.'

CXXXII.

Ὄις μονήρης λύκον ἔφευγεν ἐξαίφνης
ἰδοῦσα, σηκοῦ δ᾽ ἐντὸς ἦλθεν ἀκλείστου

---

4. Pro Vaticano ἡ χεὶρ ego ὁ χρόνος dedi. Scriba male peritus signum
tachygraphicum verbi χρόνος non intellexit.   7. Suidas servavit sub
τιττυβίζετε vocabulo.   8. Pro Vaticano ἰσθήτων magis ἐσθέων quam
εἱμάτων edidi.   15. Restituerunt Knoell et Sauppe ex Vaticano καὶ
κατοπτεύσας τὴν λάλον χελιδόνα. Huic versui in codice accedunt verba
ὑπὸ τοῦ κρύους πεσοῦσαν ὡς στρουθίον quae ego interpolata putare malo
quam cum editoribus corrigere.

CXXXII. Fabulam primus edidit Knoell ex codice Vaticano.

4. Eberhard's alteration is outrageous, πλὴν σκείραφος τὸν ἐξέδυσε καὶ
ταύτης, and his alternative πλὴν ὃν σκειράφειον ἐξέδυσε still more so. But
it appears in a Festschrift, and may have been conned after the dinner.

5. ' For ere spring came a swallow had left the Southern Thebes, and
showed itself out of its due season.'

11. The construction of νικῶμαι with an accusative of the thing which a man
loses by defeat is quite natural. Thus Phrynichus has it (App. Soph. 25, 29)
in explaining the term ἀνταποπαί-
ζειν : ὅταν τις παίζων ἀστραγάλοις ἢ
ψήφοις ἢ καρύοις, ἢ κυβείων ἐπ᾽ ἀργυρίῳ,
νικήσῃ, εἶτ᾽ αὖθις νικᾶται ἃ ἐνίκησεν,

i.c. 'is by losing deprived of his
winnings.' The prodigal's opponent in
this fable ἐνίκησε τὴν στολὴν by the
same game as the prodigal ἐνικήθη τὴν
στολήν.

12. Virgil, G. 1, 449, has 'horrida
grando,' and Pindar speaks of ὄμβροι
φρίσσοντες, P. 4, 81, 'Snow came on
and cutting hail.'

13. The word κροκύς seems to mean
the nap of cloth. Here its sense is
much more general, almost that of
'cloth' or even 'clothes.' Cp. Antipater
in Anth. Pal. 9. 567, κοιμωμένη πορ-
φυρέων ἐπὶ κροκύδων. Eberhard's conjecture of χλαίνης for καινῆς will not
commend itself.

(θυσίη γὰρ ἦν τις κατὰ τύχην ἑορταίη)·
ὁ λύκος δ᾽ ἔσω μὲν οὐ παρῆλθε τοῦ τείχους,
ἔξω δ᾽ ἐφεστὼς τὴν ὄιν καθωμίλει   5
‘ ὁρᾷς ᾽ λέγων ‘ τὸν βωμὸν αἵματος πλήρη ;
ἔξελθε, μή τις συλλάβῃ σε καὶ θύσῃ.᾽
ἡ δ᾽ εἶπε ‘ μή μου τῆς ἀσυλίης κήδου·
καλῶς ἔχει μοι· κἂν δὲ τοῦτο συμβαίνῃ,
θεοῦ γενοίμην σφάγιον ἢ λύκου θοίνη.᾽   10

CXXXIII.

Ὄνος παλιούρων ἦσθι᾽ ὀξέην χαίτην.
τὸν δ᾽ εἶδ᾽ ἀλώπηξ ἁρπάσασα δ᾽ εἰρήκει·
πῶς οὕτως ἁπαλῇ καὶ ἀνειμένη γλώσσῃ
σκληρὸν μαλάσσῃ προσφάγημα καὶ τρώγεις ;᾽

CXXXIV.

Οὐρή ποτ᾽ ὄφεως οὐκέτ᾽ ἠξίου πρώτην
κεφαλὴν βαδίζειν οὐδ᾽ ἐφείπεθ᾽ ἑρπούσῃ·
‘ κἀγὼ γάρ ᾽ εἶπεν ‘ ἐν μέρει προηγοίμην.᾽
‘ τὰ λοιπὰ δὲ μέρε ᾽ εἶπεν ‘ οὐδὲν ἡγήσῃ·

---

3. Hunc versum ego restitui ex Vaticanis sordibus θυσία γὰρ ἦν τὶς
ἑορτῆς κατὰ τύχην.

CXXXIII. Hunc fabulam a tetrastichista male perito decurtatam
primus ex codice Vaticano edidit Knoell. Talia piget emendare. Ex
ipso tetrastichista claudicant numeri. Si quis plura desideret, Eberhardi
et Gitlbaueri tentamina consulere licet. In paraphrasi nihil est auxilii.

CXXXIV. Fabulam primus Knoellius ex Vaticano codice edidit.
3. Deficientem particulam facile erat supplere, εἶπ᾽ ἂν ἐν μέρει lecto, sed
ἂν μερῶν dare pro ἐν μέρει non rectum est.

CXXXII. 3. Gitlbauer's incapacity
in making conjectures is only equalled
by his boldness. Few boys in the
highest class of a public school would
venture to write lines like those of
which Gitlbauer has printed hundreds
in his attempt to ‘ restore ᾽ the prose
paraphrases. He gives a sample of
his style here in re-writing the line—

ἑορτὶς ἔτυχε γάρ τις οὖσα καὶ θοίνη.

My own proposal is hardly a conjecture ; it is a correction. The adjective

is met with in Dionysius, Archæolog.
Romana,᾽ 4, 74, κατὰ καιρούς τινας ἑορ-
ταίους. Id. Epit. 12, 10, ἑορταίων καιρῶν.
5. ‘ Would fain talk the sheep over.᾽
9. ‘ And should it come to that, may
fate make me a god's victim rather
than a wolf's meal.᾽ The lexica will
illustrate this use of ἤ.

CXXXIV. 4. There is no reason for
reading μέλεα for μέρεα, even if the
Bodleian paraphrase has the former.
The use of μέρη for the members of the
body is common enough.

πῶς, ὦ τάλαινα, χωρὶς ὀμμάτων ἥμας   5
ἢ ῥινὸς ἄξεις, οἷς ἕκαστα τῶν ζῴων
τὰ πορευτὰ βαίνει πάντα καὶ πόδ' εὐθύνει;'
τὴν δ' οὐκ ἔπειθε, τὸ φρονοῦν δ' ἐνικήθη,
τὸ μὴ φρονοῦν δὲ λοιπὸν ἦρχε τῶν πρώτων,
οὐρὴ δ' ὄπισθεν ἡγεμὼν καθεισήκει,   10
σύρουσα τυφλῇ πᾶν τὸ σῶμα κινήσει·
κοιλὸν δὲ πέτρης εἰς βάραθρον ἠνέχθη,
καὶ τὴν ἄκανθαν ταῖς πέτραισι συντρίβει.
σαίνουσα δ' ἱκέτευεν ἡ πρὶν αὐθάδης·
' δέσποινα κεφαλή, σῶσον, εἰ θέλεις, ἥμας·   15
κακῆς γὰρ ἔριδος σὺν κακοῖς ἐπειράθην.'

CXXXV.

Πέρδικά τις πριάμενος ἐντρέχειν οἴκῳ
ἀφῆκεν· ἡδέως γὰρ εἶχε τοῦ ζῴου.

4. Ego pro Vaticano μέρη scripsi μέρε', et cum Gitlbauero οὐδὲν pro οὐχ dedi. 7. Gitlbauero duce, pro Vaticano παντάποδ' ego πάντα καὶ πόδ' summa cum fiducia edidi. 10. Sordes Vaticanas τὰ δ' ὄπισθεν οὐρῆς ego detersi. Delirat Gitlbauer, τὰ δ' ὄπισθ' ἐνωπῆς proponens. 15. Restituit Knoellius ex paraphrasi Bodleiana. δέσποινα κεφαλὴ σὺ ἡμᾶς σῶσον Vaticanus. 16. In ἐπειράθην recte desinit paraphrasis Bodleiana sed Vaticanus alios tres versus adjicit qui vix sunt accipiendi—

εἰς τὸ πρῶτον οὖν με μᾶλλον καταστάσαν
ἐγὼ προσέξω φησὶ μήποτ' ἀρχούσης
ἐμοῦ τῆς δόξης ὑστέρω κακὸν κυρεῖν,

quos ad intellectum sic possis ducere si interpolatorem multi facias—

'σοὶ δ' εἰς τὸ πρῶτον μᾶλλον αὖ καταστάσῃ
ἐγὼ προσέξω,' φησί, 'μήποτ' ἀρχούσης
ἐμοῦ σὺ δόξῃς ὕστερον κακῶν κύρειν.'

CXXXV. Edidit primus Knoellius ex Vaticano codice. 2. Eberhardo praeeunte, pro Vaticano τὸ ζῷον scripsi τοῦ ζῴου.

10. I have not thought fit to record the attempts already made to restore this line, as they seem to me of a piece with the Vatican blunders.
CXXXV. 2. ἡδέως .. ζῴου. 'For the bird took his fancy.' The construction may be illustrated by two passages of Macho, quoted by Athenaeus, 13, 577 E.—ἡ Λαμία δ' ἦν αὐλητρίς, ἧς σφόδρ' ἡδέως | σχεῖν φασὶ κνισθῆναί τε τὸν Δη-

κἀκεῖνος εὐθὺς κλαγκτὸν ἐξ ἔθους ᾄδων
πᾶσαν κατ᾽ αὐλὴν ἄχρι βημάτων ᾔει.
γαλῆ πρὸς αὐτὸν ἠπίβουλος ὡρμήθη,   5
καὶ πρῶτον εἶπε ʽ τίς μὲν εἶ; πόθεν δ᾽ ἥκεις ʼ;
ὁ δ᾽ ʽ ἠγόρασμαι ʼ φησί ʽ προσφάτως †ἤδη.ʼ

   .   .   .   .

ʽ χρόνον τοσοῦτον ἔνθ᾽ ἐγὼ διατρίβω
καί μ᾽ ἔνδον ἔτεκεν ἡ μυοκτόνος μήτηρ,
ἀλλ᾽ ἡσυχάζω καὶ πρὸς ἔσχατ᾽ ἀνδύνω·   10
σὺ δ᾽ ἄρτι πως ὠνητός, ὡς λέγεις, ἥκων
παρρησιάζῃ ʼ φησί ʽ καὶ κατακρώζεις.ʼ

CXXXVI.

Χειμῶνος ὥρῃ σῖτον ἐκ μυχοῦ σύρων
ἔψυχε μύρμηξ ὃν θέρους σεσωρεύκει.

---

3. Ut in Fab. 124, 13, κλαγκτὸν pro κλαγγὴν dedi. 7. Versui claudo ἤδη Eberhard addidit, πέρδιξ Gitlbauer. Post hunc versum lacunam notavi ; carent unus versus vel plures. 8. Vaticanum ἐγὼ χρόνον τοσοῦτον ἐνθάδε διατρίβω sic correxit Gitlbauer. χρόνον δὲ τόσσον ἔνθ᾽ ἐγὼ Knoell. 10. Pro Vaticano πρὸς ἑστίαν δύνω non sine fiducia ego πρὸς ἔσχατ᾽ ἀνδύνω edidi. Deterrimae sunt paraphrases et rationem manifeste diversam exhibent : Fur. 197, C. 291.

CXXXVI. Hanc fabulam ex Dosithei Magistri codice Vossiano primus restituit Valckenaer in Schediasmate de Hygini fragmento Dositheano apud Miscellaneas Observationes Criticas, x. 1, p. 122. Confer Δοσιθέου Ἑρμηνευμάτων Βιβλίον Γ᾽ ab E. Boecking edito p. 37. Codicis quoque Parisini 6503 collationem publicavit A. Boucherie in Ἑρμηνεύματα καὶ Καθημερινὴ Ὁμιλία de Iulius Pollux, p. 246.

μήτριον. 581 C, διὰ τό πως | τὸν Ἀνδρόνικον ἡδέως αὐτῆς ἔχειν. It is the same genitive as παράπλου in ἡ Κερκύρα καλῶς παράπλου κεῖται (is favourably placed for), as παρόδου in παρόδου χρησίμως ἔχειν (to be serviceable for), and is well known with καλῶς, εὖ, ἱκανῶς, ὁμοίως, ὡς, πῶς, ὅπη, ὡσαύτως, etc., when combined with intransitive verbs. It has nothing to do with the genitive sometimes found after ἥδεσθαι ; much less is it due to ἡδέως ἔχειν being equivalent to ἐπιθυμεῖν or one of its synonyms.

4. This meaning of βήματα is unusual, and perhaps does not occur elsewhere. Cp. Aristoph. Av. 1085, κεῖ τις ὄρνιθας τρέφει εἰργμένους ὑμῶν ἐν αὐλῇ φράζομεν μεθιέναι.
7. Certainly one or more lines have been lost here. There is not only a want of articulation as they stand, but a blank in the action.
10. ἀλλ᾽ ἡσυχάζω κτλ. ʽ But I hold my peace and slink off into corners.ʼ It is better to take ἡσυχάζω here in its late sense of σιωπῶ, as it is opposed to κλαγκτὸν ἐξ ἔθους ᾄδων. My conjecture

τέττιξ δὲ τοῦτον ἱκέτευσε λιμώττων
δοῦναί τι καὐτῷ τῆς τροφῆς ὅπως ζήσῃ.
'τί οὖν ἐποίεις' φησί 'τῷ θέρει τούτῳ;'   5
'οὐκ ἐσχόλαζον, ἀλλὰ διετέλουν ᾄδων.'
γελάσας δ' ὁ μύρμηξ τόν τε πυρὸν ἐγκλείων
'χειμῶνος ὀρχοῦ' φησίν 'εἰ θέρους ᾄδεις.'

CXXXVII.

Γάλλοις ἀγύρταις εἰς τὸ κοινὸν ἐπράθη
ὄνος τις οὐκ εὔμοιρος ἀλλὰ δυσδαίμων

---

8. Etiamsi paraphrasis Latina in codice Parisino *si aestate cantas* non dedisset, ego tamen ᾄδεις pro Vossiano ᾖσας (*cantasti*) summa cum fiducia scripsissem. Epimythium habet Georgides Gnomolog. i. 48—

κρεῖττον τὸ φροντίζειν ἀναγκαίων χρειῶν
ἢ τὸ προσέχειν νοῦν τέρψεσίν τε καὶ κώμοις.

CXXXVII. Fragmentum hoc servavit Natalis Comes (Noël Conti) in ejus de Mythologia libro, quem anno 1551 scripsit. (Lib. ix. 5, p. 968, ed. 1619 ; p. 957, ed. 1636.) Antea Tzetzes in Chiliad. xiii. 263, eadem dederat nisi quod versus tertium et quartum omisit fortasse quod corrupti in suo exemplari viderentur. Certe etiam nunc manent corrupta verba καὶ πανούργοισιν, pro quibus ego scripsi dubitanter τοῖσδε πεντάθλοις.

---

of πρὸς ἔσχατ' ἀνδύνω restores the further antithesis to ἄχρι βημάτων ᾔει. The apocope of ἀνά has led to the like corruption of Fab. 88, 10, if my conjecture is there accepted. Any lexicon will supply instances of ἔσχατος in the sense of 'inmost.' The final κατακρώζεις also may well be a corruption of some word meaning 'swagger' or 'expatiate.'

CXXXVI. 3. λιμώττω and λοιμώττω are both late formations, and as such I have left λιμώττω its taus here. This pair of verbs has its early analogues like ἀγρώσσω, ἀηθέσσω, etc., and its late like ἀγνώσσω.

CXXXVII. The best illustration of this fragment is the passage of the Pseudo-Lucian's 'Ass,' in which the hero is bought by the leader of such a band as is here described, chs. 35 fin. -41. The passage is too long to

quote, but it sheds light on all the details. The allusions of Aeschylus, Sophocles, and Plato to these ἀγύρται and ἀγύρτριαι are well known, and a fragment of Antiphanes is still extant from a play bearing the title of Μητραγύρτης. Menander also wrote a comedy with the equivalent name of Μηναγύρτης. The word ἀγερσικύβηλις was a coinage of Cratinus in ridicule of two of their knaveries—collection of alms and simulated self-mutilation. From the early days to the latest periods of ancient civilisation these vagabonds were abused and flourished. In Rome the right of begging was allowed them by the Twelve Tables. Cicero de Legibus cites the clause 'Praeter Idaeae Matris famulos eosque justis diebus ne quis stipem cogito.' The Christian Fathers are not lax in denouncing them and their abettors of both sexes.

ὅστις φέρῃ πτωχοῖσι †τοῖσδε πεντάθλοις
πείνης ἄκος δίψης τε καὶ τὰ τῆς τέχνης·
οὗτοι δὲ κύκλῳ πᾶσαν ἐξ ἔθους κώμην   5
περιόντες ἐλέγοντ' †ὄψα· τίς γὰρ ἀγροίκων
οὐκ οἶδεν Ἄττιν λευκόν, ὡς ἐπηράθη;
τίς οὐκ ὑπαρχὰς ὀσπρίων τε καὶ σίτων
ἁγνῷ φέρων δίδωσι τυμπάνῳ Ῥείης;

4. Verbum σάκος in ἄκος correxit Bentleius, κακῆς in τὰ τῆς Lachmannus. 6. περιϋόντες Dobree in περιόντες mutavit ad Porsonis Aristophanica, p. 135 (addend.), et ἔλεγον in ἐλέγοντο Bentleius. Verbum ὄψα fortasse recte adjecit Lachmannus. Desunt cetera; sed paraphrasem confer apud Coraem, p. 158.

3. My conjecture τοῖσδε πεντάθλοις is founded upon the passage of Tzetz, in which seven lines of this fragment appear. Ἀγύρται τίνες λέγονται, καὶ πόθεν, μάνθανέ μοι. Πρῶτον οἱ ὄντως ἀθληταί, καὶ τῶν φιλελευθέρων, ἀγῶνας στεφανίτας μὲν ἤθλουν, οὐχὶ δωρίτας, καὶ στέφανον ἐλάμβανον, μόνον τῆς νίκης δῶρον. εἶτα καὶ τοὺς δωρίτας δὲ μετήρχοντο ἀγῶνας, τῆς πόλεως ἢ χώρας δὴ εἴτε τινὸς τῶν δήμων, τὰ δῶρα τοῖς νικήσασιν νεμόντων ἁρμοδίως, εἴτε καὶ ἄρχοντος ἑνὸς ὡς Ἀχιλλεὺς Πατρόκλῳ. ἐπεὶ δὲ κατελύθησαν πόλεσι, χώραις, δήμοις, καὶ οὗτοι οὕσπερ ἔλεξα ἀγῶνες οἱ δωρίται, οἱ ἀθληταὶ λαμβάνειν τι χρήζοντες τοῖς ἀγῶσι, μὴ λείρια καὶ ἄνθη δὲ καὶ βοτανῶν στεφάνους, νικήσαντες διέτρεχον τὴν ἄγυριν, τὸ πλῆθος. καὶ οὕτως συνηράνιζον χρήματα τῇ ἀγύρει, καὶ κλῆσιν ἔσχον ἀγυρτῶν, ὡς ἐκ τῶν ἐν ἀγύρει ἀθροίζοντες, λαμβάνοντες δῶρα, τῆς νίκης χάριν. ἄλλος γὰρ ἄλλο τι αὐτοῖς ἐδίδου τῶν τοῦ πλήθους, ὃ εἶχεν ἡ προαίρεσις καὶ δύναμις ἑκάστου· καὶ οὗτοι καταχρήσει ἐλέγοντο ἀγύρται. Κυρίως τοὺς ἀγύρτας δὲ καὶ μηναγύρτας νύει, κἂν μᾶλλον ἐκ τῶν ἀθλητῶν οὗτοι τὴν κλῆσιν ἔσχον, οἷοι εἰσιν οἱ παρ' ἡμῖν σύμπαντες σιγνοφόροι, ὁπόσοι περιτρέχουσι χώρας καὶ προσαιτοῦσι κτλ. The reader must excuse my quoting so much of this drivelling verse (I have written it as prose and done it an honour), but I wished to show that it was a piece of erudition in decaying Greek to connect the ἀγύρται with the ἀθληταί. Clement of Alexandria, who may have been a contemporary of Babrius himself, says, in his Παιδαγωγός (2, 8), ἐν δὲ τοῖς ἀγῶσι,

πρῶτον ἡ τῶν ἀθλητῶν δόσις ἦν, δεύτερον δὲ ὁ ἐπαγερμός, τρίτον ἡ φυλλοβολία, τελειταῖον ὁ στέφανος, ἐπίδοσιν λαβούσης εἰς τρυφὴν τῆς Ἑλλάδος μετὰ τὰ Μηδικά. If a scholiast on Eurip. Hec. 574 is to be trusted, Eratosthenes at a later date said much the same thing. Ἐρατοσθένης φησὶ περὶ τῆς φυλλοβολίας ὡς πάλαι, χωρὶς ἄθλων ἀγωνιζομένων ἀνθρώπων, τῷ νικήσαντι καθάπερ ἔρανον εἰσέφεροντες ἔρριπτον τῶν θεατῶν ὅπως ἕκαστος ηὐπόρει. Διὸ δὴ σύνηθες ἐγένετο κύκλῳ περιπορευόμενον ἐπαγείρειν καὶ λαμβάνειν τὸ διδόμενον. The wording of the next line, moreover, and in fact of all the rest, aims at a certain comic elevation with which πεντάθλοις well harmonises. The whole fragment is in the strain of Εἰρωνεία in the socks; while with one eye she would make you think that πεντάθλοις was meant in a good sense, the other would wink at your taking it to mean 'jacks-of-all-trades,' a sense which the word certainly bears elsewhere. Cp. Pseudo-Lucian, 'Ass,' 37, εἶτα ἐκ τῆς πόλεως ἐξηλαύνομεν τὴν χώραν περιήειμεν. ἐπὰν δ' εἰς κώμην τινὰ εἰσέλθοιμεν, ἐγὼ μὲν ὁ θεοφόρητος ἱστάμην, ὁ δὲ αὐλητὴς ἐφύσα ὅμιλος ἔνθεον, οἱ δὲ τὰς μίτρας ἀπορρίψαντες τὴν κεφαλὴν κάτωθεν ἐκ τοῦ αὐχένος εἰλίσσοντες τοῖς ξίφεσιν ἐτέμνοντο τοὺς πήχεις καὶ τὴν γλῶτταν τῶν ὀδόντων ὑπερβάλλων ἕκαστος ἔτεμνε καὶ ταύτην κτλ.

8. Cp. id. fin., Ἐπειδὰν δὲ κατακόψειαν οὕτως ἑαυτούς, ἐκ τῶν περιεστηκότων θεατῶν συνέλεγον ὀβολοὺς καὶ δραχμάς· ἄλλος ἰσχάδας καὶ τυροὺς καὶ ὄνου κάδον ἐπέδωκε καὶ πυροῦ μέδιμνον καὶ κριθῶν τῷ ὄνῳ.

K

130 SCRIPTORES FABULARUM GRAECI.

CXXXVIII.

Ὄνῳ τις ἐπιθεὶς ξόανον εἶχε κωμήτης.

CXXXIX.

Σοφῆς ἀράχνης ἱστὸν εὗρε κωλώτης,
καὶ λεπτὸν ἐνέδυ φᾶρος ἐκτεμὼν τοίχου.

CXL.

Χὤπως ἔχῃ τι βουκόλημα τῆς λύπης,
ἀνέθηκε τοίχοις ποικίλας γραφὰς ζῴων.

CXLI.

Εἰ μὴ γὰρ ὑμεῖς στελεὰ πάντα τίκτητε
οὐκ ἂν γεωργὸς πέλεκυν ἐν δόμοις εἶχε.

CXXXVIII. Hoc fabulae initium servavit Suidas sub κωμήτης vocabulo. Ceteros versus ex paraphrasi (e.g. Bodleiana 109) restituere temptaverunt editores. Ejusmodi tentamina ego altero in volumine tractabo, in hoc ad Βάβριον αὐτότατον investigandum curiosior quam τοὺς Βαβριάζοντας. Quibus alia placent, Gitlbauerum consulere licet.

CXXXIX. Hoc fragmentum habet Suidas sub κωλώτης vocabulo.

CXL. Duos hos versus ex fabula, quam exhibent Bodleiana (No. 135) et aliae paraphrases, servavit Suidas sub βουκολήσας vocabulo unde eos deduxit scholiasta ad Aristoph. Pacem, 153. Idem ἀνέθηκε recte dat pro ἐνέθηκε quod codices Suidae ostendunt. Epimythium ex Etymologico Magno sub πεπρωμένον vocabulo addidi—

ἃ σοι πέπρωται, ταῦτα τλῆθι γενναίως
καὶ μὴ σοφίζου· τὸ χρεὼν γὰρ οὐ φεύξῃ.

CXLI. Duos hos versus deterrime corruptos habet Suidas sub στελεὸν vocabulo. De iis nihil certi decerni potest. Totius fabulae paraphrasem offert Bodleianus No. 5, et Coraes 356 et p. 407.

CXLII.

Λίβυσσα γέρανος ἠδὲ ταὼς εὐπήληξ
χλωρὴν ἀεὶ 'βόσκοντο λείμακος ποίην.

CXLIII.

Volo consulas Fab. 88, 11, et quae ibi Latine et Anglice disputavi.

CXLII. Hos versus citat Suidas sub γέρανος vocabulo ita corrupte ut dedi nisi quod χείματος pro Lewisii conjectura λείμακος exhibet. Referendi sunt ad fabulam quam graviter decurtatam et vitiatam exhibet Athous codex sexagesimam quintam. Conjecit Eberhard καὶ ταώς τις εὐπήληξ.

TOTIUS GRAECITATIS BABRIANAE
LEXICON.

TOTIUS GRAECITATIS BABRIANAE
LEXICON.

*The words within brackets belong to lines considered by me to be spurious,
or to have been altered by the tetrastichists.*

Ἀβλαβής. 46, 5, ἦν γὰρ ἀβλαβὴς γείτων. 122, 6, χάριν δέ μοι δὸς ἀβλαβῆ.

Ἀβόσκητος. 45, 10, ὁρῶν ἀβοσκήτων.

Ἄβουλος. [23, 10, ἄβουλον εὐχήν.]

Ἀβρότης. 129, 11, ἀβρότητι σὺν πάσῃ.

Ἄγαν. 43, 5, ἄγαν ηὔχει. 88, 12, οὐκ ἄγαν σπεύδει. 130, 6, τῶν ἄγαν ἀναγκαίων. [24, 10, οὐκ ἄγαν χαιρήσειν.]

Ἀγαθός. 58, 10, ἀγαθῶν ἕκαστον δώσειν. 63, 5, ἀγαθὰ δαψιλῆ ποίει. 63, 7, ἀγαθὸν οὐδ᾽ ἄν τις παράσχοι. 119, 9, ἀγαθοῖς πολλοῖς ἠμείψω. 123, 1, ὄρνιθος ἀγαθῆς τικτούσης. [47, 15, μέγ᾽ ἀγαθόν. 85, 19, μέγιστον ἀγαθόν. 94, 9, μισθὸν ἀγαθόν.]

Ἄγγελος. 1, 7, τῷ ἀγγέλῳ μου. 1, 15, οὕτω πικρὸν ἄγγελον πέμπει. 93, 1, λύκων ἄγγελοι. 95, 13, χρηστῶν ἄγγελος λέγων. 103, 6, ἄγγελος φήμη.

Ἄγγος. [27, 8, κρεῶν ἀνέψγας ἄγγος.]

Ἀγέλη. 46, 4, ἀγέλαι ποικίλων ζῴων. 124, 9, εὐωπὸν ἀγέλην ὀρνέων.

Ἀγεννής. 95, 66, ἀγεννὴς πέφυκας.

Ἀγκάλη. 34, 7, ὑγραῖς μητρὸς ἀγκάλαις.

Ἀγκυλογλώχιν. 17, 3, ἀλέκτωρ ἀγκυλογλώχιν.

Ἀγνοέω. 66, 8, ἀγνοεῖν δὲ τὰς οἴκοι.

Ἄγνοια. 49, 1, ὑπ᾽ ἀγνοίης.

Ἀγνός. 54, 2, ἀγνὸν ἧπαρ ἀπλώσας. 137, 9, ἀγνῷ τυμπάνῳ Ῥείης.

Ἀγνώμων. 95, 17, σῦς μέν ἐστιν ἀγνώμων. 101, 2, ἀγνώμων λύκος. 119, 7, φίλοισιν ἀγνώμων.

Ἀγορή. 104, 4, δι᾽ ἀγορῆς. Λ. 8, ἀγοραὶ δὲ τούτων ἦσαν.

Ἀγοράζω. 30, 2, τὸν δ᾽ ἠγόραζον ἄνδρες. 135, 7, ὁ δ᾽ ᾽ἠγόρασμαι᾽ φησί.

Ἄγρη. 103, 1, ἐπ᾽ ἄγρην βαίνειν.

Ἀγρεῖος. 61, 5, θήρην ἠρέτιζεν ἀγρείην.

Ἀγρεύω. 4, 5, τῶν δ᾽ ἰχθύων ὁ μέγας ἀγρευθείς. 6, 4, μικρὸν ἰχθὺν ἤγρευσεν. 69, 2, οὐκ ἄπειρος ἀγρεύειν. 107, 1, λέων ἀγρεύσας μῦν. 124, 3, οὐ γὰρ ἠγρεύκει. [107, 18, λέοντα μῦς ἔσωσ᾽ ἀγρευθέντα.]

Ἄγριος. 15, 12, εἶπεν ἀγρίη μούσῃ. 35, 4, θάλπουσα κόλποις ἀγρίοις. 38, 1, ἀγρίην πεύκην. 45, 5, αἶγας ἀγρίας. 82, 1, λέοντος ἀγρίης χαίτης. 95, 5, ὑπ᾽ ἀγρίαις πεύκαις. 95, 10, ὑπ᾽ ἀγρίαις ὕλαις. 97, 1, ἐπεβούλευεν ἀγρίῳ ταύρῳ. 98, 11, ἄγριος θήρ. 102, 5, τῶν ἀγρίων ἀγυρμὸς ζῴων.

Ἄγροικος. 2, 3, μή τις ἀγροίκων. 16, 1, ἀγρίκος τίτθη. 18, 2, ἀνδρὸς ἀγροίκου. 137, 6, τίς γὰρ ἀγροίκων οὐκ οἶδεν;

Ἀγρός. 2, 7, ἀγροὺς κατοικεῖν. 12, 1, ἀγροῦ χελιδὼν ἐξεπωτήθη. 12, 11, ἐλθ᾽ εἰς ἀγρόν. 37, 1, ἐν ἀγροῖς ἄφετος. 129, 7, ἐξ ἀγροῦ.

Ἀγρότης. 13, 1, παγίδας ἀγρότης πήξας. 34, 1, ὄχλος ἀγρότης. 37, 5, ἀγρόται.

Ἀγρῶστης. 115, 2, κήυξιν ἀγρώσταις.

Ἄγυια. [42, 6, εἰς τὴν ἄγυιαν.]

Ἀγυρμὸς 102, 5, ἀγυρμὸς ἐγεγόνει ζῴων.

Ἀγύρτης. 137, 1, Γάλλοις ἀγύρταις ἐπράθη.

Ἄγω. 45, 6, αἶγας ἦγε. 95, 42, ἦγεν εἰς μέσας ὕλας. 111, 9, τὸν ὄνον ἦγε. 134, 6, πῶς ἡμᾶς ἄξεις; 20, 1, ἄμαξαν ἦγε. 55, 5, τίς ἄξει τῷ γέροντι τὰ σκεύη; 108, 20, τυρὸν ἦγεν ἐκ κανισκίου σύρων. 24, 3, λιμνάδας χορούς ἦγον. 24, 2, ἦγε τῷ θεῷ κώμους. [12, 18, ἄγε δή.]

Ἀγωγός. 95, 91, ἡ δ' ἀγωγὸς εἰστήκει.

Ἀγών. 72, 3, ἀγῶνα κεῖσθαι.

Ἀδεής. 5, 8, ἀδεῶς ἀμφέβαινε.

Ἄδειπνος. 89, 11, ἀλλ' οὐκ ἄδειπνον τὸν λύκον θήσεις.

Ἀδελφός. 28, 3, παρὰ τῶν ἀδελφῶν ἐπεζήτει.

Ἄδηλος. 6, 17, ἄδηλα θηρεύειν.

Ἄδην. [106, 8, ἄδην τιθεὶς δαῖτα.]

Ἀίδης. 95, 87, δὶς τὸν αὐτὸν εἰς ᾅδην. 122, 8, εἰς ᾅδου.

Ἀδικέω. 118, 11, χελιδὼν ἠδικημένη. 127, 10, θᾶσσον ἀδικῶν.

Ἄδικος. 105, 4, ἀδίκως ἀφείλω τῶν ἐμῶν. 117, 2, ἄδικα κρίνειν.

Ἀδμής. 37, 7, μόσχος ἀδμής.

Ἄδοξος. [39, 3, ἄδοξος ἐν πολιτείαις. 65, 8, ζῆν ἀδόξως.]

Ἀδρανής. 25, 3, ἀδρανέστατοι ζῴων.

Ἀδρός. 45, 3, ἀδρῇ χιόνι. 101, 1, λύκος ἀδρός.

Ἄιδω. 12, 13, θηρίοις ᾄσεις. 135, 3, κλαγκτὸν ᾄδων. 136, 6, διετέλοιν ᾄδων. 136, 8, θέροις ᾄδεις. [116, 1, ἥδε παῖς τις εὐφώνως.]

Ἀεί. 12, 9 ; 31, 2 ; 31, 6 ; 61, 7 ; 63, 4 ; 64, 9 ; 74, 17 ; 85, 7 ; 95, 53 ; 102, 11 ; 112, 9 ; 142, 2. [129, 2 ; 22, 13 ; 22, 16 ; 35, 8 ; 39, 1 ; 41, 1 ; 44, 8 ; 64, 8.]

Ἀείδω. Β. 16, τήνδε βίβλον ἀείδω.

Ἀηδών. 12, 3, ἀηδόνα ὀξύφωνον. 12, 19, ἀηδὼν ἡμείφθη.

Ἀθηνᾶ. 59, 2, τούτοις ἥριζ' Ἀθηνᾶ.

Ἀθῆναι. 12, 22, μετὰ τὰς Ἀθήνας. 15, 7, ὁ δ' ἐξ Ἀθηνῶν.

Ἀθηναῖος. 15, 1, ἀνὴρ Ἀθηναῖος. 15, 14, Ἀθηναίοις.

Ἀθηναίη. 72, 16, χελιδών, ὡς Ἀθηναίη.

Ἄθλιος. 35, 3, ἀθλίης ὑπ' εὐνοίης.

Ἀθροίζω. 74, 13, ὄλβον ἀθροίζων.

Ἀθρόως. 111, 18, ἀθρόως δὲ τῶν σπόγγων διαβραχέντων. 130, 7, ὁ δ' ἀθρόως ἐπῆλθε.

Αἴγαγρος. 102, 8, πάρδαλις αἰγάγρῳ.

Αἴγειρος. 50, 4, κρύψον με ταύταις αἰγείροις. 50, 13, παχείης αἰγείρου. 84, 4, ποταμίης ἐπ' αἰγείρου.

Αἴγιλος. 3, 3, κόμην γλυκεῖαν αἰγίλου.

Ἀετός. 5, 7 ; 72, 14 ; 77, 5 ; 99, 1 ; 115, 4 ; 115, 5.

Αἰθριάζω. 45, 9, ὡς δ' ᾐθρίασε.

Αἴθυια. 115, 1, λιμνάσιν αἰθυίαις.

Αἰκάλλω. 50, 14, σεσηρὸς αἰκάλλουσα.

Αἰκίη. 11, 2, ξίνη περιβαλεῖν αἰκίη. 21, 7, χωρὶς αἰκίης. 93, 3, πρὸς αἰκίην.

Αἴλουρος. 17, 1, αἴλουρος ὄρνεις ἐνεδρεύων. 17, 6 ; 121, 2.

Αἷμα. 31, 2, πόλεμον αἱμάτων πλήρη. 37, 8, βωμὸν αἵματος πλήσων. 51, 6, τοὐμὸν αἷμα. 132, 6, βωμὸν αἵματος πλήρη.

Αἱματόω. 95, 54, ἔλαφος ἡματωμένη.

Αἴξ. 3, 1 ; 45, 3 ; 45, 5 ; 72, 5. [45, 13.]

Αἰπόλος. 3, 1 ; 45, 1 ; 69, 3 ; 86, 2 ; 91, 3. [45, 12.]

Αἱρέομαι. 14, 3, μᾶλλον ἡροίμην εἰ. 64, 10, καὶ σὺ μᾶλλον αἱρήσῃ. 85, 2, κύων Ἀχαιὸς ἡρέθη. 59, 5, ἡρέθη τούτοις κριτής. 31, 7, εἵλοντο τοὺς ἀρίστους. [8, 3, πότερ' ἀναβαίνειν ἢ κάτω βαίνειν αἱροῖτο.]

Αἱρετίζω. 61, 5, θήρην ὁ γριπεὺς ἡρέτιζεν.

Αἴρω. 5, 7, τὸν μὲν αἰετός τις ἄρας. 16, 9, πῶς οὐδὲν ἄρας ἦλθες ; 36, 1, δρῦν ἐξ ὄρους ἄρας. 42, 4 ; 119, 4, τοῦ σκέλους ἄρας. 105, 1, λύκος ἄρας πρόβατον. 115, 8, ὑπτίην ἄρας. 32, 6, ἠρμένου δὲ τοῦ δείπνου. 56, 4, πίθωνα σιμὸν ἠρμένη κόλποις. [47, 16, ταπεινοὺς ἦρεν εἰς ὕψος. 110, 4, ἡ δὲ κέρκον οὐρεὴν ἄρασα.]

Ἀίσσω. 72, 14, πρὸς θεοὺς ᾖξεν.

Αἰσχρός. 10, 1, αἰσχρῆς τις ἦρα δούλης. [10, 13, τοῖς αἰσχροῖς ὡς καλοῖς χαίρων.]

Αἰσχύνη. 5, 4, ὑπ' αἰσχύνης.

Αἴσωπος. Α. 15, γέροντος Αἰσώπου. Β. 5, Αἴσωπος ὁ σοφός. [40, 5, τὸν λόγον τὸν Αἰσώπου. 119, 11, θεοὺς Αἴσωπος ἐμπλέκει μύθοις.]

Αἰτέω. 10, 2, παρεῖχεν αἰτούσῃ ἅπαντα. 33, 8, εἰ τὴν σφενδόνην ποτ' ᾔτηκει. 33, 13, ἄρτον αἰτήσω. 33, 16, ἄρτον ᾔτει. 63, 8, ταῦτα τοὺς θεοὺς αἴτει. 63, 11, κἂν ἕν αἰτήσῃς. 94, 5, τὸν μισθὸν ᾔτει. 130, 4, ἐγγὺς προσελθὼν ᾔτει. Α. 12, γῆς μηδὲν αἰτούσης.

Αἰτίη. 31, 4, τῆς ἥττης αἰτίην ταύτην. 89, 12, κἂν πᾶσαν αἰτίην λύσῃς. 126, 3, διὰ τίν' αἰτίην ; [106, 19, λέων τίν' εἶχεν αἰτίην διηρώτα.]

Αἴτιος. 10, 6, ὥσπερ αἰτίην τούτων. 49, 4, αἰτίη λέγωμαι. 71, 7, οὐδὲν αἰτίη τούτων. 95, 79, αἰτίη κακῶν. 117, 4, μηδὲν αἰτίοις.

Αἰώρα. [19, 6 (note), κρεμαστῆς αἰώρας.]

Ἄκανθα. 122, 7, τὴν ἄκανθαν εἰρύσας. 134, 13, τὴν ἄκανθαν συντρίβει.

Ἀκαρνάν. 85, 10, Ἀκαρνάνων.

Ἀκίνδυνος. 93, 10, νέμεσθαι ἀκινδύνως. [31, 23, ζῆν ἀκινδύνως. 44, 7, id.]

Ἄκλειστος. 132, 2, σηκοῦ ἐντὸς ἀκλείστου.

Ἀκμαῖος. 19, 5, εἰς τριγηρὸν ἀκμαίη.

22, 8, ἡ μὲν ἀκμαίη (γυνή). 88, 3, πτεροῖσιν ἀκμαίους.
Ἀκμή. [29, 5, πρὸς τὸ τῆς ἀκμῆς γαῦρον.]
Ἀκολουθέω. 11, 8, ὁ δ' ἠκολούθει κλαίων. 33, 6, τῷ δ' ἠκολούθει παιδίσκος.
Ἄκος. 94, 4, πόνων ἄκος δοίη. 137, 4, πείνης ἄκος δίψης τε.
Ἀκούω. 2, 13, τοῦτ' ἀκούσας. 16, 3, ὁ λύκος δ' ἀκούσας. 131, 7, ταύτης ἀκούσας. 49, 2, Τύχης ἔδοξ' ἀκούειν. 33, 8, οἱ ψᾶρες ἤκουον. 71, 5, ἤκουε δ' ἡ θάλασσα. 85, 6, ἀκούσατ'. 88, 9, ἤκουσεν αὐτοῦ. 95, 32, εἴ τι ἀκούεις. 111, 2, τοὺς ἅλας ἀκούων εὐώνους. 72, 3, πᾶσι δ' εὐθὺς ἠκούσθη. 76, 11, πόλεμος ἄλλος ἠκούσθη. 128,10,ἤκουσε τούτων ἡ κύων. [73, 2, ἵππου δ' ἀκούσας. 116, 2, γυνὴ δ' ἀκούει τοῦδε.]
Ἀκραῖος. 31, 14, κάρφη μετώποις ἁρμόσαντες ἀκραίοις (conj.) 95, 40, ὄνιξιν ἀκραίοις.
Ἀκρατής. 58, 3, ὁ δ' ἀκρατὴς ἄνθρωπος.
Ἀκριβής. 66, 8, βλέπειν ἀκριβῶς.
Ἄκριτος. 33, 3, ἄκριτον πλήθει ἔθνος.
Ἄκρος. 36, 12, ἄνεμος ἄκρα κινήσῃ. 107, 6, ἄκρων ἐπιψαύσει χειλῶν. 122, 10, ὀδοῦσιν ἄκροις.
Ἀκταῖος. 25, 6, βατράχων ὅμιλον ἀκταίων.
Ἀκτίς. 88, 13, ἡλίου δ' ὑπ' ἀκτίνων.
Ἄκων. 3, 8, ἄκων ηὐστόχησα. 111, 5, ὤλισθεν ἄκων.
Ἀλαζονεύομαι. 104, 5, κύων ἠλαζονεύετο.
Ἀλαζών. 95, 19, τίγρις ἀλαζών.
Ἀλγέω. 34, 6, γαστρὸς ὄγκον ἀλγήσας. 51, 5, ἀλγοῦν πρόβατον. 103, 7, καὶ πάντες ἤλγουν. 112, 1, ὁ δ' ἐδίωκεν ἀλγήσας. 125, 4, ὡς τὸ νῶτον ἠλγήκει.
Ἀλγύνω. [106, 24, τὰ παρόντα ἀλγύνει.]
Ἀλείφω. 48, 4, ἀλείψαι βούλομαί σε.
Ἀλεκτορίσκος. 5, 1 ; 97, 9 ; 124, 12.
Ἀλέκτωρ, 17, 3 ; 65, 5.
Ἀλέξανδρος. Β. 1, ὦ παῖ βασιλέως Ἀλεξάνδρου.
Ἀλετρεύω. 129, 5, ἀλετρεύων πυρόν.
Ἀλή. 18, 11, προσῆγε τὴν ἀλὴν πλείω.
Ἀλήθεια. 57, 14, ῥῆμα τῆς ἀληθείης. 81, 4, ἔλεγχον οὐκ ἔχειν τῆς ἀληθείης. 95, 98, ἀπαιολῶσα τῆς ἀληθείης. 75, 19, ταῖς ἀληθείαις ἰατρὸς οὐκ εἶ. 126, 2, ἑστῶσαν εὗρε τὴν Ἀληθίην. [83, 3, εἰ θέλεις με ταῖς ἀληθείαις καλὸν γενέσθαι.]
Ἀληθεύω. 16, 3, τὴν γραῦν ἀληθεύειν νομίσας.

Ἀληθής. 2, 8, θεοὺς ἀληθεῖς. 20, 5, ἀληθῶς προσεκύνει. 101, 7, ἀληθῶς λέων. 103, 4, οὐκ ἀληθὲς ἀσθμαίνων.
Ἀληθινός. 53, 3, λόγους τρεῖς ἀληθινούς.
Ἀλητός. [29, 1, εἰς ἀλητὸν ἐπράθη.]
Ἁλιεύς. 4, 1 ; 6, 1 ; 9, 1.
Ἀλίπλωος. 61, 4, ἰχθύων ἁλιπλώων θήρην.
Ἁλίσκομαι. 13, 4, πελαργὸς ἡλώκει. 32, 5, ἐν μέρει γὰρ ἡλώκει. 13, 12, ἀπολῇ μεθ' ὧν ἥλως. 98, 1, λέων ἁλοὺς ἔρωτι. [31, 20, μόνοι δ' ἑάλωσαν.]
Ἀλκή. 67, 2, ἀλκῇ κρείσσων.
Ἀλκμήνη. 15, 5, υἱὸν Ἀλκμήνης.
Ἀλλά. 6, 7 ; 6, 14 ; 12, 11 ; 13, 10 ; 18, 6 ; 22, 4 ; 27, 5 ; 34, 11 ; 35, 3 ; 45, 10 ; 51, 7 ; 55, 2 ; 61, 8 ; 65, 2 ; 66, 1 ; 75, 3 ; 75, 18 ; 77, 11 ; 78, 2 ; 79, 5 ; 85, 14 ; 89, 11 ; 92, 6 ; 93, 6 ; 95, 28 ; 95, 50 ; 95, 65 ; 95, 80 ; 95, 84 ; 97, 8 ; 98, 11 ; 99, 3 ; 102, 10 ; 104, 5 ; 107, 7 ; 130, 10 ; 131, 4 ; 135, 10 ; 136, 6 ; 137, 2 ; Β. 6 ; Β. 5. [19, 9 ; 36,14 ; 39, 5 : 94, 10 ; 103, 21.]
Ἀλλαχοῦ. 88, 18, ἀλλαχοῦ φεύγειν.
Ἀλλήλους. 12, 5, ἔγνωσαν αἱ δύ' ἀλλήλας. 12, 10, χωρὶς ἦμεν ἀλλήλων. 26, 9, ἀλλήλαις ἐκραύγαζον. 31, 1, πρὸς ἀλλήλους εἶχον πόλεμον. 44, 1, ἀεὶ μετ' ἀλλήλων. 44, 5, χωρίσας ἀπ' ἀλλήλων. 47, 7, δεδεμένας σὺν ἀλλήλαις. 47, 10, ἀλλήλοις ὁμοφρονῆτε. 61, 3, συνηβόλησαν οἱ δύ' ἀλλήλοις. 64, 1, ἤριζον πρὸς ἀλλήλας. 66, 7, συμφορὰς ἀλλήλων βλέπειν. 85, 18, ὅμοια πάντ' ἔχοντες ἀλλήλοις. 93, 4, κοτοῦσιν ἀλλήλοις. 95, 43, χεῖρας ἐπεκρότησεν ἀλλήλαις. 102, 6, λαβεῖν παρ' ἀλλήλων. 108, 3, κοινῶς πρὸς ἀλλήλους. 127, 6, κεχυμένων ἐπ' ἀλλήλοις. [33, 23, πρὸς ἀλλήλους λαλεῖν. 39, 6, διαφθαρῆναι ὑπ' ἀλλήλοις. 119, 12, νουθετεῖν πρὸς ἀλλήλους.]
Ἄλλοθεν. 85, 12, ἄλλοι δ' ἄλλοθεν. 129, 20, ἄλλος ἄλλοθεν κρούων.
Ἀλλοῖος. 9, 7, σπαίροντας ἄλλον ἀλλοίους. [76, 8, φόρτον ἔφερεν ἄλλοτ' ἀλλοῖον.]
Ἄλλος. 2, 14, κλέπτας γὰρ ἄλλους πῶς ἂν εἰδείη ; 5, 6, ὁ δ' ἄλλος εὐθύς. 9, 7, σπαίροντας ἄλλον ἀλλοίους. 15, 11, 33, 6, ἄλλος οὐκ ἔχων ἴσην ἀμίλλαν. 25, 10, ἄλλους ἀσθενεστέρους ἡμῶν. 31, 17, ἄλλοι μὲν οὖν σωθέντες ἦσαν. 33, 10, εὗρε δὴ τέχνην ἄλλην. 38, 7, ἄλλος γὰρ ἄλλῃ μ' ἐμπεσὼν διαρρήσσει. 47, 13, ἢν δ' ἄλλος ἄλλου χωρὶς ἦτε.

52, 5, ἄλλων ἐπ' ὤμοις φερομένη. 57,
3, ἄλλο φῦλον ἐξ ἄλλου σχέδην ἀμείβων. 57, 10, οὐδ' ἀφῆκαν εἰς ἄλλους
προελθεῖν. 59, 14, τόποις ἄλλους
συνεξαμείβειν. 69, 5, ἄλλως ἄλλον
ἁρπάσαι. 72, 11, ἄλλο δ' ἐξ ἄλλου
πτερόν. 72, 18, τὰ δ' ἀλλ' ὁμοίως.
76, 11, πόλεμος ἄλλος ἠκούσθη. 85,
11, ἄλλοι δὲ Δόλοπες. 85, 12, ἄλλοι δ'
ἄλλοθεν. 85, 16, ἄλλοι δὲ λευκοί.
95, 48, ἄλλον τιν' εὑρεῖν δόλον. 95,
63, ἄλλους ἀλωπέκιζε. 95, 64, ἄλλους βασιλεῖς ὑπερέθιζε. 95, 96, μόνην
ἀπ' ἄλλων καρδίην. 108, 26, ἄλλο
τι προαιρήσων. 120, 7, πῶς ἄλλον
ἰήσῃ ; 129, 20, ἄλλος ἄλλοθεν κρούων.
B. 10, εἰσῆλθον ἄλλοι. [5, 11, ἄλλου
πλεῖον. 33, 23, ἄλλα μὲν πρὸς ἀλλήλους
λαλεῖν μαθόντων, ἄλλα δ' ἔργα ποιούντων. 41, 3, οὐδὲν ἄλλο. 52, 7, ἄλλων
ποιούντων. 73, 1, ἄλλην εἶχε κλαγγήν.
103, 21, ἄλλων συμφοραῖς ἐπαιδεύθη.
106, 26, εἴ τις ἄλλος, εἴτ' ἄλλος
πελάζοι.]
Ἄλλοτε. [76, 8, φόρτον ἔφερεν ἄλλοτ'
ἀλλοῖον.]
Ἀλλύω, see note on 88, 11.
Ἄλλως. 15, 4, μακρὴ μὲν ἄλλως
ῥῆσις. 19, 6, κάμνουσα δ' ἄλλως.
69, 5, ἄλλον ἄλλως ἁρπάσαι. 69, 6,
ἄλλως αὑτὸν σώζων.
Ἀλοάω. 26, 8, ἠλόησε τὰς πλείους.
129, 16, ἠλόησε τὰ σκεύη.
Ἀλοιάω. 98, 15, τὸν δ' ἔκαστος ἠλοία.
122, 13, γομφίους ἀλοιήσας.
Ἀλς. 111, 2, τοὺς ἅλας ἀκούων εὐώνους.
111, 6, συντακέντων τῶν ἁλῶν. 111,
8, τοὺς ἅλας πωλήσας. 111, 16, τοὺς
ἅλας μεμίσηκει.
Ἀλύω. [9, 11, ἀλύοντα κερδαίνειν ?]
Ἀλφιτεύς. [29, 4, καμπτῆρας ἀλφιτεῦσι
γυρεύω.]
Ἄλφιτον. 108, 16, ἀλφίτων πλήθη.
Ἀλωπεκίζω. 95, 63, ἄλλους ἀλωπέκιζε.
Ἀλώπηξ. 1, 12 ; 11, 1 ; 14, 3 ; 50,
1 ; 50, 8 ; 53, 1 ; 77, 2 ; 86, 4 ; 86,
7 ; 95, 3 ; 95, 26 ; 103, 4 ; 120, 7 ;
130, 1. [133, 2.]
Ἄλως. 11, 9, οὐδ' εἶδεν αὑτοῦ τὴν
ἄλωνα. 34, 2, ἅλω πλατεῖαν.
Ἀμαλθείη. 108, 11, τὸ κέρας τῆς Ἀμαλθείης.
Ἅμαξα. 20, 1, βοηλάτης ἅμαξαν ἦγεν.
52, 2, ἅμαξαν τετράκυκλον. 57, 1,
ἅμαξαν πληρώσας. [57, 8, ἐπισταθῆναι τὴν ἅμαξαν.]
Ἀμάω. 88, 7, ἵν' ἀμήσω.
Ἀμείβω. 32, 3, δίδωσι μορφὴν ἀμείψαι.
61, 7, τὴν θήρην ἠμειβον ἀεί. 57, 4,
ἄλλο φῦλον ἐξ ἄλλου ἀμείβων. 107,

7, conj. 12, 19, τὴν· δ' ἀηδὼν ἠμείφθη.
119, 9, ἀγαθοῖς ἡμᾶς ἠμείψω.
Ἀμείνων. 5, 9, ἀμείνονα σχῶν τἀπί-
χειρα.
Ἀμέλγω. 128, 3, γάλα ἀμέλγοντα.
Ἄμετρος. 129, 13, ἄμετρα λακτίζων.
[11, 10, μηδ' ἄμετρα θιμοῦσθαι.]
Ἀμητήρ. 88, 15, μισθὸν ἀμητῆρσιν
δώσειν.
Ἀμητός. 11, 7, καλλίπαις ἀμητός.
Ἀμηχανέω. [116, 10, ἀμηχανῶν.]
Ἄμικτος. [98, 19, ὡς ἄμικτον ἀνθρώ-
ποις ἐρᾶν λεόντων.]
Ἄμιλλα. 15, 12, ἴσην ἄμιλλαν.
Ἀμοιβή. 74, 8, ξενίης ἀμοιβὴν ἀντέ-
δωκαν.
Ἀμοχθήτως. 9, 2, ἐλπίσας ἀμοχθήτως
ἥξειν. 103, 9, λαμβάνων ἀμοχθήτως.
111, 7, παρῆν ἀμοχθήτως.
Ἄμπελος. 19, 1, βότρυς μελαίνης
ἀμπέλου. 11, 1, ἐχθρὴν ἀμπέλων.
Ἀμπελών. 2, 1, ἀνὴρ ἀμπελῶνα
ταφρεύων.
Ἀμπλάκημα. 127, 2, ἀπάντων ἀμ-
πλακήμαт' ἀνθρώπων, conj.
Ἀμφιβαίνω. 5, 3, ὁ δ' ἀμφέβαινε
θηλείαις.
Ἀμφίβολος. [87, 6, ἀμφίβολός νοῦς.]
Ἄμφω. [116, 14, ἄμφω θελόντων
δρᾶν τι.]
Ἄν. 2, 14, πῶς ὁ θεὸς ἂν εἰδείη ; 7,
6, τάχ' ἂν γενοίμην σῶος. 38, 4, πῶς
ἂν μεμφοίμην ; 46, 10, κἂν γεγηράκει.
47, 11, οὐδ' ἂν εἰς δύναιτο. 50, 16,
πῶς οὐκ ἄν ; 63, 12, οὐδ' ἂν ν
παράσχοι. 68, 2, οὐκ ἂν βάλοι τις.
85, 16, πῶς ἂν δυνηθείην ; 128, 12,
οὐκ ἂν ἔσχετε. Λ. 14, μάθοις ἄν. 95,
55, ἂν ὠδήγει. 59, 10, ὡς ἂν βλέπων
ἔτυπτε. 59, 12, ὡς ἂν βλέποι τὸ τοῦ
πέλας. 33, 12, ἤνίκ' ἂν ἔλθωσι. 49,
7, ὅσ' ἂν πίπτῃ. [4, 8, σπανίως ἴδοις
ἄν. 34, 14, πρὸς τοῦτον ἄν τις κατα-
χρέοιτο. 38, 9, οὐδὲν ἂν πάθοις. 40,
5, πόλις ἄν τις εἴποι. 42, 7, πῶς γὰρ
ἂν κρείττον ; 60, 5, τότ' ἂν λίχνος
γένοιτο. 119, 14, αὑτὸν ἂν ὠφελ ηθείης.]
Ἄν = ἐάν, vide ἤν, κἄν. [50, 20,
ἄν τις προσδοκᾷ. 63, 12, ἂν θύσῃς.
41, 4, ἂν μιμήσῃ.
Ἀναβαίνω. 125, 1, ἀναβὰς εἰς τὸ δῶμα.
[8, 2, ἀναβαίνειν.]
Ἀναγκάζω. 80, 1, κάμηλον ἠνάγκαζε
ὀρχεῖσθαι.
Ἀναγκαῖος. 15, 4, ῥῆσις ἀναγκαίη.
130, 6, τῶν ἄγαν ἀναγκαίων. 55, 2,
πτωχῶς μὲν ἀλλ' ἀναγκαίως. [83, 7,
ἀποροῦντα τῶν ἀναγκαίων. 136, 9,
ἀναγκαίων χρειῶν.]
Ἀναγράφω. 75, 16, ἀνέγραφον πάντας.

Ἀναζητέω. 2, 2, ἀνεζήτει (conj.) μή τις ἔκλεψεν. 23, 2, ταῦρον ἀνεζήτει.
Ἀναιδείη. 95, 57, ἀναιδείης ὀφρὶν ἔχουσα.
Ἀναιρέω. 4, 2, σαγήνην ἀνείλετο.
Ἀναλγής. 122, 8, πνεῦμ' ἀναλγές.
Ἀναλόω. 131, 1, οὐσίαν ἀναλώσας. [29, 6, εἰς πόνους ἀνηλώθη. 34, 12, οὐσίαν ἀναλώσας.]
Ἀναλύω. [42, 8, corrupt. Cp. ἀλλύω.]
Ἀναμιμνήσκω. 62, 6, ὄνου πατρὸς ὧν ἀνεμνήσθη. 124, 17, τίς ἔργων σ' ἀναμνήσει;
Ἀναξαίνω. 12, 24, λιπὴν ἀναξαίνει.
Ἀναπίμπλημι. 46, 9, κορώνην ἀναπλήσας.
Ἀναπλόω. 74, 3, τὰς θύρας ἀναπλώσας.
Ἀναπράσσω. 127, 5, τὰς δίκας ἀναπράξει.
Ἀνάσσω. 95, 25, ἀνάσσειν θηρίων.
Ἀνασφάλλω. 75, 8, ἐκ νόσων ἀνασφήλας. 78, 3, νόσου ἀνασφῆλαι.
Ἀνατίθημι. 140, 2, ἀνέθηκε γραφάς.
Ἄναυλος. 9, 9, ἄναυλα ὀρχεῖσθε.
Ἀναψύχω. 95, 57, δρόμων ἀναψύχουσαν.
Ἀνδύνω, conj. in 135, 10, πρὸς ἔσχατ' ἀνδύνω.
Ἀνεκτός. [39, 7, ἡμῖν διαφθαρῆναι ἀνεκτότερον.]
Ἀνέλκω. 94, 4, εἰ ἀνελκύσειε.
Ἀνέμβατος. 45, 11, ἀνέμβατον δρυμῶνα.
Ἄνεμος. 36, 1, δρῦν ἄνεμος ἄρας. 36, 12, ἄνεμος ἄκρα κινήσῃ. 71, 8, ἄνεμοι δὲ πάντως. 114, 4, ἀνέμου συρίσαντος.
Ἄνευ. [80, 4, ἄνευ γέλωτος.]
Ἀνέχω. 91, 6, ἀνέξομαι μικρὰ τῆς ἐπηρείης. 117, 10, οὐκ ἀνέξῃ;
Ἀνηλεής. 71, 4, ἀνηλεὲς στοιχεῖον.
Ἀνήρ. 2, 1, ἀνὴρ γεωργός. 15, 1, ἀνὴρ Ἀθηναῖος . . . ἀνδρὶ Θηβαίῳ. 18, 2, ἀνδρὸς ἀγροίκου. 43, 7, κυνηγέτας ἄνδρας. 32, 1, ἀνδρὸς εὐπρεποῦς. 63, 1, ἀνδρὸς εὐσεβοῦς. 22, 12, φαλακρὸν ἔθηκαν ἄνδρα, conj. 30, 2, τὸν δ' ἠγόραζον ἄνδρες. 47, 1, ἦν ἀνὴρ ὑπεργήρως. 50, 7, τὸν ἄνδρ' ἐπηρώτα. 117, 1, αὐτοῖς ἀνδράσι βυθισθείσης. 54, 4, οὐδ' ἀνὴρ φαίνῃ. 12, 22, ἄνδρα καὶ πόλιν φεύγω. 15, 6, ἀνδρῶν καὶ θεῶν. [106, 1, ἀνδρῶν βίον. 52, 6, κακοῦ ἀνδρός. 81, 5, κακοῦ ἀνδρός. 98, 18, γέροντος ἀνδρός. 116, 5; 116, 8; 119, 13.]
Ἀνθέω. 108, 5, ἀρούρης ἄρτι χλωρὸν ἀνθούσης.
Ἄνθρωπος. 1, 1; 1, 6; 2, 16; 5, 2; 7, 1; 12, 11; 12, 14; 12, 23; 21, 8; 23, 1; 26, 11; 31, 10; 33, 22; 36, 3; 49, 4; 57, 11; 58, 2; 58, 3; 58, 8; 59, 4; 59, 11; 63, 9; 66, 4;

71, 4; 74, 2; 74, 8; 100, 4; 102, 3; 108, 15; 118, 1; 118, 10; 119, 6; 125, 2; 126, 1; 126, 9; 127, 2; Λ. 1; B. 2. 14, 1, ἄρκος φιλεῖν ἄνθρωπον . . . ηὔχει. 59, 4, ἐκπρεπέστατον ζῴων ἄνθρωπον. 66, 3, δεσπότην ζῴων ἄνθρωπον. [5, 10; 22, 14; 35, 7; 38, 9; 47, 15; 60, 5; 67, 9; 70, 5; 84, 7; 85, 19; 87, 6; 98, 19; 98, 20; 107, 16.]
Ἀνίη. 122, 11, ἐκλυθεὶς ἀνίης.
Ἀνίημι. 18, 10, ἀνῆκεν αὐτὸν ἐκ ψύχους. [133, 3, ἀνειμένῃ γλώσσῃ.]
Ἀνίστημι. 69, 1, λαγωὸν ἀναστήσας κύων. 87, 1, κύων λαγωὸν ἀναστήσας. 111, 7, ῥᾴων ἀνέστη. 111, 13, κούφως ἀνέστη γαῦρος.
Ἀνοίγνυμι. 108, 21, ἀνέῳξε τὴν θύρην τις. B. 9, τῆς θύρης ἀνοιχθείσης. [27, 8, κρεῶν ἀνέῳξας ἄγγος.]
Ἀνοικτός. 59, 11, μηδ' ἀνοικτὰ τὰ στήθη.
Ἄντα. 91, 4, τὸν ταῦρον ἄντα (conj.) ἐξώθει.
Ἀντάδω. [88, 2, πρὸς ὄρθρον ἀντάδων.]
Ἀντί. [40, 6, ἀντὶ τῶν πρώτων.]
Ἀντιδίδωμι. 61, 6, τὰ δ' εἶχον ἀντέδωκαν. 74, 8, ἀμοιβὴν ἀντέδωκαν.
Ἀντιζωγρέω. 107, 15, δοὺς μισθὸν ἀντιζωγρήσας.
Ἄντρον. 45, 2, εἰς ἄντρον.
Ἀνύω. [18, 16, ἀνύσεις τι πειθοῖ.]
Ἄνω. [65, 6, οὐδ' ἄνω φαίνῃ. 58, 6, τῆς γῆς ἄνω.]
Ἄξιος. 95, 20, τυραννεῖν ἀξιωτάτην.
Ἀξιόω. 134, 1, οὐρὴ οὐκέτ' ἠξίου κεφαλὴν βαδίζειν.
Ἀοίκητος. 12, 20, πέτραις ἀοικήτοις. 45, 2, ἄντρον τῶν ἀοικήτων.
Ἀπάγω. 108, 14, ἀπῆγε τὸν μῦν.
Ἀπαιολάω. 95, 98, ἀπαιολῶσα τῆς ἀληθείης.
Ἀπαιτέω. 98, 15, τὴν παῖδ' ἀπῄτει.
Ἀπαλός. [133, 3.]
Ἀπαρτάω. 17, 2, πασσάλων ἀπηρτήθη.
Ἀπαρχή. 137, 8, ἀπαρχὰς ὀσπρίων.
Ἅπας. 95, 79, ἅπασιν ἡμῖν αἰτίη κακῶν. 114, 3, ἅπασι φέγγος λάμπει. 118, 7, ἅπαντας ἔφαγεν. 127, 2, ἁπάντων ἀνθρώπων. 129, 16, ἅπαντα τὰ σκεύη. 13, παρεῖχεν ἅπαντα. 77, 12, ἔχεις ἅπαντα. 95, 30, εἰς ἅπαντα συμβούλους. [10, 13, ἅπας ὁ χαίρων. 64, 11, ἅπας ὁ λαμπρός. 106, 8, τιθεὶς ἅπασι δαῖτα.
Ἀπατάω. 75, 4, ἀπατῶ σε (conj.) 77, 3, μύθῳ τὸν ὄρνιν ἠπάτησε.
Ἀπάτη. 57, 2, ἀπάτης πολλῆς.
Ἀπαυδάω. 7, 8, τῷ κόπῳ ἀπαυδήσας.

Ἀπειθής. 3, 2, μιῆς (αἰγὸς) ἀπειθοῦς.
Ἀπειλέω. 16, 1, ἠπείλησε νηπίῳ. 75,
14, δεινὰ πᾶσιν ἠπείλουν.
Ἄπειμι αἰίδο. 103, 17, εἰ δ' ἄπειμι,
συγγνώσῃ.
Ἀπείρητος. 95, 63, ἀλωπέκιζε τοὺς
ἀπειρήτους.
Ἄπειρος. 69, 2, οὐκ ἄπειρος ἀγρεύειν.
Ἀπελπίζω. [43, 18, μηδ' ἀπελπίσῃς.
107, 17, μηδὲ τῶν ἀπελπίζειν.]
Ἀπέρχομαι. 5, 8, ἄρας ἀπῆλθε. 16,
7, ἀπῆλθε παρεδρεύσας. 32, 10,
παίξας ἀπῆλθε. 34, 6, κἀπῆλθ' ἐς
οἴκους. 58, 5, διῆκ' ἀπελθεῖν αὐτά.
84, 4, καθεδοῦμ' ἀπελθών. 84, 6, ἢν
ἀπέλθῃς. 95, 10, ἀπῆλθε κερδώ.
109, 4, ὀρθὴν ἀπελθε. 121, 4, ἢν
ἀπέλθῃς.
Ἀπέχω. 108, 31, οὐκ ἀφέξομαι βώλου.
[100, 18, δείπνου χεῖρ' ἀποσχοῦσαν.]
Ἀπιστέω. [44, 8, ἐχθροῖς ἀπίστει.
87, 7, οἷς οὔτ' ἀπιστεῖν ἔχομεν.]
Ἀπλάνητος. [50, 19, σοφὸν τὸ θεῖον
κἀπλάνητον.]
Ἀπλήστως. 34, 4, ἐσθίων ἀπλήστως.
Ἀπλοῦς. 87, 4, ἁπλοῦν θηρίον. [59,
18, ἀρεστὸν ἀπλῶς.]
Ἀπλόω. 4, 5, εἰς τὸ πλοῖον ἡπλώθη.
54, 2, ἧπαρ ἀπλώσας (conj.)
Ἀπό. 6, 3, ὁρμῆς ἀφ' ἱππείης. 44, 5,
χωρίσας ἀπ' ἀλλήλων. 74, 9, ἀφ' ὧν
ἔξων. 76, 18, ἀφ' ἵππων μεταστήσας.
95, 39, ἀπ' εὐνῆς ἐφορμήσας. 95, 96,
μόνην ἀπ' ἄλλων. 118, 6, ἐρπύσας
ἀπὸ τρώγλης. 122, 16, ἀπ' ἀρχῆς.
129, 7, κατῆγ' ἀφ' ὕψους. [Λ. 3,
τρίτη ἀπ' αὐτῶν.]
Ἀποβάλλω. 34, 10, κἀπόβαλλε, μὴ
φείδου.
Ἀπογινώσκω. [43, 18.]
Ἀποζεύγνυμι. 37, 6, βοῦς εἰς νομὰς
ἀπεζεύχθη.
Ἀποθνήσκω. 34, 8, δυστυχὴς ἀποθνήσκω. 75, 16, οὐκ ἐῶσ' ἀποθνήσκειν.
95, 70, ὡς πατὴρ ἀποθνήσκων. 98,
17, ὥσπερ ὗς ἀποθνήσκων. 114, 7,
τὸ φέγγος οὐκ ἀποθνήσκει. 121, 4,
οὐκ ἀποθνήσκω. 75, 5, ἀποθνήσ-
κεις.
Ἀποθρηνέω. 12, 3, ἀπεθρήνει τὸν
Ἴτυν. 118, 8, συμφορὰς ἀπεθρήνει.
Ἀποιμώζω. [34, 13, ἀποιμώξῃ.]
Ἀποκλείω. [8, 4, ἡ ὀρθὴ τῶν ὁδῶν
ἀπεκλείσθη.]
Ἀποκρέμαμαι. 19, 2, βότρυς ἀπεκρέ-
μαντο ἀμπέλου.
Ἀποκροτέω. 119, 4, χαμαὶ ἀπεκρό-
τησε.
Ἀποκρύπτω. 50, 6, ἡ δ' ἀπεκρύφθη.
Ἀποκτείνω. 6, 9, μὴ μάτην μ' ἀποκ-

τείνῃς. 50, 18, δακτύλῳ ἀποκτείνας.
53, 2, γραῦν ἀποκτείνειν.
Ἀπολιχμάω. 48, 6, ἥν μοι τοῦτο μὴ
'πολιχμήσῃς τοὔλαιον.
Ἀπόλλυμι. 13, 12, ἀπολῇ μετ' αὐτῶν.
21, 1, μαγείρους ἀπολέσαι. 124, 15,
τὸν ὡρόμαντιν ἀπολέσας. 2, 2, τὴν
δίκελλαν ἀπολέσας. 23, 2, ταῦρον
κεράστην ἀπολέσας.
Ἀπόλλων. 68, 1, θεοῖς Ἀπόλλων ἔλεγε.
Ἀπόμνυμι. 75, 19, ἀπώμασ' αὐτοῖς
ὅτι σὺ ἰατρὸς οὐκ εἶ.
Ἀπονυχίζω. 98, 14, ὑπὸ σμίλης ἀπωνυχίσθη.
Ἀπόνως. [9, 11, ἀπόνως κερδαίνειν.]
Ἀποξύνω. 21, 4, κέρατ' ἀποξύνοντες.
Ἀποπηδάω. 108, 21, ἀποπηδήσας
ἔφευγε.
Ἀποπνέω. 122, 4, μέλλω ἀποπνεῖν.
Ἀποπνίγω. 35, 4, ὃν μὲν αὐτῶν ἀποπνίγει.
Ἀπορέω. [83, 7, τὸν ἀποροῦντα τῶν
ἀναγκαίων.]
Ἀποσπάω. 22, 12, τῶν τριχῶν ἀποσπῶσαι. 95, 74, βιῇ ἀποσπασθεῖσα.
105, 3, ἀπέσπασ' αὐτό.
Ἀποστατέω. 101, 4, τῶν συμφύλων
ἀποστατήσας.
Ἀποτίθημι. 2, 10, κἀπέθεντο τὰς
πήρας.
Ἀποτρώγω. 46, 6, τῆς πόης ἀποτρώ-
γων. 117, 7, ἄχνας πιρίνας ἀποτρώ-
γειν.
Ἅπτω. 11, 3, τὴν κέρκον ἅψας. 114,
5, ἐκ δειέτρης ἅπτων. 14, 4, τοῦ
ζῶντος οὐχ ἥπτου. 20, 6, τῶν τροχῶν
ἅπτου. 75, 18, ἡψάμην τῶν σκήπτρων.
Ἄπωθεν. 1, 12, οὐκ ἄπωθεν εἰστήκει.
130, 1, πάγης οὐκ ἄπωθεν.
Ἀπώμαστος. 60, 1, χύτρη ἐμπεσὼν
ἀπωμάστῳ.
Ἄρα. 89, 8, ἆρα πηγὴν ἐκπέπωκας;
92, 4, ἆρα γινώσκεις ἴχνη; [72, 19.]
Ἀράβιος. 57, 6, τῷ χώρῳ τῶν Ἀραβίων
(conj.)
Ἀραιός. 108, 6, ἀραιὰς ῥίζας.
Ἀράσσω. 115, 10, ἤραξεν ὄστρακον.
Ἀράχνη. 139, 1, ἀράχνης ἱστόν.
Ἀραψ. 57, 12, Ἄραβές εἰσιν ψεῦσται.
[8, 1, Ἀραψ κάμηλον ἀχθίσας.]
Ἀργία. [37, 13, ἀργία δὲ κίνδυνος.]
Ἀργός. 20, 3, αὐτὸς ἀργὸς εἰστήκει.
62, 1, ἀργῆς χιλὸν ἐσθίων φάτνης.
98, 17, ἔκειτο ἀργός.
Ἀρεστός. [59, 18, ἀρεστὸν ἀπλῶς.]
Ἀρετή. 104, 7, κόσμον ἀρετῆς.
Ἄρης. 68, 4, Ἄρεος ἐν κινῇ. [70, 2,
Ἄρης ἔγγμεν Ὑβριν.]
Ἀριθμέω. 2, 11, χιλίας ἀριθμήσειν.
95, 95, ἕκαστον ἐγκάτων ἀριθμήσας.

Ἄριστος. 31, 8, γνώμῃ ἀρίστους. [106, 1, ἀνδρῶν βίον ἄριστον. 106, 3, ἀρίστην φυὴν ἔγνω.]

Ἀρκέω. 94, 7, σοὶ μισθὸς ἀρκεῖ. [94, 10, ἀλλ' ἀρκέσει σοι.]

Ἄρκος. 14, 1, ἄρκος ηὔχει. 95, 18, ἄρκος νωθής.

Ἁρμόζω. 31, 14, κάρφῃ μετώποις ἁρμόσαντες. 72, 12, πτερὸν ἁρμόσας.

Ἀρνειός. 96, 2, ἀρνειὸς ἔλεγε πολλά.

Ἀρνέομαι. 2, 4, ἠρνεῖθ' ἔκαστος.

Ἀρνός. 23, 4, ἄρν' ἂν παρασχεῖν. 89, 1, λύκος ἄρνα ἰδών. 89, 10, τὸν ἄρνα συλλαβών. 102, 8, λύκος μὲν ἀρνί.

Ἀροτρεύω. 21, 5, πολλὰ γῆς ἀροτρεύσας.

Ἀροτριάω. 55, 2, ἠροτρία πτωχῶς.

Ἄρουρα. 11, 5, εἰς τὰς ἀρούρας. 26, 9, ἐκλιποῦσαι τὴν ἄρουραν. 88, 5, τῆς ἀρούρης δεσπότης. 89, 6, ἄρουραν ἣν ἔχω. 108, 5, ἐπὶ τῆς ἀρούρης.

Ἀρουραῖος. 33, 5, ὄλεθρος σπερμάτων ἀρουραίων. 108, 1, μυῶν βίον ἀρουραίων.

Ἀρουρίτης. 108, 27, μῦς ἀρουρίτης.

Ἁρπάζω. 69, 5, ἄλλον ἁρπάσαι σπεύδων. 89, 2, οὐκ ἐπῆλθεν ἁρπάξων. 95, 93, ἁρπάσασα λαθραίως. [57, 9, ἁρπάζοντες ἐμπόρου φόρτον. 133, 2].

Ἄρρην. 52, 1, ἄρρενες ταῦροι (?).

Ἄρρωστος. 75, 1, ἀρρώστῳ. 95, 73, κνίσμα χειρὸς ἀρρώστου. 103, 7, λέοντος ἀρρώστου.

Ἄρτι. 28, 4, ἄρτι γάρ, πρὸ τῆς ὥρης. 108, 5, ἄρτι ἀνθούσης. 122, 15, ἄρτι ἠρξάμην. 135, 11, ἄρτι ἥκων. [82, 9, ἀρχόμενον ἄρτι.]

Ἄρτος. 33, 13, ἄρτον αἰτήσω. 33, 14, οὐ τὸν ἄρτον σφενδόνην δέ. 33, 16, ἄρτον ἤτει. 86, 3, ἄρτων ἑώλων.

Ἀρχαῖος. 86, 1, φηγὸς ἀρχαίη.

Ἀρχή. 95, 72, ἀρχὴν λαβοῦσα. 122, 16, μαθὼν ἀπ' ἀρχῆς.

Ἄρχω. 85, 17, εἰς πόλεμον ἄρχειν τῶν ἀσυμφώνων. 134, 9, ἦρχε τῶν πρώτων. 26, 12, ἤδη ἄρχεταί τι καὶ πράσσειν. 122, 15, ἠρξάμην ἰατρεύειν. [82, 9, ἀρχόμενον ἄρτι.] 134, 17, ἀρχούσης ἐμοῦ.

Ἀσεβής. 117, 3, ἑνὸς ἀσεβοῦς.

Ἄσημος. 108, 23, ἄσημα τρίζων.

Ἀσθενέω. 121, 1, ὄρνις ποτ' ἠσθένησε.

Ἀσθενής. 25, 10, ἄλλους ἀσθενεστέρους ἡμῶν. [85, 20, τὸ δὲ στασιάζον ἀσθενές. 102, 12, φοβερὰ τἀσθενῆ θήσει.]

Ἀσθμαίνω. 103, 4, οὐκ ἀληθὲς ἀσθμαίνων.

Ἀσκόπως. 95, 39, ἀσκόπως ἐφορμήσας.

Ἀσπαίρω. 6, 5, ἱκέτευεν ἀσπαίρων.

Ἀσπίς. 76, 12, ἀσπίδα σμήχειν.

Ἄσπονδος. 31, 2, ἄσπονδον πόλεμον.

Ἀστήρ. 114, 7, τῶν ἀστέρων τὸ φέγγος.

Ἄστρον. [65, 4, ἄστρων σύνεγγυς ἵπταμαι.]

Ἄστυ. 52, 1, εἰς ἄστυ εἶλκον.

Ἀσυλίη. 132, 8, μή μου τῆς ἀσυλίης κήδου.

Ἀσύμφωνος. 85, 17, ἄρχειν τῶν ἀσυμφώνων.

Ἀσφάλαξ. 108, 13, παρεὶς ὀρύσσειν ἀσφάλαξι.

Ἀσωτεύομαι. 108, 12, ὡς θέλεις ἀσωτεύσῃ.

Ἀτάκτως. 31, 6, ἀεὶ ἀτάκτως ὑπομένουσι.

Ἄτερ. [8, 3, οὐκ ἄτερ μούσης.]

Ἀτεχνης. [75, 4, ἀτεχνῆς ἰατρός.]

Ἄτεχνος. 21, 8, εἰς ἀτέχνους ἀνθρώπους. 75, 1, ἰατρὸς ἦν ἄτεχνος.

Ἀτεχνῶς. 51, 3, ἔκειρεν ἀτεχνῶς.

Ἀτιμάζω. [119, 14, ἀτιμάσας ἂν ὠφελήθείης.]

Ἄτολμος. 25, 4, ψυχὰς ἄτολμοι.

Ἀτρέμας. 52, 1, conj.

Ἀτριβής. 37, 1, δαμάλης ἀτριβὴς ζεύγλης.

Ἄττις. 137, 7, τίς οὐκ οἶδεν Ἄττιν ;

Αὖ. 18, 11, ἔπειτα δ' αὖ προσῆγε. 27, 3, τῆς δ' αὖ λεγούσης. 30, 6, εἰς τὸν ὄρθρον αὖ δείξει. 59, 5, ὁ δ' αὖ ταῦρον ποιεῖ. 76, 11, ὡς δ' αὖ πόλεμος ἠκούσθη. 76, 14, ἐκείνους αὖ τὸν ἵππον ἐγχαλινώσας. 101, 8, ἐν δ' αὖ λεόντων συγκρίσει. 129, 4, κἀκεῖνος αὖ κατεῖχεν αὐτόν. 131, 15, χελιδόν' αὖ κατοπτεύσας.

Αὐαίνω. 24, 6, λιβάδα πᾶσαν αὐαίνει.

Αὐθάδης. 134, 14, ἡ πρὶν αὐθάδης.

Αὖθις. 76, 19, αὖθις ἵππον ἐξ ὄνου. 95, 50, αὖθις ἀλλ' ὑπουργήσω (conj.) [12, 28, ταπεινὸς αὖθις ὤν.]

Αὖλαξ. 13, 1, αὔλαξι παγίδας πήξας.

Αὐλέω. 9, 1, ἁλιεὺς σοφῶς ηὔλει. 9, 5, καὶ μάτην ηὔλει. 9, 10, ἡνίκ' εἰς χοροὺς ηὔλουν.

Αὐλή. 63, 2, ἔχων ἐν αὐλῇ τέμενος. 103, 6, θηρῶν ἐπ' αὐλάς. 129, 8, ὡς δ' ἦν ἐν αὐλῇ. 129, 13, εἰς μέσσον αὐλῆς. 135, 4, πᾶσαν κατ' αὐλήν.

Αὐλός. 9, 1, αὐλοὺς εἶχε. 9, 3, αὐλῶν ἡδυφωνίην. 80, 2, ὀρχεῖσθ' ὑπ' αὐλοῖς.

Αὔρη. 26, 5, σφενδονῶντα τὰς αὔρας.

Αὔριον. 88, 15, μισθὸν αὔριον δώσειν. 75, 6, τὴν αὔριον οὐκ ὑπερβήσῃ.

Αὖτε. 12, 19, τὴν δ' αὖτ' ἀηδὼν ἠμείφθη. [13, 18. μηδ' αὖτ' ἀπογνῷς.]

Αὖτις. 88, 13, ὡς δ' αὖτις ἦλθεν.

Αὐτόθι. [31, 20, μόνοι θ' ἑάλωσαν αὐτόθι.]
Αὐτόν. 1, 5, αὐτῷ μάχεσθαι. 69, 6, αὐτὸν ἐκ κακῶν σώζων. 72, 8, πρόσωπα δ' αὐτῶν ἐξέλουε. 88, 19, αὐτὸς αὐτῷ κού φίλοισι πιστεύει. [98, 21, αὐτός τις αὐτὸν λανθάνει.]
Αὐτός. 1, 16, = ipse, πῶς αὐτὸς φοβερός; 7, 16, τοῦτ' αὐτό μοι πᾶν ἐπιτέθεικεν ἡ χρείη. 18, 13, αὐτὸς δὲ ῥιψας. 20, 3, αὐτὸς ἀργὸς εἱστήκει. 20, 8, ὅταν τι ποιῇς καὐτός. 36, 8, αὐτὴ δὲ τόσση φηγὸς ἐξεριζώθη. 45, 6, ὧν αὐτὸς ἦγε. 67, 5, αὐτὸς λήψομαι. 88, 19, αὐτὸς αὐτῷ κού φίλοισι πιστεύει. 92, 7, αὐτὸν τὸν λέοντα δείξω. 95, 89, λέων μὲν αὐτὸς εἶχε δαῖτα. 108, 29, αὐτὸς ἐντρύφα δείπνοις. 117, 1, αὐτοῖς ἀνδράσιν. 125, 6, αὐτὸ τοῦτο ποιήσας. 130, 7, αὐτὴν σκυτάλιδ' ἔσεισε. [13, 14, κἂν μηδὲν αὐτὸς καταβλάψῃς. 45, 14, ὧν αὐτὸς εἶχεν. 52, 7, ὡσείπερ αὐτὸς κάμνων. 63, 12, αὐτὸς οἶδας ἂν θύσῃς. 98, 21, αὐτός τις αὐτὸν λανθάνει. 103, 21, ἀλλ' αὐτὸς ἐπαιδεύθη. 116, 10, αὐτὸς ἦλθεν εἰς οἶμον. 56, 9, τὸν αὐτὸς αὐτοῦ πᾶς τις εὐπρεπῆ κρίνει.]
Αὐτός = ille. 16. 6, αὐτὸς δὲ πεινῶν καὶ λύκος χανὼν ὄντως. 129, 21, καὐτὸς ὕστατ' ἐκπνέων. Oblique cases.
—1, 6; 6, 5; 6, 15; 7, 10; 7, 12; 10, 9; 11, 9; 13, 4; 13, 12; 14, 2; 16, 8; 18, 10; 21, 2; 21, 5; 22, 6; 24, 8; 26, 4; 28, 2; 30, 3; 30, 6; 31, 21; 35, 2; 35, 3; 37, 9; 38, 2; 38, 3; 40, 3; 42, 3; 44, 3; 44, 6; 48, 2; 49, 7; 51, 2; 53, 7; 55, 4; 55, 6; 56, 5; 57, 10; 58, 2; 58, 4; 58, 5; 61, 8; 63, 6; 64, 7; 72, 7; 72, 16; 74, 3; 74, 7; 74, 9; 74, 12; 75, 11; 75, 20; 87, 2; 88, 9; 94, 6; 95, 12; 95, 16; 95, 33; 95, 46; 96, 1; 99, 3; 100, 2; 100, 8; 101, 2; 104, 6; 105, 3; 106, 17; 108, 16; 113, 2; 113, 3; 114, 6; 115, 10; 117, 4; 117, 6; 124, 6; 125, 2; 125, 4; 126, 3; 127, 3; 127, 4; 129, 4; 131, 4; 135, 5; 136, 4; Λ. 3. [11, 12; 39, 5; 70, 7.]
ὁ αὐτός. 47, 14, πείσεσθε ταὐτὰ τῇ μῇ ῥάβδῳ. 68, 7, διαβὰς ταὐτὸ μέτρον. 95, 87, τὸν αὐτὸν εἰς ᾅδην. [106, 14, ταὐτὸν παρετίθει.]
Αὐχέω. 14, 1, ἄρκος φιλεῖν ἄνθρωπον ηὔχει. 114, 1, λύχνος ηὔχει ὡς φέγγος ἐκπρεπέστατον λάμπει. 85, 12, οἱ δὲ Κύπρον ἢ Θρᾴκην αὐχοῦσιν. 43, 5, ἐπὶ τοῖς κέρασιν ηὔχει.

Αὐχήν. 77, 5, θεητὸς αὐχήν, 100, 10, σίδηρος αὐχένα τρίψει.
Ἀφαιρέω. 105, 4, ἀδίκως ἀφείλω τῶν ἐμῶν.
Ἄφετος. 37, 1, ἐν ἀγροῖς ἄφετος.
Ἄφθονος. 67, 3, λείην ἄφθονον. 128, 12, ἄφθονον ποίην.
Ἀφίημι. 6, 9, νῦν οὖν ἄφες με. 79, 4, τὸ κρέας ἀφῆκε. 124, 11, ἀφῆκε τὸν πέρδικα. 126, 4, τὴν πόλιν ἀφεῖσα. 11, 4, ἀλώπεκα ἀφῆκε φεύγειν. 57, 10, οὐδ' ἀφῆκαν προελθεῖν. 135, 2, ἐντρέχειν ἀφῆκεν.
Ἄφνω. 62, 5, ἄφνω δ' ἔπαυσε τὸν δρόμον.
Ἀφόβως. 98, 9, ἀφόβως περιλαβεῖν.
Ἀφροδίτη. 10, 6, τὴν δ' Ἀφροδίτην ἐτίμα.
Ἀφύλακτος. 93, 9, ἀφύλακτος σινοικήσω.
Ἄφωνος. 77, 11, οὐκ ἦσθ' ἄφωνος.
Ἀχαιίνης. 95, 86, τὴν ἀχαιίνην ἔπεισεν.
Ἀχαιός. 85, 2, κύων Ἀχαιός.
Ἀχθίζω. [8, 1, Ἀραψ κάμηλον ἀχθίσας.]
Ἄχνη. 117, 7, ἄχνας πυρίνας ἀποτρώγειν.
Ἄχρι. 26, 3, ἄχρι πολλοῦ. 135, 4, ἄχρι βημάτων. 76, 1, ἄχρι συνεισετήκει πόλεμος. 86, 8, ἄχρι πεινήσῃς. [86, 9, ἄχρι τοιαύτην τὴν γαστέρα σχῇς.]
Ἄχυρον. 76, 9, πνεῦμα σώζων ἐπ' ἀχύροισι.
Ἄψ. 25, 9, ἄψ νῦν ἴωμεν.
Ἄωρος. 12, 4, ἄωρον ἐκπεσόντα. 118, 8, παίδων ἀώρων συμφοράς.

Βαδίζω. 134, 2, οὐκέτ' ἠξίου πρώτην κεφαλὴν βαδίζειν. [70, 4, ἕπεται βαδιζούσῃ.]
Βαθυγνώμων. 126, 5, ἡ βαθυγνώμων.
Βαθύς. 25, 7, βαθέην ἐς Ἴλιον. 93, 7, βαθείη φρικὶ μαλλὸν ὀρθώσας.
Βαθύσκιος. 92, 2, ἐν βαθυσκίοις ὕλαις.
Βαθύστρωτος. 32, 7, βαθυστρώτου κλίνης.
Βαθύσχινος. 46, 2, ἐν χλόη βαθυσχίνῳ.
Βαίνω. 75, 9, τοῖς ποσὶν βαίνων. 76, 7, βαίνων. 80, 3, ὀδῷ βαίνειν. 92, 6, σὺν θεῷ βαίνεις. 103, 1, ἐπ' ἄγρην βαίνειν. 109, 1, μὴ λοξὰ βαίνειν. 134, 7, τὰ πορευτὰ βαίνει πάντα. [106, 27, τοῦτο δ' εἰς ἔθος βαίνοι. 8, 2, κάτω βαίνειν. 40, 4, ταξύπισθέ μου βαίνει.]
Βαιός. 36, 12, βαιὸν κινήσῃ. 129, 24, βαιῷ κινιδίῳ παριοσίμην.
Βάλλω. 26, 8, λίθους δὲ βάλλων. 33, 9. καὶ πρὶν βαλεῖν ἔφευγον (?). 4, 1,

σαγήνην βεβλήκει. 9, 6, βαλὼν σαγήνην ἔλαβεν. 45, 7, ἔβαλλε θαλλόν.
68, 2, οὐκ ἂν βάλοι τις. 68, 8, ποῦ
βάλω; οὐκ ἔχω χώρην. 129, 15, εἰς
μέσον βάλλων. [9, 12, ὅταν βαλὼν δὲ
τοῦτο.]
Βάπτω. 71, 2, νῆα βάπτοισαν κῦμα.
Βάραθρον. 134, 12, κοιλὸν πέτρης
βαράθρου.
Βαρδύνω. [110, 4, πάντ' ἔχω· σὺ βαρδύνεις, conj.]
Βάρος. 111, 20, βάρος διπλοῦν ἦλθε.
Βαρύνω. 84, 3, βαρύνω τὸν τένοντα.
Βαρύς. 103, 5, φωνὴν βαρεῖαν λεπτύνων.
Βασιλεύς. 67, 6, βασιλεὺς γάρ εἰμι.
95, 64, ἄλλους βασιλεῖς ὑπερέθιζε. 95,
77, βασιλῆ τὸν λύκον καταστήσειν.
103, 12, βασιλεῦ, πῶς ἔχεις; Β. 1, παῖ
βασιλέως Ἀλεξάνδρου.
Βασιλεύω. 102, 1, λέων τις ἐβασίλευεν.
Βαστάζω. 111, 20, βαστάσας νώτοις.
Βάτος. 64, 1, ἤριζον ἐλάτη καὶ βάτος.
64, 7, βάτος πρὸς αὐτὴν εἶπε. 64, 10,
βάτος γενέσθαι αἱρήσῃ.
Βάτραχος. 24, 3, βάτραχοι χοροὺς
ἦγον. 25, 6, βατράχων ὅμιλον. 120,
2, βάτραχος παρ' εὐρίποις.
Βέβαιος. 6, 16, τὰ μικρὰ πλὴν βέβαια.
93, 2, φέροντες βέβαιον εἰρήνην. [43,
17, μηδὲν βέβαιον.]
Βέλος. 68, 6, τὸ βέλος τ' ἔπηξεν.
Βελτίων. [31, 24.]
Βῆλος. Β. 3, ἐπὶ Νίνου τε καὶ Βήλου.
Βῆμα. 135, 4, ἄχρι βημάτων.
Βίαιος. [102, 12, τοῖς βιαίοις φοβερὰ
τάσθενῆ θήσει.]
Βίβλος. Β. 16, τήνδε βίβλον ἀείδω.
Βιβρώσκω. 108, 9, κρίμνα λεπτὰ βιβρώσκων. 60, 3, βέβρωκα καὶ πέπωκα.
Βίη. 18, 5, βίη συλήσειν. 47, 6, σὺν
βίη πάσῃ. 89, 2, βίῃ ἀρπάξων. 95,
74, βίη ἀποσπαθεῖσα. 102, 2, τῇ βίῃ
χαίρων. [18, 16, πειθοῖ μᾶλλον ἢ βίᾳ.]
Βίος. 6, 2, τὸν γλυκὺν βίον σώζων. 13,
9, τίνι βίῳ χαίρεις οὐκ οἶδα. 22, 1,
βίου τὴν μέσην ὥρην. 47, 3, τὸν βίον
τελευτήσειν. 108, 1, μυῶν βίον ἀρουραίων. 108, 3, ἔθετο κοινὸν τὸν βίον.
108, 8, μύρμηκος ζῆς βίον. 126, 8, ὁ
νῦν βίος. [106, 1, ἀνδρῶν βίον ἄριστον.]
Βλάβη. [11, 12, νέμεσις βλάβην φέρουσα.]
Βλάπτω. 27, 7, βλάπτουσα μᾶλλον
ἤπερ ὠφελοῦσα. 47, 12, ὕμας βλάψαι
δύναιτο. [14, 5, ὁ ζῶντα βλάπτων.
41, 3, βλάψεις σεαυτόν.]
Βλασφημέω. 71, 6, μή με βλασφήμει.
89, 4, σὺ τοί με ἐβλασφήμεις.

Βλασφήμως. 96, 2, αὐτὸν ἔλεγε πολλὰ
βλασφήμως.
Βλέπω. 59, 10, = ccrno, ὡς ἂν βλέπων
ἔτυπτε.
= vidco, 12, 8, πρῶτον βλέπω σε
σήμερον. 22, 7, νέον βλέπειν ἐραστήν.
23, 5, καλὸν βλέπειν ταῦρον. 56, 2,
πάντα ἔβλεπε. 59, 12, ὡς ἂν βλέποι
τὸ τοῦ πέλας. 66, 8, συμφορὰς βλέπειν. 107, 14, τὸ φῶς βλέψαι. 109,
4, βλέπουσά σε. [116, 3, βλέπουσα τὸν
παῖδα.]
Βληχρός. 36, 7, λεπτός τ' ἐὼν καὶ
βληχρός.
Βληχώδης. 93, 5, ποίμνη τὰ πάντα
βληχώδης.
Βόειος. 34, 5, βοείων ἐγκάτων.
Βοηθέω. 20, 3, δέον βοηθεῖν. [94, 9,
κακοῖς βοηθεῖν.]
Βοηλάτης. 20, 1, βοηλάτης ἄμαξαν
ἦγεν. 23, 1, βοηλάτης ἄνθρωπος.
Βοιωτός. 15, 11, ὁ δ' ἄλλος, ὡς Βοιωτός.
Βολή. 1, 2, τόξου βολῆς ἔμπειρος.
Βόλος. 9, 8, τὸν βόλον πλύνων.
Βομβέω. 84, 2, κώνωψ εἶπε ταῦτα βομ-
βήσας.
Βορέης. 18, 3, βορέῃ ἡλίῳ τε ἔριν
γενέσθαι. 18, 4, βορέης ἐφύσα πρῶτος.
Βορή. [106, 18, χεῖρα βορῆς ἀποσχοῦσαν.]
Βορράς. [18, 14, Βορρᾶς ἐνικήθη.]
Βόσκω. 89, 7, οὐδ' ἐβοσκήθην χλωρόν
τι. [142, 2, χλωρῆν ἐβόσκοντο ποίην.]
Βοτάνη. [128, 7.]
Βότρυς. 19, 1, βότρυς μελαίνης ἀμ-
πέλου. 19, 8, ὀμφαξ ὁ βότρυς.
Βουδόρος. 97, 7, μαχαίρας βουδόρους.
Βουκολέω. 19, 7, βουκολοῦσα τὴν
λύπην.
Βουκόλημα. 140, 1, βουκόλημα τῆς
λύπης.
Βουλεύω. 59, 12, βλέπειν τί βουλεύοι.
95, 68, συμφέροντα βουλεύων.
Βουλή. 130, 2, βουλὰς ἐκίνει ποικίλας.
Βούλομαι. 7, 15, μετασχεῖν μικρὸν οὐκ
ἐβουλήθην. 48, 4, ἀλεῖψαι βούλομαί
σε. 111, 1, ἐβουλήθη πρίασθαι.
124, 12, συλλαβεῖν ἐβουλήθη. 126, 7,
εἰ κλύειν τι βουλήσῃ. [9, 12, ὅπερ
βούλει. 63, 7, θαυμαστὸς εἶναι βουλοίμην. 119, 12, βουλόμενος ἡμᾶς
νουθετεῖν.]
Βοῦς. 20, 7, τοὺς βόας κέντριζε. 21, 1,
βόες μαγείρους ἀπολέσαι ἐζήτουν. 21,
10, τὸν βοῦν ὁ θύσων. 23, 7, βοῦν
προσάξειν. 28, 1, γένημα φρίνου
συνεπάτησε βοῦς. 37, 4, ὁ βοῦς ἐσίγα.
37, 6, ὁ βοῦς ἀπεζεύχθη. 55, 1, ἕνα
βοῦν τις εἶχε. 55, 5, ὄνος διηρώτα
τὸν βοῦν. 74, 1, ἵππος τε καὶ βοῦς.
74, 12, ὁ βοῦς μετ' αὐτόν.

Βοώτης. 52, 3, τὸν βοώτην θυμὸς εἶχε.
Βράγχος. 74, 15, Βράγχε. Λ. 2, ὦ
Βράγχε τέκνον. Λ. 10, Βράγχε.
Βραδύνω. 85, 4, ἔμελλεν, ἐβράδυνεν
(vide βαρδύνω).
Βραδύς. 127, 7, βράδιον ἐμπίπτει
= serius.
Βραχύς. 107, 13, ὁδοῦσι βραχυτάτοις.
Βρέγμα. 33, 19, τὸ βρέγμα ἔτυψε.
Βρόχος. 107, 13, στερρὸν βρόχον
κείρας.
Βρύχω. 95, 45, τὸ στόμα βρύχων.
Βυθίζω. 117, 1, νεὼς βυθισθείσης.
Βυθός. 4, 3, εἰς βυθὸν φεύγων.
Βυσσόθεν. 95, 49, κινήσασα βυσσόθεν
γνώμην.
Βῶλος. 108, 7, μελαίνῃ βώλῳ. 108,
31, λιτῆς βώλου.
Βωμός. 37, 8, βωμὸν αἵματος πλήσων.
63, 3, στέφων βωμούς. 78, 5, βωμὸς
ἐσυλήθη. 132, 6, τὸν βωμὸν αἵματος
πλήρη.

Γαίη. 71, 10, τῆς σῆς γαίης. 128, 5,
ἡ τροφὴ γαίης πᾶσα.
Γάλα. 128, 3, τὸ γάλα πῆξαι.
Γαλῆ. 27, 1, γαλῆν τις συλλαβών. 31,
1, γαλαῖ καὶ μύες. 31, 3, γαλαῖ
ἐνίκων. 31, 12, γαλῆν μῦς προυκαλεῖτο.
32, 1, γαλῇ. 135, 5, γαλῆ. [31,
22, γαλῆς.]
Γάλλος. 137, 1, Γάλλοις ἀγύρταις.
Γαμέω. 24, 7, ἐὰν γήμας παιδίον γεννήσῃ. 32, 6, γαμεῖν ἔμελλεν. 98, 4,
δίδωμι γῆμαι. [70, 1, θεῶν γαμούντων.
70, 2, Ἄρης ἔγημεν Ὕβριν.]
Γάμος. 24, 1, γάμοι Ἡλίου. 32, 9,
γάμου δαίτῃ. 98, 10, εἰ γάμου
χρῄξεις.
Γαστήρ. 34, 6, γαστρὸς ὄγκον ἀλγήσας.
86, 5, γαστὴρ ᾠγκώθη. [86, 10, τοιαύτην γαστέρα.]
Γαῦρος. 43, 6, τὰ γαῦρα. 74, 11,
γαῦρός ἐστι τὴν γνώμην. 95, 21,
γαύρη εἶδος. 111, 13, κούφως ἀνέστη
γαῦρος. [29, 5, τὸ τῆς ἀκμῆς γαῦρον.]
Γαυρόομαι. 43, 15, κέρατα οἷς ἐγαυρούμην. [90, 6, μηδεὶς γαυρούσθω.]
Γε. 23, 8, εἰ φύγοι γε τὸν κλέπτην.
50, 16, πῶς οὖν ἂν εἶπεν ὦν γε μάρτυς
εἱστήκειν ; 93, 8, καινῆς γε ταύτης
τῆς μεσιτείης. 23, 5, εἰ λάβοι γε τὸν
κλέπτην (conj.) [22, 16 ; 23, 13 ;
36, 14.]
Γεγωνίσκω. Β. 12, μαθόντες οὐδὲν
πλείον ἢ γεγωνίσκειν.
Γεηπόνος. 108, 14, τὸν γεηπόνον
πείσας.
Γείτων. 46, 5, ἦν γὰρ ἀβλαβὴς γείτων.
95, 14, ὁ λέων ἐστί μοι γείτων.

Γελάω. 136, 7, γελάσας δ᾽ ὁ μύρμηξ.
[45, 12, γελάσας.]
Γελοῖος. [84, 7, γελοῖος ὅστις οὐδὲν ὤν.]
Γέλως. 56, 5, γέλως ἐκινήθη. [80, 5,
ἄνευ γέλωτος.]
Γεμίζω. [128, 7, βοτάνη δρόσου γεμισθεῖσα.]
Γέμω. 66, 5, πήρας πᾶσι κακῶν γεμ-
ούσας. 74, 5, ἑστίη πυρὸς γεμούσῃ.
Γενεή. Λ. 1, γενεὴ δικαίων ἀνθρώπων.
Γενειήτης. 124, 11, γενειήτην ἀλεκτορίσκον.
Γέννα. [106, 22, ὦ φέριστε θηρίων
γέννης.]
Γενναῖος. 31, 8, εἰς μάχην γενναίους.
76, 3, παραστάτην γενναῖον. 95, 80,
ἴσθι γενναίη. 111, 3, φορτίσας γενναίως τὸν ὄνον.
Γεννάω. 24, 8, παιδίον τι γεννήσῃ.
89, 5. 101, 1, ἐν λύκοις ἐγεννήθην.
128, 6, ἣν τι γεννήσῃ.
Γέννημα. 28, 1, γέννημα φρύνου.
Γένος. 31, 7, τοὺς γένει ἀρίστους. 85,
8, πολεμίων γένος ἔν ἐστι. [Λ. 5,
γένος χεῖρον. 33, 23, ἀνθρώπων γένος
πονηρόν.]
Γέρανος. 13, 2, γεράνους σποραίων
πολεμίας. 13, 5, οὐκ εἰμὶ γέρανος.
26, 1, γέρανοι κατενέμοντο τὴν χώρην.
[65, 1, τεφρὴ γέρανος. 142, 1, Λίβυσσα γέρανος. 33, 21 ; 65, 3.]
Γέρων. 6, 14, τὸν γέροντα. 7, 3, ὄνῳ
γέροντι. 21, 5, λίην γέρων. 33, 18,
ὁ δὲ γέρων. 37, 6, ὁ βοῦς ὁ γέρων.
37, 11, τὸν γέροντα (βοῦν). 55, 5,
τῷ γέροντι. 72, 11, γέρων κορώνης
υἱός. 93, 6, γέρων κριός. 118, 3,
γερόντων δικαστήρων. Λ. 15, γέροντος
Αἰσώπου. [29, 1, γέρων ἵππος. 98,
γέροντος ἀνδρός. 106, 11, γέρων
πίθηκος.]
Γεύομαι. [106, 28, οὐδ᾽ ἑώλων γεύσομαι
κρεῶν.]
Γεωργός. 2, 1, ἀνὴρ γεωργός. 12, 3,
γεωργοῖς ἄσεις. 12, 6, καῖμα τὸν
γεωργὸν εἶχεν. 26, 1, γεωργοῦ χώρην.
33, 2, καί τις γεωργός. 33, 10 ; 71,
1 ; Λ. 11. [141, 2.]
Γῆ. 9, 7, ἐπὶ γῆς. 21, 5, πολλὰ γῆς.
57, 3, διὰ γῆς. 95, 2, γυῖα γῆς ἐφαπλώσας. 108, 9, ἐν πυθμέσιν γῆς.
120, 3, εἰς γῆν παρελθών. Λ. 12,
ἐφύετ᾽ ἐκ γῆς πάντα. 66, 3, πλάσασθαι ἄνθρωπον ἐκ γῆς. [58, 6, τῆς
γῆς ἄνω.]
Γῆρας. 103, 10, γῆρας λιπαρόν. [29, 6,
τὸ γῆρας εἰς πόνους ἀνηλώθη.]
Γηράσκω. 46, 10, κἂν γεγηράκει. 74,
15, πᾶς ὁ γηράσας. 103, 2, τῷ χρόνῳ
γεγηράκει.

Γίνομαι. 6, 11, ἐπὴν μέγας γένωμαι.
7, 6, τάχ' ἂν γενοίμην σῶος. 15, 8,
ὡς κρείσσων Θησεὺς γένοιτο. 18, 2,
ἔριν γενέσθαι λέγουσιν. 38, 3, ὡς
γένοιτο πόνος ῥάων. 54, 3, πατὴρ
γίνῃ. 59, 14, ἐν τοῖς θεμελίοις γεγονέναι τροχούς. 64, 10, βάτος γενέσθαι.
80, 3, ἐμοὶ γένοιτο ἐν ὁδῷ βαίνειν.
87, 4, ἁπλοῦν θηρίον γίνου. 95, 26,
τότ' οὖν γένοιτο μνήμη. 95, 79, αἰτίη
κακῶν γίνῃ. 95, 83, οὕτω γένοιτό σοι
μόνῃ. 98, 11, νύμφιος γίνου. 100,
3, μέγας κύων ἐγένετο. 101, 8, λύκος
γίνῃ. 102, 5, ἀγυρμὸς ἐγεγόνει ζῴων.
118, 4, νεοσσῶν γίνεται μήτηρ. 132,
10, θεῶν γενοίμην σφάγιον. [Λ. 3,
ἐγενήθη. Id. 4, γενέσθαι. 35, 8, ἐχθρὸς
γίγνου. 60, 5, λιχνὸς γένοιο. 83, 4,
καλὸν γενέσθαι.]
Γινώσκω. 1, 7, γνώσῃ τί σοι ποιητέ'
ἐστίν. 1, 16, πῶς φοβερός ἐστι γινώσκω. 12, 5, ἔγνωσαν ἀλλήλας. 13,
10, τοῦτο γινώσκω. 72, 18, καὶ κολοιὸς
ἐγνώσθη. 84, 6, ὅτ' ἦλθες ἐγνώκειν.
91, 7, γνώσῃ πόσον τράγου μεταξύ.
92, 4, ἆρα γινώσκεις ἴχνη; 124, 15,
πῶς γνώσῃ πύτ' ἐννυχεύει Ὡρίων. Λ.
14, μάθοις ἂν οὕτω ταῦτ' ἔχοντα καὶ
γνοίης. [23, 9, τοῦτο γινώσκειν. 42,
8. 106, 3, φυὴν ἔγνω.]
Γλήνη. 77, 4, ὀξέη γλήνη.
Γλυκύς. 3, 3, κόμην γλυκεῖαν. 6, 2,
γλυκὺν βίον. 103, 15, δεῦρο, γλυκεῖα.
Γλύφω. 30, 1, γλύψας τις Ἑρμείην.
Γλῶσσα. 57, 13, ἐπὶ γλώσσης. 77,
10, κερτόμῳ γλώσσῃ. [133, 3.]
Γνησίως. [106, 4, φιλοφρονεῖσθαι γνησίως.]
Γνώμη. 7, 14, τῆς κακῆς γνώμης. 25,
1, γνώμῃ λαγωοὺς εἶχε. 31, 8, ῥώμῃ
γνώμῃ τ' ἀρίστους. 36, 11, μαλθακῇ
γνώμῃ. 47, 13, χωρὶς ᾖτε τὴν γνώμην.
74, 11, γαῦρός ἐστι τὴν γνώμην. 95,
49, κινήσασα βυσσόθεν γνώμην. [98,
18, ποικίλου τὴν γνώμην.]
Γόης. 57, 13, ψεύσταί τε καὶ γόητες.
Γόμος. 7, 11, τὸν γόμον λύων.
Γομόω. 111, 9, γομώσων τὸν ὄνον.
Γόμφόω. 92, 8, γομφίοις σιγκρούων.
122, 13, γομφίους ἀλοίφρας.
Γοῦν. [70, 6, μὴ γοῦν ὕβρις ἐπέλθοι.]
Γραίη. 22, 5, νέης τε καὶ γραίης. 22,
7, ἡ γραίη. 22, 11, ἡ νέη τε χἠ γραίη.
95, 31, τῆς γραίης κεφαλῆς. 104, 5,
κύων γραίη. [126, 3, γραίη (conj.)]
Γραῦς. 16, 3, τὴν γραῦν. 22, 10, ἡ
γραῦς. 53, 2, γραῦν.
Γραφή. 140, 2, ποικίλας γραφὰς ζῴων.
Γράφω. 75, 17, σὲ γράφειν ἔμελλον.
127, 1, γράφοντ' ἐν ὀστράκοισιν.

Γριπεύς. 61, 2 ; 61, 5.
Γρίφος. B. 11, ποιήσεις γρίφοις ὁμοίας.
Γρύπτω. 95, 62, καὶ γρύσαι τι τολμήσῃς.
Γυῖον. 26, 1, γυῖα κοῦφα. 95, 2,
νωθρὰ γυῖα.
Γυμνός. 56, 4, πίθωνα γυμνόν. 131,
14, γυμνὸς ἐκεῖνος.
Γυμνόω. 18, 13, ἐγυμνώθη. [22, 13,
τιλλόμενος ἐγυμνοῦτο. 22, 16, δακνό-
μενος γυμνοῦται.]
Γυναικεῖος. 32, 3, μορφὴν γυναικείην.
71, 5, γυναικείην φωνήν.
Γυνή. 16, 10, γυναικὶ πιστεύω. 22, 5,
ἦρα γυναικῶν δύο. 32, 4, καλῆς γιν-
αικός. [22, 15, εἰς γυναῖκας. 116, 2,
γυνή.]
Γυρεύω. [29, 4, καμπτῆρας γυρεύω.]
Γύψ. 122, 5.
Γωνίη. 5, 4, ἐς οἴκου γωνίην.

Δαίμων. 11, 4, ἐπίσκοπος δαίμων. 12,
9, πικρὸς δαίμων.
Δαίς. 95, 89, εἶχε δαῖτα πανθοίνην.
[106, 8, τιθεὶς ἅπασι δαῖτα. 106, 21,
δαιτὸς ψαῦσον.]
Δαίτη. 32, 9, γάμου δαίτῃ 'λέλυτο.
Δαιτρεύω. [106, 11, πίθηκος ἦν ὁ δαιτρεύων.]
Δάκνω. 77, 1, δεδηχὼς στόματι τυρόν.
87, 2, δάκνων αὐτόν. 87, 5, τί δάκνεις;
104, 1, κύων ἔδακνε. 112, 1, μῦς
ταῦρον ἔδακεν. 112, 6, δακὼν φεύγει.
117, 8, ἀφ' ἑνὸς δηχθείς. 129, 10,
δηχθεὶς θυμῷ. [22, 16, δακνόμενος.]
Δάκτυλος. 50, 9, τῷ δακτύλῳ νεύων.
50, 18, δακτύλῳ ἀποκτείνας.
Δαμάλης. 37, 1, δαμάλης ἐν ἀγροῖς
ἄφετος.
Δάπτω. 95, 91, καὶ σπλάγχνα δάπτων.
Δασυπόδης. 69, 1, λαγωὸν δασυπόδην.
Δαψιλής. 63, 5, ἀγαθὰ δαψιλῆ. 100,
4, ἄνθρωπος δαψιλής.
Δεῖ. 20, 3, δέον βοηθεῖν. 75, 5, ἕτοιμα
δεῖ σε πάντ' ἔχειν. 124, 20, ὅμως δεῖ
σχεῖν τι τὸν φίλον. [36, 14, μὴ δεῖν
μάχεσθαι. 83, 1, δεῖ τὸν φιλοῦντα
φροντίζειν.]
[Δεῖμα.] 1, 10, λέων δείσας. 75, 2, μὴ
δέδιχθι. 75, 17, ἀλλ' ἐγὼ δείσας. 82,
7, τὸν μῦν δέδοικα. 122, 2, δείσας
ὄλεθρον.
Δείκνυμι. 30, 6, δεῖξειν αὐτοῖς. 50, 10,
τὸν τόπον ἐδείκνυε. 92, 7, τὸν λέοντά
σοι δείξω. 95, 55, δεικνύων ἐν ᾠδήγει.
98, 14, τῷ πενθερῷ δείξας. 103, 19,
οὐκ ἔχεις ὅ μοι δείξεις. 108, 16, ἔδειξεν
αὐτῷ πλήθη.
Δείλαιος. 53, 1, ἀλώπηξ δειλαίη. 95,
41, τὴν δειλαίην. 118, 7, ἡ δειλαίη.

L

Some commentary

Δείλη. 113, 1, πρόβατα συλλέγων δείλης.
Δειλός. 98, 6, φρένες δειλαί. 108, 22, έφευγε δειλός.
Δεινός. 75, 14, δεινὰ πᾶσιν ἠπείλουν. 78, 3, νόσου δεινῆς. [33, 25, δεινὸν τὸ φῦλον. 38, 9, οὐδὲν οὕτω δεινόν.]
Δειπνέω. 16, 4, ὡς ἕτοιμα δειπνήσων. 107, 1, ἔμελλε δειπνήσειν. 108, 28, τοιαῦτα δειπνῶν. 122, 5, σύ με δειπνήσεις. 124, 2, μέλλοντι δειπνήσειν. 124, 20, τί δειπνήσει. 129, 17, δειπνοῦντα δεσπότην. [42, 7, κυνῶν ἐρωτώντων ὅπως ἐδείπνησε.]
Δείπνον. 6, 11, πρέπων δείπνοις. 32, 6, ἡρμένου τοῦ δείπνου. 42, 1, δεῖπνόν τις εἶχε. 42, 3, ἐλθεῖν ἐπὶ τὸ δείπνον. 61, 7, δεῖπνα εἶχον ἡδίω. 97, 3, ἐλθεῖν ἐπὶ τὸ δεῖπνον. 107, 6, μυὸς δεῖπνον. 108, 29, περισσοῖς δείπνοις. [106, 18,. δείπνου χεῖρα ἀποσχοῦσαν.]
Δελφίς. [39, 1, δελφῖνες ἀεὶ διεφέροντο.]
Δένδρον. 64, 6, δένδρων τοσούτων ἐκπρεπεστάτη. 95, 23, δένδροις ὅμοιον.
Δέομαι. 53, 2, ζωγρεῖν ἐδεῖτο.
Δεσμεύω. 107, 11, σφαλεὶς ἐδεσμεύθη.
Δεσμή. 47, 5, ῥάβδων δεσμή.
Δεσμός. 129, 12, φάτνης ὀνείης δεσμά.
Δεσμώτης. 97, 8, δεσμώτην ἀλεκτορίσκον. 129, 8, παρὰ φάτναισι δεσμώτης.
Δέσποινα. 51, 7, δέσποινα. 95, 27, id. 134, 15, δέσποινα κεφαλή.
Δεσπότης. 3, 7, τῷ δεσπότῃ. 7, 11, ὁ δεσπότης. 59, 15, συνεξαμείβειν δεσπόταισιν. 66, 2, δεσπότην ζῴων ἄνθρωπον. 76, 15, ὁ δεσπότης παρήγεν. 80, 1, κάμηλον ἠνάγκαζε δεσπότης. 88, 5, ὁ τῆς ἀρούρης δεσπότης. 95, 78, πονηροῦ δεσπότου. 104, 2, ὁ δεσπότης. 129, 3, τὸν δεσπότην. 129, 17, δεσπότην. [106, 14, τῷ δεσπότῃ.]
Δεῦρο. 103, 15, δεῦρο, γλυκεῖα.
Δεύτερος. 46, 9, κωρώνην δευτέρην. 95, 48, εὑρεῖν δεύτερον δόλον. 114, 5, ἐκ δευτέρης. B. 15, ἐκ δευτέρου. [95, 101, ἐκ δευτέρου.]
Δέχομαι. 130, 5, καὶ δέχου χαίρων.
Δέω. 27, 1, γαλῆν συλλαβών τε καὶ δήσας (conj.) 37, 8, δεθεὶς κέρατα. 47, 7, δεδεμένας σὺν ἀλλήλαις.
Δή. 9, 2, καὶ δή ποτ᾽ . . . ἐλπίσας. 12, 6, καὶ δὴ προσέπτησαν. 21, 3, καὶ δὴ συνηθροίζοντο. 79, 2, καὶ δὴ παρῄει ποταμόν. 95, 51, καὶ δ:ὴ κατ᾽ ἴχνος ἥει. 12, 18, ἄγε δή. 33, 9, εὗρε δὴ τέχνην. 43, 11, ἐπεὶ δὲ δὴ ἦλθεν. 47, 6, πειρᾶσθε δή μοι. 52, 4, τί δὴ κρώζεις; 63, 2, ἔνθα δὴ θύων.

89, 10, τότε δή. 98, 10, πρὸς ταῦτα δὴ σκόπησον. 102, 4, φασὶ δή. 124, 4, ὥρμησε δή. 47, 3, ἔμελλε γὰρ δή. [29, 3, καὶ δὴ στενάξας εἶπε. 106, 2, καὶ δὴ διατρίβων.]
Δημήτηρ. 11, 9, οὐδ᾽ εἶδεν τὴν ἄλωνα Δημήτηρ. 34, 1, Δήμητρι ταῦρον θύων. 129, 6, πυρὸν φίλης Δήμητρος.
Δῆμος. 85, 2, κυνῶν δήμου στρατηγός. [70, 6, προσγελῶσα τοῖς δήμοις.]
Διά, c. gen.—57, 3, ἥλαινε διὰ γῆς. 104, 4, δι᾽ ἀγορῆς σείων.
Διά, c. acc.—93, 4, κύνας δι᾽ οὓς μάχονται. 93, 10, ὑμῖν δι᾽ οὓς μηδὲ νέμεσθαι ἔξεστι. 100, 10, τρυφῇ δι᾽ ἣν σίδηρος αὐχένα τρίψει. 126, 3, διὰ τίν᾽ αἰτίην; [96, 6, διὰ καιρόν.]
Διαβαίνω. 40, 1, διέβαινε ποταμόν. 68, 7, διαβὰς ταὐτό. 111, 11, διέβαινε τὸν ῥοῦν.
Διαβάλλω. 75, 20, μάτην διεβλήθης.
Διαβολή. 44, 4, λόγοις ὑπούλοις διαβολαῖς τε.
Διαβρέχω. 111, 19, τῶν σπόγγων διαβραχέντων.
Διάβροχος. 108, 6, διαβρόχους σίτου ῥίζας.
Διαιρέω. 31, 9, καὶ διεῖλον εἰς ἵλας.
Διαλλακτής. [39, 7, σοῦ τυχεῖν διαλλακτοῦ.]
Διανέμω. [106, 12, διανέμων μοίρας.]
Διαξαίνω. [106, 23, μερίμνῃ καρδίην διαξαίνω.]
Διαπορέω. 112, 8, ὁ δὲ διηπορεῖτο.
Διάργεμος. 85, 15, καὶ διάργεμοι στήθη.
Διαρρήγνυμι. [41, 1, διαρραγῆναί φασι σαύραν.]
Διαρρήσσω. 38, 7, ἄλλος μ᾽ ἐμπεσών διαρρήσσει.
Διασκοπέω. 95, 17, τίς τυραννήσει διεσκοπεῖτο.
Διατελέω. 136, 6, ἄλλα διετέλουν ᾄδων.
Διατρέχω. 82, 2, διέδραμεν μῦς.
Διατρίβω. 85, 6, οὐ χάριν διατρίβω. 135, 8, ἔνθ᾽ ἐγὼ διατρίβω. [106, 2, κατὰ φωλεὸν διατρίβων.]
Διαυγής. 72, 6, ὕδωρ διαυγές.
Διαφέρω. [39, 1, δελφῖνες διεφέροντο φαλ᾽λαίναις.]
Διαφθείρω. [39, 6, διαφθαρῆναι ἀνεκτότερον.]
Διαψεύδω. 43, 13, δύστηνος ὡς διεψεύσθην. 131, 17, κἀμὲ νῦν διεψεύσω.
Διδάσκαλος. 109, 3, μήτηρ ἡ διδάσκαλος.
Διδάσκω. 33, 11, παῖδα φωνήσας ἐδίδασκε. 115, 8, τοιγὰρ διδάξω. [98, 19, σοφίῃ διδαχθείς.]
Δίδωμι. 33, 14, σφενδόνην σύ μοι δώσεις. 33, 18, τὴν σφενδόνην ἔδωκε.

36, 2, ἄνεμος δρῦν ἔδωκε ποταμῷ. 58,
10, ἀγαθῶν ἔκαστον δώσειν. 67, 8,
κακόν τι δώσει τῷ μὴ θέλοντι. 74,
14, ὁ κύων ἔδωκε τοὺς τελευταίους.
71, 16, τὸν διδόντα τὴν τροφήν. 88,
15, μισθὸν δώσειν. 88, 16, μισθὸν
δραγματηφόροις δώσειν. 94, 2, μισθὸν
ἄξιον δώσειν. 94, 4, πόνων ἄκος δοίη.
95, 71, ἐντολὴν δώσειν. 97, 11, τὸ
σύμβολον δώσω. 99, 4, δώσεις τώκυπ-
τέρω. 102, 6, δίκας δοῦναι. 107, 15,
ἐπάξιον δοὺς μισθόν. 115, 5, πόσον
μισθὸν δώσεις. 115, 7, πάντα δῶρά
σοι δώσω. 122, 6, χάριν μοι δῢς.
130, 10, εἰ τοιαῦτα δώσεις. 136, 4,
δοῦναί τι αὐτῷ. 137, 9, ἀπαρχὰς
δίδωσι τυμπάνῳ. Β. 7, δίδωμι τὸν
μυθίαμβον νέῃ μούσῃ. 32, 2, γαλῇ
δίδωσι Κύπρις μορφὴν ἀμεῖψαι. 98,
4, δίδωμι γῆμαι καὶ διδοὺς χαίρω.
Διέξειμι. 57, 6, χώρῳ ἐπῆλθε καὶ
διεξῄει. [79, 6, τὸν πόρον διεξῄει.]
Διερωτάω. 55, 4, ἡ δ' ὄνος διηρώτα.
75, 12, καὶ πῶς ἔχουσιν οἱ κάτω
διηρώτα. [106, 19, τίν' εἶχεν αἰτίαν
διηρώτα.]
Διήγησις. [59, 16, μῦθός φησιν ἐν διηγήσει.]
Δίιημι. 58, 5, διῆκ' ἀπελθεῖν αὐτά.
Διΐστημι. 1, 9, μικρὸν διαστάς. 38,
2, ὡς διασταίη.
Δίκαιος. 102, 3, δίκαιος ὥς τις ἀνθρώπων. Α. 1, γενεὴ δικαίων ἀνθρώπων.
105, 6, δικαίως ἐδωρήθη.
Δικαστήρ. 118, 3, γερόντων δικαστήρων.
Δικαστής. 117, 11, τοὺς θεοὺς εἶναι
δικαστάς.
Δίκελλα. 2, 2, δίκελλαν ἀπολέσας.
Δίκη. 102, 6, δίκας δοῦναι. 115, 11,
σὺν δίκῃ θνήσκω. 122, 14, σὺν δίκῃ
πάσχω. 127, 5, τὰς δίκας ἀναπράξει.
[50, 20, δίκην φεύγων.]
Δίκτυον. 4, 4, δικτύου πολυτρήτου.
9, 4, τὸ δίκτυον θείς. 124, 7, δικτύῳ
τί ποιήσεις ;
Δικτυόω. 107, 11, λέων ἐδικτυώθη.
Διό. 66, 7, διό μοι δοκοῦσι. 74, 15,
διὸ δυσκολαίνει.
Διόπερ. 74, 10, διόπερ γαῦρός ἐστι.
74, 12, διόπερ μοχθεῖ.
Διπλοῦς. 21, 9, διπλοῦς θάνατος. 111,
20, βάρος διπλοῦν.
Δίς. 95, 87, ἐλθεῖν δὶς εἰς ᾄδην.
Δίψα. 43, 9, δίψαν παύσας. 137, 4,
δίψης ἄκος.
Διψάω. 43, 1, ὑπὸ τὸ καῦμα διψήσας.
Διωκτήρ. 128, 14, λύκων διωκτήρων
(see note).
Διώκω. 26, 4, ἐδίωκεν αὐτάς. 69, 2,

λαγωὸν κύων ἐδίωκε. 95, 7, διώκειν
ἔλαφον. 95, 41, σπουδῇ διωχθείς.
112, 1, ὁ δ' ἐδίωκεν ἀλγήσας.
Δοκέω = videor. 66, 7, διό μοι δοκοῦσι
βλέπειν. [56, 8, ὁ λόγος δοκεῖ μοι
σημαίνειν. 71, 12, ὡς δοκεῖν φαῦλα.]
= puto, 2, 6, τῶν θεῶν δοκοῦσι τοὺς
μὲν εὐήθεις ἀγροὺς κατοικεῖν. 31, 4,
οἱ μύες τῆς ἥττης ἐδόκουν ὑπάρχειν
αἰτίην σφίσιν ταύτην. 44, 3, οὐκ ἔδοξε
νικήσειν. 49, 3, τῆς Τύχης ἔδοξ'
ἀκούειν. 95, 31, δοκῶ δὲ καὶ σὲ (σπεύσειν). [134, 19, μὴ δόξῃς κακῶν κύρειν.]
Δόλιος. 103, 4, δόλιον οὐκ ἀληθὲς
ἀσθμαίνων.
Δόλος. 27, 1, γαλῆν δόλῳ συλλαβών.
95, 48, ἄλλον εὑρεῖν δόλον θήρης. [33,
25, δόλῳ πράττειν.]
Δόλοψ. 85, 11, ἄλλοι Δόλοπες.
Δολόω. 33, 12, σοφὸν δολῶσαι φῦλον.
Δόμος. 141, 2, ἐν δόμοις. [116, 9,
δόμων εἴσω. 116, 12, εἰς δόμους.]
Δόξα. 101, 3, τὴν δόξαν οὐκ ἤνεγκε.
[4, 7, τὸν μέγαν τῇ δόξῃ. 64, 12,
δόξαν ἔσχε.]
Δορή. 82, 7, μὴ τὴν δορὴν κνίσῃ.
Δόσις. 98, 12, δόσει πιστεύσας.
Δοτήρ. 63, 10, δοτῆρες ἡμεῖς.
Δούλειος. 15, 9, δουλείης τύχης.
Δουλεύω. 95, 83, σοὶ μόνῃ δουλεύειν.
Δούλη. 10, 1, ἦρα τις δούλης. 10, 10,
φανεῖσα τῇ δούλῃ.
Δοῦλος, adj., [85, 20, ἀσθενές τε καὶ
δοῦλον].
Δραγματηφόρος. 88, 16.
Δράκων. [41, 2, δράκοντι ἐξισουμένην
σαύραν.]
Δράω. [98, 21, κακῶς δράσας. 116, 14,
ἄμφω θελόντων δρᾶν τι.]
Δρητήρ. 128, 14, see note.
Δρόμος. 1, 3, φόβῳ δρόμος πλήρης.
62, 4, οὐδὲν ἐν δρόμοις ἥττων. 62,
5, ἔπαυσε τὸν δρόμον. 69, 3, δρόμῳ
ἐλείφθη. 95, 57, δρόμον ἀναψύχουσαν.
[29, 3, ἐκ δρόμων οἴων.]
Δροσίζω. 12, 16, τί σε δροσίζει στίβῃ;
Δρόσος. [128, 7, δρόσου γεμισθεῖσαν.]
Δροσώδης. 124, 13, δροσώδης ταρσός.
Δρυμός. 95, 6, τὸν ὑλήεντα δρυμόν.
Δρυμώον. 45, 11, ἀνέμβατον δρυμῶνα.
Δρῦς. 36, 6, δρῦν αὐτόριζον. 36, 6,
θάμβος τὴν δρῦν εἶχε.
Δρυτόμος. 38, 1, δρυτόμοι τινες σχίσαντες εὑρήκαμεν. 50, 3, δρυτόμον ἰδοῦσα.
92, 8, δρυτόμῳ εἰπεῖν.
Δύναμαι. 47, 8, οὐ γὰρ ἠδύναντο. 47,
12, βλάψαι δίναιτο. 85, 16, πῶς ἂν
οἴν δυνηθείην.
Δυναστείη. 102, 4, ἐπὶ τῆς ἐκείνου
δυναστείης.

Δυνάστης. 98, 5, δυνάστη καὶ λέοντι.
Δυνατός. 112, 9, οὐχ ὁ μέγας ἀεὶ δυνατός. [67, 10, ἀνθρώπῳ δυνατωτέρῳ.]
Δύνω. 31, 19, τῆς ὁπῆν ἔσω δύνειν.
Δύο. 12, 5, ἔγνωσαν αἱ δύ' ἀλλήλας. 22, 5, γυναικῶν δύο. 61, 3, συνηβόλησαν αἱ δύ' ἀλλήλας. Vide etiam δύω.
Δύσβατος. 72, 5, πέτρης αἰγὶ δυσβάτου.
Δυσδαίμων. 129, 22, ἔτλην δυσδαίμων. 137, 2, οὐκ εὔμορφος ἀλλὰ δυσδαιμων.
Δυσήνεμος. 18, 10, τοῦ δυσηνέμου ψύχους.
Δυσκολαίνω. 74, 15, διὸ δυσκολαίνει.
Δύσκολος. 115, 13, δυσκόλως προβαινούσῃ.
Δυσμή. 33, 1, δυσμαὶ Πλειάδων.
Δύσνους. 98, 3, οὐδέν τι δύσνουν.
Δυσόργητος. [11, 12, τοῖς δυσοργήτοις.]
Δύστηνος. 43, 13, δύστηνος ὡς διεψεύσθην. 76, 9, ἐπ' ἀχύροισι δυστήνοις.
Δυστυχέω. 49, 7, ὅσ' ἂν δυστυχῇ.
Δυστυχής. 23, 7, δυστυχὴς ἐπαρᾶται. 34, 8, δυστυχὴς ἀποθνήσκω.
Δύσφωνος. 33, 4, κολοιῶν δυσφώνων.
Δύω. 35, 1, δύω υἱούς. 66, 3, δύω πήρας.
Δῶμα. 12, 15, ὁμώροφόν μοι δῶμα. 5, 5, εἰς τὸ δῶμα πηδήσας. 125, 1, ἀναβὰς εἰς τὸ δῶμα.
Δωρέω. 105, 6, ὑπὸ φίλων ἐδωρήθη.
Δῶρον. 72, 4, θείων δώρων. 115, 7, τὰ τῆς Ἐρυθρῆς πάντα δῶρα.

Ἐάν. 24, 7, ἐὰν γεννήσῃ. 84, 6, ἐὰν μείνῃς. [60, 6, ἐάν με παραιτήσῃ.] Vide κἂν.
Ἔαρ. 118, 2, ἦρος. Vide εἶαρ.
Ἑαυτόν. 2, 15, τοὺς ἑαυτοῦ φῶρας. 10, 2, δούλης ἰδίης ἑαυτοῦ. 28, 7, φύσωσ' ἑαυτήν. 43, 3, ἑαυτοῦ σκιήν θεωρήσας. 64, 2, ἐλάτης ἑαυτὴν ἐπαινούσης. 131, 2, στολὴν ἑαυτῷ κατέλιπεν. [116, 5, τὸν ἄνδρ' ἑαυτῆς.]
Ἐάω. 12, 20, ἔα μὲ ἐμμένειν. 31, 18, οὐκ εἴα δύνειν. 75, 16, οὐκ ὡσ' ἀπόθνῄσκειν.
Ἐγγυάω. 58, 10, ἐγγυωμένη δώσειν.
Ἐγγύς. 25, 5, λίμνης ἐγγύς. 49, 2, φρέατος ἐγγύς. 92, 3, ἐγγὺς πεύκης. 95, 15, ἐγγὺς τοῦ θνήσκειν. 103, 16, ἐγγὺς τῆς μοίρης. 107, 2, ἐγγὺς μόρου. 130, 4, ἐγγὺς προσελθών.
Ἐγείρω. 49, 3, οὐκ ἐγερθῇσῃ; 95, 69, ἐγείρειν τῆς νωθείης.
Ἐγκάθημαι. 12, 2, ἐγκαθημένην ἕλαις.

Ἐγκαλέω. 49, 6, ἐμοὶ ἐγκαλοῦσι πάντα.
Ἔγκατα. 34, 5, ὑπὸ τῶν ἐγκάτων ἐφυσήθη. 95, 95, ἕκαστον ἐγκάτων ἀριθμήσας.
Ἐγκλείω. 136, 7, τὸν πυρὸν ἐγκλείων.
Ἔγκλημα. 89, 3, ἔγκλημ' εὐπρόσωπον.
Ἐγχαλινόω. ᵹ 76, 14, τὸν ἵππον ἐγχαλινώσας.
Ἐγώ. 3, 10, κἂν ἐγὼ σιωπήσω. 33, 13, ἐγὼ μὲν εἶπον. 38, 6, ὧν ἐγὼ μήτηρ. 49, 5, αἰτίη ἐγώ λέγωμαι. 53, 4, ἐγὼ σε ζωγρήσω. 62, 4; 65, 2; 71, 7; 71, 8; 75, 18; 89, 5; 93, 9; 100, 8; 102, 10; 108, 31; 118, 9; 121, 3; 128, 13; 134, 3; 134, 18; 135, 8; B. 6; B. 13.
ἐμέ. 115, 3, κάμέ. 131, 18, id.
μέ. 1, 14; 3, 7; 6, 6; 6, 7; 6, 9; 6, 12; 7, 7; 12, 20; 12, 21; 13, 6; [14, 5]; 30, 10; 42, 8; 43, 14; 48, 8; 50, 5; 50, 18; 51, 5; 51, 8; 51, 10; 71, 6; 71, 9; 71, 10; 76, 18; 76, 19; 78, 3; 83, 3; 83, 4; 89, 4; 89, 9; 91, 7; 93, 11; 95, 4; 95, 29; 95, 83; 96, 4; 100, 4; 113, 14; 103, 16; 103, 18; 122, 5; 124, 15; 129, 22; 135, 9.
ἐμοί. 49, 6; 56, 7; 80, 3; 81, 2; 106, 30; 108, 10.
μοι. 7, 16; 10, 11; 12, 15; 12, 23; 33, 14; 34, 9; 47, 6; 48, 6; 48, 7; 50, 15; 53, 3; 53, 5; 53, 8; 60, 4; 62, 3; 66, 7; 84, 5; 88, 7; 92, 9; 95, 14; 95, 62; 100, 7; 103, 19; 108, 12; 115, 12; 122, 6; 131, 8; 131, 17; 132, 9. [56, 8.]
ἐμοῦ. 110, 3, μετ' ἐμοῦ. B. 9, ὑπ' ἐμοῦ. [134, 19, ἀρχούσης ἐμοῦ.]
μου. 1, 7; 7, 5; 38, 5; 40, 4; 82, 7; 89, 12; 122, 7; 122, 8; 132, 8.
ἡμεῖς, ἥμεις. 36, 11; 63, 10.
ἡμᾶς, ἥμας. 12, 9; 21, 6; 26, 11; 27, 7; 33, 11; 58, 9; 119, 8; 119, 12; 128, 2; 134, 5; 134, 15. [23, 9; 43, 19.]
ἡμέων. 90, 2.
ἡμῶν, ἥμων. 25,'10; 36, 12; 74, 11; 85, 9; 85, 14; 128, 4. [116, 12.]
ἡμίν, ἥμιν. 12, 12; 15, 4; 24, 5; 85, 13; 90, 4; 95, 30; 95, 79; 98, 7; 113, 4; 128, 5. [38, 8; 39, 5; 128, 8.]
Ἔθνος. 33, 4, μέλαν κολοιῶν ἔθνος. [70, 5, μὴ ἔθνη ὕβρις ἐπέλθοι.]
Ἔθος. [135, 3, ἐξ ἔθους ᾄδων. 137, 5, ἐξ ἔθους. [106, 27, τοῦτο εἰς ἔθος βαίνοι.]
Εἰ. 7, 6, εἰ δὲ μή. θνήσκω. 11, 4, εἰ νεκρὸν εἴλκες. 22, 10, ἔτιλλε δ' ἡ γραῦς εἰ μέλλαιναν ηὕρηκει. 23, 5, εἰ

GRAECITATIS BABRIANAE LEXICON. 149

λάβοι γε. 23, 8, εἰ φύγοι γε. 28, 7,
εἰ τοιοῦτον ἦν. 33, 8, εἰ τὴν σφενδόνην ποτ' ἠτήκει. 46, 7, οὐδ' ἐπῆcν
εἰ θνήσκει (conj.) 46, 10, εἰ φίλους
οὐκ ἔσχε. 47, 4, εἴ τις ἐστι ποῦ. 51,
7, εἰ κρεῶν χρήζεις. 51, 9, εἰ εἰρίων
χρήζεις. 63, 10, εἰ κακῶν χρήζεις.
72, 16, εἰ μὴ ἤλεγξεν. 83, 3, εἰ
θέλεις. 84, 3, εἰ βαρύνω. 87, 2, εἰ
κατειλήφει. 94, 4, εἰ ἀνελκύσειε. 95,
4, εἰ θέλεις. 95, 31, εἴ τι ἀκούεις.
98, 13, εἰ γάμου χρήζεις. 103, 17, εἰ
δ' ἄπειμι. 108, 12, εἴ μοι συνέλθῃς.
126, 8, εἰ δ' ἔστιν εἰπεῖν. 127, 8,
εἴ ποτ' εὐθύνοι. 128, 1, εἰ μὴ παρήμην. 130, 10, εἰ τοιαῦτα δώσεις.
134, 15, εἰ θέλεις. 136, 8, εἰ θέρους
ᾄδεις. 141, 1, εἰ μὴ τίκτητε (corrupt).
[39, 3, εἴ τις εἰρηνεύει. 85, 5, εἰ
μὴ προάξῃ. 106, 13, εἴ τις ἦλθεν.
106, 26, εἴ τις ἄλλος πελάζοι. 107,
18, εἰ λέοντα μῦς ἔσωσε.]
Εἶαρ. 131, 5, πρὸ εἴαρος.
Εἶδον. 9, 7, ἰδὼν σπαίροντας. 17, 3,
τὸν δ' εἶδ' ἀλέκτωρ. 17, 5, ἰδὼν ἤδη.
19, 3, ἰδοῦσα. 25, 6, βατράχων ὅμιλον
εἶδον. 30, 7, ὁ δ' εἶδεν αὐτὸν Ἑρμῆν.
32, 5, ἰδὼν δ' ἐκεῖνος. 43, 7, ἄνδρας
εἶδεν ἐξαίφνης. 43, 9, ἰδὼν ἔφευγε.
50, 3, δριτόμον ἰδοῦσα. 50, 9 ; 54,
3 ; 71, 1 ; 71, 9 ; 79, 3 ; 88, 6 ; 89,
2 ; 90, 2 ; 95, 55 ; 97, 6 ; 98, 9 :
113, 3 ; 117, 2 ; 122, 2 ; 132, 2. [4,
8 ; 116, 9 ; 129, 19 ; 133, 2.]
= viso.—11, 9, οὐδ' εἶδεν τὴν ἄλωνα
Δημήτηρ.
Εἶδος. 95, 21, γαύρη εἶδος.
Εἶεν. 30, 9, Ἑρμῆν 'εἶεν' λέγοντα (conj.)
Εἴθε. 53, 5, εἴθε μὴ συνηντήκεις. 53,
6, εἴθε ὑπηντήκεις. 53, 7, εἴθε μὴ
ἴκοιο. 71, 3, εἴθε μή ποτ' ἐπλεύσθης.
115, 3, εἴθε τις πεποιήκει. 131, 17,
εἴθε μοι τότ' οὐκ ὤφθης.
Εἰκός, vide ἔοικα.
Εἴκω. [36, 14, τοῖς κρατοῦσιν εἴκειν.]
Εἰμί. 6, 7 ; 13, 5 ; 13, 6 ; 64, 3 ; 64,
5 ; 67, 6 ; 120, 4 ; 130, 6.
εἰ. 75, 21 ; 87, 5 ; 87, 5 ; 117, 11 ;
135, 6.
ἐσσί. 77, 7 ; 119, 7.
ἐστί. 1, 8 ; 1, 16 ; 6, 16 ; 24, 5 ; 25,
3 ; 36, 2 ; 47, 4 ; 51, 8 ; 51, 10 ; 56,
7 ; 60, 4 ; 62, 3 ; 74, 11 ; 74, 13 ; 75,
3 ; 81, 2 ; 85, 9 ; 85, 13 ; 88, 11 ;
88, 18 ; 95, 14 ; 95, 15 ; 95, 17 ; 112,
9 ; 124, 18 ; 126, 8 ; 128, 3 ; 128, 9 ;
142, 1 ; B. 2. [4, 6 ; 9, 11 ; 9, 13 ;
10, 14 ; 11, 11 ; 12, 25 ; 35, 7 ; 52,
6 ; 59, 18 ; 81, 5 ; 87, 6 ; 116, 9.]
εἰσίν. 57, 12 ; 85, 10.

ᾖ. [82, 10.]
ᾖτε. 47, 13.
ἴσθι. 95, 80 ; [5, 10].
εἶναί. 2, 8 ; 5, 2 ; 85, 3 ; 99, 2 ;
104, 8 ; 112, 10 ; 117, 11 ; [4, 7 ; 11,
10 ; 65, 7] ; 82, 11.
ὤν. 39, 3 ; 40, 1 ; 53, 6 ; 57, 11 ;
62, 6 ; 74, 5 ; 84, 8 ; 89, 4 ; 103,
16 ; 107, 2 ; 107, 8 ; 120, 8 ; 131,
3. [47, 16 ; 84, 7 ; 132, 3.]
ἐών. 36, 7.
ἦν. 1, 2 ; 5, 1 ; 5, 3 ; 9, 9 ; 11, 6 ;
15, 10 ; 19, 5 ; 22, 2 ; 28, 3 ; 28, 7 ;
30, 5 ; 46, 5 ; 47, 1 ; 48, 2 ; 58, 4 ;
63, 1 ; 66, 1 ; 66, 6 ; 67, 2 ; 75, 1 ;
76, 4 ; 88, 1 ; 90, 4 ; 106, 11 ; 108,
17 ; 111, 11 ; 115, 12 ; 118, 3 ; 119,
1 ; 126, 6 ; 129, 8 ; 131, 13 ; Λ. 1.
ἦσθα. 77, 11.
ἦμεν. 12, 10.
ἦσαν. 24, 1 ; 25, 5 ; 31, 17 ; 33,
1 ; Λ. 8 ; B. 3.
ἔσῃ. 75, 3.
ἔσται. 21, 9.
Εἶμι. 25, 9, ἄψ νῦν ἴωμεν. 46, 7, ᾔει
πρὸς ὕλας. 61, 1, ᾔει κυνηγὸς ἐξ
ὄρους. 61, 2, ᾔει γριπεύς. 95, 51,
κατ' ἴχνος ᾔει. 134, 4, ἄχρι βημάτων
ᾔει.
Εἶπον. Introducing an independent sentence.—2, 13 ; 3, 10 ; 7, 7 ; 8, 4 ;
12, 7 ; 14, 3 ; 15, 12 ; 16, 10 ; 20,
6 ; 21, 6 ; 24, 4 ; 25, 8 ; 28, 9 ; 29,
3 ; 33, 13 ; 33, 22 ; 34, 10 ; 36, 9 ;
37, 10 ; 38, 4 ; 40, 3 ; 47, 10 ; 48, 3 ;
48, 9 ; 50, 9 ; 50, 15 ; 50, 16 ; 51,
5 ; 54, 3 ; 63, 7 ; 65, 3 ; 69, 5 ; 71,
3 ; 71, 6 ; 75, 13 ; 76, 17 ; 77, 11 ;
78, 1 ; 80, 3 ; 82, 6 ; 83, 3 ; 85, 6 ;
85, 17 ; 86, 8 ; 87, 4 ; 88, 6 ; 88, 11 ;
88, 17 ; 89, 11 ; 91, 5 ; 92, 4 ; 92, 6 ;
92, 10 ; 93, 8 ; 95, 49 ; 96, 3 ; 97,
11 ; 100, 4 ; 100, 5 ; 102, 10 ; 103,
13 ; 105, 5 ; 108, 8 ; 108, 28 ; 109,
3 ; 115, 11 ; 119, 6 ; 120, 7 ; 121, 2 ;
121, 4 ; 122, 9 ; 122, 14 ; 124, 7 ;
124, 19 ; 125, 5 ; 130, 5 ; 131, 8 ;
132, 8, 134, 3 ; 135, 6 ; 135, 7.
[40, 5 ; 42, 7 ; 72, 18 ; 75, 4 ; 106, 22.]
With adverb added.—56, 6, ἡ δ'
εἶπεν οὕτω. 122, 3, οὕτως εἶπεν.
95, 36, ὡς εἶπε κερδώ.
With neuter pronoun.—37, 10, τοιάδ'
εἶπε φωνήσας. 75, 7, ταῦτ' εἶπε.
95, 27, τῆς σοι τοῦτο εἰποῦσης.
With accusative of noun.—53, 3, ἢν
λόγους τρεῖς εἴπῃς. 124, 13, κλαγκτὸν
εἶπε φωνήσας. 128, 1, οἷς εἶπε μύθους πρὸς νομήσα.
With dative of person.—48, 3, κύων

τούτῳ εἶπεν. 61, 8, ἕως τις αὐτοῖς εἶπε. 72, 2, πτηνοῖσιν εἶπεν. 81, 1, κερδοῖ πίθηκος εἶπεν. 95, 4, ταύτῃ εἶπεν. 114, 6, εἶπέν τις αὐτῷ. 115, 2, κήυξιν εἶπεν ἀγρώσταις. Β. 4, εἶπε παισὶν Ἑλλήνων.
With acc. of thing and dat. of person.—Β. 5, εἶπε Λιβυστίνοις λόγους Κιβύσσης.
With πρὸς and acc. of person.—14, 3, πρὸς ἣν ἀλώπηξ εἶπεν. 55, 6; 64, 7; 99, 3; 104, 6; 113, 3.
Acc. of thing.—126, 5, πρὸς τάδ' εἶπεν. [39, 5.]
Absolutely.—126, 8, εἰ δ' ἔστιν εἰπεῖν. 131, 10, ὡς δ' εἶπεν.
With acc. and inf.—97, 4, κἀκεῖνος ἥξειν εἶπεν.
Εἰρηνεύω. 39, 4, στάσιν εἰρηνεύει.
Εἰρήνη. 76, 4, ἦν δὲ λοιπὸν εἰρήνη. 93, 2, φέροντες βέβαιον εἰρήνην. 102, 9, πάντα δ' εἶχεν εἰρήνην.
Εἴριον. 51, 9, εἰ δ' εἰρίων χρῄζεις.
Εἰρύω. 122, 7, τὴν ἄκανθαν εἰρύσσας.
Εἰς. Local.—1, 1; 1, 11; 2, 5; 3, 1; 4, 3; 4, 5; 5, 4; 5, 5; 11, 5; 12, 11; 20, 2; 23, 1; 25, 2; 25, 7; 26, 10; 33, 2; 34, 6; 35, 6; 43, 11; 45, 2; 52, 1; 57, 10; 72, 10; 74, 2; 74, 12; 76, 7; 91, 1; 95, 37; 95, 42; 95, 88; 97, 9; 108, 15; 108, 22; 111, 5; 111, 8; 112, 2; 115, 9; 120, 3; 125, 1; 126, 1; 127, 3; 129, 13; 129, 15; 134, 10. [42, 6; 45, 12; 47, 16; 95, 101; 116, 10; 116, 12.] 37, 6, εἰς νομὰς ἀπεξεύχθη. 76, 18, εἰς ὄνους μεταστήσας. 85, 17, εἰς πόλεμον ἄρχειν. 93, 1, εἰς ποίμνην ὅρκους φέροντες. 31, 9, καὶ διεῖλον εἰς ἴλας. 21, 8, ἣν εἰς ἀτέχνους ἐμπέσωμεν. 53, 1, εἰς λύκον ἀλώπηξ ἐμπεσοῦσα. 95, 8, χεῖρας εἰς ἐμὰς ἥξει. 95, 87, δὶς τὸν αὐτὸν εἰς ᾅδην. 122, 8, κατελθεῖν εἰς ᾅδου. 127, 8, ἐμπίπτει εἰς τοῦ Διὸς τὰς χεῖρας. [22, 15, εἰς γυναῖκας ἐμπίπτει. 17, 12, τρέπουσιν εἰς τὸ χεῖρον. 29, 6, εἰς πόνους. 106, 27, εἰς ἔθος βαίνειν.]
Denoting purpose.—6, 4, εἰς τάγηνον ὡραῖος. 9, 10, εἰς χορούς ἠ῀λοιν. 19, 5, εἰς τρυφηρὸν ἀκμαίη. 22, 4, εἰς ἔρωτας ἐσχόλαζε. 29, 1, εἰς ἀλητὸν ἐπράθη. 30, 2, εἰς στήλην. 31, 8, εἰς μάχην γενναίους. 37, 10, εἰς ταῦτα ἐτηρήθης. 124, 5, εἰς τὸ θηρεύειν. 137, 1, εἰς τὸ κοινὸν ἐπράθη. [31, 23, εἰς τὸ ζῆν.]
Relation.—95, 30, εἰς ἅπαντα συμβούλοις. 119, 10, εἰς σὲ εὐσέβειαν.
Time.—30, 6, συνθέμενος εἰς τὸν ὅρ-

θρον. 53, 7, μὴ σύγ' εἰς ὥρας ἵκοιο. 124, 14, πόσσον εἰς ἕω λείπει. 134, 17, εἰς τὸ πρῶτον. 95, 21, πολλὰ εἰς ἔτη ζώει.
Εἷς. 3, 2, μιῆς τρωγούσης. 21, 4, εἰς δέ τις λίην γέρων. 30, 10, ἓν γάρ με, νεκρὸν ἢ θεὸν, σὺ ποιήσεις. 47, 8, κατὰ μίην. 47, 11, οὐδ' ἂν εἰς δύναιτο. 47, 14, τῇ μιῇ ῥάβδῳ. 55, 1, ἕνα βοῦν τις εἶχε. 63, 7, οὐδ' ἂν εἷς τις ἡρώων. 63, 11, κἂν ἓν αἰτήσῃς. 85, 9, γένος ἓν ἔστιν. 85, 13, τὸ χρῶμα ἡμῖν οὐχ ἓν ἔστιν. 103, 8, εἷς ἕκαστος. 117, 3, ἑνὸς ἀσεβοῦς. 117, 8, ἰφ' ἑνὸς δηχθείς. 131, 2, μίην μοίνην. [22, 13; 22, 16; 39, 5.]
Εἰσάγω. 113, 4, τοῦτον εἰσάγων ἡμῖν.
Εἰσβαίνω. [75, 4, εἶπεν εἰσβαίνων.]
Εἰσδύνω. 45, 4, τάχιον εἰσδεδυκυίας αἴγας.
Εἴσειμι. 2, 9, εἰσιόντες τὰς πύλας. 75, 7, οὐκέτ' εἴσῃει. 103, 8, εἰς ἕκαστος εἰσῄει. [86, 10, ὅτ' εἰσῄεις.]
Εἰσελαύνω. 45, 2, εἰσήλαινε τὰς αἶγας.
Εἰσέρχομαι. Β. 10, εἰσῆλθον ἄλλοι.
Εἰστρέχω. 31, 18, τοὺς στρατηγοὺς εἰστρέχοντας. 86, 4, ἀλώπηξ εἰσόδραμοῦσα τὴν φηγόν.
Εἴσω. [116, 9, δόμων εἴσω, see ἔσω.]
Εἶτα. 1, 8, εἶτα τοξεύει. 61, 6, εἶτα τὴν θήρην ἥμειβον. 95, 12, εἶτα χαίρειν προσεῖπε. 98, 13, εἶτ' ἀπωνυχίσθη. 108, 24, εἶτ' ἔσωθεν ἐκκύψας. 117, 10, εἶτ' οὐκ ἀνέξῃ; [40, 2, εἶτ' ἔχεξε. 106, 26, ἄλλος εἶτ' ἄλλος. 116, 3, εἶτα κἀκεῖνος ἐραθύμει.]
Εἴωθα. 7, 1, τοῦτον εἰώθει παρέλκειν. 16, 9, ὥσπερ εἰώθης. 26, 7, ὡς πρὶν εἰώθει. 55, 6, ὅσπερ εἰώθει. 120, 9, ὥσπερ εἰώθει. [106, 20, ὥσπερ εἰώθας.]
Ἐκ. Local.—5, 7; 15, 7; 18, 4; 20, 1; 33, 20; 36, 1; 45, 7; 61, 1; 76, 6; 79, 1; 85, 9; 85, 10; 87, 1; 90, 1; 105, 1; 108, 20; 111, 16; 122, 7; 124, 13; 129, 7; 136, 1; Λ. 12; 66, 3, ἐκ δὲ τοῦ δύω πήρας κρέμασαι.
Change from.—29, 3, ἐκ δόμων οἴων. 57, 3, ἄλλο φίλον ἐξ ἄλλου. 72, 11, ἄλλο δ' ἐξ ἄλλου πτερόν. 76, 19, ἵππον ἐξ ὄνου με ποιήσεις. 69, 6, ἐκ κακοῦ σῴζειν. 75, 8, ἐκ νόσων ἀνασφήλας.
Of origin, of material, etc.—66, 3, πλάσασθαι ἐκ γῆς. 46, 3, χλόη ἐξ ἧς χιλὸν εἶχε. 76, 5, μισθὸν ἐκ δήμου.
Of author or occasion.—12, 5, ἐκ τοῦ μέλλονς ἔγνωσαν ἀλλήλας. 98, 16, ἐκ χερὸς παίων. Λ. 15, μάθοις ἂν . . . . ἐκ τοῦ σοφιστοῦ γέροντος.
Expressing separation from a number.—95, 81, πρόβατον οἷον ἐκ ποίμνης.

Adverbial Phrases.—29, 9, ἐκ μέσου
ῥήξεις. 41, 1, διαρραγῆναι ἐκ μέσου
νώτου. 71, 2, νῆα βάπτουσαν κῦμα
ἐκ πρώρης. 33, 7, ἐκ συνηθείης. 135,
3, ἐξ ἔθους. 137, 5, ἐξ ἔθους. 115,
4, ἐκ τύχης ἔλεξεν. 67, 7, ἐξ ἴσου
κοινωνός. 114, 5, ἐκ δευτέρης. Β. 16,
ἐκ δευτέρου. [45, 14, ἐκ πρώτης. 95,
101, ἐκ δευτέρου.]
Ἕκαστος. 2, 4, ἠρνεῖθ' ἔκαστος. 44,
6, ἔκαστον αὐτῶν εἶχε. 46, 6, ἐλθὼν
ἔκαστος. 47, 9, ἑκάστης καταγείσης.
47, 14, πείσεσθ' ἔκαστος. 57, 5, νέμων
ἑκάστῳ μικρόν. 58, 10, ἀγαθῶν ἕκαστον δώσειν. 61, 10, ἔκαστος ἃ πρὶν
εἶχε ζητήσει. 74, 11, ἔκαστος ἡμῶν
γαῦρός ἐστι. 95, 53, ἔκαστον ποιμένων ἐπηρώτα. 95, 95, ἔκαστον
ἐγκάτων. 98, 15, τὸν δ' ἔκαστος ἠλόια.
103, 8, εἷς ἔκαστος. 127, 5, ἑκάστου
τὰς δίκας. 134, 6, ἔκαστα τῶν ζώων.
Λ. 17. [31, 22, γαλῆς ἑκάστης μῦν
ἑλκούσης. 70, 1, ὡς ἔκαστος ἐξεύχθη.]
Ἑκάστοτε. 22, 8, ἑκάστοτε ἔτιλλεν.
Ἑκατέρωθεν. 36, 4, κάλαμος ἑκατέρωθεν
εἱστήκει.
Ἐκβάλλω. 35, 5, ὡς περισσὸν ἐκβάλλει.
77, 9, στόματος τυρὸν ἐκβαλών.
Ἐκδέρω. 7, 13, 'ὀνείην ἐκδείρας.
Ἔκδηλος. 31, 5, στρατηγοὺς ἐκδήλους.
Ἔκδημος. 59, 15, δεσπόταισιν ἐκδήμοις.
Ἐκδύνω. 18, 3, τὴν σίσυρναν ἐκδύσει.
86, 6, οὐκέτ' εἶχεν ἐκδῦναι. 131, 4,
αὐτὸν ὁ χρόνος ἐξέδυσε καὶ ταύτης.
Ἐκεῖ. 43, 3, ἐκεῖ τὴν σκιὴν θεωρήσας.
45, 4, εὑρὼν ἐκεῖ αἶγας. 118, 4, κἀκεῖ
γίνεται μήτηρ.
= ἐκεῖσε. 46, 4, ἤρχοντο ἐκεῖ. [58,
6, κἀκεῖ πέτεσθαι.]
Ἐκεῖνος, pronoun.—7, 4 ; 13, 9 ; 26,
7 ; 28, 10 ; 32, 5 ; 35, 6 ; 37, 9 ; 42,
4 ; 59, 7 ; 62, 4 ; 63, 6 ; 67, 6 ; 74,
3 ; 75, 8 ; 75, 12 ; 76, 14 ; 79, 5 ;
92, 6 ; 94, 6 ; 95, 45 ; 95, 75 ; 96, 3 ;
97, 4 ; 102, 4 ; 103, 13 ; 122, 9 ;
124, 19 ; 129, 4 ; 131, 14 ; 135, 3.
[13, 13 ; 106, 14 ; 116, 13.]
Adjective.—72,10, ἐκείνην εἰς κρήνην.
76, 6, ἐκεῖνος ἵππος.
Ἐκκλίνω. 91, 5, οὐ σέ, τὸν λέοντα δ'
ἐκκλίνω.
Ἐκκύπτω. 18, 9, ἥλιος ἡδὺς ἐκκύψας.
50, 13, κερδὼ ἐξέκυπτεν αἰγείρου. 96,
1, ἔνθεν ἐκκύψας. 108, 24, ἔσωθεν
ἐκκύψας. 112, 5, ἔνθεν ἐκκύψας.
Ἐκλείπω. 26, 9, ἐκλιποῦσαι τὴν ἀρου-
ραν.
Ἐκλούω. 72, 8, πρόσωπα δ' ἐξέλουε.
Ἐκλύω. 122, 11, ἐκλυθεὶς πόνων.

Ἐκπίνω. 89, 8, πηγὴν ἐκπέπωκας.
Ἐκπίπτω. 12, 4, ἄωρον ἐκπεσόντα
τῆς ὥρης. 131, 6, ἐκπεσοῦσα τῆς
ὥρης.
Ἐκπλήσσω. 36, 9, μηδὲν ἐκπλήσσου.
[116, 11, id.]
Ἐκπνέω. 60, 2, ἐκπνέων ἤδη. 129,
21, ὕστατ' ἐκπνείων.
Ἐκπρεπής. 59, 3, ἐκπρεπέστατον ζώων.
64, 6, δένδρων ἐκπρεπεστάτη. 114,
3, φέγγος ἐκπρεπέστατον.
Ἐκπωτάομαι. 12, 1, χελιδὼν ἀγροῦ
ἐξεπωτήθη.
Ἐκρίζω. 36, 8, φηγὸς ἐξεριζώθη.
Ἐκρίπτω. 42, 5, αὐτὸν ἐκτὸς ἐξέριψε
τοῦ τοίχου.
Ἐκτέμνω. 139, 2, φᾶρος ἐκτεμὼν τοίχου.
Ἐκτίνω. [34, 13, οὐσίαν ἐκτίνων.]
Ἐκτόπως. 14, 1, φιλεῖν ἐκτόπως.
Ἐκτός. 42, 5, ἐκτὸς τοῦ τοίχου.
Ἐκφανής. 3, 9, ἔργον ἐκφανές. 31,
15, παντὸς ἐκφανέστατοι πλήθους.
Ἐκφέρω. Β. 11, ἐκφέρουσι ποιήσεις.
Ἐκφεύγω. 50, 12, ἐκφυγοῦσα κινδύνου.
[4, 8, ἐκφυγόντα κίνδυνον.]
Ἐκφοβέω. 26, 11, ἐκφοβεῖν ἡμᾶς.
Ἐκφορέω. [23, 11, ἐκφορουμένης λύπης.]
Ἐκψύχω. 115, 11, ἐκψύχουσα.
Ἐκών. 111, 12, ἐκὼν κατέπεσε. 111,
18.
Ἔλαιον. 48, 7, τοὔλαιον. 114, 1,
ἐλαίῳ.
Ἐλάτη. 64, 1 ; 64, 2.
Ἐλάττων. [64, 11, τῶν ἐλαττόνων.]
Ἐλαύνω. 57, 3, ἄμαξαν ἤλαυνε.
Ἔλαφος. 43, 4, ἔλαφος κεράστης.
46, 1 ; 46, 8 ; 95, 5 ; 95, 7 ; 95,
20 ; 95, 54 ; 95, 59 ; 102, 9 ; 107,
4.
Ἐλαφρός. 36, 5, ἐλαφρὸν ὄχθης ποτα-
μίης ὕδωρ. 115, 6, ἐλαφρὴν καὶ
μετάρσιον.
Ἐλαφρύνω. 111, 6, ἐλαφρύνθη.
Ἔλεγχος. 81, 4, ἔλεγχον οὐκ ἔχουσα.
[104, 7, ἔλεγχον τῆς πονηρίης.]
Ἐλέγχω. 72, 17, αὐτὸν ἤλεγξεν.
Ἐλεεινός. [22, 15, ἐλεεινὸς ὅστις.]
Ἐλεύθερος. Α. 16, τῆς ἐλευθέρης μούσης.
Ἕλκω. 14, 4, εἰ νεκρὸν εἷλκες. 37, 7,
μόσχος εἵλκετο σχοίνῳ. 52, 2, ἄμαξαν
εἷλκον. 72, 17, ἑλκύσασα τὸ πτερόν.
94, 5, ἑλκύσας ὀστοῦν. [31, 22, γαλῆς
μῦν ἑλκούσης.]
Ἕλλην. 21, 9, οὐ γὰρ ἐλλείψει ὁ
θύσων. 21, 10, κἂν μάγειρος ἐλλείψῃ.
Ἕλλην. Β. 4, παισὶν Ἑλλήνων.
Ἐλπίζω. 9, 2, ὄψον ἐλπίσας ἥξειν.
[45, 13, ἐλπίσας τὰς κρείσσους.]
Ἐλπίς. 11, 7, ἀμητὸς ἐλπίδων πλήρη.
16, 7, νωθραῖς ἐλπίσιν. 58, 7, μόνη

δ' ἔμεινεν ἐλπίς. 58, 8, ἐλπὶς ἀνθρώποις σύνεστι.
Ἐμβαίνω. 117, 3, ἐμβεβηκότος πλοίῳ.
Ἐμέω. 34, 7, ἤμει (conj.) 34, 11, ἀλλ' ἐμεῖς τὰ τοῦ ταύρου.
Ἐμμένω. 12, 20, πέτραις ἐμμένειν.
Ἐμός. 13, 8, τὸν ἐμὸν πατέρα. 13, 11, ἔργα τἀμά. 30, 9, τἀμά. 51, 6, τοὐμὸν αἷμα. 51, 7, κρεῶν τῶν ἐμῶν. 82, 8, χαίτην τὴν ἐμήν. 95, 8, χεῖρας εἰς ἐμάς. 100, 10, τὸν ἐμὸν αὐχένα. 105, 4, τῶν ἐμῶν. 118, 9, τῆς ἐμῆς μοίρης.
Ἔμπειρος. 1, 2, τόξου βολῆς ἔμπειρος. 21, 6, χερσὶν ἐμπείροις.
Ἐμπίπτω. 20, 2, ἐμπεσούσης εἰς φάραγγα. 21, 8, εἰς ἀτέχνους ἐμπέσωμεν ἀνθρώποις. 53, 1, εἰς λύκον ἀλώπηξ ἐμπεσοῦσα. 127, 7, ἐμπίπτει εἰς τοῦ Διὸς τὰς χεῖρας. 60, 1, χύτρῃ μῦς ἐμπεσών. 107, 10, ἐμπεσὼν νεανίσκοις. 38, 7, ἐμπεσὼν διαρρήσσει με. [22, 15, εἰς γυναῖκας ἐμπίπτει.]
Ἐμπλέκω. 43, 12, κέρατα θάμνοις ἐμπλακείς. [119, 11, θεοὺς ἐμπλέκει μύθοις.]
Ἔμπορος. 111, 14, ὁ δ' ἔμπορος. [57, 9, ἐμπόρου φόρτον.]
Ἐμπρέπω. [72, 20, τοῖς ἑτέρων ἐμπρέπων.]
Ἔμπροσθεν. [40, 4, ἔμπροσθεν βαίνει.]
Ἐμφαίνω. 98, 3, οὐδέν τι δύσνοιν ἐμφήνας. [36, 13, ὁ δέ γε μῦθος ἐμφαίνει.]
Ἐν, local, in, within.—3, 2; 27, 2; 30, 8; 31, 17; 37, 1; 42, 1; 46, 2; 48, 1; 51, 1; 58, 1; 58, 4; 59, 14; 63, 2; 68, 4; 72, 2; 79, 2; 80, 3; 86, 2; 88, 1; 92, 2; 95, 1; 95, 35; 95, 56; 108, 2; 108, 9; 118, 2; 127, 1; 128, 6; 129, 4; 129, 8; 141, 2; A. 8. [129, 19.]
= amongst.—21, 5; 31, 10; 47, 1; 59, 6; 66, 4; 75, 10; 101, 1; 101, 7; 128, 7; 128, 11. [60, 5; 87, 6; 80, 5, κἂν χορῷ.]
In respect of, etc.—62, 4, ἐν δρύμοις ἥττων. 76, 3, ἐν μάχαις γενναῖος. 101, 8, ἐν λεόντων σιγκρίσει. 131, 1, ἐν κύβοισιν οὐσίην ἀναλώσας. 32, 5, ἐν μέρει ἠλώκει. [39, 3, ἄδοξος ἐν πολιτείαις. 59, 16, ἐν διηγήσει.]
Temporal.—63, 6, ἐν μέσαις ὥραις. 74, 10, ἐν χρόνοις πρώτοις. 95, 34, ἐν ἐσχάταις ὥραις.
Ἔναρθρος. A. 7, φωνὴν ἔναρθρον.
Ἔνθον. 74, 4, παρῆγεν ἔνδον. 108, 27, οἱ δ' ἔνδον ἐκρύπτοντο. 135, 9, ἔνδον μ' ἔτεκε.
Ἐνδίνω. 139, 2, ἐνέδυ φάρος.

Ἐνεδρεύω. 1, 14, οὔ με πλανήσεις οὐδ' ἐνεδρεύσεις. 17, 1, ὄρνεις ἐνεδρεύων. 75, 4, ἀπατῶ σε οὐδέν, οὐδ' ἐνεδρεύω. [85, 5, τὴν μάχην ἐνεδρεύσει.]
Ἐνείρω. 38, 2, ἐνείραν αὐτῇ σφῆνας.
Ἕνεκα. 43, 4, χηλῆς μὲν ἕνεκα.
Ἐνέχυρον. 99, 3, ἐπ' ἐνεχύρῳ δώσεις.
Ἔνθα. 63, 2, ἔνθα δὴ θύων. 135, 8, ἵνθ' ἐγὼ διατρίβω.
Ἐνθάδε. 6, 12, τότ' ἐνθάδ' ἐλθών.
Ἔνθεν. 96, 1, ἔνθεν ἐκκύψας. 112, 5, ἔνθεν ἐκκύψας. 115, 9, ἔνθεν εἰς ὄρος. 118, 11, ἔνθεν φεύγω.
Ἔνιοι. 85, 15, ἔνιοι δὲ λαμπροί.
Ἐνίοτε. [43, 19.]
Ἐννυχεύω. 124, 16, ἐννυχεύει Ὠρίων.
Ἔννυχος. 12, 16, ἔννυχος στίβη.
Ἔνοικος. 120, 1, ὁ τελμάτων ἔνοικος.
Ἐνοχλέω. 7, 7, μή μ' ἐνοχλήσῃς.
Ἐντάσσω. 76, 17, ἔντασσε πεζοῖς σαυτόν.
Ἐντεῦθεν. 57, 12, ἐντεῦθεν Ἀραβές εἰσιν ψεῦσται. [23, 9, ἐντεῦθεν ἔοικε.]
Ἐντολή. 95, 71, πᾶσαν ἐντολὴν δώσειν.
Ἐντός. 68, 6, ἐντὸς κήπων. 72, 12, ἐντὸς ὦμον. 94, 1, φάρυγος ἐντός. 132, 2, σηκοῦ ἐντός.
Ἐντρέχω. 135, 1, ἐντρέχειν οἴκῳ.
Ἐντρυφάω. 108, 29, ἐντρύφα δείπνοις.
Ἐντυγχάνω. 1, 7, ἀγγέλῳ ἐντυχών. 92, 3, δρυτόμῳ ἐντυχών.
Ἐξαιρέω. 94, 8, κεφαλὴν ἐξελεῖν. 98, 13, ἐξεῖλε τοὺς ὀδόντας. 122, 10, σκόλοπα ἐξῆρει.
Ἐξαίφνης. 18, 12, καῦμα εἶχεν ἐξαίφνης. 43, 7; 111, 5; 124, 1; 132, 1. [57, 7; 116, 8.]
Ἐξαναλίσκω. 95, 44, πόνος ἐξανηλώθη.
Ἐξανίστημι. 112, 7, ὁ δ' ἐξανιστάς. [116, 2, γυνὴ ἐξανιστᾶσα. 116, 8, ἀνὴρ ἐξανίστατο.]
Ἐξαπατάω. [75, 6, οὐκ ἐξαπατῶ σε.]
Ἔξειμι. 103, 19, ὧν ἐξιόντων.
Ἐξέρχομαι. 132, 7, ἔξελθε. [86, 9, οὐδ' ἐξελεύσῃ πρότερον. 126, 7, εἰς ἅπαντας ἐξελήλυθε θνητούς.]
Ἐξεσθίω. 86, 5, ταύτην ἀλώπηξ ἐξέφαγεν.
Ἔξεστι. 93, 11, νέμεσθαι ἔξεστι.
Ἐξετάζω. 100, 2, ὁ δ' αὐτὸν ἐξήταζε.
Ἐξευρίσκω. [21, 12, μή τι χεῖρον ἐξεύρῃ.]
Ἑξῆς. 118, 7, ἅπαντας ἑξῆς.
Ἐξίσοω. [41, 2, δράκοντι ἐξισοιμένην.]
Ἐξόλλυμι. 61, 10, τὸ χρηστὸν ἐξολεῖτε.
Ἐξόπισθε. [10, 4, ταξόπισθέ μοι.]
Ἐξοχή. 18, 8, πέτρης ἐξοχή.
Ἔξω. 132, 5, ἔξω ἐφεστώς. [4, 6, κακῶν ἔξω. 116, 6, θύρης ἔξω.]

Έξωθεν. [38, 10, τῶν ἔξωθεν.]
Ἐξωθέω. 91, 4, ταῦρον ἐξώθει.
Ἔοικα. 26, 12, ἐκφοβεῖν ἔοικεν. 15,
2, ὥσπερ εἰκός. 86, 5, id. [23, 6,
τοῦτ' ἔοικε γινώσκειν.]
Ἑορταῖος. 132, 3, θυσίη ἑορταίη (conj.)
Ἔπαθλον. 56, 1, εὐτεκνίης ἔπαθλα.
Ἐπαίδεομαι. 43, 14, πόδες οἷς ἐπηδού-
μην.
Ἐπαινέω. 64, 2, ἑαυτὴν ἐπαινούσης.
Ἔπαινος. 77, 8, ἐπαίνῳ ἐχαυνώθη.
[37, 13, ἔργοις ἔπαινος.]
Ἐπαίρω. [5, 11, τῆς τύχης ἐπαιρούσης.
·29, 5, μὴ λίαν ἐπαίρου.]
Ἐπαίω. 46, 7, οὐδ' ἐπῄεν εἰ θνήσκει
(conj.)
Ἐπανθέω. 118, 5, πτερίσκοις ἐπανθοίν-
των.
Ἐπάξιος. 107, 15, ἐπάξιον δοὺς μισθόν.
Ἐπαπειλέω. 85, 4, οἱ δ' ἐπηπείλουν.
Ἐπαράομαι. 23, 7, ἐπαρᾶται προσάξειν.
Ἔπαυλις. 3, 1, εἰς ἔπαυλιν.
Ἐπεί. With impf.—25, 5, ἐπεὶ λίμνης
ἐγγὺς ἦσαν. 37, 5, ἐπεὶ ἔμελλον θύειν.
With pluperf. = imperf.—55, 3, ἐπεὶ
τοὔργον ἐτετέλεστο.
With aor.—9, 5, ἐπεὶ φυσῶν ἔκαμε.
31, 11, ἐπεὶ δ' ἐτάχθη πάντα. 43, 11,
ἐπεὶ ἦλθεν. 67, 3, ἐπεὶ λείην ἔσχον.
76, 4, ἐπεὶ ἐπαύσατο. 95, 44, ἐπεὶ
πόνος ἐξανηλώθη. 95, 88, ἐπεὶ κατεκλείσθη.
With imper.—91, 7, ἐπεὶ παρελθέτω
με. [70, 7, ἐπεὶ πόλεμος ἥξει.]
Ἔπειτα. 18, 11, τὸ πρῶτον . . .
ἔπειτα. 48, 4, πρῶτον . . . ἔπειτα.
53, 6, πρῶτα . . . ἔπειτα. [106, 25,
τὰ νῦν παρόντα . . . τὰ δ' ἔπειτα.
34, 13, ἔπειτα ἐκτίνων.]
Ἐπελπίζω. 1, 6, μηδ' ἐπελπίσῃς νίκη.
Ἐπεμβαίνω. 129, 18, νώτοις ἐπεμβάς.
Ἐπέρχομαι. 57, 6, τῷ χώρῳ ἐπῆλθε.
86, 7, ἐπῆλθε κλαιούσῃ. 124, 1, φίλος
ἐπῆλθεν ὀρνιθοθήρῃ. 89, 2, ἐπῆλθεν
ἁρπάξων. 108, 26, ἕτερος ἐπῆλθεν
. . . προσαιρήσων. 130, 7, ὁ δ' ἀθρόως
ἐπῆλθεν. 131, 12, νιφετὸς ἐπῆλθε.
[70, 6, μὴ πόλεις ὕβρις ἐπέλθοι.]
Ἐπερωτάω. 50, 7, τὸν ἄνδρ' ἐπηρώτα
μή. 95, 53, ἕκαστον ἐπηρώτα μή.
103, 12, πῶς ἔχεις ἐπηρώτα. [8, 1,
Ἄραψ κάμηλον ἐπηρώτα πότερα.]
Ἐπέχω. 95, 59, φρὶξ ἐπέσχε νῶτα.
26, 5, ὡς ἐπέσχον σφενδονῶντα. 50,
11, ὁ δ' οὐκ ἐπισχών. 84, 2, μικρὸν
ἐπισχών. 108, 24, id.
Ἐπήν. 6, 10, ἐπὴν μέγας γένωμαι.
Ἐπηρείη. 91, 6, μικρὰ τῆς ἐπηρείης.
Ἐπί, c. gen.—9, 7, ἐπὶ γῆς σπαίροντας.
108, 5, ἐπὶ τῆς ἀρούρης. 57, 13,

ἐπὶ γλώσσης οὐδὲν κάθηται ῥῆμα.
84, 4, καθεδοῦμαι ποταμίης ἐπ' αἰγείρου.
Temporal.—102, 4, ἐπὶ τῆς ἐκείνου
δυναστείης. Λ. 6, ἐπὶ τῆς χρυσῆς
(γενεῆς). Β. 3, ἐπὶ Νίνου τε καὶ
Βήλου.
Ἐπί, c. dat.—2, 9, ἐπὶ κρήνῃ. 34, 7,
ἐφ' ὑγραῖς ἀγκάλαις πεσών. 52, 5,
ἄλλων ἐπ' ὤμοις φερομένη. 127, 6,
κεχυμένων ἐπ' ἀλλήλοις. 53, 7,
τρίτον ἐπ' αὐτοῖς. 43, 5, ἐπὶ τοῖς
κέρασιν ηὔχει. 100, 8, ἐπ' αὐτῷ
καγχάσας. 56, 5, γέλως ἐπ' αὐτῷ
ἐκινήθη. 99, 3, ἐπ' ἐνεχύρῳ δώσεις.
76, 9, πνεῦμα σώζων ἐπ' ἀχύροισι. 93,
3, φέροντες εἰρήνην ἐφ' ᾧ λάβωσι κτλ.
[24, 10, ἐφ' οἷς οὐχὶ χαιρήσειν. 91,
21, νίκη δ' ἐπ' αὐτοῖς εἰστήκει.]
Ἐπί, c. acc.—7, 12, ἐπ' αὐτὸν ἐτίθει.
10, 4, σύροισα πορφύρην ἐπὶ κνήμας.
72, 7, ἐπ' αὐτὸ φῦλον ἦλθε. 97, 5,
ἐλθὼν καὶ στὰς ἐπὶ θύρας. 103, 1,
ἐπ' ἄγρην βαίνειν. 103, 6, ἐπ' αὐλὰς
ἦλθεν. 117, 6, ἐπ' αὐτὸν ἑσμὸς
ἦλθεν. 42, 3, ἐλθεῖν ἐπὶ τὸ δεῖπνον.
97, 3, id.
Temporal.—89, 3, οὐκ ἐπ' ἔτος
ἐγεννήθην.
Ἐπί, adverbial.—102, 8.
Ἐπιβουλεύω. 97, 1, λέων ἐπεβούλευεν
ταύρῳ.
Ἐπίβουλος. 135, 5, γαλῆ ἠπίβουλος.
Ἐπιδιώκω. 32, 8, ἐπεδίωκεν ἡ νύμφη.
Ἐπιεικείη. [101, 7, κόσμον ἐπιεικείης.]
Ἐπιζέω. 95, 60, χολὴ ἐπέζει καρδίην.
Ἐπιζητέω. 28, 3, αὐτὸν ποῦ ποτ' ἦν
ἐπεζήτει. 95, 95, καρδίην ἐπεζήτει.
Ἐπικαλέω. 101, 2, λέοντα αὐτὸν ἐπε-
κάλουν.
Ἐπικροτέω. 5, 6, ἐπικροτῶν τοῖς
πτεροῖς. 95, 43, χεῖρας ἐπεκρότησεν.
Ἐπιμαρτυρέω. 27, 5, ἐπιμαρτυρῶ σοι.
Ἐπίμιξις. 12, 23, ἐπίμιξις ἀνθρώπων.
Ἐπινοέω. 111, 14, ὁ ἔμπορος ἐπενοεῖτο.
Ἐπιορκέω. [50, 20, ἐπιορκῶν.]
Ἐπισκήπτω. 47, 2, παισὶν ἐπισκήπ-
των.
Ἐπισκοπέω. 46, 6, ζῴων ἐπισκοπούν-
των. 103, 8, ἐπισκοπήσων ἕκαστον
εἰσῄει.
Ἐπίσκοπος. 11, 4, ἐπίσκοπος δαίμων.
Ἐπισκώπτω. 101, 6, ὁ κερδὼ ἐπισκώπ-
τουσα.
Ἐπιστήμη. 21, 12, πολεμίην ἐπιστήμην.
Ἐπιστήμων. 85, 3, μάχης ἐπιστήμων.
120, 4, φαρμάκων ἐπιστήμων.
Ἐπιτίθημι. 7, 2, ἐπετίθει τὸν φόρτον
ὄνῳ. 7, 16, πᾶν ἐπιτέθεικεν ἢ χρείη.
138, 1, ἵνα τις ἐπιθεὶς ξύανον.

'Επιτρέχω. 125, 3, ἐπιδραμὼν κατῆγεν.

'Επιτρύζω. 112, 8, τῷ δ' ὁ μῦς ἐπιτρύξας.

'Επίχειρον. 5, 9, τἀπίχειρα τῆς ἥττης.

'Επιχλευάζω. 82, 4, κερδὼ ἐπεχλεύαζεν.

'Επιψαύω. 107, 6, ἄκρων ἐπιψαύσει χειλῶν.

"Επομαι. [70, 4, ἕπεται ταύτῃ.]

'Εποπτεύω. 2, 8, τὰ πάντ' ἐποπτεύειν. 3, 6, ὃς νάπας ἐποπτεύει. 88, 5, τῆς ἀρούρης ἐποπτεύων.

'Επτά. 118, 4, νεοσσῶν ἐπτὰ μήτηρ.

"Εραμαι. 32, 1, ἀνδρὸς ἐρασθείσῃ. [70, 3, ταύτης ἠράσθη.]

'Εραστής. 22, 7, νέον βλέπειν ἐραστήν.

'Εράω, see ἔραμαι. 10, 1, αἰσχρῆς τις ἦρα δούλης. 22, 5, ἦρα γυναικῶν δύο. 32, 4, ἧς ἔχειν τίς οὐκ ἦρα; [98, 20, ἐρᾶν λεόντων.]

'Εργάτης. 49, 1, ἐργάτης. 74, 6, ἐργάτῃ ταύρῳ.

"Εργον. 3, 9, ἔργον ἐκφανές. 13, 11, ἔργα τἀμά. 55, 3, τοὔργον ἐτετέλεστο. 124, 17, ἔργων τίς σ' ἀναμνήσει. [37, 13, ἔργοις ἔπαινος.]

'Ερείδω. 94, 1, ὀστοῦν φάρυγος ἐντὸς ἠρείσθη.

'Ερευνάω. 45, 11, δρυμῶνα ποσσὶν ἠρεύνων. 95, 97, πᾶσαν εὐνὴν ἠρεύνα. 127, 4, ἐρευνήσας ὅπως ἀναπράξει.

'Ερημαίη. 91, 1, φεύγειν εἰς ἐρημαίην. 126, 1, ὁδοιπορῶν εἰς ἐρημαίην.

'Ερημαῖος. 1, 11, εἰς νάπας ἐρημαίας. 95, 19, τίγρις ἐρημαίη.

'Ερημίη. 35, 6, ἐλθὼν εἰς ἐρημίην. 126, 4, τὴν ἐρημίην ναίεις.

"Ερημος. 12, 2, ἐρήμοις ὕλαις. [45, 13, αἰγῶν ἔρημος.]

'Ερημόω. 27, 6, πάντα οἶκον ἠρήμους.

'Εριδαίνω. 68, 3, ὁ Ζεὺς ἠρίδαινε.

'Ερίζω. 59, 2, τούτοις ἤριζ' Ἀθηνᾶ. 64, 1, ἤριζον ἐλάτη καὶ βάτος. [66, 1, ἤριζε τεφρὴ γέρανος.]

"Ερις. 18, 2, βορέῃ ἡλίῳ τε ἔριν γενέσθαι. 134, 16, κακῆς ἔριδος.

'Ερμείης. 30, 1, λύγδινον Ἑρμείην. 48, 3, Ἑρμείη. 119, 6, Ἑρμείη. 127, 1, Ἑρμείην.

'Ερμῆς. 23, 4, Ἑρμῇ νομαίῳ. 30, 8, εἴδεν αὐτὸν τὸν Ἑρμῆν. 48, 1, Ἑρμῆς τετράγωνος. 57, 1, Ἑρμῆς ἄμαξαν πληρώσας. 68, 4, Ἑρμῆς ἔσειεν κλήρους. 117, 9, Ἑρμῆς ἐπιστάς. 119, 1, ξύλινον Ἑρμῆν.

'Ερπετόν. 95, 22, πᾶσιν ἑρπετοῖς.

"Ερπω. 7, 8, εἶρπεν σιωπῶν. 134, 2, οὐδ' ἐφείπεθ' ἑρπούσῃ. 118, 6, ὄφις ἑρπύσας ἀπὸ τρώγλης.

'Ερυθρή. 115, 7, τὰ τῆς Ἐρυθρῆς πάντα δῶρα.

'Ερύω. 68, 5, τόξ' ἔρυσσε (conj.)

"Ερχομαι, only found in the aorist except imperfect. in 46, 4, ἤρχοντο ἀγέλαι.

Aorist, absolutely.—10, 10, ἡ θεὸς ἦλθεν καθ' ὕπνους. 28, 5, ἦλθεν πάχιστον τετράπουν. 30, 7, αὐτοῖς ἐλθοῦσιν. 33, 4, κολοιῶν ἔθνος ἦλθε. 33, 13, ἥνίκ' ἂν ἔλθωσιν. 33, 15, οἱ ψάρες ἦλθον. 42, 4 ; 46, 6 ; 50, 7 ; 56, 3 ; 84, 6 ; 88, 13 ; 95, 80 ; 97, 11. [106, 13.]

Participle.—48, 7, μὴ 'πολιχμήσῃς ἐλθών. 95, 33, παρεδρεύειν ἐλθοῦσαν. 131, 10, ἐλθὼν τοῖς κύβοισιν ὡμίλει. 7, 4, ἐλθὼν πρὸς τὸν ἵππον ὡμίλει.

With following future participle.— 1, 1, ἦλθε κυνηγήσων. 108, 4, ἦλθε δειπνήσων. 129, 17, ἦλθε δεσπότην κύσσων.

Varius.—6, 12, ἐνθάδ' ἐλθών. 28, 2, ἐλθοῦσα αὐτόσε. 132, 2, σηκοῦ ἐντὸς ἦλθεν. [116, 6 ; 116, 7.] 12, 11, ἀλλ' ἔλθ' ἐς ἀγρόν. 35, 6, ἐλθὼν εἰς ἐρημίην. 43, 11, ἦλθεν εἰς ὕλην. 72, 10. ἦλθεν εἰς κρήνην. 74, 2, ἦλθον ἐς οἰκίην. 95, 37, ἦλθεν εἰς σπήλυγγα. 108, 15, εἰς οἶκον ἐλθεῖν. 129, 13, εἰς μέσσον αὐλῆς ἦλθε. 95, 87, ἐλθεῖν εἰς ᾅδην. [95, 101 ; 116, 10 ; 45, 12.] 42, 3, ἐλθεῖν πρὸς αὐτόν. 54, 1, ἦλθε πρὸς θύτην. 42, 3, ἐλθεῖν πρὸς αὐτὸν ἐπὶ τὸ δεῖπνον. 72, 7, πάντων τ' ἐπ' αὐτὸ φῦλον ἦλθεν ὀρνίθων. 97, 3, τὸν ταῦρον ἐλθεῖν ἐπὶ τὸ δεῖπνον ἠρώτα. 97, 5, ἐλθεῖν καὶ στὰς ἐπὶ θύρας. 103, 6, ἐπ' αὐλὰς ἦλθεν. 117, 6, ἐπ' αὐτὸν ἑσμὸς ἦλθε. 85, 9, ἦλθον ἐκ Κρήτης. 16, 9, πῶς οὐδὲν ἄρας ἦλθες; 95, 28, ταῦτ' ἦλθον. 111, 20, ἦλθε βαστάσας.

'Ερῶ. 71, 10, ἐρεῖς με ἠπιωτέρην γαίης. [133, 2, εἰρήκει.]

'Ερωδιός. 94, 2.

"Ερως. 22, 4, εἰς ἔρωτας ἐσχόλαζε. 98, 1, λέων ἀλύσει ἔρωτι. 32, 10, παῖξας Ἔρως ἀπῆλθε.

'Ερωτάω. 10, 8, ἤυχετ', ἱκέτευεν, ἠρώτα. 16, 8, λύκαινα αὐτὸν ἠρώτα 'πῶς' κτλ. 28, 6, ἡ φρῦνος ἠρώτα εἰ ἦν. 33, 21, τὸ συμβὰν ἠρώτων. 42, 3, ἐλθεῖν εἰ τὸ δεῖπνον ἠρώτα. 97, 3, τὸν ταῦρον ἐλθεῖν ἐπὶ τὸ δεῖπνον ἠρώτα. [42, 6, τῶν κυνῶν ἐρωτώντων ὅπως ἐδείπνησεν.]

'Es. vide is.

'Εσθής. [65, 8, πλουσίᾳ σὺν ἐσθῆτι.]

'Εσθίω. 31, 4, ἐσθίων ἀπλήστως. 62, 1, χιλὸν ἐσθίων. 89, 7, οὔπω τι χλωρὸν ἔφαγεν. [133, 1.]

"Εσθος. 131, 8, ἐσθέων χρείη.

Ἐσμός. 117, 6, πολλῶν μυρμήκων ἐσμός.
Ἑσπέρη. 16, 5, ἑσπέρης ἐκοιμήθη.
114, 1, λύχνος ἑσπέρης ηὖχει. 29, 2,
πᾶσαν ἑσπέρην.
Ἕσπερος. 68, 6, ἐντὸς Ἑσπέρου κήπων.
Ἑστιάω. [106, 7, εἰστία τε κάφίλει.]
Ἑστίη. 74, 4, παρ ἑστίῃ θάλψας.
Ἔσχατος. 70, 2, ἐσχάτῳ κλήρῳ. 95,
34, ἐν ἐσχάταις ὥραις. 129, 18, ἐσχάτου κινδύνου. 135, 10, conj. [40,
6, ἔσχατοι ἀντὶ τῶν πρώτων.]
Ἔσω. 31, 19, τῆς ὀπῆς ἔσω δύνειν.
103, 3, κοίλης ἔσω σπήλυγγος ἔκειτο.
113, 1, μάνδρης ἔσω συλλέγων. 132,
4, ἔσω οὐ παρῆλθε τοῦ τείχους.
Ἔσωθεν. 108, 24, ἔσωθεν ἐκκύψας.
Ἐσωτέρω. 2, 7, τοὺς ἐσωτέρω τείχους.
Ἑταιρείη. Α. 13, θνητῶν καὶ θεῶν ἑταιρείη.
Ἕτερος. 33, 20, τοῦ μὲν . . . τοῦ δὲ
. . . ἑτέρου. 86, 7, ἀλώπηξ . . .
ἑτέρη ἀλώπηξ. 108, 26, τις . . .
ἕτερος. [72, 20, τοῖς ἑτέρων γὰρ κτλ.]
Ἔτι. 57, 11, ἔτι προελθεῖν. 59, 6,
ἔτι γὰρ ἐν θεοῖς ᾤκει. 81, 2, πατρῴη
τ' ἐστὶ κάτι παππῴη. 111, 10, πλείω
ἔτ' ἐτίθει τὸν φόρτον.
Ἕτοιμος. 16, 4, ὡς ἕτοιμα δειπνήσων.
46, 3, ἑτοίμην χιλὸν εἶχε. 75, 5,
ἕτοιμα δεῖ σε πάντ' ἔχειν. 10, 3,
παρεῖχεν ἅπαντ' ἑτοίμως. [110, 2,
πάνθ' ἑτοιμά σοι ποιεῖ.]
Ἔτος. 74, 9, μερίσαντες αὐτῷ τῶν ἐτῶν.
89, 5, οὐκ ἐπ' ἔτος ἐγεννήθην. 95, 21,
πολλὰ εἰς ἔτη ζώει.
Εὖ. Β. 15, εὖ πυρώσας, εὖ δὲ κέντρα
πρηΰνας. [107, 16, εὖ νοοῦσιν ἀνθρώποις.]
Εὕδειν. [116, 12, ἡμῶν εἰς δόμους εὕδειν.]
Εὐήθης. 2, 6, τοὺς εὐήθεις.
Εὐθαλής. 128, 6, see note. 128, 9,
εὐθαλεῖ σίτῳ.
Εὐθενέω. [12, 27, εὐθενῶν.]
Εὐθετίζω. 118, 2, καλίην ηὐθέτιζεν.
Εὐθέως. 7, 10, ἵππον εὐθέως στήσας.
94, 5, τὸν μισθὸν εὐθέως ᾔτει. [70, 7,
πόλεμος εὐθέως ἥξει.]
Εὐθύ. 74, 10, ὁ μὲν ἵππος εὐθύ. 126, 5,
ἡ δ' εὐθὺ πρὸς τάδ' εἶπεν.
Εὔθυνα. 102, 7, ὡς ὑπέσχον εὐθύνας.
Εὐθύνω. 127, 8, εἴ ποτ' εὐθύνοι. 134, 7,
καὶ πόδ' εὐθύνει.
Εὐθύς. 5, 5, εὐθὺς ἐκεκράγει. 59, 8,
πρῶτον μὲν εὐθὺς ἔψεγεν. 62, 6, εὐθὺς
ἀνεμνήσθη. 72, 3, εὐθὺς ἠκούσθη.
75, 19, εὐθὺς προσῆλθον. 114, 4,
εὐθὺς ἐσβέσθη. 129, 16, εὐθὺς ἤλυησε.
129, 17, εὐθὺς ἦλθε. 135, 3, εὐθὺς
ᾄδων.
Εὐκαταφρόντητος. [82, 11.]

Εὐλαβοῦμαι. 85, 7, τί δ' εὐλαβοῦμαι;
Εὐμήκης. 64, 3, τὸ μέτρον εὐμήκης.
Εὔμοιρος. 137, 2, ὄνος οὐκ εὔμοιρος.
Εὐμούσως. 9, 4, ἐτερίτιξεν εὐμούσως.
Εὐνή. 95, 39, ἀπ' εὐνῆς ἐφορμήσας.
95, 97, πᾶσαν εὐνὴν ἠρείνα.
Εὐνοίη. 35, 3, ἀθλίης ὑπ' εὐνοίης. 95,
84, ὑπ' εὐνοίης.
Εὐνοῦχος. 54, 1.
Εὐπήληξ. [142, 1, ταὼς εὐπήληξ.]
Εὐπρεπής. 32, 1, ἀνδρὸς εὐπρεποῦς.
[56, 9, εὐπρεπῆ κρίνει.]
Εὐπρόσωπος. 89, 3, ἔγκλημα εὐπρόσωπον.
Εὕρεμα. Β. 2, παλαιὸν εὕρεμα.
Εὕρινος. 43, 8, σκύλαξιν εὐρίνοις.
Εὔριπος. 120, 2, ὀρυκτοῖς παρ' εὐρίποις.
Εὑρίσκω. 22, 9, ὡς ηὕρισκε λευκανθιζούσας. 12, 2, εὗρεν ἀηδόνα ἐγκαθημένην. 45, 9, τὰς μὲν εὗρε τεθνώσας.
95, 11, σκιρτῶσαν εὗρε. 95, 56, εὗρεν
ἀναψύχουσαν. 69, 4, εὑρέθη θάσσων.
126, 2, ἑστῶσαν εὗρε τὴν Ἀληθείην.
45, 4, εὑρὼν αἶγας. 79, 5, ἐκείνην
εὗρεν. 103, 10, γῆρας λιπαρὸν ηὑρήκει.
139, 1, ἱστὸν εὗρε. 22, 10, εἰ μέλαιναν ηὑρήκει. 33, 9, εὗρε τέχνην ἄλλην.
95, 48, ἄλλον τιν' εὑρεῖν δόλον. 6, 6,
τίν' ὦνον εὑρήσεις;
Εὐρύθμως. 129, 2, εὐρύθμως παίζων.
Εὐρύς. 25, 5, λίμνης εὐρείης. [106, 2,
κατ' εὐρὺν φωλεόν.]
Εὐσέβεια. 119, 10, εἰς σὲ εὐσέβειαν.
Εὐσεβής. 13, 7, πελαργὸς εὐσεβέστατον ζῴων. 63, 1, ἀνδρὸς εὐσεβοῦς.
Εὐστοχέω. 3, 8, ἄκων ηὐστόχησα.
Εὐτεκνίη. 56, 1, εὐτεκνίης ἔπαθλα.
Εὐτέλεια. [31, 24, ηὐτέλεια.]
Εὐτελής. 128, 6, see note.
Εὐφυής. [65, 1, εὐφυεῖ ταφῷ.]
Εὐφώνως. [73, 2, χρεμετίζειν εὐφώνως.
116, 1, ᾖδε παῖς τις εὐφώνως.]
Εὐχερῶς. 47, 9, ἑκάστης εὐχερῶς κατα-
γείσης. 89, 12, κἂν εὐχερῶς λύσῃς.
[81, 6, λανθάνειν εὐχερῶς.]
Εὐχή. 23, 3, ἔθηκε δ' εὐχήν. 23, 10,
ἄβουλον εὐχὴν πέμπειν.
Εὔχομαι. 10, 6, ἔθυεν, ηὔχεθ', ἱκέτευεν.
20, 8, μάτην ηὔξῃ. 63, 11, εὔχοι. 20,
7, τοῖς θεοῖς εὔχου. 72, 2, id. [102,
11, ταύτην τὴν ἡμέρην ηὐχόμην.]
Εὔωνος. 111, 2, ἅλας εὐώνους.
Εὔωπος. 124, 9, εὐωπὸν ἀγέλην.
Ἐφαπλόω. 95, 2, γυῖα γῆς ἐφαπλώσας.
Ἐφεδρεύω. 44, 2, συλλαβεῖν ἐφεδρεύων.
Ἐφεξῆς. 103, 9, τούτους ἐφεξῆς
λαμβάνων.
Ἐφέπομαι. 134, 2, οὐδ' ἐφείπεθ'
ἑρπούσῃ.
Ἐφέρπω. 112, 6, ὁ μῦς ἐφέρπει.

Ἔφηβος. [72, 21.]
Ἐφικνέομαι. [19, 6, ὡς δ' οὐκ ἐφικνεῖτο.]
Ἐφιππεύω.. 76, 15, παρῆγεν ὡς ἐφιππεύσων.
Ἐφίστημι. 20, 6, θεὸς ἐπιστὰς εἶπε. 49, 2, τῆς Τύχης ἐπιστάσης. 84, 1, ἐπιστὰς κέρατι. 117, 9, Ἑρμῆς ἐπιστάς. 132, 5, ἔξω δ' ἐφεστώς. 25, 8, ἐπεστάθησαν. [57, 8, λέγουσιν ἐπισταθῆναι ἄμαξαν.]
Ἐφορμάω. 79, 4, τῇ σκιῇ ἐφωρμήθη. 95, 39, ἀσκόπως ἐφορμῆσαι.
Ἐχθές. 125, 5, πίθηκος ἐχθὲς ἔτερπεν ὑμᾶς.
Ἐχθραίνω. 59, 7, πάντας ἐχθραίνειν.
Ἔχθρη. 85, 1, κυσίν ποτ' ἔχθρη συνειστήκει. 89, 3, ἔγκλημα ἔχθρης.
Ἐχθρός. 11, 1, ἀλώπεκ' ἐχθρὴν ἀμπέλων. 71, 4, ἐχθρὸν ἀνθρώποις. 35, 8, οἷς ἐχθρὸς γίνου. 44, 5, ἐχθροὺς ἐποίει. 87, 5, ἐχθρὸς εἶ; 95, 84, οὐδὲν ἐχθρὸν οἶδεν. [44, 8, ἐχθροῖς ἀπίστει.]
Ἔχω. 7, 1, ἄνθρωπος ἵππον εἶχε. 9, 1; 17, 6; 31, 5; 32, 4; 33, 6; 34, 3; 47, 2; 51, 1; 55, 1; 59, 11; 61, 6; 61, 10; 63, 2; 88, 3; 89, 6; 95, 3; 95, 99; 108, 1; 108, 30; 111, 1; 119, 1; 124, 20; 128, 2; 129, 1; 138, 1; 141, 2; Α. 7. 5, 9, ἀμείνονα σχὼν τἀπίχειρα. 10, 11, μή μοι χάριν σχῇς. 15, 11, οὐκ ἔχων ἴσην ἄμιλλαν. 21, 2, ἔχοντας ἐπιστήμην. 22, 1, τὴν μέσην ἔχων ὥρην. 31, 1, εἶχον πόλεμον. 33, 16, καθάπερ εἶχε συνθήκην. 44, 6, ἕκαστον εἶχε ῥαδίην θοίνην. 46, 3, ἑτοίμην χιλὸν εἶχεν. 46, 10, φίλους οὐκ ἔσχε. 61, 7, δεῖπνα εἶχον ἡδίω. 67, 3, λείην ἔσχον ἄφθονον. 68, 8, οὐκ ἔχω χώρην. 72, 4, πάντα ἔσχον ἥμερον. 75, 5, ἕτοιμα πάντ' ἔχειν. 76, 5, μισθὸν οὐκέτ' εἶχεν. 77, 12, ἔχεις ἅπαντα. 81, 4, ἔλεγχον οὐκ ἔχουσα. 85, 18, ὅμοια πάντ' ἔχοντας ἀλλήλοις. 86, 1, κοίλωμα ῥίζης φηγὸς εἶχεν. 95, 58, ἀναιδείης ὀφρὺν ἔχουσα. 95, 89, εἶχε δαῖτα πανθοίνην. 95, 94, τοῦτο κέρδος εἶχεν. 102, 9, πάντα εἶχεν εἰρήνην. 124, 3, ὁ κλωβὸς εἶχεν οὐδέν. 128, 12, ἔσχετε ἄφθονον ποίην. 140, 1, ὅπως ἔχῃ τι βουκόλημα. 2, 4, οὐκ ἔχων ὃ ποιήσει. 86, 6, οὐκέτ' εἶχεν ἐκδῦναι. 103, 19, οὐκ ἔχεις ὅ μοι δείξεις. 112, 7, οὐκ ἔχων ὃ ποιήσει. 18, 12, καῦμα τὸν γεωργὸν εἶχε. 25, 1, γνώμη λαγωοῖς εἶχε. 36, 6, θάμβος τὴν δρῦν εἶχε. 52, 3, τὸν βοώτην θυμὸς εἶχε. 95, 46, αὐτὸν λιμὸς εἶχε καὶ λύπη. 42, 1, δεῖπνόν τις εἶχε θύσας. 124, 5, πέρδικα ἡμερώσας εἶχεν. 75, 12,

πῶς ἔχουσι διήρωτα. 95, 15, ἔχει φαύλως. 103, 12, πῶς ἔχεις; 121, 2, πῶς ἔχεις; 135, 2, ἡδέως εἶχε τοῦ ζῴου. Α. 14, οὕτω ἔχοντα. 132, 9, καλῶς ἔχει μοι. [45, 14; 64, 12. 73, 1, ὀξέην εἶχε κλαγγήν. 73, 4, πρώτην φωνὴν ἔσχεν. 86, 10, ἄχρι τοιαύτην τὴν γαστέρα σχῇς. 87, 7, οὔτ' ἀπιστεῖν ἔχομεν. 95, 100; 106, 15. 106, 19, τίν' εἶχεν αἰτίην; 110, 4; 119, 13.]
Ἔωλος. 86, 3, ἄρτων ἑώλων. [106, 16, ἑώλων μοῖραν. 106, 28, ἑώλων κρεῶν.]
Ἔως. [124, 14, πόσσον εἰς ἕω λείπει.]
Ἔως. 10, 9, ἔθιεν . . . ἕως ἡ θεὸς ἦλθεν. 22, 11, ἡ μὲν ἀκμαίη ἔτιλλεν . . . ἔτιλλε δ' ἡ γραῦς ἕως φαλακρὸν ἔθηκαν. 61, 8, ἤμειβον ἀεὶ ἕως τις αὑτοῖς εἶπεν. 112, 4, ὥρυσσεν ἕως ἐκοιμήθη. 16, 5, ἔμεινεν ἕως ὁ παῖς ἐκοιμήθη. 26, 6, κατεφρόνησαν ἕως ἐκεῖνος ἤλυσεν. 95, 56, δεικνύων ἂν ὡδήγει ἕως ποθ' εὗρεν.
Ἐωσφόρος. 114, 2, ἑωσφόρου κρείσσων.

Ζάω. 14, 4, τοῦ ζῶντος οὐχ ἥττου. 17, 6, ζῶντος αἰλούρου. 74, 9, τῶν ἐτῶν ἀφ' ὧν ἔζων. 108, 8, ζῆς βίον ταλαιπώρου. 120, 2, ὁ ζῶν ὀρνκτοῖς βάτραχος παρ' εὐρίποις. 136, 4, ὅπως ζήσῃ. [14, 5, ὁ ζῶντα βλάπτων. 31, 23, τὸ ζῆν ἀκινδύνως. 44, 7, ζῆν ἀκινδύνως. 65, 8, ζῆν ἀδόξως.] See also ζώω.
Ζεύγλη. 37, 1, ἀτριβὴς ζεύγλης.
Ζεύγνυμι. [29, 2, ζευχθεὶς ὑπὸ μύλην. 70, 1, ὡς ἕκαστος ἐζεύχθη.]
Ζεύς. 45, 1, ἔνιφεν ὁ Ζεύς. 56, 2; 56, 6; 58, 1; 59, 1; 59, 3; 68, 3; 68, 7; 72, 15; 127, 1. Διός, 127, 8.
Ζηλόω. [106, 1, λέων ἀνδρῶν βίον ἐζήλου. 18, 15, πραότητα ζήλου.]
Ζητέω. 61, 10, ἃ πρὶν εἶχε ζητήσει. 89, 3, ἔγκλημα ἔχθρης ἐζήτει. 95, 29, μὴ πάλαι με ζητήσῃ. 95, 99, μὴ μάτην ζήτει. 21, 1, βόες μακρείους ἀπολέσαι ἐζήτουν. 22, 6, νέον αὑτὸν ἡ νεῆνις ἐζήτει βλέπειν. 99, 1, ἐζήτει κοινωνὸς εἶναι. 2, 16, ζητεῖ μή τις οἶδεν. [116, 9, ζητῶν ὁποῖοί.]
Ζυγός. 37, 12, τένοντα οὗ ζυγὸς τρίψει.
Ζωάγριος. 50, 15, ζωαγρίους χάριτας.
Ζωγρέω. 53, 2, ζωγρεῖν ἐδεῖτο. 53, 4, ἐγώ σε ζωγρήσω.
Ζωμός. 10, 1, ζωμοῦ χύτρη.
Ζῷον. 1, 2; 13, 7; 24, 2; 25, 3; 28, 8; 46, 4; 56, 1; 59, 3; 66, 2; 67, 3; 72, 4; 95, 85; 102, 5; 102, 7; 103, 13; 120, 3; 134, 6; 140, 2; Α. 6.
Ζώω. 12, 7, φιλτάτη, ζώεις; 25, 1,

μηκέτι ζώειν. 35, 6, ἐλθὼν εἰς ἐρημίην ζώει. 95, 25, πολλὰ εἰς ἔτη ζώει. 107, 9, παρῆκε τὸν ἱκέτην ζώειν.

Ἤ. 40, 3, ἢ κακῶς πράσσω.

Ἤ. 6, 6, τί σοι τὸ κέρδος ἢ τίν' ὦνον εὑρήσεις; 20, 8, τοῖς θεοῖς εὔχου ἢ μάτην εὔξῃ. 30, 10, νεκρὸν ἢ θεόν. 49, 7, ὅσ' ἂν δυστυχῇ ἢ πίπτῃ. 50, 8, καταδέδυκεν ἢ φεύγει. 98, 16, ῥοπάλῳ ἢ λίθῳ. 108, 17, ὀσπρίων σωρὸς ἢ πίθοι σύκων. 122, 5, γὺψ ἢ κόραξ. 134, 5, χωρὶς ὀμμάτων ἢ ῥινός. 28, 10, θᾶσσον σεαυτὴν ῥήξεις ἢ μιμήσῃ. 95, 75, μᾶλλον ἢ σύ. 122, 5, σὺ μᾶλλον ἢ γὺψ με δειπνήσεις. 132, 10, θεοῦ γενοίμην σφάγιον ἢ λύκου θοίνη. B. 12, οὐδὲν πλέον ἢ γεγωνίσκειν. [8, 2, ἀναβαίνειν ἢ κάτω βαίνειν. 35, 8; 39, 7; 65, 8; 98, 20; 136, 10.]

Ἡγεμών. 134, 10, ἡγεμὼν καθεισήκει.
Ἡγέομαι. 31, 15, οἱ στρατηγοὶ ἡγοῦντο. 134, 4, τὰ μέρεα οὐδὲν ἡγήσῃ.
Ἡδέ. [142, 1, γέρανος ἠδὲ ταώς.]
Ἤδη. 21, 3, ἤδη κέρατ' ἀποξύνοντες. 21, 1, ἤδη μέσην ἔχων ὤρην. 60, 2, ἐκπνέων ἤδη. 71, 2, βάπτουσαν ἤδη. 88, 4, λοφῶντας ἤδη. 88, 14, ἤδη ῥέοντα. 93, 6, γέρων ἤδη. 1, 16, πῶς αὐτὸς ἤδη φοβερός. 26, 12, ἤδη ἄρχεται. 92, 7, ἤδη δείξω. 17, 5, θυλάκους ἰδὼν ἤδη. 103, 2, ἤδη τῷ χρόνῳ γεγηράκει. 135, 7 (conj.) [40, 4, ἤδη βαίνει.]
Ἡδύς. 18, 9, ἡδὺς ἐκκύψας. 61, 7, δεῖπνα εἶχον ἡδίω. 135, 2, ἡδέως εἶχε τοῦ ζώου. [60, 6.]
Ἡδυφωνίη. 9, 3, πρὸς αὐλῶν ἡδυφωνίην.
Ἦθος. [35, 7, ἦθος ἀνθρώπων.]
Ἧια, see note to Fab. 88, 11.
Ἥκω. 2, 13, μάτην ἥκω. 47, 5, ἡκέ τις. 95, 13, ἄγγελος ἥκειν. 97, 4, ἥξειν εἶπεν. 130, 5, ἧκε τῇδε καὶ δέχου. 135, 6, πόθεν ἥκεις; 135, 11, ὠνητὸς ἥκων. 9, 3, πρὸς ἡδυφωνίην ἥξειν. 74, 12, εἰς μέσους ἥκων. 95, 8, χεῖρας εἰς ἐμὰς ἥξει. 110, 3, μετ' ἐμοῦ ἥξεις. [70, 7, πόλεμος ἥξει.]
Ἡλίκος. 98, 7, ἡλίκους μὲν ὄνυχας, ἡλίκους δὲ φέρεις ὀδόντας. [86, 10, τοιαύτην . . . ἡλίκην.]
Ἥλιος. 18, 1; 18, 9; 24, 1; 88, 13.
Ἡμέρη. 10, 7, καθ' ἡμέρην πᾶσαν. 119, 2, καθ' ἡμέρην θύων. 129, 6, ἡμέρης ὕλην κατήγει. [83, 2, ἐκτένιζεν ἡμέρῃ πάσῃ. 102, 11, τὴν ἡμέρην ηὐχόμην. 106, 26, καθ' ἡμέρην.]
Ἡμερόω. 124, 5, ὃν ἡμερώσας εἶχεν.
Ἡμέρως. 106, 6, ἡμέρως συνηυλίσθη.
Ἡμίονος. 62, 1.

Ἤν, with pres. subj.—6, 17; 47, 10; 47, 13; 87, 10; 127, 10. With aor. subj.—7, 5; 21, 8; 48, 6; 53, 3; 64, 7; 71, 9; 84, 6; 95, 8; 95, 62; 121, 4; 128, 6. [41, 4.]
Ἡνίκα. 9, 10, ἡνίκ' εἰς χοροὺς ἠύλουν. 33, 12, ἡνίκ' ἂν ἔλθωσι.
Ἧπαρ. 54, 2, ἁγνὸν ἧπαρ.
Ἤπερ. 27, 7, βλάπτουσα μᾶλλον ἤπερ ὠφελοῦσα.
Ἤπιος. 71, 10, ἠπιωτέρην γαίης.
Ἡρακλῆς. 15, 9; 15, 14; 20, 4.
Ἡρεμέω. 75, 13, ἠρεμοῦσι τῆς Λήθης πίνοντες.
Ἥρως. 63, 1, ἡρώων. 15, 3; 63, 4; 63, 7. [Λ. 4.]
Ἡσυχάζω. 43, 2, λίμνης ὕδωρ ἡσυχαζούσης. 135, 10, ἀλλ' ἡσυχάζω.
Ἥττα. 5, 9, τἀπίχειρα τῆς ἥττης. 31, 3, τῆς ἥττης αἰτίην.
Ἡττάομαι. 32, 10, τῇ φύσει ἡττήθη.
Ἥττων. 62, 4, οὐδὲν ἐν δρόμοις ἥττων.
Ἦχος. 124, 10, πρὸς τὸν ἦχον.
Ἰϊών. 6, 1, πᾶσαν ἠόνα ξύων.

Θάλασσα. 6, 1, θαλάσσης ἠόνα. 71, 5, ἡ θάλασσα. 111, 2, παρὰ θάλασσαν. 111, 16, ἐκ τῆς θαλάσσης.
Θαλασσαῖος. 6, 10, φυκίων θαλασσαίων.
Θαλλός. 45, 7, θαλλὸν ἐξ ὕλης.
Θάλπω. 12, 17, καῦμα θάλπει σε. 35, 4, ὃν μὲν θάλπουσα κόλποις. 74, 4, αὐτοὺς παρ' ἑστίῃ θάλψας.
Θαμβέω. 72, 15, ὁ Ζεὺς ἐθάμβει.
Θάμβος. 36, 6, θάμβος τὴν δρῦν εἶχε.
Θαμινός. 106, 5, θαμινά συνηυλίσθη.
Θάμνος. 43, 12, θάμνοις ἐμπλακείς.
Θάνατος. 21, 9, διπλοῦς θάνατος.
Θαρσέω. 1, 4, λέων προικαλεῖτο θαρσῆσαι. 1, 13, ταύτης δὲ θαρσεῖν κελευούσης. 25, 8, καί τις εἶπε θαρσῆσαι. 31, 12, μῦς προικαλεῖτο θαρσῆσαι. 34, 10, ἡ δ' εἶπε 'θάρσει.'
Θαρσύνω. 95, 33, καὶ πονοῦντα θαρσύνειν.
Θαυμάζω. 127, 9, οὐ προσῆκε θαυμάζειν.
Θαυμαστός. [65, 7, θαυμαστὸς εἶναι.]
Θεητός. 77, 5, θεητὸς αὐχήν.
Θείνω. 129, 1, ἄλλος ἄλλοθεν κρούων ἔθεινον.
Θεῖος. 15, 8, τύχης θείης. 74, 4, θείων δώρων. [50, 19, σοφὸν τὸ θεῖον. Λ. 4.]
Θέλω. 73, 4, οὔτε τὴν κρείσσω θελήσας ἔσχεν. 81, 3, ὃς θέλεις, ψεύδου. 134, 15, εἰ θέλεις. 95, 8; 108, 12. 7, 5, ἢν θελήσῃς συλλαβεῖν τι. 11, 2, θελήσας περιβαλεῖν. 51, 2; 67, 8; 83, 3; 129, 14; 95, 4. [9, 12 (corrupt); 44, 7; 116, 14.]

Θεμέλιοι. 59, 14, τροχοὺς ἐν τοῖς θεμελίοις γεγονέναι.
Θέμις. 118, 10, θέμιστες ἀνθρώπων.
Θεοβλαβής. [10, 14.]
Θεός, sing., general.—92, 6, σὺν θεῷ βαίνεις. Particular.—2, 12, ὁ θεὸς ἐσυλήθη. 2, 14; 20, 6; 24, 2; 30, 10; 48, 5; 48, 5; 119, 3; 132, 10; 10, 9, ἡ θεός. Plural.—2, 6; 15, 6; 20, 5; 20, 7; 37, 5; 50, 3; 56, 5; 58, 5; 59, 6; 63, 8; 66, 1; 68, 1; 70, 1; 72, 2; 72, 14; 78, 2; 78, 4; 97, 2; 117, 2; 117, 10; 119, 11; 120, 6; Λ. 13.
Θεράπων. 129, 10, θεράποντες ἔσωσαν.
Θερινός. 72, 6, θερινὸν ὕδωρ.
Θερμός. 50, 12, θερμοῦ κινδύνου. 122, 10, σκόλοπα θερμὸν ἐξῆρει. 97, 6, θερμοῦ χαλκία πλήρη.
Θέρος. 24, 1, θέρους ὥρῃ. 88, 6, ξηρὸν θέρος. 136, 2, ὃν θέρους σεσωρεύκει. 136, 8, εἰ θέρους ᾄδεις. 136, 5, τῷ θέρει τούτῳ.
Θεωρέω. 43, 3, τὴν σκιὴν θεωρήσας. 88, 14, τὸν σταχὺν θεωρήσας. 129, 11, σκύμνον θεωρῶν. 130, 3, ταύτην θεωρήσας.
Θῆβαι. 131, 5, τὰς κάτω Θήβας.
Θηβαῖος. 15, 1, ἀνδρὶ Θηβαίῳ. 15, 5, Θηβαῖος.
Θήγω. Β. 14, τοὺς ὀδόντας οὐ θήγω.
Θηλή. 89, 9, θηλὴ μητρῴη.
Θηλύνω. Λ. 19, conj.
Θῆλυς. 5, 8, ἀμφέβαινε θηλείαις.
Θήρ. 95, 38, σπήλυγγα θηρός. 98, 11, ἄγριος θήρ. 103, 6, θηρῶν ἐπ᾽ αὐλάς. 107, 9, γελάσας ὁ θήρ. [106, 6, θηρῶν ὅμιλος.]
Θηραγρεύτης. 107, 10, θηραγρεύταις νεηνίσκοις (conj.)
Θηράω. 27, 4, θηρῶσα μῦς. 107, 5, ἐλάφους θηρῶντα.
Θηρεύω. 6, 17, ἄδηλα θηρεύῃ. 43, 12, ἐθηρεύθη. 95, 9, λόγοις θηρευθεῖσα. 124, 5, εἰς τὸ θηρεύειν.
Θήρη. 61, 5, θήρην ἡρέτιζεν. 61, 6, τὴν θήρην ἤμειβον. 67, 1, θήρης ἐκοινώνουν. 95, 48, δεύτερον δόλον θήρης. 95, 93, ἡ δ᾽ ἀγωγὸς εἰστήκει πεινῶσα θήρης. [106, 15, νεοδρ̑όμῳ θήρῃ.]
Θηρίον. 12, 13; 77, 6; 82, 5; 87, 4; 95, 16; 95, 25; 103, 18; 106, 22.
Θησεύς. 15, 8; 15, 14.
Θιγγάνω. 19, 4, πορφυρῆς θιγεῖν ὥρης.
Θλάω. 125, 2, τὸν κέραμον ἔθλα. 129, 15, τὴν τράπεζαν ἔθλασε.
Θλίβω. 108, 23, τὸν πρόξενον θλίβων.
Θνήσκω. 7, 6, εἰ δὲ μή, θνήσκω. 25, 9, οὐκέτι χρεὼν θνήσκειν. 46, 7, οὐδ᾽

ἐπῆεν εἰ θνήσκει. 60, 4, καιρός ἐστί μοι θνήσκειν. 95, 15, ἐγγύς ἐστι τοῦ θνήσκειν. 115, 11, σὺν δίκῃ θνήσκω. 117, 4, πολλοὺς . . . θνήσκειν. 122, 3, ὦ λύκε, θνήσκω. 28, 4, τέθνηκε, μῆτερ. 45, 9, τὰς μὲν εὗρε τεθνώσας. 30, 3, προσφάτως ἐτεθνήκει. [27, 8, ὥστε τεθνήξῃ.]
Θνητός. Λ. 13, θνητῶν καὶ θεῶν.
Θοίνη. 23, 7, ταῦρον λέοντι θοίνην. 44, 6, ῥᾳδίην θοίνην. 132, 10, λύκου θοίνη.
Θράκη. 12, 8, μετὰ Θράκην. 18, 4, οἷος ἐκ Θράκης. 85, 11, Κύπρον ἢ Θράκην αὐχοῦσι.
Θρασύνη. [84, 8, ὅστις θρασύνεθ᾽ ὥς τις ὤν.]
Θρασύς. [82, 9, τὸ θρασύ.]
Θρηνέω. [14, 5, μή με νεκρὸν θρηνείτω.]
Θριγκός. 96, 1, λύκος παρῄει θριγκόν.
Θρίξ. 22, 8, τῶν τριχῶν ἔτιλλεν. 22, 12.
Θρώσκω. 82, 3, ἔθορε φωλάδος κοίτης.
Θύλακος. 17, 2; 17, 5.
Θῦμα. 97, 12, θῦμα ὅμοιον τῷ μαγειρείῳ.
Θύμβρον. 124, 2, θύμβρα δειπνήσειν.
Θυμήρης. 106, 8, δαῖτα θυμήρη.
Θυμός. 5, 2, θυμὸν οἷον ἀνθρώποις. 95, 65, τῆς δ᾽ οὐκ ἐτρέφθη θυμός. 52, 3, τὸν βοώτην θυμὸς εἶχε. 129, 10, δηχθεὶς δὲ θυμῷ.
Θυμόω. 82, 2, ὁ λέων ἐθυμώθη. 95, 75, ἐκεῖνος θυμοῦται. 119, 3, τῷ θεῷ ἐθυμώθη. [11, 10, ἄμετρα θυμοῦσθαι.]
Θυμώδης. 95, 18, πάρδαλις θυμώδης. 102, 1, λέων οὐχὶ θυμώδης.
Θύρη. 74, 3, τὰς θύρας ἀναπλώσας. 95, 42, θύρης κατιθύς. 97, 5, θύρας λεοντείους. 97, 8, πρὸς τῇ θύρῃ. 108, 21, ἀνέῳξε τὴν θύρην. 131, 14, τῆς θύρης ὑπεκκύψας. Β. 9, τῆς θύρης ἀνοιχθείσης. [116, 6, θύρης ἔξω.]
Θυρίς. [116, 3, θυρίδων προκύπτει.]
Θυρωτός. 59, 1, σχεῖν θυρωτά.
Θυσίη. 132, 3, θυσίῃ ἑορταίῃ.
Θύτης. 54, 1, εὐνοῦχος ἦλθε πρὸς θύτην. 54, 2.
Θύω. 10, 8, καθ᾽ ἡμέρην πᾶσαν ἔθυεν. 42, 1, δεῖπνόν τις εἶχε θύσας. 63, 2, ἔνθα θεῷ θύων. 119, 2, καθ᾽ ἡμέρην θύων. 21, 10, τὸν βοῦν ὁ θύσων. 34, 1, Δήμητρι ταῦρον θύων. 51, 8, θύσει με. 124, 4, πέρδικα θύων. 132, 7, μή τίς σε θύσῃ. 37, 11, παρέρπεις καὶ θύῃ. 37. 5, θεοῖς θύειν. 97, 2, μητρὶ τῇ θεῶν θύειν. [63, 12, αὐτὸς οἶδας ἂν θύσῃς.]
Θωπεύω. 6, 14, τὸν γέροντα θωπεύσειν.

Ἴαμβος. Λ. 19, πικρῶν ἰάμβων. Β. 14, τῶν ἰάμβων τοὺς ὀδόντας.

Ἰάομαι. 120, 7, πῶς ἄλλους ἰήσῃ;
Ἰατρεῖα, pl., 94, 7, μισθὸς τῶν ἰατρείων.
Ἰατρεύω. 120, 6, καὶ θεοὺς ἰατρεύει.
122, 10, ἠρξάμην ἰατρεύειν.
Ἰατρός. 75, 1, ἰατρὸς ἄτεχνος. 75, 14;
75, 20; 120, 4. [75, 4.]
Ἴδιος. 10, 2, δούλης ἰδίης ἑαυτοῦ. 45,
9, τὰς ἰδίας ἀφῆκε (corrupt). 66, 6,
κακῶν ἰδίων.
Ἰδού. 131, 9, ἰδοὺ χελιδὼν σημαίνει.
Ἱκετεύω. 3, 5, τὴν δ' ἱκέτευε. 6, 5,
αὐτὸν ἱκέτευεν. 13, 3, τοῦτον ἱκέτευε.
124, 6, αὐτὸν ἱκέτευε. 136, 3, τοῦτον
ἱκέτευε. 6, 13, τοιαῦτα μύζων ἱκέτευε.
10, 8, ἔθυεν, ηὔχεθ', ἱκέτευεν. 107, 3,
τοιοῖσδε μύθοις ἱκέτευε τονθρύζων.
134, 14, σαίνουσα δ' ἱκέτευεν.
Ἱκέτης. 107, 9, παρῆκε τὸν ἱκέτην
ζώειν.
Ἱκνέομαι. 53, 8, εἴθε μή σύγ' ἵκοιο.
Ἴκτινος. [73, 1.]
Ἱλαρός. 24, 2, ἱλαροὺς κώμους.
Ἴλη. 31, 9, σφᾶς διεῖλον εἰς ἴλας.
Ἰλύς. 25, 7, βαθέην ἐς ἰλύν.
Ἵμερος. 72, 4, ἵμερον δώρων.
Ἵνα. 88, 7, πάντας καλεῖν ἵν' ἀμήσω.
Ἵππειος. 6, 3, ὁρμῆς ἀφ' ἱππείης.
Ἱππεύς. 76, 1; 76, 5.
Ἱππεύω. 76, 10, οὐκέθ' ἱππεύων (conj.)
Ἱπποκόμος. 83, 1 (conj.)
Ἵππος. 7, 1; 7, 4; 7, 10; 7, 14; 29,
1; 62, 4; 73, 2; 74, 1; 74, 6; 74,
10; 76, 1; 76, 6; 76, 13; 76, 14;
83, 2; B. 8. 76, 18, ἀφ' ἵππων εἰς
ὄνοις. 76, 19, ἵππον ἐξ ὄνου.
Ἵπταμαι. 65, 4, ἄστρων σύνεγγυς
ἵπταμαι.
Ἴρηξ. [72, 21.]
Ἴρις. 72, 1, Ἶρις οὐρανοῖο πορφυρῆ
κῆρυξ.
Ἴσος. 15, 11, ἴσην λόγοις ἄμιλλαν.
Ἴσος. 67, 7, ἐξ ἴσου κοινωνός. 35, 2,
οὐκ ἴση μήτηρ. 107, 8, ἴσως χάριν
τίσω. [106, 16, οὐκ ἴσην μοῖραν.]
Ἵστημι. 7, 10, ἵππον ἀγήσας. 97, 5,
ἐλθὼν καὶ στὰς ἐπὶ θύρας. 103, 12,
πόρρω σταθεῖσα. 105, 3, σταθεὶς
πόρρω. 127, 4, σταθεῖσαν αὐτοῦ
πλησίην. 1, 12, οὐκ ἄπωθεν εἰστήκει.
20, 3; 31, 21; 36, 4; 48, 1; 68, 7;
74, 7; 77, 1; 95, 58; 95, 91; 122,
1; 130, 1. 72, 6, θερινὸν ὕδωρ
εἰστήκει. 33, 3, ἑστώς. 112, 3,
ὤρυσσεν ἑστώς. 110, 1, τῆς κυνὸς
ἑστώσης. 126, 2, ἑστῶσαν.
Ἱστός. 139, 1, ἱστὸν ἀράχνης.
Ἰσχάς. 108, 25, ἰσχάδος Καμειραίης.
Ἰσχύω. 47, 12, κἂν μέγιστον ἰσχύῃ.
76, 16, οὐκέτ' ἰσχύω. 112, 10,
μᾶλλον ἰσχύει. [96, 6, διὰ καιρὸν

ἰσχύων.] 19, 6, οὐκ ἴσχιε ψαύειν.
95, 7, διώκειν οὐκ ἰσχύω.
Ἴτυς. 12, 4, τὸν Ἴτυν.
Ἰχανάω. 77, 2, τυροῦ ἀλώπηξ ἰχανῶσα.
Ἰχθύς. 4, 3, τῶν ἰχθύων ὁ λεπτός. 6,
3, μικρὸν ἰχθύν. 9, 6, ἰχθύας. 61, 2,
ἰχθύων. 61, 4, ἰχθύων ἀλιπλώων.
Ἰχνεύω. 92, 2, λέοντα κυνηγὸς ἴχνευεν.
Ἴχνος. 95, 51, κατ' ἴχνος ᾔει. 92, 10,
τὸ δ' ἴχνος δείξας. 92, 5, ἴχνη λέοντος.
103, 18, πολλῶν ἴχνη θηρίων. 43, 10,
ἑτέρα πεδίον ἴχνεσιν κούφοις.

Καγχάζω. 100, 8, λύκος ἐπ' αὐτῷ
καγχάσας.
Καθάπερ. 33, 16, καθάπερ εἶχε συν-
θήκην.
Καθέζομαι. 84, 4, καθεδοῦμ' ἀπελθὼν
ἐπ' αἰγείρου.
Καθεύδω. 10, 9, αὐτῶν καθευδόντων.
49, 1, ἐκάθευδεν ἐργάτης.
Κάθημαι. 18, 8, καθῆστο. 57, 14,
ἐπὶ γλώσσης οὐδὲν κάθηται ῥῆμα.
Καθιδρύω. 30, 4, ὡς θεὸν καθιδρύσων.
Καθικετεύω. 95, 47, κερδὼ καθικέτευε
φωνήσας.
Καθιμάω. 94, 3, τὸν τράχηλον καθιμήσας.
Καθίστημι. 95, 77, βασιλῆ καταστήσειν. 134, 10, ἡγεμὼν καθειστήκει.
[134, 17, καταστάσῃ.]
Καθομιλέω. 132, 5, τὴν διν καθωμίλει.
Κάθυγρος. 72, 12, καθύγρων ὤμων.
Καινός. 93, 8, καινῆς μεσιτείης. 119,
10, καινὴν εὐσέβειαν. 131, 13, κροκύδος καινῆς.
Καίπερ. 57, 10, καίπερ ὄντας.
Καίριος. [83, 5, τῶν καιρίων φροντίζειν.]
Καιρός. 60, 4, καιρός ἐστί μοι θνήσκειν.
88, 11, οὔπω καιρός ἐστιν ἀλλύειν. [9,
13, κερτομεῖν καιρός ἐστι. 96, 6, διὰ
καίρον.]
Καίτοι. 93, 11, καίτοι τῶν κυνῶν με
τηρούντων.
Κακόρρυπος. 10, 1, κακορρύπου δούλης.
Κακός. 7, 14, τῆς κακῆς γνώμης. 27,
3, κακὴν χάριν. 49, 5, κακὴν φήμην.
134, 16, κακῆς ἔριδος. 38, 6, τοὺς
κακίστοις σφῆνας. 67, 8, κακόν τι
δώσει. 24, 7, τῶν κακῶν. 63, 9, κακῶν
δοτῆρες. 63, 10, εἰ κακῶν χρῄζεις.
66, 5; 95, 79; 134, 19. 69, 6, ἐκ
κακοῦ σώζειν. 134, 16, σὺν κακοῖς.
40, 3, κακῶς πράσσω. 127, 10, κακῶς
πράσσῃ. [4, 6, κακῶν ἔξω. 12, 25,
κακῆς μοίρης. 13, 10, κακοῖς ὁμιλῶν.
52, 6, κακοῦ ἀνδρός. 71, 11, αἱ κακαὶ
φύσεις. 81, 5, κακοῦ ἀνδρός. 94, 9,

κακοῖς βοηθῶν. 94, 10, μή τι κακόν πάσχειν. 98, 21, κακῶς δράσας.]

Κάλαμος. 6, 2, λεπτῷ καλάμῳ. 36, 4, πολὺς κάλαμος. 36, 9. [36, 18.]

Καλέω. 88, 7, πάντας καλεῖν φίλους. Λ. 2, ἣν καλοῦσι χρυσείην.

Καλιή. 118, 2, καλιὴν ηὑθέτιζεν.

Καλλίπαις. 11, 7, καλλίπαις ἀμητός.

Κάλλος. 72, 2, κάλλοις ἀγῶνα.

Κάλος. 129, 12, δεσμὰ καὶ κάλους.

Καλός. 10, 11, ὡς καλήν σε ποιούσῃ. 10, 12 ; 23, 6 ; 32, 4 ; 43, 5 ; 64, 3 ; 77, 4 ; 83, 4. 56, 7, καλλίων. 56, 3, ὡς καλὴ μήτηρ. 59, 2, καλόν τι ποιήσει. 32, 9, καλῶς παίξας. 132, 9, καλῶς ἔχει μοι. [5, 12, τὸ μὴ καλῶς πράττειν. 10, 13, αἰσχροῖς ὡς καλοῖς χαίρων. 116, 4.]

Καμειραῖος. 108, 25, ἰσχάδος Καμειραίης.

Κάμηλος. 80, 1. [8, 1 ; 8. 3 ; 40, 1.]

Κάμνω. 7, 3, πολλὰ κάμνων. 95, 94, κέρδος ὢν ἐκεκμήκει. 9, 5, φυσῶν ἔκαμε. 19, 6, κάμνουσα ἄλλως. 37, 2, κάμνοντι ταύρῳ. 50, 2, ἡ δ' ἐκεκμήκει. 74, 2, ὑπὸ ψύχους κάμνοντες. 103, 3, ὡς νόσῳ κάμνων. [19, 9, ἔκαμνε πηδῶσα. 52, 7, αὐτὸς κάμνων.]

Καμπτήρ. [29, 4, καμπτῆρας γυρεύω.]

Κάμπτω. 36, 11, ἡμεῖς καμπτόμεσθα.

Καμπύλος. 84, 1, κέρατι καμπύλῳ.

Κᾶν=καὶ ἐάν. 3, 10, κἂν ἐγὼ σιωπήσω. 21, 10, κἂν μάγειρος ἐλλείψῃ. 36, 12, κἂν κινήσῃ. 47, 12, κἂν μέγιστον ἰσχύῃ. 63, 11, κἂν ἐν αἰτήσῃς. 89, 12, κἂν λύσῃς. [13, 14, κἂν μηδὲν καταβλάψῃς. 81, 6 ; 82, 10.]

Κἄν = καὶ ἄν, vide ἄν.

Κἀν = καὶ ἐν, vide ἐν.

Κανίσκιον. 108, 20, ἐκ κανισκίου.

Καρδίη. 77, 8, καρδίην ἐχαινώθη. 95, 60, χολὴ ἐπέζει καρδίην. 95, 92, καρδίην νεβρείην. 95, 96, καρδίην ἐπεζήτει. [106, 23, καρδίην διαξαίνω. 95, 100, ποίην καρδίην ;]

Καρκίνος. 39, 2 ; 109, 1.

Κάρφος. 31, 14, λεπτὰ πηλίνων τοίχων κάρφη. 31, 19, τὰ περισσὰ κάρφη.

Κάρχαρος. 94, 6, κάρχαρόν τι μειδήσας.

Κατά. [C. gen.—κατ' ἀνθρώπων θρασύνεται.]

C. acc. (local).—46, 1, καθ' ὕλην. 63, 1, κατ' οἴκους. 106, 2, κατ' εὐρὺν φωλεὸν διατρίβων. 135, 4, πᾶσαν κατ' αὐλὴν ᾔει.

Temporal.—10, 10, ἦλθεν καθ' ὕπνους.

Distributive.—10, 7, καθ' ἡμέρην πᾶσαν ἔθυεν. 119, 1, καθ' ἡμέρην θύων. 47, 8, κατὰ μῆνν κατᾶξαι. 95, 51, κατ' ἴχνος ᾔει.

Καταβαίνω. 32, 8, βαθυστρώτου καταβᾶσα κλίνης.

Καταβλάπτω. [13, 14, τοὺς πέλας καταβλάψῃς. 60, 6, τὸ καταβλάπτον.]

Καταβρέχω. 63, 3, καταβρέχων οἴνῳ.

Καταγέλαστος. 80, 4, μὴ καταγέλαστον.

Κατάγνυμι. 3, 4, τὸ κέρας κατῆξε. 47, 7, ῥάβδους κατάξαι. 47, 9, ἑκάστης καταγείσης. 119, 5, κεφαλῆς καταγείσης.

Κατάγω. 2, 5, εἰς τὴν πόλιν κατῆγε πάντας. 76, 7, κορμοὺς παχεῖς κατῆγε. 111, 4, τὸν ὄνον κατῆγε. 111, 15, σπόγγους κατῆγεν. 125, 3, αὐτὸν κατῆγε. 129, 7, ὕλην κατῆγ' ἀφ' ὕψους (conj.)

Καταδύνω. 50, 8, τῇδ' ἀλώπηξ καταδέδυκεν. 91, 2, σπήλυγγα κατέδυ.

Καταισχύνω. 82, 8, χαίτην καταισχύνειν.

Κατακλείω. 95, 88, εἰς μυχὸν κατεκλείσθη.

Κατακναίω. 12, 17, πάντα κατακναίει σε.

Κατακρώζω. 135, 12, παρρησιάζῃ καὶ κατακρώζεις.

Καταλαμβάνω. 31, 16, φύζα τοὺς μύας κατειλήφει. 58, 7, ἐλπὶς ἣν κατειλήφει τεθὲν τὸ πῶμα. 87, 2, κατειλήφει.

Καταλείπω. 131, 2, κατέλιπεν μίην μοίνην. [116, 5, τὸν ἄνδρ' ἑαυτῆς καταλιποῦσα.]

Κατανέμω. 26, 1, γέρανοι κατενέμοντο χώρην.

Καταπίπτω. 111, 12, ἑκὼν κατέπεσε. 111, 18, id.

Καταπλήσσω. 26, 4, τῷ φόβῳ καταπλήσσων.

Κατασκέλλομαι. 46, 8, νόσῳ κατεσκλήκει.

Κατάσκιος. 95, 56, ἐν κατασκίῳ χώρῳ.

Καταστρώννυμι. 34, 2, ἄλω κατεστρώκει.

Καταφθείρω. 13, 5, οὐ σπόρον καταφθείρω.

Καταφρονέω. 26, 6, κατεφρόνησαν.

Καταχράομαι. [34, 14, καταχρῷτο τῷ μύθῳ.]

Κατάχρυσος. 65, 5, καταχρύσοις πτέρυξι.

Κατέρχομαι. 122, 8, ὥς μου κατέλθῃ πνεῦμ' εἰς ᾅδου.

Κατεσθίω. 103, 10, τούτοις κατέσθιεν.

Κατέχω. 129, 4, αὖ κατεῖχεν αὐτόν.

Κατηφέω. 62, 5, ἔπαυσε τὸν δρόμον κατηφήσας.

Κατιθύς. 95, 42, θύρης κατιθύς.

Κατισχύω. 77, 6, ὄνυξι πάντων θηρίων κατισχύεις.

Κατοικέω. 2, 7, ἀγροῖς κατοικεῖν. 12,

12, σύσκηνος ἡμῖν κατοικήσεις. 108,
11, τὸ κέρας κατοικῶ τῆς Ἀμαλθείης.
Κατοπτεύω. 131, 15, χελιδόν' αὖ κατοπτεύσας.
Κάτω. 59, 9, κάτω κεῖσθαι. 75, 12,
οἱ κάτω. 131, 5, τὰς κάτω Θήβας.
[8, 2, κάτω βαίνειν. 116, 6, κάτω
μελάθρων ἦλθε.]
Καῦμα. 12, 17, καῦμά σε θάλπει.
18, 12, καῦμα τὸν γεωργὸν εἶχεν. 43,
ὑπὸ τὸ καῦμα. 131, 9, χελιδὼν καῦμα
σημαίνει.
Καυχάομαι. 96, 4, μὴ σὺ καιχήσῃ.
Καυχήμων. [5, 10, μή ποτ' ἴσθι καυχήμων.]
Κεῖμαι. 7, 9, ἔκειτο νεκρός. 28, 5,
τετράπουν ὑφ' οὗ κεῖται. 46, 2, ἔκειτο
ἐν χλόῃ. 59, 9, κάτω κεῖσθαι. 71, 8,
ὧν ἐγὼ μέσῃ κεῖμαι. 72, 3, ἀγῶνα
κεῖσθαι. 86, 2, ἔκειτο πήρη. 95, 2,
λέων νοσήσας ἔκειτο. 98, 17, ἔκειτο
ἀργός. 103, 4, ἔσω σπήλυγγος ἔκειτο.
Κεῖνος. .37, 7, ὁ δὲ μόσχος ἀδμὴς
κεῖνος. 95, 6, κεῖνον τὸν ὑλήεντα
δρυμόν.
Κείρω. 51, 3, ἔκειρεν ἀτεχνῶς. 51, 10,
ὃς κερεῖ με. 89, 6, τὴν ἄρουραν κείρεις.
107, 13, ὀδοῦσι βρόχον κείρας. 128, 2,
κείρεις μὲν ἡμᾶς καὶ πόνους ἔχεις κέρσας.
Κελεύω. 1, 13, μένειν κελενούσης. 47,
4, ἐκέλευε δεσμὸν ἐνεγκεῖν. 88, 10,
σκοπεῖν κελεύων. 100, 9, χαίρειν
κελεύω. 127, 3, Ζεὺς Ἑρμείην ἐκέλευσεν σωρεύειν. 95, 50, χαλεπὸν
κελεύεις.
Κενός. 7, 2, ἵππον κενόν. 26, 3,
σφενδόνην κενήν.
Κενόω. 57, 10, ἐκένωσαν ἄμαξαν.
Κεντρίζω. 20, 7, τοὺς βόας κέντριζε.
Κέντρον. B. 15, εὖ δὲ κέντρα πρήνας.
Κέραμος. 125, 2, τὸν κέραμον ἔθλα.
Κέρας. 3, 4; 3, 10; 95, 22; 108, 11.
   κέρατι. 84, 1.
   κέρατα. 21, 4; 37, 8; 43, 12;
   doubtful, 43, 15.
   κέρατα. 59, 9.
   κέρασι. 91, 4; 112, 3.
   κέρασι. 43, 5.
Κεράστης. 23, 2, ταῦρον κεράστην.
43, 1, ἔλαφος κεράστης.
Κερασφόρος. 107, 4, κερασφόρους ταύρους.
Κερδαίνω. 111, 13, ὥς τι κερδήσας. [9,
11, ἀπόνως κερδαίνειν.]
Κέρδος. 6, 6, τί σοι τὸ κέρδος; 95, 94,
τοῦτο κέρδος εἶχεν.
Κερδώ. 50, 13; 81, 3; 82, 4; 95, 10;
95, 36; 95, 43; 95, 98; 101, 5;
106, 16.
   Acc.—κερδώ. 95, 47; 106, 9.

   Dat.—81, 1, κερδοῖ.
   Voc.—106, 20, κερδοῖ.
Κερδῷος. 77, 2, ἀλώπηξ κερδῴη.
Κέρκος. 11, 3, τὴν κέρκον ἄψας. [110,
3, κέρκον οὐρείην.]
Κερούχος. 45, 5, αἶγας κερούχους.
Κερτομέω. 9, 8, τοσαῦτ' ἐκερτόμησε.
17, 4, καὶ ταῦτ' ἐκερτόμησε. [9, 13,
κερτομεῖν καιρός ἐστι.]
Κέρτομος. 77, 10, κερτόμῳ γλώσσῃ.
Κεφαλή. 94, 8, κεφαλὴν ἐξελεῖν σφὴν.
95, 32, τῆς γραίης κεφαλῆς. 119, 5,
κεφαλῆς καταγελάσης. 134, 2, οὐκέτ'
ἤξίου πρώτην κεφαλὴν βαδίζειν. 134,
15, δέσποινα κεφαλή.
Κηδεύω. 98, 5, τίς οὐ λέοντι κηδεύσει;
Κήδομαι. 132, 8, μή μου τῆς ἀσυλίης
κήδου.
Κῆπος. 11, 1, ἀμπέλων τε καὶ κήπων.
68, 6, ἐντὸς Ἑσπέρου κήπων.
Κηρίον. A. 18, μελισσαγὲς κηρίον.
Κῆρυξ. 2, 11, κῆρυξ ἐφώνει. 72, 1,
Ἴρις οὐρανοῖο πορφυρῆ κῆρυξ.
Κηύξ. 115, 2, λάροις τε καὶ κήυξιν.
Κιβύσσης. B. 6, εἶπε λόγους Κιβύσσης.
Κιβωτός. 127, 3, εἰς κιβωτὸν αὐτὰ
σωρεύειν.
Κίνδυνος. 31, 6, ὑπομένουσι κινδύνους.
50, 12, θερμοῦ ἐκφυγοῦσα κινδίνου.
108, 30, μεστὰ κινδύνων. 129, 18,
ἐσχάτου κινδύνου. [4, 8, ἐκφυγόντα
κίνδυνον. 37, 13, ἀργία δὲ κινδύνοις.
64, 12, χὐπέμεινε κινδύνους.]
Κινέω. 36, 12, ἄνεμος ἄκρα κινήσῃ.
56, 5, γέλως ἐκινήθη. 58, 4, τὸ πῶμα
κινήσας. 82, 4, ὡς ἐκινήθη . . . ὁ
τυραννεύσων. 95, 49, κινήσασα βυσσόθεν γνώμην. 130, 2, βουλὰς ἐκίνει
ποικίλας.
Κίνησις. 134, 11, τυφλῇ κινήσει.
Κίσσα. [72, 19.]
Κίχλα. [72, 19.]
Κλαγγή. [73, 1, ὀξέην κλαγγήν.]
Κλαγκτός. 124, 13, κλαγκτὸν εἶπε
φωνήσας (conj.) 135, 3, κλαγκτὸν
ᾄδων (conj.)
Κλαίω. 16, 2, νηπίῳ κλαίοντι. 78, 1,
μητρὶ κλαιούσῃ. 78, 2, μὴ κλαῖε. 86,
7, ὡς ἐπῆλθε κλαιούσῃ. 98, 9, τίς
ἰδοῦσα μὴ κλαύσῃ. 11, 8, τὸν πολὺν
κόπον κλαίων. [106, 25, τὰ δ' ἔπειτα
προσκοπουμένη κλαίω.]
Κλείζω. 3, 6, αἶγάς εἰς ἔπαυλιν αἰπόλος
κλείζων.
Κλέπτης. 2, 14; 23, 5; 23, 8.
Κλέπτω. 2, 3, τήνδ' ἐκλεψεν. 79, 1,
κρέας κύων ἔκλεψεν. [83, 1, κριθάς
τις ἔκλεπτε.]
Κλῆρος. 68, 4, Ἑρμῆς ἔσειε κλήρους.
70, 2, ἐσχάτῳ κλήρῳ.

M

Κλίνη. 32, 8, βαθυστρώτου κλίνης.
Κλίνω. 18, 18, πέτρης νῶτον ἐξοχῇ κλίνας. 84, 3, βαρύνω τὸν τένοντα καὶ κλίνω.
Κλοιός. 100, 6, κλοιῷ τέτριπται.
Κλονέω. 22, 3, μιγάδας ἐκλόνει χαίτας.
Κλύω. 126, 8, κλύειν τι βουλήσῃ.
Κλωβός. 124, 3, ὁ κλωβὸς εἶχεν οὐδέν.
Κλώψ. 107, 2, ὁ οἰκότριψ κλώψ.
Κνηκίης. 122, 12.
Κνηκός. 113, 2, κνηκὸν λύκον.
Κνήμη. 10, 4, σύρουσα πορφύρην ἐπὶ κνήμας. 33, 19, τοῦ δ' ἔτυψε τὴν κνήμην. 72, 8, κνήμας ἐξέλουεν. 95, 59, φρὶξ ἐπέσχε κνήμας.
Κνίσμα. 95, 73, κνίσμα χειρὸς ἀρρώστου.
Κνίζω. 82, 7, τὴν δορὴν κνίσῃ.
Κοῖλος. 27, 2, ἐν συναγγίῃ κοίλῃ. 33, 6, σφενδόνην κοίλην. 95, 37, εἰς κοίλην σπήλυγγα. 103, 3, κοίλης ἔσω σπήλυγγος. 134, 11, κοῖλον εἰς βάραθρον.
Κοιλώδης. 20, 2, εἰς φάραγγα κοιλώδη.
Κοίλωμα. 86, 1, κοίλωμα ῥίζης.
Κοιμάω. 16, 5, ὁ παῖς ἐκοιμήθη. 82, 1, κοιμωμένου λέοντος. 112, 4, ὁ ταῦρος ἐκοιμήθη. [116, 5, τὸν ἄνδρα καταλιποῦσα κοιμᾶσθαι.]
Κοινός. 108, 3, ἔθεντο κοινὸν τὸν βίον. 137, 1, εἰς τὸ κοινὸν ἐπράθη. 15, 2, κοινῶς ὁδεύων.
Κοινωνέω. 67, 1, θήρης ἐκοινώνουν. [67, 10, μηδὲ κοινώνει.]
Κοινωνός. 67, 7, ὡς ἐξ ἴσου κοινωνός. 99, 2, κοινωνὸς εἶναι.
Κοίτη. 82, 3, φωλάδος κοίτης.
Κολοιός. 33, 4 ; 33, 22 ; 72, 10 ; 72, 18.
Κόλπος. 35, 4, θάλπουσα κύλποις. 56, 4, ἠρμένη κύλποις. 129, 4, κατεῖχεν ἐν κόλποις,
Κόμη. 3, 3, κόμην γλυκεῖαν αἰγίλου τε καὶ σχίνου. 88, 3, ληίου κόμῃ.
Κομίζω. 105, 2, πρόβατον ἐκόμιζεν οἴκαδε.
Κόπος. 7, 8, τῷ κόπῳ ἀπαυδήσας. 11, 8, τὸν πολὺν κόπον.
Κοπόω. 112, 4, ἕως κοπωθεὶς ἐκοιμήθη.
Κόπτω. 50, 4, αἷς ἔκοψας αἰγείροις. [64, 8, πελέκεων ἀεὶ κοπτόντων.]
Κόραξ. 77, 1 ; 77, 4 ; 77, 8 ; 77, 12 ; 78, 1 ; 122, 5.
Κόρη. 75, 13, ἡ Κόρη χὠ μέγας Πλούτων.
Κόρη. 98, 8, τίς κόρη σε τολμήσει περιλαβεῖν ;
Κορμός. 76, 7, κορμοὺς παχεῖς.
Κορυδαλλός. 88, 1 ; 88, 17. [72, 20.]
Κορυδός. 88, 8.

Κορύνη. 129, 20, κορύναις κροίων.
Κορώνη. 46, 9, κορώνην δειτέρην ἀναπλήσας. 72, 11, κορώνης υἱός.
Κοσμέω. 31, 9, οἱ σφᾶς ἐκόσμοιν. 72, 13, ποικίλως ἐκοσμήθη. 76, 13, ἵππους κοσμεῖν. [72, 19, κόσμον οἰκεῖον κοσμεῖν.]
Κόσμος. 104, 7, κόσμον ἀρετῆς. [72, 19, κόσμον κόσμει. 83, 6, κόσμος.]
Κοτέω. 93, 4, κοτοῦσιν ἀλλήλοις.
Κουρεύς. 51, 10, πάλιν ἐστὶ κουρεύς.
Κοῦφος. 43, 10, ἴχνεσι κούφοις. 46, 1, γυῖα κοῦφα. 111, 13, κούφως ἀνέστη. 95, 76, ἄπιστον καὶ κούφην. 122, 6, χάριν ἀβλαβῆ τε καὶ κούφην. [24, 9, τῶν ὑπερβολῇ κούφων.]
Κράζω. 65, 4, ἄστρων σύνεγγυς κράζω. 3, 10, τὸ κέρας κέκραγε. 5, 6, ἐκεκράγει. 77, 9 ; 105, 4.
Κρανέη. 129, 20, κρανέης κορύναις.
Κράσπεδον. 18, 7, χερσὶ κράσπεδα σφίγξας.
Κρατέω. [36, 14, τοῖς κρατοῦσιν. 40, 6, ἧς ἔσχατοι κρατοῦσιν.]
Κραυγάζω. 26, 10, φεύγωμεν ἐκραύγαζον.
Κρέας. 79, 1, κρέας κύων ἔκλεψεν. 79, 4, τὸ κρέας ἀφῆκε. 130, 4, τὸ κρέας λαβεῖν. 79, 3, τοῦ κρέως τὴν σκιήν. 34, 3, κρεῶν τραπέζας. 51, 7, εἰ κρεῶν χρήξεις. 51, 9. 86, 3, κρεῶν πλήρης. 106, 12, κρεῶν μοίρας. [106, 28, ἑώλων κρεῶν. 27, 8, κρεῶν ἄγγος.]
Κρείσσων. 15, 7, πολὺ κρείσσων Θησεύς. 67, 2, ποσὶν κρείσσων. 72, 14, ἀετοῦ κρείσσων. 114, 2, Ἑωσφόρου κρείσσων. 45, 6, μείζονάς τε καὶ κρείσσους. 9, 9, κρεῖσσον ἦν χορεύειν. [12, 7, πῶς γὰρ ἂν κρείττον ; 45, 13, ἐλπίσας τὰς κρείσσους. 73, 3, τὴν κρείττω φωνήν. 84, 8, ἀνθρώπων τῶν κρειττόνων. 136, 9, κρεῖττον φροντίζειν.]
Κρεμάννυμι. 66, 4, ἐκ δὲ τοῦ πήρας κρεμάσαι.
Κρεμαστός. [19, 6, κρεμαστῆς αἰώρας.]
Κρήνη. 72, 5, ἵσταξε κρήνη. 72, 10, εἰς κρήνην. 95, 82, ὄμνυμι γάρ σοι κρήνας.
Κρήτη. 85, 9, οἱ μὲν ἐκ Κρήτης.
Κριθή. 74, 6, κριθὰς ἵππῳ. 129, 9, ἔτρωγε κριθάς. [88, 1, κριθὰς ἔκλεπτε.]
Κριθιάω. 62, 2, ἡμίονος κριθιάσας.
Κριθίζω. 76, 2, τὸν ἵππον ἐκρίθιζε.
Κρίμνον. 108, 9, κρίμνα λεπτά. 108, 32, τὰ κρίμνα τρώγω.
Κρίνω. 56, 6, πάντα ἔβλεπε κρίνων. 76, 3, παραστάτην γενναῖον κρίνων. 95, 20, τυραννεῖν ἀξιωτάτην κρίνει. 117, 4, ἄδικα κρίνειν. [43, 16, ὅταν κρίνῃς. 56, 9, εὐπρεπῆ κρίνειν. 59, 17, φθόνον ἐὰν κρίνειν.]

Κριός. 93, 7, γέρων ἤδη κριός.
Κριτής. 59, 6, ᾑρέθη κριτής.
Κροκύς. 131, 13, κροκύδος καινῆς.
Κρούω. 129, 20, κορύναις κρούων. [104, 8, ἔλεγχον τῆς πονηρίης κρούεις.]
Κρύος. [131, 16, ὑπὸ τοῦ κρύους πίπτειν.]
Κρύπτω. 3, 9, ἔργον ἐκφανὲς κρύψω. 50, 4, κρύψον με. 50, 10, οὐ πανοῦργος ἐκρύφθη. 115, 9, ἔκρυψε νέφεσιν. 108, 27, οἱ δ' ἔνδον ἐκρύβοντο.
Κρώζω. 52, 4, τί δὴ κρώζεις; 77, 7, κωφός ἐσσι κοὐ κρώζεις.
Κτείνω. 21, 7, σφάζουσι καὶ κτείνουσι. 124, 6, ἱκέτευε μὴ κτείνειν.
Κτενίζω. 72, 9, ἐκτένιζε τὰς χαίτας. [83, 2, τὸν ἵππον ἐκτένιζε.]
Κτῆμα. 52, 4, ὦ παγκάκιστον κτημάτων.
Κτῆνος. 7, 12, τὴν σάγην τοῦ κτήνους.
Κύβος. 131, 1, ἐν κύβοισιν οὐσίην ἀναλώσας. 131, 10, τοῖς κύβοισιν ὡμίλει.
Κύκλος. 18, 7, πάντα κύκλῳ κράσπεδα. 137, 5, κύκλῳ περιόντες.
Κυκλόω. 68, 5, τόξ' ἔρυσσε κυκλώσας.
Κῦμα. 71, 2, βάπτουσαν κῦμα.
Κυμαίνω. 36, 2, τὴν δ' ἔσυρε κυμαίνων.
Κύμβαλον. 80, 2, κυμβάλοις χαλκείοις.
Κυνέω. 95, 12, ἔκυσσεν αὐτήν. 129, 17, δεσπότην κύσσων.
Κυνῆ. 64, 8, Ἄρεος ἐν κυνῇ.
Κυνηγέτης. 43, 7, κυνηγέτας ἄνδρας.
Κυνηγέω. 1, 1, ἦλθε κυνηγήσων. 61, 1, κυνηγήσας. 124, 8, ὅταν κυνηγῇς.
Κυνηγός. 50, 1, κυνηγὸς ἐτρόχαζεν. 50, 7; 61, 1; 61, 4; 92, 1. 50, 5, κυνηγῷ.
Κυνίδιον. 129, 24, κυνιδίῳ παρισούμην.
Κύπρις. 32, 2, σεμνὴ Κύπρις.
Κύπρος. 85, 11, οἱ δὲ Κύπρον αὐχοῦσιν.
Κύπτω. 5, 4, ἔκυπτ' ἐς οἴκου γωνίην.
Κύριος. 95, 85, πάντων κυρίην σε τῶν ζῴων.
Κυρόω. 95, 24, πλὴν ἐκυρώθης.
Κυρτός. 40, 2, κυρτὴ κάμηλος. 71, 2, κῦμα κυρτόν.
Κύρτος. 61, 2, κύρτον ἰχθύων πλήσας.
Κύρω. [134, 19, κακῶν κύρειν.]
Κύων, ὁ, ἡ. 42, 2; 48, 2; 69, 2; 74, 1; 74, 7; 74, 14; 79, 1; 85, 2; 87, 1; 95, 51; 100, 1; 100, 3; 104, 1, 104, 4; 104, 5; 113, 3. [128, 10; 129, 2.]
 κύνα. 128, 8. [129, 1.]
 κύνας. 93, 3.
 κυνί. 42, 2.
 κυνός. 110, 1.

Κυνῶν. 85, 2; 93, 11. [42, 6.]
κυσίν. 85, 1.
Κώδων. 104, 2, χαλκεύσας κώδωνα. 104, 4, κώδωνα σείων.
Κῶλον. 109, 2, πλάγια κῶλα σύρειν. Λ, 19, ἰάμβων κῶλα.
Κωλύω. 99, 2, τί κωλύει; 103, 18, ἴχνη θηρίων με κωλύει. 128, 13, πάντα κωλύω λῃστῶν. [82, 9, τὸ θρασὺ κώλυε.]
Κωλώτης. 139, 1.
Κώμη. 20, 1, ἐκ κώμης. 137, 5, πᾶσαν περιόντες κώμην.
Κωμήτης. 138, 1.
Κῶμος. 22, 4, εἰς ἔρωτας καὶ κώμους. 24, 2, ἦγε τῷ θεῷ κώμους. 136, 10, προσέχειν νοῦν κώμοις.
Κώνωψ. 84, 1.
Κωτίλλω. 95, 86, τοιαῦτα κωτίλλουσα.
Κωφός. 77, 7, κωφός ἐσσι κοὐ κρώζεις.

Λαγχάνω. 15, 9, τύχης θείης λέλογχεν. 68, 5, λαχὼν δ' ὁ Φοῖβος.
Λαγωός. 25, 1, γνώμῃ λαγωοὺς εἶχε. 87, 4. 69, 1, λαγωὸν δασυπόδην. 87, 1. [102, 10, ὁ πτὼξ λαγωός.]
Λαθραίως. 95, 93, ἁρπάσασα λαθραίως.
Λάθρη. 104, 1, λάθρη ἔδακνε. 107, 12, λάθρη προπηδήσας.
Λάθυρος. 74, 6, κριθὰς μὲν ἵππῳ λάθυρα δὲ ταύρῳ.
Δακτίζω. 122, 12, τὸν κνηκίην λακτίσας. 129, 13, ἄμετρα λακτίζων.
Λαλέω. 106, 20, λάλησον ὥσπερ εἰώθης. Α. 9, λαλεῖ δὲ πέτρη, ἐλάλει δὲ (?) νηὶ καὶ ναύτῃ. 12, 18, σοφὰ λαλοῦσα. [33, 23, ἄλλα πρὸς ἀλλήλους λαλεῖν.]
Λάλος. 131, 15, τὴν λάλον χελιδόνα.
Λαμβάνω. 9, 6, ἔλαβεν ἰχθύας. 11, 5, τοῦ λαβόντος. 13, 11, ἔλαβόν σε. 23, 5, εἰ λάβοι τὸν κλέπτην. 33, 9, πρὶν λαβεῖν ἔφευγον. 77, 10, τυρὸν λαβοῦσα. 130, 4, τὸ κρέας λαβεῖν. 51, 2, τὸν πόκον λαβεῖν μείζω. 67, 5, λήψομαι πρώτην μοῖραν. 67, 6, λήψομαι κἀκείνην. 102, 6, δίκας λαβεῖν. 103, 9, τούτους ἐφεξῆς λαβών. 32, 3, μορφὴν λαβεῖν γυναικείην. 49, 5, καὶ κακὴν λάβω φήμην. 68, 9, τόξου νίκην ἔλαβε. 95, 72, ἀρχὴν λαβεῖν. 64, 7, ἢν λάβῃς μνήμην. [94, 9, μισθὸν οὐ λήψῃ. 106, 9, κερδὼ σύνοικον εἰλήφει. 106, 13, ὃν καὶ λαβὼν παρῆγεν. 106, 15, νεοδρόμῳ λαβὼν θήρῃ.]
Λαμπρός. 42, 1, δεῖπνον λαμπρόν. 85, 15, ἔνιοι λαμπροί. [64, 11, ἅπας ὁ λαμπρός. 116, 4, λαμπρῆς σελήνης.]
Λαμπρότης. [31, 24, τῆς λαμπρότητος.]
Λάμπω. 114, 2, λύχνος φέγγος λάμπει.

Λανθάνω. [50, 20, λαθεῖν ἐπιορκῶν.
81, 6, λανθάνειν ψευδόμενος. 98, 21,
λανθάνει κακῶς δράσαι.]
Λάπτω. 95, 93, καρδίην λάπτει.
Λάρος. 115, 2, λάροις τε καὶ κήυξιν.
Λαφύσσω. 95, 90, σάρκας λαφύσσων.
Λέγω. 15, 10, λέγων ἐνίκα. 70, 3, ὡς
λέγουσιν. 135, 11, ὡς λέγεις. 27, 3,
τῆς δ᾿ αὖ λεγούσης. 30, 9, 'εἶεν' λέγοντα. 68, 1, θεοῖς 'Απόλλων ἔλεγε.
75, 2, πάντων λεγόντων. 109, 1,
ἔλεγε καρκίνῳ μήτηρ. 117, 2, ἰδὼν
τις ἔλεγεν. 118, 9, 'οἴμοι' λεγούσης
'τῆς μοίρης.' 120, 3, παρελθὼν ἔλεγε.
129, 22, 'ἔτλην' ἔλεξεν. 132, 6, 'ὁρᾷς'
λέγων. 95,24, τί σοι λέγω τὰ πολλά;
96, 2, ἔλεγε πολλὰ βλασφήμως. 115,
4, ἔλεξε ταῦτα. 117, 5, ταῖθ᾿ ὁμοῦ
λέγοντος. 15, 6, ὁ δ᾿ ἐξ 'Αθηνῶν
ἔλεγεν ὡς κρείσσων Θησεὺς γένοιτο καὶ
τύχης λέλογχεν. 18, 1, βορέῃ λέγουσιν
ἡλίῳ τε ἔριν γενέσθαι. 49, 5, μὴ αἰτίη
λέγωμαι. 137, 6, περιόντες ἐλέγοντ᾿
ὄψα. [18,15, λέγει δ᾿ ὁ μῦθος. 57, 7,
λέγουσιν αὐτοῦ ἐπισταθῆναι ἄμαξαν.]
Λείη. 67, 3, λείην εἶχον.
Λεῖμαξ. 142, 2, χλωρὴν λείμακος ποίην
(conj.)
Λείπω. 12, 14, ὕπαιθρον ὕλην λεῖπε.
131, 5, λείποισα τὰς κάτω Θήβας.
72, 12, νοῖς σοι λείπει. 124, 14,
πόσσον εἰς ἕω λείπει. 5, 3, τούτων ὁ
λειφθείς. 69, 3, δρόμῳ ἐλείφθη.
Λεόντειος. 97, 5, ἐπὶ θύρας λεοντείους.
Λεπτός. 4, 3, τῶν ἰχθύων ὁ λεπτός.
6, 2, λεπτῷ καλάμῳ. 31, 13, λεπτὰ
τοίχων κάρφη. 36, 7, λεπτὸς τ᾿ ἐὼν
καὶ βληχρός. 47, 4, λεπτῶν ῥάβδων.
13, 1, λεπτὰς παγίδας. 108, 9, κρίμνα
λεπτά. 10, 4, λεπτὴν πορφύρην.
139, 2, λεπτὸν φάρος.
Λεπτύνω. 103, 5, φωνὴν λεπτύνων.
Λευκανθίζω. 22, 9, τρίχας λευκανθιζούσας. 45, 3, αἶγας χιόνι λευκανθιζούσας.
Λευκός. 22, 3, λευκαῖς μελαίνας μιγάδας
ἐκλόνει χαίτας. 85, 16, ἄλλοι (κύνες)
λευκοί. 137, 7, 'Αττιν λευκόν. Β. 13,
λευκῇ ῥήσει.
Λευκόω. 100, 5, τράχηλος πῶς ἐλευκώθη.
Λέων. 1, 4; 1, 10; 44, 2; 67, 1;
67, 2; 67, 4; 82, 2; 90, 1; 95, 1;
95, 14; 95, 39; 95, 68; 95, 84;
95, 89; 95, 95; 97, 1; 97, 10; 98,
1; 99, 2; 101, 7; 102, 1; 103, 1;
105, 2; 105, 5; 107, 1. [106, 1;
106, 15; 106, 19.]
      λέοντα. 91, 1; 91, 5; 92, 1; 92,

7; 92, 10; 95, 29; 101, 2; 107, 14.
[107, 18.]
λέοντας. [98, 20.]
λέοντι. 23, 7; 98, 5; 99, 1.
λέοντος. 1, 10; 82, 1; 92, 5;
103, 7. [95, 101.]
λεόντων. 101, 8. [98, 20.]
λέουσιν. 101, 4.
Λήθη. 75, 13, τῆς Λήθης πίνοντες.
Λήιον. 11, 6, ἣν δὲ ληίων ὥρη. 88, 3,
ληίου κόμη θρέψας.
Λῃστής. 128, 14.
Λιβάς. 24, 6, λιβάδα πᾶσαν αἰαίνει.
Λίβυσσα. 142, 1, Λίβυσσα γέρανος.
Λιβυστῖνος. Β. 5, εἶπε καὶ Λιβυστίνος.
Λίην. 21, 4, λίην γέρων. 36, 6, λίην
λεπτός. 95, 76, λίην ἄπιστον. 101, 1,
πιμελὴς λίην. [29, 5, μὴ λίαν ἐπαίρου.
41, 4, λίαν ὑπερέχοντα. 116, 4,
καλὸν λίαν.]
Λίθος. 3, 4, μακρόθεν λίθῳ πλήξας.
3, 8, τὸν λίθον ῥίψας. 26, 8, λίθοις
βάλλων. 33, 17, λίθων πλήρη σφεν-
δόνην. 48, 2, λίθων σωρός. 98, 16,
ῥοπάλῳ ἢ λίθῳ.
Λιθουργός. 30, 5; 30, 7.
Λιμνάς. 115, 1. λιμνάσιν αἰθυίαις.
[24, 3, λιμνάδας χορούς.]
Λίμνη. 25, 2, λίμνης ὕδωρ; 43, 2, id.
25, 5, λίμνης ἐγγύς.
Λιμός. 46, 8, λιμῷ κατεσκλήκει. 95,
46, λιμὸς αὐτὸν εἶχε.
Λιμώττω. 45, 8, μακρὰ λιμώττειν.
136, 3, ἱκέτευε λιμώττων.
Λίνον. 11, 3, καὶ λίνον τι προσδήσας.
Λιπαρός. 103, 10, γήρας λιπαρόν.
Λίπος. 60, 2, τῷ λίπει πνιγόμενος.
100, 3, κύων λίπους πλήρης.
Λίσσομαι. 107, 7, ἀλλά, λίσσομαι,
φείδου.
Λιτός. 108, 31, λιτῆς βώλου.
Λίχνος. [60, 5, λίχνος μῦς.]
Λόγος. 15, 12, ἴσην λόγοις ἄμιλλαν.
44, 4, λόγοις ὑπούλοις. 50, 11, τῷ
λόγῳ πιστεύσας. 53, 3, λόγοισι τρεῖς
ἀληθινούς. 95, 9, λόγοισι θηρευθεῖσα.
95, 13, χρηστῶν λόγων. 95, 37, λόγοισι ποιητοῖσι. Α. 7, λόγοις ᾔδει.
Β. 6, λόγους εἶπε Κυβίσσης. [12,
26, λόγος σοφός. 40, 5; 56, 8.]
Λοιβή. [23, 6, ἄρνα λοιβὴν παρασχεῖν.]
Λοιδορέω. 96, 4, ὁ τόπος μ᾿ ἐλοιδόρησε.
Λοιπός. 134, 4, τὰ λοιπὰ μέρεα. Α.
6, τὰ λοιπὰ τῶν ζῴων. 95, 80, τὸ
λοιπὸν ἴσθι γενναίη. 124, 7, τὸ λοιπὸν τί ποιήσεις; 75, 7, καὶ τὸ λοιπὸν
οὐκέτ᾿ εἰσήει. 26, 6, κατεφρόνησαν
λοιπόν. 76, 4, ἢν δὲ λοιπὸν εἰρήνη.
134, 9, τὸ μὴ φρονοῦν λοιπὸν ἦρχε τῶν

πρώτων. [63, 12, πρὸς ταῦτα λοιπὸν οἶδας.]
Λοξός. 109, 1, λοξὰ βαίνειν.
Λοφάω. 88, 4, παῖδας λοφῶντας.
Λοφηφόρος. 88, 8, τῶν λοφηφόρων παίδων.
Λόχμη. 95, 88, λόχμης εἰς μυχόν.
Λόχος. 31, 10, διεῖλον εἰς λόχους.
Λύγδινος. 30, 1, λύγδινον 'Ερμείην.
Λύκαινα. 16, 3.
Λύκειος. 94, 8, λυκείου φάριγγος.
Λύκος. 16, 6, λύκος χανὼν ὄντως.
101, 7, ἐν λύκοις λέων φαίνῃ. 128, 14, λύκων διωκτήρω. 16, 2 ; 16, 3 ; 53, 1 ; 85, 1 ; 89, 1 ; 89, 11 ; 93, 1 ; 94, 1 ; 95, 77 ; 96, 1 ; 100, 1 ; 100, 8 ; 101, 8 ; 102, 8 ; 105, 1 ; 105, 3 ; 105, 5 ; 113, 2 ; 122, 2 ; 122, 3 ; 122, 14 ; 130, 3 ; 132, 1 ; 132, 4 ; 132, 10.
Λυμαίνομαι. 51, 5, μή με λιμαίνου.
Λυπέω. 43, 4, χηλῆς ἕνεκα ἐλυπήθη.
Λύπη. 12, 24, λύπην ἀναξαίνει. 19, 7, βουκολοῦσα τὴν λύπην. 24, 5, φροντίδων καὶ λύπης. 95, 46, αὐτὸν εἶχε λύπη. 140, 1, βουκόλημα τῆς λύπης. [12, 27, λύπη δ' ὅταν συνοικήσῃ. 23, 11, ἐκφορουμένης λύπης.]
Λυσσάω. 90, 1, λέων ἐλύσσα.
Λύχνος. 10, 7, τὴν 'Αφροδίτην λύχνοις ἐτίμα. 114, 1, μεθύων ἐλαίῳ λύχνος. 114, 6, φαῖνε, λύχνε.
Λύω. 7, 11, πάντα τὸν γόμον λύων. 55, 3, λύειν ἔμελλεν αὐτούς. 107, 14, ἔλυσε τὸν λέοντα. 32, 9, δαιτὴ 'λέλυτο. 89, 11, κἂν αἰτίην λύσῃς. See also note ad fab. 58, 11.

Μαγειρεῖον. 79, 1, κρέας ἐκ μαγειρείου. 97, 12, ὅμοιον θῦμα τῷ μαγειρείῳ.
Μαγειρεύω. 122, 16, μαθὼν οὐδὲν ἢ μαγειρεύειν.
Μάγειρος. 21, 10 ; 42, 5. 51, 8, μαγείρους. 21, 1.
Μαίνομαι. 90, 3, τί μεμηνὼς οὐχὶ ποιήσει ;
Μακάριος. [103, 20, μακάριος ὅστις.]
Μακρόθεν. 3, 4, μακρόθεν πλήξας. 104, 3, πρόδηλον μακρόθεν. 103, 14, μακρόθεν με σκέπτῃ.
Μακρός. 23, 1, μακρὴν ὕλην. 43, 10, μακρὸν πεδίον. 92, 2, μακρῆς πεύκης. 15, 4, μακρὴ ῥῆσις. 12, 1, ἀγροῦ μακρὸν ἐξεπωτήθη. 75, 6, τὴν αὔριον οὐ μακρὸν ὑπερβήσῃ. 45, 8, μακρὰ λιμώττειν. 68, 1, μακρὰ τοξεύων. [52, 6, μακρὸν οἰμώξειν.]
Μαλάσσω. 28, 6, χηλῇ μαλαχθέν. [133, 4.]

Μαλθακός. 36, 11, μαλθακῇ γνώμῃ. 95, 11, μαλθακῆς ποίης.
Μάλιστα. [44, 7, ὅταν μάλιστα ζῆν θέλῃς.]
Μᾶλλον. 14, 3, μᾶλλον ᾑρούμην. 18, 6, ὁ δ' οὐ μεθῆκε μᾶλλον. 27, 7, βλάπτουσα μᾶλλον ἢ ὠφελοῦσα. 64, 10, μᾶλλον αἱρήσῃ. 95, 74, σὺ δ' οὐχ ὑπέστης . . . βιῇ δ' ἀποσπασθεῖσα μᾶλλον ἐτρώθης. 112, 9, μᾶλλον ἰσχύει. 122, 5, μᾶλλον ἢ γύψ. [8, 2, ἀναβαίνειν μᾶλλον ἢ κάτω βαίνειν. 18, 16, πειθοῖ μᾶλλον ἢ βιῇ. 35, 8, ἐχθρὸς μᾶλλον ἢ φίλος. 64, 11, τῶν ἐλαττόνων μᾶλλον. 134, 17, μᾶλλον οἷν.]
Μαλλός. 51, 4, τὸν μαλλὸν ἐψάλιζεν. 93, 7, μαλλὸν ὀρθώσας.
Μάνδρη. 113, 1, μάνδρης ἔσω.
Μανθάνω. 122, 16, μαθὼν οὐδέν. 124, 14, πόθεν μαθήσῃ ; A. 14, μάθοις ἂν οὕτω ταῦτ' ἔχοντα. B. 12, μαθόντες οὐδέν. [33, 24, λαλεῖν μαθόντων.]
Μάρτυς. 50, 16, ὧν μάρτυς εἰστήκειν.
Μάταιος. 35, 5, ὡς μάταιον ἐκβάλλει. 95, 45, πόνος μάταιος ἐξανηλώθη. 6, 17, ὁ μὴ τηρήσας . . μάταιός ἐστι.
Μάτην. 2, 13, μάτην ἥκω. 6, 9, μὴ μάτην μ' ἀποκτείνῃς. 9, 5, καὶ μάτην ηὔλει. 20, 8, μάτην εὔξῃ. 75, 21, μάτην διεβλήθης. 95, 99, μὴ μάτην ζήτει.
Μάχαιρα. 97, 8.
Μάχη. 5, 1, ἀλεκτορίσκων ἦν μάχη. 16, 5, πᾶσαν μάχην συνῆπτεν. 31, 8, εἰς μάχην γενναίους. 76, 3, ἐν μάχαις. 85, 3, μάχης ἐπιστήμων. [85, 5, τὴν μάχην ἐνεδρεύσει.]
Μάχομαι. 1, 5, αὐτῷ μάχεσθαι. 36, 10, μαχομένη ταῖς πνοαῖς. 39, 4, τυράννων μαχομένων. 93, 4, δι' οὓς μάχονται. [36, 14 ; 39, 6.]
Μέγας. 4, 6, τῶν ἰχθύων ὁ μέγας. 6, 11, ἐπὴν μέγας γένωμαι. 75, 14, χὠ μέγας Πλούτων. 100, 3, μέγας ὁ κύων ἐγένετο. 112, 9, οὐχ ὁ μέγας ἀεὶ δυνατός. 45, 6, μείζονάς τε καὶ κρείσσους. 51, 2, τὸν πόκον λαβεῖν μείζω. 66, 6, πήρην, ἥτις ἦν μείζων. 79, 3, ἰδούσα τὴν σκιὴν μείζω. 15, 6, μέγιστον ἀνδρῶν. 41, 15, κἂν μέγιστον ἰσχύῃ. [4, 7, τὸν μέγαν τῇ δόξῃ. 47, 15, μέγ' ἀγαθόν. 85, 19, μέγιστον ἀγαθόν.]
Μεθίημι. 18, 6, ὁ δ' οὐ μεθῆκε. 99, 4, μεθιέναι πίστιν.
Μεθίστημι. 76, 18, ἀφ' ἵππων εἰς ὄνους μεταστήσας. 88, 10, ποῦ σφέας μεταστήσει ;
Μεθύσκω. 89, 9, θηλὴ μεθύσκει με.
Μεθύω. 114, 1, μεθύων ἐλαίῳ λύχνος.

[Μειδάω.] 94, 6, κάρχαρόν τι μειδήσας.
[106, 29, ὡς λέων μειδήσας.]
Μειλίχως.   [106, 10, μειλίχως συνεζῆκει.]
Μέλαθρον.   64, 5, στέγη μελάθρων
εἰμί. [116, 6, κάτω μελάθρων ἦλθε].
Μέλας. 19, 1, μελαίνης ἀμπέλου. 22,
3, μελαίνας χαίτας. 22, 10, id. 25,
2, μέλαν ὕδωρ. 33, 4, μέλαν κολοιῶν
ἔθνος. 85, 14, οἱ μὲν ἡμῶν (κυνῶν)
μέλανες. 108, 7, μελαίνῃ βώλῳ.
Μέλεος. 129, 24, ὁ μέλεος.
Μέλι. 108, 18, στάμνοι μέλιτος.
Μελίγλωσσος.   95, 9, λόγοισι μελιγλώσσοις.
Μελισταγής. Λ. 18, μελισταγὲς κηρίον.
Μέλλω, c. inf. praes.—37, 5, ἔμελλον
θύειν. 55, 4, λύειν ἔμελλον. 75, 18,
γράφειν ἔμελλον. 82, 8, ἔμελλε καταισχύνειν. 93, 6, πέμπειν ἔμελλεν.
95, 25, μέλλεις ἀνάσσειν. 95, 69,
μέλλων ἐγείρειν. 108, 25, ψαύειν
ἔμελλεν. 110, 1, μέλλων ὁδεύειν.
113, 1, ἔμελλε συγκλείειν. 122, 4,
μέλλω ἀποπνεῖν. [81, 6.]
C. inf. fut.—6, 14, ἔμελλε θωπεύσειν. 47, 3, ἔμελλε τελευτήσειν. 95,
71, ἔμελλε δώσειν. 107, 1, ἔμελλε
δειπνήσειν. 124, 2, μέλλοντι δειπνήσειν. [84, 10.]
Doubtful.—32, 6, γαμεῖν ἔμελλε.
85, 4, ἔμελλεν, ἐβράδυνεν. 95, 38,
τὸ μέλλον οὐκ ᾔδει. [95, 100, ποίην
ἔμελλε καρδίην ἔχειν ;]
Μέλος. 12, 5, ἐκ τοῦ μέλους.
Μέλω. 84, 5, οὐ μέλει μοι.
Μελῳδός. 124, 10, τίνος μελῳδοῦ τὸν
ἦχον.
Μεμπτός. [Λ. 5.]
Μέμφομαι. 38, 4, πῶς ἂν μεμφοίμην
τὸν πέλεκυν. 97, 10, ἐμέμφεθ' ὁ
λέων. [106, 30, ταῦτα μηδ' ἐμοὶ
μέμφου.]
Μέντοι. 37, 10, εἰς ταῦτα μέντοι.
Μένω. 1, 5, μεῖνον, εἶπε. 1, 13, μένειν
κελευούσης. 16, 4, ἔμεινεν ὡς δειπνήσων. 45, 10, αἱ δ' οὐκ ἔμειναν. 58,
7, μόνη δ' ἔμεινεν ἐλπίς. 84, 5, ἐὰν
μείνῃς. 86, 8, μεῖνον, εἶπε. 91, 8,
χωρὶς αἰπόλου μείνας. 99, 5, σοὶ μὴ
μένοντι πιστεύω. 129, 5 (conj.)
Μερίζω. 67, 4, ὁ λέων μερίζει. 74, 9,
μερίσαντες αὐτῷ τῶν ἐτῶν.
Μέριμνα. 106, 23, μερίμνῃ καρδίην
διαξαίνει.
Μέρος. 57, 4, μέρος τι νέμων ἑκάστῳ.
32, 5, ἐν μέρει. 134, 3, μέρη. 134,
4, τὰ λοιπὰ μέρεα.
Μεσιτείη. 93, 8, καινῆς μεσιτείης.
Μεσιτεύω. 39, 2, καρκίνος μεσιτεύων.

Μεσόγεως. 111, 8, εἰς τὴν μεσόγεων.
Μέσος. 41, 1, ἐκ μέσου νώτου. 71, 8,
ὧν ἐγὼ μέση κεῖμαι. 74, 12, εἰς μέσους
ἥκων. 95, 42, εἰς μέσας ὕλας. 105,
1, ἐκ μέσης ποίμνης. 128, 8, ἡμῖν ἐν
μέσοις. 128, 11, ἐν μέσοις ἐπωλεύμην.
129, 13, εἰς μέσον αὐλῆς. 129, 15,
εἰς μέσον βάλλων. Λ. 8, ἐν μέσαις
ὕλαις. 129, 19, ἐν μέσοις. 22, 1,
τὴν μέσην ἔχων ὥρην. 63, 6, ἐν
μέσαις ὥραις.
Μεσόω. [116, 1, νυκτὸς μεσούσης.]
Μεστός. 108, 30, ταῦτα μεστὰ κινδύνων.
Μετά. C. gen.—13, 12, ἀπολῇ μετ'
αὐτῶν μεθ' ὧν ἦλως. 44, 1, μετ' ἀλλήλων. 110, 3, μετ' ἐμοῦ ἥξεις. 113,
2, μετ' αὐτῶν λύκον συγκλείειν. [106,
10, μεθ' ἧς συνεζῆκει.]
Μετά. C. acc.—74, 12, ὁ βοῦς μετ'
αὐτόν. 95, 16, τίς μετ' αὐτὸν τυραννήσει ; 12, 8, μετὰ Θράκην. 12, 22,
μετὰ τὰς Ἀθήνας. [Λ. 4, μεθ' ἣν
γενέσθαι φασὶ θείαν ἡρώων. 70, 7, μετ'
αὐτὴν πόλεμος ἥξει.]
Μεταλαμβάνω.   [98, 22, ὧν μεταλαβεῖν.]
Μεταξύ. 91, 8, πόσον τράγου μεταξὺ
καὶ πόσον ταύρου.
Μετάρσιος. 115, 6, ὅστις σε μετάρσιον
θήσω.
Μεταστρέφω. 87, 3, μεταστραφεὶς
ἔσαινεν.
Μετέχω. 7, 15, οὖ γὰρ μετασχεῖν μικρὸν
οὐκ ἐβουλήθην.
Μετρέω. [67, 9, μέτρει σεαυτόν.]
Μέτρον. 64, 3, τὸ μέτρον εὐμήκης. 68,
7, ταὐτὸ μέτρον.
Μέτωπον. 31, 14, κάρφη μετώποις
ἀρμόσαντες. 95, 58, ἀναιδείης ὀφρὺν
καὶ μέτωπον. 122, 18, μέτωπα ἀλοιήσας. 130, 9, μέτωπα ἐπλήγη.
Μέχρι(ς). 15, 3, ὁ μῦθος ἦλθε μέχρις
ἡρώων. 89, 9, μέχρι νῦν.
Μή, with imperative.—28, 8, παῦε, μὴ
πρίον. 34, 10, μὴ φείδου. 48, 8,
πλέον με μὴ τίμα. 51, 5, μή με
λιμαίνου. 71, 6, μή με βλασφήμει.
75, 2, μὴ δέδιχθι. 78, 2, μὴ κλαῖε.
83, 4, τὸ τρέφον με μὴ πώλει. 92, 9,
μή μοι χαρίζου. 95, 99, μὴ μάτην
ζήτει. 132, 8, μή μου κήδου. [5,
10, μὴ ποτ' ἴσθι καυχήμων. 14, 5,
μὴ θρηνείτω. 29, 5, μὴ λίαν ἐπαίρου.
59, 17, μὴ ἔα. 138, 4, μὴ σοφίζου.]
With subj. with imperatival force.—
1, 5, μὴ σπεύσῃς. 3, 5, μή με μηνυ-
ύσῃς. 6, 9, μὴ μάτην μ' ἀποκτείνῃς.
7, 7, μή μ' ἐνοχλήσῃς. 10, 11, μή
μοι χάριν σχῇς. 12, 21, μή μ' ὀργᾶδος

χωρίσσῃς. 48, 6, μὴ πολιχμήσῃς.
50, 5, μή με μηνύσῃς. 92, 10, τὸν
λέοντα μὴ δείξῃς. 96, 4, μὴ σὺ
καυχήσῃ. [72, 18, μή με συκοφαντήσῃς.]
In negative wishes.—53, 5, εἴθε μὴ
συνηντήκεις. 53, 7, εἴθε μὴ σίγ' εἰς
ὥρας ἴκοιο, μηδέ μοι πάλιν συναντήσαις. 101, 5, μὴ φρενωθείην. [70,
5, μὴ ἔθνη . . . ὕβρις ἐπέλθοι.]
With deliberative subj.—24, 7, τί
μὴ πάθωμεν ; 98, 9, τίς δ' ἰδοῦσα μὴ
κλαύσῃ ;
In conditional sentences.—60, 6,
ἐὰν μὴ παραιτήσῃ. 72, 16, παρεῖχε
τὴν νίκην, εἰ μὴ χελιδὼν αὐτὸν ἤλεγξεν.
128, 11, εἰ μὴ παρήμην οὐκ ἂν ἔσχετε.
7, 6, εἰ δὲ μή, θνήσκω. 141, 1, εἰ μὴ
τίκτητε οὐκ ἂν εἶχεν (corrupt). [85,
5, εἰ μὴ προάξει.]
After verbs of fearing.—82, 7, δέδοικα μή μου τὴν δορὴν κνίσῃ.
Signifying from fear that, lest:—
(1) After imperatives.—16, 2, παῦσαι,
μή σε τῷ λύκῳ ῥίψω. 132, 7, ἔξελθε
μή τις συλλάβῃ σε καὶ θύσῃ. 49, 4,
οὐκ ἐγερθήσῃ μὴ αἰτίῃ ἐγὼ λέγωμαι ;
(2) 95, 29, σπεύδω μὴ πάλαι με
ζητήσῃ. 131, 3, στολὴν κατέλιπεν
μίην μὴ πάθοι τι ῥιγώσας. [134, 18,
ἐγὼ προσέξω μή ποτε δόξῃς.]
After verbs of asking. — 2, 3,
ἀνεζήτει μή τις τήνδ' ἔκλεψεν. 2, 16,
ζητεῖ μή τις οἶδεν. 50, 8, ἐπηρώτα μὴ
τῆδ' ἀλώπηξ καταδέδυκεν ἢ φεύγει.
95, 54, ἐπηρώτα μή πού τις φεύγει.
After relatives.—38, 5, πῶς ἂν μεμφοίμην τὸν πέλεκυν ὅς μου μὴ προσῆκε
τῇ ῥίζῃ ; 120, 8, πῶς ἄλλον ἴσῃ ὃς
σαυτὸν μὴ σώζεις ;
With participle.—(1) 6, 16, ὁ μὴ τὰ
μικρὰ τηρήσας. 67, 8, ἡ τρίτη αὕτη
κακόν τι δώσει μὴ θέλοντί σοι φεύγειν.
99, 5, πῶς γὰρ φίλῳ σοι μὴ μένοντι
πιστεύω ; 80, 4, ἐμοὶ γένοιτο βαίνειν
μὴ καταγέλαστον.
(2) Late usage.—37, 10, εἰς ταῦτα
μὴ πονῶν ἐτηρήθης. 46, 8, ὁ τάλας
κατεσκλήκει μή πω κορώνην δευτέρην
ἀναπλήσας. 108, 32, τὰ κρίμνα μὴ
φοβούμενος τρώγω.
Other usages. — 26, 6, ὥστε μὴ
φεύγειν. 59, 9, ἔψεγε τὸ τοῦ ταίρου
τὰ κέρατα μὴ κάτω κεῖσθαι. 99, 4,
ἐπ' ἐνεχύρῳ δώσεις . . . μὴ μεθύεται.
14, 2. σῶμ' ἔφασκε μὴ σύρειν. 109,
1, μὴ λοξὰ βαίνειν ἔλεγε καρκίνῳ μήτηρ
. . . κῶλα μὴ σύρειν. 124, 6, ἱκέτευε
μὴ κτείνειν. 134, 9, τὸ μὴ φρονοῦν.
[5, 12, τὸ μὴ καλῶς πράττειν. 21, 12,

ὁρᾶν μὴ ἐξεύρῃ. 23, 10, τοῦτ' ἔοικε
γιγνώσκειν . . . μὴ πέμπειν. 36,
14, μῦθος ἐμφαίνει μὴ δεῖν. 94, 10,
ἀρκέσει σοι μὴ πάσχειν.]
Μηδέ. 95, 81, μηδ' ἐπτόησο. 98, 11,
μηδ' ἄγριος θὴρ γίνου. 106, 30, μηδ'
ἐμοὶ μέμφου. 1, 6, μηδ' ἐπελπίσῃς.
48, 7, μηδέ μοι προσουρήσῃς. 53, 8,
μηδέ μοι συναντήσαις. 68, 9, νίκην
ἔλαβε μηδὲ τοξεύσας. 48, 4, βούλομαι,
μηδ' οὕτω παρελθεῖν. 53, 2, ζωγρεῖν
ἐδεῖτο μηδὲ ἀποκτείνειν. 59, 11, ἔψεγε
μὴ σχεῖν θυρωτὰ μηδ' ἀνοικτά. 93, 10,
δι' οὓς νέμεσθαι μηδὲ νῦν ἔξεστι. [11,
10 ; 43, 18 ; 67, 10 ; 82, 9 ; 107, 17.]
Μηδείς. 36, 9, μηδὲν ἐκπλήσσον. [13,
14, κἂν μηδὲν καταβλάψῃς. 43, 17,
μηδὲν ὑπολάβῃς. 67, 9, μηδὲν
σύναπτε. 96, 6, μηδεὶς γαυρούσθω.
116, 11, μηδὲν ἐκπλήσσον.]
Late usage.—97, 8, ὡς εἶδεν . . .
πρὸς τῇ θύρῃ δὲ μηδὲν κτε. 117, 4,
πολλοὺς μηδὲν αἰτίους. Λ. 12, γῆς
μηδὲν αἰτιούσης.
Μηκέτι. 25, 1, γνώμη λαγωοὺς εἶχε
μηκέτι ζώειν.
Μῆκος. 41, 2, δράκοντι μῆκος ἐξισουμένην.
Μηκύνω. 85, 12, τί μηκύνω ;
Μῆλον. 128, 4, μηλὰ σοι περισσεύει.
Μήν. 125, 5, καὶ μὴν πίθηκος ἕτερπεν.
Μήνυτρον. 2, 12, μήνυτρα σύλων.
Μηνύω. 3, 7, μή με μηνύσῃς. 12, 18,
σεαυτὸν μήνισον. 50, 5, μή με μηνύσῃς. 88, 9, τῷ πατρὶ μηνύεις. [38, 8.
96, 5, ὁ μῦθος μηνύει.]
Μήποτε. 71, 3, εἴθε μήποτ' ἐπλεύσθης.
Μήτηρ. 6, 8 ; 28, 2 ; 32, 2 ; 38, 6 ;
56, 3 ; 62, 3 ; 109, 1 ; 118, 4 ; 135,
9.
μῆτερ. 28, 4 ; 78, 2. 109, 3,
μῆτερ ἡ διδάσκαλος.
μητρί. 28, 8 ; 78, 1 ; 97, 2.
μητρός. 34, 7.
Μῆτι. [v. l. μῆτε. 80, 4.]
Μητρῷος. 89, 9, θηλὴ μητρῴη.
Μιγάς. 22, 3, λευκαῖς μελαίνας μιγάδας
χαίτας.
Μικρέμπορος. 111, 1.
Μικρός. 6, 3, μικρὸν ἰχθύν. 6, 16, τὰ
μικρὰ τηρήσας. 7, 5, οὐ μικρὸν μετασχεῖν. 57, 5, νέμων ἑκάστῳ μικρόν.
82, 10, κἂν μικρὸν ᾖ. 89, 4, μικρὸς
ὤν. 91, 6, ἀνέξομαί σου μικρὰ τῆς
ἐπηρείης. 95, 34, τὰ μικρὰ πείθει.
107, 8, μικρὸς ὢν τίσω. 112, 10, τὸ
μικρὸν εἶναι ἰσχύει. 131, 7, μικρὰ
τιτυβιζούσης. 1, 9, μικρὸν διαστάς.
84, 2. 108, 24, μικρὸν ἐπισχών. [4, 7,
τὸ μικρὸν εἶναι.]

Μιμέομαι. 28, 10, ποιότητα μιμήσῃ.
[73, 3, μιμούμενος τὸν ἵππον. 41, 4,
ἂν ὑπερέχοντα μιμήσῃ.]
Μισέω. 111, 16, τοὺς ἅλας μεμισήκει.
[13, 13, μισηθήσῃ.]
Μισθός. 2, 16, ζητεῖ μισθοῦ μή κτε.
76, 5, μισθὸν εἶχεν. 88, 15, μισθὸν
δώσειν. 94, 2, id. 94, 5 τὸν μισθὸν
ᾔτει. 94, 7, σοὶ μισθὸς ἀρκεῖ. 107,
15, ἐπάξιον δοὺς μισθόν. 115, 5, πόσον
μισθὸν δώσεις; [76, 8, μισθῷ φόρτον
ἔφερεν. 94, 9, μισθὸν ἀγαθόν.]
Μνήμη. 64, 7, ἢν λάβῃς μνήμην. 95,
26, γένοιτο τῆς ἀλώπεκος μνήμη. Λ. 17.
Μνηστεύω. 98, 2, παῖδα παρὰ πατρὸς
ἐμνήστευε.
Μοῖρα. 67, 4, τίθησι τρεῖς μοίρας.
103, 16, ἐγγὺς ὄντα τῆς μοίρης. 118,
9, οἴμοι τῆς μοίρης. 12, 25, τῆς κακῆς
μοίρης. [106, 12, κρεῶν διανέμων μοίρας.
106, 16, ἔφερε μοῖραν οὐκ ἴσην.]
Μόλις. 75, 10, μόλις βαίνων.
Μολοσσός. 85, 10, οἱ δ' ἐκ Μολοσσῶν
(κυνῶν).
Μονήρης. 132, 1, δὶς μονήρης.
Μόνος. 20, 4, ὃν μόνον θέων ἐτίμα.
24, 6, μόνος νῦν ἀναίνει. 58, 7, μόνη
ἔμεινεν ἐλπίς. 58, 9, ἐλπὶς μόνη
σύνεστιν. 72, 13, μόνος ἐκοσμήθη.
95, 83, σοὶ μόνῃ δουλεύειν. 95, 96,
μόνην ἀπ' ἄλλων καρδίην. 74, 16,
τὸν διδόντα . . . μόνον σαίνει. 121,
3, μόνον σώζου. [31, 20, μόνοι ἐάλ-
ωσαν.]
Μόρος. 107, 2, ἐγγὺς ὢν μόροι.
Μορφή. 32, 3, μορφὴν ἀμείψαι.
Μόσχος. 37, 7, ὁ μόσχος ἀδμής.
Μοῦνος. 131, 2, κατέλιπε μίην μούνην.
25, 4, μοῦνον εἰδότες φεύγειν. 126,
2, τὴν Ἀληθίην μούνην. [106, 24, οὐ
τὰ νῦν μοῦνον . . . τὰ δ' ἔπειτα. 106,
28, γεύσομαι κρεῶν μούνῃ.]
Μοῦσα. 15, 12, ἀγρίῃ μούσῃ. Λ. 16,
μύθους τῆς ἐλευθέρας μούσης. Β. 6,
νέῃ μούσῃ. Β. 10, σοφωτέρης μούσης.
[8, 3, οὐκ ἄτερ μούσης.]
Μοχθέω. 74, 13, μοχθεῖ φίλεργός τ'
ἐστι. 111, 10, μοχθήσας.
Μόχθος. 37, 3, μόχθον οἷον ὀτλεύεις.
Μυελός. 95, 90, μυελὸν ὀστέων πίνων.
Μύζω. 6, 13, μύζων καὶ ἀσπαίρων.
Μυθιάζομαι. Β. 13, λευκῇ μυθιάζομαι
ῥήσει.
Μυθίαμβος. Β. 8.
Μῦθος. 15, 3, ῥέων ὁ μῦθος ἦλθε. 103,
15, ποικίλοις μύθοις. 107, 3, τοιοῖσδε
μύθους. 128, 1, οἷς εἶπε μύθους πρὸς
νομῆα. Λ. 16, μύθοις τῆς ἐλευθέρης
μούσης. Β. 1, μῦθος Σύρων εὕρεμα.
77, 3, μύθῳ ὄρνιν ἠπάτησε. [18, 15;

22, 14; 34, 14; 36, 13; 38, 8; 59,
16; 96, 5; 107, 16; 119, 11.]
Μύλη. [29, 2, ζευχθεὶς ὑπὸ μύλην.]
Μυοκτόνος. 135, 9, ἡ μυοκτόνος μήτηρ.
Μύρμηξ. 136, 2; 136, 7.
μύρμηκος. 108, 8.
μυρμήκων. 117, 6; 117, 11.
Μῦς. 31, 12; 32, 7; 60, 1; 82, 2;
107, 12; 107, 18; 108, 27; 112, 1;
112, 6; 112, 8.
μῦν. 31, 22; 82, 5; 82, 6; 107,
1; 108, 14; 112, 2.
μύας. 31, 16.
μύες. 31, 1; 31, 3.
μυός. 107, 6.
μῦς. 27, 4. [60, 5.]
μυῶν. 108, 1.
Μυχός. 95, 88, λόχμης εἰς μυχόν. 108,
22, εἰς μυχὸν τρώγλης. 112, 2, id.
136, 1, ἐκ μυχοῦ. [31, 20, μυχῶν
πρόσθεν.]
Μῶμος. 59, 6, ἠρέθη τούτοις κριτὴς ὁ
Μῶμος. [59, 18, ἀρεστὸν οὐδὲν τῷ
Μώμῳ.]
Μωρός. 93, 5, μωρὴ ποίμνη.

Ναίω. 126, 4, τὴν ἐρημίην ναίεις.
Νάπη. 1, 11, εἰς νάπας ἐρημαίας. 3,
6, Πανός, ὃς νάπας ἐποπτεύει.
Ναρκάω. 46, 1, γυῖα κοῦφα ναρκήσας.
Ναῦς. 71, 1, νῆα ναυτίλων πλήρη. 117,
1, νεὼς βυθισθείσης. Α. 10, ἐλαλεῖ νηί.
Ναύτης. Α. 10, νηὶ καὶ ναύτῃ.
Ναυτίλος. 71, 1, νῆα καυτίλων πλήρη.
Νεβρεῖος. 95, 92, καρδίην νεβρείην.
Νεβρός. 90, 1.
Νεηνίς. 22, 6.
Νεηνίσκος. 107, 10, θηραγρεύταις νεην-
ίσκοις.
Νεκρός. 7, 9, πεσὼν ἔκειτο νεκρός. 14,
4, εἰ νεκρὸν εἵλκες. 14, 2, νεκρὸν
σῶμα. 30, 10, μὲ νεκρὸν ἢ θεόν συ
ποιήσεις. [14, 5, νεκρόν με.]
Νέμεσις. 43, 6, παρῆν δὲ νέμεσις
[11, 11, ἔστιν τις ὀργῆς νέμεσις].
Νέμω. 57, 5, νέμεν ἑκάστῳ μικρόν.
33, 15, ἐνέμοντο τὴν χώρην. 44, 1,
ἐνέμοντο ταῦροι μετ' ἀλλήλων. 93,
10, νέμεσθαι ἀκινδύνως.
Νεόδρομος. [106, 15, νεοδρόμῳ λαβὼν
θήρῃ.]
Νεόν. 33, 2, πυρὸν εἰς νεὸν ῥίψας.
Νέος. 22, 2, νέος οὐκ ἦν. 22, 5, γυναικῶν δύο, νέης τε καὶ γραίης. 22, 6,
νέον ἐραστήν. 22, 11, ἡ νέη τε χὴ
γραίη. 37, 11, ὁ νέος παρέρπεις τὸν
γέροντα. 131, 1, νέος οἰσίην ἀναλώσας. Β. 6, νέῃ μούσῃ.
Νεόσμηκτος. 97, 7, μαχαίρας βουόροις
νεοσμήκτους.

Νεοσσεύω. 88, 1, ἐν χλόῃ νεοσσεύων.
Νεοσσός. 118, 4, νεοσσῶν ἑπτὰ μήτηρ.
Νευρή. [68, 6, τόξοιο νευρήν.]
Νεύω. 50, 9, τῷ δακτύλῳ νεύων.
Νέφος. 64, 4, νεφῶν σύνοικος. 115, 9, ἔκριψε νέφεσιν. 115, 12, χρείη νεφῶν.
Νεωστί. 4, 1, ἢν νεωστὶ βεβλήκει. 26, 2, ἐσπαρμένην νεωστί.
Νή. 53, 4, νὴ τὸν Πᾶνα.
Νηδύς. 107, 5, νηδὺν πιαίνειν.
Νήπιος. 16, 1, ἠπείλησε νηπίῳ τίτθῃ. 88, 17, παισὶ νηπίοις. [72, 21.]
Νίζω. 2, 10, τοὺς πόδας ἔνιζον.
Νικάω. 15, 10, λέγων ἐνίκα. 15, 13, πέπαυσο, νικᾷς. 31, 3, γαλαῖ ἐνίκων. 44, 3, οὐκ ἔδοξε νικήσειν. 36, 10, μαχομένη πνοαῖς ἐνικήθης. 131, 11, σμικρὰ παίξας τὴν στολὴν ἐνικήθη. 134, 8, τὸ φρονοῦν ἐνικήθη.
Νίκη. 1, 6, μηδ' ἐπελπίσῃς νίκη. 56, 6, Ζεὺς οἶδε τὴν νίκην. 68, 9, τόξου νίκην ἔλαβε. 72, 15, παρεῖχε τὴν νίκην. [31, 21, νίκη δ' ἐπ' αὐτοῖς εἰστήκει.]
Νίνος. B. 3, ἐπὶ Νίνου.
Νιφετός. 131, 12, νιφετὸς ἐπῆλθε.
Νίφω. 41, 5, ἔνιφεν ὁ Ζεύς.
Νοέω. [107, 16, εὖ νοοῦσιν ἀνθρώποις.]
Νομαῖος. 23, 4, Ἑρμῇ νομαίῳ.
Νομεύς. 128, 1, εἶπε πρὸς νομῆα.
Νομή. 37, 6, ὁ βοῦς εἰς νομὰς ἀπεζεύχθη.
Νομίζω. 16, 4, τὴν γραῦν ἀληθεύειν νομίσας. 18, 5, νομίζων συλήσειν.
Νόμος. 118, 10, νόμοι καὶ θέμιστες ἀνθρώπων. [106, 7, ἐφίλει νόμῳ ξείνων.]
Νοσέω. 75, 16, τοὺς νοσοῦντας. 78, 1, κόραξ νοσήσας. 95, 1, λέων νοσήσας.
Νοσηλεύω. 13, 8, τιθηνῶ πατέρα καὶ νοσηλεύω.
Νόσος. 46, 8, νόσῳ κατεσκλήκει. 75, 8, ἐκ νόσων ἀνασφήλας. 78, 3, νόσου ἀνασφῆλαι. 103, 3, νόσῳ κάμνων.
Νουθετέω. [119, 12, νουθετεῖν πρὸς ἀλλήλους.]
Νοῦς. 77, 12, νοῦς σοι λείπει. 95, 36, ὁ νοῦς ἐχαυνώθη. [87, 6, ἀμφίβολος νοῦς. 136, 10, προσέχειν νοῦν τέρψεσιν.]
Νύκτωρ. 49, 1, ἐκάθευδε νύκτωρ.
Νύμφη. 23, 3, ταῖς ὀρεινόμοις νύμφαις. 92, 4, ὦ πρός σε νυμφῶν. 32, 8, ἐπεδίωκεν ἡ νύμφη.
Νύμφιος. 98, 11, νύμφιος γίνου.
Νῦν. 6, 9, νῦν οὐν ὄφες με. 9, 9, ἄναυλα νῦν ὀρχεῖσθε. 25, 9, ἀψ νῦν ἴωμεν. 88, 7, νῦν ὥρη . . . καλεῖν. 88, 18, νῦν ἐστιν ὥρη. 88, 11, οὔπω καιρός ἐστιν ἀλλύειν. 15, 6, μεγίστων ἀνδρῶν νῦν τε καὶ θεῶν. 24, 6,

μόνος νῦν αὐλίνει. 30, 9, τἀμὰ νῦν ταλαντεύῃ. 93, 10, νέμεσθαι μηδὲ νῦν. 95, 7, νῦν οὐκ ἰσχύω. 95, 61, νῦν μὲν οὔτι χαιρήσεις. 95, 75, καὶ νῦν ἐκεῖνος θυμοῦται. 101, 6, τοσοῦτον ὡς σὺ νῦν. 126, 9, ὁ νῦν βίος. 131, 18, κἀμέ νῦν διεψεύσω. 89, 9, μέχρι νῦν. Α. 17. [106, 24, τὰ νῦν παρόντα. 126, 7, νῦν δ' ἐξελήλυθε.]
Νύξ. 63, 6, νυκτὸς ἐν μέσαις ὥραις. [116, 1, νυκτὸς μεσούσης.]
Νωθείη. 95, 69, ἐγείρειν τῆς πάροιθε νωθείης.
Νωθής. 95, 18, ἄρκος νωθής. 115, 1, νωθὴς χελώνη.
Νωθρός. 16, 7, νωθραῖς ἐλπίσιν. 95, 2, νωθρὰ γυῖα.
Νῶτον. 12, 16, τί σε δροσίζει νῶτον στίβη. 18, 8, πέτρης νῶτον ἐξοχῇ κλίνας. 41, 1, ἐκ μέσου νώτου. 76, 10, σάγην νώτοις ἔφερεν. 95, 59, φρὶξ ἐπέσχε νῶτα. 111, 20, βαστάσας νώτοις. 115, 10, οὖλον ὄστρακον νώτων. 125, 4, τὸ νῶτον ἠλγήκει. 129, 18, νώτοις ἐπεμβάς.

Ξεῖνος. 106, 7, ἐφίλει νόμῳ ξείνων.
Ξενίη. 74, 8, ξενίης ἀμοιβήν.
Ξένος. 11, 2, ξένη αἰκίη. 74, 17, ξένοισιν οὐ χαίρει. [106, 27, εἴ τις ξένος πελάζοι.]
Ξηρός. 88, 6, ξηρὸν θέρος.
Ξόανον. 138, 1.
Ξουθός. 118, 1, ξουθή χελιδών.
Ξύλινος. 119, 1, ξύλινον Ἑρμῆν.
Ξύλον. 125, 3, τῷ ξύλῳ παίων.
Ξύω. 6, 1, πᾶσαν ἤονα ξύων.

Ὁ, ἡ, τό. Relative.—61, 6, τὰ δ' εἶχον ἀντέδωκαν.
Ὄγκος. 28, 7, εἰ τοιοῦτον ἢν ὄγκῳ. 34, 6, γαστρὸς ὄγκον ἀλγήσας.
Ὀγκόω. 86, 3, γαστὴρ ὠγκώθη. 111, 19, ὁ φόρτος ὠγκώθη.
Ὅδε, ἥδε, τόδε. 2, 3, μή τις παρόντων τήνδ' ἔκλεψεν. 6, 8, πρὸς τῇδε πέτρῃ. 65, 5, ταῖσδε ταῖς καταχρύσοις (πτέρυξιν). 107, 5, νηδὺν σαρκὶ τῇδε πιαίνειν. 107, 8, χάριν σοι τήνδε τίσω. 122, 14, τάδε πάσχω. 126, 5, ἡ δ' εὐθὺ πρὸς τάδ' εἶπεν. 131, 9, ἰδού, χελιδὼν ἥδε. B. 16, τήνδε βίβλον ἀείδω. 50, 3, τῇδε φεύγει. 130, 5, ἧκε τῇδε. [116, 2, γυνὴ ἀκούει τοῦδε. 116, 14, τῇδ' ἐραθύμει.]
Ὁδεύω. 15, 2, κοινῶς ὁδεύων. 100, 1, μέλλων ὁδεύειν.
Ὁδηγέω. 11, 5, εἰς ἀρούρας ὡδήγει. 95, 55, δεικνύων ἂν ὡδήγει.

Ὁδοιπορέω. 18, 3, ἀνδρὸς ὁδοιποροῦν- τος. 126, 1, ὁδοιπορῶν ἄνθρωπος.

Ὁδός. 8, 4, ἡ ὀρθὴ τῶν ὁδῶν. 48, 1, ἐν ὁδῷ τις Ἑρμῆς. 80, 3, ἐν ὁδῷ βαίνειν. 111, 4, τῆς δ' ὁδοῦ προκοπ- τούσης.

Ὁδούς. 17, 6, οὐδεὶς ὀδόντας εἶχε. 98, 8, ἠλίκους φέρεις ὀδόντας. 98, 13, ἐξεῖλε τοὺς ὀδόντας. 107, 13, ὀδοῦσι βρόχον κείρας. 122, 10, ὀδοῦσιν ἄκ- ροις. Β. 14, τῶν ἰάμβων τοὺς ὀδόντας.

Ὀθνεῖος. 66, 5, ὀθνείων κακῶν.

Ὁθούνεκα. 25, 3, πεσεῖν εἰς ὕδωρ ὁθούνεκ' εἰσίν κτε.

Οἶδα. 2, 16, μή τις οἶδεν ἀνθρώπων. 13, 10, οὐκ οἶδα. 17, 5, πολλοὺς οἶδα θυλάκους ἰδὼν ἤδη. 56, 6, Ζεὺς οἶδε τὴν νίκην. 95, 14, ὁ λέων, οἶδας, ἐστὶ γείτων, see note. 120, 5, οἴων τάχ' οὐδεὶς οἶδεν. 124, 19, οἶδα χρήσιμόν σ' ὥραις. 137, 7, τίς οὐκ οἶδεν Ἄττιν ; 2, 14, ὁ θεὸς ἂν εἰδείη. 25, 4, μοῦνον εἰδότες φεύγειν. 58, 3, εἰδέναι σπεύδων. 95, 38, τὸ μέλλον οὐκ ᾔδει. 119, 10, εὐσέβειαν οὐκ ᾔδει. Λ. 7, καὶ λόγους ᾔδει. 48, 8, χάριν εἴσομαί σοι. [63, 12, αὐτὸς οἶδας ἂν θύσῃς.]

Οἴκαδε. 105, 2, ἐκόμιζεν οἴκαδε.

Οἰκεῖος. [38, 10, ὑπ' οἰκείων. 72, 19, κόσμον οἰκεῖον.]

Οἰκέω. 12, 15, ὁμώροφόν μοι δῶμα οἴκει. 59, 6, ἐν θεοῖς ᾤκει. 95, 1, δρυμὸν οἰκούσης. 120, 6, Ὄλυμπον οἰκεῖ.

Οἰκίη. 17, 1, ὄρνεις οἰκίης. 59, 13, ἔψεγε τὸ τῆς οἰκίης. 74, 2, οἰκίην ἐς ἀνθρώπου.

Οἰκοδέσποινα. 10, 5.

Οἴκοι. 66, 8, τὰς οἴκοι συμφοράς.

Οἶκος. 5, 4, ἐς οἴκου γωνίην. 12, 11, πρὸς οἶκον ἀνθρώπων. 34, 6, κἀπηλθ' ἐς οἴκους. 58, 5, πρὸς θεῶν οἴκοις. 63, 1, κατ' οἴκους. 72, 2, ἐν θεῶν οἴκοις. 108, 15, εἰς οἶκον ἐλθεῖν. 118, 3, γέροντος οἶκος. 135, 1, ἐντρέχειν οἴκῳ. 12, 23, οἶκος πας κάπίμιξις ἀν- θρώπων. 27, 6, πάντα οἶκον ἠρήμους. 95, 97, πάντα οἶκον ἠρεύνα. 51, 1, ἐν τῷ ποτ' οἴκῳ. 59, 4, ποιεῖ Παλλὰς οἶκον. 45, 12, ἦλθεν εἰς οἴκους. [95, 101, ἦλθεν εἰς οἴκους.]

Οἰκόσιτος. 108, 4.

Οἰκότριψ. 107, 2.

Οἴμοι. 7, 14, οἴμοι τῆς κακῆς γνώμης. 95, 78 ; 118, 9. 122, 4, οἴμοι, λύκος εἶπεν.

Οἶμος. [116, 8, αὐτὸς ἦλθεν εἰς οἶμον.]

Οἰμώζω. 129, 10, περισσὸν οἰμώξας. [52, 6, μακρὸν οἰμώζων.]

Οἰνάς. 34, 2, ἄλω οἰνάσιν κατεστρώκει.

Οἶνος. 34, 3, πίθους οἴνου. 63, 3, καταβρέχων οἴνῳ.

Οἴομαι. 19, 8, ὡς ᾤμην. 97, 12, ᾤμην ὅμοιον (conj).

Οἷος. 5, 2, θυμὸν οἷον ἀνθρώποις. 18, 4, οἷος ἐκ Ὀρᾴκης. 95, 82, πρόβατον οἷον ἐκ ποίμνης. 117, 5, οἷα συμβαίνει. 117, 11, δικαστὰς οἷος εἶ σύ. 120, 5, φαρμάκων οἷων τάχ' οὐδεὶς οἶδεν. 129, 22, ἔτλην οἷα χρή με. 29, 3, ἐκ δρόμων οἷων καμπτῆρας οἷους γυρεύω. 37, 3, μύχθον οἷον ὁπλεύεις.

Οἶς. 128, 1, ὄϊς. 132, 1, ὄϊν. 132, 5.

Οἰστός. 1, 9.

Οἴχομαι. 97, 9, ᾤχετ' εἰς ὄρος.

Ὀκλαδιστί. 25, 7, ὀκλαδιστὶ πηδών- των.

Ὀκλάζω. 76, 16, ὀκλάσας ἔπιπτεν. 112, 4, ὀκλάσας ἐκοιμήθη.

Ὄλβος. 74, 13, ὄλβον ἀθροίσας.

Ὄλεθρος. 33, 5, ψάρες ὄλεθρος σπερ- μάτων. 122, 3, δείσας ὄλεθρον.

Ὀλίγος. 126, 6, παρ' ὀλίγοις ἀνθρώ- ποις.

Ὀλισθάνω. 115, 5, ὤλισθεν εἰς ῥεῖθρον.

Ὀλκή. 51, 6, πόσην ὀλκὴν αἷμα προσ- θήσει.

Ὅλος. 111, 12, καὶ πάλιν δ' ὅλους τήξας.

Ὄλυμπος. 120, 6, Ὄλυμπον οἰκεῖ.

Ὁμιλέω. 7, 4, ἐλθὼν πρὸς τὸν ἵππον ὡμίλει. 15, 2, ὡμίλει. Α. 11, πρὸς γεωργὸν ὡμίλει. 101, 4, τοῖς λέοισιν ὡμίλει. 131, 10, τοῖς κύβοισιν ὡμίλει. [13, 13, κακοῖς ὁμιλῶν.]

Ὅμιλος. 25, 6, βατράχων ὅμιλον. 106, 6, θηρῶν ὅμιλος.

Ὄμμα. 59, 9, τῶν ὀμμάτων. 134, 5, χωρὶς ὀμμάτων.

Ὄμνυμι. 50, 6, ὁ δ' οὐ προδώσειν ὤμνυ'. 95, 82, ὄμνυμί σοι φύλλα πάντα . . . ὡς οὐδὲν ἐχθρὸν οἶδεν.

Ὅμοιος. 24, 8, ὅμοιον αὐτῷ παιδίον. 95, 23, κέρας δένδροις ὅμοιον. 97, 12, ὅμοιον θῦμα τῷ μαγειρείῳ. Β. 11, γρίφοις ὁμοίας ποιήσεις. 85, 18, ὅμοια πάντ' ἔχοντες ἀλλήλοις. 72, 18, τὰ δ' ἀλλ' ὁμοίως.

Ὁμοῦ. 13, 14, ὁμοῦ αὐτοῖς ἡλώκει. 43, 8, ἄνδρας ὁμοῦ σαγήναις καὶ σκύλαξιν. 44, 3, ὁμοῦ ὄντας. 95, 46, ὁμοῦ αὐτὸν λιμὸς εἶχε καὶ λύπη. 117, 5, καὶ ταῦθ' ὁμοῦ λέγοντος.

Ὁμοφρονέω. 47, 11, ἢν ὁμοφρονῆτε.

Ὄμφαξ. 19, 8, ὄμφαξ ὁ βότρυς.

Ὁμώροφος. 12, 15, ὁμώροφόν μοι δῶμα (?).

Ὅμως. 124, 20, ὅμως δεῖ σχεῖν τι.

Ὄναγρος. 67, 1.

Ὀνείη. 7, 13, τὴν ὀνείην ἐκδείρας.

Ὄνειος. 129, 12, φάτνης ὀνείης.

Ὀνείρειος. 30, 8, ἐν πύλαις ὀνειρείαις.
Ὄνθος. [40, 2.]
Ὀνίνημι. [45, 14, οὐκ ὤνατο, vide ὠνέω.]
Ὄνος. 7, 3; 55, 1; 55, 4; 62, 6; 66, 2; 76, 18; 76, 19; 111, 1; 111, 4; 111, 8; 111, 17; 122, 1; 125, 1; 125, 4; 129, 1; 129, 5; 137, 2; 137, 13; 138, 1. [133, 1.]
Ὄντως. 15, 9, τύχης θείης ὄντως λέλογχεν. 16, 6, λύκος χανὼν ὄντως. 88, 18, ὥρη νῦν ἐστὶν ὄντως.
Ὄνυξ. 77, 6, ὄνυξι κατισχύεις. 95, 40, ὄνυξιν οὔατ᾽ ἐσπάραξεν. 98, 7, ἡλίκους ὄνυχας φέρεις.
Ὀξύνω. 76, 13, σίδηρον ὀξύνειν.
Ὀξύς. 6, 15, ὀξέῃ σχοίνῳ. 40, 1, πόταμον ὀξὺν ὄντα τῷ ῥείθρῳ. 77, 4, ὀξέῃ γλήνῃ. 17, 4, ὀξύ φωνήσας. [73, 1, ὀξέην κλαγγήν. 133, 1.]
Ὀξύφωνος. 12, 3, ἀηδόν᾽ ὀξύφωνον. 12, 19, id.
Ὀπή. 31, 19, τῆς ὀπῆς ἔσω. 112, 5, παρὰ τὴν ὀπήν.
Ὄπισθε(ν). 50, 1, τῆς δ᾽ ὄπισθε φευγούσης κυνηγὸς ἐτρόχαξεν. 66, 6, τὴν ὄπισθεν πήρην. 134, 10, οὐρὴ δ᾽ ὄπισθεν ἡγεμὼν καθειστήκει.
Ὀπίσω. [79, 6, ὀπίσω.]
Ὁπλίτης. 76, 17, ἔντασσε πεζοῖς σαυτὸν ὁπλίταις. B. 8, ἵππον ὁπλίτην.
Ὁποῖος. 95, 23, κέρας οὐχ ὁποῖα τῶν ταύρων. 128, 9, κύνα τρέφων ὁποῖα σαυτόν. 129, 14, σαίνων ὁποῖα καὶ θέλων περισκαίρειν.
Ὅπου. 12, 13, κατοικήσεις ὅπου. 91, 3, σπήλυγγα ὅπου. 118, 3, ἐν τοίχῳ ὅπου. 118, 10, ὅπου εἰσὶν . . . ἔνθεν φεύγω. 1, 15, ὅπου οὕτω πικρὸν ἄγγελον πέμπει, πῶς κτε; 112, 9, ἔσθ᾽ ὅπου τὸ μικρὸν ἰσχύει. [116, 9, ζητῶν ὅπου 'στί.]
Ὅπως. 127, 5, ἐρεινήσας ὅπως ἀναπράξει. 136, 4, δοῦναι τῆς τροφῆς ὅπως ζήσῃ. 140, 1, ὅπως ἔχῃ . . . ἐνέθηκε κτε. [42, 7, ἐρωτᾶν ὅπως ἐδείπνησεν.]
Ὁράω. 25, 10, ὁρῶ ἄλλους. 81, 1, ἣν ὁρᾷς στήλην. 85, 8, τῶν πολεμίων ὁρῶ. 132, 6, ὁρᾷς τὸν βωμόν. 131, 17, εἴθε μοι τότ᾽ οὐκ ὤφθης. [21, 12, ὁρᾶν ὀφείλει μὴ ἐξεύρῃ. 12, 27, εὐθενῶν ὀφθῇ], see εἶδον.
Ὀργάς. 12, 21, ὀρεινῆς ὀργάδος.
Ὀργή. [11, 11, ὀργῆς νέμεσις.]
Ὀρεινός. 12, 21, ὀρεινῆς ὀργάδος.
Ὀρεινόμος. 23, 3, ταῖς ὀρεινόμοις νύμφαις.
Ὀρείφοιτος. 91, 2, ποιμένων ὀρειφοίτων. 95, 25, θηρίων ὀρειφοίτων.

Ὄρθιος. 64, 4, ὀρθίη φύω.
Ὀρθός. 109, 4, ὀρθὴν ἄπελθε. [8, 4, ἡ ὀρθὴ τῶν ὁδῶν. 96, 5, ὀρθῶς μηνύει.]
Ὀρθόω. 93, 7, φρικὶ μαλλὸν ὀρθώσας.
Ὄρθρος. 30, 6, εἰς τὸν ὄρθρον. [88, 2, πρὸς ὄρθρον ἀντᾴδων.]
Ὀρίτροφος. [106, 3.]
Ὅρκος. 50, 17, τὸν Ὅρκον οὐ φεύξῃ. 93, 2, ὅρκους φέροντες.
Ὀρκόω. 2, 5, πάντας ὀρκώσων.
Ὁρμάω. 1, 11, ὥρμησε φεύγειν. 124, 4, ὥρμησε . . . θύσων. 19, 3, ὡρμήθη θιγεῖν. 135, 5, πρὸς αὐτὸν ὡρμήθη.
Ὁρμή. 6, 3, ὁρμῆς ἀφ᾽ ἱππείης.
Ὄρνεον only in gen. pl., see ὄρνις. 33, 11; 124, 9. [72, 21.]
Ὀρνιθοθήρης. 124, 1.
Ὄρνις. 77, 7; 121, 1.
ὄρνεις, acc.—17, 1; 27, 6.
ὄρνιθος. 123, 1.
ὀρνίθων. 72, 7; 124, 18.
ὄρνιν. 77, 3.
Ὄρος. 1, 1; 97, 10; 115, 9.
ὄρεσιν. 128, 6.
ὀρέων. 92, 2.
ὄρους. 36, 1; 61, 1; 87, 1.
ὀρῶν. 45, 10.
Ὀρυκτός. 120, 2, ὀρυκτοῖς εἰρίποις.
Ὀρύσσω. 108, 13, παρεὶς ἀσφάλαξιν ὀρύσσειν τὴν χώρην. 112, 3, ὤρυσσεν τοῖς κέρασι τοὺς τοίχους.
Ὀρφανός. [34, 12, ὀρφανοῦ οὐσίαν.]
Ὀρχέομαι. 9, 9, ἄναυλα ὀρχεῖσθε. 80, 2, ὀρχεῖσθαι ὑπ᾽ αὐλοῖς. 136, 8, χειμῶνος ὀρχοῦ.
Ὅς, ἥ, ὅ. 2, 12, μήνιτρα σύλων ὧν ὁ θεὸς ἐσυλήθη. 2, 15, ὁ θεὸς ὃς οὐχὶ γινώσκει. 3, 6, Πανός, ὃς ἐποπτεύει. 4, 1, σαγήνην, ἣν βεβλήκει. 5, 2, ἀλεκτορίσκων οἷς θυμὸν εἶναί φασι. 10, 12, τούτῳ χολούμαι ᾧ καλὴ φαίνῃ. 13, 12, μετ᾽ αὐτῶν μεθ᾽ ὧν ἥλως. 20, 4, τῷ Ἡρακλεῖ ὃν ἐτίμα. 22, 9, τρίχας ἃς ηὕρισκε. 27, 4, κακὴν χάριν τίνεις ὧν σ᾽ ὠφέλοιν. 28, 5, τετράφοιν ὑφ᾽ οὗ κεῖται. 32, 4, γυναικὸς ἧς τίς οὐκ ἔχειν ἦρα. 38, 6, σφῆκας ὧν ἐγὼ μήτηρ. 43, 6, νέμεσίς ἢ τὰ γαῦρα πημαίνει. 43, 14, οἱ πόδες οἷς ἐπηδοῦμην. 43, 15, τὰ κέρατα οἷς ἐγαυρούμην. 45, 6, αἶγας πλείους ὧν αὐτὸς ἦγε. 46, 3, χλόη ἐξ ἧς χιλὸν εἶχε. 46, 10, κατεσκλήκει ὃς ἂν γεγηράκει. 50, 4, ταύταις αἷς ἔκρυψεν αἰγείροις. 51, 8, μάγειρος ὃς με συντόμως θύσει. 51, 10, κουρεὺς ὃς κερεῖ με. 57, 13, γόητες ὧν ἐπὶ γλώσσης οὐδὲν κάθηται ῥῆμα. 58, 7, ἐλπίς, ἣν κατειλήφει. 61, 10, ἃ πρὶν εἶχε ζητήσει. 71, 8, ἄνεμοι ὧν ἐγὼ μέση κεῖμαι. 74, 9,

τῶν ἐτῶν ἀφ' ὧν ἔζων. 79, 5, οὔτ'
ἐκείνην εὗρεν οἶθ' ὁ βεβλήκει. 81, 1,
ἣν ὁρᾷς στήλην. 85, 6, ἀκούσαθ' οἳ
χάριν διατρίβω. 85, 8, πολεμίων ὧν
ὁρῶ γένος. 85, 12, ὃς γὰρ φίλοις
πέποιθεν οὐκ ἄγαν σπεύδει. 89, 6,
τὴν ἄρουραν ἣν ἔχω. 89, 8, πηγὴν ἣν
πίνω. 90, 4, οὗτος ὃς ἦν φορητός.
92, 9, πλεῖον οὗ χρῇζω. 93, 4, τοὺς
κύνας δι' οὓς μάχονται. 93, 10, ὑμῖν
δι' οὓς νέμεσθαι οὐκ ἔξεστι. 95, 3,
ἀλώπεχ' ᾗ προσωμίλει. 95, 94, τοῦτο
ὧν ἐκεκμήκει. 100, 7, κλοιῷ ὃν περιτέθεικε. 100, 10, τῇ τρυφῇ ταύτῃ δι'
ἣν τρίψει. 103, 19, θηρίων ἴχνη ὧν
ἐξιόντων οὐκ ἔχεις ὅ μοι δείξεις. 108,
32, βώλου ὑφ' ἣν . . τρώγω. 120, 6,
ὁ Παιήων ὃς Ὄλυμπον οἰκεῖ. 124, 5,
πέρδικα ὃν ἡμερώσας εἶχε. 134, 5,
ὀμμάτων ἢ ῥινὸς οἷς βαίνει. 136, 2,
σῖτον ὃν σεσωρεύκει. A. 2, γενεὴν ἣν
καλοῦσι χρυσείην. A. 17. B. 3,
ἀνθρώπων οἳ πρίν ποτ' ἦσαν. 24, 6,
ὃς γὰρ μόνος . . . αὐαίνει, τί μὴ πάθωμεν ἐὰν γεννήσῃ ; 7, 14, οὗ γὰρ μετασχεῖν οὐκ ἐβουλήθην, τοῦτ' αὐτό κτε.
2, 4, οὐκ ἔχων ὃ ποιήσει. 103, 19, οὐκ
ἔχεις ὅ μοι δείξεις. 112, 7, οὐκ ἔχων
ὃ ποιήσει. 16, 10, πῶς γάρ, ὃς γύναικι
πιστεύω ; 119, 8, σκαιὸς τίς ἐσσι . . .
ὃς οὐδὲν ὠφέλεις ἡμᾶς. 50, 16, πῶς
οὐκ ἂν ὧν γε μάρτυς εἱστήκειν. 38, 5,
πῶς ἂν μεμφοίμην τὸν πέλεκυν ὅς μου
μὴ προσῆκε τῇ ῥίζῃ; 120, 8, καὶ πῶς
ἄλλον λήσῃ ὃς σαυτὸν μὴ σώξεις ; 93,
3, ὅρκους φέροντες ἐφ' ᾧ λάβωσι τοὺς
κύνας.
Latin usage.—14, 3, ἄρκος . . . πρὸς
ἣν ἀλώπηξ εἶπε. 24, 4, οὓς εἶπε παύσας φρῦνος. 47, 2, οἷς ἐπισκήπτων
ἐκέλευε. 105, 2, ᾧ λέων συναντήσας.
119, 6, ὃν συλλέγων.
[A. 4, μεθ' ἣν γενέσθαι φασί. 11,
11; 12, 28; 24, 10; 35, 8; 40, 6; 45,
14; 47, 16; 87, 7; 98, 22. 42, 8, πῶς
γὰρ ἂν κρεῖττον ὃς . . . γινώσκω. 65,
3, ταύταις ὧν σὺ τὴν χρόην σκώπτεις.
106, 10, κερδώ, μεθ' ἧς συνεζήκει. 106,
13, συσσίτοισιν, ὃς εἴ τις ἦλθεν. 140, 3.]
Ὅς, demonstrative.—30, 2, ἄνδρες, ὃς
μέν . . . ὁ δέ. 35, 3, ὃν μὲν αὐτῶν
. . . τὸν δέ.
Ὅσος. 49, 7, πάντα ὅσ' ἂν πίπτῃ.
129, 7, ὅσων χρείη. [106, 3, ὅσων
φυὴν ἔγνω.]
Ὅσπερ. 55, 6, ὅσπερ εἰώθει. [9, 12,
ὅπερ βούλει. 106, 13, ὅπερ εἷλεν ὁ
λέων.]
Ὄσπριον. 108, 17, ὀσπρίων σωρός. 137,
8, ὀσπρίων τε καὶ σίτων.

Ὅστε. 63, 9, κακῶν πάντων ἅτε σύνεστιν ἀνθρώποις.
Ὄστεον. 94, 1, ὀστοῦν. 95, 90, μυελὸν ὀστέων πίνων.
Ὅστις. 66, 6, τὴν ὄπισθεν ἥτις ἦν μείζων. 92, 5, λέοντος, ὅστις ὧδε φωλ-
ειεῖ. 115, 6, πόσον αἰετῷ δώσεις ὅστις
. . . θήσω; 137, 3, ὄνος δυσδαίμων
ὅστις φέρῃ. [22, 15; 84, 7; 95, 100.
102, 11, τὴν ἡμέρην ἥτις . . . θήσει.
103, 20.]
Ὄστρακον. 115, 10, οὖλον ὄστρακον.
127, 1, γράφοντ' ἐν ὀστράκοισιν. 127,
6, ὀστράκων κεχυμένων.
Ὅταν. 20, 8, τοῖς θεοῖς εὔχου ὅταν τι
ποιῇς καὐτός, ἡ μάτην εὔξῃ. 54, 3, ὅταν
ταῦτ' ἴδω. 54, 4, ὅταν δὲ τὴν σὴν
ὄψιν ἴδω. 124, 8, ὅταν κυνηγῇς. [9,
12; 12, 27; 34, 12; 43, 16; 98, 22.]
Ὅτε. 84, 6, οὐδ' ὅτ' ἦλθες ἐγνώκειν.
88, 19, ὅτ' αὐτὸς αὐτῷ πιστεύει. 124,
18, ὅτε δροσώδης ἐστίν. [86, 10,
γαστέρα ἡλίκην ὅτ' εἰσήεις.]
Ὅτι. 31, 5, ἐδόκοιν ὑπάρχειν αἰτίην
ταύτην ὅτι στρατηγοὺς οὐκ ἔχοιεν. 75,
16, δεινὰ ἠπείλουν ὅτι τοὺς νοσοῦντας
οὐκ ἐῶσιν. 75, 19, ἀπώμασα ὅτι σὺ
ἰατρὸς οὐκ εἶ. [71, 11.]
Ὀτλεύω. 37, 3, μόχθον οἷον ὀτλεύεις.
Οὐ in litotes.—1, 12, οὐκ ἄπωθεν. 35,
2, οὐκ ἴση. 51, 3, οὐ πόρρω. 69, 2,
οὐκ ἄπειρος. 74, 17, ξένοισιν οὐ χαίρει.
88, 12, οὐκ ἄγαν. 89, 11, οὐκ ἄδειπνος.
103, 4, οὐκ ἀληθῶς. 108, 31, οὐκ
ἀφέξομαι. 130, 1, οὐκ ἄπωθεν. 139,
3, οὐκ εὔμοιρος. [8, 3, οὐκ ἄτερ μούσης.
106, 16, οὐκ ἴσην μοῖραν.]
Interrogative.—7, 7, οὐ προάξεις ;
49, 3, οὗτος, οὐκ ἐγερθήσῃ ; 117, 10,
οὐκ ἀφέξῃ ;
With verbs—the participles being
in larger figures.—1, 14 ; 2, 4 ; 6, 7 ;
6, 14 ; 7, 15 ; 13, 5 ; 13, 10 ; 15,
11 ; 18, 6 ; 19, 6 ; 21, 9 ; 22, 2 ; 28,
2 ; 30, 5 ; 31, 5 ; 31, 18 ; 32, 4 ;
33, 17 ; 36, 7 ; 44, 3 ; 45, 10 ; 46,
10 ; 47, 8 ; 50, 6 ; 50, 9 ; 50, 11 ;
50, 16 ; 50, 17 ; 51, 9 ; 68, 2 ; 68,
8 ; 75, 16 ; 75, 21 ; 77, 7 ; 78, 5 ;
81, 4 ; 84, 5 ; 88, 19 ; 89, 2 ; 91, 5 ;
95, 38 ; 95, 73 ; 95, 98 ; 97, 4 ; 98,
5 ; 101, 3 ; 104, 7 ; 103, 14 ; 103,
19 ; 112, 7 ; 112, 9 ; 114, 7 ; 119,
10 ; 121, 4 ; 122, 9 ; 124, 3 ; 127, 9 ;
128, 12 ; 129, 23 ; 131, 17 ; 132, 4 ;
134, 8 ; 136, 6 ; 137, 7 ; 137, 8 ; B.
14. [9, 11 ; 19, 9 ; 45, 14 ; 75, 6 ;
75, 7 ; 94, 9 ; 98, 22 ; 116, 9 ;
141, 2.]
With nouns.—6, 4 ; 19, 8 ; 33, 14 ;

34, 10 ; 46, 8 ; 85, 13 ; 89, 5 ; 95,
23 ; 106, 24.
Οὗ. 50, 10, τὸν τόπον ἐδείκνυ' οὗ πανοῦργος ἐκρύφθη.
Οὐδείς. 16, 9, πῶς οὐδὲν ἄρας ἦλθες ;
17, 6, οὐδεὶς ὀδόντας εἶχε. 57, 14,
οὐδὲν κάθηται ῥῆμα. 62, 4, οὐδὲν ἧτ-
των. 71, 7, οὐδὲν αἰτίη τούτων. 95,
84, οὐδὲν ἐχθρόν. 98, 3, οὐδέν τι
δύσνουν. 119, 8, οὐδὲν ὠφέλεις.
120, 5, οἷων τάχ' οὐδεὶς οὐδέν. 122,
16, οὐδὲν ἢ μαγειρεύειν. 124, 3,
κλωβὸς εἶχεν οὐδέν. 128, 5, πλέον
οὐδέν. 134, 4, οὐδὲν ἡγήσῃ. Β. 12,
μαθόντες οὐδέν. [19, 10 ; 38, 9 ; 41,
3 ; 59, 18 ; 83, 6 ; 84, 7 ; 119, 13.]
Οὐδέ. 1, 14, οὔ με πλανήσεις οὐδ' ἐνεδρεύσεις. 11, 9, οὐδ' εἶδεν τὴν ἄλωνα
Δημήτηρ. 15, 4, μακρὴ ῥῆσις οὐδ'
ἀναγκαίη. 46, 7, οὐδ' ἐπῆεν (conj.)
47, 11, οὐδ' ἂν εἰς δύναιτο. 54, 14,
οὐδ' ἀνὴρ φαίνῃ. 57, 10, οὐδ' ἀφῆκαν.
63, 7, οὐδ' ἂν εἷς τις ἡρώων. 65, 6,
οὐδ' ἄνω φαίνῃ. 68, 2, οὐδὲ τοξεύσει.
89, 7, οὐδ' ἐβοσκήθην. 89, 8, οὐδ' ἄρα
πηγὴν ἐκπέπωκας. 90, 4, οὐδὲ σωφρονῶν. 98, 3, οὐδέν τι δύσνουν οὐδ'
ἔπουλον. 104, 7, οὐ κόσμον ἀρετῆς οὐδ'
ἐπεικείης. 102, 2, οὐδ' ὠμὸς οὐδὲ
πάντα τῇ βίῃ χαίρων. 106, 28, οὐδ'
ἑώλων γεύσομαι κρεῶν. 107, 6, οὐδ'
ἄκρων χειλῶν. 120, 5, οὐδ' ὁ παιήων.
134, 2, οὐδ' ἐφείπεθ' ἑρπούσῃ. [9, 11 ;
42, 8 ; 45, 14 ; 50, 19 ; 75, 6. 86,
9, οὐδ' ἐξελεύσῃ πρότερον.]
Οὐδέπω. 22, 2, οὐδέπω πρεσβύτης. 43,
9, δίψαν οὐδέπω παύσας.
Οὐκέτι. 25, 9, οὐκέτι χρεὼν θνήσκειν.
26, 7, οὐκέθ' ὡς πρὶν εἰώθει. 26, 11,
οὐκέτ' ἐκφοβεῖν ἔοικεν. 75, 8, οὐκέτ'
εἰσῄει. 76, 5, μισθὸν οὐκέτ' εἶχεν.
76, 10, οὐκέθ' ἱππεύων. 76, 16, οὐκέτ'
ἰσχύων. 86, 6, οὐκέτ' εἶχεν ἐκδῦναι.
95, 7, διώκειν οὐκέτ' ἰσχύω. 103, 1,
οὐκέτι σθένων βαίνειν. 134, 1, οὐκέτ'
ἠξίου.
Οὔκουν. 89, 6, οὔκουν σὺ τὴν ἄροιραν
ἣν ἔχω κείρεις ;
Οὖλος. 115, 10, οὖλον ὄστρακον.
Οὖν. 6, 9, νῦν οὖν ἄφες με. 7, 10,
τὸν ἵππον οὖν στῆσας. 22, 8, τῶν οὖν
τριχῶν ἔτιλλον. 31, 17, ἄλλοι μὲν οὖν
σωθέντες ἦσαν. 85, 16, πῶς ἂν οὖν
δυνηθείην ; 87, 5, τί οὖν σαίνεις ;
95, 16, τίς οὖν τυραννήσει ; 136, 5,
τί οὖν ἐποίεις ; 95, 26 (conj.) [59,
16 ; 134, 17.]
Οὔπερ. 111, 11, διέβαινε τὸν ῥοῦν οὖπερ
ἣν πεσὼν πρῴην.
Οὔπω. 88, 11, οὔπω καιρός ἐστι (see

note). 89, 7, οὔπω τι χλωρὸν ἔφαγον.
118, 5, οὔπω ἐπανθούντων.
Οὐρανός. 72, 1, οὐρανοῖο πορφυρῇ κῆρυξ.
Οὔρειος. 110, 3, κέρκον οὐρείην (conj.)
Οὔρεος. 129, 23, παρ' οὐρήεσσιν.
Οὐρή. 134, 1, οὐρή ποτ' ὄφεως. 134,
10.
Οὖς. 95, 70, ἔψαυσεν ὠτός. 95, 40,
οὔατ' ἐσπάραξεν.
Οὐσίη. 131, 1, οὐσίην ἀναλώσας. [34,
12.]
Οὔτε. 73, 3, οὔτε τὴν κρείσσω οὔτε τὴν
πρώτην. 79, 5, οὔτ' ἐκείνην εὗρεν οὔθ'
ὃ βεβλήκει. 84, 5, οὔτ' ἐὰν μείνῃς οὔτ'
ἢν ἀπέλθῃς οὔθ' ὅτ' ἦλθες ἐγνώκειν.
[87, 7, οὔτ' ἀπιστεῖν ἔχομεν οὔτε πιστεύειν.]
Οὗτος, substantival.—1, 4, λέων δὲ τοῦτον προυκαλεῖτο. 1, 12, τούτου δ'
ἀλώπηξ οὐκ ἄπωθεν εἱστήκει. 5, 3,
τούτων ὁ λειφθείς. 7, 1, τοῦτον εἰώθει
παρέλκειν. 10, 12, τούτῳ χολοῦμαι.
13, 3, τοῦτον πελαργὸς ἱκέτευε. 21, 6,
οὗτοι ἡμᾶς σφάξουσι. 42, 2, ὁ κύων δὲ
τούτου. 44, 2, τούτους συλλαβεῖν.
48, 2 ; 56, 7 ; 59, 1 ; 59, 5 ; 66, 2 ;
71, 9 ; 75, 1 ; 86, 13 ; 90, 3 ; 103, 9 ;
111, 3 ; 113, 4 ; 118, 6 ; 119, 2 ; 136,
3 ; 137, 5 ; A. 8. [12, 28 ; 34, 14.
39, 2, τούτοις μεσιτεύων. 87, 6.]
Fem.—1, 13 ; 31, 4 ; 47, 5 ; 65, 2 ;
70, 3 ; 70, 4 ; 85, 4 ; 95, 4 ; 130, 3 ;
131, 4 ; 131, 7. [34, 13 ; 116, 8.]
Neut.—2, 13 ; 7, 16 ; 10, 6 ; 13,
10 ; 17, 4 ; 24, 5 ; 34, 8 ; 37, 10 ;
43, 13 ; 48, 6 ; 54, 3 ; 61, 8 ; 63, 8 ;
71, 7 ; 75, 8 ; 84, 2 ; 95, 27 ; 104, 7 ;
115, 4 ; 117, 5 ; 125, 6 ; 132, 9 ; A.
14. [106, 27 ; 106, 30.]
Sundry uses.—49, 3, οὗτος, οὐκ
ἐγερθήσῃ ; 95, 28, ταῦτ' ἦλθον.
98, 10, πρὸς ταῦτα δὴ σκόπησον. [9,
12 ; 22, 14 ; 23, 9 ; 38, 8 ; 56, 8.
63, 12, πρὸς ταῦτα οἶδας. 72, 20 ;
96, 5 ; 128, 10 ; 138, 3.]
Adjectival.—26, 11, ἄνθρωπος (ἄνθρωπος) οὗτος. 50, 4, κρύψόν με
ταύταις αἷς ἔκοψας αἰγείροις. 67, 7,
ἡ τρίτη δ' αὕτη. 93, 8, καινῆς γε
ταύτης τῆς μεσιτελῆς. * 95, 94, τοῦτο
κέρδος εἶχεν ὧν ἐκεκμήκει. 100, 9, τῇ
τρυφῇ ταύτῃ. 108, 30, τὰ πολλὰ ταῦτα.
128, 8, τὴν κύνα ταύτην. 122, 9,
χάριτος οὐ φθονῶ ταύτης. 136, 5, τῷ
θέρει τούτῳ. [102, 10, ταύτην τὴν
ἡμέρην.]
Οὕτω(ς). 1, 15, οὕτω πικρόν. 95, 66,
οὕτως ἀγεννής. 100, 2, οὕτως | μέγας.
120, 8, οὕτω χλωρόν. 6, 5, οὕτως
ἱκέτευεν. 19, 7, οὕτω βουκολοῦσα. 47,

10, οὕτως εἶπεν ἦν ὁμοφρονῆτε. 95,
67, οὕτω τοὺς φίλους ὑποπτεύεις ; 124,
6, οὕτως ἱκέτευε. 52, 3, ἔφη δ' οὕτως.
56, 6, ἡ δ' εἶπεν οὕτω, 'Ζεύς' κτε.
128, 10, ἔφη δ' οὕτως. 95, 60,
ἔφη δ' οὕτως. 122, 3, οὕτως εἶπεν.
95, 83, ὄμνυμι γάρ σοι . . . οὕτω
γένοιτό σοι μόνη με δουλεύειν, ὡς οὐδὲν
κτε. 48, 4, ἀλεῖψαι βούλομαί σε μηδ'
οὕτω θεὸν παρελθεῖν. Λ. 14, μάθοις
ἂν οὕτω ταῦτ' ἔχοντα. [18, 14 ; 36,
13 ; 38, 9 ; 43, 18.]
Οὐχί. 2, 15, φῶρας οὐχὶ γινώσκει. 12,
13, γεωργοῖς, οὐχὶ θηριόις, ᾄσεις. 24,
4, οὐχὶ παιάνων τοῦτ' ἐστιν. 82, 6,
οὐχὶ τὸν μῦν δέδοικα. 90, 3, τί γὰρ
οὐχὶ ποιήσει ; 92, 1, κυνηγὸς οὐχὶ
τολμήεις. 102, 1, λέων οὐχὶ θυμώδης.
95, 61, νῦν μὲν οὐχὶ χαιρήσεις. [106,
13, οὐχὶ τῆς συνηθείης. 24, 10,
μέλλουσιν οὐχὶ χαιρήσειν.]
Ὀφείλω. [21, 12, ὁρᾶν ὀφείλει μή.]
Ὀφθαλμός. 95, 35, ψυχαὶ ἐν ὀφθαλμοῖσιν.
Ὄφις. 118, 6 ; 134, 1.
Ὀφλισκάνω. 50, 15, χάριτάς μοι
ὀφλήσεις.
Ὀφρύς. 95, 58, ἀναιδείης ὀφρὺν ἔχουσα.
Ὄχθη. 36, 5. ὄχθης ποταμίης.
Ὄχθος. 23, 6, ὄχθον ὑπερβάς.
Ὄχλος. 34, 1, ὄχλος ἀγρότης.
Ὀψέ. 30, 5, ἦν δ' ὀψέ. 127, 10, ἢν
ὀψέ τις κακῶς πράσσῃ.
Ὄψις. 54, 4, ὅταν τὴν σὴν ὄψιν ἴδω.
Ὄψον. 4, 2, σαγήνη ὄψου ποικίλου
πλήρης. 9, 2, ὄψον ἐλπίσας πολὺ
ἥξειν. 137, 6 (conj.)

Πάγη. 130, 1, πάγης οὐκ ἄπωθεν.
Παγίς. 13, 1, λεπτὰς παγίδας πήξας.
Πάγκακος. 52, 4, ὦ παγκάκιστον κτημάτων.
Πάθος. 75, 3, πάθος χρόνιον.
Παιάν. 24, 4, οὐχὶ παιάνων τοῦτ'
ἐστιν.
Παιδεύω. [103, 21, συμφοραῖς ἐπαιδεύθη.]
Παιδίον. 24, 8, παιδίον τι γεννήσῃ.
Παιδίσκος. 33, 7, τῷ δ' ἠκολούθει
παιδίσκος.
Παιήων. 120, 5, οὐδ' ὁ Παιήων.
Παίζω. 32, 9, καλῶς παίξας Ἔρως.
68, 3, ὁ Ζεὺς δὲ παίζων εἶπε. 80, 4,
πυρρίχην παίζειν. 125, 1, ὄνος τις
παίζων, 131, 11, σμικρὰ παίξας. [9,
13 ; 80, 5 ; 129, 2.]
Παῖς, pucr.—16, 5, ἕως ὁ παῖς ἐκοιμήθη. 33, 10 ; 33, 11 ; 33, 17 ; 68,
8. [18, 15 ; 116, 1 ; 116, 3 ; 116,
12.]

Puella.—98, 1, ἔρωτι παιδὸς ὡραίης.
98, 6 ; 98, 15.
Liberi.—34, 4 ; 47, 2 ; 47, 10 ; 88,
3 ; 88, 8 ; 88, 17 ; 88, 18 ; 116, 18.
B. 4, παισὶν Ἑλλήνων.
Filius.—B. 1, ὦ παῖ βασιλέως
Ἀλεξάνδρου.
Παίω. 98, 16, ἐκ χερὸς παίων. 117,
9, τῷ ῥαβδίῳ παίων. 125, 3, τῷ ξύλῳ
παίων.
Πάλαι. 9, 10, κρεῖσσον ἦν ὑμας πάλαι
χορεύειν.
Παλαιός. 12, 24, παλαιῶν συμφορῶν.
47, 1, ἐν τοῖς παλαιοῖς.
Παλαιστρίτης. 48, 5, θεὸν παλαισ-
τρίτην.
Παλαμναῖος. 82, 6, ὦ παλαμναίη.
Πάλιν. 31, 16, πάλιν δὲ φύζα κατειλ-
ήφει. 53, 8, μηδέ μοι πάλιν σιναν-
τήσαις. 61, 10, πάλιν ζητήσῃ. 95,
29, μὴ πάλιν με ζητήσῃ. 95, 47,
πάλιν κερδὼ καθικέτευεν. 111, 9, πάλιν
γομώσων. 111, 12, πάλιν τήξας.
112, 16, πάλιν δακών. 51, 10, ἔστι
μάγειρος . . . πάλιν ἐστὶ κουρεύς.
Παλίουρος. [133, 1.]
Παλλάς. 59, 4.
Πάν. 3, 6, πρὸς τοῦ Πανός. 23, 4,
Ηανί. 53, 4, νὴ τὸν Πᾶνα.
Πάνθοινος. 95, 89, δαῖτα πανθοίνην.
Πανουργίη. 57, 2, πανουργίης πάσης.
95, 52, πλέκουσα πανουργίας.
Πανοῦργος. 50, 10, ὁ πανοῦργος. 111,
17, πανούργως κατέπεσεν. [128, 14,
λησταῖον πανούργων (conj.)]
Πανταχοῦ. 70, 4, πανταχοῦ βαδιζούσῃ.
Παντοῖος. 106, 5, παντοίων θηρῶν.
Πάντως. 71, 8, ἐγὼ οὐδὲν αἴτίη . . .
ἄνεμοι δὲ πάντως. 95, 99, οὐκ εἶχε
πάντως.
Παππῷος. 81, 2, στήλη παππῴη.
Παρά, c. gen.—παρὰ τῶν ἀδελφῶν ἐπ-
εξῄτει. 49, 7, ὅσ' ἂν παρ' αὐτοῦ δυστυχῇ τις. 98, 2, παρὰ πατρὸς ἐμνήστευε. 102, 6, λαβεῖν παρ' ἀλλήλων.
C. dat.—12, 14, παρ' ἀνθρώποις
οἴκει. 49, 4, αἰτίη παρ' ἀνθρώποις.
126, 6, παρ' ὀλίγοις ἀνθρώποις. 129,
23, παρ' οὔρησσιν. 58, 2, ἔθηκεν
αὐτὸν παρ' ἀνθρώπῳ. 74, 7, παρ'
αὐτῷ συντράπεζος. 74, 4, παρ' ἑστίῃ.
120, 2, παρ' ὀρυκτοῖς εὐρίποις. 129,
8, παρὰ φάτναισι.
C. acc.—7, 10, ἵππον παρ' αὐτὸν
στήσας. 111, 2, ἄλας παρὰ θάλασσαν.
112, 5, ὀκλάσας ἐκοιμήθη παρὰ τὴν
ὀπήν.
Παράγω. 74, 4, αὐτοὺς παρῆγεν ἔνδον.
76, 15, ἵππον ὁ δεσπότης παρῆγεν.
[116, 13, ὃν καὶ λαβὼν παρῆγεν.]

Παραιτέομαι. [60, 6, ἐὰν μὴ παραιτήσῃ.]

Παραμυθία. [12, 25.]

Παραστάτης. 76, 3, παραστάτην γενναῖον.

Παρατίθημι. 74, 5, παρετίθει τι τῶν ὄντων. [106, 14, ταὐτὸν παρετίθει.]

Παρατρέχω. 32, 7, παρέδραμεν μῦς.

Πάρδαλις. 95, 18; 102, 8.

Παρεδρεύω. 16, 7, νωθραῖς ἐλπίσιν παρεδρεύσας. 95, 32, παρεδρεύειν αὐτῷ.

Πάρειμι. 2, 3, μή τις παρόντων. 28, 2, οὐ παρῆν γὰρ ἡ μήτηρ. 43, 6, παρῆν δὲ νέμεσις. 93, 1, λύκων παρῆσαν ἄγγελοί ποτ' εἰς ποίμνην. 111, 7, παρῆν εἰς τὴν μεσόγεων. 114, 2, πρὸς τοὺς παρόντας ηὔχει. 122, 2, λύκον ἰδὼν παρόντα. 128, 11, εἰ μὴ παρήμην. [21, 11, τὴν παροῦσαν πημονήν. 106, 24, τὰ νῦν παρόντα.]

Πάρειμι. 79, 2, παρῆει ποταμόν. 96, 1, λύκος παρῆει θριγκόν.

Παρέλκω. 7, 2, ἵππον παρέλκειν.

Παρέρπω. 37, 11, παρέρπεις τὸν γέροντα.

Παρέρχομαι. 19, 7, παρῆλθεν οὕτω βουκολοῦσα τὴν λύπην. 39, 2, τούτοις παρῆλθε καρκίνος μεσιτεύων. 48, 5, θεὸν παρελθεῖν. 50,12, λόγῳ πιστεύσας παρῆλθε. 91, 7, ἐπεὶ παρελθέτω ἐσω. 120, 3, εἰς γῆν παρελθών. 132, 4, ἔσω οὐ παρῆλθε τοῦ τείχους.

Παρέχω. 10, 2, παρεῖχεν αἰτούσῃ ἅπαντα. 23, 4, ἄρν' ἂν παρασχεῖν. 63, 7, ἀγαθὸν οὐδ' ἂν εἰς τις παράσχοι. 63, 11, παρέξω πολλά. 72, 15, παρεῖχε τὴν νίκην. 121, 3, ἐγὼ παρέξω πάντα.

Παρηγορέω. 103, 16, καί με μύθοις παρηγόρησον.

Παρθένος. 12, 10, καὶ παρθένοι γὰρ ἦμεν. 98, 6, παρθένων τε καὶ παίδων.

Παρίημι. 107, 9, παρῆκε τὸν ἱκέτην ζώειν. 108, 13, παρεὶς ὀρύσσειν ἀσφάλαξι τὴν χώρην.

Παρισόω. 129, 24, κυνιδίῳ παρισούμην.

Πάροιθε. 95, 69, τῆς πάροιθε νωθείης.

Πάροικος. 118, 1, ἡ πάροικος ἀνθρώπων.

Παρορμάω. 108, 19, παρωρμήθη καὶ τυρὸν ἦγεν.

Παρρησιάζομαι. 135, 12, παρρησιάζῃ.

Παρωρείη. 19, 1, βότρυς παρωρείη.

Πᾶς. 6, 1, πᾶσαν ᾐόνα ξύων. 7, 16, πᾶν ἐπιτέθεικεν ἡ χρείη. 27, 7, πάντα δ' οἶκον ἤρήμους. 31, 15, παντὸς ἐκπρεπέστατον πλήθους. 47, 6, σὺν βίῃ πάσῃ. 83, 2, πᾶσαν ἡμέρην. 86, 3, πᾶσα πλήρης. 135, 1, πᾶσαν κατ' αὐλήν. 95, 97, πᾶσαν εἰνήν, πάντα δ' οἶκον. 128, 6. 2, 5, κατῆγε

πάντας. 12, 17, πάντα καὶ κατακναίει. 18, 7, πάντα κράσπεδα. 20, 4, μόνον πάντων θεῶν. 25, 2, πάντας πεσεῖν εἰς ὕδωρ. 27, 5, πάσας ἔπνιγες δρνεις. 31, 11, ἐτάχθη πάντα. 47, 11, ὁμοφρονῆτε πάντες. 49, 6, ἐμοὶ ἐγκαλοῦσι πάντα. 56, 2, πάντα δ' ἔβλεπε κρίνων. 56, 7, πάντων καλλίων. 59, 7, πάντας ἐχθραίνων. 63, 9, κακῶν πάντων. 64, 6, ἐκπρεπεστάτη πάντων. 72, 3, πᾶσι δ' ἠκούσθη. 72, 4, πάντα δώρων ἔσχεν ἵμερον. 72, 7, πάντων ὀρνίθων. 72, 13, τὰ πάντα. 75, 2, πάντων λεγόντων. 75, 14, δεινὰ πᾶσιν ἠπείλουν. 75, 5; 75, 16; 76, 12; 77, 6; 82, 5; 85, 8; 85, 18; 88, 7; 88, 16; 95, 22; 95, 52; 95, 82; 95, 85; 102, 9; 103, 7; 108, 19; 110, 2; 110, 4; 115, 7; 121, 3; 128, 13; 131, 13; 141, 1; Λ. 12. 102, 2, πάντα τῇ βίῃ χαίρων. [22, 14. 29, 2, πᾶσαν ἑσπέρην. 38, 8; 56, 8; 96, 5.]

= παντοῖος. 10, 1, πᾶσαν μάχην συνῆπτεν. 57, 2, πανουργίης πάσης. 60, 3, πάσης τρυφῆς. 122, 11, πόνων κάμῃς πάσης. 129, 11, ἁβρότητι σὺν πάσῃ.

7, 11, πᾶσαν τὸν γόμον. 74, 15, πᾶς ὁ γηράσας. 111, 19, πᾶς ὁ φόρτος. 134, 12, πᾶν τὸ σῶμα. 95, 19, τὸ πᾶν ἐρημαίῃ. [116, 7.]

2, 8, τὰ πάντ' ἐποπτεύων. 34, 9, τὰ σπλάγχνα πάντα. 56, 1, πᾶσι τοῖς ζῴοις. 58, 1, τὰ χρηστὰ πάντα. 102, 7, τὰ ζῷα πάντα. 120, 3, πᾶσι τοῖς ζῴοις. 134,7, τὰ πορευτὰ πάντα. 93, 5, τὰ πάντα βληχώδης.

10, 7, καθ' ἡμέρην πᾶσαν. 12, 23, οἶκός μοι πᾶς πάντα ἀναξαίνει. 24, 6, λιβάδα πᾶσαν αὐαίνει. 95, 71, πᾶσαν ἐντολήν. 137, 5, πᾶσαν περιόντες κώμην. [56, 9, πᾶς τις.]

Πάσσαλος. 17, 2, τί μὴ πάθωμεν ἀπηρτήθη.

Πάσχω. 24, 7, τί μὴ πάθωμεν; 47,14, πείσεσθε ταῦτα τῇ ῥάβδῳ. 131, 3, μὴ πάθοι τι ῥιγώσας. 122, 14, σὺν δίκῃ πάσχω. [38, 10; 94, 10.]

Πατέω. 122, 1, ὄνος πατήσας σκόλοπα.

Πατήρ. 13, 8, τιθηνῶ πατέρα. 54, 3, πατὴρ γίνῃ. 62, 6, ὄνου πατρὸς ὤν. 88, 9, τῷ πατρὶ μηνύει. 95, 70, ὡς πατὴρ ἀποθνήσκων. 98, 2, παρὰ πατρὸς ἐμνήστευτε.

Πατρῷος. 81, 2, στήλη πατρῴη.

Παύω. 24, 2, οὓς παύσας. 43, 9, δίψαν οὐδέπω παύσας. 62, 5, ἔπαυσε τὸν δρόμον. 76, 4, πόλεμος ἐπαύσατο. 28, 8, παῦε, μὴ πρίον. 16, 2, παῦσαι, μή σε ῥίψω. 15, 13, πέπαυσο, νικᾷς.

Παχύς. 50, 13, παχείης αἰγείρου. 76, 7, κορμοὺς παχεῖς. 28, 5, πάχιστον τετράπουν.

Πεδίον. 43, 10, μακρὸν πεδίον. 46, 2, πεδίων ἐν χλόῃ βαθυσχίνῳ.

Πεζός. 76, 17, πεζοῖς ὁπλίταις.

Πειθώ. [18, 16, ἀνύσεις τι πειθοῖ.]

Πείθω. 95, 34, τὰ μικρὰ πείθει τοὺς ἐν ἐσχάταις ὥραις. 95, 87, τὴν ἀχαιίνην ἔπεισεν ἐλθεῖν. 108, 14, τὸν μῦν πείσας ἐλθεῖν. 134, 8, τὴν δ' οὐκ ἔπειθε. 88, 12, οὐ φίλοις πέποιθεν. [116, 12, τὸν παῖδα πεῖσον εὕδειν.]

Πεινάω. 16, 6, πεινῶν καὶ λύκος χανών. 46, 3, χιλὸν εἶχε πεινήσας. 86, 8, ἄχρι πεινήσῃς. 95, 92, εἱστήκει πεινῶσα. 95, 5, πεινῶ ἔλαφον. [79, 6, πεινῶσα.]

Πείνη. 137, 4, πείνης ἄκος.

Πειράω. 95, 76, ἄπιστον πειράσας σε καὶ κούφην. 47, 6, πειρᾶσθε δή μοι κατάξαι. 47, 9, κατὰ μίην πειρᾶσθε. 106, 4, φιλοφρονεῖσθαι ἐπειρᾶτο. 134, 16, κακῆς ἔριδος ἐπειράθην. 57, 12, ὡς ἐπειράθην. [59, 17, πειρῶ τι ποιεῖν.]

Πείρω. 6, 15, πείρων αὐτὸν σχοίνῳ.

Πέλαγος. 71, 3, ὦ πέλαγος.

Πελάζω. 106, 27, εἴ τις ξένος πελάζοι.

Πελαργός. 13, 3; 13, 4; 13, 6; 13, 9. 13, 7, πτηνῶν πελαργὸς εὐσεβέστατον.

Πέλας. 59, 12, βλέπειν τὸ τοῦ πέλας. [13, 14, τοὺς πέλας.]

Πέλεκυς. 37, 12, πέλεκυς. 38, 5, τὸν πέλεκυν. 141, 2, id. [64, 8, τῶν πελέκεων.]

Πέλυξ. 64, 9, τῶν πελύκων.

Πελώριος. 36, 3, πελώριον φύτευμα.

Πέμπτος. [A. 5, πέμπτης γενεῆς, conj.]

Πέμπω. 1, 15, πικρὸν ἄγγελον πέμπει. 93, 6, πέμπειν κύνας. [23, 10, εὐχὴν πέμπειν.]

Πένης. [107, 17, σώζειν πένητας.]

Πενθερός. 98, 14.

Πένταθλος. 137, 3, πτωχοῖσι τοῖσδε πεντάθλοις (conj.)

Πέπειρος. 19, 5, (ὥρη) πέπειρος. 19, 8, ὀμφαξ ὁ βότρυς οὐ πέπειρος.

Πεποίθησις. [43, 19, αἱ πεποιθήσεις.]

Περάω. 43, 10, ἑπέρα πεδίον.

Πέρδιξ. 124, 4, πέρδικα. 124, 11; 135, 1.

Περί. [43, 16, περὶ τῶν σεαυτοῦ πραγμάτων.]

Περιβάλλω. 11, 2, ξένῃ περιβαλεῖν αἰκίῃ.

Περίειμι. 137, 6, κύκλῳ κώμην περιόντες.

Περιλαμβάνω. 98, 9, τίς κόρη σε τολμήσει περιλαβεῖν;

Πέριξ. 23, 4, τοῖς πέριξ.

Περισκαίρω. 129, 3, δεσπότην περισκαίρων. 129, 14.

Περισσεύω. 108, 10, ὑπάρχει πολλὰ καὶ περισσεύει. 128, 4, μῆλά σοι περισσεύει.

Περισσός. 31, 19, τὰ περισσὰ κάρφη. 35, 5, ὡς περισσὰ ἐκβάλλει. 108, 29, περισσοῖς δείπνοις. 131, 8, περισσῶν ἐσθίων. 129, 10, περισσὸν οἰμώξας. 70, 3, περισσῶς ἠράσθη.

Περιτίθημι. 100, 7, κλοιόν μοι περιτέθεικε.

Περιτρέχω. 128, 13, περιτρέχουσα κωλύω.

Πέρνυσι. 89, 4, σὺ δή με πέρνυσι ἐβλασφήμεις.

Περυσινός. 89, 5, ἐγὼ οὐ περισινός.

Πέταυρον. 124, 13, ἐκ πεταύρου.

Πέτομαι. [58, 6, ἐκεῖ πέτεσθαι.]

Πετραῖος. 6, 6, πρὸς τῇδε πέτρῃ. 12, 20, πέτραις ἀοικήτοις. 18, 8, πέτρης ἐξοχῇ. 72, 5, πέτρης αἰγὶ δυσβάτου. 109, 2, ὑγρῇ πέτρῃ. 134, 11, κοιλὸν πέτρης βάραθρον. 134, 13, τὴν ἄκανθαν ταῖς πέτραισι συντρίβει. A. 9, ἐλάλει πέτρῃ.

Πεύκη. 38, 1, ἀγρίην πεύκην. 95, 5, ἀγρίαις πεύκαις. 92, 3, μακρῆς πεύκης. 38, 4; A. 9.

Πηγή. 89, 8, πηγὴν ἐκπέπωκας.

Πήγνυμι. 13, 1, αὔλαξι παγίδας πήξας. 68, 6, βέλος ἔπηξεν ἐντὸς κήπων. 128, 3, γάλα πῆξαι.

Πηδάω. 5, 5, εἰς τὸ δῶμα πηδήσας. 19, 4, πηδῶσα ποσσίν. 25, 7, ὀκλαδιστὶ πηδώντων. [19, 6, ἀλλ' ἔκαμνε πηδῶσα.]

Πηλίκος. 69, 4, ὁ πηλίκος σου εὑρέθη θάσσων.

Πήλινος. 31, 13, πηλίνων τοίχων.

Πημαίνω. 43, 6, νέμεσις ἢ τὰ γαῦρα πημαίνει.

Πημονή. [21, 11, τὴν παροῦσαν πημονήν.]

Πήρη. 2, 10, ἀπέθεντο τὰς πήρας. 66, 3, δύω πήρας κρεμάσαι. 86, 2, ῥωγὰς αἰπόλου πήρη. 86, 4, τὴν πήρην.

Πηρός. [10, 14, φρένας πηρός.]

Πηρόω. 137, 7, Ἀττιν, ὡς ἐπηρώθη.

Πιαίνω. 107, 5, νηδὺν πιαίνειν.

Πίθηκος. 35, 1; 56, 3; 81, 1; 106, 11; 106, 30; 125, 5.

Πίθος. 34, 3, πίθοις οἴνου. 58, 1, ἐν πίθῳ συλλέξας. 108, 17, πίθοι σύκων.

Πίθων. 56, 4, πίθωνα γυμνὸν σιμόν.

Πικρός. 1, 15, πικρὸν ἄγγελον. 12, 9, πικρὸς δαίμων. A. 19, πικρῶν ἰάμβων.

Πιμελής. 100, 1, πιμελὴς κύων.

Πίμπλημι. 37, 8, βωμὸν αἵματος
πλῆσων. 61, 2, κύρτον ἰχθύων πλήσας.
6, 10, πλησθεὶς φυκίων. 60, 4, τρυφῆς
πέπλησμαι.
Πινντός. 17, 3, ἀλέκτωρ πινυτός.
Πίνω. 28, 1, βοῦς πίνων. 36, 5, ὕδωρ
πίνων. 43, 2, λίμνης ὕδωρ ἔπινεν.
75, 14, τῆς Λήθης πίνοντες. 80, 1,
δεσπότης πίνων. 95, 90, μυελὸν ὀστέων
πίνων. 89, 8, πηγὴν ἣν πίνω. 60, 3,
βέβρωκα καὶ πέπωκα.
Πιπράσκω. 29, 1, ἵππος εἰς ἄλητον
ἐπράθη. 137, 1, γάλλοις εἰς τὸ κοινὸν
ἐπράθη ὄνος. 30, 5, οὐκ ἐπεπράκει.
Πίπτω. 7, 9, πεσὼν ἔκειτο. 34, 7,
πεσὼν ἐπ' ἀγκάλαις. 49, 4, σοῦ πεσόντος. 95, 93, καρδίην λάπτει πεσοῦσαν. 111, 11, οὕπερ ἦν πεσών. 25,
2, εἰς μέλαν πεσεῖν ὕδωρ. 34, 9,
σπλάγχνα πάντα μοι πίπτει. 36, 8,
πῶς οὐκ ἐπεπτώκει; 49, 7, δυστυχῇ
τις ἢ πίπτῃ. 76, 16, ὁ δ' ὀκλάσας
ἔπιπτεν. [131, 16, ὑπὸ τοῦ κρύους
πεσοῦσαν.]
Πιστεύω. 16, 10, ὃς γυναικὶ πιστεύω.
50, 11, τῷ λόγῳ πιστεύσας. 88, 19,
οὐ φίλοισι πιστεύει. 98, 12, τῇ δόσει
πιστεύσας. 99, 5, σοὶ μὴ μένοντι
πιστεύω. [87, 7, οἷς πιστεύειν.]
Πίστις. [99, 4, μὴ μεθιέναι πίστιν.]
Πλάγιος. 109, 2, πλάγια κῶλα σύρειν.
Πλανάω. 1, 14, οὔ με πλανήσεις.
Πλάσσω. 66, 2, πλάσασθαι ἄνθρωπον
ἐκ γῆς.
Πλατύς. 34, 2, ἄλω πλατεῖαν.
Πλειάδες. 33, 1, δυσμαὶ Πλειάδων.
Πλεῖστος. 9, 6, ἰχθύας πλείστους.
111, 14, πλείστους σπόγγους. 26, 8,
τὰς πλείστας. 117, 8, τοὺς πλείστους.
Πλείων. 18, 11, προσθήσει τὴν ἀλήν
πλείω. 45, 2, πολὺ πλείους. 111, 9,
πλείω ἔτ' ἐπετίθει τὸν φόρτον. 128,
5, πλέον οὐδὲν ἡμῖν. 68, 2, οὐκ ἂν
βάλοι τις πλεῖον. 92, 9, μή μοι χαρίζου
πλείον. 95, 76, ἐκεῖνος πλεῖον σὺ
θυμοῦται. Β. 10, οὐδὲν πλεῖον ἢ γεγωνίσκειν. 48, 8, καὶ πλέον με μὴ τίμα.
[5, 11 ; 19, 10 ; 119, 3.]
Πλέκω. 95, 52, πλέκουσα τέχνας.
Πλέω. 71, 9, ἣν ἴδῃς μὲ καὶ πλεύσῃς.
71, 3, εἴθε μήποτ' ἐπλεύσθης.
Πλῆθος. 31, 15, παντὸς ἐκφανέστατοι
πλήθους. 33, 3, ἔθνος, ἄκριτον πλήθει.
108, 16, ἀλφίτων πλήθη. [12, 26,
φυγὴ πλήθους.]
Πλήν. 6, 16, τὰ μικρά, πλὴν βέβαια.
95, 24, πλὴν ἐκυρώθης.
Πλήρης. 1, 3, φόβου δρόμος πλήρης.
4, 2, ὄψου πλήρης. 5, 3, τραυμάτων
πλήρης. 10, 3, χρυσίου πλήρης. 11, 7,

ἐλπίδων πλήρης. 31, 2, αἱμάτων πλήρη.
33, 17, λίθων πλήρη. 71, 1, ναυτίλων
πλήρη. 86, 3, κρεῶν πλήρης. 95, 6,
φόβου πλήρη. 97, 6, θερμοῦ πλήρη.
100, 3, λίπους πλήρης. 132, 6, αἵματος
πλήρη. 19, 2, πλήρεις (βότρυς).
Πληρόω. 57, 1, ἄμαξαν πληρώσας
ψευσμάτων.
Πλήσιον. 130, 3, ταύτην πλήσιον ἰδοῦσα.
Πλήσιος. 127, 4, κίβωτον σταθεῖσαν
αὐτοῦ πλησίην.
Πλήσσω. 3, 4, μακρόθεν λίθῳ πλήξας.
130, 9, ῥῖνας ἐπλήγη.
Πλοῖον. 4, 5, εἰς τὸ πλοῖον. 64, 5,
τρόπις πλοίων. 117, 3, ἐμβεβηκότος
πλοίῳ.
Πλούσιος. 6, 11, πλουσίοις δείπνοις.
108, 2, ταμείοις πλουσίοισι. [65, 8,
πλουσίᾳ σὺν ἐσθῆτι.]
Πλουτέω. 108, 28, χαῖρε καὶ πλούτει.
Πλούτων. 75, 14, ὁ μέγας Πλούτων.
Πλύνω. 9, 8, τὸν βόλον πλύνων.
Πνεῦμα. 76, 9, τὸ πνεῦμα σώζων.
122, 8, ὥς μου κατέλθῃ πνεῦμα εἰς
ᾅδου.
Πνίγω. 27, 2, γαλῆν ἔπνιγεν. 27, 6,
ἔπνιγες ὄρνεις. 60, 2, λίπει πνιγόμενος.
Πνοή. 36, 10, μαχομένη ταῖς πνοαῖς.
114, 5, πνοῇ ῥαπισθείς.
Πόη. 46, 6, τῆς πόης ἀποτρώγων.
(See ποίη.)
Πόθεν. 124, 14, πόθεν μαθήσῃ. 135,
6, πόθεν ἥκεις;
Πόθος. 32, 2, Κύπρις ἡ πόθων μήτηρ.
Ποιέω. 2, 4, οὐκ ἔχων ὃ ποιήσει. 20, 8,
ὅταν τι ποιῇς καὶτός. 59, 2, καλόν τι
ποιήσει .. ποιεῖ Ζεὺς ἄνθρωπον. 90, 3,
τί γὰρ οὐχὶ ποιήσει; 95, 78, τί ποιήσω;
112, 7, οὐκ ἔχων ὃ ποιήσει. 124, 7,
δικτύῳ τί ποιήσεις ; 125, 6, αὐτὸ τοῦτο
ποιήσας. 130, 2, τί ποιήσει ; 136, 5,
τί ἐποίεις ; 109, 4, ὀρθὴν ἄπελθε καὶ
βλέπων σε ποιήσω. 10, 11, καλήν σε
ποιούσῃ. 30, 10, νεκρὸν μ' ἢ θεὸν
ποιήσεις. 44, 5, ἐχθροὺς ἐποίει. 76,
19, ἵππον ἐξ ὄνου με ποιήσεις. 95,
64, ἄλλους βασιλεῖς ποίει. 115, 2,
κἀμὲ πτερωτὴν πεποιήκει. 104, 3,
πρόδηλον εἶναι πεποιήκει. 63, 5, τὸν
σύνοικον ἀγαθὰ δαψιλῆ ποιεῖ. [33,
24, ἄλεα ἔργα ποιούντων. 41, 3, οὐδὲν
ἄλλο ποιήσεις. 52, 7. 116, 7, ἐποίει
τὴν προθυμίην πᾶσαν. 110, 2, πάνθ'
ἐποίει ποίει.]
Ποίη. 95, 11, μαλθακῆς ὑπὲρ ποίης.
128, 12, ἄφθονον ποίην. 142, 2, χλωρὴν λειμακος ποίην.
Ποίησις. Β. 11, ἄλλοι ἐκφέρουσι ποιήσεις.

N

Ποιητέος. 1, 8, τί σοι ποιητέ' ἐστίν.
Ποιητός. 95, 36, λόγοισι ποιητοῖς.
Ποικίλος. 124, 4, πέρδικα ποικίλον.
140, 2, ποικίλας γραφὰς ζῴων. 72,
13, ποικίλως ἐκοσμήθη. 103, 15,
ποικίλοις μύθοις. 130, 2, βουλὰς ποικίλας. 19, 2, ποικίλη κερδώ. 4, 2,
ὄψου ποικίλου. 46, 4, ποικίλων ζῴων.
129, 3, ποικίλως περισκαίρων. [98,
18, ποικίλου τὴν γνώμην.]
Ποιμήν. 91, 2, ποιμένων ὀρειφοίτων.
95, 53, ἕκαστον ποιμένων.
Ποίμνη. 89, 1, πεπλανημένον ποίμνης.
93, 1, ἄγγελοι εἰς ποίμνην. 93, 5,
μωρὴ ποίμνη. 95, 81, πρόβατον ἐκ
ποίμνης. 105, 1, ἐκ μέσης ποίμνης.
Ποῖος. [42, 8, corrupt. 95, 100,
ποίην καρδίην ;]
Ποιότης. 28, 10, τὴν ἐκείνου ποιότητα
μιμήσῃ.
Πόκος. 51, 2, τὸν πόκον λαβεῖν μείζω.
51, 9, εἰ πόκου χρῄζεις. 128, 2, πόκους κέρσας.
Πολέμιος. 13, 2, γεράνους σποραίων
πολεμίους. 21, 2, αὐτοῖς πολεμίην
ἐπιστήμην. 85, 8, τῶν πολεμίων
γένος ἕν ἐστι.
Πόλεμος. 31, 2, ἄσπονδον πόλεμον.
76, 11, πόλεμος ἄλλος ἠκούσθη. 85,
17, εἰς πόλεμον ἄρχειν τῶν ἀσυμφώνων.
[70, 7, πόλεμος ἥξει.]
Πόλις. 2, 5, εἰς τὴν πόλιν. 12, 22,
ἄνδρα καὶ πόλιν φεύγω. 42, 1, ἐν
πόλει. 76, 7, εἰς πόλιν βαίνων. 126,
4, τὴν πόλιν ἀφεῖσα. [40, 5, πόλις ἄν
τις εἴποι. 70, 5, μὴ πόλεις ὕβρις
ἐπέλθοι.]
Πολιτείη. [39, 3, ἄδοξος ἐν πολιτείαις.]
Πολλάκις. 19, 3, πολλάκις ὡρμήθη.
76. 6, πολλάκις κατῆγε.
Πολλαχῶς. 64, 2, ἑαυτὴν πολλαχῶς
ἐπαινούσης.
Πολύς. 9, 2, ὄψον πολύ. 103, 2, πολλῷ
χρόνῳ. 57, 2, ἀπάτης πολλῆς. 11, 8,
τὸν πολὺν κόπον. 15, 7, πολὺ κρείσσων.
45, 5, πολὺ πλείους. 79, 3, πολὺ μείζω.
26, 3, ἄχρι πολλοῦ. 7, 3, πολλὰ
κάμνων. 21, 5, πολλὰ γῆς ἀροτρεύσας.
36, 4, πολὺς κάλαμος εἱστήκει. 17, 5,
πολλοὺς θυλάκους. 47, 2, πολλοὺς
παῖδας. 35, 7, πολλῶν ἀνθρώπων.
95, 21, πολλὰ εἰς ἔτη. 97, 6, πολλὰ
χαλκία. 103, 18, πολλῶν θηρίων.
108, 30, ἔχων τὰ πολλὰ ταῦτα. 117,
6, πολλῶν μυρμήκων. 119, 9, ἀγαθοῖς
πολλοῖς. 63, 11, παρέξω πολλά.
95, 24, τί σοι λέγω τὰ πολλά. 96, 2,
ἔλεγε πολλὰ βλασφήμως. 108, 10,
ἐμοὶ ὑπάρχει πολλά. 117, 4, πολλοῖς
μηδὲν αἰτίους. 5, 12 ; 24, 9 ; 29, 6 ;

71, 11. [106, 5, πολὺς ὅμιλος. 106,
23, πολλῇ μερίμνῃ. 106, 10, τὰ πολλὰ
συνεζήκει].
Πολύτιμος. [57, 9, πολύτιμον φόρτον.]
Πολύτρητος. 4, 4, δικτύου πολυτρήτου.
111, 15, σπόγγοις πολυτρήτους.
Πονέω. 37, 10, μὴ πονῶν. 95, 33,
πονοῦντα θαρσύνειν.
Πονηρίη. 104, 7, ἔλεγχον τῆς πονηρίης.
Πονηρός. 33, 23, γενός πονηρόν. 95,
78, πονηροῦ δεσπότου. 126, 9, βίος
πονηρός. 127, 9, τῶν πονηρῶν τις.
Πόνος. 38, 3, γένοιτο ὁ πόνος ῥάων.
78, 3, πόνων ἀνασφῆλαι. 94, 4,
πόνων ἄκος. 95, 44, πόνος ἐξανηλώθη.
122, 11, ἐκλυθεὶς πόνων.
Πόντος. Α. 10, ἐλάλει πόντος (conj.)
Πορεῖν. [138, 3, ἅ σοι πέπρωται.]
Πορευτός. 134, 7, τὰ πορευτὰ πάντα.
Πορθέω. 13, 11, ἔργα τάμὰ πορθοῦσαις.
Πόρος. [79, 6, τὸν πόρον διεξήει.]
Πόρρω. 51, 3, τῆς σαρκὸς οὐ πόρρω.
103, 11, πόρρω σταθεῖσα. 105, 3,
σταθεὶς πόρρω.
Πορφύρη. 10, 4, λεπτὴν πορφύρην.
Πορφυροῦς. 19, 4, πορφυρῆς ὥρης.
72, 1, Ἴρις, πορφυρῆ κῆρυξ. 118, 2,
πτερίσκοις πορφυροῖς.
Ποσειδῶν. 59, 1 ; 59, 5.
Πόσος. 51, 6, πόσην ὁλκὴν αἷμα προσθήσει ; 91, 8, πόσον τράγου μεταξὺ
καὶ πόσον ταύρου. 115, 5, πόσον
μισθὸν δώσεις ;
Πόσσος. 124, 14, πόσσον εἰς ἕω λείπει ;
Ποτάμιος. 36, 5, ὄχθης ποταμίης. 84,
4, ποταμίης ἐπ' αἰγείρου.
Ποταμός. 36, 5, δρῦν ἔδωκε ποταμῷ.
40, 1, διέβαινε ποταμόν. 79, 2, παρῆει
ποταμόν.
Πότε. 124, 16, πῶς γνώσῃ πότ' ἐννυχεύει Ὠρίων ;
Ποτέ. 3, 1 ; 6, 3 ; 9, 2 ; 10, 9 ; 21, 1 ;
28, 3 ; 29, 1 ; 31, 1 ; 32, 1 ; 33, 8 ;
51, 1 ; 58, 4 ; 72, 1 ; 85, 1 ; 89, 1 ;
93, 1 ; 94, 1 ; 95, 4 ; 95, 56 ; 97, 1 ;
102, 11 ; 105, 1 ; 115, 1 ; 117, 1 ;
121, 1 ; 127, 8 ; 128, 12 ; 134, 1 ;
134, 18 ; B. 3. [5, 10 ; 106, 1 ;
106, 17.]
Πότερος. 18, 2, ἔριν γενέσθαι πότερος
. . . ἐκδύσει. 8, 2, ἐπηρώτα πότερα
ἀναβαίνειν ἢ κάτω βαίνειν αἴροιτο.
Πού. 28, 3, ποῦ ποτ' ἦν ἐπεζήτει. 68,
8, ποῦ βάλω οὐκ ἔχω χώρην. 88, 10,
σκοπεῖν ποῦ κατασπήσει. 100, 2,
ἐξήταζε ποῦ τραφεὶς . . . ἐγίνετο.
108, 16, ἐδείξε ποῦ μὲν πλήθη, ποῦ δέ
ἦν σωρός.
Πού. 47, 4, εἴ τίς ἐστί που. 95, 54,
ἐπηρώτα μή πού τις φεύγει.

Πούς. 2, 10, τοὺς πόδας ἔνιζον. 43, 4, ποδῶν ἕνεκα. 43, 14, πόδες μ' ἴσωζον. 67, 2, ποσὶν κρείσσων. 75, 9, τοῖς ποσὶν μόλις βαίνων. 122, 7, ἐκ τοῦ ποδός μου. 134, 7, πόδ' εὐθύνει. 19, 4, πηδῶσα ποσσίν. 45, 11, ποσσὶν ἠρείνων.
Πρᾶγμα. [43, 16, περὶ τῶν σεαυτοῦ πραγμάτων. 67, 9, πρᾶγμα μηδὲν σύναπτε. 71, 11, πολλὰ χρηστὰ πράγματα.]
Πρᾷος. 102, 3, πρᾷος καὶ δίκαιος. [11, 10, χρὴ πρᾷον εἶναι.]
Πρᾳότης. [18, 15, πρᾳότητα ζηλοῦ.]
Πράσσω. 26, 12, ἄρχεταί τι πράσσειν. 119, 3, ἔπρασσε φαύλως. 127, 10, κακῶς πράσσῃ. [40, 3, κακῶς πράττω. 5, 12, τὸ μὴ καλῶς πράττειν. 33, 25, τῶν δόλῳ τι πραττόντων.]
Πρέπω. 6, 11, πλουσίοις πρέπων δείπνοις. 95, 32, ἔπρεπέ σοι παρεδρεύειν. 107, 4, πρέπει σοι πιαίνειν.
Πρεσβύτης. 22, 2; 50, 14; 98, 2.
Πρηύνω. B. 15, εὖ κέντρα πρηίνας.
Πρίασθαι. 111, 3, τούτους πρίασθαι. 135, 1, πέρδικά τις πριάμενος.
Πρίν. 26, 7, ὡς πρίν. 36, 3, τῶν πρὶν ἀνθρώπων. 61, 10, ἃ πρὶν εἶχε. 134, 14, ἡ πρὶν αὐθάδης. B. 3, οἳ πρὶν ποτ' ἦσαν. 33, 9, πρὶν λαβεῖν ἔφευγον.
Πρίω. 96, 3, τὰς σιαγόνας πρίων. 28, 3, παῦε, μὴ πρίου.
Πρό. 76, 11, πρὸ τειχῶν πόλεμος. 131, 5, πρὸ εἴαρος. 28, 4, ἄρτι, πρὸ τῆς ὥρης.
Προάγω. 7, 7, οὐ προάξεις; [85, 5, εἰ μὴ προάξῃ τὴν μάχην.]
Προαιρέω. 108, 26, ἄλλο τι προαιρήσων.
Προβαίνω. 115, 13, χαμᾶζε δυσκόλως προβαινούσῃ.
Πρόβατον. 51, 4; 51, 5; 95, 81; 105, 1; 113, 1; 113, 4.
Προβουλεύω. 85, 7, χρὴ ἀεὶ προβουλεύειν.
Προγινώσκω. [43, 17.]
Πρόδηλος. 104, 3, πρόδηλον μακρόθεν.
Προδίδωμι. 43, 15, τὰ κέρατά με προύδωκεν. 50, 6, ὁ δ' οὐ προδώσειν ὤμνυεν.
Προερέω. 7, 9, ἔκειτο νεκρός, ὡς προειρήκει.
Προέρχομαι. 57, 11, ἔτι προελθεῖν. 75, 9, προῆλθεν ὠχρός.
Προηγέομαι. 134, 3, ἐν μέρει προηγοίμην.
Προθυμίη. [116, 7, ἐποίει τὴν προθυμίην πᾶσαν.]
Προκαλέω. 31, 12, γαλῆν μῦς προύκαλεῖτο.

Προκόπτω. 111, 14, τῆς δ' ὁδοῦ προκοπτούσης.
Προκύπτω. [116, 3, θυρίδων προκύπτει.]
Προλαμβάνω. [103, 20.]
Προμηθεύς. 66, 1.
Πρόξενος. 108, 23, τὸν πρόξενον θλίβων.
Προπηδάω. 107, 12, χηραμοῦ προπηδήσας.
Πρός, c. gen.—3, 6, πρὸς τοῦ σε Πανός. 50, 3, πρὸς θεῶν σε σωτήρων. 92, 4, ὦ πρός σε νυμφῶν. 108, 11, πρός σε τῆς Ἀμαλθείης. [52, 6, κακοῦ πρὸς ἀνδρός ἐστι. 81, 5, id.] C. dat.—πρὸς τῇδε πέτρῃ. 97, 8, πρὸς τῇ θύρῃ. C. acc.—12, 11, ἐλθὲ πρὸς οἶκον ἀνθρώπων. 46, 7, ᾔει πρὸς ὕλας. 58, 5, ἀπελθεῖν πρὸς θεῶν οἴκους. 135, 10, πρὸς ἔσχατ' ἀνδύνω. 42, 3, ἐλθεῖν πρὸς αὑτόν. 53, 1, πρὸς θύτην ἦλθε. 72, 14, πρὸς θεοὺς ᾔξεν. 82, 5, ἐκινήθη πρὸς μῦν. 95, 29, σπεύδω πρὸς τὸν λέοντα. 135, 5, πρὸς αὐτὸν ὡρμήθη. 9, 3, πρὸς ἡδυφωνίην ἥξειν. 85, 18, ἄρχειν πρὸς τοὺς ... ἔχοντας. 21, 3, συνηθροίζοντο πρὸς μάχην. 7, 4, πρὸς τὸν ἵππον ὡμίλει. 14, 3, πρὸς ἣν ἀλώπηξ εἶπε. 55, 6, ὁ δὲ πρὸς αὐτὴν εἶπε. 64, 7, βάτος πρὸς αὐτὴν εἶπε. 99, 3; 104, 6; 113, 3; 125, 4; 128, 1. 114, 2, πρὸς τοὺς παρόντας ᾔχει. A. 11, πρὸς τὸν γεωργὸν ὡμίλοιν. 126, 5, πρὸς τάδ' εἶπεν. 64, 1, ἤριζον πρὸς ἀλλήλας. 31, 1, πόλεμον εἶχον πρὸς ἀλλήλους. 108, 3, ἔθεντο κοινὸν τὸν βίον πρὸς ἀλλήλους. 93, 3, τοὺς κύνας λαβεῖν πρὸς αἴκλην. 98, 10, πρὸς ταῦτα δὴ σκόπησον. 124, 10, πρὸς τὸν ἦχον ὑπνώσεις; [23, 11; 29, 5. 33, 23, ἄλλα πρὸς ἀλλήλους λαλεῖν. 34, 14; 39, 5; 63, 12. 88, 2, πρὸς ὄρθρον ἀντάδων. 119, 12.]
Προσάγω. 18, 11, προσῆγε τὴν ἀλὴν. 23, 8, βοῦν προσάξειν.
Προσαρτάω. 104, 2, κυνὶ κώδωνα προσαρτήσας.
Προσγελάω. [70, 6, προσγελῶσα τοῖς δήμοις.]
Προσδέω. 11, 3, λίνον τι προσδήσας.
Προσδοκάω. [50, 20, μὴ λαθεῖν προσδόκα.]
Προσεῖπον. 95, 13, χαίρειν προσεῖπε.
Προσέρχομαι. 103, 14, τί δ' οὐ προσέρχῃ; 48, 3, κύων τοίτῳ εἶπεν προσελθών. 75, 19, εὐθὺς προσῆλθον. 95, 62, ἤν μοι προσέλθῃς. 111, 17, ὡς προσῆλθε τῷ ῥείθρῳ. 130, 4, ἐγγὺς προσελθών.

Προσεπιτίθημι. 7, 13, ὀνείην προσεπέθηκεν.
Προσεύχομαι. 20, 4, τῷ Ἡρακλεῖ προσηύχετο. 63, 4, προσηύχετ' ἀεί.
Προσέχω. [134, 18, ἐγὼ προσέξω. 136, 10, προσέχειν νοῦν τέρψεσιν.]
Προσήκω. 38, 5, προσῆκε τῇ ῥίζῃ. 127, 9, οὐ προσῆκε θαυμάζειν.
Πρόσθεν. [31, 20, μυχῶν πρόσθεν.]
Προσκοπέω. [106, 25, τὰ δ' ἔπειτα προσκοπουμένη.]
Προσκυνέω. 20, 5, ὃν μόνον θεῶν προσεκύνει. 119, 8, προσκυνοῦντας ἥμας.
Προσκύπτω. 121, 1, τῇ δὲ προσκύψας. 130, 7.
Προσομιλέω. 12, 6, προσέπτησάν τε καὶ προσωμίλουν. 95, 3, ᾗ προσωμίλει.
Προσουρέω. 48, 7, μηδέ μοι προσουρήσῃς.
Προσπέτομαι. 12, 6, καὶ δὴ προσέπτησαν. 99, 1, λέοντι προσπτάς.
Προσποιέω. 97, 2, προσποιηθεὶς θύειν.
Προσποιητός. 103, 5, φωνὴν προσποιητὰ λεπτύνων. [106, 17, προσποιητὰ σιγῶσαν.]
Προστίθημι. 51, 6, ὁλκὴν προσθήσει.
Προσφάγημα. [133, 4.]
Προσφάτως. 30, 3, προσφάτως ἐτεθνήκει. 135, 7, ἠγόρασμαι προσφάτως.
Πρόσω. 66, 5.
Πρόσωπον. 72, 8, πρόσωπα δ' αὐτῶν ἐξέλουε. [106, 21, φαιδρῷ προσώπῳ.]
Πρῴην. 6, 7, πρῴην ἔπτυσε. 75, 15; 111, 11. 125, 5, ἐχθὲς καὶ πρῴην.
Πρωινός. 124, 17, ἔργων πρωινῶν.
Πρῷρα. 71, 2, ἐκ πρῴρης.
Πρῶτος. 66, 1, θεῶν τῶν πρώτων. 67, 5, τὴν πρώτην μοῖραν. 72, 17, ἑλκύσασα τὸ πτερὸν πρώτῃ. 74, 10, ἐν χρόνοις πρώτοις. 75, 17, ἐν τοῖς πρώτοις. 134, 1, ἠξίου πρώτην κεφαλὴν βαδίζειν. 134, 9, ἦρχε τῶν πρώτων. Β. 4, πρῶτος εἶπε. Β. 9, ὑπ' ἐμοῦ πρώτου. 1, 7, πρῶτον . . . εἶτα. 18, 9, τὸ πρῶτον . . . ἔπειτα δ' αὖ. 48, 3, πρῶτον . . . ἔπειτα. 53, 5, πρῶτα . . . ἔπειτα . . . τρίτον. 59, 8, πρῶτον μὲν . . . δέ . . . δέ . . . 95, 12, πρῶτον . . . εἶτα. 126, 6, τὸ πρῶτον . . . νῦν δέ . . . 135, 6, πρῶτον . . . ὁ δέ . . . Λ. 1, τὸ πρῶτον. 12, 8, πρῶτον βλέπω σε μετὰ Ὀρίκην. 95, 27, τοῦτο πρῶτον εἰπούσης. 134, 17, εἰς τὸ πρῶτον. = class. πρότερος. —18, 4, Βορέης ἐφύσα πρῶτος. 109, 3, πρώτη ὀρθὴν ἄπελθε. [40, 6, ἀντὶ τῶν πρώτων. 45, 11, ἐκ πρώτης. 73, 4, ἴσχεν οὔτε τὴν πρώτην.]
Πταίω. [103, 20.]

Πτερίσκος. 118, 5, πτερίσκοις ἐπανθεῖν.
Πτερόν. 5, 6, ἐπικροτῶν τοῖς πτεροῖς. 72, 12, ἄλλον ἐξ ἄλλου πτερόν. 72, 17, ἑλκύσασα τὸ πτερόν. 88, 4, πτεροῖσιν ἀκμαίους. 115, 12, πτερῶν χρείη.
Πτερόω. 98, 12, ὁ δὲ πτερωθείς.
Πτέρυξ. 65, 2, χρυσᾶς πτέρυγας. 77, 4, καλαὶ πτέρυγες.
Πτερύσσομαι. 65, 6, χαμαὶ πτερύσσῃ.
Πτερωτός. 115, 3, πτερωτὴν ποιεῖν.
Πτηνός. 5, 7, πτηνῶν εὐσεβέστατον. 72, 2, πτηνοῖσιν εἶπεν.
Πτοέω. 95, 81, μηδ' ἐπτόησο.
Πτύω. 6, 8, πρὸς τῇδε πέτρῃ φυκὶς ἔπτυσ' ἡ μήτηρ.
Πτώξ. [102, 10, ὁ πτὼξ λαγωός.]
Πτωχός. 137, 3, πτωχοῖσι. 55, 2, πτωχῶς ἀλλ' ἀναγκαίως.
Πυγμαῖος. 26, 10, φεύγωμεν εἰς τὰ Πυγμαίων.
Πυθμήν. 108, 9, ἐν πιθμέσιν γῆς.
Πύλη. 2, 9, εἰσιόντες τὰς πύλας. 30, 8, ἐν πύλαις ὀνειρείαις.
Πῦρ. 11, 6, τὸ πῦρ φέρουσαν. 74, 5, ἑστίῃ πυρὸς γεμούσῃ.
Πύρινος. 26, 2, πυρίνῳ σίτῳ. 117, 7, ἄχνας πυρίνας.
Πυρός. 33, 2, πυρὸν εἰς νεὸν ῥίψας. 129, 6, πυρὸν Δήμητρος. 136, 7, τὸν πυρὸν ἐγκλείων.
Πυρόω. Β. 15, εὖ πυρώσας.
Πυρρίχη. 80, 4, πυρρίχην παίζειν.
Πώ. 48, 9, μή πω ἀναπλήσας.
Πωλέομαι. 128, 11, ἐν μέσοις ἐπωλεύμην. 129, 23, οὐκ ἐπωλεύμην.
Πωλέω. 30, 1, ἐπώλει τις Ἑρμείην. 83, 1, κριθὰς ἐπώλει. 83, 4, τὸ τρέφον με μὴ πώλει. 111, 8, τοῖς ἅλας πωλήσας.
Πῶμα. 58, 4, τὸ πῶμα κινήσας. 58, 8, τεθὲν τὸ πῶμα.
Πωμάζω. 58, 2, πίθον πωμάσας.
Πῶς, direct. —2, 14, πῶς ὁ θεὸς ἂν εἰδείη; 3, 9, πῶς ἔργον κρύψω; 16, 9, πῶς ἤλθες; 16, 10, πῶς γάρ; 38, 4, πῶς ἂν μεμφοίμην; 50, 16, πῶς οὐκ ἂν; 76, 19, πῶς ποιήσεις; 85, 16, πῶς ἂν δυνηθείην; 93, 9, πῶς σινοικήσω; 99, 5, πῶς πιστεύσω; 103, 12, πῶς ἔχεις; 105, 5, πῶς ἐλευκώθη; 113, 3, πῶς σπεύδεις; 120, 7, πῶς ἰήσῃ; 121, 2, πῶς ἔχεις; 124, 19, πῶς γνώσῃ; 130, 11, πῶς σοί τις φίλος συναυτήσει; 134, 5, πῶς ἀξεις; [42, 7, πῶς γὰρ ἂν κρεῖττον; 133, 3.] Indirect. —1, 16, πῶς φοβερός ἐστι γινώσκω. 75, 12, πῶς ἔχουσιν διηρώτα. 36, 6, θάμβος τὴν δρῦν εἶχε πῶς . . . οὐκ ἐπεπτώκει. 95, 72, ἔμελλε . . . ἐντολὴν δώσειν πῶς τηρήσεις.

Πώς. 61, 3, καί πως σννηβόλησαν.
135, 11, άρτι πως. [4, 6, σωτηρία
πώς εστι.]
Ῥαββίον. 117, 9, τῷ ῥαββίῳ παίων.
Ῥάβδος. 47, 4, ῥάβδων δεσμήν. 47,
7, ῥάβδους κατάξαι. 47, 14, τῇ μιῇ
ῥάβδῳ. 130, 9, χαλασθείσης ῥάβδου.
Ῥάδιος. 44, 6, εἶχε ῥᾳδίην θοίνην. 38,
3, πόνος ῥᾴων. 75, 3, ἔσῃ ῥᾴων.
111, 7, ῥᾴων ἀνέστη.
Ῥᾳθυμέω. [116, 14, τῇ δ᾽ ἐρᾳθύμει.]
Ῥαπίζω. 114, 5, πνοῇ ῥαπισθείς.
Ῥέζω. [18, 16, βίᾳ ῥέζων.]
Ῥείη. 139, 7, τυμπάνῳ Ῥείης.
Ῥεῖθρον. 40, 1, ὀξὺν τῷ ῥείθρῳ. 79,
2, ἐν τῷ ῥείθρῳ. 111, 5, ὤλισθεν εἰς
τὸ ῥεῖθρον. 111, 17, προσῆλθε τῷ
ῥείθρῳ.
Ῥέω. 15, 3, ῥέων ὁ μῦθος. 88, 14,
ῥέοντα τὸν στάχιν. 119, 5, χρυσὸς
ἐρρύη.
Ῥήγνυμι. 28, 9, σεαυτὴν ῥήξεις. 129,
12, δεσμὰ καὶ κάλους ῥήξας.
Ῥῆμα. 57, 14, οὐδὲν ῥῆμα.
Ῥῆσις. 15, 4, μακρή μὲν ἄλλως ῥῆσις.
Β. 13, λευκῇ ῥήσει.
Ῥήτωρ. 15, 10, στωμύλος ῥήτωρ.
Ῥιγόω. 18, 6, ῥιγώσας καθῆστο. 131,
3, μὴ πάθοι τι ῥιγώσας.
Ῥίζα. 38, 5, προσῆκε τῇ ῥίζῃ. 86, 1,
κοίλωμα ῥίζης. 108, 7, τρώγων ῥίζας.
[Α. 5, σιδηρᾶ ῥίζα.]
Ῥίπτω. 3, 8, τὸν λίθον ῥίψας. 33, 2,
πυρὸν εἰς νεὸν ῥίψας. 33, 18, ῥίψας
ἔτυψε. 115, 9, εἰς ὄρος ῥίψας. 16, 2,
μή σε τῷ λύκῳ ῥίψω. 18, 13, ῥίψας
τὴν σίσυραν ἐγυμνώθη.
Ῥίς. 122, 13, ῥῖνας ἀλοιήσας. 130, 9,
ῥῖνας ἐπλήγη. 134, 6, ὀμμάτων ἢ
ῥινός.
Ῥόπαλον. 98, 16, ἠλόια ῥοπάλῳ.
Ῥοῦς. 111, 11, διέβαινε τὸν ῥοῦν.
Ῥύομαι. [50, 16, ἐρρυσάμην σε.]
Ῥωγάς. 86, 2, ῥωγὰς ἀπόλου πήρη.
Ῥώμη. 31, 7, τοῖς ῥώμῃ ἀρίστοις.
Ῥώννυμι. 50, 17, ἔρρωσο.

Σάγη. 7, 12, ἐπ᾽ αὐτὸν ἐτίθει τὴν σάγην.
76, 10, σάγην νώτοις ἔφερεν.
Σαγήνη. 4, 1, σαγήνην βεβλήκει. 9,
6, βαλὼν σαγήνην. 43, 8, ὁμοῦ σαγήναις.
Σαίνω. 74, 16, τὸν διδόντα σαίνει.
87, 3, μεταστραφεὶς ἔσαινεν. 87, 5,
τί σαίνεις; 129, 14, σαίνων. 134,
14, σαίνουσα δ᾽ ἱκέτευεν.
Σαίρω, see σέσηρα.
Σάλπιγξ. 76, 12, σάλπιγξ ἐφώνει πᾶσιν.
Σάρξ. 51, 3, τῆς σαρκὸς οὐ πόρρω. 95,

90, σάρκας λαφύσσων. 100, 6, τέτριπται σάρκα. 107, 5, νηδὺν σαρκὶ πιαίνειν.
Σαύρα. 27, 4, μῦς τε καὶ σαύρας. [41,
2, διαρραγῆναι σαύραν.]
Σαυτόν, see σεαυτόν.
Σαφής. 122, 2, σαφῆ ὄλεθρον. [107,
16, σαφῆς ὁ μῦθος.]
Σβέννυμι. 114, 4, εὐθὺς ἐσβέσθη λύχνος.
Σεαυτόν. 12, 18, σεαυτὸν μήνυσον. 28,
9, σεαυτὴν ῥήξεις. 131, 18, σεαυτὴν
διεψεύσω. 76, 17, ἔντασσε πεζοῖς σαυτόν. 104, 7, σαυτοῦ ἔλεγχον. 120,
8, σαυτὸν σώζεις. 128, 9, τρέφων
σαυτόν. [41, 3; 43, 16; 67, 9; 72,
19. 104, 7.]
Σείω. 26, 3, σφονδόνην κενὴν σείων.
62, 3, τένοντα σείων. 65, 2, σείοντι
πτέρυγας. 68, 4, ἔσειε κλήρους. 72,
9, ἔσειε ταρσούς. 104, 4, κώδωνα
σείων.
Σελήνη. [116, 4, λαμπρῆς σελήνης.]
Σέλινον. 124, 2, σέλινα δειπνήσειν.
Σεμνός. 32, 2, σεμνὴ Κύπρις.
Σεμνύνω. 104, 6, τί σεμνύνῃ;
Σέσηρα. 50, 14, σεσηρὸς αἰκάλλουσα.
Σηκός. 132, 2, σηκοῦ δ᾽ ἐντός.
Σημαίνω. 13, 6, ἡ χρόη με σημαίνει.
131, 9, χελιδὼν καῦμα σημαίνει. [56,
8, τοῦτο σημαίνειν.]
Σήμερον. 12, 8, βλέπω σε σήμερον.
Σθένω. 103, 1, οὐκέτι σθένων βαίνειν.
Σιαγών. 96, 3, τὰς σιαγόνας πρίων.
Σιγάω. 37, 4, ὁ βοῦς ἐσίγα. 114, 6,
σίγα. [106, 17, προσποιητὰ σιγώσαν.]
Σίδηρος. 76, 13, σίδηρον ὀξύνειν. 100,
10, σίδηρος αὐχένα τρίψει.
Σιδήρειος. 59, 13, τροχοὺς σιδηρείους.
100, 6, κλοιῷ τῷ σιδηρείῳ.
Σιδηροῦς. [Α. 5, σιδηρᾶ ῥίζα.]
Σιμός. 56, 4, πίθωνα γυμνὸν σιμόν.
Σίσυρνα. 18, 3, τὴν σίσυρναν ἐκδύσει.
Σισύρα or σίσυρα. 18, 10 (see note in
loco).
Σιτεύω. 100, 4, ἄνθρωπός με σιτεύει.
Σῖτος. 26, 2, πυρίνῳ σίτῳ. 108, 6,
σίτου ῥίζας. 128, 9, εὐθαλεῖ σίτῳ.
136, 1, σῖτον ἐκ μυχοῦ σύρων. 137,
8, ὀσπρίων τε καὶ σίτων.
Σιωπάω. 3, 10, κἂν ἐγὼ σιωπήσω. 7,
8, εἶρπεν σιωπῶν. 52, 5, σιωπώντων.
Σκαιός. 119, 17, σκαιός τίς ἐσσι.
Σκέλος. 42, 4, τὸν δὲ τοῦ σκέλους ἄρας.
119, 4, τοῦ σκέλους ἄρας.
Σκέπτομαι. 103, 14, τί μακρόθεν με
σκέπτῃ;
Σκεῦος. 55, 5, τίς ἄξει τὰ σκεύη; 129,
16, ἠλόησε τὰ σκεύη.
Σκῆπτρον. 75, 19, ἡψάμην τῶν σκήπτρων.

Σκιή. 43, 3, ἑαυτοῦ τὴν σκιὴν θεωρήσας.
79, 3, ἰδοῦσα τὴν σκιήν. 79, 4, τῇ
σκιῇ ἐφωρμήθη. 120, 1, ὁ σκιῇ χαίρων.
Σκιρτάω. 95, 11, σκιρτῶσαν εὗρε.
Σκληρὸς. Α. 19, ἰάμβων σκληρὰ κῶλα.
[133, 4.]
Σκόλοψ. 122, 1, ὄνος πατήσας σκόλοπα.
122, 10, σκόλοπα θερμόν.
Σκοπέω. 88, 10, σκοπεῖν κελεύων. 98,
10, πρὸς ταῦτα δὴ σκόπησον.
Σκύλαξ. 43, 8, ὁμοῦ σκύλαξιν εὑρίνοις.
Σκύμνος. 129, 11.
Σκυταλίς. 130, 8, σκυταλίδ᾽ ἔσεισε.
Σκώπτω. 65, 3, τὴν χρόην σκώπτεις.
69, 3, αἰπόλος σκώπτων φησίν. 86, 8,
σκώπτουσα εἶπε. 105, 5, τὸν λύκον
σκώπτων.
Σμήχω. 76, 12, ἀσπίδα σμήχειν.
Σμικρός. 131, 11, σμικρὰ παίξας.
Σμίλη. 98, 13, ὑπὸ σμίλης ἀπωνυχίσθη.
Σός. 34, 11, οὐ γὰρ σά, ἀλλὰ τὰ τοῦ
ταύρου. 54, 4, τὴν σὴν ὄψιν. 71, 10,
τῆς σῆς γαίης. 95, 9, λόγοισι σοῖς
μελιγλώσσοις.
Σοφίζω. [138, 4, καὶ μὴ σοφίζου.]
Σοφίη. 98, 19, σοφίη διδαχθείς.
Σοφιστής. Α. 15, conj.
Σοφός. 33, 12, σοφὸν φῦλον. 77, 10,
ἡ σοφή. 95, 51, ὡς σοφὴ κύων. 103,
11, σοφὴ ἀλώπηξ. 139, 1, σοφῆς
ἀράχνης. Β. 5, Αἴσωπος ὁ σοφός. Β.
10, σοφωτέρης μούσης. 12, 18, σοφὰ
λαλοῦσα. 9, 1, σοφῶς ἦλθει. 36, 9,
σοφῶς εἶπε. 12, 26, λόγος σοφός.
[Α. 15, τοῦ σοφοῦ γέροντος. 50, 19,
σοφὸν τὸ θεῖον. 106, 20, κερδοῖ σοφῇ.]
Σπαίρω. 6, 13, μύζων καὶ σπαίρων.
9, 7, ἐπὶ γῆς σπαίροντας.
Σπανίως. [4, 8, σπανίως ἴδοις ἄν.]
Σπαράσσω. 95, 40, οὖατ᾽ ἐσπάραξεν.
[72, 19, τὸν δ᾽ ἐσπάραττε.]
Σπείρω. 26, 2, τὴν χώρην ἐσπαρμένην.
Σπένδω. 119, 2, σπένδων Ἑρμῇ.
Σπέρμα. 33, 5, σπερμάτων ἀρουραίων.
Σπεύδω. 58, 3, εἰδέναι σπεύδων. 69, 5,
ἁρπάσαι σπεύδων. 98, 22, μεταλαβεῖν
ὅταν σπεύδῃ. 113, 3, σπεύδεις σῶσαι.
117, 7, σπεύδοντες ἀποτρώγειν. 95,
28, σπεύδω πρὸς τὸν λέοντα. 88, 12,
οὐκ ἄγαν σπεύδει. [21, 11, φεύγειν
σπεύδων.]
Σπῆλυγξ. 91, 2, σπήλυγγα κατέδυ.
95, 38, εἰς σπήλυγγα θηρός. 103, 3,
κοίλης ἔσω σπήλιγγος. 106, 5, ὑπὸ
σπήλυγγι.
Σπλάγχνον. 34, 9, τὰ σπλάγχνα πίπτει. 95, 91, σπλάγχνα δάπτων.
Σπόγγος. 111, 15, σπόγγους πολιτρή-
τοις. 111, 18, τῶν σπόγγων διαβραχέντων.

Σποραῖος. 13, 2, σποραίων πολεμίοις.
Σπόρος. 13, 5, σπόρον καταφθείρω.
33, 1, σπόρου δ᾽ ὥρῃ.
Σπουδή. 95, 41, σπουδῇ διωχθείς.
Στάζω. 72, 5, ἔσταζε πέτρης κρήνη.
Στάμνος. 108, 18, στάμνοι μέλιτος.
Στασιάζω. [85, 20, τὸ στασίαζον ἀσ-
θενές.]
Στάσις. 39, 4, στάσιν τυράννων.
Στάχυς. 88, 14, ῥέοντα τὸν στάχυν.
Στέγη. 12, 15, στέγην οἴκει. 64, 5,
στέγη μελάθρων.
Στέγος. 5, 7, ἐκ στέγους ἄρας.
Στεινος. 108, 22, στεινῆς τρώγλης.
Στελεόν. 140, 1.
Στενάζω. 29, 3, στενάξας εἶπε. 95, 45,
κἀκεῖνος ἐστέναξε.
Στενός. 86, 6, στενῆς τρώγλης.
Στένω. 38, 4, πεύκη στένουσα εἶπε.
Στερέω. [72, 20, τούτων στερηθήσῃ.]
Στέρνον. 77, 5, στέρνον αἰετοῦ.
Στερρός. 107, 13, στερρὸν βρόχον.
Στέφω. 63, 3, στέφων βωμούς.
Στῆθος. 59, 11, ἀνοικτὰ τὰ στήθη. 85,
15, διάρχεμοι στήθη.
Στήλη. 30, 2; 81, 1.
Στίβη. 12, 16, τί σε δροσίζει στίβη;
Στοιχεῖον. 71, 4, ἀνηλεὲς στοιχεῖον.
Στολή. 131, 2, στολὴν ἑαυτῷ κατέλι-
πεν. 131, 11, τὴν στολὴν ἐνικήθη.
Στόμα. 77, 1, δεδηχὼς στόματι τυρόν.
77, 9, στόματος τυρὸν ἐκβαλών. 95,
45, τὸ στόμα βρύχων.
Στρατηγός. 31, 5; 31, 13; 31, 18;
31, 22; 85, 3.
Στρουθός. Α. 11.
Στύγημα. 95, 61, ἀλλ᾽ ὦ στύγημα.
Στωμύλος. 15, 10, στωμύλος ῥήτωρ.
Σύ. 12, 21; 30, 10; 33, 14; 36, 10;
64, 10; 65, 3; 65, 5; 75, 20; 76,
18; 89, 4; 89, 6; 95, 4; 95, 8; 95,
73; 95, 75; 96, 4; 98, 7; 101, 6;
101, 7; 110, 4; 117, 11; 122, 5;
134, 19; 135, 11.
  σε. 3, 6; 10, 11; 12, 8; 12, 16;
12, 17; 13, 11; 16, 2; 27, 4; 48,
4; 50, 3; 53, 4; 64, 8; 64, 9; 75,
18; 78, 4; 91, 5; 92, 4; 95, 31;
95, 76; 95, 85; 98, 8; 108, 11;
109, 4; 115, 6; 119, 10; 124, 17;
124, 19; 132, 7.
  σοί. 1, 8; 6, 6; 27, 5; 48, 8;
67, 8; 77, 4; 77, 12; 92, 7; 95,
24; 95, 27; 95, 32; 95, 68; 95, 71;
95, 82; 95, 83; 99, 5; 100, 5; 105,
6; 107, 4; 107, 8; 110, 2; 115, 7;
121, 3; 122, 4; 124, 8; 128, 3;
128, 4; 130, 11; B. 16.
  σοῦ. 37, 12; 49, 4; 69, 4; 78,
5; 84, 3; 91, 6; 99, 4.

σύγε. 53, 7.
ὑμᾶς. 9, 9 ; 47, 11.
ὑμᾶς. 125, 6.
ὑμεῖς. 128, 12 ; 141, 1.
ὑμῖν. 71, 7 ; 93, 9. [5, 10 ; 5,
11 ; 9, 13 ; 39, 7 ; 41, 4 ; 75, 5 ; 75,
6 ; 94, 10 ; 99, 6 ; 138, 3.]
ὑμῶν. 117, 10.
Συγγέρων. 22, 7.
Συγγινώσκω. 103, 17, εἰ δ' ἄπειμι συγγνώσῃ.
Συγκλείω. 113, 2, μετ' αὐτῶν λύκον
συγκλείειν.
Συγκρίνω. [18, 14, συγκριθεὶς ἐνικήθη.]
Σύγκρισις. 101, 8, ἐν δ' αὖ λεόντων
συγκρίσει.
Συγκρούω. 92, 8, γομφίους συγκρούων.
44, 4, διαβολαῖς συγκρούων.
Συγχωρέω. [82, 10, μὴ συγχώρει εὐκαταφρόνητον σαυτὸν εἶναι.]
Συζάω. [106,⸗10, μεθ' ἧς τὰ πολλὰ
συνεζήκει.]
Συζεύγνυμι. 55, 1, τὴν ὄνον συζεύξας.
Σῦκον. 108, 17, πίθοι σύκων.
Συκοφαντέω. [72, 18, μή με συκοφαντήσῃς.]
Συλάω. 2, 12, σύλων ὦν ὁ θεὸς ἐσυλήθη.
18, 5, τὸν φοροῦντα συλήσειν. 78, 5,
βωμὸς ἐσυλήθη.
[Σῦλον.] 2, 12, μήνυτρα σύλων.
Συλλαμβάνω. 6, 12, ὕστερόν με συλλήψῃ. 7, 5, συλλαβεῖν τι τοῦ φόρτου.
18, 2, γεράνους ἀγρότης συνειλήφει.
27, 1, γαλῆν δόλῳ τις συλλαβὼν. 44,
2, τούτους συλλαβεῖν. 89, 10, τὸν
ἄρνα συλλαβών. 124, 12, ἀλεκτορίσκον
συλλαβεῖν. 132, 7, μή τις συλλάβῃ σε.
Συλλέγω. 58, 1, χρηστὰ πάντα συλλέξας.
113, 1, πρόβατα συλλέγων. 119, 6,
χρυσὸν συλλέγων.
Συλλήβδην. 49, 6, πάντα συλλήβδην.
Συμβαίνω. 117, 5, οἷα συμβαίνει.
132, 9, κἂν δὲ τοῦτο συμβαίνῃ. [33,
21, τὸ συμβάν.]
Συμβάλλω. 122, 4, σοί συμβαλὼν
χαίρω.
Σύμβολον. 97, 11, τὸ σύμβολον δώσω.
Σύμβουλος. 95, 30, χρῆται ἡμῖν εἰς
ἅπαντα συμβούλοις.
Συμπατέω. 28, 1, γέννημα φρύνου
συνεπάτησε βοῦς. 117, 8, συνεπάτησε
τοὺς πλείστους.
Συμφέρω. 95, 68, σοί συμφέροντα
βουλεύσαιμ. [83, 6, τῶν συμφερόντων.]
Συμφορή. 12, 24, λύπην παλαιῶν
συμφορῶν. 66, 7, συμφορὰς ἀλλήλων
βλέπειν. 118, 8, παίδων συμφοράς.
103, 21, συμφοραὶς ἐπαιδεύθη.
Σύμφυλος. 101, 3, τῶν συμφύλων
ἀποστατήσας.

Συμφύρω. 108, 7, συμπεφυρμένα βώλῳ.
Συμφωνία. [85, 19, συμφωνία μέγιστον
ἀγαθόν.]
Σύν. 13, 11, ἔλαβόν σε σὺν ταῖς . . .
πορθούσαις. 47, 8, δεδεμένας σὺν
ἀλλήλαις. 117, 4, σὺν αὐτῷ θνήσκειν.
134, 16, ἔριδος σὺν κακοῖς ἐπειράθην.
92, 6, σὺν θεῷ βαίνεις. 47, 6, σὺν βίῃ
πάσῃ. 115, 11, σὺν δίκῃ θνήσκω.
122, 14, σὺν δίκῃ πάσχω. 129, 11,
ἁβρότητι σὺν πάσῃ. 130, 9, μέτωπα
σύν τε ῥῖνας ἐπλήγη. [65, 7, θαυμαστὸς σὺν τρίβωνι. 65, 8, πλοισία σὺν
ἐσθῆτι.]
Συναβολέω. 61, 3, καί πως συνηβόλησαν
οἱ δύο.
Συναγκίη. 27, 2, ἐν συναγκίῃ κοίλῃ.
Συναθροίζω. 21, 3, συνηθροίζοντο πρὸς
μάχην. 31, 11, ἐτάχθη πάντα καὶ
συνηθροίσθη. 124, 8, συναθροίσει
ἀγέλην.
Συναντάω. 33, 21, γέρανοι συνήντων.
42, 2, κινεῖ φίλῳ συναντήσας. 53, 5,
εἴθε μὴ συνηντήκεις. 53, 8, μή μοι
συναντήσας. 100, 1, λύκῳ συνῆντα
κύων. 105, 3, ᾧ λέων συναντήσας.
130, 11, πῶς σοί τις φίλος συναντήσει;
Συνάπτω. 10, 5, πᾶσαν μάχην συνῆπτεν. [67, 10, πρᾶγμα μηδὲν σύναπτε.]
Συναυλίζομαι. [106, 6, θηρῶν ὅμιλος
συνηυλίσθη.]
Σύνδενδρος. 43, 11, σύνδενδρον ὕλην.
Σύνδουλος. 3, 6, χίμαιρα συνδούλη.
Σύνεγγυς. 65, 4, ἄστρων σύνεγγυς
ἵπταμαι.
Σύνειμι. 58, 9, ἐλπίς ἀνθρώποις σύνεστι.
63, 9, ἅτε σύνεστιν ἀνθρώποις.
Συνεξαμείβω. 59, 15, τόπους ἄλλους
συνεξαμείβειν δεσπόταις.
Συνέρχομαι. 108, 12, εἴ μοι συνέλθῃς.
Συνετός. Λ. 11, συνετὰ πρὸς γεωργὸν
ὠμίλουν.
Σύνεννος. [116, 11, τῇ συνεύνῳ φησί.]
Συνηθείη. 33, 7, ἐκ συνηθείης. 61, 9,
τὸ χρηστὸν ἐξολεῖτε τῇ συνηθείῃ. [106,
13, εἴ τις ἦλθεν οὐχὶ τῆς συνηθείης.]
Συνθήκη. 33, 16, καθάπερ εἶχε συν-
θήκην.
Συνίστημι. 76, 1, συνειστήκει ὁ πόλεμος.
85, 1, κυσὶν ποτ' ἔχθρη συνειστήκει.
Συνοικέω. 93, 9, ὑμῖν πῶς ἐγὼ συνοικήσω. [12, 28, τούτοις συνοικήσῃ.]
Σύνοικος. 16, 8, λύκαινα ἡ σύνοικος.
63, 5, τὸν σύνοικον ἀγαθὰ ποιεῖ. 64,
4, νεφῶν σύνοικος. [106, 9, κερδὼ
σύνοικον εἰλήφει.]
Συντήκω. 111, 6, συντακέντων τῶν
ἀλῶν.
Συντίθημι. 39, 6, συνθέμενος δείξειν.
Συντόμως. 51, 8, ὅς με συντόμως θύσει.

Συντράπεζος. 74, 7, αὑτῷ σιντράπεζος.
Συντρίβω. 134, 13, τὴν ἄκανθαν σιντρίβει. [57, 7, σιντριβεῖσαν ἄμαξαν.]
Συρίττω. 114, 4, ἀνέμου σιρίσαντος.
Σύρος. Β. 2, Σύρων ἀνθρώπων.
Σύρω. 108, 20, τιρρὸν ἐκ κανισκίου σίρων. 136, 1, σῖτον ἐκ μιχοῦ σίρων. 36, 2, τὴν δ' ἔσιρε κιμαίνων. 37, 2, σύροντι τὴν ὔνιν ταύρῳ. 10, 4, σύρουσα πορφύρην. 14, 2, νεκρὸν σῶμα μὴ σίρειν. 109, 2, πλάγια κῶλα μὴ σίρειν. 134, 12, σύρουσα πᾶν τὸ σῶμα.
Σῦς. 95, 17, σῦς ἐστὶν ἀγνώμων.
Σύσκηνος. 12, 12, σύσκηνος ἡμῖν.
Σύσσιτος. [106, 12, συσσίτοισι διανέμων μοίρας.]
Σφάγιον. 132, 10, θεοῦ γενοίμην σφάγιον.
Σφαγίς. 97, 8, ὡς εἶδε σφαγίδας.
Σφάζω. 21, 7, σφάζουσι καὶ κτείνουσι.
Σφάλλω. 107, 11, σφαλεὶς ἐδεσμεύθη. [43, 19, σφάλλουσιν ἡμᾶς.]
Σφεῖς. 31, 4, ἐδόκουν ὑπάρχειν αἰτίην σφίσιν ταύτην. 31, 9, οἱ σφᾶς ἐκόσμοιν. 88, 10, ποῦ σφέας μεταστήσει;
Σφενδονάω. 26, 5, σφενδονῶντα τὰς αἴρας.
Σφενδόνη. 26, 3, σφενδόνην κενήν. 33, 6, σφενδόνην κοίλην. 33, 8 ; 33, 14 ; 33, 18.
Σφήν. 38, 2, ἐνεῖραν αὐτῇ σφῆνας. 38, 6, τοὺς κακίστους σφῆνας.
Σφίγγω. 18, 7, χερσὶ κράσπεδα σφίγξας.
Σχέδην. 57, 4, ἄλλο φῦλον ἐξ ἄλλου σχέδην ἀμείβων.
Σχίζω. 38, 1, δριτόμοι σχίσαντες πεύκην. 12, 9, ἡμᾶς ἔσχισεν δαίμων.
Σχῖνος. 3, 3, κόμην γλυκείαν σχίνου.
Σχοίνος. 6, 15, ὀξέη σχοίνῳ. 37, 7, μόσχος εἷλκετο σχοίνῳ.
Σχολάζω. 22, 4, εἰς ἔρωτας ἐσχόλαζε. 136, 6, οὐκ ἐσχόλαζον.
Σώζω. 43, 14, πόδες μ' ἔσωσαν. 50, 18, φωνῇ με σώσας. 51, 10, ὃς κερεῖ με καὶ σώσει. 69, 6, αὐτὸν ἐκ κακοῦ σώζων. 113, 4, τὰ πρόβατα σῶσαι. 120, 8, ὃς σαυτὸν μὴ σώζεις. 129, 19, κινδύνου ἔσωσαν. 134, 15, σῶσον ἡμᾶς. 31, 17, ἄλλοι σωθέντες ἦσαν. 75, 2, σωθήσῃ. 103, 17, σωζοιο. 121, 3, μόνον σώζοι. [51, 12 ; 107, 17 ; 107, 18.]
Σῶμα. 14, 2, νεκρὸν σῶμα. 134, 12, πᾶν τὸ σῶμα.
Σῶος. 7, 6, γενοίμην σῶος. 94, 8, κεφαλὴν ἐξελεῖν σώην.
Σώρακος. 108, 18, σώρακοι φοινίκων.
Σωρεύω. 136, 2, σῖτον θέρους σεσωρεύκει.
Σωρός. 48, 2, λίθων σωρός. 108, 17, ἐσπρίων σωρός.

Σωτήρ. 50, 3, πρὸς θεῶν σωτήρων.
Σωτηρία. [4, 6.]
Σωφρονέω. 90, 4, οὐδὲ σωφρονῶν.
Τάγηνον. 6, 4, εἰς τάγηνον ὡραῖος.
Ταλαίπωρος. 90, 2, ἡμέων ταλαιπώρων. 108, 8, μύρμηκος ταλαιπώρου.
Ταλαντεύω. 30, 9, τἀμὰ ταλαντεύῃ.
Τάλας. 37, 3, τάλας. 104, 6. ὦ τάλαν. 131, 17, τάλαινα. 134, 5, ὦ τάλαινα.
Ταμεῖον. 108, 2, ἐν ταμείοις πλουσίοισι.
Τἄν. 63, 8, ὦ τἄν.
Ταναγραῖος. 51, ἀλκτορίσκων Ταναγραίων.
Ταπεινός. 112, 10, τὸ μικρὸν εἶναι καὶ ταπεινόν. [12, 28, ταπεινὸς αἶθις ὤν. 47, 16, ταπεινοὺς ἦρεν εἰς ὕψος.]
Ταρσός. 72, 9, ἔσειε ταρσούς. 124, 18, δροσώδης ταρσός.
Τάσσω. 31, 11, ἐπεὶ ἐτάχθη πάντα. 94, 3, μισθὸν δώσειν ἔταξε (possibly corrupt).
Ταῦρος. 52, 1, ἄρρενες ταῦροι (doubtful). 74, 6, ἐργάτῃ ταύρῳ. 107, 4, κερασφόρους ταύρους. 23, 2 ; 23, 6 ; 34, 1 ; 34, 11 ; 37, 2 ; 44, 1 ; 59, 5 ; 59, 8 ; 74, 6 ; 84, 1 ; 91, 1 ; 91, 4 ; 91, 8 ; 95, 23 ; 97, 1 ; 97, 3 ; 102, 1 ; 112, 5.
Τάφος. 72, 20.
Ταφρεύω. 2, 1, ἀμπελῶνα ταφρεύων.
Τάχα. 120, 5, οἷον τάχ' οὐδεὶς οἶδεν. 7, 6, τάχ' ἂν γενοίμην σῶος. [106, 28, τάχ' οὐδ' ἑώλων γεύσομαι κρεῶν.]
Ταχύς. 69, 4. θάσσων εὑρέθη. 45, 4, τάχιον εἰσδεδύκυίας. 127, 7, τάχιον ἐμπίπτει. 28, 9, θᾶσσον ῥήξεις. 127, 10, θᾶσσον ἀδικῶν.
Ταώς. 65, 1, εὐφυεῖ ταῷ. 142, 1, ταὼς εὐπήληξ.
Τε. Frequent.
Τεῖχος. 2, 7, τοῖς ἐσωτέρω τείχοις. 132, 4, ἔσω τοῦ τείχους.
Τέκνον. 34, 11 ; 47, 6 ; 78, 4 ; 95, 31 ; 128, 4. A. 2.
Τέλειος. 6, 7, οὐκ εἰμὶ γὰρ τέλειος.
Τελευταῖος. 74, 14, τοῖς τελευταίοις χρόνοις.
Τελευτάω. 47, 3, τὸν βίον τελευτήσειν. 95, 35, ψυχαὶ τῶν τελευτώντων.
Τελέω. 55, 3, ἐπεὶ τοὔργον ἐτετέλεστο.
Τέλμα. 120, 1, ὁ τελμάτων ἔνοικος.
Τέλος. 15, 5, τέλος δέ.
Τέμενος. 63, 2, ἔχων ἐν αὐλῇ τέμενος.
Τέμνω. 64, 9. πελύκων ἀεὶ τμηγέντων.
Τένων. 37, 12, τένοντα πέλεκυς τρίψει. 62, 3, τένοντα σείων. 84, 3, βαρύνω τὸν τένοντα.
Τερετίζω. 9, 4, ἐτερέτιζεν εὐμούσως.
Τέρπω. 125, 6, πίθηκος ἔτερπεν ὑμᾶς.

105, 5, λέων δὲ τερφθείς. 108, 19,
ὡς ἑτέρφθη πᾶσι. [106, 29.]
Τέρψις. [136, 10, προσέχειν νοῦν τέρ-
ψεσιν.]
Τετράγωνος. 48, 1, Ἑρμῆς τετράγωνος.
Τετράκυκλος. 52, 1, τετράκυκλον ἅμ-
αξαν.
Τετράπους. 28, 5, πάχιστον τετράποιν.
Τέττιξ. 136, 3.
Τεφρός. 65, 1, τεφρὴ γέρανος.
Τεφρώδης. 85, 14, τεφρώδεις κύνες.
Τέχνη. 33, 9, εὗρε τέχνην ἄλλην. 95,
52, πλέκουσα τέχνας. 137, 4, τὰ τῆς
τέχνης.
Τεχνίτης. 119, 1.
Τήκω. 111, 12, γόμον τήξας.
Τηρέω. 6, 16, ὁ μὴ τὰ μικρὰ τηρήσας.
37, 10, εἰς ταῦτα ἐτηρήθης. 93, 11,
τῶν κινῶν με τηρούντων. 95, 72,
ἀρχὴν πῶς τηρήσεις; [44, 8, τοὺς φιλ-
ους τήρει.]
Τίγρις. 95, 19, τίγρις ἀλαζών. 102, 9.
Τίθημι. 7, 12, ἐπ᾽ αὐτὸν ἐτίθει γόμον.
9, 4, τὸ δίκτυον θείς. 56, 2, ἔθηκεν
ἔπαθλα. 58, 2, ἔθηκεν αὐτὸν παρ᾽
ἀνθρώποις. 58, 8, τεθὲν τὸ πῶμα.
111, 10, πλείω ἔτ᾽ ἐτίθει τὸν φόρτον.
23, 3, ἔθηκεν εὐχήν. 67, 4, τίθησι
τρεῖς μοίρας. 22, 12, φαλακρὸν ἔθηκαν
ἄνδρα. 89, 11, ἄδειπνον τὸν λύκον
θήσεις. 95, 85, τίθησι κυρίην σε τῶν
ζώων. 102, 12, φοβερὰ τἀσθενῆ θήσει.
108, 3, ἔθεντο κοινὸν βίον. 115, 6,
ὅστις σ᾽ ἐλαφρὴν θήσω. Λ. 18, q. v.
note. [106, 8, τιθεὶς ἄπαισι δαῖτα.]
Τιθηνέω. 13, 8, τὸν ἐμὸν τιθηνῶ πατέρα.
Τίκτω. 35, 2, τεκοῦσα δ᾽ αὐτοῖς ἐστὶν
οὐκ ἴση μήτηρ. 123, 1, χρυσέ᾽ ᾠὰ
τίκτειν. 135, 9, καί μ᾽ ἔτεκεν ἡ μήτηρ.
34, 9, τὰ σπλάγχνα γάρ, τεκοῦσα,
πίπτει. [141, 1, στελεὰ τίκτει.]
Τίλλω. 22, 9, χαίτας ἔτιλλεν. 22, 10.
[22, 13.]
Τιμάω. 10, 7, Ἀφροδίτην λύχνοις ἐτίμα. 20, 5, Ἡρακλέα προσεκύνει τε
κἀτίμα. 48, 8, πλέον με μὴ τίμα.
[119, 13, σκαιὸν ἄνδρα τιμήσας.]
Τίνω. 27, 3, ὡς κακὴν χάριν τίνεις. 107,
8, χάριν σοι τίνω.
Τίς. Interrogative, direct.—6, 6, τί
σοὶ τὸ κέρδος; 12, 16, τί σε δροσίζει
στίβῃ; 24, 7, τί μὴ πάθωμεν; 32,
4, ἧς τίς οὐκ ἔχειν ἦρα; 52, 4, τί δὴ
κρώξεις; 55, 5, τίς ἄξει τὰ σκεύη;
78, 4, τίς θεῶν σε σώσει; 78, 5,
τίνος βωμὸς οὐκ ἐσυλήθη; 85, 7, τί
δ᾽ εὐλαβοῦμαι; 85, 12, τί μηκύνω;
87, 5, τί δάκνεις; 87, 5, τί σαίνεις;
90, 3, τί οὐχὶ ποιήσει; 95, 16, τίς
τιραννήσει; 95, 24, τί σοι λέγω τὰ

πολλά; 95, 78, τί ποιήσω; 98, 5,
τίς οὐ λέοντι κηδείσει; 98, 8, τίς κόρη
σε τολμήσει; 78, 9, τίς δ᾽ ἰδοῦσα μὴ
κλαύσῃ; 99, 2, τί κωλύει; 104, 6,
τί σεμνύνῃ; 103, 14, τί δ᾽ οὐ προσέρχῃ; 110, 2, τί χάσκεις; 115,
12, τίς νεφῶν, τίς ἦν πτερῶν χρείη;
121, 2, τίνων χρῄζεις; 122, 15, τί
γὰρ ἠρξάμην; 124, 7, δικτύῳ τί
ποιήσεις; 124, 8, τίς σοὶ σιναθροίσει;
124, 10, τίνος πρὸς τὸν ἦχον; 124,
17, τίς σ᾽ ἀναμνήσει; 129, 23, τί γὰρ
οὐκ ἐπωλεύμην; 136, 8, τί μοι ἐσθέων
χρείη; 135, 6, τίς μὲν εἴ; 136, 5,
τί οὖν ἐποίεις; 137, 6, τίς οὐκ οἶδεν
Ἄττιν; 137, 8, τίς οὐκ ἀπαρχὰς
δίδωσι; [59, 16; 126, 3.]
Indirect.—1, 8, γνώσῃ τί σοι ποιητέ᾽
ἐστίν. 13, 9, τίνι βίῳ χαίρεις οὐκ
οἶδα. 58, 4, εἰδέναι σπεύδων τί ποτ᾽
ἦν ἐν αὐτῷ. 59, 2, ἤριζον τίς καλόν
τι ποιήσει. 106, 19, τίν᾽ εἶχεν αἰτίην
διηρώτα. 130, 2, βουλὰς ἐκίνει τί
ποιήσει. 59, 12, βλέπειν τὸ τοῦ πέλας
τί βουλεύοι.
Τίς. Indefinite.—5, 7; 9, 1; 10, 1;
12, 9; 15, 1; 17, 2; 22, 1; 25, 8;
27, 1; 30, 1; 31, 12; 33, 2; 33, 22;
34, 4; 42, 1; 45, 1; 47, 4; 47, 5;
48, 1; 49, 7; 51, 1; 55, 1; 59, 2;
61, 8; 63, 1; 66, 1; 68, 2; 69, 2;
69, 3; 69, 6; 83, 1; 88, 1; 88, 8;
91, 3; 92, 1; 93, 6; 95, 55; 98, 16;
99, 1; 101, 1; 102, 1; 102, 3; 108,
1; 108, 21; 110, 1; 111, 1; 113, 1;
114, 6; 115, 3; 117, 2; 119, 1;
119, 7; 125, 1; 125, 2; 127, 10;
129, 1; 130, 11; 132, 3; 132, 7;
133, 1; 135, 1; 137, 2; 139, 1.
[10, 14; 11, 11; 12, 25; 12, 27;
34, 12; 34, 14; 39, 3; 40, 5; 50,
19; 56, 9; 84, 3; 98, 21; 106, 11;
106, 13; 106, 26; 116, 1.]
εἴς τις. 21, 4, εἴς δέ τις γέρων.
63, 7, οὐδ᾽ ἂν εἴς τις ἡρώων.
μή τις. 2, 3; 2, 16; 95, 54.
τι. 7, 5; 11, 3; 20, 8; 24, 8;
26, 12; 57, 4; 67, 8; 74, 5; 89, 7;
94, 6; 95, 31; 95, 62; 98, 3; 108,
26; 111, 5; 111, 13; 116, 14; 124,
20; 126, 8; 128, 6; 136, 4; 140, 1.
[33, 25; 38, 10; 59, 17; 96, 6.]
μή τι. 131, 3. [21, 12; 94, 10.]
τινά. 95, 48, ἄλλον τιν᾽ εὑρεῖν
δόλον. 38, 1, δρυτόμοι τινές.
Τίτθη. 16, 1, ἄγροικος τίτθη.
Τιτρώσκω. 51, 4, ἐψάλιζεν ὥστε τιτρώσκειν. 95, 74, βίῃ ἐτρώθης.
Τιττυβίζω. 131, 7, ταύτης μικρὰ τιττυβιζούσης.

[Τλάω.] 129, 22, ἔτλην οἷα χρή με.
138, 3, ταῦτα τλῆθι γενναίως.
Τλήμων. 107, 2, ἐγγὺς ὢν μόρου τλήμων.
Τοιγάρ. 58, 8, τοιγὰρ ἐλπὶς ἀνθρώποις
μόνη σύνεστι. 63, 10, κακῶν δοτῆρες
ἡμεῖς· τοιγὰρ εἰ κακῶν χρῄζεις. 115,
8, τοιγὰρ διδάξω.
Τοιγαροῦν. 7, 3, πολλὰ τοιγαροῦν κάμνων. 13, 12, ἀπολῇ μετ' αὐτῶν τοιγαροῦν. 15, 13, νικᾷς. τοιγαροῦν
χολωθείη κτε.
Τοίνυν. 31, 7, εἵλοντο τοίνυν τοὺς ἀρίστους. 33, 12, ἥνίκ' ἂν τοίνυν ἔλθωσι.
47, 8, κατὰ μίην τοίνυν πειρᾶσθε. 50,
17, ἔρρωσο τοίνυν. 100, 8, ἐγὼ τοίνυν
χαίρειν κελεύω.
Τοῖος. 77, 7, ὁ τοῖος ὄρνις κωφός ἐστι.
Τοιόσδε. 37, 9, τοιάδ' εἶπε φωνήσας.
107, 3, τοιοῖσδε μύθοις ἱκέτευε.
Τοιοῦτος. 6, 13, τοιαῦτα ἱκέτευε. 95,
86, τοιαῦτα κωτίλλουσα. 108, 28,
τοιαῦτα δειπνῶν. 130, 10, τοιαῦτα
τοῖς φίλοις δώσεις. 28, 7, εἰ τοιοῦτον
ἦν ὄγκῳ. 18, 1, τοιαύτην ἔριν. 77,
3, μύθῳ τοιούτῳ. 128, 1, μύθους
τοιούτους (conj.) [35, 7. 86, 9, ἄχρι
τοιαύτην τὴν γαστέρα σχῇς.]
Τοῖχος. 31, 13, πηλίνων τοίχων. 42,
5, ἐκτὸς τοῦ τοίχου. 108, 15, εἰς οἶκον
ὑπό τε τοῖχον. 112, 3, ὤρυσσεν τοὺς
τοίχους. 118, 2, ἐν τοίχῳ. 139, 2 ;
140, 2.
Τολμάω. 95, 62, καὶ γρύσαι τι τολμήσῃς. 98, 8, τίς σε τολμήσει περιλαβεῖν ;
Τολμήεις. 92, 1, κυνηγὸς οὐχὶ τολμήεις.
Τονθρύζω. 107, 3, ἱκέτευε τονθρύζων
(conj.)
Τοξεύω. 1, 8, τοξεύει. 68, 1, μακρὰ
τοξεύων. 68, 2 ; 68, 8.
Τόξον. 1, 2, τόξου βολῆς ἔμπειρος. 68,
5, τόξ' ἔρυσσε κυκλώσας (conj.) 68, 9,
τόξου νίκην ἔλαβεν.
Τόπος. 50, 10, τὸν τόπον ἐδείκνυε. 59,
14, τόποις ἄλλους συνεξαμείβειν. 96,
4, ὁ τόπος μ' ἐλοιδόρησε.
Τοσοῦτος. 9, 8, τοσαῦτ' ἐκερτόμησε.
64, 6, δένδρων τοσούτων. 95, 72,
ἀρχὴν τοσαύτην. 101, 6, τοσοῦτον ὡς
σὺ νῦν. 135, 8, χρόνον τοσοῦτον.
Τόσσος. 36, 8, τόσση φηγός.
Τότε. 6, 12, ἐπὴν μέγας γίνωμαι τότ'
ἐνθάδ' ἐλθών. 21, 9, ἢν ἐμπέσωμεν,
διπλοῦς τότ' ἔσται θάνατος. 76, 5,
ἐπεὶ δ' ἐπαύσατο . . . τότε κατήγεν.
89, 10, τότε δή. 91, 7, παρελθέτω
με καὶ τότε γνώσῃ. 95, 26, τότ' αὖ
γένοιτο. 131, 13, πᾶσιν ἦν τότε χρείη.
131, 17, εἴθε μοι τότ' οὐκ ὤφθης.

Τράγος. 91, 3 ; 91, 8.
Τράπεζα. 34, 3, κρέων τραπέζας. 129,
15, τὴν τράπεζαν ἔθλασε.
Τραπεζεύς. 129, 1, κύνα τε τῶν τραπ-
εζήων (conjecture).
Τραῦμα. 5, 3, τραυμάτων πλήρης.
Τράχηλος. 94, 3, τράχηλον καθιμήσας.
100, 5, τράχηλος ἐλευκώθη.
Τρεῖς. 44, 1 ; 53, 3 ; 67, 4.
Τρέπω. 95, 65, τῆς δ' οὐκ ἐτρέφθη
θυμός. [71, 12.]
Τρέφω. 76, 2, ἵππον ἔτρεφε χόρτῳ. 83,
4, τὸ τρέφον με. 88, 3, ληΐου κόμη
θρέψας. 100, 2, ποῦ τραφεὶς οὕτως
μέγας. 128, 9, τρέφων σίτῳ.
Τρέχω. 69, 6, ἄλλως τρέχει τις.
Τρίβω. 37, 12, πέλεκυς τένοντα τρίψει.
100, 6, κλοιῷ τέτριπται σάρκα. 100,
10, σίδηρος αὐχένα τρίψει.
Τρίβων. [65, 7, σὺν τρίβωνι.]
Τρίζω. 108, 23, ἄσημα τρίζων. 52,
2, ἡ δ' ἐτερτρίγει.
Τρίτος. 53, 7, πρῶτον . . . ἔπειτα
. . . τρίτον. 59, 1, καὶ τρίτη τούτοις
Ἀθηνᾶ. 67, 7, ἡ τρίτη δ' αὕτη. [Λ.
3, τρίτη δ' ἀπ' αὐτῶν.]
Τρόπαιον. 31, 21, τρόπαιον εἱστήκει.
Τρόπις. 64, 5, τρόπις πλοίων.
Τροφεύς. 100, 7.
Τροφή. 74, 16, τὸν διδόντα τὴν τροφήν.
128, 5, τροφῆ γαίης πᾶσα. 136, 4,
δοῦναί τι τῆς τροφῆς.
Τροχάζω. 50, 2, κυνηγὸς ἐτρόχαζεν.
62, 2, κριθιάσας ἐτρόχαζε.
Τροχός. 20, 6, τῶν τροχῶν ἄπτου. 50,
12, τροχοὺς σιδηρείους.
Τρυγητός. 19, 5, εἰς τρυγητὸν ἀκμαίη.
Τρυγών. [72, 19.]
Τρυφή. 60, 4, πάσης τρυφῆς πέπλησμαι.
100, 9, τῇ τρυφῇ ταύτῃ.
Τρώγλη. 31, 17, ἐν τρώγλαις. 86, 6,
στενῆς τρώγλης. 108, 22, εἰς μυχὸν
τρώγλης. 112, 2, id. 118, 6, ἀπὸ
τρώγλης.
Τρώγω. 3, 2, αἰγὸς τρωγούσης. 89, 10,
τὸν ἄρνα τρώγων. 108, 6, τρώγων
ῥίζας. 108, 32, τὰ κρίμνα τρώγω.
129, 9, ἔτρωγε κριθάς. [133, 4.]
Τυγχάνω. 4, 2, ὄψου ἔτυχε ποικίλου
πλήρης. [39, 7.]
Τύμπανον. 137, 9, ἀγνῷ τυμπάνῳ.
Τύπτω. 33, 19, ἔτυψε τὴν κνήμην.
59, 10, ὡς ἂν βλέπων ἔτυπτε.
Τυραννεύω. 82, 5, ὁ πάντων θηρίων
τυραννεύων.
Τυραννέω. 95, 16, τίς θηρίων τυραννήσει. 95, 20, τυραννεῖν ἀξιωτάτην.
Τυρός. 77, 1 ; 77, 2 ; 77, 9 ; 108, 20.
Τυφλός. 53, 6, τυφλὸς ὤν. 134, 12,
τυφλῇ κινήσει.

Τυφόω. 101, 6, ὡς σὺ νῦν ἐτυφώθης.

Τύχη. 15, 8, τύχης θείης. 115, 4, ἐκ τύχης. 132, 3, κατὰ τύχην. 49, 2, τῆς Τύχης ἐπιστάσης. [5, 11.]

Ὑβρίζω. 119, 9, τοὺς ὑβρίσαντας ἠμείψω. [82, 9.]

Ὕβρις. [70, 2, Ἄρης ἔγημεν Ὕβριν. 70, 6.]

Ὑγρός. 109, 2, ὑγρῇ πέτρῃ. 1, 10, ὑγραῖς χολάσαν. 34, 7, ὑγραῖς ἀγκάλαις.

Ὕδωρ. 25, 2, μέλαν ὕδωρ. 43, 2, λίμνης ὕδωρ. 72, 6, θερινὸν ὕδωρ καὶ διαυγές. 27, 2, ὑδάτων ἐν συναγκίῃ κοίλῃ.

Υἱός. 15, 5, υἱὸν Ἀλκμήνης. 30, 3, υἱὸς ἐτεθνήκει. 35, 1, δύω υἱούς. 72, 11, κορώνης υἱός.

Ὑλακτέω. 74, 17, ἀεὶ δ' ὑλακτεῖ.

Ὕλη. 12, 14, ὕπαιθρον ὕλην. 23, 1, εἰς μακρὴν ὕλην. 43, 11, σύνδενδρον ὕλην. 45, 7, θαλλὸν ἐξ ὕλης. 46, 1, καθ' ὕλην. 76, 6, ἐξ ὕλης κατήγε. 90, 1, νεβρὸς ἐξ ὕλης. 12, 2, ἐρήμοις ὕλαις. 46, 7, πρὸς ὕλας. 92, 2, ἐν βαθυσκίοις ὕλαις. 95, 10, ὑπ' ἀγρίαις ὕλαις. 95, 42, εἰς μέσας ὕλας. Α. 8, ἐν μέσαις ὕλαις. 129, 6, ὕλην κατήγ' ἀφ' ὕψους.

Ὑλήεις. 95, 6, τὸν ὑλήεντα δρυμόν.

Ὑμνέω. 15, 6, μέγιστον ἀνδρῶν ὑμνεῖ.

Ὕνις. 37, 2, σύροντι τὴν ὕνιν ταύρῳ.

Ὕπαιθρος. 12, 14, ὕπαιθρον ὕλην.

Ὑπαντάω. 53, 6.

Ὑπάρχω. 31, 4, ὑπάρχειν αἰτίην. 108, 10, ἐμοὶ δ' ὑπάρχει πολλά. Α. 13, ὑπῆρχεν ἑταιρείη.

Ὑπεκδύνω. 4, 4, ὑπεξέδυνε δικτύου.

Ὑπεκκύπτω. 131, 14, τῆς θύρης ὑπεκκύψας.

Ὑπερ. 54, 1, ὑπὲρ παίδων σκεψόμενος. 95, 11, μαλθακῆς ὑπὲρ ποίης.

Ὑπερβαίνω. 23, 6, ὄχθον ὑπερβάς. 75, 6, τὴν αὔριον οὐχ ὑπερβήσῃ.

Ὑπερβολή. [24, 9, τῶν ὑπερβολῇ κούφων.]

Ὑπεργήρως. 47, 1, ἀνὴρ ὑπεργήρως.

Ὑπερεθίζω. 95, 64, βασιλεῖς ὑπερέθιξε.

Ὑπερέχω. [41, 4, λίαν ὑπερέχοντα.]

Ὑπέχω. 102, 7, ὡς ὑπέσχον εὐθύνας.

Ὕπνος. 10, 10, ἦλθεν καθ' ὕπνοις.

Ὑπνόω. 30, 7, εἶδεν ὑπνώσας. 124, 10, πρὸς τὸν ἦχον ὑπνώσεις.

Ὑπό, c. gen.—28, 5, ὑφ' οὗ κεῖται. 78, 5, ὑπὸ σοῦ ἐσυλήθη. 105, 6, ὑπὸ φίλων ἐδωρήθη. 117, 8, ὑφ' ἑνὸς δηχθείς. Β. 9, ὑπ' ἐμοῦ τῆς θύρης ἀνοιχθείσης. 34, 5, ὑπὸ τῶν ἐγκάτων ἐφυσήθη. 98, 13, ὑπὸ σμίλης ἀπωνυχίσθη.

74, 1, ὑπὸ ψύχους κάμνοντες. 88, 13, ἠλίου ὑπ' ἀκτίνων ῥέοντα. 5,' 4, ὑπ' αἰσχύνης. 49, 1, ὑπ' ἀγνοίης. 95, 84, ὑπ' εὐνοίης. [38, 9 ; 38, 10 ; 39, 6. 131, 16, ὑπὸ τοῦ κρύους πεσοῦσαν.] C. dat.—48, 2, λίθων ὑπ' αὐτῷ σωρὸς ἦν. 95, 5, ὑπ' ἀγρίαις πεύκαις. 95, 10, ὑπ' ἀγρίαις ὕλαις. 80, 2, ὀρχεῖσθαι ὑπ' αὐλοῖς. [106, 5, ὑπὸ σπήλυγγι.] C. acc.—108, 15, ἐλθεῖν ὑπὸ τοῖχον. 108, 31, βώλου ὑφ' ἣν τὰ κρίμνα τρώγω. 29, 2, ζευχθεὶς ὑπὸ μύλην. 43, 1, ὑπὸ τὸ καῦμα διψήσας.

Ὑποβλήδην. 95, 65, ὑποβλήδην φησί.

Ὑπολαμβάνω. [39, 5, εἶς δ' ὑπολαβὼν εἶπε.] 43, 17, μηδὲν βέβαιον ὑπολάβῃς.]

Ὑπομένω. 31, 6, ὑπομένουσι κινδύνους. [64, 12, χὐπέμεινε κινδύνους.]

Ὑπονοέω. 103, 11, ἀλώπηξ ὑπενόησε.

Ὑποπτεύω. 95, 67, τοὺς φίλους ὑποπτεύεις. 97, 4, οὐχ ὑποπτεύσας.

Ὑποτέμνω. 37, 4, ὑπέτεμνε τὴν χώρην.

Ὕπουλος. 44, 4, λόγοις ὑπούλοις. 98, 3, οὐδέν τι δύσνοιν οὐδ' ὕποιλον.

Ὑπουργέω. 95, 50, αὖθις ἀλλ' ὑπουργήσω.

Ὕπτιος. 115, 8, ὑπτίην ἄρας.

Ὗς. 98, 17, ἀργός, ὥσπερ ὗς.

Ὕστερος. 129, 21, ὕσται' ἐκπνείων. ὕστερον. 6, 12, ὕστερόν με συλλήψῃ. 38, 4, πόνος ὕστερον ῥάων. 97, 10, ὕστερον συναντήσας. 111, 15, σπόγγοις κατήγεν ὕστερον. [134, 19, ὕστερον κακῶν κύρειν.]

Ὑφίστημι. 95, 73, σὺ δ' οὐχ ὑπέστης κνίσμα.

Ὕψος. 129, 7, κατήγ' ἀφ' ὕψους. [47, 16, ἦρεν εἰς ὕψος.]

Φαιδρός. 106, 21, φαιδρῷ προσώπῳ.

Φαίνω. 114, 6, φαῖνε, λύχνε. 77, 5, στέρνον ἀετοῦ φαίνεις. 10, 10, φανεῖσα τῇ δούλῃ. 10, 12, ᾧ καλὴ φαίνῃ. 54, 4, οὐδ' ἀνὴρ φαίνῃ. 65, 6, οὐδ' ἄνω φαίνῃ. 101, 7, λέων φαίνῃ. 131, 6, ἐφάνη χελιδών.

Φάλαγξ. 31, 10, διεῖλον εἰς φάλαγγας.

Φαλακρός. 22, 11, φαλακρὸν ἔθηκαν ἄνδρα.

Φάλαρον. Β. 7, φαλάρῳ χρισέῳ.

Φάλλαινα. 39, 1.

Φάος. [116, 4, σελήνης ἐν φάει.]

Φάραγξ. 3, 2, ἐν φάραγγι. 20, 2, εἰς φάραγγα κοιλώδη. 95, 1, ἐν φάραγγι πετραίην.

Φάρμακον. 120, 4, φαρμάκων ἐπιστήμων.

Φᾶρος. 139, 2, φᾶρος λεπτόν.

Φάρυγξ. 94, 1, φάρυγος ἐντός. 94, 8, λυκείου φάρυγος.

Φάσκω. 14, 2, σῶμ' ἔφασκε μὴ σύρειν.
95, 14, ὁ λέων, ἔφασκεν, ἐστί μοι
γείτων. 90, 2, νεβρὸς ἔφησεν 'ἡμέων
ταλαιπώρων.' [22, 14, μῦθος φάσκει
τοῦτο.]
Φάτνη. 62, 1, ἀργῆς ἐσθίων φάτνης.
129, 8, παρὰ φάτναισι δεσμώτης.
129, 12, φάτνης ὀνείης δεσμὰ καὶ
κάλους.
Φαῦλος. 95, 13, ἔχει φαύλως. 119, 3,
ἔπρασσε φαύλως. [71, 12, ὡς δοκεῖν
φαῦλα. 82, 11, εὐκαταφρόνητον τοῖς
φαύλοις.]
Φέγγος. 114, 2, φέγγος ἐκπρεπέστατον.
114, 7, τῶν ἀστέρων τὸ φέγγος.
Φείδομαι. 34, 10, μὴ φείδου. 107, 7,
ἀλλὰ λίσσομαι, φείδου.
Φέρβω. [128, 8, φέρβεις τὴν κίνα.]
Φέριστος. 106, 22, ὦ φέριστε θηρίων
γένυης.
Φέρω. 76, 10, σάγην νώτοις ἔφερεν.
52, 5, ἐπ' ὤμοις φερομένη. 98, 8,
ἡλίκους φέρεις ὀδύντας ; 47, 5, δεσμὴν
ἐνεγκεῖν. 11, 6, τὴν δ' ὁ δαίμων
ὠδήγει τὸ πῦρ φέρουσαν. 45, 7,
φέρων ἔβαλλε θαλλόν. 47, 5, ἦκέ τις
φέρων ταύτην. 66, 4, ἐκ δὲ τοῦ δύω
πήρας κρέμασαι φέροντα. 93, 2, παρῆσαν ἄγγελοι ὄρκοις φέροντες. 137,
9, ἀπαρχὰς φέρων δίδωσι. 137, 3,
φέρῃ πτωχοῖσι πείνης ἄκος. 101, 3,
τὴν δόξαν οὐκ ἤνεγκε. 134, 11, εἰς
βάραθρον ἠνέχθη. [11, 12, αὐτοῖς βλάβην φέρουσα. 76, 8, φόρτον ἔφερεν.
106, 16, ἔφερεν οὐκ ἴσην μοῖραν.]
Φεύγω. 11, 4, ἀφῆκε φεύγειν. 25, 4,
μοῦνον εἰδότες φεύγειν. 26, 6, ὥστε
μὴ φεύγειν. 33, 9, ἔφευγον. 33, 17,
οἱ δ' οὐκ ἔφευγον. 43, 9, ἰδὼν ἔφευγε.
50, 1, ἔφευγ' ἀλώπηξ, τῆς δ' ὄπισθε
φευγούσης. 67, 8, μὴ θέλοντί σοι
φεύγειν. 88, 11, οὔπω καιρὸς φεύγειν.
112, 6, πάλιν δακὼν φεύγει. 122, 12,
λακτίσας φεύγει. 1, 11, φεύγειν εἰς
νάπας. 4, 3, εἰς βύθον φεύγων. 45,
1, φεύγειν ἐς ἄντρον. 97, 9, ὤχετ' εἰς
ὅρος φεύγων. 108, 22, ἔφευγεν εἰς
μυχόν. 112, 2, εἰς μυχὸν φεύγειν.
26, 10, φεύγω μὲν εἰς τὰ Πυγμαίων.
33, 20, ἔφευγον ἐκ χώρης. 50, 8, τῆδ'
ἀλώπηξ φεύγει. 88, 18, ἀλλαχοῦ φεύγειν. 95, 54, μή πού τις ἔλαφος
φεύγει. 118, 11, ἔνθεν φεύγω. 12,
22, ἄνδρα καὶ πόλιν φεύγω. 33, 22,
φεύγετ' ἀνθρώπων γένος. 91, 1, λέοντα
φεύγων ταῦρος. 132, 1, δὶς λύκον
ἔφευγεν. 58, 9, τῶν πεφευγότων ἦμας
ἀγαθῶν. 23, 8, εἰ φύγοις γε τὸν κλέπτην. 50, 17, τὸν Ὅρκον οὐ φεύξῃ.
82, 7, μή μοι τὴν δορὴν κνίσῃ φεύγων.

[21, 11, πημονὴν φεύγειν. 50, 20,
Δίκην φεύγει. 58, 6, πέτεσθαι τῆς τε
γῆς ἄνω φεύγειν. 81, 5, φεύγειν
ψεῦδος. 140, 4, τὸ χρεὼν οὐ φεύξῃ.]
Φηγός. 36, 8 ; 86, 1.
Φήμη. 49, 5, κακὴν λάβω φήμην.
103, 6, ἦλθεν ἄγγελος φήμη.
Φημί. 1, 14, 'οὐ με πλανήσεις' φησίν
'οὐδ' ἐνεδρεύσεις.' 10, 12 ; 13, 10 ;
27, 5 ; 50, 5 ; 53, 4 ; 60, 3 ; 65, 6 ;
67, 5 ; 68, 8 ; 69, 4 ; 75, 4 ; 78, 4 ;
84, 5 ; 92, 9 ; 94, 7 ; 95, 66 ; 95, 99 ;
98, 4 ; 100, 9 ;¹ 103, 17 ; 110, 4 ;
115, 8 ; 117, 10 ; 130, 10 ; 131, 17 ;
135, 7 ; 135, 12 ; 136, 5 ; 136, 8.
59, 1, Ζεὺς καὶ Ποσειδῶν, φασί, καὶ
τρίτη τούτοις ἦριζ' Ἀθηνᾶ. 74, 14 ;
102, 4 ; B. 4. 7, 14, οἴμοι τῆς κακῆς,
ἔφη, γνώμης. 43, 13 ; 101, 6. 6, 15,
ἔφη δὲ πείρων αὐτόν 'ὁ μὴ τὰ μικρὰ
τηρήσας μάταιός ἐστιν.' 52, 3, ἔφη δ'
οὕτως 'ὦ παγκάκιστον.' 95, 60, ἔφη
δ' οὕτως 'ἀλλ' ὦ στύγημα.' 81, 3,
κερδὼ πιθήκῳ φησίν, 'ὡς θέλεις,
ψεύδου.' 75, 11, ὁ δ' ἰατρὸς αὐτῷ
'χαῖρ' ἔφη σιναντήσας. 95, 76,
βασιλῆ δέ φησι τὸν λύκον καταστήσειν.
5, 2, οἷς θυμὸν εἶναί φασι. 66, 2,
τοῦτον πλάσασθαί φασι. 66, 4, κρεμάσαι φέροντά φασι. [A. 4, μεθ' ἦν
γενέσθαι φασί. 41, 5, διαρραγῆναί
φασιν σαύραν. 59, 16, τί οὖν ὁ μῦθός
φησι ; 106, 25 ; 116, 11, τῇ σινεύνῳ
φησὶ 'μηδὲν ἐκπλήσσου.' 126, 3, καί
φησιν αὐτῇ 'διὰ τίν' αἰτίην ναίεις ;'
134, 18.]
Φθάνω. 112, 2, φθάσαντος φυγεῖν.
[40, 3, τοῦ δ' ὄνθου φθάνοντος αὐτήν.]
Φθονέω. 122, 9, χάριτος οὐ φθονῶ ταύτης.
Φθόνος. [59, 17.]
Φιλαδελφίη. [47, 15.]
Φιλάλληλος. 124, 9, ὀρνέων φιλαλλήλων.
Φίλεργος. 74, 13.
Φιλέω. 14, 1, ἄνθρωπον φιλεῖν ἐκτόπως.
[83, 5, τὸν φιλοῦντα. 106, 7, ἑστία
τε κάφίλει.]
Φίλος. 12, 12, σύσκηνος ἡμῖν καὶ φίλη.
42, 2, κινεῖ φίλῳ σιναντήσας. 99, 5,
φίλῳ σοι πιστεύω. 106, 9, φίλην καὶ
σύνοικον. 46, 10, εἰ φίλους οὐκ ἔσχε.
87, 3, ὡς φίλῳ ψαύων. 87, 5, φίλες
εἶ. 88, 7, πάντας καλεῖν τοῖς φίλοις.
88, 12, φίλοις πέποιθεν. 88, 19, οὐ
φίλοισι πιστεύει. 95, 3, φίλην ἀλώπεκ'
εἶχεν. 95, 67, τοῖς φίλοις ὑποπτεύεις.
103, 6, ὑπὸ φίλων ἐδωρήθη. 119, 7,
φίλοισιν ἀγνώμων. 124, 1, φίλος
ἐπῆλθεν. 124, 20, τὸν φίλον. 130,

GRAECITATIS BABRIANAE LEXICON. 189

ὁ, φίλος γάρ εἰμι. 130, 10, τοῖς φίλοις δώσεις. 130, 11, σοὶ φίλος συναντήσει. 129, 6, πυρὸν φίλης Δήμητρος. 12, 7, φιλτάτη, ζώεις ; 63, 4, χαῖρε, φίλταθ' ἡρώων. 95, 28, χαῖρε, φιλτάτη. 103, 13, χαῖρε, φιλτάτη, ζώων. 128, 3, ἐστί σοι φίλον πῆξαι γάλα. [35, 8 ; 44, 8. 106, 21, ὦ φίλη.]
Φιλοφρονέομαι. [106, 4, φιλοφρονεῖσθαι ἐπειρᾶτο.]
Φοβερός. 1, 16, φοβερός ἐστι. 95, 22, φοβερὸν πᾶσιν ἑρπετοῖς. [102, 12, φοβερὰ τἀσθενῆ θήσει.]
Φοβέω. 108, 32, μὴ φοβούμενος.
Φόβος. 1, 3, φόβου δρόμος πλήρης. 26, 4, τῷ φόβῳ καταπλήσσων. 95, 60, φόβου πλήρης.
Φοῖβος. 68, 3 ; 68, 5.
Φοῖνιξ. 108, 18, σώρακες φοινίκων.
Φορέω. 18, 5, τὸν φοροῦντα συλήσειν.
Φορητός. 90, 4, ἦν φορητὸς οὐδὲ σωφρονῶν.
Φορτίζω. 111, 3, φορτίσας τὸν ὄνον.
Φόρτος. 7, 2, ἐπετίθει τὸν φύρτον ὄνῳ. 7, 5, συλλαβεῖν τι τοῦ φόρτου. 111, 16 ; 111, 19. [57, 9. 76, 8, φόρτον ἔφερεν.]
Φράζω. Λ. 16, μύθους φράσαντος.
Φρέαρ. 49, 2, φρέατος ἐγγύς.
Φρενοῦμαι, = class. φρονῶ.—101, 5, μὴ φρενωθείην τοσοῦτον.
Φρήν. 98, 6, φρένες δὲ δειλαὶ παρθένων. [10, 14, φρένας πηρός.]
Φρικώδης. 131, 12, χάλαζα φρικώδης.
Φρίξ. 93, 7, βαθείη φρικὶ μαλλὸν ὀρθώσας. 95, 59, φρὶξ ἐπέσχε νῶτα.
Φρίσσω. 82, 3, φρίξας δὲ χαίτην.
Φρονέω. 134, 8, τὸ φρονοῦν. 134, 9, τὸ μὴ φρονοῦν.
Φροντίζω. [83, 5 ; 136, 9.]
Φροντίς. 24, 5, φροντίδων καὶ λύπης.
Φρῦνος. 24, 4 ; 28, 1 ; 28, 6.
Φυγή. 1, 3, ἦν τῶν ζώων φυγή. [12, 6, φυγῇ πλήθους.]
Φύζα. 31, 16, φύζα τοὺς μύας κατειλήφει. 95, 41, τὴν δὲ φύζα ἦγεν εἰς ὕλας.
Φυή. [106, 3, ἀρίστην φυήν.]
Φυκίον. 6, 10, φυκίων θαλασσαίων.
Φυκίς. 6, 8, φυκὶς ἡ μήτηρ.
Φυλάσσω. 33, 3, πυρὸν ἐφύλασσεν ἐστώς. [11, 11, νέμεσιν ἦν φυλαττοίμην.]
Φύλλον. 95, 82, ὄμνυμί σοι πάντα φύλλα. Λ. 9, τὰ φύλλα τῆς πεύκης.
Φῦλον. 33, 12, σοφὸν φῦλον. 57, 3, ἄλλο φῦλον ἐξ ἄλλου. 72, 7, πάντων φῦλον ὀρνίθων. [33, 25.]
Φυσάω. 9, 5, φυσῶν ἔκαμε. 18, 4, βορέης ἐφύσα. 28, 7, φυσῶσ' ἑαυτήν. 34, 5, ὑπὸ τῶν ἐγκάτων ἐφυσήθη.

Φύσις. 32, 10, τῇ φύσει ἐνικήθη. [71, 11, αἱ κακαὶ φύσεις.]
Φύτευμα. 36, 3, πιλώριον φύτευμα.
Φύω. 64, 4, ὀρθίη φύω. 95, 22, κέρας φοβερὸν φύει. 95, 67, φόβου πλήρης πέφυκας. Λ. 12, ἐφύετ' ἐκ γῆς πάντα. 59, 7, κάκεῖνος ὡς πέφυκε πάντας ἐχθραίνειν. [98, 22.]
Φωλάς. 82, 3, φωλάδος κοίτης.
Φωλεός. 106, 2, κατ' εὐρὺν φωλεόν.
Φωλεύω. 92, 5, ὧδε φωλεύει. 108, 2, ἐν ταμείοις φωλεύων.
Φωνέω. 17, 4, ὀξὺ φωνήσας. 34, 8, καὶ ταῦτ' ἐφώνει. 37, 3, 'τάλας,' ἐφώνει, ' μόχθον οἷον ὀτλεύεις.' 39, 9, τοιάδ' εἶπε φωνήσας. 62, 2, ἐτρόχαζε κάφώνει. 95, 47, ἱκέτευε φωνήσας. 124, 13, κλαγκτὸν εἶπε φωνήσας. 33, 10, τὸν παῖδα φωνήσας ἐδίδασκεν. 2, 11, κῆρυξ ἐφώνει ἀριθμήσειν. 76, 12, σάλπιγξ ἐφώνει πᾶσιν ἀσπίδα σμήχειν.
Φωνή. 50, 18, φωνῇ με σώσας. 71, 6, γυναικείην λαβοῦσα φωνήν. 103, 5, φωνὴν λεπτύνων. Λ. 7, φωνὴν ἔναρθρον εἶχεν. [73, 4, τὴν κρείττω φωνήν.]
Φωνήεις. 77, 11, οὐκ ἄφωνος ἀλλὰ φωνήεις.
Φώρ. 2, 15, τοὺς ἑαυτοῦ φῶρας.
Φῶς. 107, 14, τὸ φῶς βλέψαι.

Χαίρω. 13, 9, τίνι βίῳ χαίρεις ; 74, 17, ξένοισιν οὐ χαίρει. 102, 2, τῇ βίῃ χαίρων. 120, 1, σκιῇ χαίρων. 95, 61, νῦν μὲν οὐχὶ χαιρήσεις. 98, 4, διδοὺς χαίρω. 122, 4, σοὶ συμβαλὼν χαίρω. 130, 2, δέχου χαίρων. 48, 3, χαῖρε πρῶτον, Ἑρμείη. 63, 4 ; 95, 28 ; 103, 13 ; 108, 28. 75, 11, ἰατρὸς αὐτῷ 'χαῖρ'' ἔφη. 95, 12, χαίρειν προσεῖπε. 100, 9, χαίρειν κελεύω. [10, 13 ; 24, 9 ; 24, 10. 129, 2.]
Χαίτη. 22, 3, λευκαῖς μελαίνας χαίτας. 72, 9, ἐκτένιζε τὰς χαίτας. 82, 1, ἀγρίης χαίτης. 82, 3, φρίξας δὲ χαίτην. 82, 8, χαίτην καταισχύνειν. [133, 1.]
Χάλαζα. 131, 12, χάλαζα φρικώδης.
Χαλάω. 130, 8, χαλασθείσης ῥάβδου.
Χαλεπός. 95, 50, χαλεπὸν κελεύεις.
Χαλινόω. Β. 7, φαλάρῳ χρυσέῳ χαλινώσας τὸν μυθίαμβον.
Χάλκεος. 80, 2, χαλκοῖς χαλκείοις. [Λ. 3, τρίτη γενεὴ χαλκείη.]
Χαλκεύω. 100, 7, κλοιὸν χαλκεύσας. 104, 3, χαλκεύσας κώδωνα.
Χαλκίον. 97, 6, πολλὰ χαλκία θερμοῦ πλήρη.
Χαμᾶζε. 115, 13, χαμᾶζε προσβαίνειν.

Χαμαί. 65, 6, χαμαὶ πτερύσσῃ. 119, 4, χαμαὶ ἀπεκρότησε.
Χαραδριός. 88, 2.
Χαρίζομαι. 92, 9, μή μοι χαρίζου.
Χάρις. 16, 11, μή μοι χάριν σχῇς. 27, 3, ὡς κακὴν χάριν τίνεις. 48, 9, χάριν εἴσομαί σοι. 50, 15, ζωαγρίοις χάριτας ὀφλήσεις. 107, 8, χάριν σοι τίσω. 122, 6, χάριν μοι δός. 122, 9, χάριτος οὐ φθονῶ ταύτης. 85, 6, οὐ χάριν.
Χάσκω. 110, 2, τί χάσκεις; 122, 12, τὸν κνηκίην χάσχοντα. 16, 6, λύκος χανὼν ὄντως.
Χαννόω. 77, 8, ἐπαίνῳ καρδίην ἐχαυνώθη. 95, 36, τῆς δ' ὁ νοῦς ἐχαυνώθη.
Χέζω. [40, 2, εἶτ' ἔχεζε.]
Χεῖλος. 107, 7.
Χειμών. 131, 3, χειμῶνος ὄντος. 136, 1, χειμῶνος ὥρῃ. 136, 8, χειμῶνος ὀρχοῦ.
Χείρ. 18, 7, χερσὶ κράσπεδα σφίγξας. 21, 6, χερσὶν ἐμπείροις. 95, 8, χεῖρας εἰς ἐμὰς ἥξει. 95, 43, χεῖρας ἐπεκρότησεν. 95, 73, χειρὸς ἀρρώστου. 98, 16, ἐκ χερὸς παίων. 127, 8, εἰς τοῦ Διὸς τὰς χεῖρας. [106, 18, χεῖρα βορῆς ἀποσχεῖν.]
Χειροτέχνημα. 30, 4.
Χείρων. [Λ. 5, γένος χεῖρον. 21, 12, μή τι χεῖρον ἐξεύρῃ. 71, 12, τρέπουσιν εἰς τὸ χεῖρον.]
Χελιδών. 12, 1; 12, 7; 118, 11; 131, 6; 131, 9; 118, 1, ξουθὴ χελιδών. 131, 15, χελιδόν' αὖ κατοπτεύσας.
Χέλυμνα. 115, 5.
Χελώνη. 115, 1, νωθὴς χελώνη.
Χέω. 127, 6, τῶν ὀστράκων κεχυμένων ἐπ' ἀλλήλοις.
Χηλή. 28, 6, χηλῇ μαλαχθέν. 43, 4, χηλῆς ἔνεκα.
Χηραμός. 107, 12, χηραμοῦ προπηδήσας.
Χήρη. 51, 1, πρόβατον εἶχέ τις χήρη.
Χίλιος. 2, 11, χιλίας ἀριθμήσειν.
Χιλός. 46, 3, ἑτοίμην χιλόν. 62, 1, χιλὸν ἐσθίων φάτνης.
Χίμαιρα. 3, 5; 3, 7.
Χιών. 45, 3, ἀδρῇ χιόνι.
Χλόη. 46, 2, ἐν χλόῃ βαθυσχίνῳ. 88, 2, ἐν χλόῃ νεοσσειῶν.
Χλωρός. 89, 7, οὔπω τι χλωρὸν ἔφαγον. 120, 8, οὕτω χλωρόν. 142, 2, χλωρὴν λείμακος ποίην. 108, 5, τῆς ἀρούρης ἄρτι χλωρὸν ἀνθούσης.
Χολάς. 1, 10, λέοντος ὑγραῖς χολάσιν.
Χολή. 95, 60, χολὴ ἐπέζει καρδίην.
Χολόω. 10, 12, τούτῳ χολοῦμαι. 15, 12, χολωθείη Ὀησεὺς ἡμῖν.
Χορεύω. 9, 10, πάλαι χορεύει.

Χορός. 9, 10, ἡνίκ' εἰς χορὸν ἦλθουν. 24, 3, λιμνάδας χορεὺς ἦγον. [80, 5, χορῷ παίζειν.]
Χόρτος. 76, 2, τὸν ἵππον ἔτρεφεν χόρτῳ. 129, 9, ἔτρωγε χόρτον.
Χράομαι. 95, 30, χρῆται ἡμῖν συμβούλοις.
Χρείη. 7, 16, μοι ἐπιτέθεικεν ἡ χρείη. 115, 12, τίς νεφῶν χρείη; 129, 7, ὅσων χρείη. 131, 8, ἐσθίων χρείη. 131, 13, κροκύδος πᾶσιν ἦν χρείη. [136, 9, ἀναγκαίων χρειῶν.]
Χρεμετίζω. [73, 2, ἵππου χρεμετίσαντος.]
Χρεών. 25, 9, οὐκέτι χρεὼν θνήσκειν. [138, 4, τὸ χρεὼν οὐ φεύξῃ.]
Χρή. 33, 11, χρὴ ἡμᾶς δολῶσαι φίλον. 85, 7, χρὴ δ' ἀεὶ προβουλεύειν. 129, 22, ἔτλην οἷα χρή με. [11, 10, χρὴ πρῷον εἶναι.]
Χρῄζω. 51, 7, κρεῶν χρῄζεις. 51, 9, εἰρίων χρῄζεις. 63, 10, εἰ κακῶν χρῄζεις. 92, 9, οὐ χρῄζω. 98, 10, εἰ γάμου χρῄζεις. 121, 2, τίνων χρῄζεις;
Χρήσιμος. 124, 19, οἶδα χρήσιμόν σε.
Χρηστός. 58, 1, τὰ χρηστὰ πάντα. 61, 9, τὸ χρηστὸν ἐξολεῖτε. 95, 13, χρηστῶν ἄγγελος λόγων. [71, 11, πολλὰ χρηστά.]
Χρόη. 13, 6, χῆ χρόη με σημαίνει. 65, 3, τὴν χρόην σκώπτεις.
Χρόνιος. 75, 3, πάθος χρόνιον.
Χρόνος. 75, 8, χρόνῳ ἐκεῖνος ἐκ νόσων ἀναφήλας. 103, 2, τῷ χρόνῳ γεγηράκει. 12, 3, ὁ χρόνος ἐξέδυσε καὶ ταύτης (conj.) 135, 8, χρόνον τοσοῦτον. 74, 10, ἐν χρόνοις πρώτοις.
Χρύσεις. Λ. 2,·γενεὴν καλοῦσι χρύσειην.
Χρύσεος. 123, 1, χρύσε' ᾠά. Β. 7, φαλάρῳ χρισέῳ.
Χρυσίον. 10, 3, ἡ δὲ χρυσίου πλήρης.
Χρυσός. 119, 5, χρυσὸς ἐρρίη.
Χρυσότοξος. 124, 16, χρυσότοξος Ὠρίων.
Χρυσοῦς. Λ. 6, χρυσῆς γενεῆς. 65, 2, χρυσᾶς πτέρυγας.
Χρῶμα. 85, 13, τὸ χρῶμα ἡμῖν οὐχ ἕν ἐστιν.
Χύτρη. 60, 1, ζωμοῦ χύτρη.
Χωλεύω. 13, 3, πελαργὸς χωλεύων.
Χωλός. 122, 1, ὄνος χωλός. 122, 15, χωλοῖς ἰατρεύειν.
Χώρη. 26, 1, κατενέμοντο τὴν χώρην. 33, 15, ἐνέμοντο τὴν χώρην. 37, 4, ὑπέτεμνε τὴν χώρην. 108, 13, ὀρύσσειν τὴν χώρην. 33, 20, οἱ δ' ἔφευγον ἐκ χώρης. 68, 8, οὐκ ἔχω χώρην.
Χωρίζω. 12, 20, μή μ' ὀργάδος χωρίσσῃς. 44, 5, χωρίσας ἀπ' ἀλλήλων.

Χωρίς. 12, 10, χωρὶς ἦμεν ἀλλήλων.
47, 13, ἄλλος ἄλλου χωρίς. 91, 3,
χωρὶς αἰπόλου μείνας. 71, 9, τούτων
χωρίς. 134, 5, χωρὶς ὀμμάτων. 21,
7, χωρὶς αἰκίης.
Χῶρος. 51, 7, τῷ χώρῳ 'Λράβων. 95,
56, ἐν κατασκίῳ χώρῳ.

Ψαλίζω. 51, 4, τὸν μαλλὸν ἐψάλιζεν.
Ψάρ. 33, 5 ; 33, 7 ; 33, 13.
Ψαύω. 19, 6, οὐ γὰρ ἴσχυε ψαύειν.
87, 3, ὡς φίλῳ ψαύων. 95, 70, ἔψαυ-
σεν ὠτός. 108, 25, ψαύειν ἰσχάδος.
[106, 21, δαιτὸς ψαῦσον.]
Ψέγω. 59, 8, ἔψεγεν τὸ τοῦ ταύρου.
Ψεῦδος. [81, 5, μὴ φεύγειν ψεῦδος.
126, 6.]
Ψεύδω. 81, 3, ὡς θέλεις ψεύδου. [81,
6, λανθάνειν ψευδόμενος.]
Ψεῦσμα. 57, 1, ψευσμάτων τε ἀπάτης
τε καὶ πανουργίης.
Ψεύστης. 57, 13, ψεῦσταί τε καὶ γόητες.
Ψυχή. 25, 4, ψυχὰς ἄτολμοι. 95, 35,
ψυχαὶ δ' ἐν ὀφθαλμοῖσιν.
Ψῦχος. 18, 10, τοῦ δυσηνέμου ψύχους.
74, 1, ὑπὸ ψύχους.
Ψύχω. 136, 2, σῖτον ἔψυχε μύρμηξ.

*Ω. 13, 9, ὦ πελαργέ. 33, 11, ὦ παῖ.
47, 10, ὦ παῖδες. 52, 4, ὦ παγκάκιστον κτημάτων. 63, 8, ὦ τᾶν. 71, 3,
ὦ πέλαγος. 82, 6, ὦ παλαμναίη. 95,
61, ἀλλ' ὦ στύγημα. 104, 6, ὦ τάλαν.
122, 3, ὦ λύκοι. 134, 5, ὦ τάλαινα.
Α. 2, ὦ Βράγχε τέκνον. Β. 1, ὦ παῖ
βασιλέως. [106, 21, ὦ φίλη. 106,
22, ὦ φέριστε.]
"Ω. 92, 4, ὦ πρός σε νυμφῶν.
*Ωδε. 92, 5, ὅστις ὧδε φωλεύει.
'Ωδίνω. 35, 1, ἡ πίθηκος ὠδίνει δύο
υἱούς.
'Ωκύπτερον. 99, 4, τὠκυπτέρω σου.
*Ωμος. 33, 20, ἔτυψε τὸν ὦμον. 52, 2,
ἅμαξαν ὤμοις εἷλκον. 52, 5, ἐπ' ὤμοις
φερομένη. 72, 12, καθύγρων ἐντὸς
ὤμων.
'Ωμός. 102, 2, οὐδ' ὠμὸς οὐδὲ βίῃ
χαίρων.
'Ωνέω, vox nihili.—[83, 6, ὠνήσει.]
'Ωνητός. 135, 11, ὠνητὸς ἥκων.
*Ωνος. 6, 6, τίν' ὦνον εὑρήσεις ; 57, 4,
μέρος τι τῶν ὤνων.
'Ωιόν. 123, 1, χρύσε' ᾠά.
'Ωραῖος. 6, 4, εἰς τάγηνον ὡραίων. 98,
1, παιδὸς ὡραίης. [128, 7, ὡραία
βοτάνη.]
"Ωρη. 11, 6, ἦν ληίων ὥρη. 12, 4,
ἄωρον ἐκπεσόντα τῆς ὥρης. 131, 6,

id. 19, 4, πορφυρῆς θιγεῖν ὥρης. 22,
1, τὴν μέσην ἔχων ὥρην. 24, 1, θέρους
ὥρῃ. 33, 1, σπόρου δ' ὥρῃ. 136, 1,
χειμῶνος ὥρῃ. 63, 6, νικτὸς ἐν μέσαις
ὥραις. 95, 34, ἐν ἐσχάτοις ὥραις.
28, 4, ἄρτι πρὸ τῆς ὥρης. 53, 7, μὴ
σύγ' εἰς ὥρας ἵκοιο. 124, 19, οἶδα
χρήσιμόν σ' ὥραις (conj.) 88, 6, νῦν
ὥρη καλεῖν. 88, 18, νῦν ἐστιν ὥρη
φεύγειν. [23, 11.]
'Ωρίων. 124, 16, χρυσότοξος 'Ωρίων.
'Ωρόμαντις. 124, 15, τὸν ὠρόμαντιν
ἀπολέσας με.
"Ως = so.—95, 36, ὡς εἶπε κερδώ.
'Ως = when.—2, 9, ὡς ἐνιξον κάπέθεντο.
26, 5, αἱ δ' ὡς ἐπέσχον. 45, 9, ὡς δ'
ἠθρίασε. 57, 5 ; 70, 1 ; 76, 11 ; 86,
7 ; 88, 6 ; 88, 13 ; 95, 55 ; 97, 6 ;
102, 7 ; 108, 19 ; 111, 10 ; 111, 17 ;
125, 4 ; 129, 8 (conj.) ; 130, 7 ; 131,
10. [19, 9 ; 129, 19.]
= since.— 82, 4, κερδὼ δ' ἐπεχλεύ-
αξεν ὡς ἐκινήθη. 95, 84.
= as.—7, 9, νεκρός, ὡς προειρήκει.
19, 8, οὐ πέπειρος, ὡς ᾤμην. 26, 7,
ὡς πρὶν εἰώθει. 31, 10 ; 57, 12 ; 59,
7 ; 65, 5 ; 70, 3 ; 81, 3 ; 85, 13 ; 95,
51 ; 95, 70 ; 101, 6 ; 102, 3 ; 108,
12 ; 131, 18 ; 135, 11. [106, 29.]
= as if, giving an assumed reason.
—10, 11, ὡς καλήν σε ποιούσῃ. 16,
4, ὡς ἕτοιμα δειπνήσων. 38, 6 ; 76,
15 ; 103, 3 ; 111, 13.
15, 11, ὁ δ' ἄλλος, ὡς Βοιωτός, οὐκ
ἔχων. 17, 2, ὡς [θύλακός τις. 30, 4 ;
35, 5 ; 43, 5 ; 56, 3 ; 67, 7 ; 72, 16 ;
87, 3 ; 103, 7 ; 114, 2. 101, 7, ὡς
ἀληθῶς. [10, 13 ; 13, 13 ; 38, 10 ;
39, 3, καρκίνος μεσιτεύων ὡς εἴ τις ὢν
ἄδοξος . . . εἰρηνεύει. 84, 8.]
'Ως = so that.—38, 2, ἐνείραν σφῆνας
ὡς διασταίη. 59, 12, ὡς ἂν βλέποι τὸ
τοῦ πέλας. 59, 10, ὡς ἂν βλέπων
ἔτυπτε.
= that.—15, 7, ἔλεγεν ὡς κρείσσων
γένοιτο. [38, 9, μηνύει ὡς. 98,
19.]
= ὥστε.—[71, 12, ὡς δοκεῖν φαῦλα.]
'Ως = how.—2, 13, ὡς μάτην ἥκω. 27,
3, ὡς κακὴν χάριν τίνεις. 43, 13, ὡς
διεψεύσθην.
'Ωσείπερ. [52, 7.]
"Ωσπερ. 10, 6, 'Αφροδίτην ὥσπερ
αἰτίην ἐτίμα. 98, 17, ὥσπερ ὗς ἀποθνήσκων. Β. 8, ὥσπερ ἵππον ὁπλίτην.
15, 2, ὥσπερ εἰκός. 86, 5, id. 16, 9,
ὥσπερ εἰώθης. 129, 9, ὥσπερ εἰώθει.
[57, 8, οἱ δ', ὥσπερ ἁρπάζοντες, . . .
ἐκίνωσαν αὐτήν. 106, 20, ὥσπερ
εἴωθας.]

Ὥστε.   26, 6, κατεφρόνησαν ὥστε μὴ
φεύγειν.   51, 4, ἐψάλιξεν ὥστε τιτρώσκειν.   129, 21, ἔθεινον ὥστε ἔλεξεν.
[27, 8, ὥστε τεθνήξῃ.]
Ὠφελέω.   27, 4, ὧν σ᾽ ὠφέλοιν.   27, 7,

βλάπτουσα μᾶλλον ἤπερ ὠφελοῦσα.
119, 8, οὐδὲν ὠφέλεις ἡμᾶς.   [119, 14,
ὠφεληθείης.]
Ὠχριάω.   92, 8, ὁ δ᾽ ὠχριήσας.
Ὠχρός.   75, 9, προῆλθεν ὠχρός.

I.

INDEX FABULARUM.

O

INDEX II.

INDEX III.

INDEX IV.

THE END.

Printed by R. & R. Clark, Edinburgh.

Messrs. Macmillan & Co.'s Publications.

By W. GUNION RUTHERFORD, M.A.,

Balliol College, Oxford, Assistant Classical Master in St. Paul's School.

THE NEW PHRYNICHUS.

Being a Revised Text of the Ecloga of the Grammarian Phrynichus, with Introductions and Commentary. 8vo. 18s.

"It must be at once acknowledged that his work is a credit to English scholarship. Mr. Rutherford is original, concise, and powerful in generalisations. . . . Dr. Veitch and Cobet are mainly the storehouses whence Mr. Rutherford draws his premises, though he is far from a slavish follower of their conclusions. Lastly, he has quite succeeded in catching the amusing, though somewhat aggressive, dogmatism of style of Cobet and the best critics."—*The Times.*

"His work must commend itself to all scholars, and not least to those who in some respects differ from his conclusions, for the thoroughness with which every detail is worked up, and the clear, concise language in which his arguments are expressed."—*Saturday Review.*

"We feel justified in repeating once more . . . our deliberate opinion that his work is an honour to English scholarship, and the best of its kind that has been written in England for over half a century."—*Spectator.*

"This is a sound and scholarly book, and one that will be welcomed by all who take an interest in the literature of ancient Greece."—*St. James's Gazette.*

"This book is in several respects one of the most important classical works published within late years, because it seems to indicate that the current of Greek scholarship is now setting in a new direction in England. On the one hand, it is a deliberate attempt to dethrone the German School founded by Hermann, and to return to the methods of the great English scholars, Bentley, Porson, Elmsley, and Dawes ; on the other hand, it fearlessly enunciates the first maxim of true scholarship, that anomalies must be disregarded till the rules are thoroughly understood. . . . The book, on the whole, is a remarkable one."—*Notes and Queries.*

"Mr. Rutherford has seen the new use to which his author could be applied, and the result is a monumental addition to the masterpieces of English scholarship."—*Academy.*

A FIRST GREEK GRAMMAR.

Third Edition, Revised. Extra fcap. 8vo. 1s. 6d.

"In the arrangement and selection of such outlines of grammar as are necessary for beginners, Mr. Rutherford has displayed good judgment. He has made a decided advance beyond any book of the same size and scope."—*Athenæum.*

"Mr. Rutherford's 'Greek Grammar' is a most important and interesting contribution to classical educational literature. It is not only the fruit of independent research, but is also the outcome of practical experience as a classical tutor, and as a consequence the work is compiled on a new principle and contains a considerable amount of Greek scholarship that has not yet found its way into elementary books. The work is by no means a drill book for beginners learning the elements of the language, though this is done in the earlier portion of the work, and far more completely than in most elementary Greek grammars. The system pursued is to gradually impart additional information contemporaneously with the drill in inflection, so that the pupil finds little that is left for him to learn on this score when he comes to the Second Part. In this second part, which is the most important of all, and the most distinctive part of the new Greek Grammar, many scholarly suggestions are given and rules laid down on the grammatical forms included in the First Part, while much additional matter of an advanced kind is introduced."—*School Board Chronicle.*

MACMILLAN AND CO., LONDON.

MACMILLAN'S CLASSICAL LIBRARY.

With Notes and Introductions for Higher Students.

AESCHYLUS.—*AGAMEMNON, CHOEPHORAE, AND EUMENIDES.* By A. O. PRICKARD, M.A., Fellow and Tutor of New College, Oxford. 8vo. [*In preparation.*

ANTIPHON, ANDOKIDES, LYSIAS, ISOKRATES, AND ISÆOS.—*SELECTIONS.* Edited, with Notes, by R. C. JEBB, M.A., LL.D., Professor of Greek in the University of Glasgow. 8vo. 12s. 6d.

ARISTOTLE.—*POLITICS.* After Susemihl. By R. D. HICKS, M.A., Fellow of Trinity College, Cambridge. 8vo. [*In preparation.*

MARCUS AURELIUS ANTONINUS.—*BOOK IV. OF THE MEDITATIONS.* The Greek Text revised, with Translation and Notes. By Prof. HASTINGS CROSSLEY, M.A., Professor of Greek in Queen's College, Belfast. 8vo. 6s.

CICERO.—*THE ACADEMICA.* The Text revised and explained by JAMES REID, M.A., Fellow of Caius College, Cambridge. New Edition. With Translation. 8vo. [*In the press.*

EURIPIDES.—*MEDEA.* Edited, with Introduction and Notes, by A. W. VERRALL, M.A., Fellow and Lecturer of Trinity College, Cambridge. 8vo. 7s. 6d.

HERODOTUS, Books I.-III.—*THE EMPIRES OF THE EAST.* Edited, with Notes and Introductions, by A. H. SAYCE, M.A., Fellow and Tutor of Queen's College, Oxford, and Deputy-Professor of Comparative Philology. 8vo. [*In the press.*

HOMER.—*THE ILIAD.* Edited, with Introduction and Notes, by WALTER LEAF, M.A., Fellow of Trinity College, Cambridge, and the late J. H. PRATT, M.A. 8vo. [*In preparation.*

JUVENAL.—*THIRTEEN SATIRES OF JUVENAL.* With a Commentary. By JOHN E. B. MAYOR, M.A., Kennedy Professor of Latin at Cambridge. Vol. I.—Second Edition, enlarged. Crown 8vo. 7s. 6d. Vol. II.—Crown 8vo. 10s. 6d.

MARTIAL.—*BOOKS I. AND II. OF THE EPIGRAMS.* Edited, with Introduction and Notes, by Professor J. E. B. MAYOR, M.A. 8vo. [*In the press.*

PLATO.—*PHÆDO.* Edited by R. D. ARCHER-HIND, M.A., Fellow of Trinity College, Cambridge. 8vo. [*In preparation.*

—— *PHILEBUS.* Edited, with Introduction and Notes, by HENRY JACKSON, M.A., Fellow of Trinity College, Cambridge. 8vo. [*In preparation.*

TACITUS.—*THE HISTORIES.* Edited, with Introduction and Notes, by Rev. WALTER SHORT, M.A., and Rev. W. A. SPOONER, M.A., Fellows of New College, Oxford. 8vo. [*In preparation.*

—— *THE ANNALS.* Edited, with Introductions and Notes, by G. O. HOLBROOKE, M.A., Professor of Latin in Trinity College, Hartford, U.S.A. With Maps. 8vo. 16s.

MACMILLAN AND CO., LONDON.